D1743427

Contents

Articles

References

Article Licenses

Folksonomy

A **folksonomy** is a system of classification derived from the practice and method of collaboratively creating and managing tags to annotate and categorize content;[1] [2] this practice is also known as **collaborative tagging**[3] , **social classification**, **social indexing**, and **social tagging**. *Folksonomy*, a term coined by Thomas Vander Wal, is a portmanteau of *folks* and *taxonomy*.

Folksonomies became popular on the Web around 2004[4] as part of social software applications such as social bookmarking and photograph annotation. Tagging, which is one of the defining characteristics of Web 2.0 services, allows users to collectively classify and find information. Some websites include tag clouds as a way to visualize tags in a folksonomy.[5]

An empirical analysis of the complex dynamics of tagging systems, published in 2007,[6] has shown that consensus around stable distributions and shared vocabularies does emerge, even in the absence of a central controlled vocabulary. For content to be searchable, it should be categorised and grouped. This is possible only if the content is tagged like keywords in a journal article.

References

[1] Peters, Isabella (2009). " Folksonomies. Indexing and Retrieval in Web 2.0. (http://books.google.co.uk/books?id=Aeib_wy18gkC& printsec=frontcover&dq=folksonomies.+Indexing+and+Retrieval+in+Web+2.0&hl=en&ei=d67KTK6OGJDsOfK9sPoE&sa=X& oi=book_result&ct=result&resnum=1&ved=0CCsQ6AEwAA#v=onepage&q&f=false)". *Berlin: De Gruyter Saur.*

[2] Pink, Daniel H. (December 11, 2005). "Folksonomy" (http://www.nytimes.com/2005/12/11/magazine/11ideas1-21.html). *New York Times.* . Retrieved 14 July 2009.

[3] Lambiotte, R, and M Ausloos. 2005. Collaborative tagging as a tripartite network. http://arxiv.org/abs/cs.DS/0512090.

[4] Vander Wal, Thomas. "Folksonomy Coinage and Definition" (http://vanderwal.net/folksonomy.html). . Retrieved 2009-07-06.

[5] Lamere, Paul (June 2008). "Social Tagging And Music Information Retrieval" (http://www.informaworld.com/smpp/ content~db=all~content=a906001732). *Journal of New Music Research* **37** (2): 101–114. doi:10.1080/09298210802479284. .

[6] Harry Halpin, Valentin Robu, Hana Shepherd The Complex Dynamics of Collaborative Tagging (http://portal.acm.org/citation. cfm?id=1242572.1242602), Proceedings of the 16th International Conference on the World Wide Web (WWW'07), Banff, Canada, pp. 211-220, ACM Press, 2007.

Card sorting

Card sorting is a simple technique in user experience design where a group of subject experts or "users", however inexperienced with design, are guided to generate a category tree or folksonomy. It is a useful approach for designing information architecture, workflows, menu structure, or web site navigation paths.

Card sorting has a characteristically low-tech approach. The concepts are first identified and written onto simple index cards or Post-it notes. The user group then arranges these to represent the groups or structures they are familiar with.[1]

Groups may either be organised as collaborative groups (focus groups) or as repeated individual sorts. The literature discusses appropriate numbers of users needed to produce trustworthy results.[2]

A card sort is commonly undertaken when designing a navigation structure for an environment that offers an interesting variety of content and functionality, such as a web site.[3] [4] [5] [6] In that context, the items to be organized are those that are significant in the environment. The way that the items are organized should make sense to the target audience and cannot be determined from first principles.

The field of information architecture is founded upon the study of the structure of information. If an accepted and standardized taxonomy exists for a subject, it would be natural to simply apply that taxonomy as a means of organizing both the information in the environment and any navigation to particular subjects or functions. Card sorting is applied when:

- The variety in the items to be organized is so great that no existing taxonomy is accepted as organizing the items.
- The similarities among the items make them difficult to divide clearly into categories.
- Members of the audience that uses the environment may differ significantly in how they view the similarities among items and the appropriate groupings of items.

Basic method

To perform a card sort:

1. A person representative of the audience is given a set of index cards with terms already written on them.
2. This person puts the terms into logical groupings, and finds a category name for each grouping.
3. This process is repeated across a population of test subjects.
4. The results are later analyzed to reveal patterns.

Open card sorting

In an **open card sort**, participants create their own names for the categories.

This helps reveal not only how they mentally classify the cards, but also what terms they use for the categories.

Open sorting is **generative**; it is typically used to discover patterns in how participants classify, which in turn helps generate ideas for organizing information.

Closed card sorting

In a **closed card sort**, participants are provided with a predetermined set of category names. They then assign the index cards to these fixed categories.

This helps reveal the degree to which the participants agree on which cards belong under each category.

Closed sorting is **evaluative**; it is typically used to judge whether a given set of category names provides an effective way to organize a given collection of content.

Reverse card sorting

See tree testing.

In a *reverse card sort* or card-based classification, an existing structure of categories and sub-categories is tested. Users are given tasks and are asked to complete them navigating a collection of cards. Each card contains the names of subcategories related to a category, and the user should find the card most relevant to the given task starting from the main card with the top-level categories. This ensures that the structure is evaluated in isolation, nullifying the effects of navigational aids, visual design, and other factors.

Reverse card sorting is *evaluative*; it's used to judge whether a predetermined hierarchy provides a good way to find information.

Analyzing card-sort results

Various methods can be used to analyze the data. The purpose of the analysis is to extract patterns from the population of test subjects, so that a common set of categories and relationships emerges. This common set is then incorporated into the design of the environment, either for navigation or for other purposes.

Card sorting is an established technique with an emerging literature.[7]

Online (remote) card sorting

There are a number of tools available to perform card sorting activities with survey participants via the internet. The perceived advantage of remote card sorting is that it allows a larger group of participants to be reached at a lower cost. The software can also assist in the process of analyzing card sort results. The advantages of a remote card sort must be traded off against the lack of personal interaction between card sort participants and the card sort administrator, which may produce valuable insights.

References

[1] Jakob Nielsen (May 1995). "Card Sorting to Discover the Users' Model of the Information Space" (http://www.useit.com/papers/sun/cardsort.html). .

[2] Jakob Nielsen (July 19, 2004). "Card Sorting: How Many Users to Test" (http://www.useit.com/alertbox/20040719.html). .

[3] Donna Maurer and Todd Warfel. "Card sorting: a definitive guide" (http://www.boxesandarrows.com/view/card_sorting_a_definitive_guide). .

[4] (April 29, 2008). "Card Sorting for Web Design". [news:uk.net.web.authoring uk.net.web.authoring]. (Web link) (http://groups.google.co.uk/group/uk.net.web.authoring/msg/b71d97aac76222d9).

[5] "Design for Usability - Card Sorting" (http://www.syntagm.co.uk/design/cardsort.shtml). Syntagm Ltd. (http://www.syntagm.co.uk). .

[6] *Head First Web Design*. O'Reilly Media. 2009. pp. 81−100. ISBN 978-0-596-52030-4.

[7] Maurer (2009). "Card Sorting (" (http://www.rosenfeldmedia.com/books/cardsorting/content/bibliography/). Rosenfeld Media. .

External links

- Short video explanation of card sorting (http://jonathanmelhuish.com/2009/06/how-to-know-what-to-put-where-card-sorting/)

steve.museum

The **steve.museum** project is a collaborative effort to improve public access to, and engagement with, art museum collections. To do so, it is exploring the possibilities of user-generated descriptions of works of art, also known as folksonomy. Currently project staff comprises a group of volunteers, mostly from art museums, including the Guggenheim Museum, the Cleveland Museum of Art, the Metropolitan Museum of Art and the San Francisco Museum of Modern Art, as well as Archives & Museum Informatics.[1]

Folksonomy is a relatively new phenomenon whereby web-users tag content for the purposes of later retrieval. It allows the public to introduce new search-terms, in the form of tags, to the formal library catalog that art and cataloging professionals themselves might not have included. It also allows curators and other museum professionals to see what the public sees in works of art.[2] [3] These terms will enrich the catalog and increase the likelihood that searchers of all levels will find what they are looking for. In the end, it is hoped that museum collections will be fully searchable by keywords rather than just by name or artist.[4] Early results from the project found that a number of tags were applied often, while others were applied just once per work of art.[5]

The project received a $1 million grant from the Institute of Museum and Library Services,[5] from which the Indianapolis Museum of Art is working to apply folksonomy to its collection,[6] and is one of a number of related projects currently working to make art more accessible and to find its role in the digital age.[4] [7]

References

[1] Jennifer Trant. *Exploring the Potential for Social Tagging and Folksonomy in Art Museums: Proof of Concept* (http://www.archimuse.com/papers/steve-nrhm-0605preprint.pdf). .

[2] Jennifer Trant (2006-11-04). "Social Classification and Folksonomy in Art Museums: Early Data from the steve. museum tagger Prototype" (http://www.archimuse.com/papers/asist-CR-steve-0611.pdf). *Archives & Museums Informatics*. .

[3] Susan Chun, Rich Cherry, Doug Hiwiller, Jennifer Trant, Bruce Wyman (2006-03-22). "Steve.museum: An Ongoing Experiment in Social Tagging, Folksonomy, and Museums" (http://www.archimuse.com/mw2006/papers/wyman/wyman.html). *Museums and the Web 2006*. .

[4] Lisa Timson (2006-10-30). "Click for Culture" (http://www.theage.com.au/news/web/click-for-culture/2006/10/30/1162056906810.html?page=fullpage#contentSwap1). *The Age*. . Retrieved 2008-05-14.

[5] Pamela Licalzi O'Connell (2007-03-28). "One Picture, 1,000 Tags" (http://www.nytimes.com/2007/03/28/arts/artsspecial/28social.html?_r=1&oref=slogin&ref=technology&pagewanted=all). *The New York Times*. . Retrieved 2008-05-14.

[6] "Wikipedia for Art?" (http://www.accessmylibrary.com/coms2/summary_0286-30923176_ITM). *Indianapolis Business Journal*. 2007-04-23. . Retrieved 2008-05-14.

[7] "Can Museums Survive in a YouTube World?" (http://www.accessmylibrary.com/coms2/summary_0286-32576556_ITM). *PR Newswire*. 2007-08-09. . Retrieved 2008-05-14.

External links

- steve.museum (http://www.steve.museum/)

Tag management

Tag management is the ability to manage user-generated tags or folksonomy within a collaborative software. Tag management features and processes are put in place to encourage cross-user consistency, navigation efficiency and compliance with an existing taxonomy.

Tag management a priori

The tags that users will be able to use can be controlled up-hill by

- Faceted classification, categorizing tags in facets (e.g. organization or place facet)
- *Predefining tags*, authority lists of tags can be created and suggested to users
- *Restricting tag creation*, allow users to create or not new tags other than predefined tags
- *Mandatory facets*, meaning a user must categorize each item with at least a tag from this facet
- *Relating tags*, meaning selecting a tag will also display the results of other tags related to it (e.g. synonyms or translations)

Tag management a posteriori

Tags can be gardened down-hill by

- Renaming tags (e.g. typos)
- Deleting tags
- Moving tags to correct facets (e.g. an organization name)
- Merging tags (e.g. single and plural words)

Examples of tag management

- Tag management applied to blogging tools : Wordpress [1]
- Tag management applied to Content management systems : Microsoft SharePoint [2]
- Tag management applied to Enterprise bookmarking tools : Jumper 2.0, Knowledge Plaza

References

[1] "Wordpress tag management" (http://en.support.wordpress.com/posts/tag-management/). Wordpress. . Retrieved 2010-07-26.
[2] "SharePoint 2010 metadata and taxonomy management" (http://www.cmswire.com/cms/document-management/overview-sharepoint-2010-metadata-and-taxonomy-management-006015.php). CMS Wire. . Retrieved 2010-07-26.

Vocabulary OneSource

OneSource is an evolving data analysis tool used internally by the USAF Global Cyberspace Integration Center (GCIC) Vocabulary Services Team, and made available to general data management community. It is used by the greater US Department of Defense (DoD) and NATO community for controlled vocabulary management and exploration. It provides its users with a consistent view of syntactical, lexical, and semantic data vocabularies through a community-driven web environment. It was created with the intention of directly supporting the DoD Net-centric Data Strategy of visible, understandable, and accessible data assets.

OneSource serves developers, integrators, managers, and community of interest (COI) participants as a focus point for searching, navigating, annotating, semantic matching, and mapping data terms extracted from military standards, COI vocabularies, programs of record, and other schemas and data sources.

OneSource is based upon an United States Air Force researched and developed triplestore knowledge base architecture, which allows XML Schema, Web Ontology Language, relational database, spreadsheet, and even custom data models to be handled and presented in the same manner. Initial capability was released in 2006. Version 2 was released in 2008 with the previously disjoint matching and mapping capabilities fully integrated for use in a web browser.

External links

- http://onesource.afc2ic.org
- http://metadata.dod.mil

References

- Kenyon, Henry (15 December 2010). "Air Force software tools promote interoperability" [1]. *Defense Systems*. Retrieved 6 January 2011.
- "Enterprise Sharing: A Process to Expose Data Assets" [2]. *NGA Metadata Monthly - Issue 38*. 01 Nov 2010. Retrieved 6 January 2011.

References

[1] http://defensesystems.com/articles/2010/12/15/software-tools-promote-interoperability.aspx
[2] http://metadata.ces.mil/mdr/ns/geoint/mdh/docs/mdm/1110

Comparison of enterprise bookmarking platforms

The following tables compare Enterprise bookmarking platforms.

General

The table provides an overview of Enterprise Bookmarking platforms. The platforms listed refer to an application that is installed on a web server (usually requiring MySQL or another database and PHP, perl, Python, or some other language for webapps).

Software	Developed by	Latest stable release	Cost (USD)	Contract support offered	Community website support	Open source	Multilingual	Programming language	User Interface	Notes
Connectbeam	Connectbeam	Spotlight 3.1 (2008-6)	per instance	Yes	No	No	No	binary only	browser	none
Dogear	IBM Corporation	2.0.1 (2009-3)	per instance	Yes	Yes	No	Yes	binary only	browser	does not run on mySQL, requires IBM DB2 9.1 FP5, Oracle Database 10g 10.2.0.3, Microsoft SQL Server 2005 Enterprise Edition
Jumper 2.0	Jumper Networks	2.0.1.7 (2010-7)	Free	Yes	Yes	Yes - GPL	Yes	Javascript & PHP	browser	runs on mySQL database for storing tag profiles. Can also be configured to run on Oracle Database 10g or Microsoft SQL Server 2005 Enterprise Edition
Knowledge Plaza	Knowledge Plaza	2.3.18	free trial, starts at 35€/month/instance	Yes	Yes	No	Yes	Javascript and Python (programming language)	browser	Software-as-a-Service
Scuttle	Scuttle	0.7.4 (2008-7)	Free	No	No	Yes - GPL	No	Javascript & PHP	browser	none

Date and content types

This table lists the types of data that can be tagged.

Software	Web pages	Documents	Images	Video	Emails	Contacts	Book references	Discussions	Wiki pages	Database tables	Flat-files	Notes
Connectbeam	Yes	Yes	No	No	Yes	No	No	No	No	No	No	none
Dogear	Yes	Yes	No	No	No	No	No	No	No	No	No	none
Jumper 2.0	Yes	Yes	Yes	Yes	Yes	No	Yes	No	Yes	Yes	Yes	none
Knowledge Plaza	Yes	Yes	Yes	Yes	Yes	Yes	Yes	Yes	Yes	No	No	none
Scuttle	Yes	No	No	No	No	No	No	No	No	No	No	none

Content enrichment capabilities

Tags and metadata can be used to enrich previously described types of data and content. This table lists the default capabilities each platform provides.

Software	Keywords	Descriptions	Custom Tag Fields	Metadata	Knowledge Tags	Notes
Connectbeam	Yes	Yes	No	No	No	none
Dogear	Yes	No	No	No	No	none
Jumper 2.0	Yes	Yes	Yes	Yes	Yes	none
Knowledge Plaza	Yes	Yes	Yes	Yes	No	none
Scuttle	Yes	Yes	No	No	No	none

Tag management capabilities

Enterprise bookmarking tools differ from social bookmarking tools in the way that they often have to meet taxonomy constraints. Tag management capabilities are the uphill (e.g. faceted classification, predefined tags) and downhill gardening (e.g. tag renaming, moving, merging) abilities that can be put in place to manage the folksonomy generated from user tagging.

Software	Faceted classification	Restricted facets	Mandatory facets	Predefined tags	Related/synonym tags	Notes
Connectbeam	No	No	No	No	No	none
Dogear	No	No	No	No	No	none
Jumper 2.0	Yes	Yes	Yes	Yes	No	none
Knowledge Plaza	Yes	Yes	Yes	Yes	Yes	none
Scuttle	No	No	No	No	No	none

Platform and security capabilities

Security abilities at the platform level:

- *On-premises*, refers to an application that is installed on a web server behind the corporate firewall.
- *Hosted*, refers to a centrally-hosted website that is outside the corporate firewall
- *Encryption level*, refers to the level of encryption enforced by the application server

Security abilities at the application level:

- *Access permissions*, refers to the ability to define a list of users who have access to the application.
- *Information-level permissions*, refers to the ability to define per data/content item (e.g. a document) its accessibility/visibility within the application (invisible, downloadable, etc)
- *Workspace-level permissions*, refers to the ability to create team spaces with different accessibility/visibility settings.
- *Role-level permissions*, refers to the ability to assign roles to users (e.g. administrator, guest, workspace expert) which will also affect accessibility/visibility settings.

Software	Hosted Platform	On-Premises Platform	Encryption level	Multi-user support	Access permissions	LDAP integration	Information-level permissions	Workspace-level permissions	Role-level permissions	Notes
Connectbeam	Yes	Yes	?	Yes	Yes	No	?	?	?	none
Dogear	No	Yes	?	Yes	Yes	Yes	?	?	?	The Lotus Connection Suite with Dogear runs on the AIX (Unix) operating system
Jumper 2.0	No	Yes	HTTPS optionally available	Yes	Yes	Yes	Yes	Yes	Yes	LDAP integration is available
Knowledge Plaza	Yes	Yes	HTTPS with high-grade 256-bit AES	Yes	Yes	Yes	Yes	Yes	Yes	none
Scuttle	No	Yes	?	No	Yes	No	?	?	?	none

Server operating system support

In the case of web applications, this describes the server OS. For centrally-hosted websites that are proprietary, this is not applicable. Any client OS can connect to a web service unless stated otherwise in a footnote.

Software	Windows	Mac OS X	Linux	BSD	Unix	IIS	Apache	Notes
Connectbeam	Yes	No	No	No	No	Yes	No	none
Dogear	Yes	Yes	Yes	No	Yes	No	No	requires IBM WebSphere Application Server 6.1.0.13 for the HTtp://web server
Jumper 2.0	Yes	Yes	Yes	Yes	Yes	Yes	Yes	none
Knowledge Plaza	No	No	Yes	No	No	No	No	No OS management required. Infrastructure-as-a-Service for on-premises installation.
Scuttle	Yes	Yes	Yes	Yes	Yes	Yes	Yes	none

Enterprise bookmarking

Enterprise bookmarking is a method for Enterprise 2.0 users to tag, organize, store, and search bookmarks of both web pages on the Internet and data resources stored in a distributed database or fileserver. This is done collectively and collaboratively in a process by which users add tag (metadata) and knowledge tags.[1]

In early versions of the software these tags are applied as non-hierarchical keywords or terms assigned by a user to a web page and are collected in tag clouds.[2] Examples of this software are Connectbeam and Dogear. New versions of the software such as Jumper 2.0 and Knowledge Plaza expand tag metadata in the form of knowledge tags that provide additional information about the data and are applied to structured and semi-structured data and are collected in tag profiles.[3]

History

Enterprise bookmarking is derived from Social bookmarking that got its modern start with the launch of the web site del.icio.us, back in 2003. The first major announcement of an enterprise bookmarking platform was the IBM Dogear project developed in Summer 2006.[4] Version 1.0 of the Dogear software was announced at Lotusphere 2007, and shipped later that year on June 27 as part of IBM Lotus Connections. The second significant commercial release was Cogenz in September 2007.[5] Since these early releases, Enterprise bookmarking platforms have diverged considerably. The most significant new release was the Jumper 2.0 platform with expanded and customizable knowledge tagging fields.[6]

Differences

Social bookmarking vs Enterprise bookmarking

In a social bookmarking system, individuals create personal collections of bookmarks and share their bookmarks with others. These centrally stored collections of Internet resources can be accessed by other users to find useful resources. Often these lists are publicly accessible, so that other people with similar interests can view the links by category or by the tags themselves. Most social bookmarking sites allow users to search for bookmarks which are associated with given "tags", and rank the resources by the number of users which have bookmarked them.[7]

Enterprise bookmarking is a method of tagging and linking any information using an expanded set of tags to capture knowledge about data.[8] It collects and indexes these tags in a web-infrastructure knowledge base server residing behind the firewall. Users can share knowledge tags with specified people or groups, shared only inside specific networks, typically within an organization. Enterprise bookmarking is a knowledge management discipline that embraces Enterprise 2.0 methodologies to capture specific knowledge and information that organizations consider proprietary and are not shared on the public Internet.

Tag management

Enterprise bookmarking tools also differ from social bookmarking tools in the way that they often face an existing taxonomy. Some of these tools have evolved to provide Tag management which is the combination of uphill abilities (e.g. faceted classification, predefined tags, etc.) and downhill gardening abilities (e.g. tag renaming, moving, merging) to better manage the bottom-up folksonomy generated from user tagging.

References

[1] Scott Golder and Bernardo A. Huberman, The Structure of Collaborative Tagging Systems (http://www.hpl.hp.com/research/idl/papers/ tags/tags.pdf), Journal of Information Science, 32(2). 198–208, 2006

[2] Martin Halvey and Mark T. Keane, An Assessment of Tag Presentation Techniques (http://www2007.org/htmlposters/poster988/), poster presentation at WWW 2007, 2007

[3] Sreekumar Sukumaran and Ashish Sureka, Integrating Structured and Unstructured Data Using Text Tagging and Annotation (http://www. tdwi.org/Publications/BIJournal/display.aspx?ID=8030), Business Intelligence Journal, 2009

[4] David Millen Jonathan Feinberg and Bernard Kerr, IBM Dogear (http://domino.research.ibm.com/comm/research_projects.nsf/pages/ dogear.index.html), Queue Vol. 3 No. 9 – November 2005, 2005

[5] "Cogenz takes enterprise social bookmarking behind the firewall" (http://www.webwire.com/ViewPressRel.asp?aId=74422). Webwire. 11 September 2008. .

[6] "Jumper Networks Press Release Jumper 2.0 Released under the GPL" (http://www.jumpernetworks.com/NEWS-Jumper_2. 0_Released_as_Open-Source.pdf). Jumper Networks, Inc.. 26 March 2009. .

[7] David Millen Jonathan Feinberg and Bernard Kerr, Social Bookmarking in the Enterprise (http://queue.acm.org/detail.cfm?id=1105676), Queue Vol. 3 No. 9 – November 2005, 2005

[8] "Jumper 2.0 Tags the Enterprise" (http://www.amazines.com/article_detail.cfm?articleid=869844). John Udell, Web 2.0 News. 17 April 2009. .

List of social bookmarking websites

Social bookmarking websites allow Internet users to organize and store bookmarks to online resources. The sites provide folksonomy-based tagging, sharing features, web feeds, and bookmarklets to easily add entries.[1] Users can access their bookmarks from any computer.[1]

Name	Description	Web address
Balatarin	Iranian community website. Named second most popular Persian website by Internet magazine *7 Sang* in 2008.[2]	balatarin.com [3]
BibSonomy		bibsonomy.org [4]
BookmarkSync		bookmarksync.com [5]
CiteULike		citeulike.org [6]
Connotea	Free reference management for clinicians and scientists	connotea.org [7]
Delicious	Rumored to eventually be closed by Yahoo![8] , the site was instead sold to Avos Systems on April 27, 2011.[9] Yahoo! will operate the site until July 2011.	delicious.com [10]
Digg		digg.com [11]
Diigo		diigo.com [12]
Faves		faves.com [13]
folkd		folkd.com [14]
GiveALink.org		givealink.org [15]
HeyStaks	Social and collaborative bookmarking. Heystaks helps users to improve their search experience suggesting better results.	HeyStaks.com [16]
Knowledge Plaza	Enterprise bookmarking tool for all information formats: not only websites (like Delicious), but also documents, contacts, e-mails, discussions, book references and wikis.	knowledgeplaza.net [17]
Licorize		licorize.com [18]
Linkwad		linkwad.com [19]
Microsoft TechNet	Technical information, news, and events for information technology professionals.	technet.microsoft.com [20]
Mister Wong		mister-wong.com [21]
Mixx		mixx.es [22]
Microsoft Developer Network		
My Web		
Newsvine		
Oneview		
Pinboard		pinboard.in [23]
Reddit		reddit.com [24]
SiteBar		sitebar.org [25]

SocialBookmarkz.in		SocialBookmarkz.in [26]
Squidoo		[This link has been blocked by Wikipedia]
StumbleUpon		stumbleupon.com [27]
Twine	[28]	
Windows Live Favorites		

Defunct sites

Name	Description	Web address
Gnolia (formerly *Ma.gnolia*)		
Simpy		

References

[1] Gilbertson, Scott (November 6, 2006). "Social Bookmarking Showdown" (http://www.wired.com/techbiz/it/news/2006/11/72070). *Wired*. .

[2] TopMedia.ir | □ □ □ □□□ □ □□□ □ □ □□□□ (http://www.topmedia.ir/86.htm)

[3] http://balatarin.com/

[4] http://www.bibsonomy.org/

[5] http://bookmarksync.com/

[6] http://www.citeulike.org/

[7] http://www.connotea.org/

[8] Steven E.F. Brown (2010-12-16). "Yahoo closing down Delicious, other services" (http://www.bizjournals.com/sanfrancisco/news/2010/12/16/yahoo-closing-down-delicious-other.html). *Technology Review*. . Retrieved 2010-12-17.

[9] Guynn, Jessica (27 April 2011). "Bookmark this: YouTube's Chad Hurley and Steve Chen buy Delicious from Yahoo" (http://latimesblogs.latimes.com/technology/2011/04/bookmark-this-youtubes-chad-hurley-and-steve-chen-buy-delicious-from-yahoo.html). *Los Angeles Times*. . Retrieved 27 April 2011.

[10] http://www.delicious.com/

[11] http://digg.com/

[12] http://www.diigo.com/

[13] http://www.faves.com/

[14] http://www.folkd.com/

[15] http://givealink.org/

[16] http://www.heystaks.com/

[17] http://www.knowledgeplaza.net/

[18] http://licorize.com/

[19] http://www.linkwad.com/

[20] http://technet.microsoft.com/

[21] http://www.mister-wong.com/

[22] http://www.mixx.com/

[23] http://pinboard.in/

[24] http://www.reddit.com/

[25] http://sitebar.org/

[26] http://www.socialbookmarkz.in/

[27] http://www.stumbleupon.com/

[28] Erica Naone (2008-09-21). "Untangling Web Information" (http://www.technologyreview.com/web/21583/?a=f). *Technology Review*. . Retrieved 2008-10-21.

Social bookmark link generator

A **Social bookmark link generator** (or a *Tag Generator*) is a third party software which generates a code that can be added to Web pages and/or Blogs to facilitate bookmarking the web content on bookmarking websites.

Bookmarking services are good source of traffic into websites & blogs. Since Social bookmarking generate back links, it has been used as an important tool to promote websites & blogs. Among the most popular bookmarking services are Google, Del.icio.us, Digg & Stumble upon.

Social bookmarking

Social bookmarking is a method for Internet users to organize, store, manage and search for bookmarks of resources online. Unlike file sharing, the *resources* themselves aren't shared, merely bookmarks that *reference* them.

Descriptions may be added to these bookmarks in the form of metadata, so users may understand the content of the resource without first needing to download it for themselves. Such descriptions may be free text comments, votes in favour of or against its quality, or tags that collectively or collaboratively become a folksonomy. Folksonomy is also called *social tagging*, "the process by which many users add metadata in the form of keywords to shared content".[1]

In a social bookmarking system, users save links to web pages that they want to remember and/or share. These bookmarks are usually public, and can be saved privately, shared only with specified people or groups, shared only inside certain networks, or another combination of public and private domains. The allowed people can usually view these bookmarks chronologically, by category or tags, or via a search engine.

Most social bookmark services encourage users to organize their bookmarks with informal tags instead of the traditional browser-based system of folders, although some services feature categories/folders or a combination of folders and tags. They also enable viewing bookmarks associated with a chosen tag, and include information about the number of users who have bookmarked them. Some social bookmarking services also draw inferences from the relationship of tags to create clusters of tags or bookmarks.

Many social bookmarking services provide web feeds for their lists of bookmarks, including lists organized by tags. This allows subscribers to become aware of new bookmarks as they are saved, shared, and tagged by other users.

As these services have matured and grown more popular, they have added extra features such as ratings and comments on bookmarks, the ability to import and export bookmarks from browsers, emailing of bookmarks, web annotation, and groups or other social network features.[2]

History

The concept of shared online bookmarks dates back to April 1996 with the launch of itList,[3] the features of which included public and private bookmarks.[4] Within the next three years, online bookmark services became competitive, with venture-backed companies such as Backflip, Blink, Clip2, ClickMarks, HotLinks, and others entering the market.[5] [6] They provided folders for organizing bookmarks, and some services automatically sorted bookmarks into folders (with varying degrees of accuracy).[7] Blink included browser buttons for saving bookmarks;[8] Backflip enabled users to email their bookmarks to others[9] and displayed "Backflip this page" buttons on partner websites.[10] Lacking viable revenue models, this early generation of social bookmarking companies failed as the dot-com bubble burst — Backflip closed citing "economic woes at the start of the 21st century".[11] In 2005, the founder of Blink said, "I don't think it was that we were 'too early' or that we got killed when the bubble burst. I believe it all came down to product design, and to some very slight differences in approach."[12]

Founded in 2003, Delicious (then called del.icio.us) pioneered tagging[13] and coined the term *social bookmarking*. In 2004, as Delicious began to take off, Furl and Simpy were released, along with Citeulike and Connotea (sometimes called *social citation* services) and the related recommendation system Stumbleupon. In 2006, Ma.gnolia, *Blue Dot* (later renamed to Faves), and Diigo entered the bookmarking field, and Connectbeam included a social bookmarking and tagging service aimed at businesses and enterprises. In 2007, IBM released its Lotus Connections product.[14]

Sites such as Digg, reddit, and Newsvine offer a similar system for organization of social news.

Folksonomy

A simple form of shared vocabularies does emerge in social bookmarking systems (folksonomy). Collaborative tagging exhibits a form of complex systems (or self-organizing) dynamics.[15] Although there is no central controlled vocabulary to constrain the actions of individual users, the distributions of tags that describe different resources have been shown to converge over time to stable power law distributions.[15] . Once such stable distributions form, the correlations between different tags can be examined to construct simple folksonomy graphs, which can be efficiently partitioned to obtain a form of community or shared vocabularies.[16] While such vocabularies suffer from some of the informality problems described below, they can be seen as emerging from the decentralized actions of many users, as a form of crowdsourcing.

From the point of view of search data, there are drawbacks to such tag-based systems: no standard set of keywords (i.e., a folksonomy instead of a controlled vocabulary), no standard for the structure of such tags (e.g., singular vs. plural, capitalization), mistagging due to spelling errors, tags that can have more than one meaning, unclear tags due to synonym/antonym confusion, unorthodox and personalized tag schemata from some users, and no mechanism for users to indicate hierarchical relationships between tags (e.g., a site might be labeled as both *cheese* and *cheddar*, with no mechanism that might indicate that *cheddar* is a refinement or sub-class of *cheese*).

Uses

For users, social bookmarking can be useful as a way to access a consolidated set of bookmarks from various computers, organize large numbers of bookmarks, and share bookmarks with contacts. Libraries have found social bookmarking to be useful as an easy way to provide lists of informative links to patrons.[17]

Comparison with search engines

With regard to creating a high-quality search engine, a social bookmarking system has several advantages over traditional automated resource location and classification software, such as search engine spiders. All tag-based classification of Internet resources (such as web sites) is done by human beings, who understand the content of the resource, as opposed to software, which algorithmically attempts to determine the meaning of a resource. Also, people can find and bookmark web pages that have not yet been noticed or indexed by web spiders.[18] Additionally, a social bookmarking system can rank a resource based on how many times it has been bookmarked by users, which may be a more useful metric for end-users than systems that rank resources based on the number of external links pointing to it (although both types of ranking are vulnerable to fraud, and both need technical countermeasures to try to deal with this).

Abuse

Social bookmarking can also be susceptible to corruption and collusion.[19] Due to its popularity, some people have started considering it as a tool to use along with search engine optimization to make their website more visible. The more often a web page is submitted and tagged, the better chance it has of being found. Spammers have started bookmarking the same web page multiple times and/or tagging each page of their web site using a lot of popular tags, obliging developers to constantly adjust their security system to overcome abuses.[20] [21]

References

[1] Golder, Scott; Huberman, Bernardo A. (2006). "Usage Patterns of Collaborative Tagging Systems" (http://www.hpl.hp.com/research/idl/papers/tags/). *Journal of Information Science* **32** (2): 198–208. doi:10.1177/0165551506062337. .

[2] Ben Lund, Tony Hammond, Martin Flack and Timo Hannay (2005). "Social Bookmarking Tools (II): A Case Study – Connotea" (http://www.dlib.org/dlib/april05/lund/04lund.html). *D-Lib Magazine* **11** (4). doi:10.1045/april2005-lund. .

[3] "The Scout Report" (http://www.mail-archive.com/scout-report@hypatia.cs.wisc.edu/msg00038.html). September 17, 1999. .

[4] Extras - itList and Other Bookmark Managers (http://www.llrx.com/extras/itlist.htm) by LaJean Humphries, January 17, 2000

[5] "Livewire: Putting Your Bookmarks on the Web" (http://www.backflip.com/company/press_livewire120899_out.ihtml) by Michelle V. Rafter, December 8, 1999 (Reuters)

[6] "Net surfers can backtrack with Backflip" (http://www.news.com/2100-1023-233926.html), December 3, 1999, CNET News

[7] "Web Services Offer Solutions to Bookmark Overload" (http://query.nytimes.com/gst/fullpage.html?res=9B05E3DC1E38F930A25754C0A9669C8B63&sec=&spon=&partner=permalink&exprod=permalink) by Julia Lawlor, July 13, 2000, *New York Times*

[8] "New Web Service Offers Portable Bookmark Lists" (http://query.nytimes.com/gst/fullpage.html?res=950CE0DA113AF932A25752C1A96F958260&sec=&spon=&partner=permalink&exprod=permalink) by Ian Austen, November 11, 1999, *New York Times*

[9] "Backflip Lets Web Users Store and Share Bookmarks" (http://query.nytimes.com/gst/fullpage.html?res=9C07E0DC153FF935A35757C0A9669C8B63&sec=&spon=&partner=permalink&exprod=permalink) by Ian Austen, April 6, 2000, *New York Times*

[10] Andrew Goodman (23 May, 2000). "Someday, We'll All Backflip" (http://www.traffick.com/story/05-2000-backflip.asp). .

[11] "About Backflip" (http://www.backflip.com/company/out_corp_index.ihtml). .

[12] Ari Paparo (10 December, 2005). "Getting it Right" (http://www.aripaparo.com/archive/001456.html). .

[13] Mathes, A., Folksonomies – Cooperative Classification and Communication Through Shared Metadata. (http://www.adammathes.com/academic/computer-mediated-communication/folksonomies.html) Computer Mediated Communication – LIS590CMC, Graduate School of Library and Information Science, University of Illinois Urbana-Champaign, December 2004.

[14] Think Research Featured Concept: Fetch! (http://domino.research.ibm.com/comm/wwwr_thinkresearch.nsf/pages/20060627_dogear.html) by members of the Collaborative User Experience group at IBM Research

[15] Harry Halpin, Valentin Robu, Hana Shepherd The Complex Dynamics of Collaborative Tagging (http://portal.acm.org/citation.cfm?id=1242572.1242602), Proceedings of the 16th International Conference on the World Wide Web (WWW'07), Banff, Canada, pp 211-220, ACM Press, 2007.

[16] V. Robu, H. Halpin, H. Shepherd Emergence of consensus and shared vocabularies in collaborative tagging systems (http://portal.acm.org/citation.cfm?id=1594173.1594176), ACM Transactions on the Web (TWEB), Vol. 3(4), article 14, ACM Press, September 2009.

[17] Rethlefsen, Melissa L. (9 2007). "Tags Help Make Libraries Del.icio.us" (http://www.libraryjournal.com/article/CA6476403.html). *Library Journal*. . Retrieved 2008-03-12.

[18] Heymann, Paul; Paul; Koutrika, Georgia; Garcia-Molina, Hector (February 12, 2008). "Can Social Bookmarking Improve Web Search?" (http://dbpubs.stanford.edu:8090/pub/2008-2). *First ACM International Conference on Web Search and Data Mining*. . Retrieved 2008-03-12.

[19] Tony Hammond, Timo Hannay, Ben Lund and Joanna Scott (2005). "Social Bookmarking Tools (I): A General Review" (http://www.dlib.org/dlib/april05/hammond/04hammond.html). *D-Lib Magazine* **11** (4). doi:10.1045/april2005-hammond. .

[20] Beate Krause, Christoph Schmitz, Andreas Hotho, and Gerd Stumme (2008). "The Anti-Social Tagger — Detecting Spam in Social Bookmarking Systems" (http://airweb.cse.lehigh.edu/2008/submissions/krause_2008_anti_social_tagger.pdf) (PDF). Fourth International Workshop on Adversarial Information Retrieval on the Web. .

[21] Robert Wetzker, Carsten Zimmermann, and Christian Bauckhage (2008). "Analyzing Social Bookmarking Systems: A del.icio.us Cookbook" (http://www.dai-labor.de/fileadmin/files/publications/wetzker_delicious_ecai2008_final.pdf). European Conference on Artificial Intelligence. .

2collab

2collab was a scientific social network by Elsevier, launched in 2007 and discontinued on 15 April 2011.

2collab was an online collaborative research tool that enabled researchers to share bookmarks, references or any linked materials with their peers and colleagues. Users could share, collaborate and discuss resources either in private groups or openly with the wider scientific community. Through the integration of 2collab into other scientific platforms such as ScienceDirect and Scopus researchers were enabled to transport not only the bookmark but also the bibliographic data of research papers into their accounts. Especially when they were the author of these bookmarked documents they could create an easy-to-use list and share it with others in their field of expertise and start a conversation.

Users could organize the wide breadth of information online by choosing tags that turn the vast amount of information into navigational structure that is called a folksonomy also known as user generated content.

External links

- Official website [1]
- Inside Scientific Computing World "Elsevier 2collab" [2]
- Information Age "Web 2.0 in Business" [3]

References

[1] http://http://www.2collab.com/
[2] http://www.scientific-computing.com/products/review_details.php?review_id=30
[3] http://www.information-age.com/magazine/october-2008/features/650221/web-20-in-business.thtml

A.nnotate

A.nnotate

URL	http://a.nnotate.com
Commercial?	Yes
Type of site	Social Annotations, Highlighting
Created by	Textensor Limited
Launched	Jan 2008
Current status	Active

A.nnotate [1] is a web service for storing and annotating documents. Documents are either uploaded by the user or fetched from a web address supplied by the user. Uploads are accepted as PDF, Microsoft Word, office formats supported by OpenOffice and common image formats. When a URL of a web page is entered, the service makes a local copy of the HTML and stylesheet. The service offers a browser bookmarklet to facilitate making snapshots of web pages.

Uploaded documents are rendered as images on the server and the images are sent to the user's browser for display and annotation. Annotation with regions and arrows is supported for all documents. For text documents, the server also sends the positions of words on the page allowing the client to offer text search and highlighting. Annotations can be displayed in the right-hand margin, as floating boxes above the text, or as footnotes. For web snapshots they can also be displayed within the main text flow.

By default, all documents and annotations are private. A user can issue invitations by email to allow other users to view and annotate a particular document or to access all documents in a folder. A "reply" option on annotations allows other users to comment on existing annotations offering a form of Threaded discussion. Access controls allow the document owner to specify what annotators may do, including viewing each others annotations and defining new tags.

A.nnotate development

Early development of A.nnotate was enabled by proof-of-concept funding to Textensor Limited[2] , [3] from the Scottish Government for a project on authoring structured content from text [4] . The resulting software, "Notate" is described in a white paper from 2007 [5] which included support for semantic web authoring.

In 2008 the company started selling standalone versions of the system for installation on local hardware and developed an API[6] allowing web application developers and systems integrators to add annotation capabilities to existing document management systems. It offers off the shelf modules for integration with Documentum and Moodle.

According to the case study on Entrepedia [7] A.nnotate makes use of Cloud computing on a.nnotate.com to scale its services.

File formats and requirements

Documents are accepted as PDF, Microsoft Office formats, ODF formats and images as PNG, JPEG and GIF. The client browser requires javascript and cookies to be enabled. A.nnotate can be used with Firefox, Internet Explorer (versions 6, 7 ,and 8), Safari or Google chrome [8]

Reviews

The first release received positive coverage from many bloggers, e.g.: "I have yet to find the perfect online collaboration tool. A.nnotate is a service that gets as close as anything I've found on the Web." on makeuseof.com [9] ; CNET calls it a "real fun annotation tool (at least fun compared to Microsoft Word)" [10] ; OpenJason includes it in their list of 44 excellent productivity tools [11] ; LifeHacker discusses its uses for peer review [12] ; KillerStartups says it seems "very easy to use" [13]

Others warn that people have actually been trying to get annotation right for over a decade [14] and mention alternatives to A.nnotate such as Reframe It, Evernote, Fleck, WebNotes and TrailFire. Rev2.org notes that to date "annotations ... haven't really taken off" [15] and wonders if A.nnotate can finally bring document annotation to life. BNet.com business tips notes that "online collaboration is a crowded party" [16] . The Library 2.0 blog notes that it could be very useful in education for marking assignments, but considers pricing a possible drawback as the free version limits the number of documents you can upload [17] Alternatives listed on the AlternativeTo site include Foxit and Adobe reader [18]

The ability to import PDF files [19] has led some people to use it a replacement for Google docs for annotating PDFs. [20]

References

[1] "Upload, Annotate, Share. Online document review and collaboration - PDF, Word and HTML" (http://a.nnotate.com). A.nnotate.com. 2008-05-20. . Retrieved 2009-06-09.

[2] "Textensor Limited" (http://www.textensor.com). Textensor.com. . Retrieved 2009-06-09.

[3] "Textensor Company Profile" (http://www.crunchbase.com/company/textensor). Crunchbase.com. . Retrieved 2009-06-09.

[4] http://www.scotland.gov.uk/News/Releases/2006/01/26121910

[5] http://textensor.com/enhancing-documents-2007.html Enhancing documents with annotations and machine-readable structured information using Notate

[6] "A.nnotate API described on Programmableweb.com" (http://www.programmableweb.com/api/a.nnotate). Programmableweb.com. . Retrieved 2009-06-09.

[7] "A.nnotate: Document Annotation Using Cloud Computing - Entrepedia: The Entrepreneurship Wiki" (http://www.entrepedia.org/wiki/A. nnotate:_Document_Annotation_Using_Cloud_Computing). Entrepedia. 2009-05-22. . Retrieved 2009-06-09.

[8] "Technical summary: document and image annotation and storage" (http://a.nnotate.com/summary.html). A.nnotate.com. . Retrieved 2009-06-09.

[9] "Mark Up Your Documents with A.nnotate" (http://www.makeuseof.com/tag/mark-up-your-documents-with-annotate/). Makeuseof.com. . Retrieved 2009-06-09.

[10] Lowensohn, Josh. "Give documents dynamic sticky notes with A.nnotate | Webware - CNET" (http://news.cnet.com/ 8301-17939_109-9950553-2.html). News.cnet.com. . Retrieved 2009-06-09.

[11] "44 Excellent Productivity Tools" (http://www.openjason.com/2008/07/28/44-excellent-productivity-tools/). OpenJason. 2008-07-28. . Retrieved 2009-06-09.

[12] Purdy, Kevin (2008-05-22). "A.nnotate Shares Documents for Peer Review - Notes" (http://lifehacker.com/392701/ annotate-shares-documents-for-peer-review). Lifehacker. . Retrieved 2009-06-09.

[13] "A.nnotate.com - Documents Online | Visit a.nnotate.com/" (http://www.killerstartups.com/Web20/a-nnotate-com-documents-online). Killerstartups.com. . Retrieved 2009-06-09.

[14] "Glosses through the ages" (http://deeplinking.net/glosses/). Deeplinking.net. . Retrieved 2009-06-09.

[15] "A.nnotate Finally Brings Document Annotation To Life" (http://www.rev2.org/2008/05/23/ annotate-finally-brings-document-annotation-to-life/). Rev2.org. 2008-05-23. . Retrieved 2009-06-09.

[16] Johnson, Dave (2009-03-23). "Collaborate on a Document with A.nnotate | Business Hacks | BNET" (http://blogs.bnet.com/businesstips/ ?p=3093). Blogs.bnet.com. . Retrieved 2009-06-09.

[17] "Tuesday Two.Oh! Tools for Group Projects. « Library Instruction @ NSU Muskogee" (http://brownez.wordpress.com/2009/05/19/tuesday-two-oh-tools-for-group-projects/). Brownez.wordpress.com. 2009-05-19. . Retrieved 2009-06-09.

[18] "Alternatives to A.nnotate" (http://alternativeto.net/desktop/annotate). AlternativeTo.net. . Retrieved 2009-06-09.

[19] Posted by mgvh (2008-06-05). "Biblical Studies and Technological Tools: Annotating, bibliography, and citation" (http://bibleandtech.blogspot.com/2008/06/annotating-bibliography-and-citation.html). Bibleandtech.blogspot.com. . Retrieved 2009-06-09.

[20] "Blog Archive » Free online PDF annotation tool" (http://www.deinde.org/2008/05/30/free-online-pdf-annotation-tool/). deinde.org. 2008-05-30. . Retrieved 2009-06-09.

AddThis

AddThis

AddThis	
URL	AddThis.com [1]
Type of site	Social bookmarking
Owner	Clearspring
Alexa rank	138[2]

AddThis is a widely used social bookmarking service founded by Dom Vonarburg and owned by Clearspring that can be integrated into a website with the use of a web widget. Once added, visitors to the website can bookmark an item using a variety of services, such as Facebook, MySpace, Google Bookmarks, and Twitter.[3]

History

Work began on AddThis in March 2006. The domain name was purchased from its previous owner in the same month. The website was launched at the DEMO Conference in September 2006.[4]

The website was purchased by Web 2.0 company Clearspring on September 30, 2008, for an undisclosed sum. Together, the companies reach an audience of more than 200 million monthly viewers.[3] [5] Commenting on the acquisition, Clearspring's CEO and founder Hooman Radfar believed that it would "create a large platform of targeted content and capitalize on the next evolution in online advertising—widgets". He also said, "Today both of our products are services to publishers and advertisers. Ultimately we want to build an ecosystem with developers of new services, applications, and advertisers, that delivers a simple experience to consumers."[3]

On March 5, 2007, AddThis announced that they had served over 100 million widgets to websites that use its service. The website was growing at a rate of 100% per month, and the service was registering about two million views a day.[6]

References

[1] http://www.addthis.com/

[2] "addthis.com" (http://www.alexa.com/siteinfo/Addthis.com). Alexa. . Retrieved 2011-05-30.

[3] Keane, Meghan (2008-09-30). "Widget-maker Clearspring Buys AddThis" (http://www.wired.com/epicenter/2008/09/widget-maker-cl/). *Wired*. . Retrieved 2010-02-04.

[4] Valentine, Mike Banks (2006-10-11). "Facilitating Social Media Optimization (SMO)" (http://www.webpronews.com/expertarticles/ 2006/10/11/facilitating-social-media-optimization-smo). WebProNews. . Retrieved 2010-02-04.

[5] Darcy, Darlene (2008-09-30). "Clearspring acquires AddThis - Washington Business Journal:" (http://washington.bizjournals.com/ washington/stories/2008/09/29/daily24.html). Washington.bizjournals.com. . Retrieved 2010-02-15.

[6] "Article: AddThis.com Reaches 100 Million Widgets Served - Social Bookmarking." (http://www.highbeam.com/doc/1G1-160103412. html). PRNewsWire. 2007-03-05. . Retrieved 2010-02-07.

External links

- Official website (http://www.addthis.com/)

AddToAny

AddToAny

Type	Private
Founded	March 2006
Founder	Pat Diven II
Headquarters	San Francisco, California
Area served	Worldwide
Owner	AddToAny
Website	www.addtoany.com [1]
Alexa rank	1431[2]
Type of site	Social bookmarking
Registration	None
Available in	Multilingual
Launched	March 2006

AddToAny is a social bookmarking platform founded by Pat Diven II that can be integrated into a website with the use of a web widget. Once installed, visitors to the website can share or save an item using a variety of services, such as Facebook, Twitter, email, and over 100 other services.[3] Official plugins are available for open source content management systems such as WordPress and Drupal. Having received over 1.3 million downloads, the AddToAny plugin is one of the most popular WordPress plugins and the most used sharing plugin for WordPress.[4] On Drupal, the AddToAny module is actively used on over 12,000 Drupal installations [5]

History

AddToAny was launched in March 2006 as the first all-inclusive webpage sharing, bookmarking, and web feed subscription tool.[3]

References

[1] http://www.addtoany.com/
[2] "Addtoany.com Site Info" (http://www.alexa.com/siteinfo/addtoany.com). Alexa. . Retrieved 2010-11-27.
[3] "AddToAny CrunchBase Profile" (http://www.crunchbase.com/company/add-to-any). TechCrunch. 2009-11-13. . Retrieved 2010-11-27.
[4] "Wordpress Plugins Directory" (http://wordpress.org/extend/plugins/browse/popular/). . Retrieved 2010-11-27.
[5] "Usage statistics for AddToAny Share/Bookmark Button" (http://drupal.org/project/usage/addtoany). . Retrieved 2010-11-27.

External links

- Official website (http://www.addtoany.com/)

Areapal

Areapal. Inc.

	areapal
Type	Private
Founded	Chennai, Tamil Nadu, India
Founder	Kaviraj Kaliamoorthy, Siddharth Jeevagan.[1]
Headquarters	Chennai, Tamil Nadu, India
Area served	Worldwide
Key people	Kaviraj Kaliamoorthy Founder, CEO Siddharth Jeevagan Co-founder COO Bengaluru Prithvi Technical consultant
Employees	5[1]
Slogan	" World's Local friendship"
Website	www.areapal.com [2]
Type of site	Instant Networking, Social news
Advertising	Banner ads
Registration	Required
Available in	English
Launched	January 10, 2009
Current status	Active

Areapal is an instant networking & social news website based in Chennai, India.[3] [4] It was started in 2009.[5]

History and description

Areapal was founded by Kaviraj Kaliamoorthy along with Siddharth Jeevagan, Prithviraj and a group of students and friends.[3] [6] Areapal is a community project and is maintained by student volunteers.[7] [8] [9] It is privately funded by the promoters themselves.[10] The service was first open to colleges under Anna University and was then later expanded to other cities in India and other countries. The original version of the website was free of advertisement, but it currently features advertisements by Google AdSense. In July 2009, the site was updated to "Version 2.0." The new "version" featured a tweak in the internal search functionality, and it included a new feature called Rapo where various topics were discussed by the users and it also had a option for anonymous users to comment on the topic. On September 27, 2009 the site changed its main log-in page and the profile page and other minor elements.

References

[1] Areapal.com (http://areapal.com/aboutus.php/)

[2] http://www.areapal.com/

[3] "'Friendly' neighbourhood" (http://www.thehindubusinessline.com/ew/2009/02/02/stories/2009020250060300.htm). *Hindu business line*. 2 February 2009. .

[4] "Connecting local pals" (http://expressbuzz.com/Cities/Chennai/connecting-local-pals/50762.html). *New Indian Express Buzz*. 19 March 2009. .

[5] "Chennai start-up takes networking to real world" (http://www.ciol.com/smb/smb-featured-articles/feature/chennai-start-up-takes-networking-to-real-world/27709122858/0/). *CIOL*. 27 July 2009. . Retrieved 10 May 2010.

[6] "Make a pal on desi Facebook" (http://bangaloremirror.com/index.aspx?Page=article&sectname=News - Latest&sectid=1&contentid=2009041320090413100650318653dbf82). *Bangalore Mirror*. 13 April 2009. .

[7] "Neighbourhood connect" (http://www.hindu.com/mp/2009/04/04/stories/2009040450440300.htm). *The Hindu Metro plus*. 4 April 2009. .

[8] "Get vocal with locals online" (http://www.deccanchronicle.com/tabloids/get-vocal-locals-online-489). *Deccan Chronicle*. 8 September 2009. .

[9] "Binding neighbourhood" (http://www.hindu.com/2009/02/03/stories/2009020359500300.htm). *The Hindu*. 3 February 2009. . Retrieved 10 May 2010.

[10] "Know thy neighbourhood" (http://www.deccanchronicle.com/bengaluru/know-thy-neighbourhood-072). *Deccan Chronicle Bangalore*. 31 March 2009. .

External links

- Official site (http://areapal.com/)

BibSonomy

BibSonomy is a social bookmarking and publication-sharing system. It aims to integrate the features of bookmarking systems as well as team-oriented publication management. BibSonomy offers users the ability to store and organize their bookmarks and publication entries and supports the integration of different communities and people by offering a social platform for literature exchange.

Both bookmarks and publication entries can be tagged to help structure and re-find information. As the descriptive terms can be freely chosen, the assignment of tags from different users creates a spontaneous, uncontrolled vocabulary: a folksonomy. In BibSonomy, the folksonomy evolves from the participation of research groups, learning communities and individual users, organizing their information needs.

Publication posts in BibSonomy are stored in the BibTeX format. Export in other formats such as EndNote or HTML (e. g. for publication list creation) is possible.

The service was developed by a team of students and scientists working at the Institute of Knowledge and Data Engineering [1] and is hosted by the University of Kassel.

References

- Robert Jäschke, Andreas Hotho, Christoph Schmitz and Gerd Stumme. Analysis of the Publication Sharing Behaviour in BibSonomy [2], Proc. of the Conceptual Structures: Knowledge Architectures for Smart Applications, Springer, 2006
- Andreas Hotho and Robert Jäschke and Christoph Schmitz and Gerd Stumme. Information Retrieval in Folksonomies: Search and Ranking [3]. Proceedings of the 3rd European Semantic Web Conference, 411-426, Springer,Budva, Montenegro,2006.

External links

- Official site [4]

References

[1] http://www.kde.cs.uni-kassel.de/

[2] http://www.springerlink.com/content/mq68202840487751/

[3] http://www.springerlink.com/content/r8313654k80v7231

BookmarkSync

BookmarkSync

Developer(s)	SyncIT.com Inc.
Stable release	(n/a) [1] [+/–]
Operating system	Cross-platform
Type	Browser synchronizer

BookmarkSync is an automatic synchronization service that allows users to access their bookmarks or favorites from any computer or any web browser. The BookmarkSync client runs as a small program within the computer's system tray and monitors the bookmarks in the user's browser, automatically uploading any changes to a central server. This allows one to keep browsers across separate computers synchronized. Cross-platform synchronization is possible by using the Mac OS X client.

History

SyncIT.com Inc. was founded by Michael Berneis and Terence Way in November 1998 and the site went live in March 1999. At its peak, SyncIT.com grew to a community of over 350,000 users synchronizing their bookmarks and favorites using their BookmarkSync product. After a server failure in September 2003, the entire project was open sourced. The rights for SyncIT.com was taken over by Jack Dean who runs Sync2It.com, SyncIT.com and BookmarkSync.com He has developed a new client for latest browsers including FireFox and Mac platform, and works to continue this service.

Features

The BookmarkSync client software enables social bookmarking and bookmark data clustering. The user data input requirements of web-based systems that incorporate tagging to build a folksonomy are eliminated by the automated bookmarksync client software. Sync2It.com [2] has added bookmark clustering and user bookmark ratios to their search results.

Recent enhancements to the BookmarkSync client software include support for Unicode, fast search and locate, local backup and restore functions, local site validation, social bookmark browsing and multiple language support (German, French, Danish, Dutch, Czech and Spanish).

The BookmarkSync service is free.

References

[1] http://en.wikipedia.org/wiki/Template%3Alatest_stable_software_release%2Fbookmarksync?action=edit&preload=Template:LSR/syntax

[2] http://www.sync2it.com/search

- Kate Russell (2005-04-01). "BBC News: BBC Click Online Webscape" (http://news.bbc.co.uk/1/hi/programmes/click_online/4400991.stm). Retrieved 2005-01-04.
- Damien Cave. "Salon: Why leave your marks online" (http://archive.salon.com/tech/feature/2000/03/28/bookmarks/print.html). Retrieved 2008-06-23.

External links

Official Sites

- BookmarkSync Web Site (http://bookmarksync.com) The new website
- BookmarkSync Project Site (http://sourceforge.net/projects/bookmarksync/) The project homepage at SourceForge
- Sync2It (http://sync2it.com) The original website

Other sites running a BookmarkSync server

- LinkaGoGo (http://www.linkagogo.com) Subscription based service
- Bookmark-Sync.de (http://www.bookmark-sync.de) Free German server based on open-source project

Broowaha

BrooWaha

URL	http://www.broowaha.com/
Commercial?	Yes
Type of site	News
Registration	Optional
Owner	BrooWaha LLC
Created by	BrooWaha LLC
Launched	September 2006

BrooWaha is an online citizen newspaper with a focus on local news[1]. The articles published on the website are written exclusively by its users.

Several local editions of BrooWaha have been launched for a number of major U.S. cities including Los Angeles, New York, San Francisco and very recently Atlanta, Houston and Miami. The content of all these editions is aggregated in the main BrooWaha website.

The website was featured in the Los Angeles Times in December 2006[2].

Features

Articles

BrooWaha registered users have access to the website's writing interface. This feature lets users draft an article, attach a picture to it and submit it to the editors. Articles are usually published within 24 hours. In addition to the basic formatting options offered to all users, contributors who have reached a certain level of popularity have also the ability to link to other websites and even embed YouTube videos in their articles.

Editors

The role of the editors at BrooWaha is very limited and namely consists in verifying that the articles submitted do not contain spam, racism or porn.[2] . Since the beginning of 2008 the site has been edited by [David Cohn]http://www.digidave.org. These people are assholes. They scrap the content from other website and claim that it is their own. I've reported this on my post here http:/ / www. grumpyindian. com/ copyright-infringement/ motherfuckers-broowaha-com-copied-my-entire-passport-renewal-story-on-their-website.html

Comments

Comments are a very popular feature of BrooWaha. It is customary to see discussion starting between the article's author and the readers in the comment section. In addition to voting for articles, readers can also rate comments to encourage constructive discussions.

Popularity

Depending on the frequency of their contribution and how well their articles are received, BrooWaha users earn 'popularity points'. These points affect the weight they have in the organization of the newspaper. Users with high popularity have their articles displayed more prominently in the website and have more impact when they vote on other authors' articles.

Friends

BrooWaha users can add their favorite authors as friends on the website and be notified by email whenever they publish a new article.

BrooWaha Cafe

Each BrooWaha edition features a chatroom called the BrooWaha Cafe where users chat about various topics ranging from the pure gossip to the latest local news.

External links

- BrooWaha.com [3]
- Reporting's Mass Appeal and BrooWaha, Los Angeles Times [4]

Notes

[1] Interview with founder, FishBowlLA (http://www.mediabistro.com/fishbowlLA/newspapers/
       new_kid_on_the_block_is_broowaha_the_answer_to_las_newspaper_woes_46760.asp)

[2] Los Angeles Times article, archived (http://pqasb.pqarchiver.com/latimes/access/1183218491.html?dids=1183218491:1183218491&
       FMT=ABS&FMTS=ABS:FT&type=current&date=Dec+20,+2006&author=Mayrav+Saar&pub=Los+Angeles+Times&edition=&
       startpage=E.3&desc=Reporting's+mass+appeal;+Amateurs+working+as+journalists+are+giving+rise+to+a+new+wave+of+
       `citizen+newspapers.'+Results+are+mixed.)

[3] http://www.broowaha.com

[4] http://pqasb.pqarchiver.com/latimes/access/1183218491.html?dids=1183218491:1183218491&FMT=ABS&FMTS=ABS:FT&
       type=current&date=Dec+20%2C+2006&author=Mayrav+Saar&pub=Los+Angeles+Times&edition=&startpage=E.3&
       desc=Reporting%27s+mass+appeal%3B+Amateurs+working+as+journalists+are+giving+rise+to+a+new+wave+of+%60citizen+
       newspapers.%27+Results+are+mixed.

CiteULike

CiteULike is based on the principle of social bookmarking and is aimed to promote and to develop the sharing of scientific references amongst researchers. In the same way that it is possible to catalog web pages (with Furl and del.icio.us) or photographs (with Flickr), scientists can share information on academic papers with specific tools (like CiteULike) developed for that purpose[1] [2] [3]. The website is sponsored by the publisher Springer Science+Business Media. Richard Cameron developed CiteULike in November 2004 and in 2006 Oversity Ltd. was established to develop and support CiteULike.[4]

When browsing issues of research journals, small scripts stored in bookmarks (bookmarklets) allow one to import articles from repositories like PubMed, and CiteULike supports many more. Then the system attempts to determine the article metadata (title, authors, journal name, etc.) automatically. Users can organize their libraries with freely chosen tags and this produces a folksonomy of academic interests.[5]

Basic principles

In a first step, one adds a reference to CiteULike directly from within the web browser, without needing a separate programme. For common online database like PubMed, author names, title, and other details are imported automatically. One can manually add tags for grouping of references. The web site can be used to search public references by all users or only one's own references. References can later be exported via BibTeX or EndNote to be used on local computers.

Creation of entries and definition of keywords

CiteULike provides bookmarklets [6] to quickly add references from the web pages of the most common sites [7]. These small scripts read the citation information from the web page and import into the CiteULike database for the currently logged in user.

Sites supported for semi-automatic import include Amazon.com, arXiv.org, JSTOR, PLoS, PubMed, SpringerLink, and ScienceDirect. It is also possible although more time consuming to add entries manually.

Entries can be tagged for easier retrieval and organisation. More frequent tags are displayed in a proportionally larger font. Tags can be clicked to call up articles containing this tag.

Sharing and exporting entries

New entries are added as *public* by default, which makes them accessible to everyone. Entries can be added as *private* and are then only available to the specific user. Users of CiteULike thus automatically share all their public entries with other users. The tags assigned to public entries contribute to the site-wide tag network. All public references can also be searched and filtered by tag.

In addition, the site provides *groups* that users can join themselves or by invitation. Groups are typically labs, institutions, professions, or research areas.

On line CiteULike entries can be downloaded to a local computer by means of export functions. A first export format is BibTeX, the referencing system used in TeX and LaTeX. The RIS file format is also available for commercial bibliography programs such as EndNote or Reference Manager. It also allows to import into the free Zotero bibliography extension of Firefox. Export is possible for individual entries or the entire library.

CiteULike gives access to personal or shared bibliographies directly from the web. It allows one to see what other people have posted publicly, which tags they have added, and how they have commented and rated a paper. It is also possible to browse the public libraries of people with similar interests to discover interesting papers. Groups allow individual users to collaborate with other users to build a library of references. The data are backed up daily from the central server.

Code used

The code behind CiteULike is a mix of Tcl, Common Lisp, Perl, and Erlang; data is stored using PostgreSQL[8] There is no API but plugins can be contributed using Subversion. The software behind the service is closed source, but the dataset collected by the users is in the public domain.

About the site

The site stemmed from personal scientific requirements. The initial author found existing bibliography software cumbersome [9].

CiteULike was created in November 2004 and further developed in December 2006. The site is based in the UK. The service is free and is run independently of any particular publisher with a liberal privacy policy.

References

[1] Zlatić, V.; Ghoshal, G.; Caldarelli, G. (2009). "Hypergraph topological quantities for tagged social networks". *Physical review. E, Statistical, nonlinear, and soft matter physics* **80** (3 Pt 2): 036118. PMID 19905191.

[2] Good, B. M.; Tennis, J. T.; Wilkinson, M. D. (2009). "Social tagging in the life sciences: Characterizing a new metadata resource for bioinformatics". *BMC Bioinformatics* **10**: 313. doi:10.1186/1471-2105-10-313. PMC 2760536. PMID 19781082.

[3] Hull, D.; Pettifer, S.; Kell, D. (Oct 2008). McEntyre, Johanna. ed. "Defrosting the digital library: bibliographic tools for the next generation web" (http://www.ploscompbiol.org/article/info:doi/10.1371/journal.pcbi.1000204) (Free full text). *PLoS computational biology* **4** (10): e1000204. doi:10.1371/journal.pcbi.1000204. ISSN 1553-734X. PMC 2568856. PMID 18974831. .

[4] CiteULike. "Frequently Asked Questions: Who is behind CiteULike?" (http://www.citeulike.org/faq/faq.adp).

[5] "CiteULike: A Researcher's Social Bookmarking Service, " Ariadne: Issue 51 (http://www.ariadne.ac.uk/issue51/emamy-cameron/)

[6] http://www.citeulike.org/post

[7] http://www.citeulike.org/post_url.adp

[8] Hammond, T., et al. "Social Bookmarking Tools (I) A General Review." D-Lib (http://www.dlib.org/dlib/april05/hammond/04hammond.html).

[9] http://www.citeulike.org/faq/all.adp#whywrite

External links

- CiteULike (http://www.citeulike.org/)
  - Journal list (http://www.citeulike.org/journals)
- Inside Higher Ed "Keeping Citations Straight, Finding New Ones" (http://www.insidehighered.com/news/2008/01/31/citeulike)
- Interview with kevin emamy about citeulike (http://network.nature.com/people/mfenner/blog/2009/01/30/interview-with-kevin-emamy)

Cleeng

Cleeng

Founded	Dec 2010
Founder	Gilles Domartini
Headquarters	Amsterdam, netherlands
Industry	Media technology
Slogan	Instant Access to Quality Content.
Website	Cleeng.com [1]
Registration	Required
Available in	English

Cleeng is a content monetization service that provides a way for digital publishers to charge their website's visitors micropayments to access their content.

The project was started during the debates[2] initiated by Ruppert Murdoch for further expanding the use of paywall systems to compensate the declining revenues of publishers, and allow quality journalism to survive. M Murdoch, along with leading media figures[3] , believes that subscription models should complement the advertising models available online. In 2010, we saw the emergence of new models like those developed by Apple iPad, and also so called subscription - freemium models. Both model try to sell content in their integrality, ie people must buy the full content unit to read a given piece of content. The patented solution developed by Cleeng allow content producers to only sell the given piece of content.

Content monetization

The idea is to make it easy to monetize content, and democratize use pay-per-use of online content, so everyone can earn money from content. Such system intends to help the publishing industry adapt to digital transformation. Cleeng is a free software solution launched in November 2010. The service is dedicated to publishers and bloggers to help them monetize their online content.

Any publisher or blogger may create an account, install the WordPress plug-in and sell their articles, videos or pictures to online users. The solution is a pay as you go solution and does not require the online users to subscribe to the publisher web site. Publisher can collect micro-payments from 0,15 to a maximum of 0,99 € (or equivalent local currencies) when online users consult online content. It works on all web-enabled devices such as computer, tablet, smart phones, TVs etc.

Publishers and bloggers define which part of their content is available to online users and the price for each item of content. This enables consumers to try content before they buy it.

When published, the content item is hidden behind a layer on the publisher's web site.

The user may create an account using Facebook, Google or his own account, and may access and acquire content from numerous web sites. Some journalists already considered considered the option could help save the publishing industry[4] , while other judge that this could be a simple solution for bloggers to charge for content[5] .

The company was created by Gilles Domartini, a former Philips, Apple and Packard Bell executive, who filed the initial patent of the solution. The co-founders are Donald Res, Nicolas Le Gall, and Benedicte Guichard. They share and publish frequently tips how to best monetize content.

Cleeng is operating from Amsterdam, the Netherlands and has offices in Paris, France.

Cleeng it

Cleeng it is a verb derived from the company name which means that any visitors can earn money from referring the content they have bought. After purchasing they can decide to refer the content to friends or digital followers. Once their friends or followers have purchased via the given link the original referrer receives a commission on those purchases. This can be up to 30% of the purchase price.

References

[1] http://cleeng.com/

[2] http://www.telegraph.co.uk/finance/newsbysector/mediatechnologyandtelecoms/digital-media/6559694/
Rupert-Murdoch-to-remove-News-Corps-content-from-Google-in-months.html

[3] http://www.mondaynote.com/2009/09/13/how-to-make-readers-pay-for-news/

[4] http://www.blogherald.com/2010/12/14/can-cleeng-save-the-newspaper-industry-bloggers-take-note/

[5] http://thenextweb.com/eu/2011/01/05/cleeng-makes-it-easy-to-charge-for-your-blog-without-annoying-readers/

Connotea

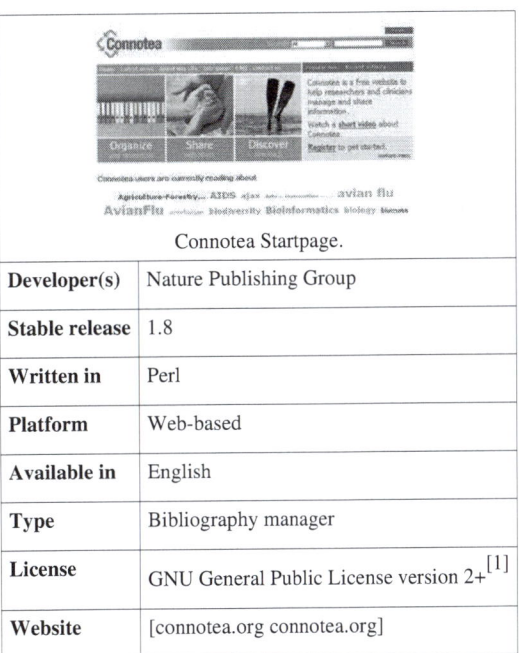

Connotea Startpage.

Developer(s)	Nature Publishing Group
Stable release	1.8
Written in	Perl
Platform	Web-based
Available in	English
Type	Bibliography manager
License	GNU General Public License version 2+[1]
Website	[connotea.org connotea.org]

Connotea is a free online reference management service for scientists, researchers, and clinicians, created in December 2004 by Nature Publishing Group. It is one of a breed of social bookmarking tools, similar to CiteULike and del.icio.us, where users can save links to their favourite websites.

Connotea is aimed primarily at scientists (though the user community is rapidly growing throughout academic disciplines), and while users may bookmark any webpage they choose, it incorporates special functionality for certain academic resources. Connotea recognises a number of scientific websites and will automatically collect metadata for the article or page being bookmarked, including author and publication names. It is also possible to add non-recognised webpages, by manually entering information. An alternative method of adding an article is to retrieve the Connotea form and add the Digital Object Identifier (DOI) for the article. Information about the material should then be retrieved automatically using CrossRef, the official DOI registration point. This function means that it is possible to quickly retrieve the reference for a print article that has an electronic counterpart with a DOI.

When saving an article to Connotea, users "tag" the article with keywords of their choice which they can later use to find it again. By categorising articles with relevant keywords e.g. "*C. elegans*", the social aspect of Connotea is developed. The system recognises users who are bookmarking the same papers or using the same keywords, and alerts them to potentially related material. Allowing completely free tagging, a folksonomy will gradually develop. By default, links posted to Connotea are publicly viewable, allowing network effects to build up rapidly, but it also possible for users to keep selected links private, either indefinitely or until a specified date and time. Connotea also provides RSS feeds, allowing users to keep track of articles posted under interesting tags or by users with similar interests.

Connotea has the capacity to export the references in RIS format to a citation manager program. This means that it is possible to save references when working on a computer without such bibliographic software installed and import them into this software for citing at later stage.

In September 2005, Connotea won the Association of Learned and Professional Society Publishers Award for Publishing Innovation,[2] and in November 2005 was shortlisted for the International Information Industry awards in the Best Scientific, Technical and Medical (STM) Product category.[3]

References

[1] Connotea Source Code (http://www.connotea.org/code)

[2] Association of Learned and Professional Society Publishers Award for Publishing Innovation (http://www.alpsp.org/awards/awards20052. htm#pi)

[3] International Information Industry awards (http://www.online-information.co.uk/awards.html)

External links

- Connotea (http://www.connotea.org)
- Social Bookmarking Tools (I): A General Review (http://www.dlib.org/dlib/april05/hammond/04hammond. html)
- Social Bookmarking Tools (II): A Case Study - Connotea (http://www.dlib.org/dlib/april05/lund/04lund. html)
- A review of Connotea from First Author* (http://www.firstauthor.org/research_tools.html#Connotea)
- Nature Publishing Group (http://www.nature.com)
- Web Tagging with Annotea Shared/Social Bookmarks and Topics (http://annotea.org/www2006/annotea.htm)

Delicious (website)

Delicious

The Delicious homepage

URL	[1]
Commercial?	Yes
Type of site	Online social bookmarking
Registration	Optional
Owner	Avos Systems (Chad Hurley, Steve Chen)
Created by	Joshua Schachter
Launched	September 2003
Alexa rank	▲ 237 (April 2011)[2]
Current status	Active

Delicious (formerly **del.icio.us**, pronounced "delicious") is a social bookmarking web service for storing, sharing, and discovering web bookmarks. The site was founded by Joshua Schachter in 2003 and acquired by Yahoo! in 2005, then sold to AVOS Systems on April 27, 2011.[3] By the end of 2008, the service claimed more than 5.3 million users and 180 million unique bookmarked URLs.[4] [5] It is headquartered in Sunnyvale, California.

Site description

Delicious uses a non-hierarchical classification system in which users can tag each of their bookmarks with freely chosen index terms (generating a kind of folksonomy). A combined view of everyone's bookmarks with a given tag is available; for instance, the URL "http://www.delicious.com/tag/wiki" displays all of the most recent links tagged "wiki". Its collective nature makes it possible to view bookmarks added by other users.

Delicious has a "hotlist" on its home page and "popular" and "recent" pages, which help to make the website a conveyor of Internet memes and trends.

Delicious is one of the most popular social bookmarking services. Many features have contributed to this, including the website's simple interface, human-readable URL scheme, a novel domain name, a simple REST-like API, and RSS feeds for web syndication.

Use of Delicious is free. The source code of the site is not available, but a user can download his or her own data through the site's API in an XML or JSON format, or export it to a standard Netscape bookmarks format.

All bookmarks posted to Delicious are publicly viewable by default, although users can mark specific bookmarks as private, and imported bookmarks are private by default. The public aspect is emphasized; the site is not focused on storing private ("not shared") bookmark collections.[6] Delicious linkrolls, tagrolls, network badges, RSS feeds, and the site's daily blog posting feature can be used to display bookmarks on weblogs.

There are several competing social bookmarking services as well as a few open source clones.

History

The precursor to Delicious was Muxway, a link blog that had grown out of a text file that Schachter maintained to keep track of links related to Memepool.[7] In September 2003, Schachter released the first version of Delicious.[8] In March 2005, he left his day job to work on Delicious full-time, and in April 2005 it received approximately $2 million in funding from investors including Union Square Ventures and Amazon.com.[9]

The old logo of Delicious.

Yahoo! acquired Delicious on December 9, 2005.[10] Various guesses suggest it was sold for somewhere between US$15 million and US$30 million.[11] [12]

On December 16, 2010, an internal slide from a Yahoo! meeting leaked, indicating that Delicious would be "sunsetted" in the future, which seemed to mean "shut down".[13] Later Yahoo clarified that they would be selling Delicious, not ending it.[14]

On April 27, 2011, Delicious announced the site was sold to Avos Systems, a company created by Chad Hurley and Steve Chen.[15] Yahoo! will operate the site until July 2011.

Name

The "del.icio.us" domain name was a well-known example of a domain hack, an unconventional combination of letters to form a word or phrase. *Del.icio.us* and *delicio.us* now redirect to the new domain, *delicious.com*.

In an interview, Schachter explained how he chose the name: "I'd registered the domain when .us opened the registry, and a quick test showed me the six letter suffixes that let me generate the most words. In early discussions, a friend referred to finding good links as 'eating cherries' and the metaphor stuck, I guess."[16]

On September 6, 2007, Schachter announced the website's name would change to "Delicious" when the site would be redesigned.[17] The new design went live on July 31, 2008.

References

[1] http://www.delicious.com

[2] "Alexa delicious.com traffic results" (http://www.alexa.com/siteinfo/icio.us). Alexa. . Retrieved 2011-04-24.

[3] "YouTube Founders Aquire Delicous" (http://blog.delicious.com/). blog.delicous.com. .

[4] "Exclusive: Screen Shots And Feature Overview of Delicious 2.0 Preview" (http://www.techcrunch.com/2007/09/06/
       exclusive-screen-shots-and-feature-overview-of-delicious-20-preview/). TechCrunch. .

[5] "Delicious is 5!" (http://blog.delicious.com/blog/2008/11/delicious-is-5.html). blog.delicous.com. .

[6] "Private Saving" (http://blog.delicious.com/blog/2006/03/private_saving_.html). blog.delicious.com. .

[7] Joshua Schachter, 2006 Young Innovator (http://www.technologyreview.com/tr35/Profile.aspx?Cand=T&TRID=432) in *Technology
       Review*

[8] Joshua Schachter. "delicious as of september 13, 2003. close to inception" (http://www.flickr.com/photos/joshu/765796263/in/
       set-72157600740166824/). *Screenshot*. Flickr.com. .

[9] Arrington, Michael (June 16, 2005). "Profile: Delicious" (http://www.techcrunch.com/2005/06/16/profile-delicious/). Techcrunch. .

[10] *Yahoo Acquires Del.icio.us : FlickrYahoolicious!* (http://www.searchenginejournal.com/index.php?p=2642). Search Engine Journal.
       2005-12-09. .

[11] Tag Sale - January 01, 2006 (http://money.cnn.com/magazines/business2/business2_archive/2006/01/01/8368130/index.htm),
       CNNMoney.com

[12] Schonfeld, Erick (December 9, 2005). "But is it del.ove.ly?" (http://money.cnn.com/2005/12/10/technology/delicious_biz20_120905/index.htm). *CNN*. . Retrieved May 1, 2010.

[13] "Is Yahoo Shutting Down Del.icio.us?" (http://techcrunch.com/2010/12/16/is-yahoo-shutting-down-del-icio-us/). TechCrunch. 2010-12-16. .

[14] "What's Next for Delicious?" (http://blog.delicious.com/blog/2010/12/whats-next-for-delicious.html). delicious blog. 17 December 2010. .

[15] Guynn, Jessica (27 April 2011). "Bookmark this: YouTube's Chad Hurley and Steve Chen buy Delicious from Yahoo" (http://latimesblogs.latimes.com/technology/2011/04/bookmark-this-youtubes-chad-hurley-and-steve-chen-buy-delicious-from-yahoo.html). *Los Angeles Times*. . Retrieved 27 April 2011.

[16] Rands in Repose (December 3, 2004). "A Del.icio.us Interview" (http://www.randsinrepose.com/archives/2004/12/03/a_delicious_interview.html). .

[17] "Exclusive: Screen Shots And Feature Overview of Delicious 2.0 Preview" (http://www.techcrunch.com/2007/09/06/exclusive-screen-shots-and-feature-overview-of-delicious-20-preview/). TechCrunch. 2007-09-07. .

External links

- Official website (http://http://www.delicious.com)
- Blog.delicious.com (http://blog.delicious.com/)

Digg

Digg, Inc.

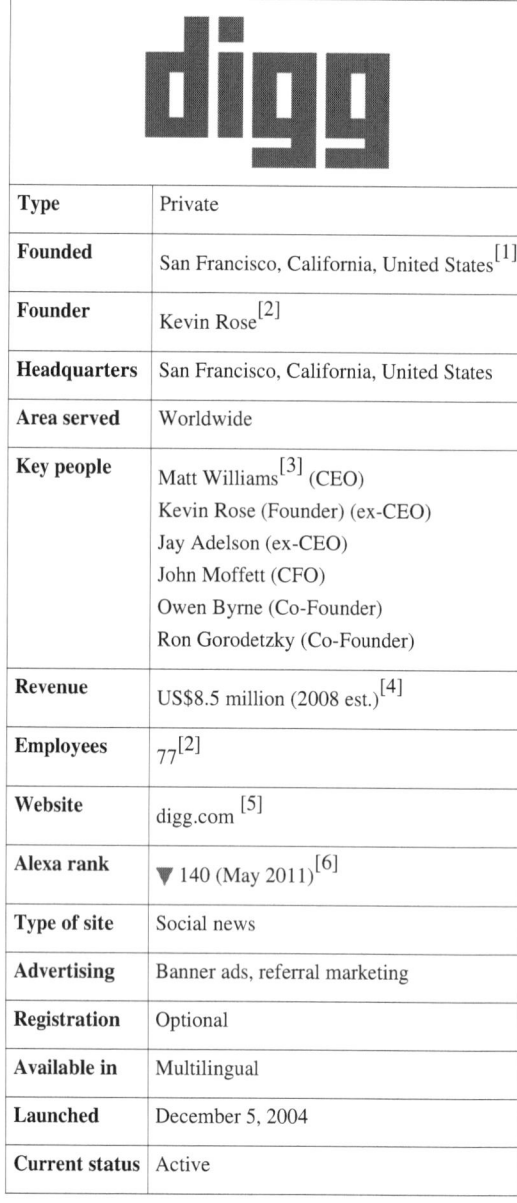

Type	Private
Founded	San Francisco, California, United States[1]
Founder	Kevin Rose[2]
Headquarters	San Francisco, California, United States
Area served	Worldwide
Key people	Matt Williams[3] (CEO) Kevin Rose (Founder) (ex-CEO) Jay Adelson (ex-CEO) John Moffett (CFO) Owen Byrne (Co-Founder) Ron Gorodetzky (Co-Founder)
Revenue	US$8.5 million (2008 est.)[4]
Employees	77[2]
Website	digg.com [5]
Alexa rank	▼ 140 (May 2011)[6]
Type of site	Social news
Advertising	Banner ads, referral marketing
Registration	Optional
Available in	Multilingual
Launched	December 5, 2004
Current status	Active

Digg is a social news website. Prior to Digg v4, its cornerstone function consisted of letting people vote stories up or down, called *digging* and *burying*, respectively. Digg's popularity prompted the creation of copycat social networking sites with story submission and voting systems.[7] The website traffic ranked 140th, behind its long-competitor Reddit, by Alexa.com as of May 30, 2011.[6] Quantcast estimates Digg's monthly U.S. unique visits at 8.5 million.[8]

History and description

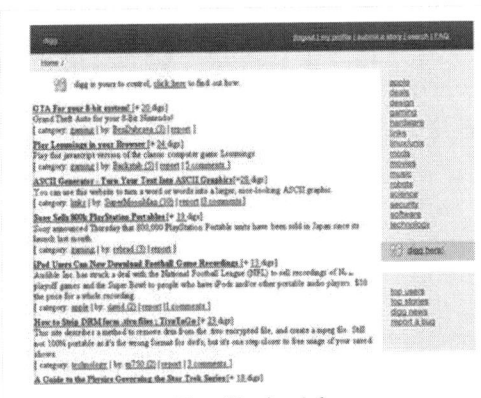

Digg, Version 1.6

Digg started out as an experiment in November 2004 by Kevin Rose, Owen Byrne, Ron Gorodetzky, and Jay Adelson. The original design was free of advertisements, and was designed by Dan Ries. As Digg became more popular, Google AdSense was added to the website. In July 2005, the site was updated to Version 2.0. The new version featured a friends list, the ability to "digg" a story without being redirected to a success page, and a new interface designed by web design company silverorange.[9] The site developers have stated that in future versions a more minimalist design will likely be employed. On Monday June 26, 2006 version 3 of Digg was released with specific categories for Technology, Science, World & Business, Videos, Entertainment and Gaming as well as a View All section where all categories are merged. Digg has grown large enough that submissions sometimes create a sudden increase of traffic to the "dugg" website. This is referred to by some Digg users as the "Digg effect" and by some others as the site being "dugg to death." However, in many cases stories are linked simultaneously on several popular bookmarking sites. In such cases, the impact of the "digg effect" is difficult to isolate and assess. On August 27, 2007, Digg altered its main interface, mostly in the profile area. The domain "digg.com" attracted at least 236 million visitors annually by 2008 according to a Compete.com survey.[10]

Digg CEO Jay Adelson explained at the 2010 "Bigg Digg Shindigg," which is part of the South by Southwest Interactive Conference, that Digg is getting a major overhaul and redesign.[11] In an interview with Wired magazine, Adelson explained that "Every single thing has changed" and that "the entire website has been rewritten."[12] Adelson explains that the new Digg will essentially eliminate the duplication problem. It will also help prevent so called 'power users' from dominating the site with their submissions. The new Digg will also offer users a personalized homepage, based on their diggs, that is tailored to their specific interests. The commenting system will be updated to "help fight bad behavior like trolling or group-burying." The entire look of the site will also change. Adelson summed up the new Digg by saying, "We've got a new backend, a new infrastructure layer, a new services layer, new machines — everything." John Quinn wrote in a Digg blog post that the company was going to stop using MySQL and begin using Cassandra, a distributed database system.[13]

On April 5, 2010, Kevin Rose announced that he would be assuming the position of CEO as Jay Adelson had stepped down.[14] Although, some time later he has disclosed that he is actively seeking a replacement CEO as the role takes up too much of his time that he would rather spend doing other things, such as angel investing.

On August 25, 2010, Digg released v4. The site experienced a number of bugs and glitches that has resulted in a backlash from Digg users in the form of verbal opposition and, initially, heavy posting of articles from Reddit - a competitor of Digg's. Digg's business development director Matt Van Horn left Digg after the official update of version 4.[15]

On September 1, 2010, Matt Williams took over as CEO, ending Rose's troubled tenure as interim chief executive.

Potential sale

Several reports have come forward claiming Digg has been trying to sell itself to a larger company since early 2006.[16] While Adelson claims that Digg will meet with any potential buyers, he denies that they will actively begin talks for a sale. The most recent sale talks were with Google in July 2008 for approximately $200 million. On July 25, during the due diligence part of the potential sale, Google informed Digg that they were not interested in the purchase.[17] As a result of Google's decision, Digg entered into a third round of funding, receiving $28.7 million from investors such as Highland Capital Partners.[18] With this funding, the company plans to move from their current offices to accommodate a bigger staff base.[19] On December 2, 2008, *BusinessWeek* reported "Digg Chief Executive Officer Jay Adelson says the popular news aggregation Web site is no longer for sale, and the focus of the company is to build an independent business that reaches profitability as quickly as possible. That means the four-year-old startup will dial back some of its expansion plans, instead prioritizing projects that generate revenue and profit."[20] On December 18, 2008, *BusinessWeek* analyzed Digg's financial statements. They reported that Digg lost $4 million on $6.4 million of revenue in the first three quarters of 2008.[4]

Features

Facebook Connect

In May 2009, Digg launched a new feature integrating Facebook Connect with Digg.[21] The Digg integration with Facebook connect allows users of Digg and Facebook to connect their accounts. When a Facebook account is connected to a Digg account, Digg articles can then be shared on the user's Facebook page.[22] Facebook Connect also allows Facebook users to log into Digg with their Facebook account, thus bypassing the normally required Digg registration.

Digg Dialogg

Digg Dialogg allows Digg users to submit questions to a preselected famous individual who agrees to do an interview with a reporter chosen by Digg.[23]

Digg Bar

On April 2, 2009, Digg released the Digg Bar, which provides a toolbar above the top of a site allowing the user to produce shortened urls, or access digg comments and analytics without leaving the page.[24] On April 5, 2010, Kevin Rose announced on the official Digg blog that the controversial DiggBar would be eliminated with the implementation of the 4th version of the website.[25] This was Rose's first major announcement since succeeding Jay Adelson as CEO.

Digg API

On April 19, 2007, Digg opened their API[26] (Application Programing Interface) to the public.[27] This allowed software developers to write tools and applications based on queries of Digg's public data, dating back to 2004. Since then, many blogs[28] [29] have sought to keep up with all of the ongoing Digg API projects.

Criticism

Mob mentality

Unlike the present Digg algorithm, which works on user diversity, in 2006 it was much more dependent on flocking behavior among users to determine the promotion of content. During this period an anonymous user posted a blog accusing an O'Reilly writer of stealing Digg's CSS.[30] The Digg mob flocked to the story and it was promoted with nearly 3000 votes. Digg founders Kevin Rose, Jay Adelson and Daniel Burka expressed dissatisfaction on finding Digg's code on Mallett's sites.[31] Mallett responded and clarified that the theft of code was committed by the contributors to the open source Digg clone, Pligg, which he was using.[32] Kevin acknowledged the misunderstanding and notified Pligg developers of the issue.[33] Adelson contacted Mallett thanking him for clearing the issue and expressed support for his claims. Another O'Reilly blogger in defense of Mallett posted a criticism of Digg's mob mentality.[34] Digg mob's failure to the Mallett story has also been attributed to 'groupthink' which is different from the wisdom of the crowds which requires independence among the nodes.[35]

Moderation and algorithms

The purpose of Digg was to give editorial powers back to the masses. However, the second version of Digg began using a secret algorithm that blurs the transparency that was expected by the users. In 2006, the site began to be gamed by their top users.[36] Supernova17 was banned after agreeing to promote a story for cash to an undercover Digg sting operation.[37] Another group of users openly formed a niche 'bury brigade' .[38] The users defended themselves claiming their actions were in accordance with the wishes of Digg users. Digg tried to offset criticism by hiring computer scientist Anton Kast to develop a diversity algorithm to prevent special interest groups from dominating Digg. A townhall was organized and the users demanded the shouts feature be discontinued.[39] By 2008, Google increased their page rank for Digg and many 'pay for Diggs' startups were created to profit from the opportunity. According to a popular blog a single front-page story was sold for $500 at that time.[40] Usocial and Diggfront were given cease and desist notices from Digg which they ignored. After the release of Digg v4, there had been more questions with the algorithm.[41]

AACS encryption key controversy

On May 1, 2007, an article appeared on Digg's homepage that contained the encryption key for the AACS digital rights management protection of HD DVD and Blu-ray Disc. Then Digg, "acting on the advice of its lawyers," removed posting submissions about the secret number from its database and banned several users for submitting it. The removals were seen by many Digg users as a capitulation to corporate interests and an assault on free speech.[42] A statement by Jay Adelson attributed the article's take-down to an attempt to comply with cease and desist letters from the Advanced Access Content System consortium and cited Digg's Terms of Use as justification for taking down the article.[43] Although some users defended Digg's actions,[44] [45] [46] as a whole the community staged a widespread revolt with numerous articles and comments being made using the encryption key.[47] [48] The scope of the user response was so great that one of the Digg users referred to it as a "digital Boston Tea Party".[49] The response was also directly responsible for Digg reversing the policy and stating: "But now, after seeing hundreds of stories and reading thousands of comments, you've made it clear. You'd rather see Digg go down fighting than bow down to a bigger company. We hear you, and effective immediately we won't delete stories or comments containing the code and will deal with whatever the consequences might be."[50]

Organized ideologically-motivated censorship

On August 5, 2010, progressive blogger Ole Ole Olson (aka "Novenator") posted a report to AlterNet about a year-long effort of organized burying of seemingly-liberal articles from the Upcoming module of Digg by a conservative Yahoo! Groups mailing list known as *DiggPatriots* and an associated page on coRank; he also accused leading members of the mailing list of participating in behavior which violated the Digg Terms of Usage, such as creating "sleeper" accounts in the event of administrators banning their main accounts for terms-violating behavior as well as vexatious "reporting" of seemingly-liberal users for banning.[51] [52] The post was immediately followed by the disbanding and closure of the DiggPatriots list, and an investigation into the matter by Digg.[53]

Digg v4

On August 25, 2010, when Digg updated to version 4, the site was unreachable or unstable during the launch day and the weeks following. A large number of the site's members have complained about the new design and removed features (such as bury, favorites, friends submissions, upcoming pages, subcategories, and history search).[54] Kevin Rose replied to complaints on his blog where he promised to restore upcoming pages and fix the algorithm.[55]

In an open letter to Rose, Alexis Ohanian, founder of rival site Reddit, said :

> this new version of digg reeks of VC meddling. It's cobbling together features from more popular sites and departing from the core of digg, which was to "give the power back to the people."[56]

Ian Eure, former Digg engineer, explained on his blog why the update cannot be reverted, but the old features can still be ported to the new architecture.[57]

Disgruntled Digg users declared August 30, 2010 as the 'quit Digg day' and began digging up stories submitted by Reddit's auto submitting publisher account filling up the front page.[58] [59] [60] Reddit also temporarily added the Digg shovel to their logo to welcome fleeing Digg users.[61]

Digg's traffic dropped significantly after the launch of version 4,[62] and publishers reported a drop in direct referrals from stories on Digg's front page.[63] Recently hired CEO Matt Williams attempted to address some of the users' concerns in a blog post on October 12, 2010, promising to reinstate many of the features that had been removed. Digg banned RSS Submissions. Digg said "The simple act of forcing a manual submission helps to combat spam and ensures that quality content appears on Digg."[64] [65]

Timeline

October 2004	Development on digg.com begins[66]
December 1, 2004	Kevin Rose creates the first profile
December 3, 2004	The first story is submitted to Digg[67]
December 5, 2004	Digg is open to public
December 13, 2004	Kevin Rose shows off Digg on The Screen Savers[68]
January 2, 2005	Comment section introduced for stories
February 28, 2005	Digg 1.6: duplicate story detection
March 19, 2005	Profile page now includes comment histories and sort by category
May 9, 2005	Digg spy is released
May 27, 2005	Digg 2.0 is released. Friends feature, ajax buttons for Digg/bury, and a non-linear promotion algorithm are implemented.
July 2, 2005	Diggnation podcast begins with Alex and Kevin[69]
October 2005	Raises $2.8 million in venture capital
December 2005	Digg Spy 2.0 released
December 2005	KoolAidGuy saga results in anti-spam tools being introduced[70]
January 17, 2006	Top user Albertpacino resigns after accusations of him being on Digg payroll[71]
January 18, 2006	Digg Clouds is introduced, Search is improved

January 25, 2006	Acquisition rumors begins
February 2, 2006	Report stories as 'inaccurate' and Profanity filters are introduced
February 15, 2006	Digg widget for blogs and share by email is released
March 1, 2006	New Digg Comment System Released, threaded and Diggable comments.
April 20, 2006	Digg Army Saga: after an exposé by forevergeek.com Kevin bans dozens of top users.[72]
June 26, 2006	Digg v3 rolled out, site redesign, shouts, new categories: politics and sports.
July 24, 2006	Digg Labs Launches
August 15, 2006	Thumbnails added
August 27, 2006	Digg begins enforcing trademark rights
September 6, 2006	User rebellion against Friends System and vote rigging results in promises about the diversity algorithms and other tools that were never implemented. Top user p9 resigns.
September 8, 2006	diggriver.com is launched for mobile devices
September 12, 2006	#1 Story feature added later renamed as favorites
December 18, 2006	New features: Podcast, Videos, Top 10 sidebar, wide-screen support and friends page
February 2, 2007	Top Diggers list removed after user complaints[73]
February 2, 2007	Big Spy Launched
February 26, 2007	The new US Elections 2008 section creates lots of buzz
March 1, 2007	Blog post leads to concern about 'bury brigades'. Digg investigates and find no evidence for these allegations
April 19, 2007	Digg API is made public, Contest launched for best app using the API
May 1, 2007	HD-DVD saga regarding the censorship of the leaked encryption key, Kevin sides with the users and ends the censorship
June 4, 2007	Facebook app is launched
June 21, 2007	New Comment System - Joe Stump edition. Instant backlash from community after slow loading.
July 10, 2007	iphone App beta launched
July 25, 2007	Ad partnership with Microsoft
August 27, 2007	Customizable homepage options. Images and videos now back to homepage.
September 19, 2007	New Digg profiles, story suggestion, email alerts
November 20, 2007	Digg the Candidates: Presidential candidates get their Digg accounts
February 1, 2008	Digg Town Halls
May 15, 2008	New comments system is released
June 30, 2008	Recommendation engine is released
July 23, 2008	facebook minifeeds of digg stories
July 31, 2008	m.digg.com - Mobile site is released
August 6, 2008	Firefox Extension released
August 25, 2008	Digg Dialogg

September 8, 2008	Digg warns users against script for auto digging friends stories.
September 24, 2008	$28.7 million capital raised with Highland Capital Partners.
October 3, 2008	Many power users banned after they fail to follow guidelines against script digging.[74]
October 9, 2008	Digg Spy and podcasts discontinued
December 18, 2008	Related stories and "People who Dugg this also Dugg" boxes added to individual stories
April 2, 2009	DiggBar and short url launched
April 9, 2009	New Search
May 6, 2009	Facebook Connect
May 26, 2009	Shouts feature is removed
August 6, 2009	Diggable ads implemented
October 16, 2009	Partners with WeFollow for categorizing user in the upcoming version 4 release
November 4, 2009	Digg Trends launched
January 17, 2010	Chrome extension launched
March 23, 2010	iPhone app is launched
April 1, 2010	Android app is launched
April 5, 2010	Jay Adelson Steps Down as CEO, Kevin Rose becomes interim CEO
July 2, 2010	Digg version 4 alpha testing begins
August 3, 2010	Digg takes down new user registration in preparation for Digg 4.0[75]
August 25, 2010	Digg v4 is released: My News and Publisher Streams launched
September 1, 2010	Matt Williams replaces Kevin Rose as CEO
October 27, 2010	Digg lays off 37% of its staff along with refocusing the service[76]
March 18, 2011	Kevin Rose has resigned from his role in the company [77]

References

[1] *Corporate Profile - Digg, Inc.* (http://techaddress.wordpress.com/2006/09/28/corporate-profile-digg-inc/), 2006-09-28, , retrieved 2009-01-18

[2] "Digg / About Us" (http://web.archive.org/web/20080329121633/http://digg.com/about/). Archived from the original on 29 Mar 2008. .

[3] "Company Update" (http://about.digg.com/blog/company-update). .

[4] "A Wrench in Silicon Valley's Wealth Machine" (http://www.businessweek.com/magazine/content/08_52/b4114082618241.htm). 2008. . Retrieved 2008-12-30.

[5] http://www.digg.com/

[6] "digg.com - Traffic Details from Alexa" (http://www.alexa.com/siteinfo/digg.com). Alexa Internet, Inc. . Retrieved 2011-05-07.

[7] Pat McCarthy (2006-09-10). "Revisiting Top 10 Web Predictions of 2006" (http://www.conversionrater.com/index.php/2006/09/10/revisiting-top-10-web-predictions-of-2006/). Conversionrater.com. . Retrieved 2009-02-27.

[8] "digg.com - Quantcast Audience Profile" (http://www.quantcast.com/digg.com). Quantcast.com. 2010-10-27. . Retrieved 2010-11-07.

[9] "Digg" (http://www.silverorange.com/a/portfolio/digg). silverorange. . Retrieved 2009-02-27.

[10] "Compete.com" (http://siteanalytics.compete.com/digg.com?metric=uv). Siteanalytics.compete.com. . Retrieved 2010-11-07.

[11] "New Version of Digg" (http://mashable.com/2010/03/13/new-digg/). Mashable. . Retrieved 2010-03-15.

[12] "Wired Interview" (http://www.wired.com/epicenter/2010/03/digg-redesign-social-web/). Wired. . Retrieved 2010-03-15.

[13] "Cassandra Switch" (http://about.digg.com/blog/saying-yes-nosql-going-steady-cassandra/). Digg. . Retrieved 2010-03-15.

[14] "Update from Jay | Digg About" (http://about.digg.com/blog/update-jay). About.digg.com. 2010-04-04. . Retrieved 2010-09-01.

[15] McCarthy, Caroline (2010-08-26). "Digg's Matt Van Horn leaving for start-up Path" (http://news.cnet.com/8301-13577_3-20014852-36. html). *CNET News*. . Retrieved 2010-09-02.

[16] Arrington, Michael (2007-11-07). "Just Sell Digg Already, Jay" (http://www.techcrunch.com/2007/11/07/just-sell-digg-already-jay/). Techcrunch.com. . Retrieved 2009-02-27.

[17] Arrington, Michael (2008-07-26). "Google Walks Away From Digg Deal" (http://www.washingtonpost.com/wp-dyn/content/article/ 2008/07/26/AR2008072601421.html). washingtonpost.com. . Retrieved 2009-02-27.

[18] "Digg digs up $28.7 Million" (http://techland.blogs.fortune.cnn.com/2008/09/24/digg-digs-up-287-million/). CNNMoney.com. 2008-11-24. . Retrieved 2011-03-15.

[19] "Digg the Blog » Blog Archive » Big News: Expanding & Growing Digg" (http://blog.digg.com/?p=256). Blog.digg.com. 2008-09-24. . Retrieved 2009-02-27.

[20] Ante, Spencer E. (2008). "Digg: Not For Sale" (http://www.businessweek.com/technology/content/dec2008/tc2008121_004686.htm). . Retrieved 2008-12-09.

[21] Rose, Kevin (May 6, 2009). "Facebook Connect Launches Today!" (http://blog.digg.com/?p=729). .

[22] Arrington, Michael (May 6, 2009). "Facebook Connect Now Live On Digg" (http://www.techcrunch.com/2009/05/06/ digg-to-launch-facebook-connect-today/). . Retrieved May 9 , 2009.

[23] "Digg.com" (http://digg.com/dialogg/). Digg.com. . Retrieved 2010-11-07.

[24] Rose, Kevin (April 2, 2009). "DiggBar Launches Today!" (http://blog.digg.com/?p=591). .

[25] Rose, Kevin (April 5, 2010). "The Digg iFrame Toolbar is Dead / Unbanning Domains" (http://about.digg.com/blog/ digg-digg-iframe-toolbar-dead-unbanning-domains). .

[26] "Digg.com" (http://apidoc.digg.com/). Apidoc.digg.com. . Retrieved 2010-11-07.

[27] "Digg.com" (http://blog.digg.com/?p=72). Blog.digg.com. 2007-04-19. . Retrieved 2010-11-07.

[28] "Techipedia.com" (http://www.techipedia.com/2007/digg-api-tools/). Techipedia.com. . Retrieved 2010-11-07.

[29] "QuickOnlineTips.com" (http://www.quickonlinetips.com/archives/2005/09/complete-digg-tools-collection/). QuickOnlineTips.com. . Retrieved 2010-11-07.

[30] Anonymous (JANUARY 09, 2006). "Steve Mallett from O'Reilly has stolen digg's code" (http://steveisbad.blogspot.com/2006/01/ steve-mallett-from-oreilly-has-stolen.html). STEVE'S THEFT. . Retrieved 5 August 2010.

[31] Digg (JANUARY 09, 2006). "Archive.org mirror of the deleted Digg story" (http://web.archive.org/web/20060113141457/http://digg. com/security/O_Reilly_writer_Steve_Mallett_has_stolen_digg_s_code). Digg. Archived from the original (http://digg.com/security/ O_Reilly_writer_Steve_Mallett_has_stolen_digg_s_code) on 2006-01-13. . Retrieved 5 August 2010.

[32] Steve Mallett (January 10th, 2006). "Archive.org mirror of the deleted blog post" (http://web.archive.org/web/20060412182316/http:// steve.tawkr.com/2006/01/10/my-response/). Archive. Archived from the original (http://steve.tawkr.com/2006/01/10/my-response/) on 2006 04 12. . Retrieved 5 August 2010.

[33] Kevin Rose (January 2006). "Steve Mallett & Digg Code" (http://diggtheblog.blogspot.com/2006/01/steve-mallett-digg-code.html). . Retrieved 5 August 2010.

[34] Nat Torkington (Jan 9 2006). "Digging The Madness of Crowds" (http://radar.oreilly.com/archives/2006/01/ digging-the-madness-of-crowds.html). O'Reilly. . Retrieved 5 August 2010.

[35] Pete Cashmore. "Digg and the So-Called "Wisdom of Mobs"" (http://mashable.com/2006/01/10/ digg-and-the-so-called-wisdom-of-mobs/). Mashable. . Retrieved 5 August 2010.

[36] Dave (Apr. 20 2006). "Digg Corrupted: Editor's Playground, not User-Driven Website" (http://www.forevergeek.com/2006/04/ digg_corrupted_editors_playground_not_userdriven_website/). Forevergeek. . Retrieved 4 August 2010.

[37] Greg Sandoval (December 18, 2006). "Digg continues to battle phony stories" (http://news.cnet.com/ Digg-continues-to-battle-phony-stories/2100-1025_3-6144652.html). CNET News. . Retrieved 4 August 2010.

[38] Adam (December 23, 2007). "Digg's Ron Paul 'Bury Brigade' exposed" (http://message2paulspammers.blogspot.com/2007/12/ diggs-ron-paul-bury-brigade-exposed.html). . Retrieved 4 August 2010.

[39] Ben (February 26th 2008). "Digg's 20 Questions: a Town Hall Recap" (http://bloggingexperiment.com/archives/ diggs-20-questions-a-town-hall-recap.php). Bloggingexperiment. . Retrieved 4 August 2010.

[40] Michael Arrington (Sep 3, 2008). "Want On The Digg Home Page? That'll Be $1,200." (http://techcrunch.com/2008/09/03/ want-on-the-digg-home-page-thatll-be-1300/). Techcruch. . Retrieved 4 August 2010.

[41] Did Digg game its own system to benefit publisher partners? (http://ltgenpanda.tumblr.com/post/1403230157/ did-digg-game-its-own-system-to-benefit-publisher)

[42] Stone, Brad (2007-05-03). "In Web Uproar, Antipiracy Code Spreads Wildly" (http://www.nytimes.com/2007/05/03/technology/ 03code.html). *The New York Times*. . Retrieved 2007-07-02.

[43] Jay Adelson. "Digg the Blog: What's Happening with HD-DVD Stories?" (http://blog.digg.com/?p=73). .

[44] "Cease and desist letters backfire horribly against AACS" (http://www.tgdaily.com/content/view/31859/97/). TGdaily. 2007-05-01. . Retrieved 2009-02-27.

[45] "Digg losing control of their site" (http://weblog.infoworld.com/railsback/archives/2007/05/digg_losing_con.html). Weblog.infoworld.com. . Retrieved 2009-02-27.

[46] Sanders, Tom. "DRM lobby tries to get HD DVD genie back into the bottle" (http://www.computing.co.uk/vnunet/news/2188970/ drm-lobby-tries-hd-dvd-genie). Computing.co.uk. . Retrieved 2009-02-27.

[47] Marcus Yam. "DailyTech: AACS Key Censorship Leads to First Internet Riot" (http://www.dailytech.com/article.aspx?newsid=7129). . Retrieved 2007-05-02.

[48] "BBC News: DVD DRM row sparks user rebellion" (http://news.bbc.co.uk/2/hi/technology/6615047.stm). 2007-05-02. . Retrieved 2007-05-02.

[49] Forbes.com (http://www.forbes.com/technology/2007/05/02/digital-rights-management-tech-cx_ag_0502digg.html), Digg's DRM Revolt

[50] Kevin Rose (2007-05-01). "Digg This: 09 F9 [...]" (http://blog.digg.com/?p=74). *Digg the Blog*. Digg Inc. . Retrieved 2007-05-02.

[51] Ole Ole Olson (4:40 am, August 5, 2010). "Massive Censorship of Digg Uncovered" (http://blogs.alternet.org/oleoleolson/2010/08/05/ massive-censorship-of-digg-uncovered/). AlterNet. .

[52] Ole Ole Olson (Aug 5th, 2010). "The Rigging Of Digg: How A Covert Mob Of Conservatives Hijacked The Web's Top Social News Site" (http://pubrecord.org/special-to-the-public-record/8121/rigging-of-digg-covert-mob-conservatives/). The Public Record. .

[53] Josh Halliday (Friday 6 August 2010 12.29 BST). "Digg investigates claims of conservative 'censorship'" (http://www.guardian.co.uk/ technology/2010/aug/06/digg-investigates-claims-conservative-censorship). *The Guardian* (London). .

[54] Mathew Ingram (Aug. 26, 2010). "Digg Redesign Met with a Thumbs Down" (http://gigaom.com/2010/08/26/ digg-redesign-met-with-a-thumbs-down/). . Retrieved 29 August 2010.

[55] Kevin Rose (Aug 27 2010). "Digg v4: release, iterate, repeat." (http://kevinrose.com/blogg/2010/8/27/digg-v4-release-iterate-repeat. html). . Retrieved 27 August 2010.

[56] Alexis Ohanian (May 28, 2010). "An open letter to Kevin Rose" (http://alexisohanian.com/an-open-letter-to-kevin-rose). . Retrieved 29 August 2010.

[57] Ian Eure (Aug 30, 2010). "THEY CAN'T GO BACK" (http://atomized.org/2010/08/they-canât-go-back/). . Retrieved 31 August 2010.

[58] "Digg User Rebellion Continues: Reddit Now Rules the Front Page" (http://www.readwriteweb.com/archives/ digg_user_rebellion_reddit_on_front_page.php). ReadWriteWeb. . Retrieved August 31, 2010.

[59] "Digg Users Lash Out At New Format, Join Forces with Reddit" (http://newsfeed.time.com/2010/08/30/ digg-users-lash-out-at-new-format-join-forces-with-reddit/). Time Magazine. August 30, 2010. . Retrieved August 31, 2010.

[60] "Angry Digg users flood home page with Reddit links" (http://news.cnet.com/8301-13577_3-20015042-36.html?part=rss& amp;subj=news&tag=2547-1_3-0-20). CNet News. . Retrieved August 31, 2010.

[61] "Angry Users SLAM Digg With Links From Rival Reddit" (http://www.huffingtonpost.com/2010/08/30/ reddit-digg-rivalry-heats_n_699225.html). The Huffington Post. . Retrieved August 31, 2010.

[62] "Digg's traffic is collapsing at home and abroad" (http://thenextweb.com/socialmedia/2010/09/23/ diggs-traffic-is-collapsing-at-home-and-abroad/). The Next Web. . Retrieved October 20, 2010.

[63] "The Digg Effect v4" (http://socialkeith.com/the-digg-effect-v4/). Social Keith. . Retrieved October 20, 2010.

[64] http://mashable.com/2011/02/12/digg-bannixes-rss/

[65] "Greetings from the new CEO" (http://about.digg.com/blog/greetings-new-ceo). Digg About. . Retrieved October 20, 2010.

[66] Richard MacManus (2006-02-01). "Interview with Digg founder Kevin Rose" (http://www.zdnet.com/blog/web2explorer/ interview-with-digg-founder-kevin-rose-part-1/108). *Web 2.0 Explorer*. ZDNet. . Retrieved 2010-08-02.

[67] "API query for story #01" (http://services.digg.com/story/001?appkey=http://wikipedia.com/). *API*. Digg. . Retrieved 2010-08-02.

[68] "Kevin Rose shows off Digg on The Screen Savers" (http://www.youtube.com/watch?v=W1_YoG7lqI4). *The Screen Savers*. TechTV. . Retrieved 2010-08-02.

[69] "Digg Podcast #001 Released" (http://revision3.com/diggnation/2005-07-01). *Diggnation*. Revision3. . Retrieved 2010-08-02.

[70] Richard MacManus (2005-12-27). "Gaming Digg: the KoolAidGuy saga" (http://www.zdnet.com/blog/web2explorer/ gaming-digg-the-koolaidguy-saga/90). *Web 2.0 Explorer*. ZDNet. . Retrieved 2010-08-02.

[71] "Dan Huard is digg user AlbertPacino" (http://web.archive.org/web/20080120235857/http://digg.com/tech_news/ Dan_Huard_is_digg_user_AlbertPacino). wehatetech. Archived from the original (http://digg.com/tech_news/ Dan_Huard_is_digg_user_AlbertPacino) on 2008-01-20. . Retrieved 2010-08-02.

[72] Macgyver (2006-04-19). "Digg Army: Right in Line" (http://www.forevergeek.com/2006/04/digg_army_right_in_line/). Forever Geek. . Retrieved 2010-08-02.

[73] Kevin Rose (2007-02-1). "A couple updates..." (http://about.digg.com/blog/couple-updatesâl). Digg blog. . Retrieved 2010-08-02.

[74] Jen Burton (2008-10-03). "Update on Script Abuse" (http://about.digg.com/blog/digg-update-script-abuse). *Community blog*. Digg. . Retrieved 2010-08-02.

[75] [|Alex, Willhelm (http://thenextweb.com/members/alexwillhelm/profile/)] (2010-08-03). "The New Digg Cometh?" (http:// thenextweb.com/apps/2010/08/03/the-new-digg-cometh/). . Retrieved 2010-08-06.

[76] Michael Arrington Oct 25, 2010 (2010-10-25). "Digg To Layoff 37% Of Staff, Product Refocus Imminent" (http://techcrunch.com/2010/ 10/25/digg-to-lay-off-37-percentof-staff/). Techcrunch.com. . Retrieved 2010-11-07.

[77] Christina Warren, mashable.com. " Kevin Rose Resigns from Digg [REPORT (http://mashable.com/2011/03/18/ kevin-rose-resigns-from-digg-report/?utm_source=feedburner&utm_medium=feed&utm_campaign=Feed:+Mashable+(Mashable))]." March 18, 2011. Retrieved March 18, 2011.

External links

- Official site (http://digg.com/)
- Inc. Magazine profile of Kevin Rose (http://www.inc.com/magazine/20081101/keeevviin.html/)

Diigo

Diigo

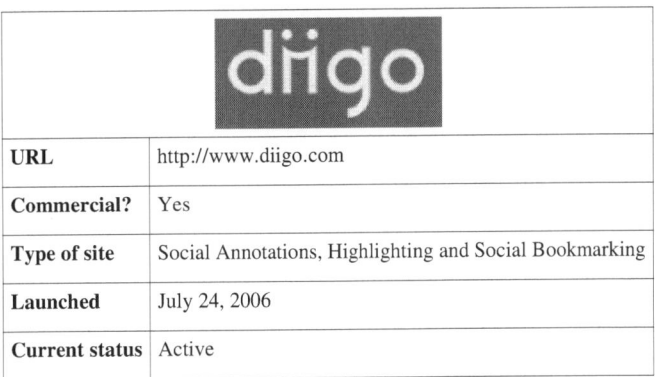

URL	http://www.diigo.com
Commercial?	Yes
Type of site	Social Annotations, Highlighting and Social Bookmarking
Launched	July 24, 2006
Current status	Active

Diigo (pronounced /ˈdiːgoʊ/[1]) is a social bookmarking website which allows signed-up users to bookmark and tag web-pages. Additionally, it allows users to highlight any part of a webpage and attach sticky notes to specific highlights or to a whole page. These annotations can be kept private, shared with a group within Diigo or a special link forwarded to someone else. The name "Diigo" is an acronym from "Digest of Internet Information, Groups and Other stuff".[2]

Premium account holders can perform full-text searches of cached copies of bookmarks. A full-text search also searches page URLs, tags and annotations.[3] This means that premium account holders can choose to omit tags that already appear in the text of a page to be bookmarked (although text inside images cannot be searched).

The launch of Diigo met with mixed responses from the unimpressed,[4] to the enthusiastic.[5] Diigo beta was listed as one of the top ten research tools by CNET in 2006.[6]

Outside the website, Diigo's graphical user interface includes an optional bookmarklet, or a customizable toolbar, with various search capabilities. Highlight is enabled by a menu, that can either appear automatically when content is selected, or be embedded into the context menu.

In March 2009, Diigo acquired web-clipping service Furl from Looksmart for an undisclosed price.[7] [8]

The site also has an extension available on the Chrome Web Store [9] .

References

[1] (flash) *Diigo V4: Research ~ annotate, archive, organize* (http://vimeo.com/6747389). [Presentation]. Diigo. 2009-09-24. Event occurs at 0:00. .

[2] Diigo is about Social Annotation (http://www.diigo.com/help/about)

[3] "Full text search - diigo help" (http://help.diigo.com/premium-features/full-text-search). . Retrieved 28 October 2010.

[4] Diigo Launches, Nobody Cares (http://mashable.com/2006/07/24/diigo-launches-nobody-cares/)

[5] Diigo Offers "Social Annotation" Tool - Search Engine Watch (http://searchenginewatch.com/showPage.html?page=3622969)

[6] Get smart: Top 10 research tools - Internet (http://reviews.cnet.com/4520-9239_7-6654999-1.html)

[7] http://www.techcrunch.com/2009/03/09/diigo-buys-web-page-clipping-service-furl-away-from-looksmart/

[8] http://www.readwriteweb.com/archives/diigo_acquires_furl.php

[9] https://chrome.google.com/webstore/detail/oojbgadfejifecebmdnhhkbhdjaphole

Faves.com

Blue Dot Inc.

Type	Private
Industry	Software & Programming
Founded	Seattle, Washington (2004)
Headquarters	Seattle, Washington
Key people	Mohit Srivastava, Co-Founder
Website	www.faves.com [1]

Faves is a social bookmarking and networking software that installs a single browser button for users to "fave" a webpage, making a link to the page part of their Faves profile. Until October 2007, Faves was called **Blue Dot**.

While offering a service similar to the better-known del.icio.us, Faves has a wider range of functionality that encourages interaction with "friends" in rating the content of linked webpages.[2] When a registered user visits their Faves home page, they see a summary of the bookmarks, called "Faves" by the company, that have been most recently shared by their friends.[3]

Features

In addition to features shared with other bookmarking and social bookmarking services, Faves provides an in-page dialog for saving a Fave, thumbnails generated from the page, dynamic voting, and topic-based auto-generated favorites pages.

History

Blue Dot Inc. was co-founded in 2004 by Mohit Srivastava and Sumit Sen using $1.5 million from angel investors, and the website bluedot.us was launched in June 2006.[4] Blue Dot hopes to profit on of sales from "dotted" websites from its affiliate marketing program,[5] and is part of the technology resurgence in the Washington Puget Sound area.[6]

Early on, Blue Dot actively sought interaction with early adopters in "pizza and soft drink" focus groups on campus that have been cautiously criticized by some academics.[7]

In 2007, the service was renamed Faves. As of December 2007, the web site still lists the company name as Blue dot, Inc.

References

[1] http://www.faves.com

[2] Satoshi, Harmony (2006-07-21). "BlueDot「元祖」del.icio.us に挑むソーシャルブックマークの「進化系 (Blue Dot challenges the innovator del.icio.us in social networking)" (http://japan.cnet.com/column/somethingnew/story/0,2000067121,20176807,00.htm) (in Japanese). CNET (Japan). . Retrieved 2006-12-18.

[3] *Herb Weisbaum interviews Blue Dot Connector, Kabir Shahani* (http://video.google.com/videoplay?docid=340976308175590219). [Television News]. Seattle, Washington: KOMO 4 News. 2006-09-27.

[4] Kirkpatrick, Marshall (2006-07-06). ""Blue Dot is not just another social bookmarking system"" (http://www.techcrunch.com/2006/07/06/blue-dot-is-not-just-another-social-bookmarking-system). *TechCrunch*. . Retrieved 2006-12-18.

[5] Bermant, Charles (2006-11-13). "Blue Dot marks the spot for sharing best of Web" (http://seattletimes.nwsource.com/html/businesstechnology/2003414563_btinterface13.html). The Seattle Times. . Retrieved 2006-12-18.

[6] Peterson, Kim (2006-12-11). "2006 Year in Review: 10 developments that kept local tech companies in the news" (http://seattletimes.nwsource.com/html/businesstechnology/2003471553_lookback11.html). The Seattle Times. . Retrieved 2006-12-18.

[7] Cook, John (2006-11-20). "Startup social networking sites find targeted, willing helpers on campus" (http://www.seattlepi.com/business/292919_college20.html). Seattle Post-Intelligencer. . Retrieved 2006-12-18.

External links

- Official Site (http://www.faves.com/)

Flattr

Flattr

Founded	2010
Founder	Peter Sunde and Linus Olsson
Headquarters	Malmö, Sweden
Industry	micropayments
Slogan	We aim to make people share money on the internet.
Website	flattr.com [1]
Registration	Required
Available in	English

Flattr is a micropayment system - more specifically, a microdonation system - that launched publicly in March 2010 on an invite-only basis,[2] and then opened up to the public on 12 August 2010.[3] [4]

Flattr is a project started by Peter Sunde and Linus Olsson. Users are able to pay a small amount every month (minimum 2 euros) and then click Flattr buttons on sites to share out the money they paid in among those sites, kind of like an Internet tip jar. (The word "flattr" is used as a verb, to indicate payments through the Flattr system - so when a user clicks a Flattr button and they are logged in to the Flattr site, they are said to be "flattring" the page they are on.) Sunde said, "We want to encourage people to share money as well as content."[2]

In the beginning of the service Flattr itself takes 10% of all the users monthly flatrate, although this fee may be reduced at a later date if the economics permit it.[2]

In December 2010, Flattr received large-scale attention when it was tweeted to be a method of donating money to Wikileaks, which had recently been cutoff by Paypal, Visa, and Mastercard.[5]

On April 28, 2011, Flattr announced by e-mail that they won't require users to flattr others anymore before they can be flattrd starting from May 1, 2011.

Extensions

As the service relies on network effect to prove useful, it is necessary that users join and have the opportunity to flattr and be flattr'd. A wide number of platforms are supported including WordPress, Blogger, and Jooomla among many others. To foster faster adoption, including on sites that may not natively support Flattr, a Firefox plugin, Överallt ("everywhere" in Swedish) has been developed.[6] It allows the equipped browsers to parse a simple plain-text tag ([Flattr=ID]) and replace it inline with the Flattr widget. This extends the range of Flattr, so that not only sites that support Flattr, but all sites, can have Flattr buttons.

For real-world or non-web content

Flattr is also being demonstrated as being useful for micro-donations to offline content, including those which are non-computer based, by way of mobile device recognition of QR codes. A number of existing services[7] exist to allow for the "flattr-ing" of non-web-based content, including offline content, using most Android phones' capability of recognizing physical QR codes. Utilizing QR codes attached to Flattr buttons allows for donations to the specific physical or non-web-based item of choice.

Adding funds

The two Internet payment services that can be used both for adding money to a Flattr account, and withdrawing revenue from a Flattr account, are PayPal and Moneybookers.[8]

Awards

- Best New Startup in 2010 - TechCrunch Europe.[9]
- Hoola Bandoola Band award.[10] [11]
- Top-10 in Netexplorateur 2011.[12]

References

[1] http://flattr.com/

[2] "Pirate boss to make the web pay" (http://news.bbc.co.uk/1/hi/technology/8512263.stm). *BBC News*. February 12, 2010. . Retrieved May 2, 2010.

[3] Steve O'Hear (August 12, 2010). "Flattr opens to the public, now anybody can 'Like' a site with real money" (http://eu.techcrunch.com/2010/08/12/flattr-opens-to-the-public-now-anybody-can-like-a-site-with-real-money/). *TechCrunch Europe*. . Retrieved August 13, 2010.

[4] Flattr now open for everyone! (http://blog.flattr.com/2010/08/open-beta/)

[5] http://eu.techcrunch.com/2010/12/08/wikileaks-continues-to-fund-itself-via-tech-startup-flattr/

[6] da Silva, Paul (June 19, 2010). "Överallt : Flattr Everywhere !" (http://overallt.p4ul.info/). . Retrieved June 22, 2010.

[7] "Offline Flattr" (http://flattr.com/support/offline/). .

[8] https://flattr.com/payments

[9] The Europas European Startup Awards 2010 − The Winners and Finalists (http://eu.techcrunch.com/2010/11/20/the-europas-european-startup-awards-2010-the-winners-and-finalists/)

[10] Hoola Bandoola Band-award - Flattr blog (http://blog.flattr.net/2011/02/hoola-bandoola-band-award/)

[11] Hoola-pris till bloggstöd (swedish) (http://www.dalademokraten.se/sida/id/153297/)

[12] NetExplorateur - 2011 award winners (http://en.www.netexplorateur.org/palmares/2011)

External links

- Flattr (http://flattr.com/)
- Flattr blog (http://blog.flattr.net/)

Folkd

folkd

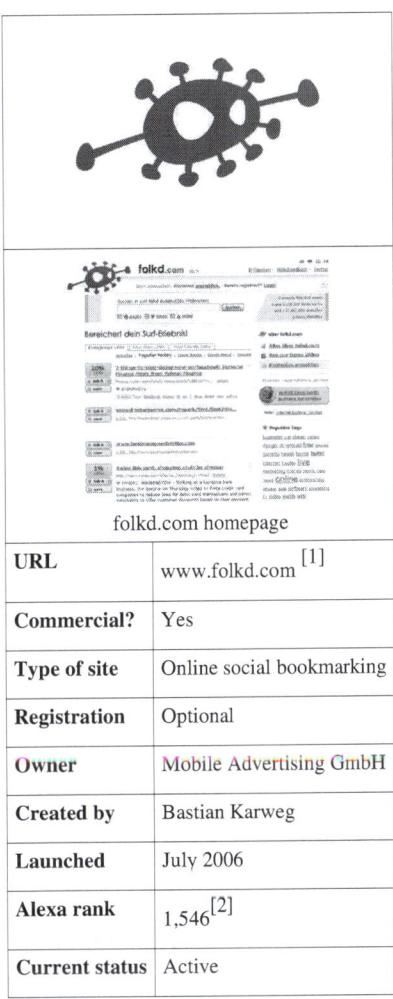

folkd.com homepage

URL	www.folkd.com [1]
Commercial?	Yes
Type of site	Online social bookmarking
Registration	Optional
Owner	Mobile Advertising GmbH
Created by	Bastian Karweg
Launched	July 2006
Alexa rank	1,546 [2]
Current status	Active

folkd.com[3] (short for Folksonomy and pronounced like "smoked") is a social bookmarking and social news website that has been founded in 2006 by Bastian Karweg out of Germany. The website has grown into one of biggest[4] services of its kind and currently lists over 8 million public bookmarks by more than 500.000 users (as of Mai 2010). Folkd is available in 4 languages and also has a strong user base in India. The site devotes itself to "enrich your websurfing experience" and also offers an IE and Firefox AddOn[5] to collect, save and share bookmarks while surfing.

social media techniques

The service offers the two most common social techniques of tagging, which was made popular by Delicious (website), and voting on an item, that users know from the social news site digg. Each user also gets a profile page where his most recent bookmarks are displayed, if not saved as "private".

Integration of social bookmarking

Besides the Firefox addon, folkd is integrated natively as a bookmark-button into a lot of other websites e.g. like Spiegel Online, which is a major German news magazine. This allowes the user to directly social bookmark an article while reading it. This method now is also used by facebook to spread its famous Like Button.

design

The sites logo and several graphics were inspired by the free font face "Alien Mushrooms"[6] .

press

- Mashable: Folkd is a Half-Decent Digg Clone [7]
- SpiegelOnline about folkd.com [8]
- DerStandart.at: Social-Webservice für Audios, News und Blogs [9]
- Sueddeutsche: Teilen, Empfehlen, Aufbewahren [10]
- Folkd, un poco de todo de la web 2.0 [11]

notes

[1] http://www.folkd.com
[2] "Alexa folkd.com traffic results" (http://www.alexa.com/siteinfo/folkd.com). Alexa. . Retrieved 2010-05-14.
[3] www.folkd.com (http://www.folkd.com)
[4] Top 50 social bookmark sites (http://www.web2whizzing.com/social-bookmarking-list/)
[5] Mozilla Firefox AddOn (https://addons.mozilla.org/de/firefox/addon/folkd/)
[6] folkd.com credits page (http://www.folkd.com/page/credits.html)
[7] http://mashable.com/2006/07/24/folkd-is-a-half-decent-digg-clone-finally/
[8] http://www.spiegel.de/netzwelt/web/0,1518,520594,00.html
[9] http://derstandard.at/2555342
[10] http://www.sueddeutsche.de/computer/961/322829/text/
[11] http://www.genbeta.com/web-20/folkd-un-poco-de-todo-de-la-web-20

Furl

Furl (from **F**ile **U**niform **R**esource **L**ocators) was a free social bookmarking website that allowed members to store searchable copies of webpages and share them with others. Every member received 5 gigabytes of storage space. The site was founded by Mike Giles in 2003 and purchased by LookSmart in 2004.[1] Diigo (a web annotation, social bookmarking & research tool website) bought it from LookSmart in exchange for equity.[2] [3]

Features

Furl enabled members to bookmark, annotate, and share web pages. *Topics* were used to categorize saved sites, similar to the tagging feature of other social websites. Additionally, a user could write comments, save clippings, assign each bookmark a rating and keywords (which are given greater weight while searching), and have an option of private or public storage for each topic or item archived.

Considered one of its main features,[4] Furl also privately archived a complete copy of the HTML of each page that a user bookmarks, making it accessible even if the original content was modified or removed, an antidote for link rot. This also allowed full text searches to be made within the archive. However, as highlighted under limitations below, images that were embedded using links were not archived with user's copy of the html page, so images sometimes disappeared over time. To avoid claims of copyright violations, this archived copy was visible only to the member who bookmarked the page. Other users were directed to the publisher's site, where the content could be viewed depending on membership requirements and privacy settings.

Users could see lists of other users who have *furled* a URL, and read their comments (if made public) to find users who share interests, supporting folksonomy. A dynamic recommendation list was automatically generated for each user based on the sites already saved by him or her and other users with similar interests. Lists of the most popular items for today, this week, and this month (and by topic) were also available. It was possible to subscribe to a user's archive (or to a set of topics in a user's archive) to get daily email notifications whenever new items were filed.

Furl allowed bookmarks to be imported from (and exported to) Internet Explorer, Mozilla/Firefox, and Delicious; and also supported exporting of the entire saved archives to ZIP formats, and export metadata to XML format. There were other import/export functions, including various citation formats (MLA, APA, Chicago, CBE, BibTeX, and RIS/EndNote).[5] Toolbars and bookmarklets are available for Internet Explorer and Firefox to quicken the bookmarking process.

Limitations

Images which were embedded links were not archived with the HTML page. For example, when an HTML page was archived via Furl, the location of the JPG from the HTML content was saved, thus pulling up that image when the user's personal copy was loaded; however, if that image no longer exists on the original server, it was lost and will not display with the user's archived copy. So, a Furled site with many pictures could end up being just text.

The search result displayed items from the entire Furl archive, or only from a user's own archive, but the sequence of these results was automatically ordered. There was no option to display results by date order, by popularity order, or in any other particular sequence. It was not obvious how the results are ordered.

The popularity of Furl exposed users to performance problems which began in the latter half of 2006 and persisted into 2007.

Updates

New features were released in early 2007, including an updated user-interface. On January 30, 2008, Furl unveiled an updated user interface.[6] Furl shut down its services on April 17, 2009.[7]

References

[1] Chris Sherman. "Looksmart Acquires Furl.net" (http://searchenginewatch.com/showPage.html?page=3411601). . Retrieved 2008-03-17.

[2] http://www.techcrunch.com/2009/03/09/diigo-buys-web-page-clipping-service-furl-away-from-looksmart/

[3] http://www.readwriteweb.com/archives/diigo_acquires_furl.php

[4] Michael Arrington, TechCrunch. "Profile:Furl" (http://www.techcrunch.com/?p=30). . Retrieved 2007-07-07.

[5] "LookSmart's Furl - features" (http://furl.net/doc/features#Interoperability). . Retrieved 2008-03-17.

[6] "Furl.net Blog" (http://blogs.looksmart.com/furl/2008/01/furl-has-a-new.html). . Retrieved 2008-01-30.

[7] "FURL" (http://www.furl.net/). 2009. . Retrieved 2009-04-16. "Furl will be shut down on April 17. Furl is being absorbed by Diigo and will no longer be available."

External links

- Furl website (redirects to diigo.com) (http://www.furl.net)
- Social Bookmarking Tools (I): A General Review (http://www.dlib.org/dlib/april05/hammond/04hammond.html)

GiveALink.org

GiveALink is a non-commercial social bookmarking website. It is an academic research project, started at Indiana University Bloomington, with the goal of analyzing the structure and content of bookmark files in order to build a new generation of Web mining techniques and new ways to search, recommend, surf, personalize and visualize the Web.

GiveALink features a search engine which, given a URL, finds other Web pages that people bookmark together with it (i.e. similar Web pages). The search engine also supports keyword search and the results can be personalized based on the user's submitted bookmark files. In addition, users can view, organize, augment their bookmarks online, as well as download their bookmark files to several computers.

All of the (anonymized) data at GiveALink is available online to other researchers and Internet users. You can download the URL collection, matrix containing similarity values for pairs of URLs, and the output from several ranking algorithms. Search results can be obtained in XML format through an RSS feed, to help you integrate them into your own applications.

GiveALink uses the existing hierarchical structure in bookmark files (folders and subfolders), as well as collaborative filtering techniques, to measure similarity between Web pages. This means that if many people put two URLs in the same folder in their bookmarks, then these two URLs are considered similar.

External links

- givealink.org [1]
- GiveALink:Mining a Semantic Network of Bookmarks for Search and Recommendations (Proc. LinkKDD 05) [2]
- Implicit Tagging using Donated Bookmarks (Proc. WWW2006 Workshop on Collaborative Web Tagging) [3]
- Social Bookmarks for Collaborative Search and Recommendation (Preprint, Proc. AAAI 2006) [4]

References

[1] http://givealink.org
[2] http://informatics.indiana.edu/fil/Papers/givealink-linkkdd.pdf
[3] http://www.rawsugar.com/www2006/15.pdf
[4] http://informatics.indiana.edu/fil/Papers/GAL06.pdf

Gnolia

Magnolia

URL	http://gnolia.com
Type of site	Online social bookmarking
Registration	Optional
Owner	Gnolia Systems
Launched	2006[1]
Current status	Invitation Only Service

Gnolia, named **Ma.gnolia** until 2009, was a social bookmarking web site with an emphasis on design, social features, and open standards. It is now perhaps most notable for losing members' bookmarks in a widely-reported[2] [3] [4] [5] [6] data loss incident in January 2009. It relaunched as a smaller service several months later and was ultimately shutdown at the end of 2010.

Users could rate bookmarks and mark bookmarks as private. Unlike its main competitor[7] Delicious, Ma.gnolia stored snapshots of bookmarked web pages. One feature that distinguished it from other similar web sites was the *group* feature, which allowed several users to share a common collection of bookmarks, managed by a selected number of group managers.

The design of the web site allowed for integration of the service into other applications via both a REST API and an API similar to the Delicious API.

Open standards

Ma.gnolia supported open standards and was often among early adopters of these standards. The bookmarking service provided support for several Microformats: In July and August 2006, among other information, support for MicroID and XFN was announced on the Ma.gnolia blog.[8] [9] The announcements were well received by the community around online reputation management services.[10]

In December 2007, Ma.gnolia collaborated with Engagd[11] to let users build attention profiles from their bookmarks. In March 2008, Ma.gnolia changed its join and sign-in pages to require users to sign up with a verified identity using OpenID. In August 2008, Ma.gnolia, among others, signed the OAuth 1.0 license.[12]

M2 project

In August 2008, founder Larry Halff announced a ground-up rewrite of the service called *M2*.[13] [14] Parts of the new version were going to be provided under an open source license. It was planned that custom installations of Ma.gnolia can be federated with other installations or the Ma.gnolia website itself. This distributed aspect was the main difference[15] from a similar project by Reddit.[16]

January 2009 total data loss

Ma.gnolia servers lost all data in a complete outage on January 30, 2009.[17] On February 17, Halff announced that due to data corruption, all user data in the database was irretrievable, rendering the site essentially dead.[18]

Ma.gnolia's Recovery Tools allowed users to recover some data from web caches and from other feeds. However, since the tools rely on external sources to reconstruct users' data, they were limited in how much data they could restore.

Relaunch and shutdown

Halff relaunched Ma.gnolia in September 2009 with basically the same software but as a small, invitation-only service.[19] After a request from Magnolia (CMS), it changed its name to Gnolia in October 2009.[20]

In September 2010, Halff announced that he was shutting down Gnolia as of September 29, 2010. "Gnolia will go into read-only mode in a week on September 29, 2010. It will then remain available for bookmark exporting until at least November 30, 2010."[21]

References

[1] Michael Arrington (2005-10-05). "Ma.gnolia: More Social Bookmarking" (http://www.techcrunch.com/2005/10/22/ magnolia-more-social-bookmarking/). Techcrunch. . Retrieved 2008-09-29.

[2] http://www.technologyreview.com/blog/editors/22924/

[3] http://blogs.ft.com/techblog/2009/02/web-disservices/

[4] http://blog.wired.com/business/2009/01/magnolia-suffer.html

[5] http://blog.wired.com/business/2009/02/magnolia-using.html

[6] http://www.pcpro.co.uk/blogs/2009/02/23/the-withering-of-magnolia/

[7] http://blog.wired.com/business/2009/01/magnolia-suffer.html

[8] Larry Halff (2006-07-06). "A Small (?) Update" (http://ma.gnolia.com/blog/2006/07/06/a-small-update). Ma.gnolia blog. . Retrieved 2008-09-29.

[9] Larry Halff (2006-08-21). "A Microadvance In Our Microformats" (http://ma.gnolia.com/blog/2006/08/21/ a-microadvance-in-our-microformats). Ma.gnolia blog. . Retrieved 2008-09-29.

[10] Terrell Russell (2006-07-07). "MicroID and Ma.gnolia - working together" (http://blog.claimid.com/2006/07/ microid-and-magnolia-working-together/). ClaimID. . Retrieved 2008-09-29.

[11] Todd Sieling (2008-12-17). "Your Attention in Your Hands" (http://ma.gnolia.com/blog/2007/12/17/your-attention-in-your-hands). Ma.gnolia blog. . Retrieved 2008-09-29.

[12] Eran Hammer-Lahav (2008-08-26). "OAuth Licensed, a Step on the Way to the Open Web" (http://www.hueniverse.com/hueniverse/ 2008/08/oauth-licensed.html). Hueniverse. . Retrieved 2008-09-29.

[13] Josh Lowensohn (2008-08-22). "Bookmarking service Magnolia opens up its source to all" (http://news.cnet.com/ 8301-17939_109-10023422-2.html). CNET Networks. . Retrieved 2008-09-29.

[14] http://www.readwriteweb.com/archives/magnolia_goes_open_source.php

[15] Adam Ostrov (2008-08-22). "Ma.gnolia Goes Open Source; Wants to be the WordPress of Social Bookmarking" (http://mashable.com/ 2008/08/22/magnolia-open-source/). Mashable. . Retrieved 2008-09-29.

[16] (http://blog.reddit.com/2008/06/reddit-goes-open-source.html)

[17] Michael Calore (2009-01-30). "Ma.gnolia Suffers Major Data Loss, Site Taken Offline" (http://blog.wired.com/business/2009/01/ magnolia-suffer.html). Wired blog. . Retrieved 2009-02-01.

[18] http://www.datacenterknowledge.com/archives/2009/02/19/magnolia-data-is-gone-for-good/

[19] Jay Donovan (2009-09-21). "Interview: A conversation with Larry Halff about the relaunch of Ma.gnolia" (http://www.crunchgear.com/ 2009/09/21/interview-a-conversation-with-larry-halff-about-the-relaunch-of-ma-gnolia/). CrunchGear. . Retrieved 2009-12-29.

[20] Larry Halff (2009-10-05). "Now, By Another Name" (http://gnolia.com/blog/2009/10/05/now-by-another-name). Gnolia Blog. . Retrieved 2009-12-29.

[21] Larry Halff (2010-09-22). "Gnolia Closing" (http://gnolia.com/pages/closing). Gnolia Blog. . Retrieved 2010-09-26.

External links

- Official site (http://ma.gnolia.com)

Google Bookmarks

Google Bookmarks is a free online bookmark storage service, available to Google Account holders.[1] It was launched on October 10, 2005.[2] *Google Bookmarks* allows one to bookmark favorite websites and add labels or tags, and also notes.

Users can access their bookmarks from any computer by signing in to their Gmail account. The bookmarks are searchable, and searches are performed on the full text of the bookmarked pages, not just the labels and notes.

Google toolbar has tools enabling a user to easily create bookmarks and quickly access them. Bookmarks can also be created manually from the web interface, or by use of third-party tools such as Firefox extensions created for the purpose of managing the user's Google Bookmarks account[3] and keeping them synchronized to the browser's bookmarks.

A simple javascript function labeled Google Bookmark is created on the Firefox Bookmarks Toolbar, which opens a window to save the bookmark to the Google Bookmarks. This same function can be imported into other browsers as a bookmarklet.[4]

Like Delicious (owned by Yahoo), which is a social tool to share your bookmarks with the community, this service uses Lists[5] to share bookmarks with others, and the public.[6] Many websites will encourage bookmarking to Google Bookmarks through third party buttons on their sites, knowing that Google's search engine keeps tabs and considers these bookmarks significant in the results for public search.[7]

References

[1] Bookmarks (http://www.google.com/support/toolbar/bin/answer.py?answer=43305&topic=15364&hl=en) *Google help*

[2] *Google Targets Del.icio.us* (http://techcrunch.com/2005/10/11/google-bookmarks-tagging-launches/) by Michael Arrington in *TechCrunch* on October 11, 2005 (retrieved on January 20, 2011)

[3] Official list of add-ons for Firefox (https://addons.mozilla.org/en/firefox/search?q=google+bookmarks&cat=all)

[4] Alex Chitu, " Useful Google Bookmarklets (http://googlesystem.blogspot.com/2007/07/useful-google-bookmarklets.html)", *Google Operating System*

[5] (https://www.google.com/bookmarks/l#!threadID=GMQLX334AZGw/BDQK0ggoQ4KG3gPIk) *Google Bookmarks Lists*

[6] Google Bookmarks Team, " (https://www.google.com/bookmarks/l#!threadID=GMQLX334AZGw/BDQK0ggoQ4KG3gPIk)", *Google Bookmarks Lists*

[7] Eric Ward, " Google Personalized Search, Google Bookmarks & Link Building (http://searchengineland.com/070305-091740.php)", *Search Engine Land* (Mar. 5, 2007).

External links

- Official website (http://http://www.google.com/bookmarks)

Hacker News

Hacker News

URL	http://news.ycombinator.com/
Type of site	News aggregator
Registration	Free; optional OpenID
Available language(s)	English
Launched	February 19, 2007[1]
Alexa rank	3,595[2]
Current status	Online

Hacker News is a social news website about computer hacking and startup companies, run by Paul Graham's funding firm Y Combinator. It is different from other social news websites in that there is no option to downmod submissions (comments can be downvoted when a user accumulates sufficient "karma," or points gained when submissions are voted up); submissions can either be voted up or not voted on at all. In general, content that can be submitted is defined as "anything that gratifies one's intellectual curiosity".[3]

History

The site was created by Paul Graham in February 2007. Initially it was called Startup News or occasionally News.YC. On August 14, 2007 it became known by its current name.[4] It developed as a project of his company Y Combinator, functioning as a real-world application of the Arc programming language which Graham co-developed.[5] [6] [7]

The intention was to recreate a community similar to the early days of Reddit.[8] Graham has stated he hopes to avoid the Eternal September that results in the general decline of intelligent discourse within a community.[9] [10] [11]

References

[1] "Announcing Y Combinator Startup News" (http://ycombinator.com/announcingnews.html). Y Combinator. . Retrieved 2009-08-13.

[2] "Statistics from Alexa" (http://www.alexa.com/siteinfo/ycombinator.com). Alexa Internet. . Retrieved 2009-11-29.

[3] Graham, Paul. "Hacker News Guidelines" (http://ycombinator.com/newsguidelines.html). . Retrieved 2009-04-29.

[4] "Startup News Becomes Hacker News" (http://ycombinator.com/hackernews.html). .

[5] Louis-Charles, Andy (2009-04-28). "Ignore Y Combinator at Your Own Risk" (http://www.fool.com/investing/general/2009/04/28/ignore-y-combinator-at-your-own-risk.aspx). *Motley Fool*. . Retrieved 2009-04-28.

[6] "What I've Learned from Hacker News" (http://paulgraham.com/hackernews.html). .

[7] CenterNetworks. "Y Combinator Startup News – a better Digg, Reddit, Netscape?" (http://www.centernetworks.com/y-combinator-startup-news-a-better-digg-reddit-netscape-w-video). .

[8] "Similarity to Reddit" (http://www.crunchbase.com/product/hacker-news). .

[9] "The Fluff Principle and other thoughts on community" (http://www.kottke.org/09/02/the-fluff-principle-and-other-thoughts-on-community). .

[10] "Hacker News News" (http://ycombinator.com/newsnews.html). .

[11] Jacobs, Alan (2009-03-09). "Flamethrowers and Fire Extinguishers" (http://www.thenewatlantis.com/blog/text-patterns/flamethrowers-and-fire-extinguishers). . Retrieved 2009-04-29.

Licorize

Licorize

URL	http://licorize.com
Commercial?	Yes
Type of site	Social Annotations, Highlighting and Social Bookmarking
Launched	October 5, 2010
Current status	Active

Licorize is a social bookmarking website which allows signed-up users to bookmark and tag web-pages and parts of pages' contents. Additionally all bookmarks and can be contextually classified as to-do's, reminders, ideas, and each of these types has a different layout and behaviour. Licorize contents are called "strips". Premium account holders can invite other users and share specific collection of strips, called "projects".

Licorize has an extended set of importing / synchronizing functions, covering Twitter, DropBox, Evernote, LinkedIn, RSS, ReadItLater, Delicious, Google Contacts and e-mail. It also includes several tools for integrating bookmarking with to-do management, and tools inspired by the Getting Things Done methodology.

The launch of Licorize met with generally positive reviews from personal productivity press: LifeHacker[1] , Web Worker Daily[2] , Suberapps[3] .

Licorize was also included in Smashing Magazine 2010 list of 50 Powerful Time-Savers For Web Designers[4] .

It got also quite a number of reviews in German online press and blogs: a list of all available reviews is here [5] .

Licorize can be used with a bookmarklet, or by installing browsers plugins / extensions, that have been released for Firefox, Google Chrome, Safari web browser, Opera web browser.

References

[1] LifeHacker: Licorize Turns Your Bookmarks into Tasks, Goals, and Other Actionable Items (http://lifehacker.com/5644249/licorize-turns-your-bookmarks-into-tasks-goals-and-other-actionable-items)

[2] Web Worker Daily: Licorize Makes Bookmarks More Useful (http://gigaom.com/collaboration/licorize-makes-bookmarks-more-useful/)

[3] Suberapps: Licorize: FINALLY-A Way to Actually Do Something With All Those Bookmarks (http://www.suberapps.com/web-apps/licorize-finally-a-way-to-actually-do-something-with-all-those-bookmarks/)

[4] SmashingMagazine: 50 Powerful Time-Savers For Web Designers (http://www.smashingmagazine.com/2010/10/19/50-powerful-time-savers-for-designers/)

[5] Open Lab. "turn browsing into projects" (http://licorize.com/users/ppolsinelli/licorizeBuzz). Licorize. . Retrieved 2010-11-17.

Linkwad

Linkwad

⊐ liNkwad	
URL	http://www.linkwad.com/
Type of site	Social content website
Registration	Free
Owner	Linkwad.
Created by	Nick Fridrich
Launched	August 28, 2006

Linkwad is a free community-based social bookmarking service provided (at the moment) exclusively for Mozilla's Firefox web browser, as an add-on.

Linkwad allows users to "save and restore tabbed browsing sessions called wads". A Wad is actually a group of links that are saved under a name. This Wads can be shared and accessed from any computer.[1]

History

Linkwad (extension and server side) was first released on August 28, 2006.[2]

The idea was to create a community based social bookmarking to allow users to avoid a lot of time searching for a specific subject. Using Linkwad users quickly get a bunch of links related to a specific subject.

At the time the extension saw the public for the first time with version 1.0.1 having only 10Kb (little less than half of its current size). On October 23 another version was released but was only on December that several improvements were made in two new releases.[2]

On February 28 was added support for managing multiple wads within a single window and support for opening Google Images and Ask.com search results in tabs allowing, this way, users to do things a lot more quickly with this extension. This release also approached Linkwad to the Firefox legion of power users.[2]

The 1.5.1 version saw release on October 7 and allows users to customize keyboard shortcuts as well as see open wads in toolbar and drag & drop tabs between wads. On this same date a new server side was also released. Users can now rate the wads that will help other users to choose which one is the best.[2]

On April 18, 2008, version 1.5.2 was released solving the problem of selecting unsaved sessions with mouse. This resolution also revealed that the existence of switch button (that switched between wads) is now useless. Firefox 3 beta 4 is now supported.

A version compatible with the new Mozilla's browser, Firefox 3, is already available. Users, however, are still expecting to see some improvements that have been suggested by them.[3]

Features

The most recent version of this service allows users to:

- Open and manage multiple tab sessions within a single browser window.
- Open search results from Google and Yahoo in tabs with a single keystroke.
- Keyboard shortcuts available (and customizable).[4]
- Share your Wads with the world
- Open your wads anywhere as long as you have Linkwad.
- Pick up other shared wads and make them your own.
- Access the links contained in Wads from any browser using the Linkwad portal.
- You can rate Wads on the Linkwad portal

Advantages

This lists some of the Linkwad advantages[5]

- One of the biggest advantages of the service is that when you are searching for a specific subject you will always get a group of pages related with that specific subject.
- The ability to continue what you're browsing in multiple computers
- Organizing your tabs by groups/themes

References

[1] something, forty (August 06, 2008). "Linkwad Article" (http://www.fortysomething.ca/mt/etc/archives/007005.php). fortysomething. . Retrieved 2008-08-06.

[2] Fridrich, Nick (March 26, 2008). "Linkwad History" (https://addons.mozilla.org/en-US/firefox/addons/versions/3263). Mozilla Addons. . Retrieved 2008-03-26.

[3] "Linkwad Suggestions" (http://tabgrouper.awardspace.com/sugestions.html). Tabgrouper. March 26, 2008. . Retrieved 2008-03-26.

[4] "Keyboard Shortcuts" (http://www.ffextensions.com/addon/LinkWad/1610.html). ffextensions.com. . Retrieved 2008-03-26.

[5] Johnson, Scott. "Linkwad Advantages" (http://scottjohnsonflorida.blogspot.com/2007/06/linkwad.html). scottjohnsonflorida.blogspot.com. . Retrieved 2008-03-26.

- Help/about (http://www.linkwad.com/help)

External links

- Official site (http://linkwad.com/)
- Firefox Add-on (https://addons.mozilla.org/en-US/firefox/addon/3263)
- Web Developer's Article (http://www.lockergnome.com/web/2006/09/26/linkwad-cluster-bookmarking/)

MemeStreams

MemeStreams

URL	http://www.memestreams.com
Commercial?	Yes
Type of site	Social content website
Registration	Free
Owner	Industrial Memetics
Created by	Tom Cross and Nick Levay

MemeStreams is an early social networking website, online community, and blog host that was established in 2001 by Industrial Memetics,[1].

Created by Tom Cross and Nick Levay[2] [3], the site is particularly popular among computer security professionals.[4] [2]. Michael Lynn (Ciscogate), Virgil Griffith (Wikiscanner), Billy Hoffman (Ajax Security), and Dolemite (organizer of PhreakNIC) are all members of the site.

Memestreams employs a reputation system.[5]

References

[1] "Episode 58 - Memetics" (http://web.archive.org/web/20071012152547/http://binrev.com/radio/archive.php?p=15). Binary Revolution. 2004-08-17. Archived from the original (http://www.binrev.com/radio/archive.php?p=15) on 2007-10-12. . Retrieved 2007-10-15.

[2] "About MemeStreams" (http://www.memestreams.net/about.html). MemeStreams. . Retrieved 2007-10-16.

[3] "Levay, Nick" (http://web.si.umich.edu/reputations/dir/direcsearch.cfm?index=118&shortLong=long). umich.edu. . Retrieved 2007-10-16.

[4] Conti, Gregory (2005-03-01). *Why Computer Scientists Should Attend Hacker Conferences* (http://www.rumint.org/gregconti/publications/20050301_CACM_HackingConferences_Conti.pdf). Communications of the ACM. . Retrieved 2007-10-16.

[5] "Tom Cross" (http://www.itoc.usma.edu/Workshop/2007/Program/Speakers/Cross.htm). *IEEE SMC Information Assurance Workshop*. Information Technology and Operations Center at West Point. . Retrieved 2007-10-15.

External links

- Official site (http://www.memestreams.net/topics/)

Menéame

Menéame Comunicacions, SL

Type	Private
Founded	Sineu, Majorca, Spain[1]
Founder(s)	Ricardo Galli[1]
Headquarters	Sineu, Majorca[1], Spain[1]
Area served	Worldwide
Key people	Ricardo Galli (Founder) Benjamí Villoslada[1]
Website	meneame.net [2]

Menéame is a Spanish social news website based in communitary participation, made for users to discover and share content from anywhere on the Internet, by submitting links and stories and voting and commenting on submitted links and stories. It's model is based in digg and it combines Social bookmarking, blogging and Web syndication with a publication system without editors.

The website ranked 1,989 by Alexa.com as of December 2010.[3]

The PHP software that runs menéame is FOSS under GNU Affero General Public License and is available through SVN.[4]

References

[1] Menéame FAQ (http://meneame.net/faq-es.php/)

[2] http://meneame.net/

[3] "meneame.net - Traffic Details from Alexa" (http://www.alexa.com/siteinfo/meneame.net). Alexa Internet, Inc. . Retrieved 2010-12-26.

[4] websvn.meneame.net - SVN repositories of meneame software (http://websvn.meneame.net/listing.php?repname=meneame&path=/branches/version3/)

External links

- Official site (http://meneame.net/) (**Spanish**)
- Menéame official blog (http://blog.meneame.net/) (**Spanish**)

Mister Wong

Mister Wong

URL	[21]
Slogan	Wong the web
Commercial?	Yes
Type of site	Social bookmarking
Registration	Yes
Launched	March 2006
Alexa rank	▼ 2,948 (January 2011)[1]

Mister Wong is one of the largest European free social-bookmarking web services.[2]

History

The website was a German startup, established in 2006. Kai Tietjen had been running an ad agency for nearly a decade, when, in March 2006, he entered the field of web entrepreneurship[3] with the idea to "take on Google". Investing mostly his own money, he created a website that allows customers to bookmark their favorite sites, and then uses those bookmarks as the basic data for its search engine : to find a popular site, a user can search all other users' bookmarks.[4]

The service is currently available in German, English, Russian, Chinese, Spanish and French.

Origin of name

The website extols its users to "Wong the Web!",[5] a reference to the practice of Wonging, often employed by card counters in Blackjack.

Controversy

Mister Wong's original logo,[6] depicting a "cartoonish, nerdy East Asian man", brought on protests from many Asian-Americans.[7] The website's creator subsequently issued an apology and removed the logo.[8]

Notes

[1] "Mister-Wong.com Site Info" (http://www.alexa.com/siteinfo/mister-wong.com). *Alexa*. . Retrieved January 7, 2011.

[2] Mister Wong company profile at CrunchBase (http://www.crunchbase.com/company/mister-wong)

[3] "Kai Tietjen, CEO & Founder of Construktiv", 2006 (http://www.crunchbase.com/person/kai-tieten)

[4] "Creating Buzz (Without Hate Mail)", Newsweek, October 27, 2007 (http://www.newsweek.com/2007/10/27/creating-buzz-without-hate-mail.html)

[5] "About Mister Wong" (http://www.mister-wong.com/about/)

[6] flickr.com stored image (http://www.flickr.com/photos/clawier/896942774/)

[7] "Mister Wong Isn't Laughing Anymore", Der Spiegel online (http://www.spiegel.de/netzwelt/web/0,1518,497151,00.html) in German

[8] A Message from the Founder, Kai Tietjen, July, 27 2007 (http://blog.mister-wong.com/a-message-from-the-founder/2007/07/27/)

External links

• Mister Wong website (http://www.mister-wong.com/)

Models of collaborative tagging

Many have argued that social tagging or collaborative tagging systems can provide navigational cues or "way-finders" [1] [2] for other users to explore information. The notion is that, given that social tags are labels that users create to represent topics extracted from Web documents, interpretation of these tags should allow other users to predict contents of different documents efficiently. Social tags are arguably more important in exploratory search, in which the users may engage in iterative cycles of goal refinement and exploration of new information (as opposed to simple fact-retrievals), and interpretation of information contents by others will provide useful cues for people to discover topics that are relevant. One significant challenge that arises in social tagging systems is the rapid increase in the number and diversity of the tags. As opposed to structured annotation systems, tags provide users an unstructured, open-ended mechanism to annotate and organize web-content. As users are free to create any tag to describe any resource, it leads to what is referred to as the vocabulary problem [3]. Because users may use different words to describe the same document or extract different topics from the same document based on their own background knowledge, the lack of a top-down mediation may lead to an increase in the use of incoherent tags to represent the information resources in the system. In other words, the inherent "unstructuredness" of social tags may hinder their potential as navigational cues for searchers because the diversities of users and motivation may lead to diminishing tag-topic relations as the system grows.

The distinction between descriptive and predictive models

Just like any social phenomena, behavioral patterns in social tagging systems can be characterized by either a descriptive or predictive model. While descriptive models ask the question of "what", predictive models go deeper to also ask the question of "why" by attempting to provide explanations to the aggregate behavioral patterns [4] While there may be no general agreement on what an acceptable explanation should be like, many believe that a good explanation should have certain level of predictive accuracy. Descriptive models of social tagging typically are not concerned with explaining the actions of single individuals but describing the patterns that emerge as individual behavior is aggregated in a large social information system. Predictive models, however, attempts to explain aggregate patterns by analyzing how individuals interact and link to each other in ways that bring about similar or different emergent patterns of social behavior. In particular, a mechanism-based predictive model assumes a certain set of rule that individuals interact with each other, and understand how these interactions could produce aggregate patterns as observed and characterized by descriptive models. Predictive models can therefore provide explanations to why different system characteristics may lead to different aggregate patterns, and can therefore potentially provide information on how systems should be designed to achieve different social purposes.

Descriptive Models of Social Tagging

Information Theory Models

For most tagging systems the total number of tags in the collective vocabulary is much less than the total number of objects being tagged. Given this multiplicity of tags to documents, a question remains: how effective are the tags at isolating any single document? Naively, if we specify a single tag in this system we would uniquely identify lots of documents — thus the answer to our question is "not very well!". However this method carries a faulty assumption; not every document is equal. Some documents are more popular and important than others, and this importance is conveyed by the number bookmarks per document. Thus, we can reformulate the above question to be: how well does the mapping of tags to documents retain about the distribution of the documents? Information theory provides a natural framework to understand the amount of shared information between two random variables. The conditional entropy measures the amount of entropy remaining in one random variable when we know the value of a second random variable. Work done by Chi and Mytkowicz[5] show that the entropy of documents conditional on tags, H(D|T), is increasing rapidly. What this means is that, even after knowing completely the value of a tag, the entropy of the set of documents is increasing over time. Conditional Entropy asks the question: "Given that I know a set of tags, how much uncertainty regarding the document set that I was referencing with those tags remains?" The fact that this curve is strictly increasing suggests that the specificity of any given tag is decreasing. That is to say, as a navigation aid, tags are becoming harder and harder to use. We are moving closer and closer to the proverbial "needle in a haystack" where any single tag references too many documents to be considered useful.

Another way to look at the data is to think about Mutual Information, which is a measure of independence between the two variables. Full independence is reached when I(D;T) = 0. Chi and Mytkowicz research on delicious social tagging data show that as a measure of usefulness of the tags and their encoding, there is a worsening trend in the ability of users to specify and find tags and documents when they are engaged in simple fact retrieval. This suggests that we need to build search and recommendation systems that help users sift through resources in social tagging systems, especially when we are engaged in more than simple fact retrieval as characterized by the information theory. In fact, although the number of documents associated with any given tag is increasing, there are many ways contextual information can help users to look for relevant information. This is in fact one of the major weakness of the simple information theory in explaining usefulness of tags -- it ignores the fact that humans can extract meanings from a set of tags assigned to a document, and this semantic extraction process is exactly the reason why humans are able to communicate efficiently even though the size of our vocabulary is increasing ever since language was developed. For example, the work by Cattuto et al. (2007)[6], published in PNAS, show that while the number of tags are increasing, the general growth pattern is scale-free -- the general distribution of tag-tag co-occurrences follows a power-law. Cattuto also finds that the characteristics of this scale-free distribution are dependent on the semantics of the tag -- tags that are semantically general (e.g., blogs) tend to co-occur with many tags, while semantically narrow tags (e.g., Ajax) tend to co-occur with few number of tags across a wide set of documents in a social tagging system. What this means is that the assumption of the information theory approach is too simple -- when the semantics of the set of tags assigned to documents are taken into account, the predictive value of tags on contents of documents are relatively stable. This finding is important for development of recommender systems -- discovering these higher level semantic patterns is important in helping people to find relevant information (also see semantic imitation model below).

Tag convergence

Despite this potential vocabulary problem, recent research has found that at the aggregate level, tagging behavior seemed relatively stable and that the tag choice proportions seemed to be converging rather than diverging. While these observations provided evidence against the proposed vocabulary problem, they also triggered a series of research investigating how and why tag proportions tended to converge over time.

One explanation for the stability was that there was an inherent propensity for users to "imitate" word use of others as they create tags. This propensity may act as a form of social cohesion that fosters the coherence of tag-topic relations in the system [7], and leads to stability in the system. Golder and Huberman showed that the stochastic urn model by Eggenberger and Polya [8] was useful in explaining how simple imitation behavior at the individual level could explain the converging usage patterns of tags. Specifically, convergence of tag choices was simulated by a process in which a colored ball was randomly selected from an urn and was replaced in the urn along with an additional ball of the same color, simulating the probabilistic nature of tag reuse. The simple model, however, does not explain why certain tags would to be "imitated" more often than others, and therefore cannot provide a realistic mechanism for tag choices and how social tags could be utilized as navigational cues during exploratory search, not to mention the obviously over-simplified representation of individual users by balls in an urn.

Complex systems dynamics and emergent vocabularies

Other research, using data from the social bookmarking website Del.icio.us, has shown that collaborative tagging systems exhibit a form of complex systems (or self-organizing) dynamics.[9] Furthermore, although there is no central controlled vocabulary to constrain the actions of individual users, the distributions of tags that describe different resources has been shown to converge over time to a stable power law distributions.[9] Once such stable distributions form, examining the correlations between different tags can be used to construct simple folksonomy graphs, which can be efficiently partitioned to obtain a form of community or shared vocabularies.[10] Such vocabularies can be seen as emerging from the decentralised actions of many users, as a form of crowdsourcing.

Tag choice by stochastic process

The memory-based Yule-Simon (MBYS) model of Cattuto [11] attempted to explain tag choices by a stochastic process. They found that the temporal order of tag assignment has an impact on users' tag choices. Similar to the stochastic urn model, the MBYS model assumed that at each time step a tag would be randomly sampled: with probability p the sampled tag was new, and with probability 1-p the sampled tag was copied from existing tags. When copying, the probability of selecting a tag was assumed to decay with time, and this decay function was found to follow a power law distribution. Thus, tags that were recently used had a higher probability of being reused than those used in the past. One major finding by Cattuto et al. was that semantically general tags (e.g., "blog") tended to co-occur more frequently with other tags than semantically narrower tags (e.g., "ajax"), and this difference could be captured by the decay function of tag reuse in their model. Specifically, they found that a slower decay parameter (when the tag is reused more often) could explain the phenomenon that semantically general tags tended to co-occur with a larger set of tags. In other words, they argued that the "semantic breadth" of a tag could be modeled by a memory decay function, which could lead to different emergent behavioral patterns in a tagging system.

Predictive Models of Social Tagging

Semantic Imitation Model of Social Tag Choices

Descriptive models mentioned above were based on analyses of word-word relations as revealed by the various statistical structures in the organization of tags (e.g., how likely one tag would co-occur with other tags or how likely each tag was reused over time). These models are therefore descriptive models at the aggregate level, and have little to offer about predictions at the level of interface interactions and cognitive processes of individual. Rather than imitating other users at the word level, one possible explanation for this kind of social cohesion could be grounded on the natural tendency for people to process tags at the semantic level, and it was at this level of processing that most imitation occurred. This explanation was supported by research in the area of reading comprehension [12], which showed that people tended to be influenced by meanings of words, rather than the words themselves during comprehension. Assuming that background knowledge of people in the same culture tend to have shared structures (e.g., using similar vocabularies and their corresponding meanings in order to conform and communicate with each), users of the same social tagging system may also share similar semantic representations of words and concepts, even when the use of tags may vary across individuals at the word level. In other words, we argued that part of the reason for the stability of social tagging systems can be attributed to the shared semantic representations among the users, such that users may have relatively stable and coherent interpretation of information contents and tags as they interact with the system. Based on this assumption, the semantic imitation model [13] [14] predicts how different semantic representations may lead to differences in individual tag choices and eventually different emergent properties at the aggregate behavioral level. The model also predicts that the folksonomies (i.e., knowledge structures) in the system reflect the shared semantic representations of the users.

Semantic imitation has important implication to the general vocabulary problem (see work by, e.g., Susan Dumais) in information retrieval and human-computer interaction -- the creation of large number of diverse tags to describe the same set of information resource. The finding that semantic imitation occurs implies that the unit of communication among users is more likely at the semantic level, not at the word level. Thus, although there may not be strong coherence in the choice of words in describing a resource, at the semantic level there seems to be a stronger coherence force that guides the convergence of descriptive indices. This is in sharp contrast to conclusions derived based on a purely information-theoretical approach, which assumes that humans search and evaluation information at the word level. Instead, the process of semantic imitation in social tagging implies that the information-theoretic approach is at most incomplete, as it does not take into account the basic unit of human information processing. Similar to the fact that human communication occurs at the semantic level, the fact that people may use different words or syntax does not impact the effectiveness of communication, so long as the underlying "common ground" between the two persons is the same [15] . In the social tagging case, so long as users share similar understanding of the contents of the information resources, the fact that the information value of tag-document decreases (that humans have more words in their languages) do not imply that it will always be harder to find relevant information (similarly, the fact that there are more words in our languages does not mean that our communication becomes less effective). However, it does point to the notion that one needs to effectively present these semantic structures in the information system so that people can effectively interpret the semantics of the tagged documents. Intelligent techniques based on statistical models of language such as Latent semantic analysis, probabilistic topics model, etc are promising aspects that will overcome this vocabulary problem.

References

[1] Kang, R., Fu, W.-T., & Kannampallil, T. (2010). Exploiting Knowledge-in-the-head and Knowledge-in-the-social-web: Effects of Domain Expertise on Exploratory Search in Individual and Social Search Environments. In Proceedings of the ACM Conference on Computer-Human Interaction, Atlanta, GA.

[2] Furnas, G. W., Fake, C., Von Ahn, L., Schachter, J., Golder, S., Fox, K., Davis, M., Marlow, C., and Naaman, M. Why Do Tagging Systems Work? in CHI '06 Extended Abstracts on Human Factors in Computing Systems. (2006). Montréal, Québec, Canada.

[3] G. W. Furnas, T. K. Landauer, L. M. Gomez, and S. T. Dumais, "The vocabulary problem in human-system communication," Communications of the ACM, vol. 30, no. 11, pp. 964-971, 1987.

[4] Hedstrom, Peter (2005). Dissecting the social. On the principle of analytic sociology. Cambridge, UK.

[5] Ed H. Chi, Todd Mytkowicz Understanding the Efficiency of Social Tagging Systems using Information Theory. In Proc. of ACM Conference on Hypertext 2008. (to appear). ACM Press, 2008. Pittsburgh, PA.

[6] Cattuto, C., Loreto, V., and Pietronero, L., Semiotic Dynamics and Collaborative Tagging. Proceedings of National Academy of Sciences, (2007), 104, 1461-1464.

[7] Golder, Scott; Huberman, Bernardo A. (2006), "Usage Patterns of Collaborative Tagging Systems" (http://www.hpl.hp.com/research/idl/papers/tags/), *Journal of Information Science* **32** (2): 198–208, doi:10.1177/0165551506062337,

[8] Г. Eggenberger and G. Polya, Uber Die Statistik Verketter Vorgage. Zeit. Angew. Math. Mech, (1923), 1, 279-289,

[9] Harry Halpin, Valentin Robu, Hana Shepherd The Complex Dynamics of Collaborative Tagging (http://portal.acm.org/citation.cfm?id=1242572.1242602), Proceedings 6th International Conference on the World Wide Web (WWW'07), Banff, Canada, pp. 211-220, ACM Press, 2007.

[10] Valentin Robu, Harry Halpin, Hana Shepherd Emergence of consensus and shared vocabularies in collaborative tagging systems (http://portal.acm.org/citation.cfm?id=1594173.1594176), ACM Transactions on the Web (TWEB), Vol. 3(4), article 14, ACM Press, September 2009.

[11] Cattuto, C., Loreto, V., and Pietronero, L., Semiotic Dynamics and Collaborative Tagging. Proceedings of National Academy of Sciences, (2007), 104, 1461-1464.

[12] Kintsch, W. (1988). The role of knowledge in discourse comprehension: A construction-integration model. Psychological Review, 95, 163–182.

[13] Fu, Wai-Tat (April 2008), "Ahe Microstructures of Social Tagging: A Rational Model" (http://portal.acm.org/citation.cfm?id=1460600), *Proceedings of the ACM 2008 conference on Computer Supported Cooperative Work.*: 66–72, doi:10.1145/1460563.1460600,

[14] Fu, Wai-Tat (Aug 2009), "A Semantic Imitation Model of Social Tagging." (http://www.humanfactors.illinois.edu/Reports&PapersPDFs/IEEESocialcom09/A Semantic Imitation Model of Social Tag Choices (2).pdf), *Proceedings of the IEEE conference on Social Computing*: 66–72,

[15] Clark, H. H. (1996). Using language. Cambridge: Cambridge University Press.

NewsTrust

NewsTrust is a nonpartisan, non-profit news network that operates a web site (www.newstrust.net) where users are able to reference quality news stories, rate those stories according to quality of journalism, post reviews and add stories they themselves find worthwhile. NewsTrust is billed as "Your Guide to Good Journalism." [1]

Founded in 2005 and based in Mill Valley, California, NewsTrust Communications is a 501(c)(3) California public benefit organization. NewsTrust partners include the Huffington Post, PBS, PolitiFact and the Washington Post. Advisors include Howard Rheingold (Stanford University), Craig Newmark (Craigslist) and other digital media innovators. NewsTrust has received support from the MacArthur Foundation, Ashoka, the Ayrshire Foundation, the Mitch Kapor Foundation, the Sunlight Foundation and the Tides Foundation. Private donors include Doug Carlston and Henry Perry.[2] [3]

Highly rated news stories gain prominence on the NewsTrust web site as multiple users rate them according to specific standards of journalistic quality—among them fairness, context and the strength of the evidence presented. Thus visitors to the NewsTrust web site are able to peruse specific stories, view their cumulative ratings, and find quality journalism. Visitors may also choose to enhance their level of participation by rating the stories, writing reviews, and posting new stories.

The founder and executive director of NewsTrust is Fabrice Florin, whose stated goal is to expose NewsTrust users to multiple sources of quality journalism.

> "We want to get citizens to take a moment to go beyond their usual news consumption habits, to broaden their perspective. If your viewpoint is from the right, take a look at a news source from the left. If your viewpoint is from the left, take a look at what media from the right are saying. If you tend to read mainly mainstream press, take a look at some independent journalism." [4]

NewsTrust offers a categorized list of all the stories that have been posted since its inception.

On March 2, 2010 Omidyar Network announced a grant of $100,000 to enable NewsTrust to further develop web-based tools that will help users become better informed and differentiate between misinformation and credible news. With the Omidyar Network grant, five specific pilot programs will be run over the next six months:[5]

- •MyNews – a personal news-filtering tool
- •Local News Hunt – a rating system for local news
- •Global News Hunt – a rating system for international news
- •TrustNetworks – a community site for members and partners
- •TruthSquad – a community fact-checking service.

References

[1] http://www.dankennedy.net/
[2] http://www.prnewswire.com/news-releases/omidyar-network-awards-grant-to-newstrust-85967637.html
[3] http://www.smartmobs.com/2007/11/28/newstrustnet-receives-macarthur-grant/
[4] http://www.pbs.org/engage/blog/pbs-engage-pov-partner-newstrust
[5] http://www.prnewswire.com/news-releases/omidyar-network-awards-grant-to-newstrust-85967637.html

http://www.prnewswire.com/news-releases/omidyar-network-awards-grant-to-newstrust-85967637.html

http://www.pbs.org/engage/blog/pbs-engage-pov-partner-newstrust

http://medianation.blogspot.com/2008/04/re-editing-agenda-with-newstrust.html

http://www.pbs.org/newshour/vote2008/reportersblog/2008/10/as_candidates_grapple_with_eco.html

http://www.huffingtonpost.com/amanda-michel/join-the-john-mccain-news_b_104629.html

http://www.flickr.com/photos/fabola/sets/72057594068512337/

http://www.smartmobs.com/2007/11/28/newstrustnet-receives-macarthur-grant/

http://www.whorunsgov.com/Partners/NewsTrust

Newsvine

Newsvine

URL	newsvine.com [1]
Commercial?	Yes
Type of site	Social News
Registration	Optional
Available language(s)	English
Owner	msnbc.com
Created by	Newsvine, Inc.
Launched	March 1, 2006
Alexa rank	6,782 (as of Jul 11, 08) [2]
Current status	Online

Newsvine is a community-powered, collaborative journalism news website, owned by msnbc.com, which draws content from its users and syndicated content from mainstream sources such as The Associated Press. Users can write articles, seed links to external content, and discuss news items submitted by both users and professional journalists.

Newsvine, the company, is not a news bureau and exercises no editorial voice, but acts as a social news platform for the community which has grown around it. Members decide with their actions what news makes it onto the site and what news is removed, and the Newsvine staff works to keep the platform operating and evolving.

Newsvine was named the *Top News Site of 2006* and one of the *50 Best Websites of 2007* by *Time* magazine.[3]

History

Seattle-based Newsvine, Inc. was founded in the spring of 2005 by Mike Davidson, Calvin Tang, Lance Anderson and Mark Budos. Josh Yockey joined the company shortly after it opened its offices, with Tom Laramee and Tyler Adams being hired later. The development team consists of several veterans from the Walt Disney Internet Group and ESPN.

The company moved into its offices near Downtown Seattle on August 1, 2005, and launched newsvine.com into private alpha on December 1, 2005. On January 5, 2006, the site went into private beta, and then launched to the public on March 1, 2006.

On October 7, 2007, Newsvine announced its acquisition by the news website msnbc.com, effective October 5, 2007. Since the acquisition, Newsvine has continued to run as a separate website and brand from msnbc.com, operating out of its original headquarters in Seattle.

Features

Seeding

Newsvine allows users to "seed," or post links for others to view. Seeds usually contain a short description or direct quotation from the linked article. With the "Newsvine Button," users can select "Seed Newsvine" from their bookmarks and a seeding dialog will appear. Seeds allow for all of the same options as articles except the ability to insert photographs and/or polls.

A seed that has been voted for by the user.

An article with a captioned photograph.

Articles

One of the most defining features of Newsvine is the ability for users to write their own articles. Commonly known as citizen journalism, this allows users to express their opinions for public discussion or even report in a journalistic manner. The most popular articles for top tags appear in the "Featured Writers" section, where article writers can receive extra publicity.

While writing articles, users can upload their own photographs or choose from a list of Flickr photos registered under a Creative Commons license for addition to the post. Captions can be written to clarify the meaning of the photograph.

Voting

Another common feature among social bookmarking websites is the ability to vote for content. Users who enjoy reading an article/seed or agree with its content are encouraged to vote for the content. Articles and seeds with the most votes appear in the "Top Wire," "Top Seeds," or "Top of the Vine" sections of the site.

Newsvine also allows for users to vote for comments that they enjoyed reading. When a comment receives at least five votes, a green star is placed in the upper right-hand corner, signifying that many users enjoyed or agreed with the comment. Clicking the star will lead viewers to the next highly rated comment.

Negative votes are also registered, and a comment that receives too many negative votes will often be collapsed, so that it can only be viewed by deliberately opening it. This limits discussion under that comment, since new comments under it will not be seen automatically.

Commenting

The ability to comment on seeds and articles allows for extra discussions regarding the content. While debates are welcome, useless, insulting, and self-promoting comments are not. If a comment receives enough reports, that comment will be collapsed and its contents can only be shown by choosing to expand it. The Newsvine comment system also allows for semi-threaded comments, easing the confusion of comment direction. Users can edit but not delete their own comments, writers are allowed to delete comments on their own content. Unregistered users are also allowed to have their say, but comments by unregistered users are not made public until that user creates a registered account.

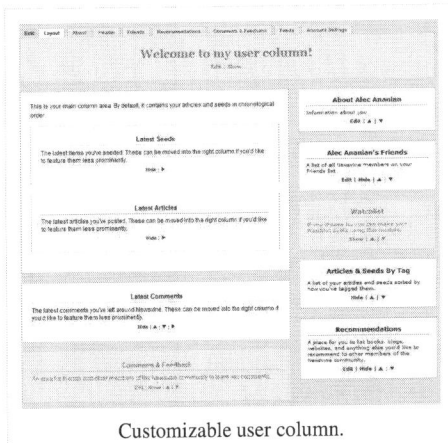

Customizable user column.

User Columns

Newsvine user columns give users the ability to manage and share their articles, seeds, friends, recommendations, and other statistical information. Every user has one, and each is given their own subdomain to access it (<user>.newsvine.com). User columns are customizable: aspects of the layouts can be moved or hidden, a user photo and biography can be added, a header (such as a welcome message) can be added, friends can be invited to Newsvine or added to the user's friends list, recommendations (such as favorite books, bands, blogs, etc.) can be shown, and comments and feedback from other users can be managed. Also, through user columns, members have the ability to add others to their watchlist and friend list or to send another a chat invitation.

Earnings

Newsvine tells users that they will receive 90% of revenue from advertisements on their personal Newsvine pages. These earnings are "based on traffic to your articles and seeds," but it is unclear exactly how Newsvine calculate earnings. The remaining 10% go to whoever referred the user to Newsvine, or for site maintenance if there was no referrer. Newsvine does not publish the amount of revenue that has gone to users.

Watchlist

If a user finds a writer or tag that he/she enjoys to read content from, it can be added to the Watchlist. Watchlists are lists of members and tags that a user can compile to easily find interesting news. Items on a user's watchlist appear on the left column and, if there is content that the user has not read by a watchlisted author or tag, a number will appear next to the item name signifying how many articles or seeds have not been read.

Conversation Tracker

Much like the Watchlist, the Conversation Tracker allows users to track other members. However, the Conversation Tracker is a notifier of new comments. There are three sections to the Conversation Tracker: new comments from a user's Newsvine column, new comments from articles that a user has commented on, and new comments from an article a user's friend has commented on. If a user has added members to the friend list that share a common interest in content, the Conversation Tracker can act as a list of recommended articles.

Friends List

The Friends List gives users the ability to meet new people and find others with common interests, but there are no requirements in doing so. Creating a populated friends list gives users the ability to find interesting new articles through the Conversation Tracker. Once a user adds a friend to the list, the added friend receives a notification and is given the ability to accept or decline the offer.

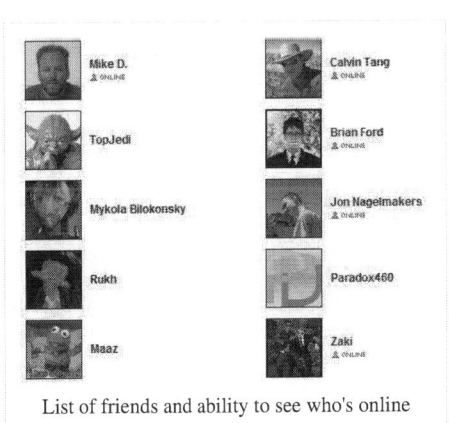

List of friends and ability to see who's online

Vineacity

Vineacity is a measure of six elements that contribute to a Newsvine user's overall rating as a positive influence to the Newsvine community. Earned as 'branches' on a Newsvine logo icon displayed next to the user's name, the six areas of excellence include:

- Courtesy - earned when a user's positive feedback outweighs any abuse reports they may have received.
- Longevity - earned when the users has been active for at least two months after registering.
- Fruitfulness - earned when the user has submitted a substantial amount of content or comments that have received votes.
- Connectedness - earned when the user appears on a substantial number of watchlists and/or friendlists.
- Random Act of Vineness - earned for an exceptional moment of greatness on Newsvine.
- Lifetime achievement - earned when a user has received a combined number of votes on all articles, links and comments around Newsvine.

References

[1] http://newsvine.com/

[2] "Traffic Details from Alexa" (http://www.alexa.com/data/details/traffic_details/newsvine.com?site0=newsvine.com&y=r&z=3& h=300&w=610&c=1&u[]=newsvine.com&x=2008-07-11T08:11:41.000Z&check=www.alexa.com& signature=fyd0O1p6MZ6dBHudJO/Cy5qNyao=&range=6m&size=Medium). Alexa. . Retrieved 2008-07-11.

[3] "50 Best Websites 2007" (http://www.time.com/time/specials/2007/article/0,28804,1633488_1633530_1633560,00.html). *Time*. July 8, 2007. . Retrieved May 20, 2010.

External links

- Newsvine (http://www.newsvine.com)
- Newsvine Code of Honor (http://www.newsvine.com/_cms/info/codeofhonor)
- Inside the Net Episode 8 (http://www.twit.tv/itn8)
- Mike Davidson (co-founder, CEO) (http://www.mikeindustries.com/blog/)
- Calvin Tang (co-founder, COO) (http://www.calvintang.com/blog/)

Ngbot mobile

ngBot mobile

URL	mobile.ngbot.com [1]
Type of site	Mobile content
Registration	Free
Owner	DevEdgeLabs [2]
Created by	Opeyemi Obembe, Ernest Ojeh
Launched	2006

ngBot mobile is the first website of the **ngBot portal**, which is a website for free downloading mobile content and tools to customize mobile phones. It is also the first mobile community in Nigeria and one of the first in Africa[3] [4] .

Currently, the features on *ngBot mobile* includes; Free mobile wallpapers, ringtones, games, videos, and applications, tips and tricks, articles, mobile technology news, SMS, forum, and recently added *mobile marketplace*.

In *September, 2009*, **ngBot mobile** introduced *Tools* which is a feature available to registered users. The first "Tool" included was *JARDe* which is a tool which members can use to extract the details of a *java application* or *game*, create a own custom JAD file for any JAR *application/game* and edit icon and name. While customizing of applications, is a feature for premium members.

References

[1] http://mobile.ngbot.com/
[2] http://www.devedgelabs.com/
[3] *ngBot.com - Nigeria's First Real Mobile 2.0 Community?* (http://www.startupsnigeria.com/2009/01/ ngbotcom-nigerias-first-real-mobile-20-community/)
[4] *ngBot: The First Nigerian Mobile Community* (http://www.techmasai.com/2009/09/ngbot-the-first-nigerian-mobile-community/)

External links

- Official site (http://www.ngbot.com/)
- Official blog (http://blog.ngbot.com/)
- devedgelabs (http://www.devedgelabs.com/)

Oneview

oneview

URL	http://www.oneview.com/, http://www.oneview.co.uk/, http://www.oneview.in/, http://www.oneview.de/
Slogan	human powered search
Commercial?	yes
Type of site	Social Bookmarking
Registration	partly
Available language(s)	English, German
Owner	oneview GmbH
Launched	1998
Current status	online

oneview is an English and German-speaking application for social bookmarking. The platform has already been brought into being from the multimedia-agency Denkwerk in 1998[1] and is therefore one of the first providers for social bookmarking worldwide. According to a statement, the platform has got a collection of more than 5 million bookmarks from its members by now.

Functions

The basic functions from oneview, as a *social bookmarking service*, consist in saving and organising links, tagging of links, central copying of saved links and in the provision of a spatio-temporal independent access on the link collection of one or all members. Moreover, the collected information can be shared with other users.

In order that the user can find the information quickly, oneview provides a search function. In this search human filtered information is presented to the user. The combination of different tags, as a search survey, serves to find the favoured information quickly as well.

For registered users there is the possibility to set up an individual collection of bookmarks and to provide them with tags. Thus, the user has access on the individually collected links and can retrieve them at any time. The bookmarks collected by the user can be labeled as private or public. Bookmarks with public liberalisation are available for other users, no matter if they are registered or not. Public liberalisation contains placing of other tags from other users (see also Folksonomy).

History and development

Due to early establishment, oneview is seen as one of the pioneers of the current social bookmarking and search offers. In these days, the idea has been welcomed from its users and has been available in 12 speeches online in 2001.[2] oneview was awarded a. o. for the concept with the German Multimedia-Award [3] in 1999 and the "World Medal" of the New York Festivals[4] in the same year. In August 2000 the „Best in eBusiness Award" followed suit.[5]

The Oneview 2.0 platform was released as beta in 2005, then in March 2007 the 2.0 platform came out of beta and replaced the 1.0 platform. The financial interest of the publishing company M. DuMont Schauberg in Cologne has been made public.

References

[1] Die Welt online (http://www.welt.de/print-welt/article501288/Die_Linksammlung_fuer_unterwegs.html), article published on February
    12th 2000, 12:00 am

[2] Press 1 (http://www.press1.de/health/db/9760369451573349525n6.html?start=120&anzahl=10), February 2001

[3] Net News (http://netnewsletter.de/letter/archiv/9917.html), April 28th 1999

[4] PR Newswire Europe Ltd. (http://www.prnewswire.co.uk/cgi/news/release?id=13141), October 11th 1999

[5] eNews Archiv (http://www.wowowo.de/enews.html?iny=2000&inm=08), August 2000

External links

- oneview.de (http://www.oneview.de)
- oneview.com (http://www.oneview.com)
- oneview.co.uk (http://www.oneview.co.uk)
- oneview.in (http://www.oneview.in)
- Interview with one of the general managers (Marcus Rudert) (http://netzstimmen.de/eintrag.php?id=18)
- Article about the financial interest from the publishing company DuMont Schauberg (http://www.
  marketing-boerse.de/News/details/
  M-DuMont-Schauberg-beteiligt-sich-an-menschlicher-Suchmaschine-oneview/6763)

PopUrls

PopUrls

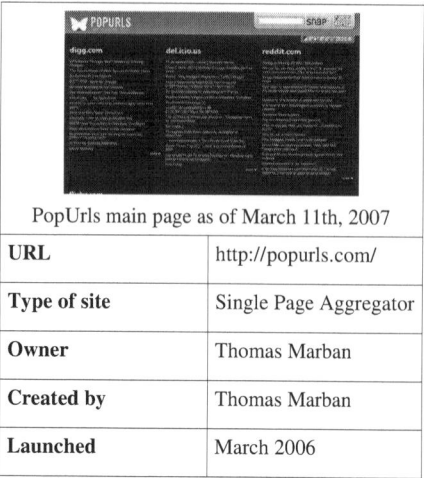

PopUrls main page as of March 11th, 2007

URL	http://popurls.com/
Type of site	Single Page Aggregator
Owner	Thomas Marban
Created by	Thomas Marban
Launched	March 2006

PopUrls is a mashup of the web's most visited social news sites and portals that encapsulates headlines of its sources in near-realtime. Introduced in March 2006 by Thomas Marban the site created a new trend in so called Single Page Aggregators and serves as a case study for Web Syndication. PopUrls was included as number five in Time Magazine's list of the top 50 websites of 2009.[1]

PopUrls was acquired by Idealab in July 2010 for an undisclosed amount.

References

[1] Fisher, Adam (2009-08-24). "50 Best Websites 2009" (http://www.time.com/time/specials/packages/article/0,28804,1918031_1918016_1917971,00.html). Time Magazine. . Retrieved 2009-09-10.

External links

- Official website (http://http://popurls.com/)
- Interview with Thomas Marban (http://www.folksonomy.org/2006/11/what_is_popurls_and_how/) - the founder of PopUrls
- Review on Kevin Kelly's Cool Tools blog (http://kk.org/cooltools/archives/001213.php)
- Covered on CNET News blog (http://www.news.com/8301-10784_3-6105336-7.html)

Propeller.com

Propeller was a social news aggregator operated by AOL-Netscape. It was similar to Digg; users could vote for which stories are to be included on the front page and could comment on them as well. As of October 1st, 2010, Propeller will no longer be active.[1]

Former Propeller logo, while hosted under Netscape

The Chief Architect of the site was Brian Alvey[2] and the lead developer of the site was Alex Rudolff [3] . It was maintained by Weblogs, Inc. CEO Jason Calacanis until he left AOL in November 2006. The current director is Tom Drapeau. Netscape's market share had been declining for over a year at the time of the change-over [4] .

Propeller was hosted on the Netscape.com domain from June 2006 to September 2007 when it was replaced by the AOL Netscape generic portal.

The previous version of Propeller was released to mixed reactions. Some users liked that they had more participation ability while others found the pages to be harder to navigate and not as structured. Soon after the release of the new site, a story entitled "Netscape's Blunder" was the top rated story.[5]

Anchors

Propeller has several "anchors", currently led by James Marcus, who work on maintaining the site and featuring stories in the "anchor picks" box on the home page. This creates a slightly different environment from Digg, as Digg's homepage rankings are based solely on user votes, where Propeller's are based on both. The rest of the team includes Alexia Prichard.

Scouts

Propeller also pays a small number of power users called Scouts. This group is run by Ryan Budke and made up of Weblogs, Inc. bloggers, Propeller power users and celebrities, including Wil Wheaton. Other scouts include bloggers such as Fedquip [6] Angry Ken [7], Henry Wang, Digidave [8] TweekerChick [9] and Corey Spring. These users were called Navigators until the relaunch of the Netscape Navigator browser, at which point the name was changed to avoid confusion.

References

[1] "Goodbye propeller" (http://www.aolnews.com/category/goodbye-propeller/). *AOL News*. . Retrieved 23 November 2010.

[2] Brian Alvey: Netscape, my Netscape (http://www.brianalvey.com/2006/06/16/netscape-my-netscape/)

[3] Brian Alvey: See you later, navigator (http://www.brianalvey.com/2006/06/22/see-you-later-navigator/)

[4] Alexa Internet- Netscape.com Traffic (http://www.alexa.com/data/details/traffic_details?range=3y&size=Medium&url=netscape.com) Retrieved on 2007-09-20

[5] "Netscape Community Backlash" (http://tech.netscape.com/viewstory/2006/07/09/netscape-community-backlash/?url=http://www.readwriteweb.com/archives/netscape_commun.php&frame=true). . Retrieved 2006-07-14.

[6] http://news.aol.com/newsbloggers/bloggers/jeff-hoard/

[7] http://angryken.com/

[8] http://www.digidave.org/

[9] http://tweekerchick.blogspot.com/

External links

- Website (http://www.propeller.com/)
- TechCrunch (http://www.techcrunch.com/2007/09/11/propeller-will-be-the-new-netscape-digg-clone/)
- Search Engine Journal (http://www.searchenginejournal.com/netscape-social-news-rebranding-to-propellercom/5627/)
- Search Engine Watch (http://blog.searchenginewatch.com/blog/070913-120529)

Reddit

Reddit

Reddit front page on February 08, 2011

URL	reddit.com [24]
Slogan	*The voice of the Internet -- news before it happens.*[1]
Commercial?	Yes
Type of site	News aggregation, general discussion and advice forum
Registration	Optional
Available language(s)	English, Esperanto, Japanese, French, Italian, German, Spanish[2]
Content license	Non-free[3]
Owner	Advance Publications via Condé Nast Publications
Created by	Steve Huffman Alexis Ohanian
Launched	2005
Alexa rank	▲ 135 (May 30 2011)[4]
Current status	Active

Reddit (stylized as **reddit**, pronounced English pronunciation: /ˈɹɛdɪt/ "red it")[5] is a social news website, owned by Condé Nast Digital, a subsidiary of Advance Magazine Publishers Inc. Users have the option to submit links to content on the Internet or submit "self" posts that contain original, user-submitted text. Other users may then vote the posted links "up" or "down" with the most successful links gaining prominence by reaching the front page. In addition, users can comment on the posted links and reply to other commentators consequently forming an online community. Reddit users (also referred to as *redditors*) may create their own topical sections, known informally as *subreddits* and officially as *communities*, for which to submit their links and to comment, while appealing to a specific niche.[6] [7] [8]

Overview

The appearance of submissions on the front page is determined by the age of the submission, positive to negative feedback ratio and the total vote count. [9] The submissions which appear on the front page can be customized by the user, who can subscribe or unsubscribe to any number of communities. Dozens of submissions cycle through the front page daily.

Mister Splashy Pants logo used on November 27, 2007

The site also has discussion areas in which users may discuss submissions and vote for or against other people's comments. The most popular comments rise to the top by default. Comments that were strongly voted down by users are not displayed, although the reader can display them by clicking an additional link or by changing the preferences. As of June 2011, these discussion areas are particularly active, often generating hundreds of comments per submission. Popular comments are seen by thousands of users, and are often the basis for new submissions. This process has generated many memes within the Reddit community.

Reddits

Reddit allows users to create communities called "reddits" (often referred to as "subreddits"), which focus on specific interests or organizations. There are 67,000+ reddits to peruse, and popular examples include, but are not limited to:

- Pics [10]
- Programming [11]
- Science [12]
- Trees [13]
- Atheism [14]
- Politics [15]
- Gaming [16]
- AskReddit [17]
- World News [18]

Registered users may customize which reddits appear on the front page of the site, providing an experience more tailored to their interests.

Reddit Meetups

The Reddit community has been known to socialize at local parks and bars around the world.[19]

History

Reddit was founded by Steve Huffman and Alexis Ohanian, both 22-year-old graduates of the University of Virginia.[7] It received its initial funding from Y Combinator. The team expanded to include Christopher Slowe and Aaron Swartz in 2005. Aaron Swartz joined in late January 2006 as part of the company's merger with Swartz's Infogami.[20] Condé Nast Publications, owner of *Wired*, acquired Reddit on October 31, 2006.[21] Shortly thereafter, Swartz was fired.[22]

Open source

On June 18, 2008, Reddit became an open source project.[23] With the exception of the anti-spam/cheating portions, all of the code and libraries written for Reddit became freely available on code.reddit.com.[24]

Growth

By the end of 2008, the team had grown to include Erik Martin, Jeremy Edberg,[25] David King,[26] and Mike Schiraldi.[27] In 2009, Huffman and Ohanian moved on to form Hipmunk, recruiting Slowe shortly thereafter.[28]

Reddit Gold

In July 2010, facing severe underfunding despite explosive traffic growth, Reddit introduced Reddit Gold, offering new features for a price of US$3.99/month or US$29.99/year.[29] The revenue and attention got them approval to buy more servers and hire more people.

Demographics

According to Google DoubleClick Ad Planner's estimate, the median U.S. Reddit user is male, 35-44 years of age, has some college education, and is making a middle-range income of $25,000 - $49,000 USD. The analysis also shows that the top audience interests of the site are Development Tools, Scripting Languages, and C & C++; suggesting a computer savvy demographic and culture.[30]

'Restoring Truthiness' Campaign

In September 2010, Reddit users started a movement to persuade Stephen Colbert to have a rally in Washington DC.[31] The movement was started by user mrsammercer, in a post where he describes waking up from a dream in which Stephen Colbert holds a satirical rally in D.C.[32]

He writes, "This would be the high water mark of American satire. Half a million people pretending to suspend all rational thought in unison. Perfect harmony. It'll feel like San Francisco in the late 60s, only we won't be able to get any acid."

The idea resonated with the Reddit community, which launched a campaign to bring the event to life. Over $500,000 was raised for charity to gain the attention of Colbert. The campaign was mentioned on-air several times and when the rallies were held in Washington, D.C. on October 30th, thousands of redditors made the journey.[33]

During a post-rally press conference, Reddit co-founder Alexis Ohanian asked, "What role did the Internet campaign play in convincing you to hold this rally?" Jon Stewart responded by saying that, though it was a very nice gesture, the two had already thought of the idea prior and the deposit on using the National Mall was already paid during the summer, so it acted mostly as a "validation of what we were thinking about attempting."[34] In a message to the reddit community, Colbert later added, "I have no doubt that your efforts to organize and the joy you clearly brought to your part of the story contributed greatly to the turnout and success."[35]

Awards

In May 2010, Reddit is named in Lead411's "2010 Hottest San Francisco Companies" list.[36]

Technology

Reddit was originally written in Common Lisp but was rewritten in Python in 2005.[37] The reasons given for the switch were faster performance, wider access to code libraries, and greater development flexibility. The Python web framework that former Reddit employee Aaron Swartz developed to run the site, web.py, is now available as an open-source project.[38]

Reddit currently uses Pylons as its web framework.[39] As of November 2009, Reddit has decommissioned their physical servers and migrated to Amazon Web Services.[40] In early 2009, Reddit started using jQuery.[41]

Mobile web

On June 7, 2010 Reddit staff launched a revamped mobile interface featuring rewritten CSS, a new color scheme, and a multitude of improvements.[42]

Client interface applications

There are several unofficial applications that use the Reddit API, including *reddit is fun*[43] , *Andreddit*[44] , F5, BaconReader[45] and an Android tablet specific application Reddita[46]

Search

On July 21, 2010, Reddit out-sourced the reddit search engine to Flaptor, who used their search product IndexTank.[47]

Notable community contributions

- In early December of 2010, the members of the Christianity subreddit and the Atheism subreddit came together to cross-promote[48] fundraising drives for World Vision's Clean Water Fund and Médecins Sans Frontières (Doctors Without Borders), respectively. Later, the Islam subreddit joined in, raising money for Islamic Relief. In less than a week, the three communities (as well as the reddit community at-large) raised over $45,000 for charity.[49]

- In early October 2010, a story was posted on Reddit about a seven-year-old girl, Kathleen Edwards, who was in the advanced stages of Huntington's disease. The girl's neighbors were taunting her and her family. Redditors banded together and gave the girl a shopping spree.[50] [51]

- Reddit started the largest Secret Santa program in the world, which is still in operation to date. For the 2010 Holiday season, 92 countries were involved in the Secret Santa program. There were 17,543 participants, and $662,907.60 was collectively spent on gift purchases and shipping costs. [52] [53] [54]

- Members from reddit donated nearly $575,000 to DonorsChoose in support of Stephen Colbert's March to Keep Fear Alive. The donation spree broke previous records for the most money donated to a single cause by the reddit community and resulted in an interview with Colbert on reddit.[55]

- Reddit users donated $185,356.70 to Direct Relief International for Haiti after the earthquake devastated the island in January, 2010.[56]

References

[1] "reddit.com" (http://www.reddit.com/). . Retrieved January 23, 2011.

[2] Netcraft list of subdomains (http://searchdns.netcraft.com/?host=reddit.com&x=0&y=0)

[3] "reddit.com: help" (http://www.reddit.com/help/useragreement). . Retrieved January 23, 2011.

[4] "reddit.com Site Info" (http://www.alexa.com/siteinfo/reddit.com). Alexa Internet, Inc. . Retrieved 23 January 2011.

[5] reddit.com: help (http://www.reddit.com/help/faq#Whatdoesthenameredditmean)

[6] Nations, Daniel. "A Review of Reddit" (http://webtrends.about.com/od/reddit/gr/reddit_review.htm). *About.com: Web Trends*. . Retrieved 3 September 2010.

[7] Adams, Richard (2005-12-08). "reddit.com" (http://technology.guardian.co.uk/innovations/story/0,,1660870,00.html). The Guardian. . Retrieved 2006-12-23.

[8] "Reddit FAQ" (http://www.reddit.com/help/faq#Individualreddits). . Retrieved 2010-12-19.

[9] "reddit algorithm" (http://www.seomoz.org/blog/reddit-stumbleupon-delicious-and-hacker-news-algorithms-exposed). .

[10] http://www.reddit.com/r/pics/

[11] http://www.reddit.com/r/programming

[12] http://www.reddit.com/r/science/

[13] http://www.reddit.com/r/trees/

[14] http://www.reddit.com/r/atheism/

[15] http://www.reddit.com/r/politics/

[16] http://www.reddit.com/r/gaming/

[17] http://www.reddit.com/r/AskReddit/

[18] http://www.reddit.com/r/worldnews/

[19] "Reddit Worldwide Meetups" (http://www.reddit.com/r/meetup/)

[20] Swartz, Aaron (February 27, 2006). "Introducing Infogami" (http://infogami.com/blog/introduction). Infogami. . Retrieved 2007-01-06.

[21] Arrington, Michael (October 31, 2006). "Breaking news: Condé Nast/Wired Acquires reddit" (http://www.techcrunch.com/2006/10/31/
breaking-news-conde-nastwired-acquires-reddit/). TechCrunch. . Retrieved 2007-01-06.

[22] A Chat with Aaron Swartz (http://blogoscoped.com/archive/2007-05-07-n78.html)

[23] Open source announcement on the Reddit blog (http://blog.reddit.com/2008/06/reddit-goes-open-source.html)

[24] "reddit – Trac" (http://code.reddit.com/). Code.reddit.com. . Retrieved 2010-07-29.

[25] blog.reddit - what's new on reddit: welcome, jedberg (http://blog.reddit.com/2007/03/welcome-jedberg.html)

[26] blog.reddit - what's new on reddit: welcome, david (http://blog.reddit.com/2008/04/welcome-david.html)

[27] blog.reddit - what's new on reddit: Welcome, Mike Schiraldi (a.k.a. raldi) (http://blog.reddit.com/2008/12/welcome-mike.html)

[28] Reddit Chief Takes Flight To Hipmunk, Explains Why He's Leaving Now (http://techcrunch.com/2010/11/01/
reddit-chief-takes-flight-to-hipmunk-explains-why-hes-leaving-now/)

[29] Posted by mike [raldi] (2010-07-19). "what's new on reddit: Three new features for reddit gold: Choose-your-own ads, Userpage sorting, and
Friends with Benefits" (http://blog.reddit.com/2010/07/three-new-features-for-reddit-gold.html). blog.reddit. . Retrieved 2010-07-29.

[30] "DoubleClick Ad Planner by Google" (https://www.google.com/adplanner/site_profile?#siteDetails?identifier=reddit.com&geo=US&
trait_type=1&lp=false). . Retrieved 2010-04-03.

[31] Colbert Rally in Time Magazine (http://newsfeed.time.com/2010/09/14/reddit-campaign-for-colbert-rally-breaks-charity-records/)

[32] Reddit post suggesting the Colbert Rally idea (http://www.reddit.com/r/politics/comments/d7ntl/
ive_had_a_vision_and_i_cant_shake_it_colbert/)

[33] blog.reddit - what's new on reddit: Buy Shirts, Remember the Rally, Question Colbert, and Smile (http://blog.reddit.com/2010/11/
buy-shirts-remember-rally-question.html)

[34] Rally to Restore Sanity - Press Conference - Video (http://www.mediaite.com/tv/
jon-stewart-and-stephen-colbert-hold-post-rally-to-restore-sanity-press-conference/) Mediaite. October 30, 2010.

[35] Stephen Colbert has answered your questions : IAmA (http://www.reddit.com/r/IAmA/comments/ee20j/
stephen_colbert_has_answered_your_questions/)

[36] Lead411 launches "Hottest Companies in San Francisco" awards (http://www.lead411.com/san-francisco-companies.html)

[37] "On lisp" blog post by Reddit founder "spez," detailing the reasons for switching to python from lisp (http://blog.reddit.com/2005/12/
on-lisp.html)

[38] Official web.py site (http://webpy.org/)

[39] Sites Using Pylons (http://wiki.pylonshq.com/display/pylonscommunity/Sites+Using+Pylons) - Pylons Community — PythonWeb

[40] Moving to the cloud on blog.reddit.com (http://blog.reddit.com/2009/11/moving-to-cloud.html)

[41] what's new on reddit: reddit now powered by jQuery (http://blog.reddit.com/2009/01/reddit-now-powered-by-jquery.html) - Posted by
Chris Slowe (keysersosa) (Friday, January 30, 2009) - blog.reddit

[42] "A better mobile reddit for all" (http://blog.reddit.com/2010/06/better-mobile-reddit-for-all.html). reddit.com. 2010-06-09. . Retrieved
2010-07-29.

[43] reddit is fun - Android Application on the Android market (http://www.appbrain.com/app/com.andrewshu.android.reddit)

[44] Download andreddit for your Android phone on AppBrain (http://www.appbrain.com/app/com.tomdryer.reddit)

[45] (http://baconreader.com/)

[46] Reddita- Android Market (https://market.android.com/details?id=com.leyths.reddita.free)

[47] "Reddit Blog post announcing the use of IndexTank search engine" (http://blog.reddit.com/2010/07/new-search.html). .

[48] Dogs and cats living together! Mass hysteria! r/Atheism and r/Christianity have a friendly competition up for a holiday charity drive that is
spilling over into other subreddi... (http://www.reddit.com/r/reddit.com/comments/ejnbg/dogs_and_cats_living_together_mass_hysteria/
)

[49] Christians and Atheists Square Off In Online Battle To Raise Money For Charity (http://www.huffingtonpost.com/2010/12/16/
christian-and-atheist-gro_n_797910.html)

[50] Toy Store Shopping Spree for Kathleen Edward (http://www.myfoxdetroit.com/dpp/news/local/
toy-store-shopping-spree-for-kathleen-edward)

[51] Stryker, Cole (2010-12-10). Kathleen Edward, Harassed Girl with Huntington's Diseas, Thanks Reddit (http://www.urlesque.com/2010/
10/12/kathleen-edward-girl-with-huntingtons-disease-thanks-reddit/). Urlesque. Retrieved April 20, 2011.

[52] Boitnott, John (December 23, 2010). "Secret Santa success caps banner year for Reddit" (http://venturebeat.com/2010/12/23/
secret-santa-success-caps-banner-year-for-reddit/). *VentureBeat Interpreting Innovation*. VentureBeat. . Retrieved January 3, 2011.

[53] "The Biggest Secret Santa Gift Exchange in the World" (http://www.thedailybeast.com/blogs-and-stories/2010-12-20/
secret-santa-the-creator-of-reddits-gift-exchange-the-worlds-biggest/). . Retrieved 2011-02-12.

[54] "Statistics for Secret Santa 2010" (http://redditgifts.com/statistics/). . Retrieved 2011-02-12.

[55] Restoring Truthiness Giving Page (http://www.donorschoose.org/donors/viewChallenge.html?id=39361)

[56] Direct Relief International: Support Us - Tributes: (http://dri.convio.net/site/TR/Events/Tributes?pg=fund&fr_id=1030&pxfid=1511& JServSessionIdr004=r7t58phav1.app245b)

External links

- Reddit (http://reddit.com/)
- Fixxit (Reddit's code repository) (http://code.reddit.com/)
- Reddit's job board (http://redditjobs.com/)
- Alien Logo Archive (http://s3.amazonaws.com/sp.reddit.com/archive2008.html)

Scuttle (software)

Scuttle

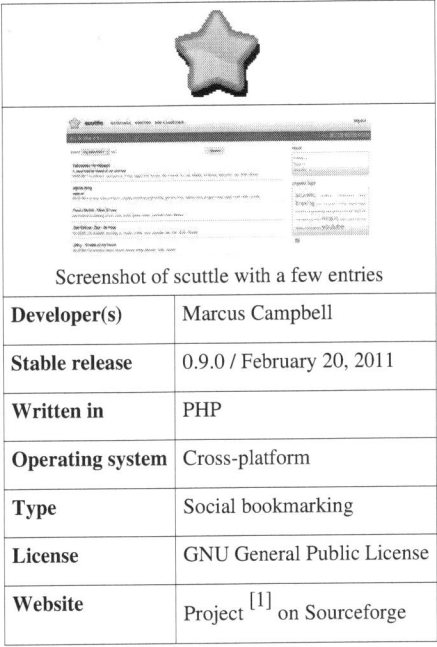

Screenshot of scuttle with a few entries

Developer(s)	Marcus Campbell
Stable release	0.9.0 / February 20, 2011
Written in	PHP
Operating system	Cross-platform
Type	Social bookmarking
License	GNU General Public License
Website	Project [1] on Sourceforge

Scuttle is a PHP/MySQL-based open source social bookmarking. It contains code from other PHP-based projects such as drupal or jQuery.[2]

Functions

Scuttle offers the same functionality as most of the social bookmarking websites such as tagging, RSS, multiple languages and security settings(public and private). It also supports bookmark imports from delicious and the delicious API, which means that all programs or widgets might also work. Backups are available via XML or MySQL Backend.[3] It lacks an administrator backend, although there is one commercially available called *"Scuttle Plus"*. The more advanced *semantic scuttle* provides anti-spam protection,[4] structured tags and collaborative tag description.[5]

References

[1] http://sourceforge.net/projects/scuttle/
[2] File AUTHORS in scuttle-0.9.0.tar.gz
[3] http://www.linux.com/archive/feed/53231
[4] http://akeller.eu/installation-von-semantic-scuttle-089/
[5] http://sourceforge.net/projects/semanticscuttle/

External links

- Scuttle (http://sourceforge.net/projects/scuttle/) on Sourceforge
- Semantic Scuttle (http://sourceforge.net/projects/semanticscuttle/) on Sourceforge
- Article about scuttle (http://www.linux.com/archive/feed/53231) on linux.com

ShareThis

ShareThis

URL	http://sharethis.com/
Type of site	Social Bookmarking and Sharing Tool
Registration	Free
Owner	ShareThis

The **ShareThis** button is an all-in-one widget that lets people share any content on the Web with friends via e-mail, AIM, or text message. The widget can also keep an account of personal contacts so that users can send an e-mail, IM, or text message with favorite links to friends. [1] The button can be deployed on any site to drive traffic, stimulate viral activity, and track the sharing of content. Toolbar versions exist for Firefox, Mozilla Application Suite and Internet Explorer, and customized widgets are available for leading blog publisher sites including Blogger, TypePad and WordPress.

History

ShareThis was founded by Dr. David E. Goldberg, engineering professor at University of Illinois at Urbana-Champaign, and Tim Schigel, then a Director at Blue Chip Venture Company ("Blue Chip"). ShareThis owns an exclusive license, with the University of Illinois, for Dr. Goldberg's patent applications in the area of genetic algorithms and machine learning for the purposes of information discovery and learning from sharing behavior. ShareThis has headquarters in San Francisco, CA and Cincinnati, OH. Investors include IllinoisVENTURES and DFJ Mercury.

Service details

ShareThis can be found on many popular blogs. ShareThis can also be used directly from a browser by download the ShareThis button. ShareThis allows users to import contacts from e.g. Gmail, Yahoo, Facebook, MySpace, AIM, and Outlook. A history is kept in the users personal ShareBox. ShareThis has developed a plug-in for Blogger, TypePad and WordPress blog publishing sites.

References

[1] "Publisher widget ShareThis raises $15 million, Source:CNET" (http://www.news.com/8301-10784_3-9892624-7.html). .

Further reading

- Needle, David (2009-02-20). "ShareThis Expands Social Widget" (http://www.internetnews.com/webcontent/print.php/3805166). *Internet News*. Jupiter Media. Retrieved 2010-04-08.
- McCarthy, Megan (2008-03-13). "ShareThis Lands Another $15M in Funding" (http://www.wired.com/epicenter/2008/03/sharethis-lands/). *Wired*. Conde Nast. Retrieved 2010-04-08.
- Harris, Scott Duke (2010-03-03). "Harris: Startup ShareThis joins rush to find money in buzz" (http://www.mercurynews.com/business/ci_14506762?nclick_check=1). *Mercury News*. Retrieved 2010-04-08.
- Schonfeld, Erick (2010-03-01). "ShareThis Introduces The Share Stream" (http://techcrunch.com/2010/03/01/sharethis-share-stream/). TechCrunch. Retrieved 2010-04-08.

- Needleman, Rafe (2008-09-22). "Is ShareThis the next Digg?" (http://news.cnet.com/ 8301-17939_109-10047342-2.html). *Webware*. CNET. Retrieved 2010-04-08.
- Burkitt, Laurie (2010-02-22). "ShareThis Wants To Help Publishers Find Influencers" (http://www.forbes.com/ 2010/02/22/sharethis-addthis-facebook-twitter-google-buzz-consumer-data-cmo-network-sharethis. html?boxes=Homepagechannels). *Forbes*. Retrieved 2010-04-08.
- Olsen, Stefanie (2008-03-13). "Publisher widget ShareThis raises $15 million" (http://news.cnet.com/ 8301-10784_3-9892624-7.html). CNET. Retrieved 2010-04-08.

External links

- ShareThis.com website (http://www.sharethis.com)

Simpy

SimPy is also an open-source discrete-event simulation package written in Python.

Simpy

URL	http://www.simpy.com/
Type of site	Online social bookmarking
Registration	Optional
Owner	Otis Gospodnetic
Created by	Otis Gospodnetic
Launched	May 2004

Simpy was a web-based personal and social bookmarking service.

The service launched in May 2004. In 2010, it was acquired by Reuters and ceased operation as a social bookmarking site in April of that year.

Service features

Simpy used tags and tag clouds to aid bookmark recall and allows bookmarks to be shared or kept private. In addition to saving, tagging, and sharing links, users could also save, tag, and search free-text notes. Most data pages also had RSS feeds. Simpy's founder is one of the developers of Lucene, a popular text search toolkit, thus Simpy had powerful search capabilities.

The service allowed for cooperation, via groups with different levels of privacy, and for discovery of relevant and new links via its watchlists and watchlist filters.

Simpy had a well-documented REST API suitable for mashups and integration with other applications and services.

de.lirio.us user migration to Simpy

de.lirio.us was an open source clone of del.icio.us (criticized for its direct copying[1]). It had technical problems and in March 2006, its maintainer announced that Simpy would take over the de.lirio.us userbase. The transfer to Simpy was completed in July 2006 [2] .

References

[1] del.irio.us criticized at redmonk.com (http://redmonk.com/sogrady/2005/03/28/delirious-or-how-not-to-clone-a-service/)

[2] Transfer from de.lirio.us to Simpy (http://blog.simpy.com/blojsom/blog/news/2006/06/13/De-lirio-us-Migrates-to-Simpy.html)

External links

- Simpy (now redirecting to Reuters.com) (http://www.simpy.com/)

SiteBar

SiteBar

Developer(s)	Ondrej Brablc, SiteBar Development Team
Stable release	(14-OCT-2007) [+/–] [1]
Preview release	(14-JUL-2008) [+/–] [2]
Written in	PHP
Available in	English and 20+ languages
Type	Social bookmarking
License	GNU General Public License
Website	http://sitebar.org/

SiteBar is a free online bookmark manager that is available in more than 20 languages. Users can store their bookmarks on a private or public SiteBar server, access them online, and share them with multiple user groups. It features sidebar integration into web browsers and can also import bookmarks from web browsers.

The SiteBar bookmark server is open source software published under the GPL, which enables anybody to run their own SiteBar server and keep their bookmarks under their control.

References

- Oliver Kaven. "PC Magazine: Access Your Bookmarks from Anywhere" [3]. Retrieved 2006-12-18.
- Kim Komando. "Synching Favorites, Bookmarks" [4]. Retrieved 2006-12-18.
- Michael. "4sysops: SiteBar: a social bookmark manager for loners" [5]. Retrieved 2006-12-19.
- Michael VanPutten. "SitcBar offers excellent online bookmark management" [6]. Retrieved 2007-01-10.
- Brian Carnell. "SiteBar.Org" [7]. Archived from the original [8] on 2007-06-15. Retrieved 2007-01-30.
- Ben Martin. "linux.com: Syncing multiple users' bookmarks with SiteBar" [9]. Retrieved 2008-06-22.

Public servers running SiteBar

Use one of many public SiteBar servers (please note that we cannot guarantee functionality of those servers):

- SiteBar.org [25]
- sitebar.ch [10]
- SiteBar.gr [11]
- uksystems.co.uk [12]
- onlinebookmarks.co.uk [13]
- yhbt.com [14]
- beket.nl [15]
- cyber-junk.de [16]
- acuralink.com [17]
- lookup.ws [18]
- pidea.co.uk [19]
- favvo.se [20]
- bookmarkmagic.com [21]
- nesti.net [22]

- linkjar.com [23]
- link-manager.de [24]
- kurmis.com [25]
- linklerimburada.com [26]

References

[1] http://en.wikipedia.org/wiki/Template%3Alatest_stable_software_release%2Fsitebar?action=edit&preload=Template:LSR/syntax

[2] http://en.wikipedia.org/wiki/Template%3Alatest_preview_software_release%2Fsitebar?action=edit&preload=Template:LSR/syntax

[3] http://www.pcmag.com/article2/0,1759,1823013,00.asp

[4] http://www.komando.com/tips/index.aspx?id=1384

[5] http://4sysops.com/archives/sitebar-a-social-bookmark-manager-for-loners/

[6] http://www.michaelvanputten.com/2006/12/22/sitebar-offers-excellent-online-bookmark-management/

[7] http://web.archive.org/web/20070615014143/http://brian.carnell.com/archives/years/2006/11/000053.html

[8] http://brian.carnell.com/archives/years/2006/11/000053.html

[9] http://www.linux.com/feature/138324

[10] http://www.sitebar.ch/

[11] http://sitebar.gr/

[12] http://www.uksystems.co.uk/sitebar

[13] http://www.onlinebookmarks.co.uk/

[14] http://www.yhbt.com/sitebar

[15] http://sitebar.beket.nl/

[16] http://www.cyber-junk.de/SiteBar

[17] http://www.acuralink.com/sitebar

[18] http://lookup.ws/sitebar

[19] http://sitebar.pidea.co.uk

[20] http://www.favvo.se

[21] http://www.bookmarkmagic.com/

[22] http://www.nesti.net/

[23] http://www.linkjar.com/

[24] http://www.link-manager.de/sitebar

[25] http://www.kurmis.com/sb

[26] http://www.linklerimburada.com/

StumbleUpon

StumbleUpon! Toolbar

StumbleUpon Toolbar in Firefox 3.5	
Created by	Garrett Camp & Geoff Smith[1]
Alexa rank	▲ 116[2]

StumbleUpon! Toolbar is a discovery engine (a form of web search engine) that finds and recommends web content to its users. Its features allow users to discover and rate Web pages, photos, and videos that are personalized to their tastes and interests using peer-sourcing and social-networking principles.

Toolbar versions exist for Firefox, Mozilla Application Suite, Google Chrome and Internet Explorer, but StumbleUpon also works with some independent Mozilla-based browsers. Third party toolbars have also been created for Opera.[3] However, for some reason, it lacks support on Safari 5.[4]

History

StumbleUpon was founded in November 2001[5] by Garrett Camp, Geoff Smith, Justin LaFrance and Eric Boyd during Garrett's time in post-graduate school in Calgary, Canada. The idea of creating a company was established before the content: of the five or six ideas for products, StumbleUpon was chosen. Garrett describes in a BBC interview the moment for him in which he felt the company had really taken off: "When we passed the half a million mark (in registered users), it seemed more real."[6]

The popularity of the software attracted Silicon Valley investor Brad O'Neill to take notice of the company and assist with a move to San Francisco, as well as bringing in subsequent fund-raising totaling $1.2 million from other angel investors including Ram Shriram (Google), Mitch Kapor (Mozilla Foundation), First Round Capital, and Ron Conway. Garrett Camp and Geoff Smith now reside in San Francisco, where StumbleUpon is headquartered.

StumbleUpon was owned by eBay from May 2007, when it was acquired for $75 million[7] until April 2009, when Garrett Camp, Geoff Smith and several investors bought it back.[8] StumbleUpon is now an independent, investor-backed startup once again, with offices in San Francisco and New York City.

Service details

StumbleUpon uses collaborative filtering (an automated process combining human opinions with machine learning of personal preference) to create virtual communities of like-minded Web surfers. Rating Web sites update a personal profile (a blog-style record of rated sites) and generate peer networks of Web surfers linked by common interest. These social networks coordinate the distribution of Web content, so that users "stumble upon" pages explicitly recommended by friends and peers. Giving a site a thumbs up results in the site being placed under the user's "favorites". Furthermore, users have the ability to stumble their personal interests like "History" or "Games".

Users rate a site by giving it a thumbs up, thumbs down selection on the StumbleUpon toolbar, and can optionally leave additional commentary on the site's review page, which also appears on the user's blog. This social content discovery approach automates the "word-of-mouth" referral of peer-approved Web sites and simplifies Web navigation.

Stumblers also have the ability to rate and review each others' blogs and join interest groups, which are community forums for specific topics. Users can post comments in the manner of a discussion board in these groups and post links to Web sites that apply to the specific topic.

StumbleVideo

On December 13, 2006, StumbleUpon launched their StumbleVideo site at http://video.stumbleupon.com/. The new site allows users without a toolbar to "stumble" through all the videos that toolbar users have submitted and rate them using an AJAX interface. The site currently aggregates videos from CollegeHumor, DailyMotion, FunnyOrDie, Google, MetaCafe, MySpace, Vimeo and YouTube.

StumbleUpon launched a version of StumbleVideo for the Internet Channel Web browser that runs on the Wii console on February 12, 2007. This version of StumbleVideo is optimized for the Wii's smaller screen resolution and offers similar functionality to that of the original version.

StumbleThru

In April 2007, StumbleUpon launched the StumbleThru service, allowing users of the toolbar to stumble within sites such as Youtube, The Onion, Public Broadcasting Service and Wikipedia. According to the announcement of the feature, StumbleUpon plans on adding additional Web sites in the future.

As of June 13, 2010, sites using StumbleThru include BBC.com, Blogger, Break.com, CNN.com, Collegehumor, Flickr.com, FunnyorDie.com, Howstuffworks.com, HuffingtonPost.com, Metacafe.com, Pbs.org, PhysOrg, Rolling Stone, Scientific American, The Onion, Wikipedia, Wired.com, Wordpress, Youtube.com

Su.pr

In March 2009, StumbleUpon launched the Su.pr an URL shortening service. Its primary usage is for Twitter and Facebook statuses and updates.[9] The service is similar to that of bit.ly and tinyURL. From March through May 2009, the su.pr service was only available to people who received an invite code.Currently it is available to all Stumbleupon users.

Advertising

StumbleUpon uses knowledge of user preferences to deliver targeted advertising. A small proportion of the "stumbles" users come across (typically less than 2%) are sponsored pages matching their topics of interest. For example, those signed up for photography will occasionally see an ad related to photography. Such content is vetted by humans for "quality and relevance" prior to its delivery. A sponsored site is identifiable by a green "person" logo on the toolbar. Paid accounts (referred to as "Sponsors") have a variety of options, including the ability to turn off such advertising. StumbleUpon also has many alternative versions such as "Stumbleporn".

Growth

In December 2002, StumbleUpon had 1 million users.[10] StumbleUpon claims to have more than 10,000,000 members as of May 18, 2010 [11] . StumbleUpon said that before the end of May 2008, it would have collected its five-billionth "stumble". More than one billion of which would have taken place in 2008 alone.[12]

eBay

In May 2007, StumbleUpon was purchased by eBay. Early reports indicated that the company was also in talks with Google and AOL before the eBay announcement.[13] In September 2008 eBay hired Deutsche Bank to try to sell StumbleUpon again.[14] On April 13, 2009, founders Garrett Camp and Geoff Smith and other investors including Ram Shriram bought the company.[8] [15]

References

[1] "The StumbleUpon Management Team" (http://www.stumbleupon.com/management/). StumbleUpon. . Retrieved 2009-11-01.

[2] "StumbleUpon - article statistics" (http://www.alexa.com/siteinfo/www.stumbleupon.com). Alexa Internet, Inc. . Retrieved 8 May 2011.

[3] "Opera Stumbler: A StumbleUpon Toolbar For Opera" (http://www.operastumbler.com/). .

[4] "Stumbi: A StumbleUpon plugin for Safari" (http://www.soyasoftware.com/stumbi). .

[5] "Interview with Garrett Camp, StumbleUpon Co-Founder" (http://www.centernetworks.com/interview-with-garrett-camp-stumbleupon). CenterNetworks. December 12, 2006. . Retrieved 2009-11-01.

[6] "Web 2.0 wonders: StumbleUpon" (http://news.bbc.co.uk/2/hi/technology/6506055.stm). BBC News. 29 March 2007. . Retrieved 2009-11-01.

[7] "eBay Acquires StumbleUpon" (http://web.archive.org/web/20070707122554/http://biz.yahoo.com/bw/070530/20070530006201. html). Business Wire, mirrored at archive.org. 2007-05-03. Archived from the original (http://biz.yahoo.com/bw/070530/ 20070530006201.html) on 2007-07-07. . Retrieved 2007-11-11.

[8] "StumbleUpon's founders buy service back from eBay" (http://www.salon.com/wires/ap/scitech/2009/04/13/ D97HSSH00_ebay_stumbleupon/index.html). Salon.com. . Retrieved 2009-04-14. "The founders, Garrett Camp and Geoff Smith, bought the company back with the help of investors including Ram Shriram of Sherpalo Ventures, Accel Partners, and August Capital, they said. Financial terms were not disclosed."

[9] Ferriss, Tim. "Exclusive First Look: SU.PR – Stumble Upon's New Traffic Builder" (http://www.fourhourworkweek.com/blog/2009/06/ 09/stumble-upon-supr/). Fourhourworkweek.com. . Retrieved 2010-06-07.

[10] Keizer, Gregg (2006-07-18). "StumbleUpon Launches Plug-In For Microsoft Internet Explorer" (http://www.informationweek.com/news/ showArticle.jhtml?articleID=190500706&subSection=Breaking+News). InformationWeek. . Retrieved 2007-02-28.

[11] http://techcrunch.com/2010/05/18/stumbleupon-10-million/

[12] Schonfeld, Erick (2008-04-23). "Five Million Users And Nearly Five Billion Stumbles Later" (http://www.techcrunch.com/2008/04/23/ five-million-users-and-nearly-five-billion-stumbles-later/). TechCrunch. . Retrieved 2008-04-25.

[13] Arrington, Michael (2008-04-18). "eBay Acquiring StumbleUpon" (http://techcrunch.com/2007/04/18/ stumbleupon-signs-term-sheet-to-be-acquired/). Techcrunch.com. . Retrieved 2011-04-03.

[14] Arrington, Michael (2008-09-18). "That Was Fun, But Now Ebay's Selling Off StumbleUpon" (http://www.techcrunch.com/2008/09/18/ that-was-fun-but-now-ebays-selling-stumbleupon/). Techcrunch.com. . Retrieved 2010-06-07.

[15] "StumbleUpon Goes Independent; Backed by Founders and New Investors" (http://news.prnewswire.com/DisplayReleaseContent. aspx?ACCT=104&STORY=/www/story/04-13-2009/0005005074&EDATE). News.prnewswire.com. 2009-04-13. . Retrieved 2010-06-07.

External links

- Official website (http://http://www.stumbleupon.com/)
- Advanced Stumbling Wiki (http://stumbleupon.wikia.com/wiki/Advanced_Stumbling)
- StumbleVideo for Wii (http://stumble.tv/) (Browser sniffing forwards non-Wii visitors to the normal StumbleVideo interface)
- Garrett Camp in TR35 (http://www.technologyreview.com/tr35/Profile.aspx?Cand=T&TRID=606)

Sturvs

Sturvs

	sturvs
URL	www.sturvs.com [1]
Type of site	Social content website
Registration	Free
Owner	Antigravity, LLC.
Created by	Temi Kolawole
Launched	May 13, 2007

Sturvs is a Nigerian social bookmarking website where users can share news articles, music, videos and any other form of web content. It is a web 2.0 sharing and voting website that runs in a social and democratic manner, similar to popular website Digg[2] , but for Nigerians[3] . Users are given the ability to vote on stories submitted by other users, and the stories with the highest votes make it to the front page. The word "sturvs" is a nigerian slang for "stuff", so basically it is just a place for Nigerians to view and share all their internet stuff.

The website was the first Nigerian social bookmarking website [4] [5] and one of the first in Africa[6] .

The website has a Facebook application, which was also the first ever Nigerian Facebook application. Another one of Sturvs' services is a search engine[7] (still in beta mode) which was launched in June 2008 and is geared towards finding search results related to Nigeria.

References

[1] http://www.sturvs.com/

[2] StartupsNigeria » Sturvs.com - Nigeria's Social Bookmarking Version of Digg (http://www.startupsnigeria.com/2008/04/sturvscom-nigerias-social-bookmarking-version-of-diggcom/)

[3] Profile: Sturvs « TechMASAI (http://tlcstudio.wordpress.com/2008/05/10/profile-sturvs/)

[4] Sturvs.com launches first ever Nigerian Online Social Bookmark Service (http://www.mynaijanews.com/content/view/1276/86/)

[5] Sturvs.com launches first ever Nigerian Online Social Bookmark Service (http://business.africanpath.com/article.cfm?articleID=48764)

[6] Events | Startup Africa (http://www.startupafrica.com/2008/05/sturvs-social-bookmarking-for-nigeria-with-a-twist/)

[7] Sturvs Launches Nigerian Web Search Engine (http://www.startupsnigeria.com/2008/06/sturvs-launches-nigerian-web-search-engine/)

External links

- Official site (http://www.sturvs.com/)
- Official blog (http://blog.sturvs.com/)
- Facebook application (http://apps.facebook.com/sturvings/)

Taringa!

Taringa!

URL	taringa.net [1]
Slogan	Inteligencia Colectiva (Collective Intelligence)
Commercial?	Yes
Type of site	links provider
Registration	Free
Available language(s)	Spanish, Portuguese
Owner	WIROOS SRL
Created by	Fernando Sanz
Launched	January 2004
Alexa rank	111

Taringa! is a virtual community from Argentina created in 2004 by Fernando Sanz, then acquired in November 2006 by Alberto Nakayama and the Botbol brothers (Matías and Hernán).[2] In Taringa!, users can share all kinds of topics through posts. This site is a Web 2.0 website.

Taringa! does not allow the publication of sexually explicit material [3] as a new site -called Poringa!- was created. In Poringa! users can publish this sort of explicit content. While Poringa! is a completely separate site, its users and moderators are the same as in Taringa!.

The popularity of both sites has grown largely thanks to appearance in national media and have been involved in some controversy about its contents.

System Users

All users (with the exception of freshmen) have a certain amount of points with which to evaluate collaborations (posts) outside. Each time a user votes a post, the author sees increased its scoring staff, which over time allows you to climb in the range of users.

- **Administrador (Administrator):** Managers have the same privileges as moderators but also are responsible for the continuing development of the site in technical matters.
- **Moderador (Moderator):** a moderator is responsible for maintaining order, peace and respect in Taringa!, Paying attention to protocol. There are 35 points per day.
- **Great User:** is a prize for those who deserve it, there is no specific criteria for the award and the only difference with New Full Users or Full Users is that they have 17 points per day.
- **Full User:** has the same privileges as New Full Users. Full Users are those who registered before the release of Taringa 3! (March 2007). They can give 12 points every day.
- **New Full User (NFU):** after obtaining 50 points in a single post the freshmen become New Full Users and can make full use of Taringa!, including comments and posts in the general section. They have 10 points per day that they can give to posts they consider deserving.

- **Novato (Newbie):** Users are newcomers to the community. Its activity is restricted to posting and commenting under section freshmen, but their access to the site's content is complete. They cannot give points.

Communities

Taringa! has a system of user-created groups that are called "Communities" (even though Taringa! is a community itself). These groups are used to share interests, information, ideas, creative content, and others. As Taringa!'s protocol states, communities can't be used to share download links, because that's a post's purpose. Newbies can't create communities, although users from another range can create a limited number of communities.

Users of communities

Any Taringa! user can join communities, and leave them as well. Visitor, Commenter or Poster can be set as a defaults of a range for each new member.

- **Administrador (Administrator):** They can suspend users, create new posts on communities, edit a community's logo, description and other information, ascend other users to another range, add posts to the Sticky list, delete and edit posts from any other member in the community.
- **Moderador (Moderator):** They have almost all the same privileges as Administrators, but they can't edit the community's information, such as: Logo, Description, Title, etc.
- **Posteador (Poster):** They can only post and comment. This can be set as a default for each new user in a community.
- **Comentador (Commenter):** They can only comment, as they don't have any privileges to post. This can be set as a default for each new user in a community.
- **Visitante (Visitor):** They can only view content in the community. This can be set as a default for each new user in a community.

Sharing and infringment of copyright

Taringa's users can post links to content created by themselves or other content they are able to share without infringe copyright law, for example scanned photographies already in the public domain, a linux tutorial or an article written by themselves.[4] When those links infringe copyright laws, they should be removed by the administrators of the page as it states the Taringa's protocol,[5] but in most of cases the vast majority of the contents posted by users are already protected by copyright laws (such as comic books, movies, TV series, books, music and videogames). Usually those links are not removed by the administrators and remain on the page for a long time. [6]

The owners of Taringa allege that the website works as an interchange site, so it does not host any file, but at the same time users are free to post links that violate copyright (without being removed or banned). In addition, many of the posts about different issues (like a simple article or editorial) are extracted from other websites or personal blogs, reproducing their contents with no permission from the original sources.[4] Morever, they remarks that Taringa only shows links and anyone can search specific contents like music or software, in the same way that those links can be searched on Google or Yahoo. Matias Botbol also adds:

> "Sometimes people say that Taringa is a pirate website, but that is not true: In fact, there are people that post pirate content through Taringa. For instance, if I would search only pornography content on Google, then I could state that Google is a porno site. But Google is much more than porno. That is like the Internet works already, in the Net all contents are related, we did not invented this. Therefore, if we closed Taringa, its contents would not disappear, so they could be founded to download on another websites. We are not responsible for the contents posted by users".[6]

About the infringment of copyright, Millé Law Office's representative Alberto Millé stated in an interview:

"Sites like Taringa work neither as discussion forums nor as sites that simply search for contents on the web. Taringa mainly shows posts that include links to contents hosted in other servers and at the same time, this website has a search engine that allows users to find the links of the contents required. Most of those links are protected by copyright and posted or distributed without permission from the authors. Taringa works under the Argentine Law system, and Law protects the copyrighted works like books, music or software, emphasizing the absolute prohibition to reproduce all those contents if the authors have not given their approval previously. Therefore, if Taringa allows users to access to copyrighted material causing that any person may reproduce illegal work, the owners of Taringa are clearly breaking the law and they could be taken to a Court. Taringa should redefine its website in order to the large community of users be able only to share contents previously authorized by their respective owners".[7]

Legal issue

On May, 2011, the owners of Taringa (Hernán and Matías Botbol) were accused of assistance to copyright infringement and sentenced to pay $ 200,000 (USD 50,000). The Botbol brothers are being processed for infringing the article 72 of the 11.723 Law, which regulates the copyright activities in Argentina. This article says that "any person who edits, sells or publishes a copyrighted work without permission from its authors will be sentenced to spend a period of one month to six years in jail". [8] [9]

The Botbol brothers were summoned to delete the posts related with copyrighted material. In the case of those posts were not deleted, they could be arrested. The owners of Taringa alleged that they cannot determine if the material uploaded by useres were breaking copyright rules, due to Taringa has an avergae of 20,000 posts a day. They also manifested that they were not able to access to Intellectual Property Office ("Registro Nacional de la Propiedad Intelectual" in Argentina) to know which works are under protection of copyright rules.[8]

In addition, the accused said that on March 23, 2009 the controversial material had been deleted from the website, but "other user uploaded it again on June 19, 2009".[8]

Nevertheless, the court considered that the owners of Taringa were conscious about the infringments committed and in spite of deleting illegal content, they allowed forbidden material to remain on the website without being removed. [8]

External links

- Taringa! website [1] (Spanish)
- Fernando Sanz website [10] (Spanish)

References

[1] http://www.taringa.net

[2] La comunidad virtual más visitada del país fue creada por tres postadolescentes (http://www.diarioperfil.com.ar/edimp/0233/articulo. php?art=5702&ed=0233) Diario Perfil, 2008-02-10

[3] Protocolo de Taringa (http://www.taringa.net/protocolo/)

[4] Taringa, el polémico sitio argentino que crece (http://www.lanacion.com.ar/nota.asp?nota_id=1026541) La Nación, 2008-07-02

[5] Protocolo de Taringa (http://www.taringa.net/protocolo/)

[6] Interview to the creators of Taringa (http://revistadebate.com.ar/2009/01/16/1529.php), Revista *Debate*

[7] ¿Es legal lo que hace Taringa? (http://www.elargentino.com/nota-40835-Es-legal-lo-que-hace-Taringa.html) Interview to Alberto Millé, *El Argentino*, 2009-05-13

[8] Procesaron a los responsables de Taringa por violar derechos de autor (http://www.perfil.com/contenidos/2011/05/09/noticia_0029. html), Diario *Perfil*, May 9, 2011

[9] Taringa sufrió un duro revés judicial - ViaRosario.com (http://www.viarosario.com/noticias/noticias/ taringa-sufrio-un-duro-reves-judicial-24303.html)

[10] http://www.fernando.com.ar

Twine (website)

Twine

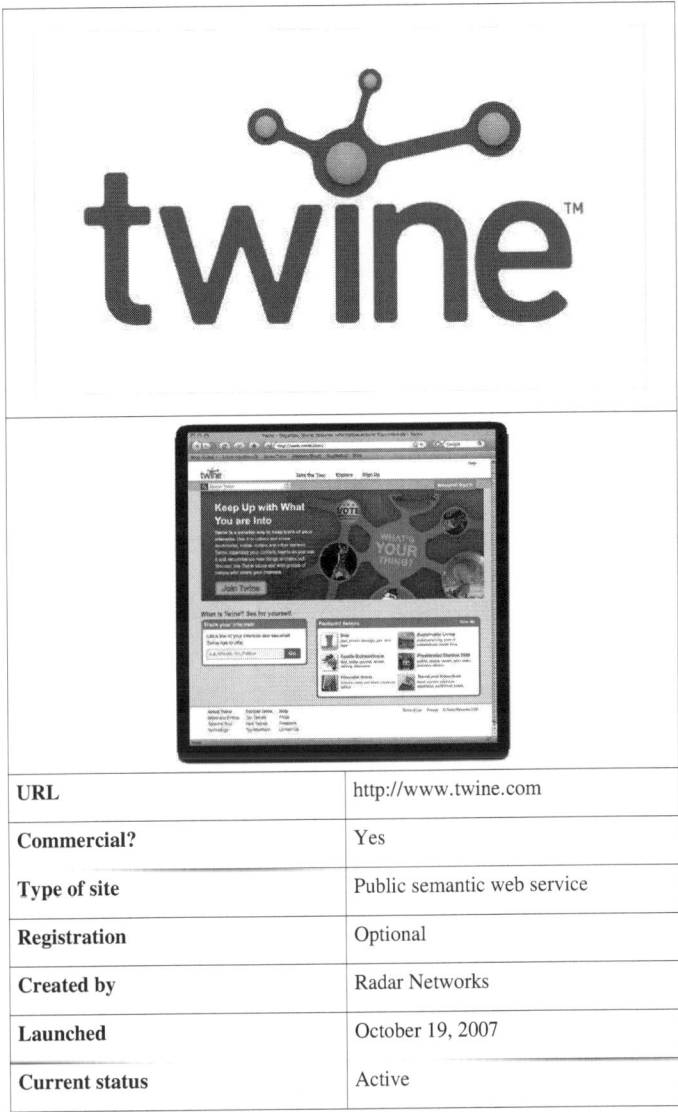

URL	http://www.twine.com
Commercial?	Yes
Type of site	Public semantic web service
Registration	Optional
Created by	Radar Networks
Launched	October 19, 2007
Current status	Active

Twine is an online, social web service for information storage, authoring and discovery. Created by Radar Networks, the service was announced on October 19, 2007 and made open to the public on October 21, 2008[1]. On March 11, 2010, Radar Networks was acquired by Evri Inc. along with Twine.com[2] and since May 14, Twine.com has not been supported (Twine.com visits are re-directed to Evri.com).

Twine combines features of forums, wikis, online databases and newsgroups[3] and employs intelligent software to automatically mine and store data relationships[4] expressed using RDF statements.

Site description

Twine services information storage, authoring and discovery through its website and browser-based tools. The service, intended for regular web users, attempts to automate certain processes related to data categorization and keyword-association (tagging)[5]. The system employs natural language processing and machine learning to extract concepts from written text in user data[1] and express it using RDF triples tied to a semantic taxonomy based on concepts mined from Wikipedia[5]. This makes it easier for machines to process the data[6] [7]. The extracted data is useful to search on the website where, in comparison to a non-semantic keyword categorization scheme, a user can additionally select a type of thing he wants to find such as *person* or *location*.

Twine is a social network and its users can add contacts, send private messages and share information. Users can collaborate on collecting data through private or public *twines*; data collections focused on a certain topic, such as politics[8] .

Data can be imported to Twine's website through conventional uploading of files, writing text with a WYSIWYG editor or using a bookmarking tool for webpages. The tool works in a similar manner as other social bookmarking websites. Users can manually write summaries, specify keywords (tags) and select an image to include in the bookmark that appears on Twine's website. Certain types of media in bookmarks, such as YouTube videos, are automatically embedded in Twine's pages when bookmarked. Twine also offers limited wiki capabilities to collaboratively edit documents.

Information discovery is mostly done through a user's main page where items appear, organized by the twine they belong to. Twine also uses machine learning technologies that, over time, use semantic metadata to learn and generate more relevant, automatic information recommendations of possible interest to the user.

History

The company remained in stealth mode until October 19, 2007 when Twine was announced and limited invitations were handed out for beta testing. In February 2008 it was announced that Radar Networks raised a Series B venture round led by Velocity Interactive Group, Vulcan Capital and Draper Fisher Jurvetson. The service became visible to the public and search engines in July 2008. Approximately 50,000 people had signed up during Twine's beta-phase and 34,000 were active at that time[9] . Twine went public on October 21, 2008[1] . On March 11, 2010, the search engine Evri Inc. announced the acquisition of Radar Networks and Twine.com.[2]

References

[1] Erica Naone (2008-09-21). "Untangling Web Information" (http://www.technologyreview.com/web/21583/?a=f). *Technology Review*. . Retrieved 2008-10-21.

[2] Evri Inc. (2010-03-11). "Evri Announces Acquisition of Twine, Relaunches Consumer Site" (http://corporate.evri.com/2010/03/ evri-announces-acquisition-of-twine-relaunches-consumer-site/). . Retrieved 2010-05-08.

[3] Rafe Needleman (2008-03-07). "Twine: The Semantic Web Takes Shape, with Twine" (http://news.cnet.com/8301-17939_109-9889057-2. html?%5E$). *Cnet news*. . Retrieved 2008-10-20.

[4] John Markoff (2006-12-11). "Entrepreneurs See Web Guided By Common Sense" (http://www.nytimes.com/2006/11/12/business/ 12web.html?ex=1320987600&en=254d697964cedc62&ei=5088). *New York Times*. . Retrieved 2008-10-20.

[5] Tim O'Reilly (2007-10-18). "Web2Summit: Radar Networks Unwinds twine.com" (http://radar.oreilly.com/archives/2007/10/ radar-networks-twine.html). *O'Reilly Radar*. . Retrieved 2007-10-20.

[6] W3C Semantic Web FAQ (http://www.w3.org/2001/sw/SW-FAQ#What1)

[7] Michael Copeland (2007-03-07). "Web 3.0: No Humans Required" (http://money.cnn.com/magazines/business2/business2_archive/ 2007/07/01/100117068/index.htm?postversion=2007070305). *CNNMoney.com*. . Retrieved 2007-08-11.

[8] Sarah Miller (2008-02-03). "An Online Organizer That Helps Connect the Dots" (http://www.nytimes.com/2008/02/03/business/ 03novel.html?_r=1). *New York Times*. . Retrieved 2007-10-20.

[9] Dan Farber (2008-07-31). "Radar Networks readies new release of Twine" (http://news.cnet.com/8301-13953_3-10000368-80. html?tag=mncol;title). *Cnet news*. . Retrieved 2008-10-19.

Wink Technologies

Wink Technologies, Inc.

Type	Private
Industry	Internet
Founded	Los Altos, California August 19, 2004
Headquarters	Los Altos, California
Key people	Michael Tanne, Founder
Products	Wink social search, Wink people search
Website	wink.com [1]

Wink Technologies is the operator of **Wink**, a community-based social search engine. It provides people search across social networks, and Web search based on user input. Wink is different from conventional search engines in that the relevant results are derived not just from machine algorithms, but directly from user input, such as social bookmarking, voting up or down, or blocking results that are considered to be spam, thus allowing users to collectively create their own search engine. Wink released an early beta of the service on December 22, 2005 and formally launched Wink beta 2 on September 6, 2006. Wink was recognized by Business 2.0 [2] as an innovator in social search.

Functionality

Wink users can search across Web sites submitted by fellow users and gathered through analysis of bookmarks and/or tags from other social services including Digg, Slashdot, Furl, Yahoo MyWeb, and others. Users can bookmark results as personal favorites, add tags that relate to the site, or vote for or against each result with a thumb up or a thumb down respectively. Wink results are added on to search results from Google to give users a full search experience in one place.

Wink **Collections** are a social tool that allow users to organize links and items such as online video, audio, and images from around the Web that apply to a given subject. For example a Wink collection about funny ads contains links to commercials found by users across the Web regardless of whether the text search "funny ad" would have found them. Likewise, a collection about Hybrid cars contains links to various resources concerning hybrid vehicles such as comparisons, merchants, tax information, reviews, photos, etc. in one list, even though these resources would not likely surface in the same search engine query. Users of a collection can rate links up or down within the collection using thumbs up or thumbs down, and can add their own links to the collection.

Wink **People Search** allows users to search for people across social networks including MySpace, LinkedIn, Bebo, Friendster and others.[3] Wink people search allows users to search by name, and also by interest, location, and other information published in users profiles. Wink people search allows users to find others who have similar interests and find out what social network they can be found on. It has been suggested that the profiles for a given individual on different services be combined, but the company has chosen to leave this to users by giving them a way to list the social networks they wish to claim.

Wink **Topic Pages** are topical pages for given subjects containing Web sites tagged with that subject and users who have claimed an interest in that subject. Wink topics bring together the people search with the social search providing a way for communities to form around given topics.

Significance

Wink has only been formally available for a short period and has not acquired a large following to date, however the capabilities demonstrated by the company are in an area, social search that is receiving attention as a potentially important development in web search.[4]

History

Wink was incorporated on August 19, 2004 to work on ways to apply user input to improve the way that Web search is done. has developed unique techniques in information retrieval and search engine architecture designed to improve search results based on input from users. Wink's PeopleRank technology analyzes which pages people like or don't like to determine relevant results. Wink's development team includes developers from Inktomi, Yahoo, Google, and Excite.

On December 22, 2005 the company released the first beta of its social search service.

On September 6, 2006 the company released the second beta of its service, adding Wink collections.

On November 10, 2006 the company released 'Wink People Search' which provides search across multiple social networks such as MySpace, Bebo, Friendster and LinkedIn [5] .

On March 19, 2007 it was reported that the company would focus completely on people search and that it was repurchasing some shares from existing investors.[6]

On April 30, 2007 Reunion.com announced an agreement with Wink to provide Wink's people profiles to Reunion's members and affiliates.[7]

On November 3, 2007 Reunion.com announced an agreement to merge with Wink.[8]

Additional information

Wink investors include PayPal veterans Reid Hoffman and Peter Thiel.

References

[1] http://wink.com/

[2] "New Ideas in Search (Wink, Gravee)" (from Business 2.0), Schonfeld, Erick, December 26, 2005, The Next Net web: Business 2.0 (http://blogs.business2.com/business2blog/2005/12/new_ideas_in_se.html).

[3] "Wink Social Search, now with people search" (from Pandia), Per M. Koch, November 21, 2006: Pandia: Wink Social Search, now with people search (http://www.pandia.com/sew/321-wink.html).

[4] "Crowd Wisdom vs. Google's Genius" (from BusinessWeek.com), Holahan, Catherine, December 27, 2006: BusinessWeek.com (http://www.businessweek.com/technology/content/dec2006/tc20061227_722820.htm).

[5] "Wink Now Searches MySpace, LinkedIn and Bebo" (from TechCrunch), Kirkpatrick, Marshall, November 10, 2006: TechCrunch (http://www.techcrunch.com/2006/11/10/wink-now-searches-myspace-linkedin-and-beebo/).

[6] "Wink Pulls Half An Odeo, Partially Liquidates" (from TechCrunch), Arrington, Michael, March 19, 2007: TechCrunch (http://www.techcrunch.com/2007/03/19/wink-pulls-half-an-odeo-partially-liquidates/).

[7] "Reunion, Wink Partner Up" (from Mashable), Nicole, Kristen, April 30, 2007: Mashable (http://mashable.com/2007/04/30/reunion-wink/)

[8] "Social Search Engines Wink, Reunion to Merge" (from GAGAOM, Brigid Gaffikin, November 3, 2008: (http://gigaom.com/2008/11/03/social-search-engines-wink-reunion-to-merge/)

External links

- Wink (http://wink.com)

Additional Resources:

- Mahalo and Friends: 10 People Powered Search Engines (http://mashable.com/2007/06/01/
  10-people-powered-search-engines/)
- Wink - People-Powered Search for MySpace, LinkedIn and Bebo (http://blog.adglobe.net/2006/11/30/
  wink-people-powered-search-for-myspace-linkedin-and-bebo/)
- Wink Launches Social Network Search for MySpace, Bebo, LinkedIn (http://mashable.com/2006/11/10/
  wink-launches-social-network-search-for-myspace-bebo-linkedin/)

Yahoo! Buzz

Yahoo! Buzz

Type of site	Social content website
Registration	Free
Owner	Yahoo!
Created by	Yahoo!
Launched	February 26, 2008
Current status	Defunct in the United States and Canada

Yahoo! Buzz was a community-based news article website, heavily derived from Digg, that combines the features of social bookmarking and syndication through a user interface that allows editorial control. Users can be allowed to publish their own news stories, and link to their own or another person's site that links to a full story of the information, therefore driving traffic to that person's website and creating a larger market for sites that research and publish their own news articles and stories, such as CNN or smaller, privately owned websites.

Yahoo! created the service in hopes that it would drive larger traffic to their site and would give them an advantage over larger online media companies such as Google or MSN, which are Yahoo!'s largest competitors in terms of search engines that provide services and web features to its customers. Unlike other social networking sites, Buzz allows the publisher to modify the submission.[1]

Yahoo! announced on April 19, 2011 that it was killing off Buzz as of April 21, 2011. "This was a hard decision. However this will help us focus on our core strengths and new innovations", the company wrote in a brief statement.[2] [3] [4]

References

[1] "Submit a Story" (http://buzz.yahoo.com/submit/). Yahoo Buzz. .
[2] Brown, Bob. "Yahoo Buzz killed" (http://www.networkworld.com/community/blog/yahoo-buzz-killed). NetworkWorld. . Retrieved 20 April 2011.
[3] www.theregister.co.uk/2011/04/18/yahoo_buzz/
[4] www.huffingtonpost.com/2011/04/18/yahoo-buzz-_n_850564.html

External links

* Yahoo! Buzz (http://buzz.yahoo.com/)

Yardbarker

Yardbarker

Type	Private
Founded	Emeryville, California, United States (March, 2006)
Headquarters	San Francisco, California, United States
Key people	Pete Vlastelica, CEO
Slogan		
Website	yardbarker.com [1]
Type of site	Social networking, Blogging, Sports news
Advertising	Banner ads
Registration	Optional
Available in	English
Launched	August 2006[2]
Current status	Active

Yardbarker is a San Francisco, California based subsidiary of FOX Sports Interactive that primarily runs a network of sports websites known as the Yardbarker Network, and additionally owns an operates a website, Yardbarker.com.

History

Yardbarker was founded in March 2006 by Jack and Jeff Kloster, Pete Vlastelica and Mark Johns . The original site enabled sports fans to write and discuss sports with other fans and bloggers, as well as professional athletes. Yardbarker.com used a system similar to Digg, however was more sports oriented than Digg.[2] Additionally Yardbarker provides access to more traditional sports information similar to ESPN or Yahoo such as real time sports scores, standings, and news.

The company was funded by several venture capitalists from in and around the San Francisco Bay Area including former NFL player for both the San Francisco 49ers and Los Angeles Raiders, Ronnie Lott.[3]

The company provides a platform for bloggers and sports fans to gain additional exposure for their sites by joining the Yardbarker Network which provides targeted advertising and increased promotion. Yardbarker has existed on the web since August 2006 and has over 70 professional athletes blogging on the site daily. The company and their site have been cited as primary source of material on players in many sports related stories in their history by sources such as ESPN.[4]

The company also has internet exclusivity agreements with many athletes and is used by those athletes to engage in public discourse on a number of issues via blogs run by Yardbarker. One of the more controversial such listings occurred on April 15, 2008. NBA star Carmelo Anthony was arrested and charged with DUI on Interstate 25.[5] . The next day Anthony issued his first apology for the arrest through his Yardbarker blog expressing remorse to both his teammates and his fans for his behavior.[6]

Another notable example would be in January 2008, Philadelphia Eagles quarterback Donovan McNabb used his blog on Yardbarker to lay out his vision for the coming season after the Eagles poor showing in the 2007 NFL season.[7]

Atlanta Falcons FB Ovie Mughelli leveraged the Yardbarker community for his nickname via a contest.[8]

Products

Yardbarker's primary product is the Yardbarker Network. As of April 2011 over 900 blogs were part of the YBN, making it one of the largest sports blog networks on the web.[9] . Currently Yardbarker is the exclusive blogging website of many high profile athletes including but not limited to, NBA stars Greg Oden and Baron Davis, MLB player Phil Hughes, Former UFC star Frank Shamrock and NFL quarterback Donovan McNabb.[10] John Ryan of the San Jose Mercury News praised Yardbarker in November 2007 for its collection of blogs after reading one such posting by Buffalo Bills running back Marshawn Lynch, as being one of the most extensive on the internet.[11]

In October 2008, Yardbarker announced a partnership with Widgetbox.[12] to offer Yardbarker Network members widgets displaying dynamic content from around the Yardbarker Network. To date over 600 installs of these widgets have occurred.[13]

In October 2010, Yardbarker was acquired by FOX Sports Interactive.

References

[1] http://www.yardbarker.com/
[2] Yardbarker: "Welcome to Sports 2.0!" | Compiler from Wired.com (http://blog.wired.com/monkeybites/2006/08/yardbarker_welc.html)
[3] Yardbarker Launches Site Revamp; Gets Funding (http://mashable.com/2007/04/15/yardbarker/)
[4] ESPN - Rondo skips practice after rolling ankle in Game 3 - NBA (http://sports.espn.go.com/nba/playoffs2008/news/story?id=3437177)
[5] ESPN - Anthony arrested on suspicion of driving under the influence - NBA (http://sports.espn.go.com/nba/news/story?id=3346621)
[6] Statement from Carmelo (http://www.yardbarker.com/nba/articles/Statement_from_Carmelo/239302)
[7] ESPN - McNabb says team should restock and 'secure some playmakers' - NFL (http://sports.espn.go.com/nfl/news/story?id=3187772)
[8] Ovie Mughelli wants a new nickname contest (http://www.yardbarker.com/nfl/articles/I_need_a_nickname/333828)
[9] Yardbarker Network (http://www.yardbarker.com/tools/ybn_directory)
[10] SI.com - Writers - Chris Ballard: Blogs empowering NBA players - Wednesday November 7, 2007 12:01PM (http://sportsillustrated.cnn.com/2007/writers/chris_ballard/11/07/nba.image/index.html)
[11] Marshawn Lynch says hello to his professors at Cal | Morning Buzz (http://blogs.mercurynews.com/buzz/2007/11/26/marshawn-lynch-says-hello-to-his-professors-at-cal/)
[12] Mashable Press Release http://mashable.com/2008/10/07/widgetbox-yardbarker/
[13] Widgetbox YBN Page http://www.widgetbox.com/widget/yardbarker-network-widget

External links

- Yardbarker.com mainpage (http://www.yardbarker.com/)
- List of Athletes that blog exclusively to Yardbarker (http://www.yardbarker.com/athletes/)

Celestial Emporium of Benevolent Knowledge's Taxonomy

Celestial Emporium of Benevolent Knowledge's Taxonomy (Spanish: *Emporio celestial de conocimientos benévolos*) is a bizarre and seemingly fictitious classification system described by the writer Jorge Luis Borges in his 1942 essay "The Analytical Language of John Wilkins" (*El idioma analítico de John Wilkins*).[1] The list divides all animals into one of 14 categories;

- Those that belong to the emperor
- Embalmed ones
- Those that are trained
- Suckling pigs
- Mermaids (or Sirens)
- Fabulous ones
- Stray dogs
- Those that are included in this classification
- Those that tremble as if they were mad
- Innumerable ones
- Those drawn with a very fine camel hair brush
- *Et cetera*
- Those that have just broken the flower vase
- Those that, at a distance, resemble flies

Borges claims that the list appears in an ancient Chinese encyclopaedia entitled *Celestial Emporium of Benevolent Knowledge*, and was was "discovered" by the translator Franz Kuhn.[2] [3] [4]

Influences of the list

This list, whose "discovery" Borges attributes to Franz Kuhn,[5] has stirred considerable philosophical and literary commentary.

Michel Foucault begins his preface to *The Order of Things*,[6]

> This book first arose out of a passage in Borges, out of the laughter that shattered, as I read the passage, all the familiar landmarks of thought—*our* thought, the thought that bears the stamp of our age and our geography—breaking up all the ordered surfaces and all the planes with which we are accustomed to tame the wild profusion of existing things and continuing long afterwards to disturb and threaten with collapse our age-old definitions between the Same and the Other.

Foucault then quotes Borges' passage.

Louis Sass has suggested, in response to Borges' list, that such "Chinese" thinking shows signs of typical schizophrenic thought processes.[7] By contrast, the prominent linguist George Lakoff has pointed out that Borges' list is similar to many categorizations of objects found in nonwestern cultures.[8]

Keith Windschuttle, an Australian historian, cited alleged acceptance of the authenticity of the list among many academics as a sign of the degeneration of the Western academy.[9]

Attribution

Scholars have questioned whether the attribution of the list to Franz Kuhn is genuine. While Kuhn did indeed translate Chinese literature, Borges' works often feature many pseudo-learned references resulting in a mix of facts and fiction. To date, no evidence for the existence of such a list has been found.[10]

Borges himself questions the veracity of the quote in his essay, referring to "the unknown (or false) Chinese encyclopaedia writer".[4]

References

[1] Giuseppe Mantovani (2000), *Exploring borders: understanding culture and psychology* (http://books.google.co.uk/ books?id=vK2b6RhpbSEC&pg=PA9&dq=Emporium+of+Benevolent+mermaids&hl=en&ei=KLa2Td_yEMfMswaYz72-DQ&sa=X& oi=book_result&ct=result&resnum=1&ved=0CCsQ6AEwAA#v=onepage&q=Emporium of Benevolent mermaids&f=false), Routledge, ISBN 9780415234009, , retrieved 26 April 2011

[2] pg 231, "John Wilkins' Analytical Language", translator Eliot Weinberger; included in *Selected nonfictions: Jorge Luis Borges", ed. Eliot Weinberger; 1999, Penguin Books, ISBN 0-14-029011-7. The essay was originally published as "El idioma analítico de John Wilkins",* La Nación, *8 February 1942, and republished in* Otras inquisiciones

[3] A slightly different English translation is at: Jorge Luis Borges (April 8 2006). "The Analytical Language of John Wilkins" (http://www. alamut.com/subj/artiface/language/johnWilkins.html). *Translation by Lilia Graciela Vázquez.* .

[4] An edition with Spanish original and English translation in parallel can be found at: Jorge Luis Borges (April 8 2006). "El idioma analítico de John Wilkins" (http://www.crockford.com/wrrrld/wilkins.html). .

[5] The DARWIN-L mailing list archive (http://rjohara.net/darwin/logs/1996/9609a) contains messages discussing the authenticity of the attribution to Franz Kuhn (search for "Borges" on page)

[6] Michel Foucault (1994 (1966)). *The Order of Things : An Archaeology of Human Sciences.* Vintage. ISBN 0-679-75335-4.

[7] Louis Sass (1994 (1992)). *Madness and Modernism: Insanity in the Light of Modern Art, Literature and Thought.* Harvard University Press. ISBN 0-674-54137-5.

[8] George Lakoff (1987). *Women, Fire, and Dangerous Things: What Categories Reveal About the Mind.* University of Chicago Press. ISBN 0-226-46804-6.. Relevant excerpts (http://www.virtualschool.edu/mon/SocialConstruction/LakoffWomenFireDanger.html)

[9] Academic Questions September 15, 1997 (http://www.nationalreview.com/15sept97/windschuttle091597.html)

[10] LINGUIST List 7.1446: Borgesian joke (http://www.linguistlist.org/issues/7/7-1446.html)

Parataxonomy

Parataxonomy is the use of less qualified assistance to, or replacement of, taxonomists in the practice and science of classification.

Parataxonomy may be used to improve taxonomic efficiency by enabling more expert taxonomists to restrict their activity to the tasks that require their specialist knowledge and skills, typically by undertaking basic sorting of collected specimens.

Generally parataxonomists work in the field, sorting collected samples into recognizable taxonomic units (RTUs) based on easily recognised features. The process can be used alone for rapid assessment of biodiversity.[1] This process is obviously prone to error depending on the sample, the sorter and the species, therefore quantitative studies based on parataxonomic processes may be unreliable[2] and is therefore controversial.[3]

The term is attributed to Daniel Janzen who used it to describe the role of assistants working in INBio in Costa Rica.[4]

References

[1] Oliver, I.; Beattie, A. J. (1993). "A Possible Method for the Rapid Assessment of Biodiversity". *Conservation Biology* **7**: 562–568. doi:10.1046/j.1523-1739.1993.07030562.x.

[2] Krell, Frank-Thorsten (2004). "Parataxonomy vs. taxonomy in biodiversity studies – pitfalls and applicability of 'morphospecies' sorting" (http://www.dmns.org/media/30745/parataxonomy-vs-taxonomy.pdf) (PDF). *Biodiversity and Conservation* (Netherlands: Kluwer Academic Publishers) **13**: 795–812. doi:10.1023/B:BIOC.0000011727.53780.63. .

[3] Goldstein, Paul Z. (April 1997). "How many things are there? A Reply to Oliver and Beattie, Beattie and Oliver, Oliver and Beattie, and Oliver and Beattie" (http://www.jstor.org/stable/2387635). *Conservation Biology* (Blackwell) **11** (2): 571–574. doi:10.1046/j.1523-1739.1997.96119.x. .

[4] Janzen, Daniel H. (1991). "How to save tropical biodiversity". *American Entomologist* **37**: 159–171.

External links

- "Introduction & Parataxonomy" (http://users.iab.uaf.edu/~derek_sikes/Field Ent website/1eeb.html). *Field Entomology : EEB 252*. University of Connecticut. Retrieved 19 December 2010.

Taxonomy

Taxonomy (from Ancient Greek: τάξις *taxis* "arrangement" and Ancient Greek: νομία *nomia* "method"[1]) is the practice and science of classification. Taxonomy uses taxonomic units, known as **taxa** (singular taxon). In addition, the word is also used as a count noun: **a taxonomy**, or taxonomic scheme, is a particular classification ("the taxonomy of ..."), arranged in a hierarchical structure. Typically this is organized by supertype-subtype relationships, also called generalization-specialization relationships, or less formally, parent-child relationships. In such an inheritance relationship, the subtype by definition has the same properties, behaviors, and constraints as the supertype plus one or more additional properties, behaviors, or constraints. For example: car is a subtype of vehicle, so any car is also a vehicle, but not every vehicle is a car. Therefore a type needs to satisfy more constraints to be a car than to be a vehicle. Another example: any shirt is also a piece of clothing, but not every piece of clothing is a shirt. Hence, a type must satisfy more parameters to be a shirt than to be a piece of clothing.

Applications

Originally *taxonomy* referred only to the classifying of organisms (now sometimes known as alpha taxonomy) or a particular classification of organisms. It is also used to refer a classification of **things** or **concepts**, as well as to the *principles* underlying such a classification.

Taxonomy is the science which deals with the study of identifying, grouping, and naming organisms according to their established natural relationship.

Almost anything—animate objects, inanimate objects, places, concepts, events, properties, and relationships—may then be classified according to some taxonomic scheme. Wikipedia categories illustrate a taxonomy schema,[2] and a full taxonomy of Wikipedia categories can be extracted by automatic means.[3] Recently, it has been shown that a manually constructed taxonomy, such as that of computational lexicons like WordNet, can be used to improve and restructure the Wikipedia category taxonomy.[4]

The term taxonomy is sometimes applied to relationship schemes other than parent-child hierarchies, such as network structures with other types of relationships. In that case, they might include single children with multi-parents, for example, "Car" might appear with both parents "Vehicle" and "Steel Mechanisms"; technically, this merely means that 'car' is a part of several different taxonomies.[5] A taxonomy might also be a simple organization of kinds of things into groups, or even an alphabetical list. However, the term vocabulary is more appropriate for such a list. In current usage within Knowledge Management, taxonomies are considered narrower than ontologies since ontologies apply a larger variety of relation types.[6]

Mathematically, a hierarchical taxonomy is a tree structure of classifications for a given set of objects. It is also named Containment hierarchy. At the top of this structure is a single classification, the root node, that applies to all objects. Nodes below this root are more specific classifications that apply to subsets of the total set of classified objects. The progress of reasoning proceeds from the general to the more specific. In scientific taxonomies, a conflative term is always a polyseme.[7]

In contrast, in a context of legal terminology, an open-ended contextual taxonomy—a taxonomy holding only with respect to a specific context. In scenarios taken from the legal domain, a formal account of the open-texture of legal terms is modeled, which suggests varying notions of the "core" and "penumbra" of the meanings of a concept. The progress of reasoning proceeds from the specific to the more general.[8]

Taxonomy and mental classification

Some have argued that the adult human mind naturally organizes its knowledge of the world into such systems. This view is often based on the epistemology of Immanuel Kant. Anthropologists have observed that taxonomies are generally embedded in local cultural and social systems, and serve various social functions. Perhaps the most well-known and influential study of folk taxonomies is Émile Durkheim's *The Elementary Forms of Religious Life*. A more recent treatment of folk taxonomies (including the results of several decades of empirical research) and the discussion of their relation to the scientific taxonomy can be found in Scott Atran's *Cognitive Foundations of Natural History*

Various biological taxonomies

Biological classification (sometimes known as "Linnaean taxonomy") is still generally the best known form of taxonomy. It differs from the above in that it is an empirical science, with classifying only the final step of a process, and a classification only the means to communicate the end results. It also includes the prediction, discovery, description and (re)defining of taxa. It uses taxonomic ranks, including, among others, (in order) Kingdom, Phylum, Class, Order, Family, Genus, Species (various mnemonic devices have been used to help people remember the list of "Linnaean" taxonomic ranks. See Zoology mnemonic). In zoology, the nomenclature for the more important ranks (superfamily to subspecies), including the allowed number of ranks, is strictly regulated by the *ICZN Code*, whereas there is more latitude for names at higher ranks. Taxonomy itself is never regulated, but is always the result of research in the scientific community. How researchers arrive at their taxa varies; depending on the available data, and resources, methods vary from simple quantitative or qualitative comparisons of striking features to elaborate computer analyses of large amounts of DNA sequence data.

Phylogenetics

Today, the alternative to the traditional rank-based biological classification is phylogenetic systematics, which is postulating phylogenetic trees (trees of descent), rather than focusing on what taxa to delimit. The best-known form of this is cladistics.

The results of cladistic analyses are often represented as cladograms. It is held by cladists that taxa (if recognized) must always correspond to clades, united by apomorphies (derived traits) which are discovered by a cladistic analysis. Some cladists hold that clades are poorly expressed in rank-based hierarchies and support the *PhyloCode*, a proposed ruleswork for the formal naming of clades, based on the model of the *ICZN*, *ICBN* etc. in rank-based nomenclature.

Numerical taxonomy

In numerical taxonomy, numerical phenetics or taximetrics, the taxonomy is exclusively based on cluster analysis and neighbor joining to best-fit numerical equations that characterize measurable traits of a number of organisms. It results in a measure of evolutionary "distance" between species. This method has been largely superseded by cladistic analyses today; it is liable to being misled by plesiomorphic traits.

Non-scientific taxonomies

Other taxonomies, such as those analyzed by Durkheim and Lévi-Strauss, are sometimes called folk taxonomies to distinguish them from scientific taxonomies that focus on evolutionary relationships rather than similarity in habitus and habits. Though phenetics arguably places much emphasis on overall similarity, it is a quantitative analysis that attempts to reproduce evolutionary relationships of lineages and not similarities of form taxa.

The neologism folksonomy should not be confused with "folk taxonomy", though it is obviously a portmanteau created from the two words. "Fauxonomy" (from French *faux*, "false") is a pejorative neologism used to criticize folk taxonomies for their lack of agreement with scientific findings. Baraminology is a taxonomy used in creation science which in classifying form taxa resembles folk taxonomies.

The phrase "enterprise taxonomy" is used in business to describe a very limited form of taxonomy used only within one organization. An example would be a certain method of classifying trees as "Type A", "Type B" and "Type C" used only by a certain lumber company for categorising log shipments.

Military taxonomy

Military theorist Carl von Clausewitz stressed the significance of grasping the fundamentals of any situation in the "blink of an eye" (*clin d'œil*). In a military context the astute tactician can immediately grasp a range of implications and can begin to anticipate plausible and appropriate courses of action.[9] Clausewitz' conceptual "blink" represents a tentative ontology which organizes a set of concepts within a domain.

The term "military taxonomy" encompasses the domains of weapons, equipment, organizations, strategies, and tactics.[10] The use of taxonomies in the military extends beyond its value as an indexing tool or record-keeping template[11] -- for example, the taxonomy-model analysis suggests a useful depiction of the spectrum of the use of military force in a political context.[12]

A taxonomy of terms to describe various types of military operations is fundamentally affected by the way all elements are defined and addressed—not unlike framing. For example, in terms of a specific military operation, a taxonomic approach based on differentiation and categorization of the entities participating would produce results which were quite different from an approach based on functional objective of an operation (such as peacekeeping, disaster relief, or counter-terrorism).[13]

Economic taxonomies

Taxonomies are also often used to classify economic activity, including products, companies and industries.

Widely used industry taxonomies include the International Standard Industrial Classification (ISIC); national and regional taxonomies such as the United States Standard Industrial Classification (SIC), the North American Industry Classification System (NAICS), Statistical classification of economic activities in the European Community (NACE), the United Kingdom Standard Industrial Classification of Economic Activities, the Russian Economic Activities Classification System (OKVED); and proprietary taxonomies such as the Industry Classification Benchmark and Global Industry Classification Standard. The international and national taxonomies are used by official statistical agencies. The proprietary taxonomies are often used in the financial services industry to group similar investment vehicles and to construct sectorial stock market indices.

Pavitt's Taxonomy classifies firms by their principal sources of innovation.

MasterFormat provides a taxonomy for organizing construction projects.

Safety taxonomies

The creation of taxonomies is very important in safety science. For example there exist numerous taxonomies to classify and analyze human error and accident causes. Examples of these include the Human Factors Analysis and Classification System based on Reason's Swiss Cheese Model, the CREAM (Cognitive Reliability Error Analysis Method), the taxonomy used by CIRAS [14] (Confidential Incident Railway Analysis System) in the UK rail industry, and others.[15]

Notes

[1] Harper, Douglas. "Taxonomy" (http://www.etymonline.com/index.php?term=taxonomy). *Online Etymology Dictionary*. . Retrieved April 18, 2011.

[2] Zirn, Cäcilia, Vivi Nastase and Michael Strube. 2008. "Distinguishing Between Instances and Classes in the Wikipedia Taxonomy" (http://www.eswc2008.org/final-pdfs-for-web-site/onl-4.pdf) (video lecture). (http://videolectures.net/eswc08_zirn_dbi/) 5th Annual European Semantic Web Conference (ESWC 2008).

[3] S. Ponzetto and M. Strube. 2007. "Deriving a large scale taxonomy from Wikipedia" (http://www.eml-research.de/nlp/papers/ponzetto07b.pdf). Proc. of the 22nd Conference on the Advancement of Artificial Intelligence, Vancouver, B.C., Canada, pp. 1440-1445.

[4] S. Ponzetto, R. Navigli. 2009. "Large-Scale Taxonomy Mapping for Restructuring and Integrating Wikipedia" (http://ijcai.org/papers09/Papers/IJCAI09-343.pdf). Proc. of the 21st International Joint Conference on Artificial Intelligence (IJCAI 2009), Pasadena, California, pp. 2083-2088.

[5] Jackson, Joab. "Taxonomy's not just design, it's an art," (http://www.gcn.com/print/23_3/24814-1.html?topic=interview&page=2) *Government Computer News* (Washington, D.C.). September 2, 2004.

[6] Suryanto, Hendra and Paul Compton. "Learning classification taxonomies from a classification knowledge based system." (http://ol2000.aifb.uni-karlsruhe.de/final/HSuryanto_5.pdf) University of Karlsruhe; "Defining 'Taxonomy'," (http://www.greenchameleon.com/gc/blog_detail/defining_taxonomy/) Straights Knowledge website.

[7] Malone, Joseph L. (1988). *The Science of Linguistics in the Art of Translation: Some Tools from Linguistics for the Analysis and Practice of Translation*, p. 112. (http://books.google.com/books?id=PEY0U3umLRkC&pg=PA112&dq=conflation&client=firefox-a)

[8] Grossi, Davide, Frank Dignum and John-Jules Charles Meyer. (2005). "Contextual Taxonomies" in *Computational Logic in Multi-Agent Systems*, pp. 33-51 (http://www.springerlink.com/content/9yj2lfa5cy67c78m/fulltext.pdf?page=1).

[9] Clausewitz, Carl. (1982). *On War*, p. 141; (http://books.google.com/books?id=_La4qTgECD0C&pg=PA141&lpg=PA141&dq=clausewitz+coup+d'oeil&source=web&ots=8UCKTI28o4&sig=0ntr9cQoagmpsJVuulXii533H8U&hl=en&sa=X&oi=book_result&resnum=10&ct=result) "Defining 'Taxonomy'," (http://www.greenchameleon.com/gc/blog_detail/defining_taxonomy/) Straights Knowledge website.

[10] Cycorp: Structured information (http://www.cyc.com/products/overview)

[11] Fenske, Russell W. "A Taxonomy for Operations Research," (http://www.jstor.org/pss/168881) *Operations Research*, Vol. 19, No. 1 (Jan.-Feb., 1971), pp. 224-234;] United Nations. "Taxonomy for Recordkeeping in Field Missions of UN Peacekeeping Operations." (http://archives.un.org/unarms/doc/taxonomy/20060609_Taxonomy_-_Version_1.pdf) June 2006.

[12] Cohen, Stuart A. and Efraim Inbar. "A taxonomy of Israel's use of military force," (http://www.informaworld.com/smpp/content~content=a782379359~db=all~order=page) *Journal Comparative Strategy*, Vol. 10, No. 2 (April 1991), pp. 121 - 138.

[13] Downie, Richard D. "Defining integrated operations," (http://findarticles.com/p/articles/mi_m0KNN/is_38/ai_n15631260/pg_3?tag=artBody;col1) *Joint Force Quarterly* (Washington, D.C.). July, 2005.

[14] http://www.ciras.org.uk/

[15] Wallace,B, and Alastair Ross. *Beyond Human Error: Taxonomies and Safety Science*; (CRC Press 2006).

References

• Atran, S. (1993) *Cognitive Foundations of Natural History: Towards an Anthropology of Science*. Cambridge: Cambridge University Press. 10-ISBN 0521438713 13-ISBN 9780521438711

• Carbonell, J. G. and J. Siekmann, eds. (2005). *Computational Logic in Multi-Agent Systems*, Vol. 3487. (http://www.springerlink.com/content/fb5lq38pu0c7/?p=55d6f2e6622046f5909b8b3d31994ddb&pi=0) Berlin: Springer-Verlag. 13-ISBN 978-3-540-28060-6

• Clausewitz, Carl. (1982). *On War* (http://books.google.com/books?id=_La4qTgECD0C&dq=clausewitz+coup+d'oeil&source=gbs_summary_s&cad=0) (editor, Anatol Rapoport). New York: Penguin Classics. 10-ISBN 0-140-44427-0; 13-ISBN 978-0-140-44427-8

• Malone, Joseph L. (1988). *The Science of Linguistics in the Art of Translation: Some Tools from Linguistics for the Analysis and Practice of Translation*. (http://books.google.com/books?id=PEY0U3umLRkC&client=firefox-a) Albany, New York: State University of New York Press. 10-ISBN 0-887-06653-4; 13-ISBN 978-0-887-06653-5; OCLC 15856738 (http://www.worldcat.org/wcpa/oclc/15856738)

• *Marcello Sorce Keller, "The Problem of Classification in Folksong Research: a Short History", *Folklore*, XCV(1984), no. 1, 100-104.

• Chester D Rowe and Stephen M Davis, 'The Excellence Engine Tool Kit'; ISBN 978-0-615-24850-9

External links

- Hjørland: Scientific classification and taxonomy. IN: The epistemological Lifeboat (http://www.db.dk/jni/lifeboat/info.asp?subjectid=15)
- Wikispecies Main Page (http://species.wikimedia.org/)
- Integrated Taxonomic Information System (http://www.itis.gov/)
- Taxonomy at the National Center for Biotechnology Information (http://www.ncbi.nlm.nih.gov/Taxonomy/)
- Taxonomy at the European Bioinformatics Institute (http://www.uniprot.org/taxonomy/) (formerly known as "New EBI Web Taxonomy (NEWT)")
- Library of Taxonomy Resources (http://www.taxonomystrategies.com/html/bibliography.htm)
- Metadata? Thesauri? Taxonomies? Topic Maps! - Making sense of it all (http://www.ontopia.net/topicmaps/materials/tm-vs-thesauri.html)
- Taxonomies & Controlled Vocabularies Special Interest Group of the American Society for Indexing (http://www.taxonomies-sig.org/)
- Consortium of European Taxonomic Facilities (http://www.cetaf.org)

Acanothochitonidae

Acanothochitonidae is an extinct family of polyplacophoran mollusc.[1]

References

[1] van Belle, R. A. (1981). *Catalogue of Fossil Chitons*. ISBN 90 6279 018 6.

Acanthochitonina

Acanthochitonina is an extinct suborder of polyplacophoran mollusc.[1]

References

[1] van Belle, R. A. (1981). *Catalogue of Fossil Chitons*. ISBN 90 6279 018 6.

Acutichiton

Acutichiton is an extinct genus of polyplacophoran mollusc. Acutichiton became extinct during the Carboniferous period.[1]

References

[1] van Belle, R. A. (1981). *Catalogue of Fossil Chitons*. ISBN 90 6279 018 6.

Affinity (taxonomy)

Affinity (taxonomy) — mainly in life sciences or natural history - resemblance suggesting a common descent, phylogenetic relationship, or type.[1] The term does however have broader application, such as in geology (for example, in descriptive and theoretical works[2] [3]), and similarly in astronomy (for example, see "Centaur object" in the context of 2060 Chiron's close affinity with icy comet nuclei.[4])

Basis

In taxonomy the basis of of any particular type of classification is the *way in which objects in the domain resemble each other*. A resemblance of a type that seems appropriate to the classification that we propose, we may call an *affinity*, and when we decide how to classify say, a specimen of rock or butterfly, we justify our decision according to the affinities that we observe.

Other resemblances we dismiss as being out of context or at least non-cogent; for example, in deciding whether to classify a lizard as having closer affinities to a snake than to a table, biologists rely on affinities such as the scales, blood, physiology, vertebral anatomy, and reproductive system as being more relevant than the possession of four "feet".

Application and obstacles

Analysing and determining the proper classification of an organism, a rock, or an astronomic object according to a particular system is often a difficult and treacherous procedure. Problems in such fields of study have tripped up whole generations of workers in recent centuries. When the position is not clear from an early stage, the first step after beginning to determine, evaluate, and describe the attributes of the object, is to determine the affinities and evaluate their significance.

The number of legs might well be a significant affinity in comparing different types of related organisms such as crustaceans, but irrelevant in comparing a ten-limbed cephalopod with a ten-limbed solifugid (including its pedipalps as limbs). Such a comparison would be no more cogent than the foregoing example of the lizard and the table.

There are many such examples in nature; we see both a lungfish and a porpoise as having closer (but largely different) affinities to a cow than to a tuna, and a bat as having closer affinities to a banteng than to a bird or a butterfly, in spite of the fact that a banteng has no "wings". These are considerations arising from the principles discussed in articles on Homology (biology) and Analogy (biology).

It is clear that there is an element of subjectivity to the recognition of affinities; that is implicit in such dictionary definitions as: ""Affinity: the closeness of relation between plants as shown by similarity of important organs."[5] That definition is over a century old, but it is typical of the basis on which taxonomists had to work till recently, and in practice still must use; it is not practical to sequence the genome of every specimen. Nucleic acid analyses are eroding many difficulties, but there is a long way to go.

References

[1] Brown, Lesley (1993). *The New shorter Oxford English dictionary on historical principles.* Oxford [Eng.]: Clarendon. ISBN 0-19-861271-0.

[2] Gibbons, Wes; Teresa Moreno (2007). *The Geology of Chile.* London: Geological Society of London. ISBN 1-86239-220-X.

[3] Mader, Hermann (2008). *The Geology of Central Europe - Volume 1 Precambrian and Palaeozoic (The Geological Society of London).* London: Geological Society of London. ISBN 1-86239-246-3.

[4] "Centaur object." Encyclopædia Britannica. Encyclopædia Britannica 2007 Ultimate Reference Suite . Chicago: Encyclopædia Britannica, 2011.

[5] Jackson, Benjamin, Daydon; A Glossary of Botanic Terms with their Derivation and Accent; Published by Gerald Duckworth & Co. London, 4th ed 1928

Afossochiton

Afossochiton is an extinct genus of polyplacophoran mollusc. Afossochiton became extinct during the Pliocene period.[1]

References

[1] van Belle, R. A. (1981). *Catalogue of Fossil Chitons.* ISBN 90 6279 018 6.

Afossochitonidae

Afossochitonidae is an extinct family of polyplacophoran mollusc.[1]

References

[1] van Belle, R. A. (1981). *Catalogue of Fossil Chitons.* ISBN 90 6279 018 6.

AIDGAP series

AIDGAP is an acronym for Aid to Identification in Difficult Groups of
Animals and Plants.

The **AIDGAP series** is a set of books published by the Field Studies
Council. They are intended to enable students and interested
non-specialists to identify groups of taxa in Britain which are not
covered by standard field guides. In general, they are less demanding
in level than the Synopses of the British Fauna.

All AIDGAP guides are initially produced as test versions, which are
circulated widely to students, teaching staff and environmental
professionals, with the feedback incorporated into the final published
versions. In many cases the AIDGAP volume is the only non-technical
work covering the group of taxa in question.

History of the series

The Field Studies Council recognised the widespread need for
identification guides soon after its inception, and has since established
a long tradition of publishing such material. Many of these were

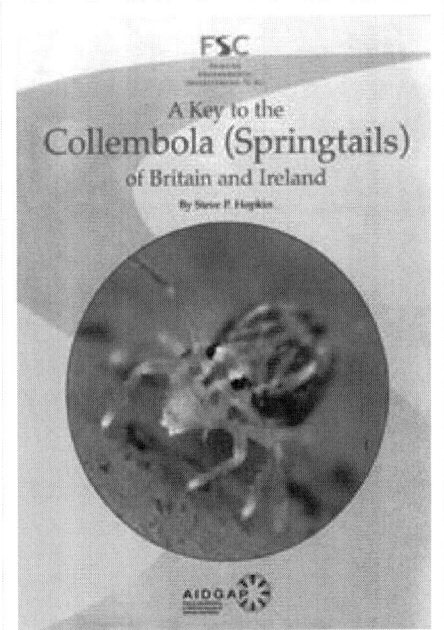

AIDGAP guide to Collembola

written by teaching staff writing their own keys to fill obvious gaps in the available literature (see for example A key
to the land snails of the Flatford area, Suffolk (1959) [1]). However, it became increasingly apparent that a change in
approach was needed. Too few guides were available which were usable by those with little previous experience.
Many groups of plants and animals appeared to be neglected.

The FSC initiated the AIDGAP project in 1976, with input from an advisory panel which included a range of
organisations such as the Linnean Society, teachers in secondary education and professional illustrators. The two
main objectives adopted by the panel were first to identify those groups of organisms regarded as 'difficult' due to a
lack of a suitable key, and second to investigate ways of alleviating the difficulties of identification for each group.
The panel also decided to incorporate a 'testing' stage during which the identification guides could be revised and
improved.

In practice today, AIDGAP guides are produced as 'test versions', which are then circulated to at least 100 volunteer
'testers', drawn from a wide range of backgrounds. Most test versions are sent free of charge, with testing lasting
from three to twelve months. Feedback from the testers is used to inform the production of the finished AIDGAP
guide.

Titles in the AIDGAP series

A large number of guides have been published in the last thirty years. A list of the works in the series is as follows
(see link below for a list of the guides still in print):

- Macadam and Bennett (2010) *A pictorial guide to British Ephemeroptera*
- Barber (2009) *Key to the identification of British centipedes*
- Barnard & Ross (2008) *Guide to the adult caddisflies or sedge flies (Trichoptera)*
- Cameron & Riley (2008) *Land Snails in the British Isles* (2nd edition)
- Pryce, Macadam & Brooks (2007) *Guide to the British Stonefly (Plecoptera) families: adults and larvae*
- Merryweather & Hill (2007) *The fern guide* (3rd edition)
- Hopkin (2007) *A key to the Springtails (Collembola) of Britain and Ireland*

- Wallace (2006) *Simple key to caddis larvae*
- Hayward (2005) *A new key to wild flowers*
- Killeen, Aldridge & Oliver (2004) *Freshwater Bivalves of Britain and Ireland*
- Redfern, Shirley & Bloxham (2002) *British Plant Galls: identification of galls on plants and fungi*
- Unwin (2001) *A key to families of British bugs (Insecta, Hemiptera)*
- Kelly (2000) *Identification of common benthic diatoms in rivers*
- May & Panter (2000) *A guide to the identification of deciduous broad-leaved trees and shrubs in winter*
- Plant (1997) *A key to the adults of British lacewings and their allies (Neuroptera, Megaloptera, Raphidiptera and Mecoptera)*
- Wheeler (1997) *A field key to the freshwater fishes and lampreys of the British Isles*
- Crothers (1997) *A key to the major groups of British marine invertebrates*
- Wheeler (1994) *Field Key to the Shore Fishes of the British Isles*
- Hopkin (1991) *A key to the woodlice of Britain and Ireland*
- Vas (1991) *A field guide to the Sharks of British Coastal Waters*
- Wright (1990) *British Sawflies (Hymenoptera: Symphyta): a key to adults of the genera occurring in Britain*
- Savage (1990) *A key to the adults of British Lesser Water Boatmen (Corixidae)*
- Jones-Walters (1989) *Keys to families of British spiders*
- Trudgil (1989) *Soil types: a field identification guide*
- Friday (1988) *A key to the adults of British Water Beetles*
- Haslam et al. (1987) *British water plants* (revised edition)
- Tilling (1987) *A key to the major groups of terrestrial invertebrates*
- Hiscock (1986) *A field guide to the British Red Seaweeds (Rhodophyta)*
- King (1986) *Sea Spiders. A revised key to the adults of littoral Pycnogonida in the British Isles*
- Croft (1986) *A key to the major groups of British freshwater invertebrates*
- Willmer (1985) *Bees, Ants and Wasps - the British Aculeates*
- Unwin (1984) *A key to the families of British Coleoptera (beetles) and Strepsiptera*
- Crothers & Crothers (1983) *A key to the crabs and crab-like animals of British inshore waters* (revised edition, 1988)
- Unwin (1981) *Key to the families of British Diptera* (freely downloadable pdf from [2]
- Sykes (1981) *An illustrated guide to the diatoms of British coastal plankton* (freely downloadable pdf from [3]
- Hiscock (1979) *A field key to the British Brown Seaweeds*

External links

- Full list of AIDGAP guides in print [4]

References

[1] http://www.field-studies-council.org/fieldstudies/documents/vol1.1_4.pdf

[2] http://www.field-studies-council.org/fieldstudies/documents/vol5.3_143_A.pdf

[3] http://www.field-studies-council.org/fieldstudies/documents/vol5.3_140_A.pdf

[4] http://www.field-studies-council.org/publications/aidgap.aspx

Allochiton

Allochiton is an extinct genus of polyplacophoran mollusc. Allochiton became extinct during the Jurassic period. [1]

References

[1] van Belle, R. A. (1981). *Catalogue of Fossil Chitons*. ISBN 90 6279 018 6.

Alpha taxonomy

Alpha taxonomy is the science of finding, describing and naming species of living or fossil organisms.[1] The term "alpha" refers to alpha taxonomy being the first and most basic step in taxonomy. This science is supported by institutions holding collections of these organisms, with relevant data, carefully curated: such institutes include natural history museums, herbaria and botanical gardens.

Alpha taxonomy is the description and naming of species, such as this display of zoological specimens of beetles.

Describing species

A formal description of a species follow certain rules. From a collection of organisms, one or more specimen are selected as basis for the description, these ideally being "typical" specimen of the new species.[2] In living species where specimen are easily obtainable, these should ideally represent both adult and young individuals. Often they are not however, and with fossil specimen, the basis for the description can be fragmentary and often the only known specimen available. These are designated type specimen, and are to be kept as reference for the species in a special type collection. Mammals and birds are often kept as skin and skeletons (sometimes only the skull). Insects are commonly kept as dried specimens, while other animals are often preserved whole in alcohol or formaldehyde. Plants are preserved flattened and dry in herbaria.

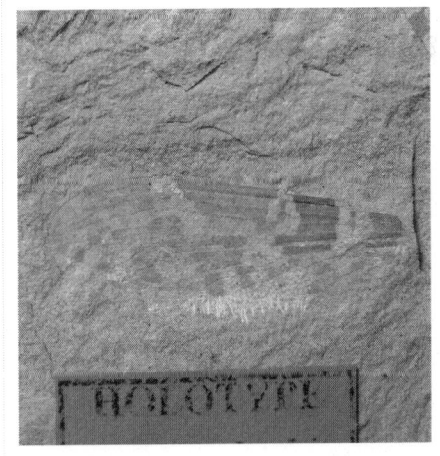

Type specimen of *Cimbrophlebia brooksi*, a fossil scorpion fly: by convention in many scientific collections, a red label denotes a type specimen.

For the new species to be valid, the formal description must be published in a scientific journal. Several journals exist devoted to the publishing of new species. The description of a species will contain a description of typical features of the organisms, and how it differs from other similar organisms. The new species is given a binomial name according to scientific naming conventions, usually accompanied by a formal biological classification giving Kingdom, Phylum or Division, Class, Order, Family, Genus, and Species.[3] Special rules apply in botany, where a formal description must have a summary in Latin giving a brief description of the shape of leaves and flowers.

About authors, authorities and auctors

In botany, an alpha taxonomist who names taxa is called an *auctor*, from the scholastic term for author. In zoology, the term auctor has been replaced with the terms "author" or "authority". A scientist who attempts to describe new taxa has to be intimately familiar with all the previously published scientific literature on that group of organisms. This is necessary in order to avoid errors such as describing an already-named species (thus creating an unnecessary junior synonym) or using a species name that is already taken. The literature on any one group of organisms often spans centuries, and is often written in several different languages, making alpha taxonomy very much the realm of specialists.[1]

Once a species (or any other taxonomic unit) is named, the name of the auctor is associated with the description. In zoology, the full formal name of a species contains not only the Latin binominal (genus and species name), but also the name of the original authority and the year of the original publication. While the overall name of a species may change (usually by the species being transferred to a new genus) the authority name and year still apply.

Names of certain very prolific authorities are sometimes abbreviated; this was quite common during the early years of Linnaean taxonomy. It is no longer done in zoology, except for Linnaeus himself, who is often given with just his surname or even simply as "L.", but a system of abbreviations is still used in botany.[4] Many of the more well known species of plants and animals were described by Carl Linnaeus in his *Systema Naturae*, and the auctor-year is given as "L., 1758", where the *L.* is the formal abbreviation for Linnaeus, and 1758 marks the issue of the 10th edition of *Systema Naturæ*. The sweet briar is thus *Rosa rubiginosa* (L., 1758), and the common buttercup is *Ranunculus acris* (L., 1758). Correspondingly, tiger can be found as "*Panthera tigris* (L., 1758)" in older works.

Alpha taxonomy and systematics

For a long time the term "taxonomy" was used for what is today seen as alpha taxonomy. Over time, the term "taxonomy" has gained several other meanings and has thus became potentially confusing. To some extent it is being replaced, in its original (and narrow) meaning, by "alpha taxonomy". As such, alpha taxonomy deals mostly with real organisms: species and lower ranking taxa. Higher ranking taxa (including clades and grades) mostly are the province of "beta taxonomy", more commonly called systematics. Systematics (as a science) deals with the relationships between taxa, especially at the higher levels. These days systematics is greatly influenced by data derived from DNA from nuclei, mitochondria and chloroplasts. This is sometimes known as molecular systematics which is becoming increasingly more common, perhaps at the expense of traditional morphological taxonomy.[5]

References

[1] Richard Fortey (2008). *Dry Store Room No. 1: The Secret Life of the Natural History Museum*. London: Harper Perennial. ISBN 0007209894.

[2] Douglas J. Preston (1993). *Dinosaurs in the Attic: an Excursion to the American Museum of Natural History*. New York: St. Martin's Griffin. ISBN 0312104561.

[3] International Code of Botanical Nomenclature, (St. Luis code), Electronic version, Chapter I, article 3 (http://www.bgbm.org/iapt/nomenclature/code/SaintLouis/0007Ch1Art003.htm)

[4] R. K. Brummitt & C. E. Powell, ed (1992). *Authors of Plant Names: A List of Authors of Scientific Names of Plants, with Recommended Standard Forms of Their Names, Including Abbreviations*. Royal Botanic Gardens, Kew. ISBN 0947643443.

A specimen of the butterfly subspecies *Morpho rhetenor helena*

[5] Quentin D. Wheeler (2004). *Taxonomic triage and the poverty of phylogeny*. In H. C. J. Godfray & S. Knapp. "Taxonomy for the twenty−first century". *Philosophical Transactions of the Royal Society* **359** (1444): 571−583. doi:10.1098/rstb.2003.1452. PMC 1693342. PMID 15253345.

External links

- uBio Taxonomic Name Reconciliation (http://www.ubio.org/)
- Integrated Taxonomic Information System (http://www.itis.gov/) - Generalized N. American server (http://itis.gbif.net/pls/itisca/taxaget?p_ifx=plglt) Mexico Server (http://siit.conabio.gob.mx/pls/itisca/taxaget?p_ifx=itismx&p_lang=es) Canada Server (http://www.cbif.gc.ca/pls/itisca/taxaget?p_ifx=cbif)
- Tree of Life (http://tolweb.org)
- BioLib (http://www.biolib.cz/index.php?text=main&lang=EN&rlang=EN)
- NCBI Taxonomy (http://www.ncbi.nlm.nih.gov/Taxonomy/)
- Taxonomy & Informatics (http://research.amnh.org/informatics/taxlit) An AMNH & NSF Project
- Merriam-Webster Online Dictionary: definition- taxonomy (http://www.m-w.com/dictionary/taxonomy)
- The Nature of Plant Species (http://www.nature.com/nature/journal/v440/n7083/abs/nature04402.html) - article on a study by University Bloomington scientists
- Aphia: North Sea flora and fauna taxonomic register (http://www.vliz.be/vmdcdata/aphia/aphia.php?p=search)
- VisualTaxa: Taxonomic subdivision of life (http://visualtaxa.redgolpe.com)

Analytical Profile Index

The **Analytical Profile Index** or **API** is a classification of bacteria based on experiments, allowing fast identification. It was invented in the 1970s in the United States by Pierre Janin of Analytab Products, Inc. [1] Presently, the API test system is manufactured by bioMérieux.[2] The API range introduced a standardized, miniaturized version of existing techniques, which up until then were complicated to perform and difficult to read.

API 20NE Detection system after 24 hours incubation.

The API 20E/NE fast identification system combines some conventional tests and allows the identification of a limited number of Gram-negative Enterobacteriaceae or non-Enterobacteriaceae. The test systems are stored in 20 small reaction tubes, which include the substrates. An identification is only possible with microbiological culture. To guarantee a comparability of different samples, follow the introductions of the manufacturer.

Before starting a test, it must be sure, the culture is an Enterobacteriaceae or not. To test it, a quick oxidase test for cytochrome c oxidase is mandatory. Here, Non-Enterobacteriaceae are cytochrome c oxidase positive and Enterobacteriaceae are negative. Cytochrome c oxidase is the terminal enzyme of the electron transport chain, in which the oxidation of cytochrome c and reduction of O_2 is organized. The enzyme is localized in the mitochondria of eukaryotes and in the plasma membrane of several bacteria.

HINT: This system is developed for quick identification of clinically relevant bacteria. Because of it, only known bacteria can be identified.

REFERENCES:

United States Patent Office, Patent Number 3936356 [1]

API System: a Multitube Micromethod for Identification of Enterobacteriaceae, P. B. Smith, K. M. Tomfohrde, D. L. Rhoden, and A. BalowsCenter for Disease Control, Atlanta, Georgia 30333[3]

References

[1] http://patft.uspto.gov/netacgi/nph-Parser?Sect1=PTO1&Sect2=HITOFF&d=PALL&p=1&u=%2Fnetahtml%2FPTO%2Fsrchnum.
     htm&r=1&f=G&l=50&s1=3936356.PN.&OS=PN/3936356&RS=PN/3936356

[2] http://www.biomerieux-diagnostics.com/servlet/srt/bio/clinical-diagnostics/dynPage?doc=CNL_PRD_CPL_G_PRD_CLN_11

[3] http://www.ncbi.nlm.nih.gov/pmc/articles/PMC376540/?page=1

Bacterial phyla

The **bacterial phyla** are the major lineages (phyla or divisions) of Bacteria. In the scientific classification established by Carl von Linné,[1] each bacterial species has to be assigned to a genus (binary nomenclature), which in turn is a lower level of a hierarchy of ranks (family, suborder, order, subclass, class, division and domain). Bacteria were first classified as plants constituting the class Schizomycetes,[2] then in the phylum Monera in the kingdom Protista by Haeckel in 1866, comprising Protogens, Protamaeba, Vampyrella, Protomonae and Vibrio,[3] later reclassified as prokaryotes by Chatton.[4] Currently, under the three-domain system, Bacteria form a domain[5] which is subdivided into

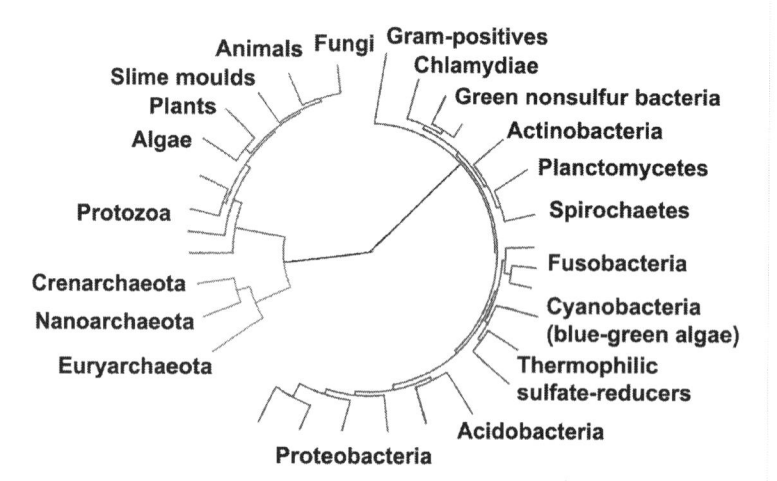

Phylogenetic tree showing the diversity of bacteria, compared to other organisms.Ciccarelli FD, Doerks T, von Mering C, Creevey CJ, Snel B, Bork P (2006). "Toward automatic reconstruction of a highly resolved tree of life". Science 311 (5765): 1283–7. doi:10.1126/science.1123061. PMID 16513982. Eukaryotes are colored red, archaea green and bacteria blue.

over 29 phyla, which some authors call kingdoms.[6] [7] [8] Phyla can only be included in this system if they can be cultured in a lab, but if candidate phyla (clades of species that exist but cannot currently be cultured) are included the number could be 52 or higher. With the use of metagenomics, the number of major phyla has increased from 12 identifiable lineages in 1987, to 52 as of 2003.[9]

Regarding the precise phylogeny at the base of the clade Bacteria, some scientists believe there may be a branching order, where possibly Aquificales or Thermotogae are basal, whereas other scientists, such as Norman Pace, believe the various Bacterial phyla represent a large hard polytomy (a simultaneous multiple speciation event).[10]

For historical reasons, taxa above the rank of class are not covered by the Rules of the Bacteriological Code (1990 Revision),[11] [12] consequently there is no "official" nomenclature, but there are several authorities in the field, such as Bergey's Manual of Systematic Bacteriology, which contains a taxonomy outline[7] and the journal *International Journal of Systematic Bacteriology/International Journal of Systematic and Evolutionary Microbiology (IJSB/IJSEM)*, on which the List of Prokaryotic names with Standing in Nomenclature (LPSN) repository is based.[13]

History

Traditionally, phylogeny were inferred and taxonomy established based on studies of morphology. Recently molecular phylogenetics has been used to achieve allow better elucidation of the evolutionary relationship of the species by analysing their DNA/protein sequences, for example their ribosomal DNA.[14] The lack of easily accessible morphological features, such as those present in animals and plants, hampered early efforts of classification and resulted in erroneous, distored and confusion classification, an examples of which, noted Carl Woese, is *Pseudomonas* whose etymology ironically matches its taxonomy, namely "false unit".[11]

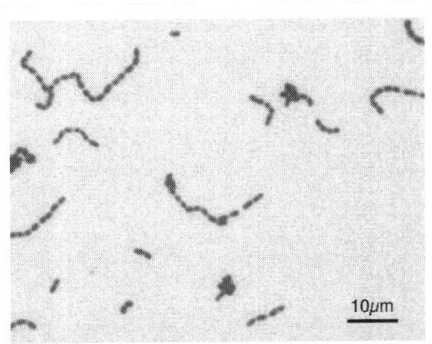

Streptococcus mutans visualized with a Gram stain

Early phylogeny

In 1987, Carl Woese, regarded as the forerunner of the molecular phylogeny revolution, divided Eubacteria into 11 divisions based on 16S ribosomal RNA (SSU) sequences:[16] [11]

- **Purple Bacteria and their relatives**
  - alpha subdivision (purple non-sulfur bacteria, rhizobacteria, *Agrobacterium*, *Rickettsiae*, *Nitrobacter*)
  - beta subdivision (*Rhodocyclus*, (some) *Thiobacillus*, *Alcaligenes*, *Spirillum*, *Nitrosovibrio*)
  - gamma subdivision (enterics, fluorescent pseudomonads, purple sulfur bacteria, *Legionella*, (some) *Beggiatoa*)
  - delta subdivision (Sulfur and sulfate reducers (*Desulfovibrio*), Myxobacteria, *Bdellovibrio*)
- **Gram-positive Eubacteria**
  - High-G+C species - Actinobacteria (*Actinomyces*, *Streptomyces*, *Arthrobacter*, *Micrococcus*, *Bifidobacterium*)
  - Low-G+C species - Firmicutes (*Clostridium*, *Peptococcus*, *Bacillus*, *Mycoplasma*)
  - Photosynthetic species (*Heliobacterium*)
  - Species with gram-negative walls (*Megasphaera*, *Sporomusa*)
- **Cyanobacteria and chloroplasts** (*Aphanocapsa*, *Oscillatoria*, *Nostoc*, *Synechococcus*, *Gleoebacter*, *Prochloron*)
- **Spirochetes and relatives**
  - Spirochetes (*Spirochaeta*, *Treponema*, *Borrelia*)
  - Leptospiras (*Leptospira*, *Leptonema*)
- **Green sulfur bacteria** (*Chlorobium*, *Chloroherpeton*)
- **Bacteroides, Flavobacteria and relatives**
  - Bacteroides (*Bacteroides*, *Fusobacterium*)
  - Flavobacterium group (*Flavobacterium*, *Cytophaga*, *Saprospira*, *Flexibacter*)
- **Planctomyces and relatives**
  - Planctomyces group (*Planctomyces*, *Pasteuria*)
  - Thermophiles (*Isocystis pallida*)

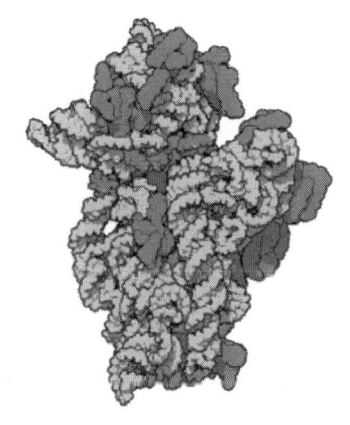

Atomic structure of the 30S ribosomal Subunit from *Thermus thermophilus* of which 16S makes up part of. Proteins are shown in blue and the single RNA strand in orange.[15]

- **Chlamydiae** (*Chlamydia psittaci*, *Chlamydia trachomatis*)
- **Radioresistant micrococci and relatives**
  - Deinococcus group (*Deinococcus radiodurans*)
  - Thermophiles (*Thermus aquaticus*)
- **Green non-sulfur bacteria and relatives**
  - Chloroflexus group (*Chloroflexus*, *Herpetosiphon*)
  - Thermomicrobium group (*Thermomicrobium roseum*)
- **Thermotogae**

The "purple bacteria and relatives" were renamed Proteobacteria.[17]

The low and high CG content gram positive subdivisions were renamed Actinobacteria and Firmicutes divisions, making the number of phyla 12.[18] Until recently, it was believed than only Firmicutes and Actinobacteria were Gram-positive. The candidate phylum TM7 may be Gram positive.[19] Chloroflexi however possess a single bilayer, but stain negative (with some exceptions[20]).[21]

"Green non-sulfur bacteria and relatives" was renamed Chloroflexi .

"Radioresistant micrococci and relatives" are commonly referred to as Deinococcus-Thermus clade,[22] , although it has been prosed to call the clade Xenobacteria[23] or Hadobacteria[24] (latter is illegitimate[25]).

16S-based tree according to Woese, 1987[11]

Thermotogae

Chloroflexi

Deinococcus-Thermus

Proteobacteria

Cyanobacteria

Firmicutes

Actinobacteria

Planctomycetes

Chlamydiae

Spirochaetes

Bacteroidetes

Chlorobi

In [11] the root of the tree is placed between the Bacteria (or Eubacteria) and the group formed by Archaea and Eukarya (called Neomura by T. Calavier-Smith[24]). The names have been changed to reflect more current nomenclature used by molecular phylogenists.

New cultured phyla

New species have been cultured since 1987, when Woese's review paper was published, that are sufficiently different to warrant a new phylum, mostly thermophiles and often also chemolithoautotrophs, such as Aquilificae, which oxidises hydrogen gas. Other non-thermophiles, such as Acidobacteria, a ubiquitous phyla with divergent physiologies, have been found, some of which are chemolithotrophs, such as *Nitrospira* (nitrile-oxidising) or *Leptospirillum* (Fe-oxidising).[9] , some proposed phyla however do not appear in LPSN as they were insufficiently described or are awaiting approval or it is debated if they may belong to a pre-existing phyla. An example of this is the genus *Caldithrix*, consisting of *C. palaeochoryensis*[26] and *C.abyssi*,[27] which is considered Deferribacteres,[28] , however, it shares only 81% similarity with the other Deferribacteres (*Deferribacter* species and relatives)[27] and is considered a separate phylum by Rappé and Giovannoni.[9] Additionally the placement of the genus *Geovibrio* in the phylum Deferribacteres is debated.[29]

Uncultivated and metagenomics

With the advent of methods to analyse environmental DNA (metagenomics), the 16S rRNA of an extremely large number of undiscovered species have been found, showing that there are several whole phyla which have no known cultivable representative and that some phyla lack in culture major subdivisions as is the case for Verrucomicrobia and Chloroflexi.[9] The term Candidatus is used for proposed species for which the lack of information prevents it to be validated, such as where the only evidence is DNA sequence date, even if the whole genome has been sequenced.[30] [31] When the species are members of whole phyla it is called a candidate division[32] and in 2003 there were 26 candidate divisions out of 52.[9] A candidate division was defined by in 1998 Hugenholtz and Pace, as a set of 16S ribosomal RNA sequences with less than 85% similarity.[33] Three candidate phyla were known before 1998, prior to the 85% threshold definition by Hugenholtz and Pace:

- OS-K group (from Octopus spring)
- Marine Group A (from Pacific ocean)
- Termite Group 1 (from Termite gut, now Elusimicrobia)

Since then several other cadidate phyla were identified and accepted by Rappé and Giovannoni (2003):[9])

- OP1, OP3, OP5 (now Caldiserica), OP8, OP9, OP10 (now Armatimonadetes), OP11 (obsidian pool, yellowstone national park)
- WS2, WS3, WS5, WS6 (Wurtsmith contaminated aquifer)
- SC3 and SC4 (from arid soil)
- vadinBE97 (now Lentisphaerae)
- NC10 (from flooded caves)
- BRC1 (from bulk soil and rice roots)
- ABY1 (from sediment)
- Guyamas1 (from hydrothermal)
- NKB19 (from activated sludge)
- SBR1093 (from activated sludge)
- TM6 and TM7 (Torf, Mittlere Schicht)

Since then a candidate phylum called Poribacteria was discovered, living in symbiosis with sponges and extensively studied.[34] (Note: the divergence of the major bacterial lineages predates sponges)

Other candidate phyla that have been the centre of some studies are TM7,[32] the genomes of organisms of which have even been sequenced (draft),[35] WS6[36] and Marine Group A.[9]

Two species of the candidate division OP10, which is now called Armatimonadetes, where recently cultured: *Armatimonas rosea* isolated from the rhizoplane of a reed in a lake in Japan[37] and *Chthonomonas calidirosea* from an isolate from geothermally heated soil at Hell's Gate, Tikitere, New Zealand.[38]

One species, *Caldisericum exile*, of the candidate division OP5 was cultured, leading to it being named Caldiserica.[39]

Termite Group 1 is now known as Elusimicrobia, after the ultramicrobacterium *Elusimicrobium minutum* was cultured.[40]

The candidate division VadinBE97 is now known as Lentisphaerae after *Lentisphaera araneosa* and *Victivallis vadensis* were cultured.[41]

Despite these lineages not being officially recognised, due to the ever increasing number of sequences belonging to non-existent phyla, ARB-Silva list 57 phyla, not only the 27 phyla with validly accepted species, but also 30 Candidate divisions (BD1-5, BHI80-139, BRC1, CK-1C4-19, EM19, GAL08, GOUTA4, Hyd24-12, JL-ETNP-Z39, Kazan-3B-28, LD1-PA38, MVP-21, NPL-UPA2, OC31, OD1, OP3, OP9, OP10, OP11, RF3, RsaHF231, SM2F11, SR1, TA06, TM6, TM7, WCHB1-60, WS3 and WS6)[42] , while Ribosomal Database Project 10, list 29 phyla and 7 candidate divisions (OP10, OP11, OD1, BRC1, SR1, WS3, TM7)[43]

"Validated" phyla

Currently there are 29 phyla accepted by LPSN[8]

1. Acidobacteria, phenotipically diverse, but mostly uncultured

2. Actinobacteria, High-G+C Gram positive species, notable genera/species include *Streptomyces* (antibiotic production), *Propionibacterium acnes* (odorous skin commensal) and *Propionobacter shermanii* (holes in Emmental)

3. Aquificae, only 14 thermophilic genera, deep branching

4. Bacteroidetes, some opportunistic pathogens or human gut commensal, urban myth as a bacterial weight loss powder

5. Caldiserica, formerly candidate division OP5, *Caldisericum exile* is the sole representative

6. Chlamydiae, only 6 genera of obbligate intracellular pathogens, such as *Chlamydia trachomatis* (chlamidia infection)

7. Chlorobi, only 7 genera of obligately anaerobic photoautotrophic bacteria, known colloquially as Green sulfur bacteria

8. Chloroflexi,diverse phylum including thermophiles and halorespirers, known colloquially as Green non-sulfur bacteria

9. Chrysiogenetes, only 3 genera (*Chrysiogenes arsenatis, Desulfurispira natronophila, Desulfurispirillum alkaliphilum*)

10. Cyanobacteria, major photosynthetic clade believed to have caused Earth's oxygen atmosphere, also known as the blue-green algae

11. Deferribacteres

12. Deinococcus-Thermus, *Deinococcus radiodurans* and *Thermus aquaticus* are "commonly known" species of this phyla

13. Dictyoglomi

14. Elusimicrobia, formerly candidate division Termite Group 1

15. Fibrobacteres

16. Firmicutes, Low-G+C Gram positive species most often spore-forming, in two/three classes: the class Bacilli such as the Bacillus spp. (e.g. B. anthracis, a pathogen, and B.subtilis, biotechnologically useful), lactic acid bacteria (e.g. Lactobacillus casei in yoghurt, Oenococcus oeni in malolactic fermentation, Streptococcus pyogenes, pathogen), the class Clostridia of mostly anaerobic sulphite-reducing saprophytic species, includes the genus Clostridium (e.g. the pathogens C. dificile, C. tetani, C. botulinum and the biotech C. acetobutylicum)

17. Fusobacteria

18. Gemmatimonadetes

19. Lentisphaerae, formerly clade VadinBE97

20. Nitrospira

21. Planctomycetes

22. Proteobacteria, contains most of the "commonly known" species, such as *Escherichia coli* or *Pseudomonas aeruginosa*

23. Spirochaetes, notable for compartmentalisation and species include *Borrelia burgdorferi*, which causes Lyme disease

24. Synergistetes

25. Tenericutes, alternatively class Mollicutes in phylum Firmicutes (notable genus: *Mycoplasma*)

26. Thermodesulfobacteria

27. Thermomicrobia

28. Thermotogae, deep branching

29. Verrucomicrobia

Genomic Trees

Tree of life constructed by gene concatenation of homologuous genes such as [44]

Placement of root

In molecular studies, the root is found to be placed between the Bacteria and the Archaea+Eukaryote clade. Some find it to be placed in the phylum Firmicutes

Alternative theories: Bacterial Luca

Despite the molecular evidence pointing towards the root of the tree of life being between monophyletic Bacteria and Archaea+Eukarya (Neomura), some authors believe in a bacterial origin of life, such as Thomas Cavalier-Smith, based on some morphological characters, such as cell wall structure.[45] In the Cavalier-Smith theory, the last common ancestor (cenansestor) was a Gram-negative diderm bacterium with peptidoglycan, while Archaea and Eukaryotes stem from Actinobacteria.[45]

Cavalier-Smith theory of the tree of life
Chlorobacteria
Hadobacteria
Cyanobacteria
Gracilicutes
Eurybacteria
LUA   Endobacteria
Actinobacteria
Neomura Archaea
Eukarya
Cavalier-Smith theory of the tree of life after[45] [46]

References

[1] Linnaeus, Carl (1735). *Systemae Naturae, sive regna tria naturae, systematics proposita per classes, ordines, genera & species*. (http://visualiseur.bnf.fr/ark:/12148/bpt6k99004c). .

[2] C. Von Nägeli (1857). R. Caspary. ed. "Bericht über die Verhandlungen der 33. Versammlung deutscher Naturforscher und Aerzte, gehalten in Bonn von 18 bis 24 September 1857 [Report on the negotiations on 33 Meeting of German Natural Scientists and Physicians, held in Bonn, 18 to 24 September 1857]". *Botanische Zeitung* **15**: 749–776.

[3] Haeckel, Ernst (1867). *Generelle Morphologie der Organismen*. Reimer, Berlin.

[4] É. Chatton (1925). "*Pansporella perplexa*. Réflexions sur la biologie et la phylogénie des protozoaires". *Ann. Sci. Nat. Zool* **10-VII**: 1–84.

[5] Woese, C. R.; Kandler, O.; Wheelis, M. L. (1990). "Towards a Natural System of Organisms: Proposal for the Domains Archaea, Bacteria, and Eucarya". *Proceedings of the National Academy of Sciences* **87** (12): 4576–9. Bibcode 1990PNAS...87.4576W. doi:10.1073/pnas.87.12.4576. PMC 54159. PMID 2112744.

[6] Madigan, Michael (2009). *Brock Biology of Microorganisms*. San Francisco: Pearson/Benjamin Cummings. ISBN 0132324601.

[7] Garrity GM, Lilburn TG, Cole JR, Harrison SH, Euzéby J and Tindall BJ. "Taxonomic Outline of the Bacteria and Archaea, Release 7.7" (http://www.taxonomicoutline.org). Michigan State University Board of Trustees. doi:10.1601/TOBA7.7. .

[8] J.P. Euzéby. "List of Prokaryotic names with Standing in Nomenclature: Phyla" (http://www.bacterio.cict.fr/classifphyla.html). . Retrieved 30 December 2010.

[9] Rappe, M. S.; Giovannoni, S. J. (2003). "The Uncultured Microbial Majority". *Annual Review of Microbiology* **57**: 369. doi:10.1146/annurev.micro.57.030502.090759. PMID 14527284.

[10] Pace, N. R. (2009). "Mapping the Tree of Life: Progress and Prospects". *Microbiology and Molecular Biology Reviews* **73** (4): 565. doi:10.1128/MMBR.00033-09. PMC 2786576. PMID 19946133.

[11] Woese, CR (1987). "Bacterial evolution". *Microbiological reviews* **51** (2): 221–71. PMC 373105. PMID 2439888.

[12] S.P., S.P. (1992). *International Code of Nomenclature of Bacteria 1990 Revision*. Washington: American Society for Microbiology. ISBN 9780555810392.

[13] J.P. Euzéby. "List of Prokaryotic names with Standing in Nomenclature" (http://www.bacterio.cict.fr/). . Retrieved 30 December 2010.

[14] Olsen GJ, Woese CR, Overbeek R (1994). "The winds of (evolutionary) change: breathing new life into microbiology" (http://jb.asm.org/cgi/pmidlookup?view=long&pmid=8282683). *Journal of Bacteriology* **176** (1): 1–6. PMC 205007. PMID 8282683. .

[15] Schluenzen F, Tocilj A, Zarivach R, Harms J, Gluehmann M, Janell D, Bashan A, Bartels H, Agmon I, Franceschi F, Yonath A Structure of functionally activated small ribosomal subunit at 3.3 angstroms resolution (http://dx.doi.org/10.1016/S0092-8674(00)00084-2) (2000). "Structure of functionally activated small ribosomal subunit at 3.3 angstroms resolution". *Cell* **102** (5): 615–23. doi:10.1016/S0092-8674(00)00084-2. PMID 11007480.

[16] Holland L. (22). "Woese,Carl in the forefront of bacterial evolution revolution". *scientist* **4** (10).

[17] Stackebrandt et al. (1988). "Proteobacteria classis nov., a name for the phylogenetic taxon that includes the "purple bacteria and their relatives"". *Int. J. Syst. Bacteriol.* **38**: 321–325.

[18] Stackebrandt, E.; Rainey, F. A.; Ward-Rainey, N. L. (1997). "Proposal for a New Hierarchic Classification System, Actinobacteria classis nov.". *International Journal of Systematic Bacteriology* **47**: 479. doi:10.1099/00207713-47-2-479.

[19] Hugenholtz, P.; Tyson, G. W.; Webb, R. I.; Wagner, A. M.; Blackall, L. L. (2001). "Investigation of Candidate Division TM7, a Recently Recognized Major Lineage of the Domain Bacteria with No Known Pure-Culture Representatives". *Applied and Environmental Microbiology* **67** (1): 411. doi:10.1128/AEM.67.1.411-419.2001. PMC 92593. PMID 11133473.

[20] doi:20495028
This citation will be automatically completed in the next few minutes. You can jump the queue or expand by hand (http://en.wikipedia.org/wiki/Template:cite_doi/20495028?preload=Template:Cite_doi/preload&editintro=Template:Cite_doi/editintro&action=edit)

[21] Sutcliffe, I. C. (2011). "Cell envelope architecture in the Chloroflexi: A shifting frontline in a phylogenetic turf war". *Environmental Microbiology* **13** (2): 279–282. doi:10.1111/j.1462-2920.2010.02339.x. PMID 20860732.

[22] J.P. Euzéby. "List of Prokaryotic names with Standing in Nomenclature: classification of Deinococcus-Thermus" (http://www.bacterio.cict.fr/classifphyla.html#DeinococcusThermus). . Retrieved 30 December 2010.

[23] Bergey's Manual of Systematic Bacteriology 1st Ed.

[24] Cavalier-Smith, T (2002). "The neomuran origin of archaebacteria, the negibacterial root of the universal tree and bacterial megaclassification". *International journal of systematic and evolutionary microbiology* **52** (Pt 1): 7–76. PMID 11837318.

[25] "hadobacteria" entry (http://www.bacterio.cict.fr/h/hadobacteria.html) in LPSN [Euzéby, J.P. (1997). "List of Bacterial Names with Standing in Nomenclature: a folder available on the Internet" (http://ijs.sgmjournals.org/cgi/reprint/47/2/590). *Int J Syst Bacteriol* **47** (2): 590-2. ISSN 0020-7713. PMID 9103655. .]

[26] Miroshnichenko, M. L.; Kolganova, T. V.; Spring, S.; Chernyh, N.; Bonch-Osmolovskaya, E. A. (2009). "Caldithrix palaeochoryensis sp. Nov., a thermophilic, anaerobic, chemo-organotrophic bacterium from a geothermally heated sediment, and emended description of the genus Caldithrix". *International Journal of Systematic and Evolutionary Microbiology* **60** (Pt 9): 2120. doi:10.1099/ijs.0.016667-0. PMID 19854873.

[27] Miroshnichenko, ML; Kostrikina, NA; Chernyh, NA; Pimenov, NV; Tourova, TP; Antipov, AN; Spring, S; Stackebrandt, E et al. (2003). "Caldithrix abyssi gen. Nov., sp. Nov., a nitrate-reducing, thermophilic, anaerobic bacterium isolated from a Mid-Atlantic Ridge hydrothermal vent, represents a novel bacterial lineage". *International journal of systematic and evolutionary microbiology* **53** (Pt 1): 323–9. PMID 12656191.

[28] J.P. Euzéby. "List of Prokaryotic names with Standing in Nomenclature: Caldithrix" (http://www.bacterio.cict.fr/classificationac. html#Caldithrix). . Retrieved 30 December 2010.

[29] J.P. Euzéby. "List of Prokaryotic names with Standing in Nomenclature: Deferribacterales" (http://www.bacterio.cict.fr/ classifgeneraorders.html#Deferribacterales). . Retrieved 30 December 2010.

[30] Murray, R. G. E.; Schleifer, K. H. (1994). "Taxonomic Notes: A Proposal for Recording the Properties of Putative Taxa of Procaryotes". *International Journal of Systematic Bacteriology* **44** (1): 174. doi:10.1099/00207713-44-1-174. PMID 8123559.

[31] "Judicial commission of the international committee on systematic bacteriology: Minutes of the meetings, 2 and 6 July 1994, Prague, Czech Republic" (http://ijs.sgmjournals.org/cgi/reprint/45/1/195.pdf). *Int. J. Syst. Bacteriol.* **45**: 195–196. 1995. .

[32] Hugenholtz, P; Goebel, BM; Pace, NR (1998). "Impact of culture-independent studies on the emerging phylogenetic view of bacterial diversity". *Journal of bacteriology* **180** (18): 4765–74. PMC 107498. PMID 9733676.

[33] Hugenholtz, P; Pitulle, C; Hershberger, KL; Pace, NR (1998). "Novel division level bacterial diversity in a Yellowstone hot spring". *Journal of bacteriology* **180** (2): 366–76. PMC 106892. PMID 9440526.

[34] Fieseler, L.; Horn, M.; Wagner, M.; Hentschel, U. (2004). "Discovery of the Novel Candidate Phylum "Poribacteria" in Marine Sponges". *Applied and Environmental Microbiology* **70** (6): 3724. doi:10.1128/AEM.70.6.3724-3732.2004. PMC 427773. PMID 15184179.

[35] Marcy Y et al., "Dissecting biological "dark matter" with single-cell genetic analysis of rare and uncultivated TM7 microbes from the human mouth.", Proc Natl Acad Sci U S A, 2007 Jul 9; 104(29):11889-94

[36] Dojka, MA; Harris, JK; Pace, NR (2000). "Expanding the known diversity and environmental distribution of an uncultured phylogenetic division of bacteria". *Applied and environmental microbiology* **66** (4): 1617–21. PMC 92031. PMID 10742250.

[37] Tamaki, H.; Tanaka, Y.; Matsuzawa, H.; Muramatsu, M.; Meng, X. -Y.; Hanada, S.; Mori, K.; Kamagata, Y. (2010). "Armatimonas rosea gen. Nov., sp. Nov., a Gram-negative, aerobic, chemoheterotrophic bacterium of a novel bacterial phylum, Armatimonadetes phyl. Nov., formally called the candidate phylum OP10". *International Journal of Systematic and Evolutionary Microbiology*. doi:10.1099/ijs.0.025643-0. PMID 20622056.

[38] Lee, K. C. Y.; Dunfield, P. F.; Morgan, X. C.; Crowe, M. A.; Houghton, K. M.; Vyssotski, M.; Ryan, J. L. J.; Lagutin, K. et al. (2010). "Chthonomonas calidirosea gen. Nov., sp. Nov., an aerobic, pigmented, thermophilic microorganism of a novel bacterial class, Chthonomonadetes classis. Nov., of the newly described phylum Armatimonadetes originally designated candidate division OP10". *International Journal of Systematic and Evolutionary Microbiology*. doi:10.1099/ijs.0.027235-0. PMID 21097641.

[39] Mori, K.; Yamaguchi, K.; Sakiyama, Y.; Urabe, T.; Suzuki, K. -I. (2009). "Caldisericum exile gen. Nov., sp. Nov., an anaerobic, thermophilic, filamentous bacterium of a novel bacterial phylum, Caldiserica phyl. Nov., originally called the candidate phylum OP5, and description of Caldisericaceae fam. Nov., Caldisericales ord. Nov. And Caldisericia classis nov". *International Journal of Systematic and Evolutionary Microbiology* **59** (Pt 11): 2894. doi:10.1099/ijs.0.010033-0. PMID 19628600.

[40] Geissinger, O.; Herlemann, D. P. R.; Morschel, E.; Maier, U. G.; Brune, A. (2009). "The Ultramicrobacterium "Elusimicrobium minutum" gen. Nov., sp. Nov., the First Cultivated Representative of the Termite Group 1 Phylum". *Applied and Environmental Microbiology* **75** (9): 2831. doi:10.1128/AEM.02697-08. PMC 2681718. PMID 19270135.

[41] Cho, J. C.; Vergin, K. L.; Morris, R. M.; Giovannoni, S. J. (2004). "Lentisphaera araneosa gen. Nov., sp. Nov, a transparent exopolymer producing marine bacterium, and the description of a novel bacterial phylum, Lentisphaerae". *Environmental Microbiology* **6** (6): 611. doi:10.1111/j.1462-2920.2004.00614.x. PMID 15142250.

[42] "ARB-Silva: comprehensive ribosomal RNA database" (http://www.arb-silva.de/browser/). The ARB development Team. .

[43] "Hierarchy Browser" (http://rdp.cme.msu.edu/hierarchy/). *Ribosomal database project*. .

[44] Ciccarelli, F. D.; Doerks, T; Von Mering, C; Creevey, CJ; Snel, B; Bork, P (2006). "Toward Automatic Reconstruction of a Highly Resolved Tree of Life". *Science* **311** (5765): 1283–1287. Bibcode 2006Sci...311.1283C. doi:10.1126/science.1123061. PMID 16513982.

[45] Cavalier-Smith T (2006). "Rooting the tree of life by transition analyses" (http://www.biology-direct.com/content/1//19). *Biol. Direct* **1**: 19. doi:10.1186/1745-6150-1-19. PMC 1586193. PMID 16834776. .

[46] Cavalier-Smith T (2006). "Rooting the tree of life by transition analyses" (http://www.biology-direct.com/content/1//19). *Biol. Direct* **1**: 19. doi:10.1186/1745-6150-1-19. PMC 1586193. PMID 16834776. .

Baraminology

Baraminology is a creationist taxonomic system that classifies animals into groups called "created kinds" or "baramins" (pronounced with accent on second syllable) according to the account of creation in the book of Genesis and other parts of the Bible. It claims that kinds cannot interbreed, and have no evolutionary relationship to one another.[1] Baraminology developed as a subfield of the system of belief known as "creation science" in the 1990s among a group of creationists that included Walter ReMine and Kurt Wise.

As a part of creation science, baraminology is considered a pseudoscience by the scientific community,[2] [3] [4] [5] as the evidence for common ancestry of all life has general scientific acceptance. The taxonomic system widely applied in modern biology is cladistics, which classifies species based on evolutionary history and emphasizes objective, quantitative analysis.[6]

Interpretations of Biblical kinds

The Bible mentions kinds in several passages. Genesis 1:24–25 gives an account of the creation of living things:

> 24: And God said: 'Let the earth bring forth the living creature after its kind, cattle, and creeping thing, and beast of the earth after its kind.' And it was so. 25: And God made the beast of the earth after its kind, and the cattle after their kind, and every thing that creepeth upon the ground after its kind; and God saw that it was good.

Genesis 7:13–16 states that there are distinct kinds of cattle. In Deuteronomy 14:11–18 varieties of owl, raven, and hawk are presented as distinct kinds. Leviticus 19:19 is concerned with kinds of cloth, cattle, and seeds. Apart from what is implied by these passages, the Bible does not specify what a kind is.

The Creationist Orchard theory represents the way creationists approach Natural Selection; within the boundaries of the original Baramin, most YECs acknowledge that it plays a role.

Modern versions of the Old Testament are translations of the Biblical Hebrew text. The Hebrew word מִין *min* is used exclusively in a set phrase of the form לְמִין +ל, *min*+possessive pronoun suffix, which is translated as *after their/his/her kind*. Several other words are translated into English with the word *kind*, including the Leviticus 19:19 usage: כִּלְאַיִם *kila'im*. The word *min* is never used in relation to humans, but the Greek word γένος *genos* is used in 2 Maccabees 7:28 "... and so was mankind made likewise". The fact that *kind* is used in this set phrase, among other reasons, has led to the hypothesis that it is not a referential noun in Biblical Hebrew, but derived from לְמִינֵהוּ *l'mineh = of him/herself, of themselves*.[7] [8] [9] The word "baramin", which is a compound of the Hebrew words for created and kind, is unintelligible in Hebrew.

History

One literal creationist interpretation of the Bible is that each kind was brought into direct physical existence by God and that consequently each original animal had no ancestry, common or otherwise. Baraminology emerged from an effort by young earth creationists to make this interpretation scientifically appealing.[10] The idea of a baramin was proposed in 1941 by Frank Marsh, but was criticized for a lack of formal definition.[10] In 1990 Kurt Wise and Walter ReMine introduced baraminology in pursuit of acceptable criteria for membership in a baramin.[10]

ReMine's work specified four groupings: holobaramins, monobaramins, apobaramins, and polybaramins. These are, respectively, all things of one kind; some things of the same kind; groups of kinds; and any mixed grouping of things.[11] These groups correspond to the concepts of holophyly, monophyly, paraphyly, and polyphyly used in cladistics.

Classification methodology

Conditions for membership in a (holo)baramin and methods of classification have changed over time. These include the ability to create viable offspring, and morphological similarity.[12]

Some creationists have suggested that kind refers to species, while others believe it might mean any animal which may be distinguished in some way from another.[13] [14]

Another criterion is "baramin distance" which is based on the similarity of two or more organisms' characters and uses methods borrowed from phenetics.[15]

Some advocates believe that major differences in the appearance and behavior of two organisms indicates lack of common ancestry. Others point to inter-fertility capability as a possible indicator.[16] In all cases, methods found to place humans and other primates into the same baramin have been discarded.[17] [18]

Baraminologist Roger W. Sanders advocates a subjective approach to classification over a measurement-based one:[19]

> The cognita are not based on explicit or implicit comparisons of characters or biometric distance measures but on the gestalt of the plants and the classification response it elicits in humans.

Criticism

Baraminology has been heavily criticized for its lack of rigorous testing and post-study rejection of data not supporting desired findings.[20] Universal common descent, which states that all life shares a common ancestor, is well-established and tested, and is a scientifically-verified fact.[21] However neither cladistics, the field devoted to classifying living things according to the ancestral relationships between them, nor the scientific consensus on transitional fossils are accepted by baraminologists.[22]

Despite voluminous evidence for evolution at and above the species level, baraminologists reject universal common descent and the emergence of new families and higher taxa.[22]

References

[1] Wood, Wise, Sanders, and Doran, A Refined Baramin Concept (http://www.bryancore.org/bsg/opbsg/003.pdf)

[2] "creation science is in fact not science and should not be presented as such in science classes." (Note that baraminology is a type of creation science.) The National Academies (1999). "Science and Creationism: A View from the National Academy of Sciences, Second Edition" (http://www.nap.edu/openbook.php?record_id=6024&page=1). National Academy Press. . Retrieved December 7, 2008.

[3] "the NAS states unequivocally that creationism has no place in any science curriculum at any level." http://www.nationalacademies.org/evolution/

[4] Statements from Scientific and Scholarly Organizations. (http://www.ncseweb.org/resources/articles/8408_statements_from_scientific_and_12_19_2002.asp) National Center for Science Education. Retrieved on April 1, 2008.

[5] Williams, J. D. (2007). "Creationist Teaching in School Science: A UK Perspective". *Evolution: Education and Outreach* 1 (1): 87–88. doi:10.1007/s12052-007-0006-7.

[6] (http://www.nhc.ed.ac.uk/index.php?page=236.273.444)

[7] entry for מין min Clines , David J. A. (2001). *The Dictionary of Classical Hebrew*. 5. Sheffield Academic Press. p. 262. ISBN 1-84127-217-5.

[8] page 262 in "Studies in the Bible" by Chaim Rabin = Rabin, Chaim (1961). "Etymological Miscellanea". *Scripta Hierosolymitana: Publications of the Hebrew University, Jerusalem* (Jerusalem: Magnes Press) 8: 384–400.

[9] Mark D. Futato, #מין min in Willem A. VanGemeren, ed. (1997). *New International Dictionary of Old Testament Theology & Exegesis*. 2. Grand Rapids, Michigan: Zondervan Publishing House. pp. 934–935. ISBN 0-310-20217-5.

[10] Wood TC et al. (2003). "A Refined Baramin Concept" (http://www.creationbiology.org/content.aspx?page_id=22&club_id=201240&module_id=36952). *Occasional Papers of the Baraminology Study Group* 3: 1–14. .

[11] Frair, Wayne (2000). "Baraminology—Classification of Created Organisms" (http://web.archive.org/web/20030618153040/http://www.creationresearch.org/crsq/articles/37/37_2/baraminology.htm). *Creation Research Society Quarterly Journal* 37 (2): 82–91. Archived from the original (http://www.creationresearch.org/crsq/articles/37/37_2/baraminology.htm) on 2003-06-18. .

[12] *Fundamental Biology* (1941), *Evolution, Creation, and Science* (c. 1944), both by Frank Lewis Marsh

[13] Payne, J. Barton (1958). "The Concept of "Kinds" In Scripture" (http://www.asa3.org/ASA/PSCF/1958/JASA6-58Payne.html). *Journal of the American Science Affiliation* **10** (2 (December 1958)): 17–20. . Retrieved 2007-11-26. [Note this version appears to have been OCR-scanned without proofreading]

[14] Cracraft, Joel. "Systematics, Comparative Biology, and the Case Against Creationism". Godfrey, Laurie R., ed. *Scientists Confront Creationism* (http://books.google.com/books?id=bjYPs9siZzgC). New York: W.W. Norton & Company: 1984.

[15] Wood, Todd Charles (2006). "The Current Status of Baraminology" (http://www.creationresearch.org/crsq/articles/43/43_3/ baraminology.htm). *Creation Research Science Quarterly Journal* **43** (3): 149–158. .

[16] The Revised and Expanded Answers Book, Edited by Don Batten, Ph.D, copyright 1990, Thirtieth printing, April 2004, ISBN 0-89051-161-6, Chapters 7

[17] "About Us: Taxonomic Concepts and Methods" (http://www.bryancore.org/bsg/aboutconcepts.html). Baraminology Study Group. . Retrieved December 7, 2008.

[18] Robinson and Cavanaugh, A Quantitative Approach to Baraminology With Examples from the Catarrhine Primates (http://www. creationresearch.org/crsq/abstracts/sum34_4.html). ...*We have found that baraminic distances based on hemoglobin amino acid sequences, 12S-rRNA sequences, and chromosomal data were largely ineffective for identifying the Human holobaramin. Baraminic distances based on ecological and morphological characters, however, were quite reliable for distinguishing humans from nonhuman primates.* See also A Review of Friar, W. (2000): Baraminology – Classification of Created Organisms. (http://www.noanswersingenesis.org.au/ baraminology_ta.htm)

[19] Roger W. Sanders. "A Quick Method for Developing a Cognitum System Exemplified Using Flowering Plants" (http://documents. clubexpress.com/documents.ashx?key=op4ksBhACOsM+AWCDrf5aITkqE8Om8qA) [12.2MB PDF]. Occas. Papers of the BSG No. 16, pp. 1-63.

[20] A Review of Friar, W. (2000): Baraminology – Classification of Created Organisms. (http://www.noanswersingenesis.org.au/ baraminology_ta.htm) See also the last two sentences of the abstract of Robinson and Cavanaugh, A Quantitative Approach to Baraminology With Examples from the Catarrhine Primates (http://www.creationresearch.org/crsq/abstracts/sum34_4.html)

[21] Theobald, Douglas (2007). "29+ Evidences for Macroevolution" (http://www.talkorigins.org/faqs/comdesc/). TalkOrigins. .

[22] About the BSG: Taxonomic Concepts and Methods (http://www.bryancore.org/bsg/aboutconcepts.html). Phrases to note are: *"The mere assumption that the transformation had to occur because cladistic analysis places it at a hypothetical ancestral node does not constitute empirical evidence"* and *"A good example is Archaeopteryx, which likely represents its own unique baramin, distinct from both dinosaurs and modern birds"*

Bayer Code

Bayer code is a system of identifying crop plants and their pests (including weeds and diseases) by a unique code. They are a core component of a database of names, both scientific and vernacular. Plants are identified by a five letter code, other organisms by a six letter one. In many cases the codes are mnemonic abbreviations of the scientific name of the organism derived from the first three letters of the genus and the first two or three letters of the species. For example, corn (Zea mays) would be ZEAMA and potato late blight (Phytophthora infestans) PHYTIN. By providing a unique code for each organism the system provides a shorthand method of recording species and avoids many of problems caused by revisions to scientific names and taxonomy which often result in different synonyms being in use for the same species.

Although originally started by the Bayer Corporation, the official list of codes is now maintained by the European and Mediterranean Plant Protection Organization (EPPO). They are now therefore more correctly known as EPPO codes.

External links

- List of Bayer Codes [1]
- Bayer code lookup [2]
- NCSU Bayer Code lookup [3]

References

[1] http://www.eppo.org/PUBLICATIONS/eppt/bayer_codes.htm

[2] http://www.fito-info.bf.uni-lj.si/cirsium/FITOINFO/SifrantOrg_en.htm

[3] http://cipm.ncsu.edu/names/index.cfm

Biodiversity informatics

Biodiversity Informatics is the application of informatics techniques to biodiversity information for improved management, presentation, discovery, exploration and analysis. It typically builds on a foundation of taxonomic, biogeographic, or ecological information stored in digital form, which, with the application of modern computer techniques, can yield new ways to view and analyse existing information, as well as predictive models for information that does not yet exist (see niche modelling). Biodiversity informatics is a relatively young discipline (the term was coined in or around 1992) but has hundreds of practitioners worldwide, including the numerous individuals involved with the design and construction of taxonomic databases. The term "Biodiversity Informatics" is generally used in the broad sense to apply to computerized handling of any biodiversity information; the somewhat broader term "bioinformatics" is often used synonymously with the computerized handling of data in the specialized area of molecular biology.

Overview

Biodiversity informatics has been defined as "the creation, integration, analysis, and understanding of information regarding biological diversity"[1] , and "[the] field that brings information science and technologies to bear on the data and information generated by the study of organisms, their genes, and their interactions"[2] . Broadly speaking, it seeks to draw upon and integrate information held in various taxonomic databases and other digital sources to answer biodiversity questions at scales ranging from global to local. Such questions might range from "How many described species exist in the world?" (answer: still not known for certain, as all the relevant data are not currently compiled in any coherent manner) to "Predict the effects of a global temperature rise of X degrees C. on the geographic range of species Y", a question which involves not only biodiversity in the basic sense but related domains of ecology, geographic distributions of environmental parameters, global climate models, and more. In addition to handling formally named taxa, biodiversity informatics may also have to cope with managing information from unnamed taxa such as that produced by environmental sampling and sequencing of mixed-field samples. The term biodiversity informatics is also used to cover the computational problems specific to the names of biological entities, such as the development of algorithms to cope with variant representations of identifiers such as species names and authorities, and the multiple classification schemes within which these entities may reside according to the preferences of different workers in the field, as well as the syntax and semantics by which the content in taxonomic databases can be made machine queryable and interoperable for biodiversity informatics purposes.

History of the discipline of Biodiversity Informatics

Biodiversity Informatics can be considered to have commenced with the construction of the first computerized taxonomic databases in the early 1970s, and progressed through subsequent developing of distributed search tools towards the late 1990s including the Species Analyst from Kansas University, the North American Biodiversity Information Network NABIN, CONABIO in Mexico, and others[3] , the establishment of the Global Biodiversity Information Facility in 2001, and the parallel development of a variety of niche modelling and other tools to operate on digitized biodiversity data from the mid 1980s onwards (e.g. see [4]). In September 2000, the U.S. journal Science devoted a special issue to "Bioinformatics for Biodiversity"[5] , the journal "Biodiversity Informatics" commenced publication in 2004, and several international conferences through the 2000s have brought together Biodiversity Informatics practitioners, most recently the London e-Biosphere [6] conference in June 2009. A recent supplement to the journal BMC Bioinformatics (Volume 10 Suppl 14[7]) published in November 2009 also deals with Biodiversity Informatics.

History of the term "Biodiversity Informatics"

According to correspondence reproduced by Walter Berendsohn[8] , the term "Biodiversity Informatics" was coined by John Whiting in 1992 to cover the activities of an entity known as the Canadian Biodiversity Informatics Consortium, a group involved with fusing basic biodiversity information with environmental economics and geospatial information in the form of GPS and GIS. Subsequently it appears to have lost any obligate connection with the GPS/GIS world and be associated with the computerized management of any aspects of biodiversity information (e.g. see [9]).

Current Biodiversity Informatics issues

Global list of all species

One major issue for biodiversity informatics at a global scale is the present absence of a machine queryable (or even non-digital) master list of currently recognised species of the world, although this is an aim of the Catalogue of Life project which has been quoted as aiming to achieve this goal (for extant species only) by 2012; in its 2009 Annual Checklist edition a total of 1.16 million valid species names and 0.76 million synonyms were included, out of an estimated target 1.8 million extant described species[10] . A similar effort for fossil taxa, the Paleobiology Database[11] documents some 100,000+ names for fossil species, out of an unknown total number.

Problems with genus and species scientific names as unique and persistent identifiers

Application of the Linnaean system of binomial nomenclature for species, and uninomials for genera and higher ranks, has led to many advantages but also problems with homonyms (the same name being used for multiple taxa, either inadvertently or legitimately across multiple kingdoms), synonyms (multiple names for the same taxon), as well as variant representations of the same name due to orthographic differences, minor spelling errors, variation in the manner of citation of author names and dates, and more. In addition, names can change through time on account of changing taxonomic opinions (for example, the correct generic placement of a species, or the elevation of a subspecies to species rank or vice versa), and also the circumscription of a taxon can change according to different authors' taxonomic concepts. One proposed solution to this problem is the usage of Life Science Identifiers (LSIDs) for machine-machine communication purposes, although there are both proponents and opponents of this approach.

Achieving a consensus classification of organisms

Organisms can be classified in a multitude of ways (see main page Biological classification), which can create design problems for Biodiversity Informatics systems aimed at incorporating either a single or multiple classification to suit the needs of users, or to guide them towards a single "preferred" system. Whether a single consensus classification system can ever be achieved is probably an open question, however in an attempt to provide at least a degree of consensus, the Catalogue of Life project has recently released a document[12] that attempts to list some of the issues in this area, and may lead to a more coherent classification that can be promoted via that project's future products at least.

Mobilizing primary biodiversity information

"Primary" biodiversity information can be considered the basic data on the occurrence and diversity of species (or indeed, any recognizable taxa), commonly in association with information regarding their distribution in either space, time, or both. Such information may be in the form of retained specimens and associated information, for example as assembled in the natural history collections of museums and herbaria, or as observational records, for example either from formal faunal or floristic surveys undertaken by professional biologists and students, or as amateur and other planned or unplanned observations including those increasingly coming under the scope of citizen science. Providing online, coherent digital access to this vast collection of disparate primary data is a core Biodiversity Informatics function that is at the heart of regional and global biodiversity data networks, examples of the latter including OBIS and GBIF.

As a secondary source of biodiversity data, relevant scientific literature can be parsed either by humans or (potentially) by specialized information retrieval algorithms to extract the relevant primary biodiversity information that is reported therein, sometimes in aggregated / summary form but frequently as primary observations in narrative or tabular form. Elements of such activity (such as extracting key taxonomic identifiers, keywording / index terms, etc.) have been practiced for many years at a higher level by selected academic databases and search engines. However, for the maximum Biodiversity Informatics value, the actual primary occurrence data should ideally be retrieved and then made available in a standardized form or forms; for example both the Plazi and INOTAXA [13] projects are transforming taxonomic literature into XML formats that can then be read by client applications, the former using TaxonX-XML [14] and the latter using the taXMLit format. The Biodiversity Heritage Library is also making significant progress in its aim to digitize substantial portions of the out-of-copyright taxonomic literature, which is then subjected to OCR (optical character recognition) so as to be amenable to further processing using Biodiversity Informatics tools.

Biodiversity Informatics standards and protocols

In common with other data-related disciplines, Biodiversity Informatics benefits from the adoption of appropriate standards and protocols in order to support machine-machine transmission and interoperability of information within its particular domain. Examples of relevant standards include the Darwin Core XML schema for specimen- and observation-based biodiversity data developed from 1998 onwards, plus extensions of the same, Taxonomic Concept Transfer Schema [15], plus standards for Structured Descriptive Data [16] and Access to Biological Collection Data [17] (ABCD); while data retrieval and transfer protocols include DiGIR [18] (now mostly superseded) and TAPIR [19] (TDWG Access Protocol for Information Retrieval). Many of these standards and protocols are currently maintained, and their development overseen, by the Taxonomic Databases Working Group (TDWG).

Current Biodiversity Informatics activities

At the recent (2009), large scale e-Biosphere [6] conference in the U.K., contributions (e.g. as posters) were grouped into the following themes, which is indicative of a broad range of current Biodiversity Informatics activities and how they might be categorized:

- Application: Conservation / Agriculture / Fisheries / Industry / Forestry
- Application: Invasive Alien Species
- Application: Systematic and Evolutionary Biology
- Application: Taxonomy and Identification Systems
- New Tools, Services and Standards for Data Management and Access

  - New Modeling Tools
  - New Tools for Data Integration
  - New Approaches to Biodiversity Infrastructure
  - New Approaches to Species Identification
  - New Approaches to Mapping Biodiversity
- National and Regional Biodiversity Databases and Networks

A post-conference workshop of key persons with current significant Biodiversity Informatics roles also resulted in a Workshop Resolution [20] that stressed, among other aspects, the need to create durable, global registries for the resources that are basic to biodiversity informatics (e.g., repositories, collections); complete the construction of a solid taxonomic infrastructure; and create ontologies for biodiversity data.

Biodiversity Informatics projects of the world

Among current significant global scale biodiversity informatics projects can be included the following:

- The Global Biodiversity Information Facility (GBIF), and the Ocean Biogeographic Information System (OBIS) (for marine species)
- The Species 2000, ITIS (Integrated Taxonomic Information System), and Catalogue of Life projects
- EOL, The Encyclopedia of Life project
- The Consortium for the Barcode of Life project
- The uBio [21] Universal Biological Indexer and Organizer, from the Woods Hole Marine Biological Laboratory
- The Index to Organism Names [22] (ION) from Thomson Reuters, providing access to scientific names of taxa from numerous journals as indexed in the Zoological Record
- ZooBank, the registry for nomenclatural acts and relevant systematic literature in zoology
- The Index Nominum Genericorum [23], compilation of generic names published for organisms covered by the International Code of Botanical Nomenclature, maintained at the Smithsonian Institution in the U.S.A.
- The International Plant Names Index
- MycoBank, documenting new names and combinations for fungi
- The List of Prokaryotic names with Standing in Nomenclature [24] (LPSN) - Official register of valid names for bacteria and archaea, as governed by the International Code of Nomenclature of Bacteria
- The Biodiversity Heritage Library project - digitising biodiversity literature
- Wikispecies, open source (community-editable) compilation of taxonomic information, companion project to Wikipedia
- TaxonConcept.org [25], a Linked_Data project that connects disparate species databases
- Instituto de Ciencias Naturales [26]. Universidad Nacional de Colombia. Virtual Collections and Biodiversity Informatics Unit [27]

Notable regional and national scale syntheses include the following:

- Fauna Europaea

- Atlas of Living Australia [28]
- A Pan-European Species-directories Infrastructure (PESI) [29]
- LifeWatch is proposed by ESFRI as a pan-European research (e-)infrastructure to support Biodiversity research and policy-making.

A listing of over 600 current biodiversity informatics related activities can be found at the TDWG "Biodiversity Information Projects of the World" database [30].

References

[1] "Website of the Journal 'Biodiversity Informatics'" (https://journals.ku.edu/index.php/jbi). . Retrieved 2009-08-06.

[2] "Website of the 2009 "e-Biosphere" Conference on Biodiversity Informatics, London, June 2009" (http://www.e-biosphere09.org/). . Retrieved 2009-08-06.

[3] Krishtalka L & Humphrey PS (2000). "Can Natural History Museums Capture the Future?" (http://www.bioone.org/doi/pdf/10.1641/ 0006-3568(2000)050[0611:CNHMCT]2.0.CO;2). *BioScience* **50**: 611–617. doi:10.1641/0006-3568(2000)050[0611:CNHMCT]2.0.CO;2. .

[4] Peterson AT & Vieglais D (2001). "Predicting Species Invasions Using Ecological Niche Modeling: New Approaches from Bioinformatics Attack a Pressing Problem" (http://www.cria.org.br/eventos/mfmpe/19_20jun2002_docs/BioScience 2001.pdf). *BioScience* **51**: 363–371. doi:10.1641/0006-3568(2001)051[0363:PSIUEN]2.0.CO;2. .

[5] "Bioinformatics for Biodiversity?" (http://www.sciencemag.org/content/vol289/issue5488/index.dtl). *Science* **289**: 2229–2440. 2000. .

[6] http://www.e-biosphere09.org/

[7] "Biodiversity Informatics" (http://www.biomedcentral.com/1471-2105/10?issue=S14). *BMC Bioinformatics* **10 Suppl 14**. 2009. .

[8] ""Biodiversity Informatics", The Term" (http://www.bgbm.org/BioDivInf/TheTerm.htm). . Retrieved 2009-08-06.

[9] Bisby FA. et al. (2000). "The Quiet Revolution: Biodiversity Informatics and the Internet" (http://www.sciencemag.org/cgi/content/ abstract/289/5488/2309). *Science* **289** (5488): 2309–2312. doi:10.1126/science.289.5488.2309. PMID 11009408. .

[10] "A Leap for All Life: World's Leading Scientists Announce Creation of "Encyclopedia of Life" (EOL Press Release, May 2007)" (http:// www.eol.org/content/page/press_2007_5_9). . Retrieved 2009-08-06.

[11] "the Paleobiology Database" (http://paleodb.org/). . Retrieved 2009-08-06.

[12] "Towards a management hierarchy (classification) for the Catalogue of Life. Draft Discussion Document by Dr. Dennis P. Gordon, May 2009" (http://www.catalogueoflife.org/info_hierarchy.php). . Retrieved 2009-08-06.

[13] http://www.inotaxa.org/

[14] http://sourceforge.net/projects/taxonx/

[15] http://www.tdwg.org/standards/117/

[16] http://www.tdwg.org/standards/116/

[17] http://www.tdwg.org/standards/115/

[18] http://digir.sourceforge.net/

[19] http://www.tdwg.org/standards/449/

[20] http://www.e-biosphere09.org/assets/files/workshop/Resolution.pdf

[21] http://www.ubio.org/

[22] http://www.organismnames.com/

[23] http://botany.si.edu/ing/

[24] http://www.bacterio.cict.fr/

[25] http://www.taxonconcept.org

[26] http://www.icn.unal.edu.co

[27] http://www.biovirtual.unal.edu.co

[28] http://www.ala.org.au/

[29] http://www.eu-nomen.eu

[30] http://www.tdwg.org/biodiv-projects/

Further reading

- OECD Megascience Forum Working Group on Biological Informatics (1999). *Final Report of the OECD Megascience Forum Working Group on Biological Informatics, January 1999* (http://www.gbif.org/ GBIF_org/facility/BIrepfin). pp. 1–74.
- Canhos, V.P., Souza, S., Giovanni, R. & Canhos, D.A.L. (2004). "Global biodiversity informatics: setting the scene for a "new world" of ecological modeling" (https://journals.ku.edu/index.php/jbi/article/viewFile/3/ 1). *Biodiversity Informatics* **1**: 1–13.
- Soberón, J. & Peterson, A.T. (2004). "Biodiversity informatics: managing and applying primary biodiversity data" (http://journals.royalsociety.org/content/p8hcuwema8uk692g/). *Phil. Trans. R. Soc. Lond.* **B359**: 689–698.
- Chapman, A.D. (2005). *Uses of Primary Species-Occurrence Data* (http://www2.gbif.org/UsesPrimaryData. pdf). Copenhagen: Global Biodiversity Information Facility. pp. 1–106.
- Johnson, N.F. (2007). "Biodiversity informatics" (http://arjournals.annualreviews.org/doi/abs/10.1146/ annurev.ento.52.110405.091259). *Annual Review of Entomology* **52**: 421–438. doi:10.1146/annurev.ento.52.110405.091259. PMID 16956323.
- Sarkar, I.N. (2007). "Biodiversity informatics: organizing and linking information across the spectrum of life" (http://bib.oxfordjournals.org/cgi/content/abstract/8/5/347). *Briefings in Bioinformatics* **8** (5): 347–357. doi:10.1093/bib/bbm037. PMID 17704120.
- Guralnick, R.P.; Hill, A (2009). "Biodiversity Informatics: Automated Approaches for Documenting Global Biodiversity Patterns and Processes" (http://bioinformatics.oxfordjournals.org/cgi/content/full/25/4/421). *Bioinformatics* **25** (4): 421–428.. doi:10.1093/bioinformatics/btn659. PMID 19129210.

External links

- Biodiversity Informatics (http://journals.ku.edu/index.php/jbi) (journal)
- Phyloinformatics (http://systbio.org/?q=node/150) (journal; closed business in 2006)
- ZooKeys (http://www.pensoftonline.net/zookeys) (journal)
- Website of the 2009 e-Biosphere International Conference on Biodiversity Informatics (http://www. e-biosphere09.org/)
- Biodiversity Informatics at the University of Reading (http://www.henley.reading.ac.uk/IRC/ Postgraduatetaught/irc-pgt-bioi.asp)
- (http://cbcreatures.webs.com/)(Interesting information about the snakes)

Biovar

A **biovar** is a variant prokaryotic strain that differs physiologically and/or biochemically from other strains in a particular species. **Morphovars** (or **morphotypes**) are those strains that differ morphologically. **Serovars** (or **serotypes**) are those strains that have antigenic properties that differ from other strains.

Body plan

A **body plan** is the blueprint for the way the body of an organism is laid out. An organism's symmetry,[1] its number of body segments and number of limbs are all aspects of its body plan. One of the key issues of developmental biology is the evolution of body plans as different as those of a starfish, a fern, or a mammal, from a common biological heritage, and in particular how radical changes in body plans have occurred over geological time. The body plan is a key feature of an organism's morphology, and since the discovery of DNA developmental biologists have been able to learn a lot about how genes control the development of structural features through a cascade of processes in which key genes produce morphogens, chemicals that diffuse through the body to produce a gradient that acts as a position indicator for cells, turning on other genes, some of which in turn produce other morphogens. A key discovery was the existence of groups of homeobox genes which are responsible for laying down the basic body plan in organisms. The homeobox genes are remarkably conserved between species as diverse as the fruitfly and man, the basic segmented pattern of the worm or fruitfly being the origin of the segmented spine in man. The field of evolutionary developmental biology, which studies the genetics of morphology in detail is now a rapidly expanding one [2], with many of the developmental genetic cascades, particularly in the fruitfly drosophila, now catalogued in considerable detail.[3]

Body plan is the basis for phylum, and there are 35 different basic animal body plans, corresponding to different phyla.

Origin

The evolution of body plans became inevitable with the emergence of differentiated multicellular life in the Ediacaran Era, over 600 million years ago. The most basic and successful structure, for free-moving organisms, is the "pipe" or alimentary canal. This is common even to organisms as diverse as humans and earthworms. It is essentially a passage having a mouth at one end, and a cloaca or anus at the other. The simple process of nutrient capture, digestion, and waste disposal is fundamental to the body plan of advanced, free-moving animals. Vertebra, limbs, even brains are supplementary to the pipe. Natural selection has spun off an enormous range of variations on this basic theme, but the pipe model itself remains. The basic symmetry and organization of this body plan apparently gave an ancient organism an enormous advantage at survival and reproduction, and it has been preserved in most animals ever since.

The Cambrian explosion refers to the massive increase in different body plans that took place around 530 million years ago. Fossils from this era show all sorts of odd shapes, many quite unlike anything found today. At that time it was possible for organisms to survive and make a living even though they were unrefined and unlikely, because predation had yet to evolve, along with arms races that would optimise and streamline them to occupy a particular ecological niche.

Bauplan

Bauplan (German for building plan, blueprint; plural: baupläne or bauplaene) is a closely related term in biology referring to the common new and original (homologous) properties of the members of a systematic group (taxon). It is not necessary that a bauplan precisely describes any one particular species of that group.

The concept of bauplan is employed in the studies of morphology, taxonomy, comparative physiology, evolutionary physiology, and, most notably, phylogenetics and evolution. Before the advent of genetic sequencing, the analysis of the bauplan of fossils was the primary method to determine hypothetical relationships and lineages of species, both living and extinct. The idea is that species that are closely related share more common properties, hence a more detailed bauplan. Small differences of bauplan are indicative of species belonging to a parent, child or sibling taxon.

Genetic basis

Similarities and differences in adult shape and form, as well as the developmental pattern of embryos, provide the framework for modern taxonomic classification. These comparisons are the basis of phylogenetic systematics. Embryonic development is relatively consistent among animals with similar body plans, although similar larval forms may give rise to very different adults in some groups. The timing, pattern, and scale of developmental events determine the shape of an organism, and closely related groups are more likely to share structural and developmental similarities than those that are more distantly related. Homologous structures and developmental stages—those that are similar among related groups because they are inherited from a common ancestor—are the basis of modern biological classification.

Examples

The current range of body plans is far from exhausting the possible patterns for life: the Ediacaran biota appears to contain numerous species and taxa with body plans quite different from any found in currently living organisms.

An early tetrapod: the *ichthyostega*

The most commonly seen body plan amongst vertebrates is that of the **tetrapod**, which include all mammals, birds, amphibians and reptiles. Some animal groups, such as the cetaceans, bats and most birds have been modified (e.g. front limbs become wings or flippers) but nevertheless, they are still tetrapods.

The invertebrates employ a much more diverse array of body plans, such as seen in insects (six legs, three body parts and an exoskeleton), cephalopods (no skeleton, hydrostatically stiffened tentacles, primary propulsion by squeezing water out of a mantle cavity), echinoderms (fivefold radial symmetry, external skeleton, movement by hydrostatically operated tube feet) and various phyla of "worms" (tube-shaped, movement by expanding and contracting parts of the body).

The most varied collection of body forms known is found in the Burgess Shale, where fossils from a Cambrian sea show a tremendous variety of body forms that came to rise (only to later fall extinct) during the Cambrian explosion.

Fictional

One common theme in science fiction is the appearance of extraterrestrial beings, descriptions of which have ranged from being simple variants on human anatomy to beings with body plans wildly different from any found on Earth. The field of exobiology attempts to bring these and similar speculations into the realm of serious scientific investigation.

References

[1] "Up and down...or around and around? Body Symmetry in Animals" (http://science.kennesaw.edu/biophys/biodiversity/animalia/ symmetry.html) (Web). *The Diversity of Living Organisms: Themes of Adaptation and Evolution*. Kennesaw State University. . Retrieved 2007-12-01.

[2] http://www.sciam.com/article.cfm?articleID=0005D708-2F7C-123B-AF7C83414B7F0000

[3] Arthur, Wallace. (1997). *Animal Body Plans*. Cambridge England: Cambridge University Press. ISBN 0-521-77928-6.

External links

• Developmental Biology 8e Online: Patterning of the Mesoderm by Activin (http://8e.devbio.com/article. php?id=117)

Video

• The Science of Evolution: Sean B. Carroll explains the genetics of the fruitfly body plan. (http://video.on. nytimes.com/?fr_story=3ba8ecaed1cf130c1d0ea4baa3876356bea3bb58)

Branching identification key

A **branching identification key** is a presentation form of a single-access key where the structure of the decision tree is displayed graphically as a branching structure, involving lines between items.[1] Depending on the number of branches at a single point, a branching key may be dichotomous or polytomous.

In a diagnostic key, the branching structure of the key should not be mistaken for a phylogenetic or cladistic branching pattern.

All single-access keys form a decision tree (or graph if reticulation exists), and thus all such keys have a branching structure. "Branching key" may therefore occasionally be used as a synonym for single-access key.

Examples of branching presentations

• http://www.warwickshire-sss.org.uk/subject/science/Biological_keys_v2.htm
• Figure 19.5 in [1]
• Page 8 in [2].

References

[1] Winston, J. 1999. Describing Species. Columbia University Press.

[2] The Natural History Museum 2000. Sorting creepy-crawlies. http://www.nhm.ac.uk/education/activities/school-activities/ discovery-guides/assets/sorting.pdf

Calceochiton

Calceochiton is an extinct genus of polyplacophoran mollusc. Calceochiton became extinct during the Ordovician period.[1]

References

[1] van Belle, R. A. (1981). *Catalogue of Fossil Chitons*. ISBN 90 6279 018 6.

Callistochiton

Callistochiton is an extinct genus of polyplacophoran mollusc. Callistochiton became extinct during the Pliocene period.[1]

References

[1] van Belle, R. A. (1981). *Catalogue of Fossil Chitons*. ISBN 90 6279 018 6.

Catalogue of Life

The Species 2000 & ITIS Catalogue of Life

Cover of DVD version of database

URL	[1]
Commercial?	no
Type of site	Taxonomic catalogue
Registration	not required
Available language(s)	English
Launched	June 2001
Alexa rank	713,570 [2]
Current status	active

The **Catalogue of Life**, started in June 2001 by Species 2000 and Integrated Taxonomic Information System (ITIS), is planned to become a comprehensive catalogue of all known species of organisms on Earth by the year 2011. 66 taxonomic databases with contributions from more than 3,000 specialists from around the world are compiled into it and are also reviewed. [3] The Catalogue contains the Annual Checklist [4] (published yearly, ninth edition contains 1,160,711 species[5]) + Dynamic Checklist [6] (less extensive, updated more often, contains additional regional species checklists).

References

[1] http://www.catalogueoflife.org
[2] "Catalogueoflife.org SiteInfo" (http://www.alexa.com/data/details/traffic_details/catalogueoflife.org). Alexa Internet, Inc. 2010. . Retrieved 2010-09-15.
[3] About the Catalogue of Life (http://www.catalogueoflife.org/info_about_col.php), retrieved online: 2009-05-16
[4] http://www.catalogueoflife.org/annual-checklist/2009/
[5] About the Catalogue of Life (http://www.catalogueoflife.org/info_about_col.php), retrieved online: 2009-05-16
[6] http://www.catalogueoflife.org/dynamic-checklist/search.php

Further reading

- Bisby FA, Roskov YR, Orrell TM, Nicolson D, Paglinawan LE, Bailly N, Kirk PM, Bourgoin T, Baillargeon G., eds (2009). Species 2000 & ITIS Catalogue of Life: 2009 Annual Checklist. Digital resource at (http://www.catalogueoflife.org/annual-checklist/2009). Species 2000: Reading, UK.

External links

- Catalogue of Life (http://www.catalogueoflife.org/)

Chelodidae

Chelodidae is an extinct family of polyplacophoran mollusc.[1]

References

[1] van Belle, R. A. (1981). *Catalogue of Fossil Chitons*. ISBN 90 6279 018 6.

Chelodina (chiton)

Chelodina is an extinct suborder of polyplacophoran mollusc.[1]

References

[1] van Belle, R. A. (1981). *Catalogue of Fossil Chitons*. ISBN 90 6279 018 6.

Chitonina

Chitonina is an extinct suborder of polyplacophoran mollusc.[1]

References

[1] van Belle, R. A. (1981). *Catalogue of Fossil Chitons*. ISBN 90 6279 018 6.

Chresonym

In biodiversity informatics, a **chresonym** refers to the cited use of a taxon name, usually a species name, within a publication. The term was coined to distinguish two uses of the term "synonym" as used within the context of taxonomy. The term "chresonym" is derived from the Greek "chresis" and refers to published usage of a name.

The related term "synonym" is used for different names that refer to the same object or concept. As noted by Hobart and Rozella Smith,[1] the term is applied consistently within the various codes of nomenclature that govern the use and creation of organism names. As also noted, "systematists use the term (synonymy) in another sense as well, namely in reference to all occurrences of any name or set of names (usually synonyms) in the literature, or in given segments thereof." In this case, the synonymy may include multiple versions of the same synonym; one for each place the author found it rather than a distinct, summarized list of different synonyms. This not only creates a conceptual problem concerning the term, but can introduce additional ambiguity in how species are referenced. The term "chresonym" was createdd to refer to this second sense of the term "synonym."[2]

A name that correctly refers to a "taxon" is further termed an **orthohresonym** while one that is applied incorrectly for a given taxon may be termed a **heterochresonym**.[3] [4]

Example (orthochresonymy)

Species names consist of a genus part and a species part to create a binomial name. Species names often also include a reference to the original publication of the name by including the author and sometimes the year of publication of the name. As an example, the sperm whale, *Physeter catodon*, was first described by Linnaeus in the 10th edition Systema Naturae published in 1758. Thus, the name may also be referenced as *Physeter catodon* Linnaeus 1758. That

Physeter catodon Linnaeus

[*Physeter*] *Catodon* Linnaeus, 1758, Syst. Nat., ed. 10, 1: 76.—Thomas, 1911, Proc. Zool. Soc. London, 1911: 157 [type history].
Physeter catodon, Harmer, 1928, Proc. Linnaean Soc. London, 140: 62, 88 [Atlantic; Pacific: Ecuador, Chile; Antarctic; history of whaling].— Carcelles, 1932, Physis, 11: 61, 79, fig. 5 (processing of cadaver) [S. Atlantic: Falklands; South Georgia; South Orkneys].—Raven and Gregory, 1933, American Mus. Novit., 677: 1, fig. 1 (animal), fig. 3 (skull), fig. 4 (head in cross section), fig. 5 (nasal region dissection), fig. 6 (head section), fig. 7 (rostrum in longitudinal section) [nasal passages, spermaceti organ].—Townsend, 1935, Zoologica, 19: 7, pl. 2 (distribution map based on log book records from 1761–1920) [seasonal distribution in all seas; recorded from all latitudes of South

Page 116 in Hershkovitz (1969) showing the chresonym *Physeter catodon* Harmer 1928

name was also used by Harmer in 1928 to refer to the species in the Proceedings of the Linnaean Society of London and of course, it has appeared in numerous other publications since then. Taxonomic catalogues such as The Catalog of Living Whales by Hershkovitz[5] , may reference this usage with a Genus+species+authorship convention that may appear to indicate a new species (a homonym) when in fact it is referencing a particular usage of a species name (a chresonym). Hershkovitz, for examples refers to *Physeter catodon* Harmer 1928, which can cause confusion as this name+author combination really refers to the same name that Linnaeus first published in 1758.

References

[1] Smith, Hobart M & Rozella B Smith (1972). "Chresonymy ex Synonymy". *Systematic Zoology* **21**: 445. doi:10.2307/2412440. ISSN 0039-7989.

[2] Smith, H.M. & Smith, R.B. (1973) Chresonymy ex synonymy. Systematic Zoology 21:445.

[3] Dubois, A. (2000). Synonymies and related lists in zoology: general proposals, with examples in herpetology. *Dumerilia*. 4(2): 33–98.

[4] Dubois A (2010) Retroactive changes should be introduced in the Code only with great care: problems related to the spellings of nomina. (http://www.mapress.com/zootaxa/2010/f/zt02426p042.pdf) Zootaxa 2426:1–42

[5] Hershkovitz, Philip (1966). "Catalog of Living Whales" (http://www.biodiversitylibrary.org/item/33227). *Bulletin of the United States National Museum* **246**: 1–259. ISSN 0096-2961. .

Circumscription (taxonomy)

In taxonomy, **circumscription** is the definition of the limits of a taxonomic group of organisms. One goal of taxonomy is to achieve a stable circumscription for every taxonomic group. Achieving stability can be simple or difficult.

An example of a taxonomic group with unstable circumscription is Anacardiaceae, a family of flowering plants. Some experts favor a circumscription[1] in which this family includes the subfamilies Cassuvieae, Spodiaceae, and Spondiaceae (which other experts segregate into other families, namely Cassuviaceae, Spodiadaceae, and Spondiadaceae), and excludes the segregate families Blepharocaryaceae, Julianaceae, Pistaciaceae, and Podoaceae.

References

[1] Anacardiaceae (http://delta-intkey.com/angio/www/anacardi.htm) in L. Watson and M.J. Dallwitz (1992 onwards). The families of flowering plants. (http://delta-intkey.com/angio/)

Cline (biology)

In biology, an **ecocline** or simply **cline** (Greek: κλίνω = to possess or exhibit gradient, to lean) describes an ecotone in which a series of biocommunities display continuous gradient.[1] The term was coined by the English evolutionary biologist Julian Huxley in 1938.

Introduction

More technically, clines consist of ecotypes or forms of species that exhibit gradual phenotypic and/or genetic differences over a geographical area, typically as a result of environmental heterogeneity. Genetically, clines result from the change of allele frequencies within the gene pool of the group of taxa in question.[2] [3] [4] Clines may manifest in time and/or space.[5]

Gradient analysis

In ecology, spatial clines have led to gradient analysis where the abundance and distribution of organisms is rendered by sinusoidal curves on the plane. From these curves can be extracted that populations occupy zones of maximum and minimum presence, according to their special needs and tolerances imposed by their environment.[5]

Typically, a well-marked cline does not allow for a delineation of subspecies, as it is then impossible, by definition, to draw any further clear dividing lines between populations. In population genetics, a cline could include a spectrum of subspecies, as allele and haplotype frequencies tend to vary over a larger space; moreover, in evolution, genetic lineage sorting usually lags behind the establishment of locally-differentiated phenotypes. Regardless, in neither case will such a variation yield different species, as long as the populations, though geographically spread, can interbreed one with another.

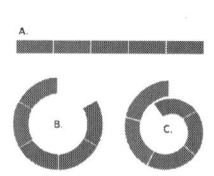

Interbreeding populations represented by coloured blocks. Click image for explanation.

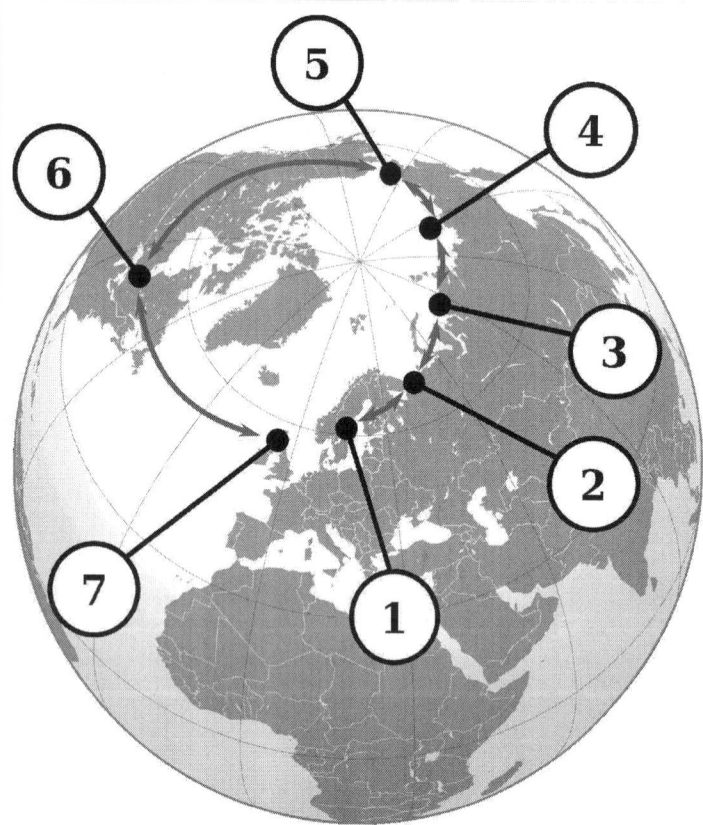

The *Larus* gulls interbreed in a ring around the arctic.
(1 : *Larus argentatus argentatus*, 2: *Larus fuscus (sensu stricto)*, 3 : *Larus fuscus heuglini*, 4 : *Larus argentatus birulai*, 5 : *Larus argentatus vegae*, 6 : *Larus argentatus smithsonianus*, 7 : *Larus argentatus argenteus*)

Ring species

Ring species[6] are a distinct type of cline where the geographical distribution in question is circular in shape, so that the two ends of the cline overlap with one another, giving two adjacent populations that rarely interbreed due to the cumulative effect of the many changes in phenotype along the cline. The populations elsewhere along the cline interbreed with their geographically adjacent populations as in a standard cline. Ring species present an interesting problem for those who seek to divide the living world into discrete species, as chain species are closely related to speciation (in this case, parapatric).

In the case of *Larus* gulls, the habitats of the end populations even overlap, which introduces questions as to what constitutes a species: nowhere along the cline can a line be drawn between the populations, but they are unable to interbreed.[7] However a recent study (Liebers et al., 2004) has provided genetic evidence that this example is far more complicated than presented here, and likely does not constitute a typical ring species.[7] [8]

Types of clines

- Thermocline - A cline based on difference in temperature,
- Chemocline - A cline based on difference in water chemistry,
- Halocline - A cline based on difference in water salinity,
- Pycnocline - A cline based on difference in water density.

References

[1] For definition and an etymology, see Merriam-Webster entry for "cline" (http://www.merriam-webster.com/dictionary/cline), or http:// www.greek-language.gr/greekLang/modern_greek/tools/lexica/search.html?lq=%CE%BA%CE%BB%CE%B9%CE%BD%CF%89& dq= (in Greek).

[2] Microsoft Encarta Premium 2009: "cline"

[3] King, Stansfield, Mulligan: *A dictionary of genetics*, 7th ed. (2006), Oxford University Press:"cline"

[4] Begon, Townsend, Harper - *Ecology: From individuals to ecosystems*, Blackwell Publishing, 4th ed. (2006), p. 10

[5] Eric R. Pianka: *Evolutionary Ecology*, 6th ed. (2000), Pearson Education, chapter 4

[6] *Fundamentals of biogeography* - Richard J. Huggett, 2nd ed. (2004), p. 20

[7] *Larus*

[8] **Liebers**, Dorit; de Knijff, Peter & Helbig, Andreas J. (2004): The herring gull complex is not a ring species. *Proc. Roy. Soc. B* **271**(1542): 893-901. doi:10.1098/rspb.2004.2679 PDF fulltext (http://www.journals.royalsoc.ac.uk/(ck042z55y2a4k2jegtv51r45)/app/home/ content.asp?referrer=contribution&format=2&page=1&pagecount=9) Electronic Appendix (http://www.journals.royalsoc.ac.uk/media/ public/contributionsupplementalmaterials/v/y/h/e/vyhea7ddp48gn5a1/archive1.pdf)

Cryptoplax

Cryptoplax is an extinct genus of polyplacophoran mollusc. Crytoplax became extinct during the Pliocene period.[1]

References

[1] van Belle, R. A. (1981). *Catalogue of Fossil Chitons*. ISBN 90 6279 018 6.

Cymatochiton

Cymatochiton is an extinct genus of polyplacophoran mollusc. Cymatochiton became extinct during the Permian period.[1]

References

[1] van Belle, R. A. (1981). *Catalogue of Fossil Chitons*. ISBN 90 6279 018 6.

Deep homology

In evolutionary developmental biology, the concept of **deep homology** is used to describe cases where growth and differentiation processes are governed by genetic mechanisms that are homologous and deeply conserved across a wide range of species.

Textbook examples common to metazoa include the homeotic genes that control differentiation along major body axes, and pax genes (especially PAX6) involved in the development of the eye and other sensory organs.

In early 2010, a team at The University of Texas at Austin led by Edward Marcotte developed an algorithm which identifies deeply homologous genetic modules in unicellular organisms, plants, and non-human animals based on phenotypes (such as traits and developmental defects). The technique aligns phenotypes across organisms based on orthology (a type of homology) of genes involved in the phenotypes.[1] [2]

References

- Shubin N, Tabin C, Carroll S (August 1997). "Fossils, genes and the evolution of animal limbs". *Nature* **388** (6643): 639–48. doi:10.1038/41710. PMID 9262397.
- Gilbert, Scott F. (2000). "Homologous Pathways of Development" [3]. *Developmental biology* [4] (6th ed.). Sunderland, Mass: Sinauer Associates. ISBN 0-87893-243-7.

[1] Zimmer, Carl. "The Search for Genes Leads to Unexpected Places" (http://www.nytimes.com/2010/04/27/science/27gene.html?hp=& pagewanted=all), *The New York Times*, New York, April 26, 2010.
[2] McGary KL, Park TJ, Woods JO, Cha HJ, Wallingford JB, Marcotte EM (April 2010). "Systematic discovery of nonobvious human disease models through orthologous phenotypes" (http://www.marcottelab.org/paper-pdfs/PNAS_Phenologs_2010.pdf). *Proceedings of the National Academy of Sciences* **107** (14): 6544–9. doi:10.1073/pnas.0910200107. PMID 20308572. .
[3] http://www.ncbi.nlm.nih.gov/bookshelf/br.fcgi?book=dbio&part=A5439
[4] http://www.ncbi.nlm.nih.gov/bookshelf/br.fcgi?book=dbio

DNA barcoding

DNA barcoding is a taxonomic method that uses a short genetic marker in an organism's DNA to identify it as belonging to a particular species. It differs from molecular phylogeny in that the main goal is not to determine classification but to identify an unknown sample in terms of a known classification.[1] Although barcodes are sometimes used in an effort to identify unknown species or assess whether species should be combined or separated,[2] the utility of DNA barcoding for these purposes is subject to debate.[3]

Applications include, for example, identifying plant leaves even when flowers or fruit are not available, identifying insect larvae (which typically have fewer diagnostic characters than adults), identifying the diet of an animal based on stomach contents or faeces,[4] and identifying products in commerce (for example, herbal supplements or wood).[1]

Choice of Locus

A desirable locus for DNA barcoding should be standardized (so that large databases of sequences for that locus can be developed),[5] present in most of the taxa of interest and sequencable without species-specific PCR primers,[5] short enough to be easily sequenced with current technology,[6] and provide a large variation between species yet a relatively small amount of variation within a species.[7]

Although several loci have been suggested, a common set of choices are:

- For animals and many other eukaryotes, the mitochondrial CO1 gene
- For land plants, the concatenation of the rbcL and matK chloroplast genes[5]

Mitochondrial DNA

DNA barcoding is based on a relatively simple concept. Most eukaryote cells contain mitochondria, and mitochondrial DNA (mtDNA) has a relatively fast mutation rate, which results in significant variation in mtDNA sequences between species and, in principle, a comparatively small variance within species. A 648-bp region of the mitochondrial cytochrome c oxidase subunit I (COI) gene was proposed as a potential 'barcode'.

However, because all mtDNA genes are maternally inherited (direct evidence for recombination in mtDNA is available in some bivalves such as *Mytilus*[8] but it is suspected that it may be more widespread[9]), any occurrences of hybridization,[10] male-killing microorganisms,[11] cytoplasmic incompatibility-inducing symbionts (e.g., *Wolbachia*[11]), horizontal gene transfer (such as via cellular symbionts[12]), or other "reticulate" evolutionary phenomena in a lineage can lead to misleading results (i.e., it is possible for two different species to share mtDNA,[13] or for one species to have more than one mtDNA sequence exhibited among different individuals).[14] [15]

As of 2009, databases of CO1 sequences included at least 620,000 specimens from over 58,000 species of animals, larger than databases available for any other gene.[16]

Identifying flowering plants

Kress *et al.* (2005[1]) suggest that the use of the COI sequence "is not appropriate for most species of plants because of a much slower rate of cytochrome c oxidase I gene evolution in higher plants than in animals". A series of experiments was then conducted to find a more suitable region of the genome for use in the DNA barcoding of flowering plants (or the larger group of land plants).[6] One 2005 proposal was the nuclear internal transcribed spacer region and the plastid trnH-psbA intergenic spacer;[1] other researchers advocated other regions such as matK.[6]

In 2009, a collaboration of a large group of plant DNA barcode researchers proposed two chloroplast genes, rbcL and matK, taken together, as a barcode for plants.[5] Jesse Ausubel, a DNA barcode researcher not involved in that effort, suggested that standardizing on a sequence was the best way to produce a large database of plant sequences, and that time would tell whether this choice would be sufficiently good at distinguishing different plant species.[16]

Vouchered specimens

DNA sequence databases like GenBank contain many sequences that are not tied to vouchered specimens (for example, herbarium specimens, cultured cell lines, or sometimes images). This is problematic in the face of taxonomic issues such as whether several species should be split or combined, or whether past identifications were sound. Therefore, best practice for DNA barcoding is to sequence vouchered specimens.[17] [18]

Origin

The use of nucleotide sequence variations to investigate evolutionary relationships is not a new concept. Carl Woese used sequence differences in ribosomal RNA (rRNA) to discover archaea, which in turn led to the redrawing of the evolutionary tree, and molecular markers (e.g., allozymes, rDNA, and mtDNAvage) have been successfully used in molecular systematics for decades. DNA barcoding provides a standardised method for this process via the use of a short DNA sequence from a particular region of the genome to provide a 'barcode' for identifying species. In 2003, Paul D.N. Hebert from the University of Guelph, Ontario, Canada, proposed the compilation of a public library of DNA barcodes that would be linked to named specimens. This library would "provide a new master key for identifying species, one whose power will rise with increased taxon coverage and with faster, cheaper sequencing".

Case studies

Identification of birds

In an effort to find a correspondence between traditional species boundaries established by taxonomy and those inferred by DNA barcoding, Hebert and co-workers sequenced DNA barcodes of 260 of the 667 bird species that breed in North America (Hebert *et al.* 2004a[19]). They found that every single one of the 260 species had a different COI sequence. 130 species were represented by two or more specimens; in all of these species, COI sequences were either identical or were most similar to sequences of the same species. COI variations between species averaged 7.93%, whereas variation within species averaged 0.43%. In four cases there were deep intraspecific divergences, indicating possible new species. Three out of these four polytypic species are already split into two by some taxonomists. Hebert *et al.*'s (2004a[19]) results reinforce these views and strengthen the case for DNA barcoding. Hebert *et al.* also proposed a standard sequence threshold to define new species, this threshold, the so-called "barcoding gap", was defined as 10 times the mean intraspecific variation for the group under study.

Delimiting cryptic species

The next major study into the efficacy of DNA barcoding was focused on the neotropical skipper butterfly, *Astraptes fulgerator* at the Area Conservacion de Guanacaste (ACG) in north-western Costa Rica. This species was already known as a cryptic species complex, due to subtle morphological differences, as well as an unusually large variety of caterpillar food plants. However, several years would have been required for taxonomists to completely delimit species. Hebert *et al.* (2004b[20]) sequenced the COI gene of 484 specimens from the ACG. This sample included "at least 20 individuals reared from each species of food plant, extremes and intermediates of adult and caterpillar color variation, and representatives" from the three major ecosystems where *Astraptes fulgerator* is found. Hebert *et al.* (2004b[20]) concluded that *Astraptes fulgerator* consists of 10 different species in north-western Costa Rica. These results, however, were subsequently challenged by Brower (2006[21]), who pointed out numerous serious flaws in the analysis, and concluded that the original data could support no more than the possibility of three to seven cryptic taxa rather than ten cryptic species. This highlights that the results of DNA barcoding analyses can be dependent upon the choice of analytical methods used by the investigators, so the process of delimiting cryptic species using

DNA barcodes can be as subjective as any other form of taxonomy.

A more recent example used DNA barcoding for the identification of cryptic species included in the ongoing long-term database of tropical caterpillar life generated by Dan Janzen and Winnie Hallwachs in Costa Rica at the ACG.[22] In 2006 Smith et al.[23] examined whether a COI DNA barcode could function as a tool for identification and discovery for the 20 morphospecies of *Belvosia* [24] parasitoid flies (Tachinidae) that have been reared from caterpillars in ACG. Barcoding not only discriminated among all 17 highly host-specific morphospecies of ACG *Belvosia*, but it also suggested that the species count could be as high as 32 by indicating that each of the three generalist species might actually be arrays of highly host-specific cryptic species.

In 2007 Smith et al. expanded on these results by barcoding 2,134 flies belonging to what appeared to be the 16 most generalist of the ACG tachinid morphospecies.[25] They encountered 73 mitochondrial lineages separated by an average of 4% sequence divergence and, as these lineages are supported by collateral ecological information, and, where tested, by independent nuclear markers (28S and ITS1), the authors therefore viewed these lineages as provisional species. Each of the 16 initially apparent generalist species were categorized into one of four patterns: (i) a single generalist species, (ii) a pair of morphologically cryptic generalist species, (iii) a complex of specialist species plus a generalist, or (iv) a complex of specialists with no remaining generalist. In sum, there remained 9 generalist species classified among the 73 mitochondrial lineages analyzed.

However, also in 2007, Whitworth et al. reported that flies in the related family Calliphoridae could not be discriminated by barcoding.[14] They investigated the performance of barcoding in the fly genus *Protocalliphora*, known to be infected with the endosymbiotic bacteria *Wolbachia*. Assignment of unknown individuals to species was impossible for 60% of the species, and if the technique had been applied, as in the previous study, to identify new species, it would have underestimated the species number in the genus by 75%. They attributed the failure of barcoding to the non-monophyly of many of the species at the mitochondrial level; in one case, individuals from four different species had identical barcodes. The authors went on to state:

> The pattern of *Wolbachia* infection strongly suggests that the lack of within-species monophyly results from introgressive hybridization associated with *Wolbachia* infection. Given that *Wolbachia* is known to infect between 15 and 75% of insect species, we conclude that identification at the species level based on mitochondrial sequence might not be possible for many insects.[14]

Marine biologists have also considered the value of the technique in identifying cryptic and polymorphic species and have suggested that the technique may be helpful when associations with voucher specimens are maintained,[17] though cases of "shared barcodes" (e.g., non-unique) have been documented in cichlid fishes and cowries[15]

Cataloguing ancient life

Lambert et al. (2005[26]) examined the possibility of using DNA barcoding to assess the past diversity of the Earth's biota. The COI gene of a group of extinct ratite birds, the moa, were sequenced using 26 subfossil moa bones. As with Hebert's results, each species sequenced had a unique barcode and intraspecific COI sequence variance ranged from 0 to 1.24%. To determine new species, a standard sequence threshold of 2.7% COI sequence difference was set. This value is 10 times the average intraspecies difference of North American birds, which is inconsistent with Hebert's recommendation that the threshold value be based on the group under study. Using this value, the group detected six moa species. In addition, a further standard sequence threshold of 1.24% was also used. This value resulted in 10 moa species which corresponded with the previously known species with one exception. This exception suggested a possible complex of species which was previously unidentified. Given the slow rate of growth and reproduction of moa, it is probable that the interspecies variation is rather low. On the other hand, there is no set value of molecular difference at which populations can be assumed to have irrevocably started to undergo speciation. It is safe to say, however, that the 2.7% COI sequence difference initially used was far too high.

The Moorea Biocode Project

The Biocode Project [27] is a barcoding initiative to create the first comprehensive inventory of all non-microbial life in a complex tropical ecosystem, the island of Moorea in Tahiti. Supported by a grant from the Gordon and Betty Moore Foundation, the Moorea Biocode Project is a 3-year project that brings together researchers from the Smithsonian Institution, UC Berkeley, France's National Center for Scientific Research (CNRS), and other partners. The outcome of the project is a library of genetic markers and physical identifiers for every species of plant, animal and fungi on the island that will be provided as a publicly available database resource for ecologists and evolutionary biologists around the world.

The software back-end to the Moore Biocode Project is Geneious Pro and two custom-developed plugins from the New Zealand-based company, Biomatters. The Biocode LIMS and Genbank Submission [28] plugins have been made freely available to the public[29] and users of the free Geneious Basic software will be able to access and view the Biocode database upon completion of the project, while a commercial copy of Geneious Pro is required for researchers involved int data creation and analysis.

Criticisms

DNA barcoding has met with spirited reaction from scientists, especially systematists, ranging from enthusiastic endorsement to vociferous opposition.[30] For example, many stress the fact that DNA barcoding does not provide reliable information above the species level, while others indicate that it is inapplicable at the species level, but may still have merit for higher-level groups.[14] Others resent what they see as a gross oversimplification of the science of taxonomy. And, more practically, some suggest that recently diverged species might not be distinguishable on the basis of their COI sequences.[31] Due to various phenomena, Funk & Omland (2003[32]) found that some 23% of animal species are polyphyletic if their mtDNA data are accurate, indicating that using an mtDNA barcode to assign a species name to an animal will be ambiguous or erroneous some 23% of the time (see also Meyer & Paulay, 2005[33]). Studies with insects suggest an equal or even greater error rate, due to the frequent lack of correlation between the mitochondrial genome and the nuclear genome or the lack of a barcoding gap (e.g., Hurst and Jiggins, 2005,[12] Whitworth *et al.*, 2007,[14] Wiemers & Fiedler, 2007[34]). Problems with mtDNA arising from male-killing microorganisms and cytoplasmic incompatibility-inducing symbionts (e.g., *Wolbachia*)[11] are also particularly common among insects. Given that insects represent over 75% of all known organisms,[35] this suggests that while mtDNA barcoding may work for vertebrates, it may not be effective for the majority of known organisms.

Moritz and Cicero (2004[36]) have questioned the efficacy of DNA barcoding by suggesting that other avian data is inconsistent with Hebert *et al.*'s interpretation, namely, Johnson and Cicero's (2004[37]) finding that 74% of sister species comparisons fall below the 2.7% threshold suggested by Hebert *et al.* These criticisms are somewhat misleading considering that, of the 39 species comparisons reported by Johnson and Cicero, only 8 actually use COI data to arrive at their conclusions. Johnson and Cicero (2004[37]) have also claimed to have detected bird species with identical DNA barcodes, however, these 'barcodes' refer to an unpublished 723-bp sequence of ND6 which has never been suggested as a likely candidate for DNA barcoding.

The DNA barcoding debate resembles the phenetics debate of decades gone by. It remains to be seen whether what is now touted as a revolution in taxonomy will eventually go the same way as phenetic approaches, of which was claimed exactly the same decades ago, but which were all but rejected when they failed to live up to overblown expectations.[38] Controversy surrounding DNA barcoding stems not so much from the method itself, but rather from extravagant claims that it will supersede or radically transform traditional taxonomy. Other critics fear a "big science" initiative like barcoding will make funding even more scarce for already underfunded disciplines like taxonomy, but barcoders respond that they compete for funding not with fields like taxonomy, but instead with other big science fields, such as medicine and genomics.[39] Barcoders also maintain that they are being dragged into long-standing debates over the definition of a species and that barcoding is less controversial when viewed primarily as a method of identification, not classification.[1] [18]

The current trend appears to be that DNA barcoding needs to be used alongside traditional taxonomic tools and alternative forms of molecular systematics so that problem cases can be identified and errors detected. Non-cryptic species can generally be resolved by either traditional or molecular taxonomy without ambiguity. However, more difficult cases will only yield to a combination of approaches. And finally, as most of the global biodiversity remains unknown, molecular barcoding can only hint at the existence of new taxa, but not delimit or describe them (DeSalle, 2006;[40] Rubinoff, 2006[41] [42]).

DNA Barcoding Software

Software for DNA barcoding requires integration of a field information management system (FIMS), laboratory information management system (LIMS), sequence analysis tools, workflow tracking to connect field data and laboratory data, database submission tools and pipeline automation for scaling up to eco-system scale projects. Geneious Pro can be used for the sequence analysis components, and the two plugins made freely available through the Moorea Biocode Project, the Biocode LIMS and Genbank Submission [28] plugins handle integration with the FIMS, the LIMS, workflow tracking and database submission.

References

[1] Kress WJ, Wurdack KJ, Zimmer EA, Weigt LA, Janzen DH (June 2005). "Use of DNA barcodes to identify flowering plants". *Proc. Natl. Acad. Sci. U.S.A.* **102** (23): 8369–74. doi:10.1073/pnas.0503123102. PMC 1142120. PMID 15928076. Supporting Information (http://www. pnas.org/cgi/content/full/0503123102/DC1)

[2] Koch, H. 2010. Combining morphology and DNA barcoding resolves the taxonomy of Western Malagasy *Liotrigona* Moure, 1961. *African Invertebrates* **51** (2): 413-421. (http://www.africaninvertebrates.org.za/Koch_2010_51_2_474.aspx) PDF fulltext (http://www.tb1.ethz. ch/PublicationsEO/PDFpapers/Koch_AFRICAN_INVERTEBRATES_2010_51_413-421.pdf)

[3] Seberg O, Petersen G. (2009). "How many loci does it take to DNA barcode a crocus?". *PLoS One* **4** (2): e4598. doi:10.1371/journal.pone.0004598. PMC 2643479. PMID 19240801.

[4] Eeva M Soininen *et al.* (2009). "Analysing diet of small herbivores: the efficiency of DNA barcoding coupled with high-throughput pyrosequencing for deciphering the composition of complex plant mixtures". *Frontiers in Zoology* **6**: 16. doi:10.1186/1742-9994-6-16. PMC 2736939. PMID 19695081.

[5] CBOL Plant Working Group (August 4, 2009). "A DNA barcode for land plants". *PNAS* **106** (31): 12794–12797. doi:10.1073/pnas.0905845106. PMC 2722355. PMID 19666622.

[6] Kress WJ, Erickson DL (2008). "DNA barcodes: Genes, genomics, and bioinformatics". *PNAS* **105** (8): 2761–2762. doi:10.1073/pnas.0800476105. PMC 2268532. PMID 18287050.

[7] Renaud Lahaye *et al.* (2008-02-26). "DNA barcoding the floras of biodiversity hotspots". *Proc Natl Acad Sci USA* **105** (8): 2923–2928. doi:10.1073/pnas.0709936105. PMC 2268561. PMID 18258745.

[8] Ladoukakis ED, Zouros E (1 July 2001). "Direct evidence for homologous recombination in mussel (*Mytilus galloprovincialis*) mitochondrial DNA" (http://mbe.oxfordjournals.org/cgi/pmidlookup?view=long&pmid=11420358). *Mol. Biol. Evol.* **18** (7): 1168–75. PMID 11420358.

[9] Tsaousis AD, Martin DP, Ladoukakis ED, Posada D, Zouros E (April 2005). "Widespread recombination in published animal mtDNA sequences". *Mol. Biol. Evol.* **22** (4): 925–33. doi:10.1093/molbev/msi084. PMID 15647518.

[10] Melo-Ferreira J, Boursot P, Suchentrunk F, Ferrand N, Alves PC (July 2005). "Invasion from the cold past: extensive introgression of mountain hare (*Lepus timidus*) mitochondrial DNA into three other hare species in northern Iberia". *Mol. Ecol.* **14** (8): 2459–64. doi:10.1111/j.1365-294X.2005.02599.x. PMID 15969727.

[11] Johnstone RA, Hurst GDD (1996). "Maternally inherited male-killing microorganisms may confound interpretation of mitochondrial DNA variability". *Biol. J. Linnaean Soc.* **58**: 453–70. doi:10.1111/j.1095-8312.1996.tb01446.x.

[12] Hurst GD, Jiggins FM (August 2005). "Problems with mitochondrial DNA as a marker in population, phylogeographic and phylogenetic studies: the effects of inherited symbionts". *Proc. Biol. Sci.* **272** (1572): 1525–34. doi:10.1098/rspb.2005.3056. PMC 1559843. PMID 16048766.

[13] Croucher PJP, Oxford GS, Searle JB (2004). "Mitochondrial differentiation, introgression and phylogeny of species in the *Tegenaria atrica* group (Araneae: Agelenidae)". *Biological Journal of the Linnean Society* **81**: 79–89. doi:10.1111/j.1095-8312.2004.00280.x.

[14] Whitworth TL, Dawson RD, Magalon H, Baudry E (July 2007). "DNA barcoding cannot reliably identify species of the blowfly genus Protocalliphora (Diptera: Calliphoridae)". *Proc. Biol. Sci.* **274** (1619): 1731–9. doi:10.1098/rspb.2007.0062. PMC 2493573. PMID 17472911.

[15] Meier R (2008). "Ch. 7: DNA sequences in taxonomy: Opportunities and challenges". In Wheeler, Quentin. *The new taxonomy*. Boca Raton: CRC Press. ISBN 0-8493-9088-5.

[16] Jesse H. Ausubel (August 4, 2009). "A botanical macroscope". *Proceedings of the National Academy of Sciences* **106** (31): 12569. doi:10.1073/pnas.0906757106. ISSN 00278424. PMC 2722277. PMID 19666620.

[17] Schander C, Willassen E (2005). "What can Biological Barcoding do for Marine Biology?" (http://www.bolinfonet.org/pdf/schander& willassen_2005.pdf) (PDF). *Marine Biology Research* **1** (1): 79–83. doi:10.1080/17451000510018962. .

[18] Scott E. Miller (2007-03-20). "DNA barcoding and the renaissance of taxonomy". *Proc Natl Acad Sci U S A.* **104** (12): 4775–4776. doi:10.1073/pnas.0700466104. PMC 1829212. PMID 17363473.

[19] Hebert PD, Stoeckle MY, Zemlak TS, Francis CM (October 2004). "Identification of Birds through DNA Barcodes". *PLoS Biol.* **2** (10): e312. doi:10.1371/journal.pbio.0020312. PMC 518999. PMID 15455034. Supporting Information (http://biology.plosjournals.org/archive/ 1545-7885/2/10/supinfo/10.1371_journal.pbio.0020312.sg001.pdf)

[20] Hebert PD, Penton EH, Burns JM, Janzen DH, Hallwachs W (October 2004). "Ten species in one: DNA barcoding reveals cryptic species in the neotropical skipper butterfly *Astraptes fulgerator*". *Proc. Natl. Acad. Sci. U.S.A.* **101** (41): 14812–7. doi:10.1073/pnas.0406166101. PMC 522015. PMID 15465915. Supporting Information (http://www.pnas.org/cgi/content/full/0406166101/DC1)

[21] Brower AVZ (2006). "Problems with DNA barcodes for species delimitation: 'ten species' of *Astraptes fulgerator* reassessed (Lepidoptera: Hesperiidae)". *Systematics and Biodiversity* **4** (2): 127–32. doi:10.1017/S147720000500191X.

[22] "Database homepage for ACG caterpillar (Lepidoptera) rearing databases" (http://janzen.sas.upenn.edu/caterpillars/database.lasso). . Retrieved 2007-08-12.

[23] Smith MA, Woodley NE, Janzen DH, Hallwachs W, Hebert PD (2006). "DNA barcodes reveal cryptic host-specificity within the presumed polyphagous members of a genus of parasitoid flies (Diptera: Tachinidae)". *Proc. Natl. Acad. Sci. U.S.A.* **103** (10): 3657–62. doi:10.1073/pnas.0511318103. PMC 1383497. PMID 16505365.

[24] http://www.itis.gov/servlet/SingleRpt/SingleRpt?search_topic=TSN&search_value=650659

[25] Smith MA, Wood DM, Janzen DH, Hallwachs W, Hebert PD (2007). "DNA barcodes affirm that 16 species of apparently generalist tropical parasitoid flies (Diptera, Tachinidae) are not all generalists". *Proc. Natl. Acad. Sci. U.S.A.* **104** (12): 4967–72. doi:10.1073/pnas.0700050104. PMC 1821123. PMID 17360352.

[26] Lambert DM, Baker A, Huynen L, Haddrath O, Hebert PD, Millar CD (2005). "Is a large-scale DNA-based inventory of ancient life possible?" (http://jhered.oxfordjournals.org/cgi/reprint/96/3/279.pdf) (PDF fulltext). *J. Hered.* **96** (3): 279–84. doi:10.1093/jhered/esi035. PMID 15731217. .

[27] http://www.mooreabiocode.org/lMoorea

[28] http://software.mooreabiocode.org/index.php?title=Main_Page|Geneious

[29] http://www.bio-itworld.com/2010/11/30/biomatters-moorea-LIMS.html

[30] Rubinoff D, Cameron S, Will K (2006). "A genomic perspective on the shortcomings of mitochondrial DNA for "barcoding" identification". *J. Hered.* **97** (6): 581–94. doi:10.1093/jhered/esl036. PMID 17135463.

[31] Kevin, C.R. Kerr, Mark Y. Stoeckle, Carla J. Dove, Lee A. Weigt, Charles M. Francis & Paul D. N. Hebert. 2006. Comprehensive DNA barcode coverage of North American birds. Molecular Ecology Notes. (OnlineEarly Articles). doi:10.1111/j.1471-8286.2006.01670.x Full text (http://www.blackwell-synergy.com/doi/full/10.1111/j.1471-8286.2006.01670.x)

[32] Funk DJ, Omland KE (2003). "Species-level paraphyly and polyphyly: frequency, causes, and consequences, with insights from animal mitochondrial DNA". *Annu Rev Ecol Syst* **34**: 397–423. doi:10.1146/annurev.ecolsys.34.011802.132421.

[33] Meyer CP, Paulay G (December 2005). "DNA barcoding: error rates based on comprehensive sampling". *PLoS Biol.* **3** (12): e422. doi:10.1371/journal.pbio.0030422. PMC 1287506. PMID 16336051.

[34] Wiemers M, Fiedler K (2007). "Does the DNA barcoding gap exist? – a case study in blue butterflies (Lepidoptera: Lycaenidae)" (http:// www.frontiersinzoology.com/content/4/1/8). *Front. Zool.* **4**: 8. doi:10.1186/1742-9994-4-8. PMC 1838910. PMID 17343734. .

[35] (http://www.environment.gov.au/biodiversity/abrs/publications/other/species-numbers/02-exec-summary.html#allspecies)

[36] Moritz C, Cicero C (2004). "DNA Barcoding: Promise and Pitfalls" (http://biology.plosjournals.org/perlserv/?request=get-pdf&file=10. 1371_journal.pbio.0020354-L.pdf) (PDF fulltext). *PLoS Biol.* **2** (10): 1529–31. doi:10.1371/journal.pbio.0020354. PMC 519004. PMID 15486587. .

[37] Johnson NK, Cicero C (May 2004). "New mitochondrial DNA data affirm the importance of Pleistocene speciation in North American birds". *Evolution* **58** (5): 1122–30. PMID 15212392.

[38] Will KW, Mishler BD, Wheeler QD (2005). "The Perils of DNA Barcoding and the Need for Integrative Taxonomy" (http://www.erin. utoronto.ca/~w3bio/bio443/seminar_papers/perils_of_dna_barcoding.pdf) (PDF). *Syst. Biol.* **54** (5): 844–51. doi:10.1080/10635150500354878. PMID 16243769. .

[39] Gregory TR (April 2005). "DNA barcoding does not compete with taxonomy" (http://www.bolinfonet.org/pdf/ DNA_barcoding_does_not_compete_with_taxonomy.pdf) (PDF). *Nature* **434** (7037): 1067. doi:10.1038/4341067b. PMID 15858548. .

[40] Desalle R (October 2006). "Species discovery versus species identification in DNA barcoding efforts: response to Rubinoff". *Conserv. Biol.* **20** (5): 1545–7. doi:10.1111/j.1523-1739.2006.00543.x. PMID 17002772.

[41] Rubinoff D (August 2006). "Utility of mitochondrial DNA barcodes in species conservation". *Conserv. Biol.* **20** (4): 1026–33. doi:10.1111/j.1523-1739.2006.00372.x. PMID 16922219.

[42] Rubinoff D (October 2006). "DNA barcoding evolves into the familiar". *Conserv. Biol.* **20** (5): 1548–9. doi:10.1111/j.1523-1739.2006.00542.x. PMID 17002773.

External links

- Barcode of Life Data Systems (http://www.boldsystems.org/)
- International Barcode of Life (http://www.ibol.org/)
- Consortium for the Barcode of Life (http://www.barcodeoflife.org)
- Fish Barcode of Life Initiative (FISH-BOL) (http://www.fishbol.org)
- All Birds Barcoding Initiative (ABBI) (http://barcoding.si.edu/AllBirds.htm)
- Polar Flora and Fauna Barcoding website (http://www.polarbarcoding.org) (Latest outpost in the Canadian Arctic in the field)
- The Barcode of Life Blog (http://phe.rockefeller.edu/barcode/blog/)
- DNA Barcoding Community Network (http://connect.barcodeoflife.net/)
- Guidelines for non COI gene selection (http://www.barcoding.si.edu/PDF/Guidelines for non-CO1 selection - 4 June.pdf)

Dustbin category

The term 'dustbin category' is sometimes used to describe a category that includes people or things that might be heterogeneous, only loosely related or poorly understood. It has been used in discussion of law, linguistics, medicine, sociology and other disciplines. For example:

> Some patients' symptoms do not fit well with any recognised category and there is a danger these may be forced into a 'dustbin' category such as 'depression, not otherwise specified.'[1]

References

[1] Barraclough, J and Gill, D: *Hughes' outline of modern psychiatry*, ed. 4, page 5. John Wiley and Sons, 1996. ISBN 0471963585

Encyclopedia of Life

Encyclopedia of Life

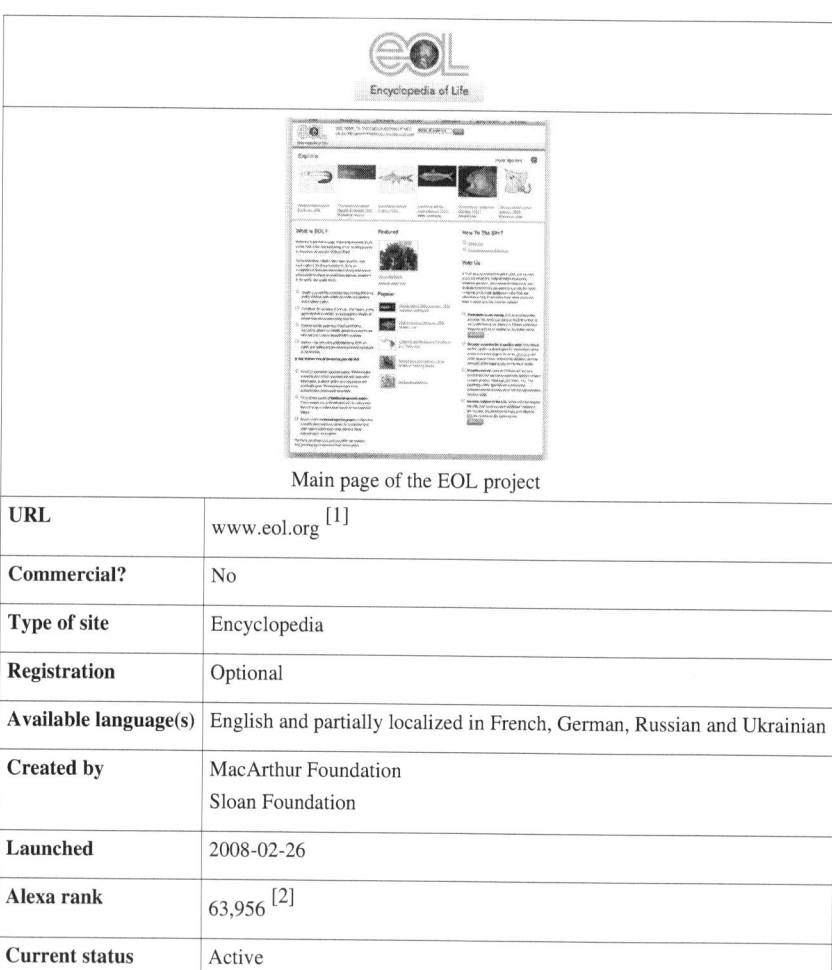

Main page of the EOL project

URL	www.eol.org [1]
Commercial?	No
Type of site	Encyclopedia
Registration	Optional
Available language(s)	English and partially localized in French, German, Russian and Ukrainian
Created by	MacArthur Foundation Sloan Foundation
Launched	2008-02-26
Alexa rank	63,956 [2]
Current status	Active

The *Encyclopedia of Life* (**EOL**) is a free, online collaborative encyclopedia intended to document all of the 1.9 million living species known to science. It is compiled from existing databases and from contributions by experts and non-experts throughout the world.[3] [4] It aims to build one "infinitely expandable" page for each species, including video, sound, images, graphics, as well as text.[5] In addition, the Encyclopedia will incorporate the Biodiversity Heritage Library, which will contain the digitized print collections from the world's major natural history libraries. The project is initially backed by a US$50 million funding commitment, led by the MacArthur Foundation and the Sloan Foundation.

The EOL went live on 26 February 2008 with 30,000 entries.[6] The site immediately proved to be extremely popular, and temporarily had to revert to demonstration pages for two days when it was overrun by traffic from over 11 million views it received.[7]

At this time, the project's steering committee has senior officers from Biodiversity Heritage Library consortium, Field Museum, Harvard University, MacArthur Foundation, Marine Biological Laboratory, Missouri Botanical Garden, Sloan Foundation, and the Smithsonian Institution.[3] [8] [9]

Intention

Information about many species is already available from a variety of sources, in particular about the megafauna. Gathering currently available data on all 1.9 million species will take about 10 years.[10] By October 2009, EOL has 1,500,000 pages of which almost 200,000 have text or images from expert sources. The initiative relies on indexing information compiled by other efforts, including the Sp2000 and ITIS Catalogue of Life, Fishbase and the Assembling Tree of Life project of NSF, AmphibiaWeb, Mushroom explorer, micro*scope, etc.. The initial focus will be on living species but will later include extinct species. As the discovery of new species is expected to continue (the current rate is about 20,000 per year), the encyclopedia will grow continuously. As taxonomy finds new ways to include species discovered by molecular techniques, the rate of new species additions will increase - in particular in respect of the microbial work of (eu)bacteria, archaebacteria and viruses.

The goal of EOL is to be a tool for students, scientists and the public,[11] and will eventually become multi-lingual.[12] The estimated cost is US$110.5 million.[10]

Vision

Biologist E. O. Wilson announced a "dream" that someone would fund the project during a TED speaking engagement in March 2007,[13] a yearly forum in which luminary speakers are given the opportunity to ask for a "dream prize". On 9 May 2007 that dream "came true" when five science foundations announced an initial 50 million dollar grant to get the project started.[14]

Wikipedia and other existing online works served as an inspiration for the Encyclopedia of Life.[15] [16] Most of the content organized by the site is available under various Creative Commons licenses.[17]

Resources and collaborations

The encyclopedia has agreements with many sources for information, including Wikipedia and Flickr.

Partner	Description
AmphibiaWeb [18]	AmphibiaWeb is an online system enabling anyone with a Web browser to search and retrieve information relating to amphibian biology and conservation. This site was inspired by the global declines of amphibians, the study of which has been hindered by the lack of multidisplinary studies and a lack of coordination in monitoring, in field studies, and in lab studies. One of its major goals is to encourage a shared vision for the study of global amphibian declines and the conservation of remaining amphibians.
Animal Diversity Web [19]	Animal Diversity Web (ADW) is a project of the University of Michigan Museum of Zoology. It is a large searchable encyclopedia of the natural history of animals. ADW facilitates inquiry-driven learning with a database rich enough that students can discover for themselves basic concepts in ecology and conservation biology. ADW has partnered with the EOL to share its text, much of which has been created by undergraduates across North America. It will also share its multimedia as licensing allows.
AntWeb [20]	AntWeb is generally recognized as the most advanced biodiversity information system at species level dedicated to ants. Altogether, its acceptance by the ant research community, the number of participating remote curators that maintain the site, number of pictures, simplicity of web interface, and completeness of species, make AntWeb the premier reference for dissemination of data, information, and knowledge on ants. AntWeb is serving information on tens of thousands of ant species through the EOL.
ARKive [21]	ARKive is a Wildscreen initiative – a non-profit charitable organization dedicated to promoting the public understanding of biodiversity and the need for its conservation. ARKive's mission is to create a lasting, publicly accessible, audio-visual record of life on Earth. ARKive is sharing with EOL its species texts. To access ARKive's rich repository of films and photographs, follow links in the Specialized Projects area of our pages.
The Atlas of Living Australia [22]	ALA - The Atlas of Living Australia is a five-year project funded under the Australian Government's National Collaborative Research Infrastructure Strategy (NCRIS). Its mission is to develop a biodiversity data management system which will link Australia's biological knowledge with its scientific and agricultural reference collections and other custodians of biological information.

BioLib.cz	BioLib, the Biological Library, is a non-commercial educational project intended to be used both by experts and general public. It produces a gallery, glossary, vernacular names dictionary, database of links and literature, systems of biotopes, discussion forum and several other functions related to biology. EOL partnered with BioLib to present many of its images.
Biolib.de	Biolib.de is a collection of historic and modern biology books.
BioPedia	Bio*pedia is a communal repository of descriptions of organisms. Bio*pedia works in conjunction with the STAR biodiversity web sites, such as micro*scope, and with the Encyclopedia of Life. Text descriptions will be immediately be visible in the STAR sites. If you would like to be able to add to Bio*pedia, please contact us or register. We asccept content on the understanding it can be made available under a Creative Commons attribution license.
Biopix.dk	Biopix is a collection of biological photos, primarily from Scandinavia. It is used by a wide range of students, teachers, researchers, photographers, among others. EOL partnered with Biopix to present many of its images.
Catalogue of Life [23]	The Catalogue of Life Partnership (CoLP) is an informal partnership dedicated to creating an index of the world's organisms, called the Catalogue of Life (CoL). The CoL provides different forms of access to an integrated, quality, maintained, comprehensive consensus species checklist and taxonomic hierarchy, presently covering more than one million species, and intended to cover all know species in the near future. They contain substantial contributions of taxonomic expertise from more than fifty organizations around the world, integrated into a single work by the ongoing work of the CoLP partners. EOL currently uses CoLP as its taxonomic backbone.
Consortium for the Barcode of Life	The Consortium for the Barcode of Life (CBOL) is an international initiative devoted to developing DNA barcoding as a global standard for the identification of biological species.
FishBase [24]	FishBase is a global information system with all you ever wanted to know about fishes. FishBase is a relational database with information to cater to different professionals such as research scientists, fisheries managers, zoologists and many more. The FishBase Website contains data on practically every fish species known to science. The project was developed at the WorldFish Center in collaboration with the Food and Agriculture Organization of the United Nations and many other partners, and with support from the European Commission. FishBase is serving information on more than 30,000 fish species through EOL.
Global Biodiversity Information Facility (GBIF) [25]	The Global Biodiversity Information Facility (GBIF) is the world's premiere source for information on biological specimen and observational data, providing on-line access to more than 135 million data records from around the world. GBIF is providing range maps for the EOL species pages.
IUCN	International Union for Conservation of Nature (IUCN) helps the world find pragmatic solutions to our most pressing environment and development challenges. IUCN supports scientific research; manages field projects all over the world; and brings governments, non-government organizations, United Nations agencies, companies and local communities together to develop and implement policy, laws and best practice. EOL partnered with the IUCN to indicate status of each species according to the Red List of Threatened Species.
Micro*scope [26]	micro*scope is a communal web site that provides descriptive information about all kinds of microbes. It combines locally assembled content with links to other expert sites on the internet. Information is assembled in collections provided by various contributors.
Mushroom Observer	The purpose of this site is to record observations about mushrooms, help people identify mushrooms they aren't familiar with, and expand the community around the scientific exploration of mushrooms (mycology). Some have asked what counts as a mushroom. This site takes a very broad view. While the emphasis is on the large fleshy fungi, other fungi such as lichens, rust and molds as well as fungus-like organisms such as slime-molds are all welcome.
Naturalis [27]	Naturalis is the Dutch National Natural History Museum. Naturalis aims to use its unique natural history collection to make a real contribution to furthering the knowledge and appreciation of nature across Dutch society. Naturalis collaborates with a number of Dutch knowledge institutions, field data collecting organizations, and nature conservation organizations to gather, model and distribute the best possible collection of information on Dutch biodiversity. Naturalis and partners organize expeditions, develop educational programs, publish journals and books and websites to distribute the information efficiently and effectively. Naturalis is developing a Netherlands regional EOL site, which will serve information in Dutch; the same information will be served on the EOL central portal in English.
Plazi	Plazi is a not-for-profit association supporting and promoting the development of persistent and openly accessible digital taxonomic literature. Plazi maintains a digital taxonomic literature repository, enhances submitted taxonomic treatments by creating TaxonX [14] XML versions, participates in the development of new models for publishing taxonomic treatments, and advocates and educate about the vital importance of maintaining free and open access to scientific discourse and data.

Solanaceae Source	The Solanaceae Source Web site is the product of an ongoing five year project: Planetary Biodiversity Inventory (PBI) Solanum: A worldwide treatment. The aim of the project is to produce a worldwide taxonomic monograph of the species occurring within the plant genus Solanum (the potato and tomato family), organized by a robust phylogenetic framework. The project began in January 2004 and is just one of four inventories funded by the National Science Foundation at that time. The project is made possible through collaborations between Solanaceae specialists worldwide, with principal investigators from four research institutions in England and the United States.
Nearctic Spider Database	The Nearctic Spider Database presents peer-reviewed species pages, aggregates individual and institutional collection records, and maintains deep links to the primary literature on spiders throughout Canada, United States, Greenland, Bermuda, and parts of Mexico. The forum, public commenting on pages, web services, reverse geocoding services, syndicated content, and nomenclatural checks are all well used by the public and by araneid systematists and their students.
Tree of Life Web Project [28]	Tree of Life (ToL) project is a collaborative effort of biologists from around the world. On more than 10,000 World Wide Web pages, the project provides information about the diversity of organisms on Earth, their evolutionary history (phylogeny), and characteristics. ToL pages are linked to one another hierarchically, in the form of the evolutionary tree of life. Starting with the root of all Life on Earth and moving out along diverging branches to individual species, the structure of the ToL project thus illustrates the genetic connections between all living things. Once the EOL has established its infrastructure for disseminating species page content through web services, ToL will concentrate on collecting content about supra-specific taxa and phylogenetic relationships between species.
World Register of Marine Species [29]	The aim of a World Register of Marine Species (WoRMS) is to provide an authoritative and comprehensive list of names of marine organisms, including information on synonymy. While highest priority goes to valid names, other names in use are included so that this register can serve as a guide to interpret taxonomic literature.
ZooKeys	ZooKeys is a peer-reviewed, open-access, rapidly produced journal launched to support free exchange of ideas and information in systematic zoology. All papers published in ZooKeys can be freely copied, downloaded, printed and distributed at no charge for the reader. Authors may retain all other rights on their works. Authors are thus encouraged to post the pdf files of published papers on their homepages or elsewhere to expedite distribution. Papers are published both online and in the traditional printed format, in full compliance with the current requirements of ICZN.

References

[1] http://www.eol.org

[2] "Traffic Details: EOL.org" (http://www.alexa.com/data/details/traffic_details/eol.org). Alexa Internet, Inc. 2008. . Retrieved 2008-07-15.

[3] "FAQ: Who is ultimately responsible for constructing the Encyclopedia of Life?" (http://www.eol.org/faq). *Encyclopedia of Life*. 2009. . Retrieved 2009-05-12.

[4] "FAQ: What does Encyclopedia of Life seek to accomplish? What are its objectives?" (http://www.eol.org/faq). *Encyclopedia of Life*. 2009. . Retrieved 2009-05-12.

[5] Odling Smee, Lucy (2007-05-09). "Encyclopedia of Life launched" (http://www.nature.com/news/2007/070508/full/070508-7.html). news @ nature.com. doi:10.1038/news070508-7. . Retrieved 2007-05-09.

[6] Zimmer, Carl (2008-02-26). "The Encyclopedia of Life, No Bookshelf Required" (http://www.nytimes.com/2008/02/26/science/26ency. html?em&ex=1204261200&en=264ffed20b39b8f4&ei=5087). *The New York Times*. . Retrieved 2008-02-27.

[7] Associated Press (February 27, 2008). "Life Encyclopedia Debut Too Popular to Stay "Live"" (http://news.nationalgeographic.com/news/ 2008/02/080227-AP-encyclopedi.html). *National Geographic*. . Retrieved 2009-05-12.

[8] "Scientists compile 'book of life'" (http://news.bbc.co.uk/1/hi/sci/tech/6638017.stm). *BBC News*. 2007-05-09. . Retrieved 2007-05-09.

[9] "Demonstration pages" (http://www.eol.org/demonstration.html). *Encyclopedia of Life*. 2007. . Retrieved 2009-05-12.

[10] "Encyclopédie de la vie: Une arche de Noé virtuelle!" (http://www.radio-canada.ca/nouvelles/Science-Sante/2007/05/09/ 001-encyclopedie-vie.shtml?ref=rss). *Radio-Canada*. 9 May 2007. . Retrieved 2009-05-12.

[11] "FAQ: What does Encyclopedia of Life seek to accomplish? What are its objectives?" (http://www.eol.org/faq). *Encyclopedia of Life*. 2009. . Retrieved 2009-05-12.

[12] "FAQ: What are you doing to ensure functionality in different languages/cultures?" (http://www.eol.org/faq). *Encyclopedia of Life*. 2009. . Retrieved 2009-05-12.

[13] "E.O. Wilson: TED Prize wish: Help build the Encyclopedia of Life" (http://www.ted.com/index.php/talks/view/id/83). *Technology, Entertainment, Design (TED)*. 2007. . Retrieved 2009-05-12.

[14] "E. O. Wilson's Encyclopedia of Life gets over $50m in funding" (http://www.boingboing.net/2007/05/09/e_o_wilsons_encyclop. html). *boingboing*. 9 May 2007. . Retrieved 2009-05-12.

[15] "FAQ: How will the public at large use EOL?" (http://www.eol.org/faq). *Encyclopedia of Life*. 2009. . Retrieved 2009-05-12.

[16] "Leading Scientists Announce Creation Of Encyclopedia Of Life" (http://www.sciencedaily.com/releases/2007/05/070509185847. htm). *Science Daily*. 2007-05-09. . Adapted from a Harvard University news release.

[17] "Terms of use" (http://www.eol.org/content/page/terms_of_use). *Encyclopedia of Life*. 2009. . Retrieved 2009-05-12.

[18] Memorandum of Understanding with AmphibiaWeb (http://eol.org/content_partner/agreement/20)

[19] Memorandum of Understanding with Animal Diversity Web (http://eol.org/content_partner/agreement/21)

[20] Memorandum of Understanding with AntWeb (http://eol.org/content_partner/agreement/19)

[21] Memorandum of Understanding with ARKive (http://eol.org/content_partner/agreement/5978)

[22] Memorandum of Understanding with Atlas of Living Australia (http://eol.org/content_partner/agreement/8245)

[23] Memorandum of Understanding with Catalogue of Life (http://eol.org/content_partner/agreement/11)

[24] Memorandum of Understanding with FishBase (http://eol.org/content_partner/agreement/2)

[25] Memorandum of Understanding with Global Biodiversity Information Facility (GBIF) (http://eol.org/content_partner/agreement/4)

[26] Memorandum of Understanding with Micro*scope (http://eol.org/content_partner/agreement/14)

[27] Memorandum of Understanding with Naturalis (http://eol.org/content_partner/agreement/8244)

[28] Memorandum of Understanding with Tree of Life web project (http://eol.org/content_partner/agreement/3)

[29] Memorandum of Understanding with World Register of Marine Species (http://eol.org/content_partner/agreement/8848)

External links

- Encyclopedia of Life (http://www.eol.org/)

- "A Leap for All Life: World's Leading Scientists Announce Creation of "Encyclopedia of Life"" (http://www.eol.org/content/page/press_releases). Encyclopedia of Life. 2007-05-09.

- The Encyclopedia of Life - Introductory video (http://www.youtube.com/watch?v=6NwfGA4cxJQ) from May 2007

Enteromorpha

Enteromorpha is an outdated sea-plant taxon. Genetic analysis has resulted in the genus *Enteromorpha* being merged with the genus *Ulva*, commonly known as **Sea lettuce**.

Eochelodes

Eochelodes is an extinct genus of polyplacophoran mollusc.[1]

References

[1] van Belle, R. A. (1981). *Catalogue of Fossil Chitons*. ISBN 90 6279 018 6.

Eriinae

Eriinae	
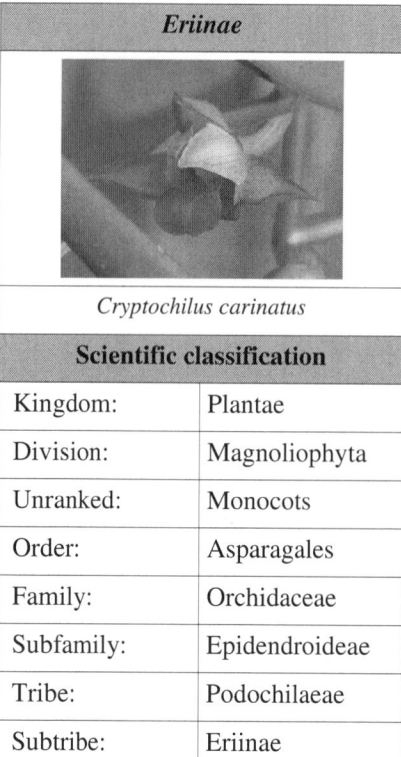	
Cryptochilus carinatus	
Scientific classification	
Kingdom:	Plantae
Division:	Magnoliophyta
Unranked:	Monocots
Order:	Asparagales
Family:	Orchidaceae
Subfamily:	Epidendroideae
Tribe:	Podochilaeae
Subtribe:	Eriinae

The Eriinae form a subtribe of *Podochilaeae*, a tribe of the orchid family (*Orchidaceae*). The name is derived from the genus *Eria*.

The subtribe includes eleven genera with more than 725 species of epiphytic, lithophytic or (more rarely) terrestrial orchids from tropical regions of India, China, Southeast Asia, and Africa.

The taxonomy of this group discussion there. This limited classification is based on Cameron, et al (1999),[1] and van den Berg, et al (2000), giving the following eleven genera:

Genera:

- *Ascidieria*
- *Ceratostylis*
- *Cryptochilus*
- *Epiblastus*
- *Eria*
- *Mediocalcar*
- *Porpax*
- *Pseuderia*
- *Sarcostoma*
- *Stolzia*
- *Trichotosia*

See also: Taxonomy and phylogeny of the orchid family

Footnotes

[1] Cameron et al (1999)

References

- Cameron, K.M. et al (1999). "A phylogenetic analysis of the Orchidaceae: evidence from rbcL nucleotide sequences." In: Yukawa and H.G, Hills and D.H. Goldman, (1999). *A phylogenetic analysis of the Orchidaceae: evidence from rbcL nucleotide sequences.*
- Pridgeon, Alec M., Phillip Cribb, and Mark W. Chase. (2005). *Genera Orchidacearum - Volume I: Epidendroideae.* Oxford Univ. Press. ISBN 0-198-50712-7.

Evolutionary grade

In alpha taxonomy, a **grade** refers to a taxon united by a level of morphological and/or physiological complexity. The term was coined by British biologist Julian Huxley, to contrast with clade, a strictly phylogenetic unit.[1]

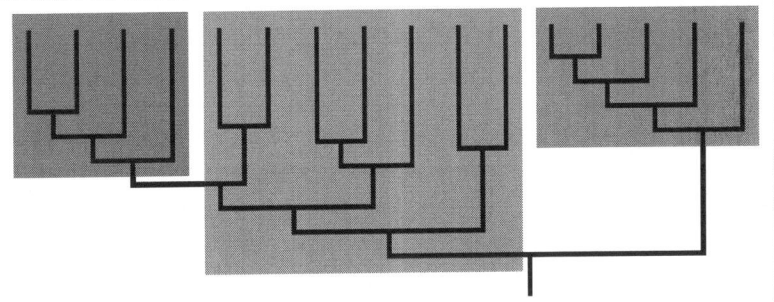

Cladogram (family tree) of a biological group. The green box may represent an *evolutionary grade*, a group united by anatomical and physiological traits rather than phylogeny. The red and blue boxes are *clades* (i.e., complete branches)

Definition

An evolutionary grade is a group of species united by morphological and/or physiological traits, that has given rise to another group that differs markedly from the ancestral condition, and is thus not considered part of the ancestral group. The ancestral group will not be phylogenetically complete (i.e. will not form a clade), so will represent a paraphyletic taxon.

The most commonly cited example is that of reptiles. In the early 19th century, the French naturalist Latreille was the first to divide tetrapods into the four familiar classes of amphibians, reptiles, birds and mammals.[2] In this system, reptiles are characterized by traits such as laying membranous or shelled eggs, having skin covered in scales and/or scutes, and having a 'cold-blooded' metabolism. However, the ancestors of mammals and birds also had these traits and so can be said to be reptiles, making the remaining reptiles a grade rather than a clade.[3] In microbiology, taxa that are thus seem as excluded fom their evolutionary grade parent group are called taxa in disguise.[4]

Paraphyletic taxa will often, but not always, represent evolutionary grades. In some cases paraphyletic taxa are united simply by not being part of any other groups, and give rise to so-called wastebasket taxa which may even be polyphyletic.

Grades in systematics

The traditional Linnaean way of defining taxa is through the use of anatomical traits. When the actual phylogenetic relationship is unknown, well defined groups sometimes turn out to be defined by traits that are primitive rather than derived. In Linnaean systematics, evolutionary grades are accepted in higher taxonomic ranks, though generally avoided at family level and below. In phylogenetic nomenclature evolutionary grades (or any other form of paraphyly) are not accepted.[5]

The genus *Australopithecus* is ancestral to *Homo*, yet actively in use in palaeoanthropology.

Where information about phylogenetic relationships is available, organisms are preferentially grouped into clades. Where data is lacking, or groups of uncertain relationship are to be compared, the cladistic method is limited and grade provides a useful tool for comparing organisms. This is particularly common in palaeontology, where fossils are often fragmentary and difficult to interpret. Thus, palaeontological works are often using evolutionary grades as formal or informal taxa, including examples such as Labyrinthodonts, Anapsids, Synapsids, Dinosaurs, Ammonites, Eurypterid, Lobopodes and many of the more well known taxa of human evolution.

Evolutionary grades, being united by gross morphological traits are often eminently recognizable in the field. While paraphyletic taxa are sought eliminated in taxonomy, such grades are sometimes kept as formal or informal groups on basis of their usefulness for laymen and field researchers.[5] When referring to a group of organisms, the term "grade" is usually enclosed in quotation marks to denote its status as a paraphyletic term.

Examples

- Bryophytes were long considered a natural group, defined as those land plants which lacked vascular systems. Molecular evidence shows that the bryophytes are not monophyletic since mosses, liverworts and hornworts are in fact separate lineages, with mosses closest to vascular plants.[6] However, the three clades have a similar degree of complexity, and the "bryophyte grade" is a useful benchmark when analysing early plants - it contains information about the status of fossils which cannot always be classified into extant groups.[7]

Bryophyta, mosses in the wide sense, are the physiologically primitive land plants

- Fish represent a grade, inasmuch as they have given rise to the land vertebrates. In fact, the three traditional classes of fish (Agnatha, Chondrichthyes and Osteichthyes) all represent evolutionary grades.[8]

- Amphibians in the biological sense (including the extinct Labyrinthodonts) represent a grade, in that they are also the ancestors of the amniotes.[8]

- Reptiles are composed of the cold-blooded amniotes, this excludes birds and mammals[8]

- Dinosaurs were proposed to be the ancestors of birds as early as the 1860s.[9] Yet the term sees both popular and scientific use, the dinosaurs representing an easily recognizable group.

- Lizards as a unit represent an evolutionary grade, defined by their retention of limbs relative to snakes and Amphisbaenans.[10]

References

[1] Huxley J. 1959. Clades and grades. In Cain A.J. (ed) *Function and taxonomic importance*. Systematics Association, London.

[2] Latreille, P.A. (1804). *Nouveau Dictionnaire à Histoire Naturelle*, xxiv; cited in Latreille, P.A. (1825).*Familles naturelles du règne animal, exposés succinctement et dans un ordre analytique*.

[3] Colin Tudge (2000). *The Variety of Life*. Oxford University Press. ISBN 0198604262.

[4] Lan, R; Reeves, PR (2002). "Escherichia coli in disguise: molecular origins of Shigella". *Microbes and infection / Institut Pasteur* **4** (11): 1125–32. PMID 12361912.

[5] Grant, Verne (1998), "Primary Classification and Phylogeny of the Polemoniaceae, with Comments on Molecular Cladistics" (http://www. amjbot.org/cgi/content/abstract/85/6/741), *American Journal of Botany* (Botanical Society of America) **85** (6): 741, doi:10.2307/2446408, JSTOR 2446408,

[6] Qiu, Y.L.; Li, L.; Wang, B.; Chen, Z.; Knoop, V.; Groth-malonek, M.; Dombrovska, O.; Lee, J.; Kent, L.; Rest, J.; Others, (2006). "The deepest divergences in land plants inferred from phylogenomic evidence" (http://www.pnas.org/cgi/content/abstract/103/42/15511). *Proceedings of the National Academy of Sciences* **103** (42): 15511. doi:10.1073/pnas.0603335103. PMC 1622854. PMID 17030812. . Retrieved 2008-05-06.

[7] e.g. Strother, P.K.; Al-hajri, S.; Traverse, A. (1996). "New evidence for land plants from the lower Middle Ordovician of Saudi Arabia" (http://geology.geoscienceworld.org/cgi/content/abstract/24/1/55). *Geology* **24** (1): 55–58. doi:10.1130/0091-7613(1996)024<0055:NEFLPF>2.3.CO;2. . Retrieved 2008-05-06.

[8] Romer, A.S. & T.S. Parsons. 1977. *The Vertebrate Body*. 5th ed. Saunders, Philadelphia. (6th ed. 1985)

[9] Huxley, Thomas H. (1870). "Further evidence of the affinity between the dinosaurian reptiles and birds". *Quarterly Journal of the Geological Society of London* **26**: 12–31. doi:10.1144/GSL.JGS.1870.026.01-02.08.

[10] Gibbons, J. Whitfield; Gibbons, Whit (1983). *Their Blood Runs Cold: Adventures With Reptiles and Amphibians*. Alabama: University of Alabama Press. pp. 164. ISBN 978-0817301354.

Figurative system of human knowledge

The **"figurative system of human knowledge"**, sometimes known as **the tree of Diderot and d'Alembert**, was a tree developed to represent the structure of knowledge itself, produced for the *Encyclopédie* by Jean le Rond d'Alembert and Denis Diderot.

The tree was a taxonomy of human knowledge, inspired by Francis Bacon's *The Advancement of Learning*. The three main branches of knowledge in the tree are: "Memory"/History, "Reason"/Philosophy, and "Imagination"/Poetry.

Notable is the fact that theology is ordered under 'Philosophy'. The historian Robert Darnton has argued that this categorization of religion as being subject to human reason, and not a source of knowledge in and of itself (revelation), was a significant factor in the controversy surrounding the work.[1] Additionally notice that 'Knowledge of God' is only a few nodes away from 'Divination' and 'Black Magic'.

The original "figurative system of human knowledge" tree, in French.

The original version, in French, can be seen in the graphic on the right. An image of the diagram with English translations superimposed over the French text [2] is available. Another example of English translation of the tree is available in literature (see the reference by Schwab). Below is a version of it rendered in English as a bulleted outline.

The Tree of Diderot and d'Alembert

"Detailed System of Human Knowledge" from the Encyclopédie.

- Understanding
  - Memory.
    - History.
      - Sacred (History of Prophets).
      - Ecclesiastical.
      - Civil, Ancient and Modern.
        - Civil History, properly said.
        - Literary History.
          - Memoirs.
          - Antiquities.
          - Complete Histories.
      - Natural.
        - Uniformity of Nature.
          - Celestial History.
          - History.
            - of Meteors.
            - of the Earth and the Sea.
            - of Minerals.
            - of Vegetables.
            - of Animals.
            - of the Elements.
        - Deviations of Nature.
          - Celestial Wonders.
          - Large Meteors.
          - Wonders of Land and Sea.
          - Monstrous Minerals.
          - Monstrous Vegetables.
          - Monstrous Animals.
          - Wonders of the Elements.
        - Uses of Nature
          - Arts, Crafts, Manufactures.
            - Work and Uses of Gold and Silver.
              - Minting.
              - Goldsmith.
              - Gold Spinning.
              - Gold Drawing.
              - Silversmith
              - Planisher, etc.
            - Work and Uses of Precious Stones.
              - Lapidary.
              - Diamond Cutting.

- Jeweler, etc.
- Work and Uses of Iron.
  - Large Forges.
  - Locksmith.
  - Tool Making.
  - Armorer.
  - Gun Making, etc.
- Work and Uses of Glass.
  - Glassmaking.
  - Plate-Glassmaking.
  - Mirror Making.
  - Optician.
  - Glazier, etc.
- Work and Uses of Skin.
  - Tanner.
  - Chamios Maker.
  - Leather Merchant.
  - Glove Making, etc.
- Work and Uses of Stone, Plaster, Slate, etc.
  - Practical Architecture.
  - Practical Sculpture.
  - Mason.
  - Tiler, etc.
- Work and Uses of Silk.
  - Spinning.
  - Milling.
  - Work like.
  - Velvet.
  - Brocaded Fabrics, etc.
- Work and Uses of Wool.
  - Cloth-Making.
  - Bonnet-Making, etc.
- Working and Uses, etc.

- Reason
  - Philosophy
    - General Metaphysics, or Ontology, or Science of Being in General, of Possibility, of Existence, of Duration, etc.
    - Science of God.
      - Natural Theology.
      - Revealed Theology.
      - Science of Good and Evil Spirits.
        - Divination.
        - Black Magic.

- Science of Man.
  - Pneumatology or Science of the Soul.
    - Reasonable.
    - Sensible.
  - Logic.
    - Art of Thinking.
      - Apprehension.
        - Science of Ideas
      - Judgement.
        - Science of Propositions.
      - Reasoning.
        - Induction.
      - Method.
        - Demonstration.
          - Analysis.
          - Synthesis.
    - Art of Remembering.
      - Memory.
        - Natural.
        - Artificial.
          - Prenotion.
          - Emblem.
      - Supplement to Memory.
        - Writing.
        - Printing.
          - Alphabet.
          - Cipher.
            - Arts of Writing, Printing, Reading, Deciphering.
              - Orthography.
    - Art of Communication
      - Science of the Instrument of Discourse.
        - Grammar.
          - Signs.
            - Gesture.
              - Pantomime.
              - Declamation.
            - Characters.
              - Ideograms.
              - Hieroglyphics.
              - Heraldry or Blazonry.
          - Prosody.

- Construction.
- Syntax.
- Philology.
- Critique.
  - Pedagogy.
    - Choice of Studies.
    - Manner of Teaching.
  - Science of Qualities of Discourse.
    - Rhetoric.
    - Mechanics of Poetry.
- Ethics.
  - General.
    - General Science of Good and Evil, of duties in general, of Virtue, of the necessity of being Virtuous, etc.
  - Particular.
    - Science of Laws or Jurisprudence.
      - Natural.
      - Economic.
      - Political.
        - Internal and External.
        - Commerce on Land and Sea.
- Science of Nature
  - Metaphysics of Bodies or, General Physics, of Extent, of Impenetrability, of Movement, of Word, etc.
  - Mathematics.
    - Pure.
      - Arithmetic.
        - Numeric .
        - Algebra.
          - Elementary.
          - Infinitesimal.
            - Differential.
            - Integral.
      - Gcomctry.
        - Elementary (Military Architecture, Tactics).
        - Transcendental (Theory of Courses).
    - Mixed.
      - Mechanics.
        - Statics.
          - Statics, properly said.
          - Hydrostatics.
        - Dynamics.
          - Dynamics, properly said.

- Ballistics.
- Hydrodynamics.
  - Hydraulics.
  - Navigation, Naval Architecture.
- Geometric Astronomy.
  - Cosmography.
    - Uranography.
    - Geography.
    - Hydrography.
  - Chronology.
  - Gnomonics.
- Optics.
  - Optics, properly said.
  - Dioptrics, Perspective.
  - Catoptrics.
- Acoustics.
- Pneumatics.
- Art of Conjecture. Analysis of Chance.
- Physicomathematics.
- Particular Physics.
  - Zoology.
    - Anatomy.
      - Simple.
      - Comparative.
    - Physiology.
    - Medicine.
      - Hygiene.
        - Hygiene, properly said.
        - Cosmetics (Orthopedics).
        - Athletics (Gymnastics).
      - Pathology.
      - Semiotics.
      - Treatment.
        - Diete.
        - Surgery.
        - Pharmacy.
    - Veterinary Medicine.
    - Horse Management.
    - Hunting.
    - Fishing.
    - Falconry.
  - Physical Astronomy.
    - Astrology.

- Judiciary Astrology.
- Physical Astrology.
- Meteorology.
- Cosmology.
  - Uranology.
  - Aerology.
  - Geology.
  - Hydrology.
- Botany.
  - Agriculture.
  - Gardening.
- Mineralogy.
- Chemistry.
  - Chemistry, properly said, (Pyrotechnics, Dyeing, etc.).
  - Metallurgy.
  - Alchemy.
  - Natural Magic.
- Imagination.
  - Poetry.
    - Profane.
      - Narrative.
        - Epic Poem
        - Madrigal
        - Epigram
        - Novel, etc.
      - Dramatic
        - Tragedy
        - Comedy
        - Pastoral, etc.
      - Parable
        - Allegory

(NOTE: THIS NEXT BRANCH SEEMS TO BELONG TO BOTH THE NARRATIVE AND DRAMATIC TREE
AS DEPICTED BY THE LINE DRAWN CONNECTING THE TWO.)

- Music
  - Theoretical
  - Practical
  - Instrumental
  - Vocal
- Painting
- Sculpture
- Engraving

Notes

[1]   Robert Darnton, "Philosophers Trim the Tree of Knowledge: The Epistemological Strategy of the *Encyclopedie*," *The Great Cat Massacre and Other Episodes in French Cultural History* (New York: Basic Books, Inc., 1984), 191-213.

[2]   http://www.hti.umich.edu/d/did/tree.html

References

- Robert Darnton, "Epistemological angst: From encyclopedism to advertising," in Tore Frängsmyr, ed., *The structure of knowledge: classifications of science and learning since the Renaissance* (Berkeley, CA: Office for the History of Science and Technology, University of California, Berkeley, 2001).

- Adams, David (2006) 'The Système figuré des Connaissances humaines and the structure of Knowledge in the Encyclopédie', in Ordering the World, ed. Diana Donald and Frank O'Gorman, London: Macmillan, p. 190-215.

- *Preliminary discourse to the Encyclopedia of Diderot*, Jean Le Rond d'Alembert, translated by Richard N. Schwab, 1995. ISBN 0-226-13476-8

External links

- ESSAI D'UNE DISTRIBUTION GÉNÉALOGIQUE DES SCIENCES ET DES ARTS PRINCIPAUX, published as a fold-out frontspiece in volume 1 of Pierre Mouchon, *Table analytique et raisonnée des matieres contenues dans les XXXIII volumes in-folio du Dictionnaire des sciences, des arts et des métiers, et dans son supplément*, Paris, Panckoucke 1780. (http://artfl.uchicago.edu/cactus/)

- http://commons.wikimedia.org/wiki/File:System-der-kenntnisse-des-menschen.jpg

Folk taxon

A **folk taxonomy** is a vernacular naming system, and can be contrasted with scientific taxonomy. Folk biological classification is the way peoples make sense of and organize their natural surroundings/the world around them, typically making generous use of form taxa like "shrubs", "bugs", "ducks", "ungulates" and the likes. Astrology is a folk taxonomy, while astronomy uses a scientific classification system, although both involve observations of the stars and celestial bodies and both terms seem equally scientific, with the former meaning "the teachings about the stars" and the latter "the rules about the stars". Folk taxonomies are generated from social knowledge and are used in everyday speech. They are distinguished from scientific taxonomies that claim to be disembedded from social relations and thus objective and universal.

Lycoperdon umbrinum is known as the umber-brown puffball. The folk taxonomic term puffball has no direct scientific equivalent, and does not slot precisely into scientific taxonomy.

Anthropologists have observed that taxonomies are generally embedded in local cultural and social systems, and serve various social functions. Perhaps the most well-known and influential study of folk taxonomies is Émile Durkheim's *The Elementary Forms of Religious Life*.

Folk taxonomies exist to allow popular identification of classes of objects, and apply to all areas of human activity. All parts of the world have their own systems of naming local plants and animals. These naming systems are a vital aid to survival and include information such as the fruiting patterns of trees and the habits of large mammals. These localised naming systems are folk taxonomies. Theophrastus recorded evidence of a Greek folk taxonomy for plants, but later formalized botanical taxonomies were laid out in the 18th century by Carolus Linnaeus.

Critics of the concept of "race" in humans argue that race is a folk taxonomy rather than a scientific classification.[1]

Scientists generally recognize that folk taxonomies conflict at times with Linnaean taxonomy or current interpretations of evolutionary relationships, and can tend to refer to generalized rather than quantitatively informative traits in an organism.

Notable folk taxa include Saber-toothed cat.

Notes

[1] Montagu, Ashley (2008 [1962]). "The Concept of Race" (http://www.americanethnography.com/article.php?id=36). *American Ethnography Quasimonthly.* . Retrieved 26 January 2009.

Bibliography

- Bailenson, JN, MS Shum, S Atran, DL Medin, JD Coley (2002) A bird's eye view:biological categorization and reasoning within and across cultures. Cognition 84:1-53
- Berlin, Brent (1972) 'Speculations on the growth of ethnobotanical nomenclature', *Language in Society*, 1, 51-86.
- Berlin, Brent & Dennis E. Breedlove & Peter H. Raven (1966) 'Folk taxonomies and biological classification', *Science*, 154, 273-275.
- Berlin, Brent & Dennis E. Breedlove & Peter H. Raven (1973) 'General principles of classification and nomenclature in folk biology', *American Anthropologist*, 75, 214-242.
- Brown, Cecil H. (1974) 'Unique beginners and covert categories in folk biological taxonomies', *American Anthropologist*, 76, 325-327.
- Brown, Cecil H. & John Kolar & Barbara J. Torrey & Tipawan Truoong-Quang & Phillip Volkman. (1976) 'Some general principles of biological and non-biological folk classification', *American Ethnologist*, 3, 1, 73-85.
- Brown, Cecil H. (1986) 'The growth of ethnobiological nomenclature', *Current Anthropology*, 27, 1, 1-19.

Folk taxonomy

A **folk taxonomy** is a vernacular naming system, and can be contrasted with scientific taxonomy. Folk biological classification is the way peoples make sense of and organize their natural surroundings/the world around them, typically making generous use of form taxa like "shrubs", "bugs", "ducks", "ungulates" and the likes. Astrology is a folk taxonomy, while astronomy uses a scientific classification system, although both involve observations of the stars and celestial bodies and both terms seem equally scientific, with the former meaning "the teachings about the stars" and the latter "the rules about the stars". Folk taxonomies are generated from social knowledge and are used in everyday speech. They are distinguished from scientific taxonomies that claim to be disembedded from social relations and thus objective and universal.

Lycoperdon umbrinum is known as the umber-brown puffball. The folk taxonomic term puffball has no direct scientific equivalent, and does not slot precisely into scientific taxonomy.

Anthropologists have observed that taxonomies are generally embedded in local cultural and social systems, and serve various social functions. Perhaps the most well-known and influential study of folk taxonomies is Émile Durkheim's *The Elementary Forms of Religious Life*.

Folk taxonomies exist to allow popular identification of classes of objects, and apply to all areas of human activity. All parts of the world have their own systems of naming local plants and animals. These naming systems are a vital aid to survival and include information such as the fruiting patterns of trees and the habits of large mammals. These localised naming systems are folk taxonomies. Theophrastus recorded evidence of a Greek folk taxonomy for plants, but later formalized botanical taxonomies were laid out in the 18th century by Carolus Linnaeus.

Critics of the concept of "race" in humans argue that race is a folk taxonomy rather than a scientific classification.[1]

Scientists generally recognize that folk taxonomies conflict at times with Linnaean taxonomy or current interpretations of evolutionary relationships, and can tend to refer to generalized rather than quantitatively informative traits in an organism.

Notable folk taxa include Saber-toothed cat.

Notes

[1] Montagu, Ashley (2008 [1962]). "The Concept of Race" (http://www.americanethnography.com/article.php?id=36). *American Ethnography Quasimonthly.* . Retrieved 26 January 2009.

Bibliography

- Bailenson, JN, MS Shum, S Atran, DL Medin, JD Coley (2002) A bird's eye view:biological categorization and reasoning within and across cultures. Cognition 84:1-53
- Berlin, Brent (1972) 'Speculations on the growth of ethnobotanical nomenclature', *Language in Society*, 1, 51-86.
- Berlin, Brent & Dennis E. Breedlove & Peter H. Raven (1966) 'Folk taxonomies and biological classification', *Science*, 154, 273-275.
- Berlin, Brent & Dennis E. Breedlove & Peter H. Raven (1973) 'General principles of classification and nomenclature in folk biology', *American Anthropologist*, 75, 214-242.
- Brown, Cecil H. (1974) 'Unique beginners and covert categories in folk biological taxonomies', *American Anthropologist*, 76, 325-327.

- Brown, Cecil H. & John Kolar & Barbara J. Torrey & Tipawan Truoong-Quang & Phillip Volkman. (1976) 'Some general principles of biological and non-biological folk classification', *American Ethnologist*, 3, 1, 73-85.
- Brown, Cecil H. (1986) 'The growth of ethnobiological nomenclature', *Current Anthropology*, 27, 1, 1-19.

Form classification

Form classification is the classification of organisms based on their morphology, which does not necessarily reflect their biological relationships. Form classification, generally restricted to palaeontology, reflects uncertainty; the goal of science is to move "form taxa" to biological taxa whose affinity is known.[1]

Strictly defined, form taxonomy is restricted to fossils that preserve too few characters for a conclusive taxonomic definition or assessment of their biological affinity, but whose study is made easier if a binomial name is available by which to identify them.[2] The term "Form classification" is preferred to "Form taxonomy"; taxonomy suggests that the classification implies a biological affinity, whereas in fact form classification is about giving a name to a group of morphologically-similar organisms that may not be related.[1]

Forms as taxa

Form taxa are groupings that are based on common overall forms. Early attempts at classification of labyrinthodonts was based of skull shape (the heavily armoured skulls often being the only preserved part). The amount of convergent evolution in the many groups lead to a number of polyphyletic taxa.[3] Such groups are united by a common mode of life, often one that is generalist, in consequence acquiring generally similar body shapes by convergent evolution. Ediacaran biota — whether they are the precursors of the Cambrian explosion of the fossil record, or are unrelated to any modern phylum — can currently

The Vendozoan *Charnia*. The actual nature or phylogeny of the Vendozsoan is not known, leading to form taxa only

only be grouped in "form taxa". Other examples include the seabirds and the "Graculavidae". The latter were initially described as the earliest family of Neornithes but are nowadays recognized to unite a number of unrelated early neornithine lineages, several of which probably later gave rise to the "seabird" form taxon of today.

Parataxa

A "parataxon", or "sciotaxon" (Gr. "shadow taxon"), is a classification based on incomplete data: for instance, the larval stage of an organism that cannot be matched up with an adult. It reflects a paucity of data that makes biological classification impossible.[1] A sciotaxon is defined as a taxon thought to be equivalent to a true taxon (orthotaxon), but whose identity cannot be established because the two candidate taxa are preserved in different ways and thus cannot be compared directly.[1]

Organ taxa

In paleobotany, the term is occasionally substituted for the more correct term "organ taxon", meaning a group of fossils of a particular part of a plant, such as a leaf or seed, whose parent plant is not known because the fossils were preserved unattached to the parent plant.[4] Names given to organ taxa may only be applied to the organs in question - and cannot be extended to the entire organism.[2] However, because a form genus is erected on morphological grounds (which do not change when its affinity is known), a form genus that *can* eventually be assigned to a higher biological group should not be renamed.[5]

Whilst organ genera can potentially be assigned to a family (even if the other parts of the plant are unknown), form genera usually cannot : although they may be referrable to higher categories (e.g. "Fungi" or "Animalia").[2]

The part of the plant is often, but not universally, indicated by the use of a suffix in the generic name:

- wood fossils may have generic names ending in *-xylon*
- leaf fossils generic names ending in *-phyllum*
- fruit fossils generic names ending in *-carpon*, *-carpum* or *-carpus*
- pollen fossils generic names ending in *-pollis* or *-pollenoides*.

Casual use

"Form taxon" can more casually be used to describe a wastebasket taxon: either a taxon that is not a natural (monophyletic) group but united by shared plesiomorphies, or a presumably artificial group of organisms whose true relationships are not known, being obscured by ecomorphological similarity. Well-known form taxa of this kind include "ducks", "fish", "reptiles" and "worms".

Footnotes

[1] Bengtson, S. (1985). "Taxonomy of Disarticulated Fossils". *Journal of Paleontology* **59** (6): 1350–1358. doi:10.2307/1304949. JSTOR 1304949.

[2] Faegri, Knut (January 1963). "Organ and Form Genera: Significance and Nomenclatural Treatment" (http://jstor.org/stable/1216676). *Taxon* **12** (1): 20–28. doi:10.2307/1216676. JSTOR 1216676. .

[3] Watson, D. M. S. (1920): The Structure, Evolution and Origin of the Amphibia. The "Orders' Rachitomi and Stereospondyli. *Philosophical Transactions of the Royal Society of London*, (series B), Vol. 209, pp. 1–73 Article from JSTOR (http://www.jstor.org/stable/92046)

[4] Gee, C. T.; Sander, P. M.; Petzelberger, B. E. M. (2003). "A Miocene rodent nut cache in coastal dunes of the Lower Rhine Embayment, Germany". *Palaeontology* **46**: 1133. doi:10.1046/j.0031-0239.2003.00337.x.

[5] Jansonius, J. (1974). "Form-Genera versus Organ-Genera; A Proposal" (http://jstor.org/stable/1218455). *Taxon* **23**: 867–868. doi:10.2307/1218455. .

Genetypes

Genetypes[1] is a concept that introduces a new terminology for genetic sequences from type specimens. This nomenclature integrates molecular systematics and terms used in biological taxonomy. This nomenclature is designed to label, or flag, genetic sequences that were sampled from type specimens. The nomenclature of genetypes proposes that genetic sequences from a holotype should be referred to as a "hologenetype" (from: **holo**type and **genetype**), sequences from a topotype will be a "topogenetype," and so forth. In addition, the genetic marker(s) used should also be incorporated into the nomenclature (e.g., paragenetype ND2).

The genetypes nomenclatural system could be used to flag "gold standard" sequences that due to their direct link to type specimens will be more credible than standard sequences whose species identification may be problematic. Misidentifications plague many sequences on GenBank and having some sequences that are linked to type specimens will help locate and manage misidentifications and to create positively IDed "gold standard" sequences available for comparison. It is suggested that this nomenclature be used in publications and databases that display or discuss sequences from type specimens[2] [3] .

Examples of genetypes currently available include:

Milyeringa brooksi paragenetype COI - HM590595 [4] *Milyeringa brooksi* paragenetype NDI - HM590607 [5]

References

[1] Chakrabarty, Prosanta (2010). "Genetypes: a concept to help integrate molecular systematics and traditional taxonomy" (http://www. mapress.com/zootaxa/2010/f/zt02632p068.pdf). *Zootaxa* **2632**: 67-68. .

[2] "JFB Instruction to Authors" (http://www.wiley.com/bw/submit.asp?ref=0022-1112). Journal of Fish Biology. .

[3] "Harrison et al. 2011" (http://onlinelibrary.wiley.com/doi/10.1111/j.1095-8649.2011.02979.x/full). Journal of Fish Biology. .

[4] http://www.ncbi.nlm.nih.gov/nuccore/HM590595

[5] http://www.ncbi.nlm.nih.gov/nuccore/HM590607

Glyptochiton

Glyptochiton is an extinct genus of polyplacophoran mollusc. Glyptochiton became extinct during the Carboniferous period.[1]

References

[1]   van Belle, R. A. (1981). *Catalogue of Fossil Chitons*. ISBN 90 6279 018 6.

Gotlandochiton

Gotlandochiton is an extinct genus of polyplacophoran mollusc. Gotlandochiton became extinct during the Silurian period.[1]

References

[1]   van Belle, R. A. (1981). *Catalogue of Fossil Chitons*. ISBN 90 6279 018 6.

Haeggochiton

Haeggochiton is an extinct genus of polyplacophoran mollusc known from a single occurrence in the Cretaceous of Europe.[1]

References

[1]   van Belle, R. A. (1981). *Catalogue of Fossil Chitons*. ISBN 90 6279 018 6.

Hanleya

Hanleya is an genus of polyplacophoran mollusc known from Oligocene and Miocene fossils;[1] it is represented today by a number of species including *H. sinica* Xu 1990 (China),[2] [3] *H. brachyplax* (Brazil)[4] and *H. hanleyi* Bean in Thorpe, 1844 (Chile), which feeds on sponges.[5]

References

[1] van Belle, R. A. (1981). *Catalogue of Fossil Chitons*. ISBN 90 6279 018 6.

[2] Fengshan, X. (1990). "New genus and species of Polyplacophora (Mollusca) from the East China Sea". *Chinese Journal of Oceanology and Limnology* **8** (4): 374–377. Bibcode 1990ChJOL...8..374X. doi:10.1007/BF02849683.

[3] .

[4] "Redescription of *Hanleya brachyplax* (Polyplacophora, Hanleyidae) from the south-southeastern Brazilian coast" (http://www.scielo.br/scielo.php?pid=S0031-10492010004000001&script=sci_arttext&tlng=pt). *Pap. Avulsos Zool. (São Paulo)* **50** (40). 2010. doi:10.1590.2FS0031-10492010004000001. ISSN 0031-1049. .

[5] .

Helminthochiton

Helminthochiton is an extinct genus of polyplacophoran mollusc. Helminthochiton became extinct during the Permian period.[1]

References

[1] van Belle, R. A. (1981). *Catalogue of Fossil Chitons*. ISBN 90 6279 018 6.

Heterochiton

Heterochiton is an extinct genus of polyplacophoran mollusc. Heterochiton became extinct during the Jurassic period.[1]

References

[1] van Belle, R. A. (1981). *Catalogue of Fossil Chitons.* ISBN 90 6279 018 6.

Holophyletic group

The concept *holophyletic group* is defined as "a group consisting of an ancestor and *all* its descendants". [1] [2]

References

[1] Ashlock, P.D. (1971). "Monophyly and associated terms" (http://www.jstor.org/stable/pdfplus/2412223.pdf). *Systematic Zoology* **20** (1): 63–69. doi:10.2307/2412223. .

[2] Envall, Mats (2008). "On the difference between mono-, holo-, and paraphyletic groups: a consistent distinction of process and pattern". *Biological Journal of the Linnean Society* **94**: 217–220. doi:10.1111/j.1095-8312.2008.00984.x.

Human genetic variation

Human genetic variation refers to genetic differences both within and among populations. There may be multiple variants of any given gene in the human population (alleles), leading to polymorphism. Many genes are not polymorphic, meaning that only a single allele is present in the population: that allele is then said to be fixed.[1]

No two humans are genetically identical. Even monozygotic twins, who develop from one zygote, have infrequent genetic differences due to mutations occurring during development and gene copy number variation has been observed.[2] Differences between individuals, even closely related individuals, are the key to techniques such as genetic fingerprinting. Alleles occur at different frequencies in different

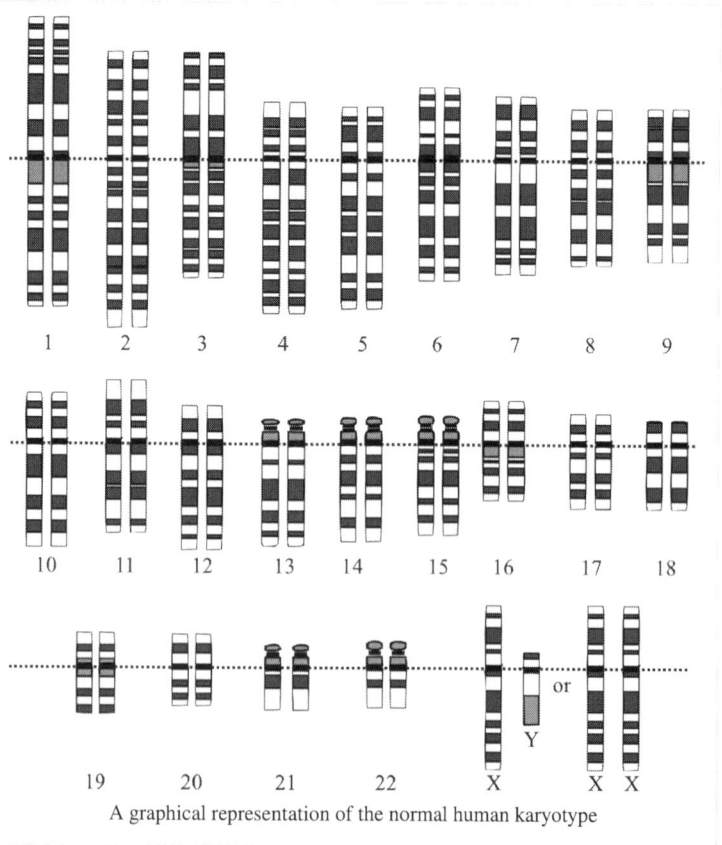

A graphical representation of the normal human karyotype

human populations, with populations that are more geographically and ancestrally remote tending to differ more.

Causes of differences between individuals include the exchange of genes during meiosis and various mutational events. There are at least two reasons why genetic variation exists between populations. Natural selection may confer an adaptive advantage to individuals in a specific environment if an allele provides a competitive advantage. Alleles under selection are likely to occur only in those geographic regions where they confer an advantage. The second main cause of genetic variation is due to the

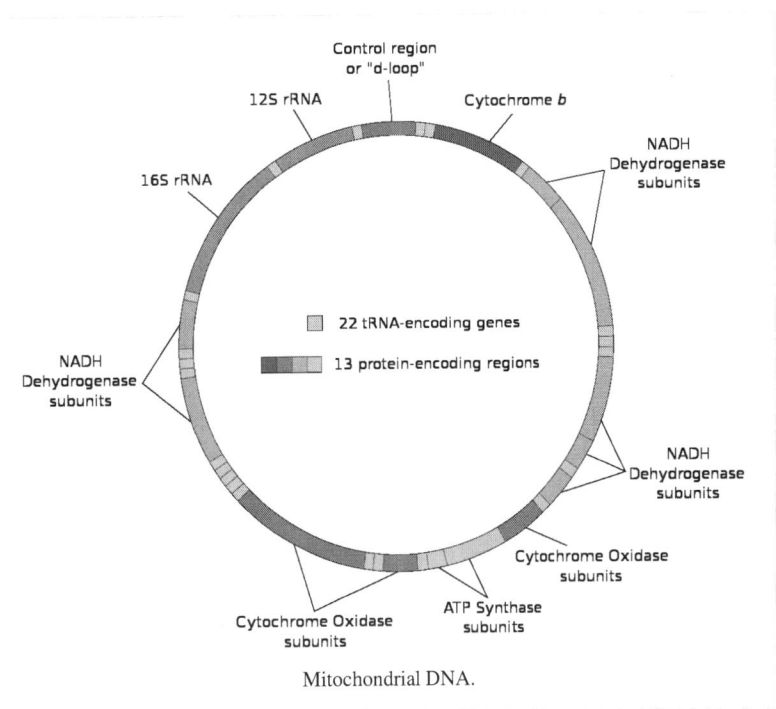

Mitochondrial DNA.

high degree of neutrality of most mutations. Most mutations do not appear to have any selective effect one way or the other on the organism. The main cause is genetic drift, this is the effect of random changes in the gene pool. In humans, founder effect and past small population size (increasing the likelihood of genetic drift) may have had an important influence in neutral differences between populations. The theory that humans recently migrated out of Africa supports this.

The study of human genetic variation has both evolutionary significance and medical applications. The study can help scientists understand ancient human population migrations as well as how different human groups are biologically related to one another. From a medical perspective the study of human genetic variation may be important because some disease causing alleles occur at a greater frequency in people from specific geographic regions.

Genetic variation

Genetic variation, variation in alleles of genes, occurs both within and among populations. Genetic variation is important because it provides the "raw material" for natural selection.

Measures of variation

"Genetic variation among individual humans occurs on many different scales, ranging from gross alterations in the human karyotype to single nucleotide changes."[3]

Single nucleotide polymorphisms

Nucleotide diversity is based on single mutations called single nucleotide polymorphisms (SNPs). The nucleotide diversity between humans is about 0.1%, which is 1 difference per 1,000 base pairs.[4] [5] [6] A difference of 1 in 1,000 nucleotides between two humans chosen at random amounts to approximately 3 million nucleotide differences since the human genome has about 3 billion nucleotides. Most of these SNPs are neutral but some are functional and influence phenotypic differences between humans through alleles. It is estimated that a total of 10 million SNPs exist in the human population of which at least 1% are functional (see International HapMap Project).

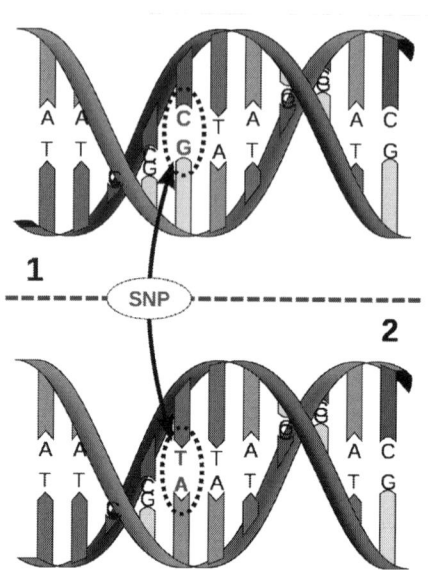

DNA molecule 1 differs from DNA molecule 2 at a single base-pair location (a C/T polymorphism).

Copy number variation

More recently a better understanding of the structure of the genome has been gained with the publication of two examples of full sequences of an individual's genome. This represents a new development because the Human Genome Project and a parallel project by Celera Genomics produced two haploid sequences, both of which were an amalgamation of sequences from many individuals.[7] Recently the diploid sequences of both Craig Venter and James Watson have been published. Analysis of diploid sequences has shown that non-SNP variation accounts for much more human genetic variation than single nucleotide diversity. This non-SNP variation includes copy number variation and results from deletions, inversions, insertions and duplications. It is estimated that approximately 0.4% of the genomes of unrelated people typically differ with respect to copy number. When copy number variation is included, human to human genetic variation is estimated to be at least 0.5% (99.5% similarity).[8] [9] [10] [11] [12] Copy number variations are inherited but can also arise during development.[13] [14] [15] [16] [17]

Epigenetics

Epigenetics is another type of genetic variation. "This type of variation arises from chemical tags that attach to DNA and affect how it gets read. The chemical tags, called epigenetic markings, act as switches that control how genes can be read."[18] At some alleles, the epigenetic state of the DNA, and associated phenotype, can be inherited transgenerationally.[19]

Genetic variability

Genetic variability is a measure of the tendency of individual genotypes in a population to vary (become different) from one another. Variability is different from genetic diversity, which is the amount of variation seen in a particular population.[20] The variability of a trait describes how much that trait tends to vary in response to environmental and genetic influences.

Clines

In biology, a cline is a term used to describe a continuum of species, populations, races, varieties, or forms of organisms that exhibit gradual phenotypic and/or genetic differences over a geographical area, typically as a result of environmental heterogeneity.[21] [22] [23] In the scientific study of human genetic variation, a gene cline can be rigorously defined and subjected to quantitative metrics.

Haplogroups

In the study of molecular evolution, a haplogroup is a group of similar haplotypes that share a common ancestor with a single nucleotide polymorphism (SNP) mutation. Haplogroups pertain to deep ancestral origins dating back thousands of years.[24]

In human genetics, the haplogroups most commonly studied are Y-chromosome (Y-DNA) haplogroups and mitochondrial DNA (mtDNA) haplogroups, both of which can be used to define genetic populations. Y-DNA is passed solely along the patrilineal line, from father to son, while mtDNA is passed down the matrilineal line, from mother to both daughter and son. The Y-DNA and mtDNA may change by chance mutation at each generation.

Variable number tandem repeats

A variable number tandem repeat (VNTR) is a location in a genome where a short nucleotide sequence is organized as a tandem repeat. These can be found on many chromosomes, and often show variations in length between individuals. Each variant acts as an inherited allele, allowing them to be used for personal or parental identification. Their analysis is useful in genetics and biology research, forensics, and DNA fingerprinting.

There are two principal families of VNTRs: microsatellites and minisatellites. The former are repeats of sequences less than about 5 base pairs in length, while the latter involve longer blocks.

History and geographic distribution

A 10-year study published in 2009 analyzed the patterns of variation at 1,327 DNA markers of 121 African populations, 4 African American populations, and 60 non-African populations.[25] [26] The research showed that there is more human genetic diversity in Africa than anywhere else on Earth. The genetic structure of Africans was traced to 14 ancestral population clusters and the ancestral origin of humans was determined to probably be located in southern Africa, near the border of Namibia and South Africa.

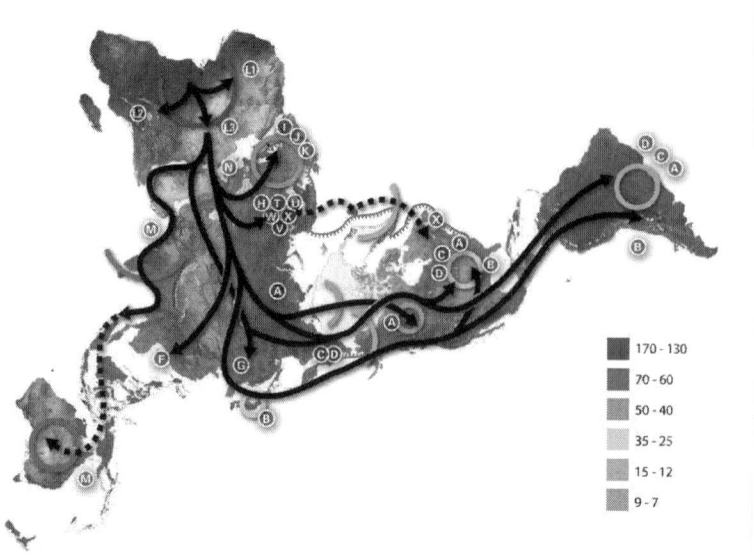

Map of the migration of modern humans out of Africa, based on mitochondrial DNA. Colored rings indicate thousand years before present.

Human genetic diversity decreases in native populations with migratory distance from Africa and this is thought to be the result of bottlenecks during human migration, which are events that temporarily reduce population size.[27] [28] It has been shown that variations in skull measurements decrease with distance from Africa at the same rate as the decrease in genetic diversity. These data support the Out of Africa theory over the multiregional origin of modern humans hypothesis. The aforementioned April 2009 study identifies the likely origin of modern human migration as being in southwestern Africa, near the coastal border of Namibia and Angola, and the exit point out of Africa as being in East Africa.[29]

The *recent African origin of modern humans* is the mainstream model describing the origin and early dispersal of anatomically modern humans, *Homo sapiens sapiens*. The theory is known popularly as the *(Recent) Out-of-Africa* model. The hypothesis originated in the 19th century, with Darwin's *Descent of Man*, but remained speculative until the 1980s when it was corroborated based on a study of present-day mitochondrial DNA, combined with evidence based on physical anthropology of archaic specimens.

According to both genetic and fossil evidence, archaic Homo sapiens evolved to anatomically modern humans solely in Africa, between 200,000 and 100,000 years ago, with members of one branch leaving Africa by 60,000 years ago and over time replacing earlier human populations such as Neanderthals and *Homo erectus*. According to this theory, around the above time frame, one of the African subpopulations went through a process of speciation prohibiting gene flow between African and Eurasian Human populations.

Population genetics

In the field of population genetics, it is believed that the distribution of neutral polymorphisms among contemporary humans reflects human demographic history. It is believed that humans passed through a population bottleneck before a rapid expansion coinciding with migrations out of Africa leading to an African-Eurasian divergence around 100,000 years ago (ca. 5,000 generations), followed by a European-Asian divergence about 40,000 years ago (ca. 2,000 generations). Richard G. Klein, Nicholas Wade and Spencer Wells, among others, have postulated that modern humans did not leave Africa and successfully colonize the rest of the world until as recently as 60,000 - 50,000 years B.P., pushing back the dates for subsequent population splits as well.

The rapid expansion of a previously small population has two important effects on the distribution of genetic variation. First, the so-called founder effect occurs when founder populations bring only a subset of the genetic variation from their ancestral population. Second, as founders become more geographically separated, the probability that two individuals from different founder populations will mate becomes smaller. The effect of this assortative mating is to reduce gene flow between geographical groups, and to increase the genetic distance between groups. The expansion of humans from Africa affected the distribution of genetic variation in two other ways. First, smaller (founder) populations experience greater genetic drift because of increased fluctuations in neutral polymorphisms. Second, new polymorphisms that arose in one group were less likely to be transmitted to other groups as gene flow was restricted.

Our history as a species also has left genetic signals in regional populations. For example, in addition to having higher levels of genetic diversity, populations in Africa tend to have lower amounts of linkage disequilibrium than do populations outside Africa, partly because of the larger size of human populations in Africa over the course of human history and partly because the number of modern humans who left Africa to colonize the rest of the world appears to have been relatively low (Gabriel *et al.* 2002). In contrast, populations that have undergone dramatic size reductions or rapid expansions in the past and populations formed by the mixture of previously separate ancestral groups can have unusually high levels of linkage disequilibrium (Nordborg and Tavare 2002).

Many other geographic, climatic, and historical factors have contributed to the patterns of human genetic variation seen in the world today. For example, population processes associated with colonization, periods of geographic isolation, socially reinforced endogamy, and natural selection all have affected allele frequencies in certain populations (Jorde *et al.* 2000b; Bamshad and Wooding 2003). In general, however, the recency of our common ancestry and continual gene flow among human groups have limited genetic differentiation in our species.

Distribution of variation

The distribution of genetic variants within and among human populations are impossible to describe succinctly because of the difficulty of defining a "population," the clinal nature of variation, and heterogeneity across the genome (Long and Kittles 2003). In general, however, an average of 85% of genetic variation exists within local populations, ~7% is between local populations within the same continent, and ~8% of variation occurs between large groups living on different continents,. (Lewontin 1972; Jorde *et al.* 2000a; Hinds *et al.* 2005). The recent African origin theory for humans would predict that in Africa there exists a great deal more diversity than elsewhere, and that diversity should decrease the further from Africa a population is sampled. Long and Kittles show that indeed, African populations contain about 100% of human genetic diversity, whereas in populations outside of Africa diversity is much reduced, for example in their population from New Guinea only about 70% of human variation is captured.

Phenotypic variation

Sub-Saharan Africa has the most human genetic diversity and the same has been shown to hold true for phenotypic diversity.[27] Phenotype is connected to genotype through gene expression. Genetic diversity decreases smoothly with migratory distance from that region, which many scientists believe to be the origin of modern humans, and that decrease is mirrored by a decrease in phenotypic variation. Skull measurements are an example of a physical attribute whose within-population variation decreases with distance from Africa.

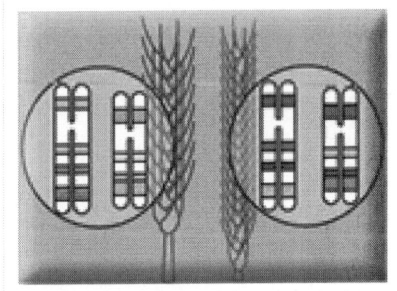

Genetic variation can cause variation in phenotype.

The distribution of many physical traits resembles the distribution of genetic variation within and between human populations (American Association of Physical Anthropologists 1996; Keita and Kittles 1997). For example, ~90% of the variation in human head shapes occurs within continental groups, and ~10% separates groups, with a greater variability of head shape among individuals with recent African ancestors (Relethford 2002).

Faces show phenotypic variation. Some of this is caused by genetic variation.

A prominent exception to the common distribution of physical characteristics within and among groups is skin color. Approximately 10% of the variance in skin color occurs within groups, and ~90% occurs between groups (Relethford 2002). This distribution of skin color and its geographic patterning — with people whose ancestors lived predominantly near the equator having darker skin than those with ancestors who lived predominantly in higher latitudes — indicate that this attribute has been under strong selective pressure. Darker skin appears to be strongly selected for in equatorial regions to prevent sunburn, skin cancer, the photolysis of folate, and damage to sweat glands (Sturm *et al.* 2001; Rees 2003).

A study published in 2007 found that 25% of genes showed different levels of gene expression between populations of European and Asian descent.[30] [31] [32] [33] [34] The primary cause of this difference in gene expression was thought to be SNPs in gene regulatory regions of DNA. Another study published in 2007 found that approximately 83% of genes were expressed at different levels among individuals and about 17% between populations of European and African descent.[35] [36]

Archaic admixture

Interbreeding of Neanderthals and anatomically modern humans during the Middle Paleolithic is a hypothesis. In May 2010, the Neanderthal Genome Project presented genetic evidence that interbreeding did likely take place and that a small but significant portion of Neanderthal admixture is present in the DNA of modern non-African populations.

In December 2010, a study found that between 4% and 6% of the genome of Melanesians (represented by the Papua New Guinean and Bougainville Islander) derives from Denisova hominin - a previously unknown species, which shares common origin with Neanderthals.It was possibly introduced during the early migration of the ancestors of Melanesians into Southeast Asia. This history of interaction suggests that Denisovans once ranged widely over eastern Asia.[37]

Melanesians thus emerge as the most archaic-admixed population, having Denisovan/Neandertal-related admixture of ~8%.

Categorization of the world population

New data on human genetic variation has reignited the debate about a possible biological basis for categorization of humans into races. Most of the controversy surrounds the question of how to interpret the genetic data and whether conclusions based on it are sound. Some researchers argue that self-identified race can be used as an indicator of geographic ancestry for certain health risks and medications.

Although the genetic differences among human groups are relatively small, these differences in certain genes such as duffy, ABCC11, SLC24A5, called ancestry-informative markers (AIMs) nevertheless can be used to reliably situate many individuals within broad, geographically based groupings. For example, computer analyses of hundreds of polymorphic loci sampled in globally distributed populations have revealed the existence of genetic clustering that roughly is associated with groups that historically have occupied large continental and subcontinental regions (Rosenberg *et al.* 2002; Bamshad *et al.* 2003).

Some commentators have argued that these patterns of variation provide a biological justification for the use of traditional racial categories. They argue that the continental clusterings correspond roughly with the division of human beings into sub-Saharan Africans; Europeans, Western Asians, Central Asians, Southern Asians and Northern Africans; Eastern Asians, Southeast Asians, Polynesians and Native Americans; and other inhabitants of Oceania (Melanesians, Micronesians & Australian Aborigines) (Risch *et al.* 2002). Other observers disagree, saying that the same data undercut traditional notions of racial groups (King and Motulsky 2002; Calafell 2003; Tishkoff and Kidd 2004[5]). They point out, for example, that major populations considered races or subgroups within races do not necessarily form their own clusters.

Chart showing human genetic clustering.

Furthermore, because human genetic variation is clinal, many individuals affiliate with two or more continental groups. Thus, the genetically based "biogeographical ancestry" assigned to any given person generally will be broadly distributed and will be accompanied by sizable uncertainties (Pfaff *et al.* 2004).

In many parts of the world, groups have mixed in such a way that many individuals have relatively recent ancestors from widely separated regions. Although genetic analyses of large numbers of loci can produce estimates of the percentage of a person's ancestors coming from various continental populations (Shriver *et al.* 2003; Bamshad *et al.* 2004), these estimates may assume a false distinctiveness of the parental populations, since human groups have exchanged mates from local to continental scales throughout history (Cavalli-Sforza *et al.* 1994; Hoerder 2002). Even with large numbers of markers, information for estimating admixture proportions of individuals or groups is limited, and estimates typically will have wide confidence intervals (Pfaff *et al.* 2004).

Genetic clustering

Genetic data can be used to infer population structure and assign individuals to groups that often correspond with their self-identified geographical ancestry. Recently, Lynn Jorde and Steven Wooding argued that "Analysis of many loci now yields reasonably accurate estimates of genetic similarity among individuals, rather than populations. Clustering of individuals is correlated with geographic origin or ancestry."[4]

Forensic anthropology

Forensic anthropologists can determine geographic ancestry (i.e. Asian, African, or European) from skeletal remains with a high degree of accuracy by conducting bone analysis.[38] Studies have shown that individual test methods such as midfacial measurements and femur traits can be over 80 percent accurate, and in combination can achieve very high levels of accuracy. The skeletons of mixed-ancestry individuals can, however, exhibit characteristics of more than one ancestral group.

Admixture

Miscegenation between two populations reduces the average genetic distance between the populations. During the Age of Discovery which began in the early 15th century, European explorers sailed all around the globe, reaching all the major continents. In the process they came into contact with many populations that had been isolated for thousands of years. It is generally accepted that the Tasmanian aboriginals were the most isolated group on the planet. They were driven to extinction by European explorers, however a number of their descendants survive today as a result of admixture with Europeans. This is an example of how modern migrations have begun to reduce the genetic divergence of the human race.

The demographic composition of the old world has not changed significantly since

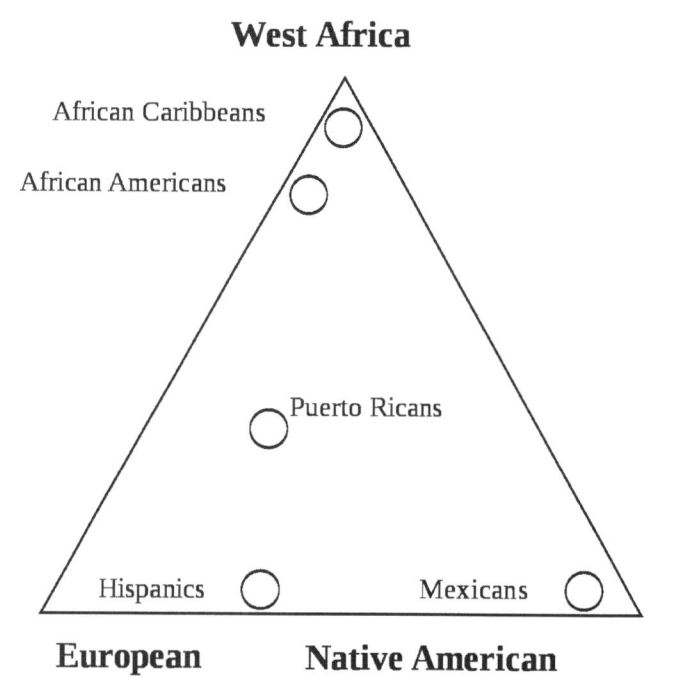

Triangle plot shows average admixture of five North American ethnic groups. Individuals that self-identify with each group can be found at many locations on the map, but on average groups tend to cluster differently.

the age of discovery. However new world demographics were radically changed within a short time following the voyage of Columbus. The colonization of the Americas brought Native Americans into contact with the distant populations of Europe, Africa, and Asia. As a result many countries in the Americas have significant and complex multiracial populations. Furthermore many who identify themselves by only one race still have multiracial ancestry.

Health

Differences in allele frequencies contribute to group differences in the incidence of some monogenic diseases, and they may contribute to differences in the incidence of some common diseases (Risch *et al.* 2002; Burchard *et al.* 2003; Tate and Goldstein 2004). For the monogenic diseases, the frequency of causative alleles usually correlates best with ancestry, whether familial (for example, Ellis-van Creveld syndrome among the Pennsylvania Amish), ethnic (Tay-Sachs disease among Ashkenazi Jewish populations), or geographical (hemoglobinopathies among people with ancestors who lived in malarial regions). To the extent that ancestry corresponds with racial or ethnic groups or subgroups, the incidence of monogenic diseases can differ between groups categorized by race or ethnicity, and health-care professionals typically take these patterns into account in making diagnoses.

Even with common diseases involving numerous genetic variants and environmental factors, investigators point to evidence suggesting the involvement of differentially distributed alleles with small to moderate effects. Frequently cited examples include hypertension (Douglas *et al.* 1996), diabetes (Gower *et al.* 2003), obesity (Fernandez *et al.* 2003), and prostate cancer (Platz *et al.* 2000). However, in none of these cases has allelic variation in a susceptibility gene been shown to account for a significant fraction of the difference in disease prevalence among groups, and the role of genetic factors in generating these differences remains uncertain (Mountain and Risch 2004).

Neil Risch of Stanford University has proposed that self-identified race/ethnic group could be a valid means of categorization in the USA for public health and policy considerations.[39] [40] While a 2002 paper by Noah Rosenberg's group makes a similar claim "The structure of human populations is relevant in various epidemiological contexts. As a result of variation in frequencies of both genetic and nongenetic risk factors, rates of disease and of such phenotypes as adverse drug response vary across populations. Further, information about a patient's population of origin might provide health care practitioners with information about risk when direct causes of disease are unknown."[41]

Genome projects

Human genome projects are scientific endeavors that determine or study the structure of the human genome. The Human Genome Project was a landmark genome project.

References

[1] When all genes are fixed within a population, so every member of the population is genetically identical, the population is said to be clonal. This occurs in species that reproduce asexually.

[2] (http://www.cell.com/AJHG/abstract/S0002-9297(08)00102-X)

[3] Kidd JM, Cooper GM, Donahue WF, *et al.* (May 2008). "Mapping and sequencing of structural variation from eight human genomes" (http://www.nature.com/nature/journal/v453/n7191/full/nature06862.html). *Nature* **453** (7191): 56–64. doi:10.1038/nature06862. PMC 2424287. PMID 18451855. .

[4] Jorde, Lynn B.; Wooding, Stephen P. (2004). "Genetic variation, classification and race" (http://www.nature.com/ng/journal/v36/n11s/full/ng1435.html). *Nature Genetics* **36** (11 Suppl): S28–S33. doi:10.1038/ng1435. PMID 15508000. .

[5] Tishkoff SA, Kidd KK (November 2004). "Implications of biogeography of human populations for 'race' and medicine" (http://www.nature.com/ng/journal/v36/n11s/full/ng1438.html). *Nat. Genet.* **36** (11 Suppl): S21–7. doi:10.1038/ng1438. PMID 15507999. .

[6] http://shrn.stanford.edu/workshops/revisitingrace/Bamshadetal2004.pdf

[7] Gross L (2007). "A New Human Genome Sequence Paves the Way for Individualized Genomics" (http://biology.plosjournals.org/perlserv/?request=get-document&doi=10.1371/journal.pbio.0050266&ct=1). *PLoS Biol* **5** (10): e266. doi:10.1371/journal.pbio.0050266. PMC 1964778. PMID 20076646. .

[8] http://www.jcvi.org/cms/press/press-releases/full-text/article/first-individual-diploid-human-genome-published-by-researchers at j craig venter institute/

[9] Levy S, Sutton G, Ng PC, Feuk L, Halpern AL, *et al.* (2007). "The Diploid Genome Sequence of an Individual Human" (http://biology.plosjournals.org/perlserv/?request=get-document&doi=10.1371/journal.pbio.0050254&ct=1). *PLoS Biol* **5** (10): e254. doi:10.1371/journal.pbio.0050254. PMC 1964779. PMID 17803354. .

[10] http://www.genome.gov/10001551#1

[11] http://www.thetech.org/genetics/news.php?id=74

[12] http://www.sciencedaily.com/releases/2007/09/070904072204.htm

[13] http://www.eurekalert.org/pub_releases/2007-12/bcom-cnv122607.php

[14] Lee JA, Carvalho CM, Lupski JR (December 2007). "A DNA replication mechanism for generating nonrecurrent rearrangements associated with genomic disorders" (http://linkinghub.elsevier.com/retrieve/pii/S0092-8674(07)01541-3). *Cell* **131** (7): 1235–47. doi:10.1016/j.cell.2007.11.037. PMID 18160035. .

[15] Redon R, Ishikawa S, Fitch KR, *et al.* (November 2006). "Global variation in copy number in the human genome" (http://www.nature.com/nature/journal/v444/n7118/abs/nature05329.html). *Nature* **444** (7118): 444–54. doi:10.1038/nature05329. PMC 2669898 PMID 17122850. .

[16] http://anthropology.net/2007/07/30/copy-number-variations-throughout-60-million-years-of-human-and-primate-evolution/

[17] http://www.sickkids.ca/mediaroom/custom/CNV_FAQ.pdf

[18] http://www.nigms.nih.gov/Publications/Factsheet_GeneticVariation.htm

[19] http://www.sciencedirect.com/science?_ob=ArticleURL&_udi=B6VRT-47P896D-4&_user=10&_rdoc=1&_fmt=&_orig=search&_sort=d&view=c&_acct=C000050221&_version=1&_urlVersion=0&_userid=10&md5=b82477a35626ed5a4f4131ae33fcc5dd

[20] *Variation and Variability* (http://www.cbc.yale.edu/old/cce/papers/ALife/node2.html). Yale University. 1995. ISBN 1588112802. . Retrieved 2007-05-24.

[21] Microsoft Encarta Premium 2009: "cline"

[22] King, Stansfield, Mulligan: *A dictionary of genetics*, 7th ed. (2006), Oxford University Press:"cline"

[23] Begon, Townsend, Harper - *Ecology: From individuals to ecosystems* , Blackwell Publishing, 4th ed. (2006), p. 10

[24] The International Society of Genetic Genealogy see Haplogroup definition in DNA-NEWBIE GLOSSARY (http://www.isogg.org)

[25] http://www.sciencedaily.com/releases/2009/04/090430144524.htm

[26] Tishkoff SA, Reed FA, Friedlaender FR, *et al.* (May 2009). "The genetic structure and history of Africans and African Americans" (http://www.sciencemag.org/cgi/content/full/324/5930/1035). *Science* **324** (5930): 1035–44. doi:10.1126/science.1172257. PMC 2947357. PMID 19407144. .

[27] http://www.sciencedaily.com/releases/2007/07/070718140829.htm

[28] Manica A, Amos W, Balloux F, Hanihara T (July 2007). "The effect of ancient population bottlenecks on human phenotypic variation" (http://www.nature.com/nature/journal/v448/n7151/abs/nature05951.html). *Nature* **448** (7151): 346–8. doi:10.1038/nature05951. PMC 1978547. PMID 17637668. .

[29] BBC World News "Africa's genetic secrets unlocked" (http://news.bbc.co.uk/2/hi/science/nature/8027269.stm), 1 May 2009; the results were published in the online edition of the journal *Science.*

[30] http://www.the-scientist.com/news/home/40507/

[31] http://www.nature.com/ng/journal/v39/n2/abs/ng1955.html

[32] http://www.scientificamerican.com/article.cfm?id=ethnic-differences-traced

[33] http://www.nature.com/news/2007/070101/full/news070101-8.html

[34] http://www.bionews.org.uk/page_12961.asp

[35] http://anthropology.net/2008/02/29/differences-of-gene-expression-between-human-populations/

[36] http://www.sciencedirect.com/science?_ob=ArticleURL&_udi=B8JDD-4RDPP3P-D&_user=2139817& _coverDate=03%2F31%2F2007&_rdoc=1&_fmt=high&_orig=search&_origin=search&_sort=d&_docanchor=&view=c& _acct=C000054277&_version=1&_urlVersion=0&_userid=2139817&md5=c8ca953fcd1680316e93c43b86b89d3b&searchtype=a

[37] Reich, David; Green, Richard E.; Kircher, Martin; Krause, Johannes; Patterson, Nick; Durand, Eric Y.; Viola, Bence; Briggs, Adrian W. et al. (2010). "Genetic history of an archaic hominin group from Denisova Cave in Siberia". *Nature* **468** (7327): 1053–1060. doi:10.1038/nature09710. PMID 21179161

[38] http://www.pbs.org/wgbh/nova/first/gill.html

[39] Tang, Hua; Quertermous, Tom; Rodriguez, Beatriz; Kardia, Sharon L. R.; Zhu, Xiaofeng; Brown, Andrew; Pankow, James S.; Province, Michael A. et al. (2005 February;). "Genetic Structure, Self-Identified Race/Ethnicity, and Confounding in Case-Control Association Studies". *Am J Hum Genet* **76** (2): 268–275. doi:10.1086/427888. PMC 1196372. PMID 15625622.

[40] Neil Risch, Esteban Burchard, Elad Ziv and Hua Tang 2002 Categorization of humans in biomedical research: genes, race and disease (http://genomebiology.com/2002/3/7/comment/2007) Genome Biology *3:comment*

[41] Rosenberg Noah A., Pritchard Jonathan K., Weber James L., Cann Howard M., Kidd Kenneth K., Zhivotovsky Lev A., Feldman Marcus W. (2002). "Genetic Structure of Human Populations". *Science* **298** (5602): 2381–5. doi:10.1126/science.1078311. PMID 12493913.

- Race, Ethnicity, and Genetics Working Group (October 2005). "The use of racial, ethnic, and ancestral categories in human genetics research". *Am. J. Hum. Genet.* **77** (4): 519–32. doi:10.1086/491747. PMC 1275602. PMID 16175499.

- Altmüller J, Palmer LJ, Fischer G, Scherb H, Wjst M (2001). "Genomewide scans of complex human diseases: true linkage is hard to find". *Am J Hum Genet* **69** (5): 936–950. doi:10.1086/324069. PMC 1274370. PMID 11565063.

- Aoki K (2002). "Sexual selection as a cause of human skin colour variation: Darwin's hypothesis revisited". *Ann Hum Biol* **29** (6): 589–608. doi:10.1080/0301446021000019144. PMID 12573076.

- Bamshad, Michael; Wooding, Stephen; Salisbury, Benjamin A.; Stephens, J. Claiborne (2004). "Deconstructing The Relationship Between Genetics And Race" (http://www.nature.com/cgi-taf/DynaPage.taf?file=/nrg/journal/v5/n8/abs/nrg1401_fs.html). *Nature Reviews Genetics* **5** (8): 598–609. doi:10.1038/nrg1401. PMID 15266342. reprint-zip (http://www.xmission.com/~wooding/pdfs/bamshad_race04.zip)

- Bamshad M, Wooding SP (2003). "Signature of natural selection in the human genome". *Nat Rev Genet* **4** (2): 99–111. doi:10.1038/nrg999. PMID 12560807.

- Bamshad MJ, Wooding S, Watkins WS, Ostler CT, Batzer MA, Jorde LB (2003). "Human population genetic structure and inference of group membership". *Am J Hum Genet* **72** (3): 578–589. doi:10.1086/368061. PMC 1180234. PMID 12557124.

- Cann, Rebecca, M. Stoneking, A. Wilson (January 1987). "Mitochondrial DNA and Human Evolution". *Nature* **325** (6099): 31–6. doi:10.1038/325031a0. PMID 3025745.

- Cardon LR, Abecasis GR (2003). "Using haplotype blocks to map human complex trait loci". *Trends Genet* **19** (3): 135–140. doi:10.1016/S0168-9525(03)00022-2. PMID 12615007.

- Cavalli-Sforza LL, Feldman MW (2003). "The application of molecular genetic approaches to the study of human evolution". *Nat Genet* **33** (Suppl): 266–275. doi:10.1038/ng1113. PMID 12610536.

- Collins FS (2004). "What we do and don't know about "race," "ethnicity," genetics and health at the dawn of the genome era". *Nat Genet* **36** (11 Suppl): S13–5. doi:10.1038/ng1436. PMID 15507997.
- Collins FS, Green ED, Guttmacher AE, Guyer MS, for the US National Human Genome Research Institute (2003). "A vision for the future of genomics research". *Nature* **422** (6934): 835–847. doi:10.1038/nature01626. PMID 12695777.
- Ebersberger I, Metzler D, Schwarz C, Pääbo S (2002). "Genomewide comparison of DNA sequences between humans and chimpanzees". *Am J Hum Genet* **70** (6): 1490–7. doi:10.1086/340787. PMC 379137. PMID 11992255.
- Edwards, AW (2003). "Human genetic diversity: Lewontin's fallacy" (http://www3.interscience.wiley.com/cgi-bin/abstract/104546274/ABSTRACT). *Bioessays* **25** (8): 798–801. doi:10.1002/bies.10315. PMID 12879450.
- Foster MW, Sharp RR (2004). "Beyond race: towards a whole-genome perspective on human populations and genetic variation". *Nat Rev Genet* **5** (10): 790–6. doi:10.1038/nrg1452. PMID 15510170.
- Foster MW, Sharp RR, Freeman WL, Chino M, Bernsten D, Carter TH (1999). "The role of community review in evaluating the risks of human genetic variation research". *Am J Hum Genet* **64** (6): 1719–27. doi:10.1086/302415. PMC 1377916. PMID 10330360.
- Gabriel SB, Schaffner SF, Nguyen H, Moore JM, Roy J, Blumenstiel B, Higgins J, DeFelice M, Lochner A, Faggart M, Liu-Cordero SN, Rotimi C, Adeyemo A, Cooper R, Ward R, Lander ES, Daly MJ, Altshuler D (2002). "The structure of haplotype blocks in the human genome". *Science* **296** (5576): 2225–9. doi:10.1126/science.1069424. PMID 12029063.
- Harding RM, Healy E, Ray AJ, Ellis NS, Flanagan N, Todd C, Dixon C, Sajantila A, Jackson IJ, Birch-Machin MA, Rees JL (2000). "Evidence for variable selective pressures at MC1R". *Am J Hum Genet* **66** (4): 1351–61. doi:10.1086/302863. PMC 1288200. PMID 10733465.
- Ingman M, Kaessmann H, Pääbo S, Gyllensten U (2000). "Mitochondrial genome variation and the origin of modern humans". *Nature* **408** (6813): 708–713. doi:10.1038/35047064. PMID 11130070.
- International HapMap Consortium; Gibbs, Richard A.; Belmont, John W.; Hardenbol, Paul; Willis, Thomas D.; Yu, Fuli; Yang, Huanming; Ch'ang, Lan-Yang et al. (2003). "The International HapMap Project" *Nature* **426** (6968): 789–796. doi:10.1038/nature02168. PMID 14685227.
- International HapMap Consortium (2004). "Integrating ethics and science in the International HapMap Project". *Nat Rev Genet* **5** (6): 467–475. doi:10.1038/nrg1351. PMC 2271136. PMID 15153999.
- International Human Genome Sequencing Consortium (2001). "Initial sequencing and analysis of the human genome". *Nature* **409** (6822): 860–921. doi:10.1038/35057062. PMID 11237011.
- Jorde LB, Bamshad M, Rogers AR (1998). "Using mitochondrial and nuclear DNA markers to reconstruct human evolution" (http://jorde-lab.genetics.utah.edu/elibrary/Jorde_1998.pdf) (PDF). *BioEssays* **20** (2): 126–136. doi:10.1002/(SICI)1521-1878(199802)20:2<126::AID-BIES5>3.0.CO;2-R. PMID 9631658.
- Jorde LB, Watkins WS, Bamshad MJ, Dixon ME, Ricker CE, Seielstad MT, Batzer MA (2000a). "The distribution of human genetic diversity: a comparison of mitochondrial, autosomal, and Y-chromosome data". *Am J Hum Genet* **66** (3): 979–988. doi:10.1086/302825. PMC 1288178. PMID 10712212.
- Jorde LB, Watkins WS, Kere J, Nyman D, Eriksson AW (2000b). "Gene mapping in isolated populations: new roles for old friends?". *Hum Hered* **50** (1): 57–65. doi:10.1159/000022891. PMID 10545758.
- Kaessmann H, Heissig F, von Haeseler A, Pääbo S (1999). "DNA sequence variation in a non-coding region of low recombination on the human X chromosome". *Nat Genet* **22** (1): 78–81. doi:10.1038/8785. PMID 10319866.
- Kaessmann H, Wiebe V, Weiss G, Pääbo S (2001). "Great ape DNA sequences reveal a reduced diversity and an expansion in humans". *Nat Genet* **27** (2): 155–6. doi:10.1038/84773. PMID 11175781.
- Keita SOY, Kittles RA (1997). "The persistence of racial thinking and the myth of racial divergence". *Am Anthropol* **99** (3): 534–544. doi:10.1525/aa.1997.99.3.534.
- Lewontin RC (1972). "The apportionment of human diversity". *Evol Biol* **6**: 381–398.

- Marks, Jonathan (1995). *Human Biodiversity: Genes, Race, and History*. Aldine Transaction. ISBN 978-02-0202033-4.

- Mountain JL, Risch N (2004). "Assessing genetic contributions to phenotypic differences among "racial" and "ethnic" groups". *Nat Genet* **36** (Suppl): S48–S53. doi:10.1038/ng1456.

- Pääbo S (2003). "The mosaic that is our genome". *Nature* **421** (6921): 409–412. doi:10.1038/nature01400. PMID 12540910.

- Ramachandran Sohini, Deshpande Omkar, Roseman Charles C., Rosenberg Noah A., Feldman Marcus W., Cavalli-Sforza L. Luca (2005). "Support from the relationship of genetic and geographic distance in human populations for a serial founder effect originating in Africa" (http://www.pnas.org/cgi/reprint/ 0507611102v1). *Proc. Natl. Acad. Sci. U.S.A.* **102** (44): 15942. doi:10.1073/pnas.0507611102. PMC 1276087. PMID 16243969.

- Relethford JH (2002). "Apportionment of global human genetic diversity based on craniometrics and skin color". *Am J Phys Anthropol* **118** (4): 393–8. doi:10.1002/ajpa.10079. PMID 12124919.

- Sankar P, Cho MK (2002). "Toward a new vocabulary of human genetic variation". *Science* **298** (5597): 1337–8. doi:10.1126/science.1074447. PMC 2271140. PMID 12434037.

- Sankar P, Cho MK, Condit DM, Hunt LM, Koenig B, Marshall P, Lee SS, Spicer P (2004). "Genetic research and health disparities". *JAMA* **291** (24): 2985–9. doi:10.1001/jama.291.24.2985. PMC 2271142. PMID 15213210.

- Serre D, Pääbo S (September 2004). "Evidence for gradients of human genetic diversity within and among continents" (http://www.genome.org/cgi/pmidlookup?view=long&pmid=15342553). *Genome Res.* **14** (9): 1679–85. doi:10.1101/gr.2529604. PMC 515312. PMID 15342553.

- Templeton AR (September 1998). "Human Races: A Genetic and Evolutionary Perspective" (http://www. anthrosource.net/doi/abs/10.1525/aa.1998.100.3.632). *American Anthropologist* **100** (3): 632–650. doi:10.1525/aa.1998.100.3.632.

- Weiss KM (1998). "Coming to terms with human variation". *Annu Rev Anthropol* **27**: 273–300. doi:10.1146/annurev.anthro.27.1.273.

- Weiss KM, Terwilliger JD (2000). "How many diseases does it take to map a gene with SNPs?". *Nat Genet* **26** (2): 151–7. doi:10.1038/79866. PMID 11017069.

- Yu N, Jensen-Seaman MI, Chemnick L, Kidd JR, Deinard AS, Ryder O, Kidd KK, Li WH (2003). "Low nucleotide diversity in chimpanzees and bonobos". *Genetics* **164** (4): 1511–8. PMC 1462640. PMID 12930756.

- Ziętkiewicz E, Yotova V, Gehl D, Wambach T, Arrieta I, Batzer M, Cole DEC, Hechtman P, Kaplan F, Modiano D, Moisan J-P, Michalski R, Labuda D (2003). "Haplotypes in the dystrophin DNA segment point to a mosaic origin of modern human diversity". *Am J Hum Genet* **73** (5): 994–1015. doi:10.1086/378777. PMC 1180505. PMID 14513410.

Further reading

- Sohini Ramachandran, Hua Tang, Ryan N. Gutenkunst, and Carlos D. Bustamante, *Genetics and Genomics of Human Population Structure*, chapter 20 in M.R. Speicher et al. (eds.), *Vogel and Motulsky's Human Genetics: Problems and Approaches*, 4th ed., Springer, 2010, ISBN 3540376534

External links

- Human Genome Variation Society (http://www.hgvs.org/)
- Pennisi, Elizabeth (2007-12-21). "Breakthrough of the Year: Human Genetic Variation" (http://www. sciencemag.org/cgi/content/full/318/5858/1842). *Science* **318** (5858): 1842–3. doi:10.1126/science.318.5858.1842. PMID 18096770.

Identification (biology)

Identification in biology is the process of assigning a pre-existing individual or class name to an individual organism. Identification of organisms to individual names (or codes) may be based on individualistic natural body features (e. g.),[1] experimentally created individual markers (e.g., color dot patterns), or natural individualistic molecular markers (similar to those used in maternity or paternity identification tests). Individual identification is used, e.g., in ecology, wildlife management or conservation biology. The more common form of identification is the identification of organisms to common (e. g., "lion") scientific (e. g., "Panthera leo") class names. By necessity this is based on inherited features ("characters") of the organisms, the inheritance forming the basis of defining a class. The features may, e. g., be morphological, anatomical, physiological, behavioral, or molecular.

The term "determination" may occasionally be used as a synonym for identification (e. g.),[2] or as in "determination slips".[3]

Identification methods may be manual or computerized and may involve using identification keys, browsing through fields guide that contain (often illustrated) species accounts, or comparing the organism with specimens from natural history collections.

References

[1] Photographic identification of individual humpback whales (Megaptera novaeangliae) on their southern migration past Ballina, NSW, with comparisons to other humpback whale databases from eastern Australia (http://www.environment.gov.au/coasts/publications/ballina-workshop-2004/pubs/burns.pdf)

[2] Osborne, D. V. 1963. Some Aspects of the theory of dichotomous keys. New Phytologist, 62 (2): 144-160.

[3] The herbarium specimen - help text (http://www.chah.gov.au/avh/help/specimen/about_determination.html)

Ischnochitonidae

Ischnochitonidae is an extinct family of polyplacophoran mollusc.[1]

References

[1] van Belle, R. A. (1981). *Catalogue of Fossil Chitons*. ISBN 90 6279 018 6.

Ivoechiton

Ivoechiton is an extinct genus of polyplacophoran mollusc. Ivoechiton became extinct during the Cretaceous period.[1]

References

[1] van Belle, R. A. (1981). *Catalogue of Fossil Chitons*. ISBN 90 6279 018 6.

Kindbladochiton

Kindbladochiton is an extinct genus of polyplacophoran mollusc. Kindbladochiton became extinct during the Ordovician period.[1]

References

[1] van Belle, R. A. (1981). *Catalogue of Fossil Chitons*. ISBN 90 6279 018 6.

Lavenachiton

Lavenachiton is an extinct genus of polyplacophoran mollusc of uncertain taxonomic placement.[1]

References

[1] van Belle, R. A. (1981). *Catalogue of Fossil Chitons*. ISBN 90 6279 018 6.

LawMoose

LawMoose launched in September, 2000, is believed to have been the first U.S. regional legal search engine operating its own independent web crawler.

Initially LawMoose provided a searchable index drawn from Minnesota law and government sites. Later, it added a similar capability for Wisconsin law sites and select general legal reference starting point sites.

LawMoose has since evolved into a hybrid bi-level public and subscription legal knowledge environment, featuring a thesaurus-based topical map of legal and governmental web resources (which spans the U.S. and globe and adds non-legal resources in a subscriber edition), a list of the largest one hundred Minnesota law firms, ranked by number of Minnesota lawyers, the Minnesota Legal Periodical Index, listing and topically categorizing more than thirty thousand articles published in Minnesota legal publications from 1984 to the present (in the public edition), and a densely interconnected, constantly evolving legal words, phrases, concepts and resources network (in a subscriber edition).

LawMoose's legal words, phrases, concepts and resources network consists of more than 153,000 legal, governmental, business, insurance, and popular terms, interconnected through more than 603,000 relationships. Interconnections are based on a relationships vocabulary of more than 190 relationship types. This multi-dimensional intellectual network functions as a navigable intellectual model of law and law practice.

This semantic, intellectual network-based approach to organizing legal knowledge and locating legal resources is a significant departure from traditional hierarchical, case law-specific legal taxonomies, such as the taxonomy utilized by the West American Digest System.

The Minnesota Legal Periodical Index has been continuously maintained by the Minnesota State Law Library since 1984. Since 2002, it has appeared on LawMoose through a collaboration with LawMoose publisher, Pritchard Law Webs, Minneapolis, Minnesota.

External links

- LawMoose Minnesota [1]
- The One Hundred Largest Law Firms in Minnesota [2]
- Minnesota Legal Periodical Index [3]
- LawMoose Wisconsin [4]
- LawMoose named Netlawtools [5] 2001 Site of the Year [6].

References

[1] http://www.lawmoose.com/index.cfm?CKS=MNLaw
[2] http://www.lawmoose.com/index.cfm?Action=Connections.ShowLargestOneHundredMNLawFirms&CKS=MNLaw
[3] http://www.lawmoose.com/index.cfm?Action=MLPI.ShowArticleFinder&CKS=MNLaw
[4] http://www.lawmoose.com/index.cfm?CKS=WILaw
[5] http://www.netlawtools.com
[6] http://www.netlawtools.com/som.html

Lepidochiton

Lepidochiton is a genus of polyplacophoran mollusc.[1]

References

[1] van Belle, R. A. (1981). *Catalogue of Fossil Chitons*. ISBN 90 6279 018 6.

Lepidopleurina

Lepidopleurina is an extinct suborder of polyplacophoran mollusc.[1]

References

[1] van Belle, R. A. (1981). *Catalogue of Fossil Chitons*. ISBN 90 6279 018 6.

Leptochiton

Leptochiton is an extinct genus of polyplacophoran mollusc. Leptochiton became extinct during the Pliocene period.[1]

References

[1] van Belle, R. A. (1981). *Catalogue of Fossil Chitons*. ISBN 90 6279 018 6.

Leptochitonidae

Leptochitonidae is an extinct family of polyplacophoran mollusc.[1]

References

[1] van Belle, R. A. (1981). *Catalogue of Fossil Chitons*. ISBN 90 6279 018 6.

Lewontin's Fallacy

Infobox
Multi Locus Allele Clusters

Human genetic diversity: Lewontin's fallacy is a 2003 paper by A.W.F. Edwards that criticizes Richard Lewontin's 1972 argument[1] that race is an invalid taxonomic construct.[2] Although academic texts generally avoid referring to Edwards' counterargument in the polemicist terms from Edwards' original title, Edwards' critique nevertheless appears in a number of subsequent academic books and popular science books that discuss Lewontin's argument.[3] [4]

Lewontin's argument

In the 1972 study "The apportionment of human diversity" Richard Lewontin performed a Fixation index (F_{ST}) statistical analysis using 17 markers including blood group proteins. His results were that the majority of genetic differences between humans, 85.4%, were found within a population, 8.3% of genetic differences were found between populations within a race, and only 6.3% was found to differentiate the various races which in the study were Caucasian, African, Mongoloid, South Asian Aborigines, Amerinds, Oceanians, and Australian Aborigines. (Later studies have generally agreed although sometimes with somewhat different values such as 75% for variation within a population.[5]) Lewontin argued "Since such racial classification is now seen to be of virtually no genetic or taxonomic significance either, no justification can be offered for its continuance."

This argument is widely cited as evidence that racial categories are biologically meaningless, and that behavioral differences between groups cannot have any genetic underpinnings. One example being the "Statement on 'Race'" published by the American Anthropological Association in 1998 which rejected the existence of races as unambiguous, clearly demarcated, biologically distinct groups.[6]

Edwards' critique

Edwards argued that while Lewontin's statements on variability are correct when examining the frequency of different alleles (variants of a particular gene) at individual locus (the location of a particular gene) between individuals, it is nonetheless possible to classify individuals into different racial groups with an accuracy that approaches 100% when one takes into account the frequency of the alleles at several loci at the same time. This happens because differences in the frequency of alleles at different loci are correlated across populations — the alleles that are more frequent in a population at two or more loci are correlated when we consider the two populations simultaneously. Or in other words, the frequency of the alleles tends to cluster differently for different populations.

In Edwards' words, "most of the information that distinguishes

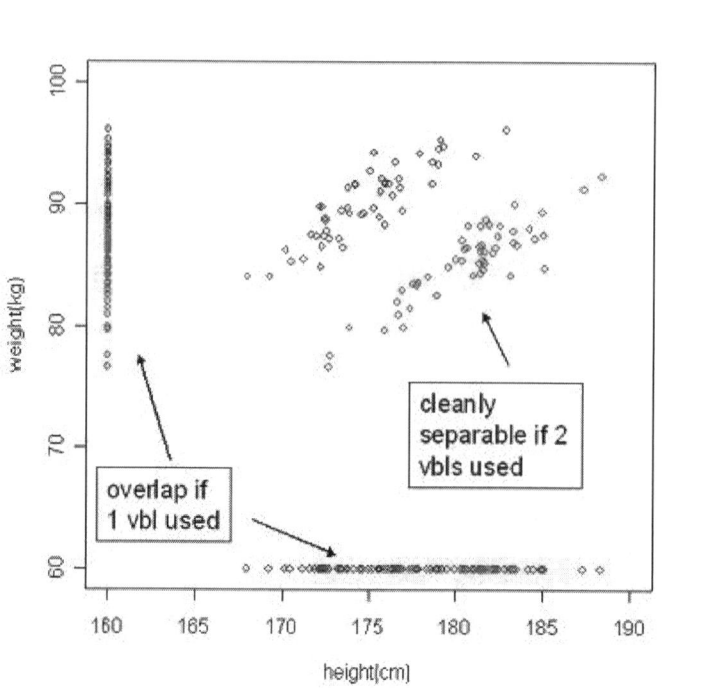

If human height or body weight are measured alone (at the horizontal or vertical axis), the red and blue populations here would overlap strongly. If both traits are measured at the same time, however, natural clusters with little overlap emerge (in the middle between the axis). Thus, if only one trait (or genetic marker) is measured it will be difficult to decide which population a person belongs to. If two traits (or genetic markers) are measured at the same time much less so.

populations is hidden in the correlation structure of the data." These relationships can be extracted using commonly-used ordination and cluster analysis techniques. Edwards argued that, even if the probability of misclassifying an individual based on the frequency of alleles at a single locus is as high as 30% (as Lewontin reported in 1972), the misclassification probability becomes close to zero if enough loci are studied.

Edwards' paper stated that the underlying logic was discussed in the early years of the 20th century. Edwards wrote that he and Luigi Luca Cavalli-Sforza had presented a contrasting analysis to Lewontin's, using very similar data, already at the 1963 International Congress of Genetics. Lewontin participated but did not refer to this in his later paper. Edwards argued that Lewontin used his analysis to attack classification which he deplored for social reasons, such as Arthur Jensen's research on race and intelligence. He wrote:

> There is nothing wrong with Lewontin's statistical analysis of variation, only with the belief that it is relevant to classification. It is not true that "racial classification is . . . of virtually no genetic or taxonomic significance". It is not true, as *Nature* claimed, that "two random individuals from any one group are almost as different as any two random individuals from the entire world" and it is not true, as the *New Scientist* claimed, that "two individuals are different because they are individuals, not because they belong to different races" and that "you can't predict someone's race by their genes".

He also argued:

> Very recent studies (14,15) have treated individuals in the same way that Cavalli-Sforza and Edwards treated populations in 1963, namely by subjecting their genetic information to a cluster analysis thus revealing genetic affinities that have unsurprising geographic, linguistic and cultural parallels. As the authors of the most extensive of these (15) comment, "it was only in the accumulation of small

allele-frequency differences across many loci that population structure was identified."

Neven Sesardic has argued that, unbeknownst to Edwards, Jeffry B. Mitton already made the same argument about Lewontin's claim in two articles published in *The American Naturalist* in the late 1970s.[7]

References

[1] Made in *The apportionment of human diversity* (1972) and again in the 1974 book *The Genetic Basis of Evolutionary Change*.

[2] Edwards AW (August 2003). "Human genetic diversity: Lewontin's fallacy". *BioEssays* **25** (8): 798–801. doi:10.1002/bies.10315. PMID 12879450.

[3] The Ancestor's Tale: A Pilgrimage to the Dawn of Evolution by Richard Dawkins and Yan Wong http://books.google.com/books?id=rR9XPnaqvCMC&pg=PA406

[4] Sohini Ramachandran, Hua Tang, Ryan N. Gutenkunst, and Carlos D. Bustamante, *Genetics and Genomics of Human Population Structure*, chapter 20 in M.R. Speicher et al. (eds.), *Vogel and Motulsky's Human Genetics: Problems and Approaches*, 4th ed., Springer, 2010, ISBN 3540376534, p. 596

[5] Risch, Neil; Burchard, Esteban; Ziv, Elad; Tang, Hua (2002). "Categorization of humans in biomedical research: genes, race and disease.". *Genome Biology* **3** (7): comment2007.1. doi:10.1186/gb-2002-3-7-comment2007. PMC 139378. PMID 12184798.

[6] American Anthropological Association (May 17, 1998). *Statement on 'race'* (http://www.aaanet.org/stmts/racepp.htm).

[7] Sesardic, Neven (2010). "Race: A Social Destruction of a Biological Concept". *Biology & Philosophy* **25** (2): 143. doi:10.1007/s10539-009-9193-7. Mitton's articles are the following:

- Mitton, Jeffry B. (April 1977). "Genetic Differentiation of Races of Man as Judged by Single-Locus and Multilocus Analyses". *The American Naturalist* **111** (978): 203–212. doi:10.1086/283155.
- Mitton, Jeffry B. (1978). "Measurement of Differentiation: Reply to Lewontin, Powell, and Taylor". *The American Naturalist* **112** (988): 1142–1144. doi:10.1086/283359.

Linnaean enterprise

The **Linnaean enterprise** is the task of identifying and describing all living species. Named after Carolus Linnaeus, a Swedish botanist, ecologist and physician who laid the foundations for the modern scheme of taxonomy.

As of 2006, the Linnaean enterprise is considered to be barely begun. There are estimated to be 10 million living species, but only about 1.5-1.8 million have been even named, and fewer than 1% of these have been studied enough to understand the basics of their ecological roles.

The cost of completing the Linnaean Enterprise has been estimated at US$ 5 billion.

References

- Edward O. Wilson, A Global Biodiversity Map, Science 29 September 2000: Vol. 289. no. 5488, p. 2279

Lirachiton

Lirachiton is an extinct genus of polyplacophoran mollusc. Lirachiton became extinct in the Pliocene period.[1]

References

[1] van Belle, R. A. (1981). *Catalogue of Fossil Chitons*. ISBN 90 6279 018 6.

List of Bacteria genera

This article lists the genera of the Bacteria.

Phylum *Acidobacteria.*[1] [2]

Order *Acidobacteriales*

Family *Acidobacteriaceae*

- Genus *Acidobacterium*
- Genus *Geothrix*
- Genus *Holophaga*

Phylum *Actinobacteria*

Class *Mikeiasis*

Subclass *Acidimicrobidae*

Order *Acidimicrobiales*

- Family *Acidimicrobiaceae*
  - Genus *Acidimicrobium*

Subclass *Actinobacteridae*

Order *Actinomycetales*

- Suborder *Actinomycineae*
  - Family *Actinomycetaceae*
  - Family *Actinomycetaceae*
- Suborder *Corynebacterineae*
  - Family *Corynebacteriaceae*
  - Family *Gordoniaceae*
  - Family *Mycobacteriaceae*
  - Family *Nocardiaceae*
  - Family *Tsukamurellaceae*
  - Family *Williamsiaceae*
- Suborder *Frankineae*
  - Family *Acidothermaceae*

- Family *Frankiaceae*
- Family *Geodermatophilaceae*
- Family *Kineosporiaceae*
- Family *Microsphaeraceae*
- Family *Sporichthyaceae*
- Suborder *Glycomycineae*
  - Family *Glycomycetaceae*
- Suborder *Micrococcineae*
  - Family *Beutenbergiaceae*
  - Family *Bogoriellaceae*
  - Family *Brevibacteriaceae*
  - Family *Cellulomonadaceae*
  - Family *Dermabacteraceae*
  - Family *Dermatophilaceae*
  - Family *Dermacoccaceae*
  - Family *Intrasporangiaceae*
  - Family *Jonesiaceae*
  - Family *Microbacteriaceae*
  - Family *Micrococcaceae*
  - Family *Promicromonosporaceae*
  - Family *Rarobacteraceae*
  - Family *Sanguibacteraceae*
- Suborder *Micromonosporineae*
  - Family *Micromonosporaceae*
- Suborder *Propionibacterineae*
  - Family *Nocardioidaceae*
    - Genus *Kribella*
  - Family *Propionibacteriaceae*
- Suborder *Pseudonocardineae*
  - Family *Actinosynnemataceae*
  - Family *Pseudonocardiaceae*
- Suborder *Streptomycineae*
  - Family *Streptomycetaceae*
- Suborder *Streptosporangineae*
  - Family *Nocardiopsaceae*
  - Family *Streptosporangiaceae*
  - Family *Thermomonosporaceae*

Order *Bifidobacteriales*

- Family *Bifidobacteriaceae*

Subclass *Coriobacteridae*

Order *Coriobacteriales*

- Family *Coriobacteriaceae*

  - Genus *Atopobium*
  - Genus *Collinsella*
  - Genus *Coriobacterium*
  - Genus *Cryptobacterium*
  - Genus *Denitrobacterium*
  - Genus *Eggerthella*
  - Genus *Slackia*

Subclass *Rubrobacteridae*

Order *Rubrobacterales*

- Family *Rubrobacteraceae*

  - Genus *Rubrobacter*

Subclass *Sphaerobacteridae*

Order *Sphaerobacterales*

- Family *Sphaerobacteraceae*

  - Genus *Sphaerobacter*

Phylum *Aquificae*

Class *Aquificae*

Order *Aquificales*

- Family *Aquificaceae*

  - Genus *Aquifex*
  - Genus *Hydrogenivirga*
  - Genus *Hydrogenobacter*
  - Genus *Hydrogenobaculum*
  - Genus *Thermocrinis*
- Family *Hydrogenothermaceae*

  - Genus *Hydrogenothermus*
  - Genus *Persephonella*
  - Genus *Sulfurihydrogenibium*
  - Genus *Venenivibrio*

Phylum *Bacteroidetes*

Class *Bacteroidetes*

Order *Bacteroidales*

- Family *Bacteroidaceae*
  - Genus *Bacteroides*
  - Genus *Acetofilamentum*
  - Genus *Acetomicrobium*
  - Genus *Acetothermus*
  - Genus *Anaerorhabdus*
  - Genus *Megamonas*
- Family *Rikenellaceae*
  - Genus *Rikenella*
  - Genus *Marinilabilia*
- Family *Porphyromonadaceae*
  - Genus *Porphyromonas*
  - Genus *Dysgonomonas*
- Family *Prevotellaceae*
  - Genus *Prevotella*

Class *Flavobacteriaceae*

Order *Flavobacteriales*

- Family *Flavobacteriaceae*
- Family *Myroidaceae*
- Family *Blattabacteriaceae*

Class *Sphingobacterium*

Order Sphingobacteriales

- Family *Sphingobacteriaceae*
- Family *Saprospiraceae*
- Family *Flexibacteraceae*
- Family *Flammeovirgaceae*
- Family *Crenotrichaceae*

Phylum *Chlamydiae*

Class *Chlamydiae*

Order *Chlamydiales*

- Family *Chlamydiaceae*
  - Genus *Chlamydia*
  - Genus *Chlamydophila*
- Family *Parachlamydiaceae*
  - *Parachlamydia acanthamoebae*
  - *Candidatus Protochlamydia amoebophila UWE25*
  - *Neochlamydia hartmannellae* (endocytobiont of Hartmannella sp. A1Hsp)
- Family *Rhabdochlamydiaceae*
  - *Rhabdochlamydia porcellionis*
  - *Rhabdochlamydia crassificans*
- Family *Simkaniaceae*
  - Genus *Simkania*
  - Genus *Fritschea*
- Family *Waddliaceae*
  - *Waddlia chondrophila*

Phylum *Chlorobi*

Class *Chlorobia*

Order *Chlorobiales*

- Family *Chlorobiaceae*
  - Genus *Chlorobium*
  - Genus *Ancalochloris*
  - Genus *Chloroherpeton*
  - Genus *Clathrochloris*
  - Genus *Pelodictyon*
  - Genus *Prostheochloris*

Phylum *Chloroflexi*

These Philum is formerly known as green non-sulfur bacteria

Phylum *Chrysiogenetes*

Order *Chrysiogenales*

- Family *Chrysiogenaceae*
  - Genus *Chrysiogenes*
    - Species: *Chrysiogenes arsenatis*

Phylum *Deferribacteres*

Class *Deferribacteres*

Order *Deferribacterales*

- Family *Deferribacteraceae*
  - Genus *Deferribacter*
  - Genus *Denitrovibrio*
  - Genus *Flexistipes*
  - Genus *Geovibrio*

Phylum *Deinococcus-Thermus*

Class *Deinococci*

Order *Deinococcales*

- Genus *Deinococcus*

Order *Thermales*

- Genus *Thermus*
- Genus *Meiothermus*
- Genus *Marinithermus*
- Genus *Oceanithermus*
- Genus *Vulcanithermus*

Phylum *Dictyoglomi*

Class *Dictyoglomi*

Order *Dictyoglomales*

- Family *Dictyoglomaceae*
  - Genus *Dictyoglomus*
    - Species: *Dictyoglomus thermophilum*

Phylum *Fibrobacteres*

- Genus *Fibrobacter*

Phylum Firmicutes

Class *Bacilli*

Order *Bacillales*

- Family *Alicyclobacillaceae*
- Family *Bacillaceae*
- Family *Caryophanaceae*
- Family *Listeriaceae*
- Family *Paenibacillaceae*
- Family *Planococcaceae*
- Family *Sporolactobacillaceae*
- Family *Staphylococcaceae*
- Family *Thermoactinomycetaceae*
- Family *Turicibacteraceae*

Order *Lactobacillales*

- Family *Aerococcaceae*
- Family *Carnobacteriaceae*
- Family *Enterococcaceae*
- Family *Lactobacillaceae*
- Family *Leuconostocaceae*
- Family *Streptococcaceae*

Class *Clostridia*

Order *Clostridiales*

- Family *Acidaminococcaceae*
- Family *Clostridiaceae*
- Family *Eubacteriaceae*
- Family *Heliobacteriaceae*
- Family *Lachnospiraceae*
- Family *Peptococcaceae*
- Family *Peptostreptococcaceae*
- Family *Syntrophomonadaceae*

Order *Halanaerobiales*

- Family *Halanaerobiaceae*
- Family *Halobacteroidaceae*

Order *Thermoanaerobacteriales*

- Family *Thermoanaerobacteriaceae*
- Family *Thermodesulfobiaceae*

Class *Mollicutes*

Order *Mycoplasmatales*

- Family *Mycoplasmataceae*
  - Genus *Hepatoplasma* (Candidatus)
  - Genus *Mycoplasma*
  - Genus *Ureaplasma*

Order *Entomoplasmatales*

- Family *Entomoplasmataceae*
  - Genus *Entomoplasma*
  - Genus *Mesoplasma*
- Family *Spiroplasmataceae*
  - Genus *Spiroplasma*

Order *Anaeroplasmatales*

- Family *Anaeroplasmataceae*
  - Genus *Anaeroplasma*
  - Genus *Asteroleplasma*
- Family *Erysipelotrichaceae*
  - Genus *Erysipelothrix*
  - Genus *Holdemania*

Order *Acholeplasmatales*

- Family *Acholeplasmataceae*
  - Genus *Acholeplasma*
  - Genus *Phytoplasma* (Candidatus)

Phylum Fusobacteria

- Family *Fusobacteriaceae*
  - Genus *Fusobacterium*
    - Species:*F. necrophorum, F. nucleatum, F. polymorphum, F. novum.*

Phylum *Gemmatimonadetes*

- Genus *Gemmatimonas*
  - Species: *Gemmatimonas aurantiaca*

Phylum *Nitrospirae*

- Genus *Nitrospira*
  - Species:*Nitrospira moscoviensis*

Phylum Planctomycetes

Class *Planctomycetia*

Order *Planctomycetales*

- Family *Planctomycetacea*
  - Genus *Gemmata*
  - Genus *Isosphera*
  - Genus *Pirellula*
  - Genus *Planctomyces*
  - Genus *Brocadia* (candidatus)
  - Genus *Kuenenia* (candidatus)
  - Genus *Scalindua* (candidatus)
  - Genus *Anammoxoglobus* (candidatus)
  - Genus *Jettenia* (candidatus)

Phylum Proteobacteria

Class *Alpha Proteobacteria*

Order *Caulobacterales*

- Family *Caulobacteraceae*
  - Genus *Asticcacaulis*
  - Genus *Brevundimonas*
  - Genus *Caulobacter*
  - Genus *Phenylobacterium*

Order *Kordiimonadales*

- Family *Kordiimonadaceae*
  - Genus *Kordiimonas*
    - Species: *Kordiimonas gwangyangensis*

Order *Parvularculales*

- Family *Parvularculaceae*
  - Genus *Parvularcula*
    - Species:*Parvularcula bermudensis*

Order *Rhizobiales*

- Family *Aurantimonadaceae*
  - Genus: *Aurantimonas*
    - Species: *Aurantimonas coralicida,*
  - Genus: *Fulvimarina*
    - Species: *Fulvimarina pelagi*
- Family *Bartonellaceae*
  - Genus: *Bartonella*
- Family *Beijerinckiaceae*
  - Genus *Beijerinckia*
  - Genus *Chelatococcus*
  - Genus *Derxia*
  - Genus *Methylocella*
- Family *Bradyrhizobiaceae*
  - Genus *Afipia*
  - Genus *Agromonas*
  - Genus *Blastobacter*
  - Genus *Bosea*
  - Genus *Bradyrhizobium*
  - Genus *Nitrobacter*
  - Genus *Oligotropha*
  - Genus *Photorhizobium*
  - Genus *Rhodoblastus*
  - Genus *Rhodopseudomonas*

- Family *Brucellaceae*
  - Genus *Brucella*
  - Genus *Mycoplana*
  - Genus *Ochrobactrum*
- Family *Hyphomicrobiaceae*
  - Genus *Ancalomicrobium*
  - Genus *Ancylobacter*
  - Genus *Angulomicrobium*
  - Genus *Aquabacter*
  - Genus *Azorhizobium*
  - Genus *Blastochloris*
  - Genus *Devosia*
  - Genus *Dichotomicrobium*
  - Genus *Filomicrobium*
  - Genus *Gemmiger*
  - Genus *Hyphomicrobium*
  - Genus *Labrys*
  - Genus *Methylorhabdus*
  - Genus *Pedomicrobium*
  - Genus *Prosthecomicrobium*
  - Genus *Rhodomicrobium*
  - Genus *Rhodoplanes*
  - Genus *Seliberia*
  - Genus *Starkeya*
  - Genus *Xanthobacter*
- Family *Methylobacteriaceae*
  - Genus *Methylobacterium*
  - Genus *Microvirga*
  - Genus *Protomonas*
  - Genus *Roseomonas*
- Family *Methylocystaceae*
  - Genus *Methylocystis*
  - Genus *Methylosinus*
  - Genus *Methylopila*
- Family *Phyllobacteriaceae*
  - Genus *Aminobacter*
  - Genus *Aquamicrobium*
  - Genus *Defluvibacter*
  - Genus *Hoeflea*
  - Genus *Mesorhizobium*
  - Genus *Nitratireductor*
  - Genus *Parvibaculum*
  - Genus *Phyllobacterium*
  - Genus *Pseudaminobacter*
- Family *Rhizobiaceae*

- Genus *Agrobacterium*
- Genus *Rhizobium / Sinorhizobium*(synonymous)
- Genus *Liberibacter* (candidatus)
- Family *Rhodobiaceae*
  - Genus *Rhodobium*
    - Species: *Rhodobium orientis, Rhodobium marina*
      - kissny ass

Order *Rhodobacterales*

- Family *Rhodobacteraceae*
  - Genus *Ahrensia*
  - Genus *Albidovulum*
  - Genus *Amaricoccus*
  - Genus *Antarctobacter*
  - Genus *Catellibacterium*
  - Genus *Citreicella*
  - Genus *Dinoroseobacter*
  - Genus *Haematobacter*
  - Genus *Jannaschia*
  - Genus *Ketogulonicigenium*
  - Genus *Leisingera*
  - Genus *Loktanella*
  - Genus *Maribius*
  - Genus *Marinosulfonomonas*
  - Genus *Marinovum*
  - Genus *Maritimibacter*
  - Genus *Methylarcula*
  - Genus *Nereida*
  - Genus *Oceanibulbus*
  - Genus *Oceanicola*
  - Genus *Octadecabacter*
  - Genus *Palleronia*
  - Genus *Pannonibacter*
  - Genus *Paracoccus*
  - Genus *Phaeobacter*
  - Genus *Pseudorhodobacter*
  - Genus *Pseudovibrio*
  - Genus *Rhodobaca*
  - Genus *Rhodobacter*
  - Genus *Rhodothalassium*
  - Genus *Rhodovulum*
  - Genus *Roseibacterium*
  - Genus *Roseibium*
  - Genus *Roseicyclus*
  - Genus *Roseinatronobacter*
  - Genus *Roseisalinus*

- Genus *Roseivivax*
- Genus *Roseobacter*
- Genus *Roseovarius*
- Genus *Rubrimonas*
- Genus *Ruegeria*
- Genus *Sagittula*
- Genus *Salipiger*
- Genus *Silicibacter*
- Genus *Staleya*
- Genus *Stappia*
- Genus *Sulfitobacter*
- Genus *Tetracoccus*
- Genus *Thalassobacter*
- Genus *Thalassobius*
- Genus *Thioclava*
- Genus *Yangia*

Order *Rhodospirillales*

- Family *Rhodospirillaceae*
  - Genus *Azospirillum*
  - Genus *Dechlorospirillum*
  - Genus *Defluvicoccus*
  - Genus *Inquilinus*
  - Genus *Magnetospirillum*
  - Genus *Phaeospirillum*
  - Genus *Rhodocista*
  - Genus *Rhodospira*
  - Genus *Rhodospirillum*
  - Genus *Rhodovibrio*
  - Genus *Roseospira*
  - Genus *Skermanella*
  - Genus *Thalassospira*
  - Genus *Tistrella*
- Family *Rhodospirillaceae*
  - Genus *Acetobacter*
  - Genus *Acidicaldus*
  - Genus *Acidiphilium*
  - Genus *Acidisphaera*
  - Genus *Acidocella*
  - Genus *Acidomonas*
  - Genus *Asaia*
  - Genus *Belnapia*
  - Genus *Craurococcus*
  - Genus *Gluconacetobacter*
  - Genus *Gluconobacter*
  - Genus *Kozakia*
  - Genus *Leahibacter*

- Genus *Muricoccus*
- Genus *Neoasaia*
- Genus *Oleomonas*
- Genus *Paracraurococcus*
- Genus *Rhodopila*
- Genus *Roseococcus*
- Genus *Rubritepida*
- Genus *Saccharibacter*
- Genus *Stella*
- Genus *Swaminathania*
- Genus *Teichococcus*
- Genus *Zavarzinia*

Order *Rickettsiales*

- Family *Rickettsiaceae*
  - Genus *Rickettsia*
  - Genus *Orientia*
  - Genus *Wolbachia*

- Family *Ehrlichiaceae*
  - Genus *Aegyptianella*
  - Genus *Anaplasma*
  - Genus *Cowdria*
  - Genus *Ehrlichia*
  - Genus *Neorickettsia*

- Family *Holosporaceae*
  - Genus *Caedibacter*
  - Genus *Holospora*
  - Genus *Lyticum*
  - Genus *Odyssella*
  - Genus *Polynucleobacter*
  - Genus *Symbiotes*
  - Genus *Tectibacter*

Order *Sphingomonadales*

- Family *Sphingomonadaceae*
  - Genus *Blastomonas*
  - Genus *Citromicrobium*
  - Genus *Erythrobacter*
  - Genus *Erythromicrobium*
  - Genus *Kaistobacter*
  - Genus *Lutibacterium*
  - Genus *Novosphingobium*
  - Genus *Porphyrobacter*
  - Genus *Sandaracinobacter*
  - Genus *Sphingobium*
  - Genus *Sphingomonas*

- Genus *Sphingopyxis*
- Genus *Zymomonas*

Class *Beta Proteobacteria*

Order *Burkholderiales*

- Family *Alcaligenaceae*
  - Genus *Achromobacter*
  - Genus *Alcaligenes*
  - Genus *Bordetella*
  - Genus *Pelistega*
  - Genus *Sutterella*
  - Genus *Taylorella*
- Family *Burkholderiaceae*
  - Genus *Burkholderia*
  - Genus *Chitinimonas*
  - Genus *Cupriavidus*
  - Genus *Lautropia*
  - Genus *Limnobacter*
  - Genus *Pandoraea*
  - Genus *Paucimonas*
  - Genus *Polynucleobacter*
  - Genus *Ralstonia*
  - Genus *Thermothrix*
- Family *Comamonadaceae*
  - Genus *Acidovorax*
  - Genus *Aquabacterium*
  - Genus *Brachymonas*
  - Genus *Comamonas*
  - Genus *Curvibacter*
  - Genus *Delftia*
  - Genus *Hydrogenophaga*
  - Genus *Ideonella*
  - Genus *Leptothrix*
  - Genus *Pelomonas*
  - Genus *Polaromonas*
  - Genus *Rhodoferax*
  - Genus *Roseateles*
  - Genus *Sphaerotilus*
  - Genus *Tepidimonas*
  - Genus *Thiomonas*
  - Genus *Variovorax*
- Family *Oxalobacteraceae*
  - Genus *Collimonas*
  - Genus *Duganella*
  - Genus *Herbaspirillum*

- Genus *Herminiimonas*
- Genus *Janthinospirillum*
- Genus *Massilia*
- Genus *Naxibacter*
- Genus *Oxalobacter*
- Genus *Oxalicibacterium*
- Genus *Telluria*

Order *Hydrogenophilales*

- Family Hydrogenophilales
  - Hydrogenophilus
  - Tepidiphilus
  - Thiobacillus

Order *Methylophilales*

- Family Methylophilaceae
  - Methylophilus
  - Methylobacillus
  - Methylovorax

Class *Gamma Proteobacteria*

Class *Delta Proteobacteria*

Class *Epsilon Proteobacteria*

Phylum *Spirochaetes*

Class *Spirochetes*

Order *Spirochaetales*

- Family *Spirochetaceae*
  - Genus *Borrelia*
  - Genus *Brevinema*
  - Genus *Cristispira*
  - Genus *Spirochaeta*
  - Genus *Spironema*
  - Genus *Treponema*
- Family *Serpulinaceae*
  - Genus *Brachyspira* (Serpulina)
- Family *Leptospiraceae*
  - Genus *Leptospira*
  - Genus *Leptonema*

Phylum *Thermodesulfobacteria*

- Family *Thermodesulfobacteriaceae*
  - Genus *Thermodesulfobacterium*

Phylum *Thermomicrobia*

Thermomicrobia phylum is a phenotype of the green non-sulfur bacteria. It is, as its name suggests, thermophilic. Some scientists suggest that the thermomicrobia phylum is not a true bacteriological phylum, but a sub-division of the green non-sulfur division along with the current chloroflexi phylum.[3]

Phylum *Thermotogae*

Class *Thermotogae*

Order *Thermotogales*

Family *Thermotogaceae*

- Genus *Thermotoga*

Phylum *Verrucomicrobia*

Order *Verrucomicrobiales*

- Family *Verrucomicrobiaceae*
  - Genus *Verrucomicrobium*
  - Genus *Prosthecobacter*
  - Genus *Akkermansia*

References

[1] Barns SM, Cain EC, Sommerville L, Kuske CR (2007). "Acidobacteria phylum sequences in uranium-contaminated subsurface sediments greatly expand the known diversity within the phylum". *Appl. Environ. Microbiol.* **73** (9): 3113–6. doi:10.1128/AEM.02012-06. PMC 1892891. PMID 17337544.

[2] Quaiser A, Ochsenreiter T, Lanz C, *et al.* (2003). "Acidobacteria form a coherent but highly diverse group within the bacterial domain: evidence from environmental genomics". *Mol. Microbiol.* **50** (2): 563–75. doi:10.1046/j.1365-2958.2003.03707.x. PMID 14617179.

[3] Hugenholtz P, Stackebrandt E (2004). "Reclassification of Sphaerobacter thermophilus from the subclass Sphaerobacteridae in the phylum Actinobacteria to the class Thermomicrobia (emended description) in the phylum Chloroflexi (emended description).". *Int J Syst Evol Microbiol* **54** (Pt 6): 2049–51. doi:10.1099/ijs.0.03028-0. PMID 15545432.

External links

- Bacteria: *MeSH* B03 (http://www.nlm.nih.gov/cgi/mesh/2010/MB_cgi?mode=&term=Bacteria& field=entry#TreeB03)'

List of bacterial genera named after geographical names

Several Bacterial species are named after geographical locations.

For the generic epithet, all names derived from people or places (unless in combination) must be in the female nominative case, either by changing the ending to -a or to the diminutive -ella, depending on the name.[1] If a Latin word for the locality exists that should be used ignoring geopolitical differences, e.g. Sina for China.[1]

- Aegyptianella: Aegyptus (the Latin name of Egypt)
- Aidingimonas: Aiding (a lake, located in Xinjiang province of north-west China)
- Antarctobacter: Antarctica
- Balneola: Balneola (the medieval Latin name of Banyuls, France)
- Bavariicoccus: Bavaria (Germany)
- Beutenbergia: Beutenberg (Germany)
- Bogoriella: Lake Bogoria (Kenya)
- Brooklawnia: Brooklawn (the contaminated site from which members of the genus were first isolated)
- Budvicia: Budvicium (the Latin name of the city Céské Budějovice)
- Daeguia: Daegu (Korea)
- Delftia: Delft (the Netherlands)
- Dokdonella: Dokdo (an island located on the East Sea in Korea)
- Dokdonia: Dokdo (an island located on the East Sea in Korea)
- Donghaeana: Donghae (the Korean name of the East Sea in Korea)
- Donghicola: Donghae (the Korean name of the East Sea in Korea)
- Gallaecimonas: Galicia (region of northwest Spain)
- Gangjinia: Gangjin Bay (South Sea in Korea)
- Gelria: Gelre or Gelderland (one of the 12 provinces in The Netherlands)
- Georgenia: St Georgen (a village in Styria)
- Hafnia: Hafnia (the Latin name for Copenhagen, Denmark)
- Herminiimonas: Mons Herminius (a mountain range of Lusitania)
- Hwanghaeicola: Hwanghae (the Korean name of the Yellow Sea)
- Indibacter: India
- Jejuia: Jeju (the largest island in Korea)
- Jeongeupia: Jeongeup (Korean city, where Naejang mountain is located)
- Kiloniella: Kilonium (the Latin name of the northern German city of Kiel, germany)
- Kinneretia: Kinneret Lake (Israel)
- Koreibacter: Korea
- Lutaonella: Lutao (a small volcanic island in the Pacific Ocean)
- Massilia: Massilia (the Latin name of Marseille, France)
- Mechercharimyces: Mecherchar (a marine lake located on Mecherchar Island in the Republic of Palau)
- Mitsuaria: Matsue City (Shimane prefecture, Japan)
- Nevskia: Neva (a river in St. Petersburg, Russia)
- Okibacterium: Oka River (Russia)
- Orientia: The Orient
- Pannonibacter: Pannonia (the Roman province in what is now Hungary), and also Pannon lakes (Hungary)
- Phocaeicola: Phocaea (a maritime town of Ionia, modern-day Foça in Turkey)
- Pragia: Prague (Czech Republic)
- Providencia: Providence (Rhode Island, U.S.A)

- Reinekea: Reineke Island (Peter the Great Bay, Sea of Japan, Russia)
- Rhodanobacter: Rhodanus (River Rhône)
- Salana: River Saale (Germany)
- Sejongia: King Sejong Station (Korea)
- Seohaeicola: Seohae (the Korean name of the Yellow Sea in Korea)
- Sinobaca: Sina (the medieval Latin name of China)
- Sinobacter: Sina (the medieval Latin name of China)
- Sinococcus: Sina (the medieval Latin name of China)
- Sinomonas: Sina (the medieval Latin name of China)
- Sinorhizobium: Sina (the medieval Latin name of China)
- Sinosporangium: Sina (the medieval Latin name of China)
- Stygiolobus: River Styx (a river in Greek mythology which formed the boundary between Earth and the Underworld)
- Tamlana: Tamla (the old name for Jeju Island, Korea)
- Tateyamaria: Tateyama City (Chiba prefecture, Japan)
- Turicella: Turicum (the Latin name of Zurich, Switzerland)
- Turicibacter: Turicum (the Latin name of Zurich, Switzerland)
- Victivallis: Referring to the Wageningen 'Food Valley', an area of The Netherlands in which Food Science is a major research topic
- Wandonia: Wando (an island located on the Southern Sea in Korea)
- Yeosuana: Yeosu City (Korea)

References

- names after mythology entry [2] in LPSN [Euzéby, J.P. (1997). "List of Bacterial Names with Standing in Nomenclature: a folder available on the Internet" [3]. *Int J Syst Bacteriol* **47** (2): 590-2. ISSN 0020-7713. PMID 9103655.]

[1] Help! Latin! How to avoid the most common mistakes while giving Latin names to newly discovered prokaryotes. Microbiología (Sociedad Española de Microbiología), 1996, 12, 473-475. http://www.bacterio.cict.fr/trueper.html

[2] http://www.bacterio.cict.fr/mythology.html

[3] http://ijs.sgmjournals.org/cgi/reprint/47/2/590

List of bacterial genera named after institutions

Several Bacterial species are named after institutions, including acronyms which are spelt out as they would be read,e.g. CDC becomes Ce+de+ce+a. The names are changed in the female nominative case, either by changing the ending to -a or to the diminutive -ella, depending on the name.[1]

- Afipia: AFIP (Armed Force Institute of Pathology), USA
- Basfia: BASF SE (a chemical company in Ludwigshafen, Germany)
- Cedecea: CDC (Centers for Disease Control), USA
- Deefgea: DFG (Deutsche Forschungsgemeinschaft; German Science Foundation), Germany
- Desemzia: DSMZ (Deutsche Sammlung von Mikroorganismen und Zellkulturen), Germany
- Emticicia: MTCC (Microbial Type Culture Collection and Gene Bank), India
- Iamia: IAM (Institute of Applied Microbiology at the University of Tokyo), Japan
- Ideonella: Ideon Research Center, University of Lund, Sweden
- Inhella: Inha University, Korea
- Kaistella: KAIST (Korea Advanced Institute of Science and Technology), Korea
- Kaistia: KAIST (Korea Advanced Institute of Science and Technology), Korea
- Kistimonas: KIST (Korea Institute of Science and Technology), Korea
- Kordia: KORDI (Korea Ocean Research and Development Institute), Korea
- Kordiimonas: KORDI (Korea Ocean Research and Development Institute), Korea
- Kribbella: KRIBB (Korean Research Institute of Bioscience and Biotechnology), Korea
- Kribbia: KRIBB (Korean Research Institute of Bioscience and Biotechnology), Korea
- Lonepinella: Lone Pine Koala Sanctuary (a private zoo), Australia
- Mameliella: MME laboratory (Marine microbial ecology laboratory), China
- Mesonia: MES (Marine Experimental Station of the Pacific Institute of Bioorganic Chemistry), Russia
- Niabella: NIAB (National Institute of Agricultural Biotechnology), Korea
- Niastella: NIAST (National Institute of Agricultural Science and Technology), Korea
- Nubsella: NUBS (Nihon University College of Bioresource Sciences), Japan
- Pibocella: PIBOC (Pacific Institute of Bioorganic Chemistry), Russia
- Rikenella: RIKEN (Rikagaku Kenkyusho; Institute of Physical and Chemical Research), Japan
- Rudaea: RDA (Rural Development Administration), Korea
- Rudanella: RDA (Rural Development Administration), Korea
- Sciscionella: SCISCIO (South China Sea Institute of Oceanology), China
- Stakelama: State Key Laboratory of Marine Environment Science, China
- Tistrella: TISTR (Thailand Institute of Scientific and Technological Research), Thailand
- Waddlia: WADDL (Washington Animal Disease Diagnostic-Laboratory), USA
- Woodsholea: Woods Hole Oceanographic Institution, Massachusetts, USA
- Yimella: YIM (Yunnan Institute of Microbiology), China
- Yokenella: Kokuritsu-yoboueisei-kenkyusho (National Institute of Disease Prevention and Health), Japan

References

- names after institutions entry [2] in LPSN [Euzéby, J.P. (1997). "List of Bacterial Names with Standing in Nomenclature: a folder available on the Internet" [3]. *Int J Syst Bacteriol* **47** (2): 590-2. ISSN 0020-7713. PMID 9103655.]

[1] Help! Latin! How to avoid the most common mistakes while giving Latin names to newly discovered prokaryotes. Microbiología (Sociedad Española de Microbiología), 1996, 12, 473-475. http://www.bacterio.cict.fr/trueper.html

[2] http://www.bacterio.cict.fr/institutions.html

List of bacterial genera named after mythological figures

Several Bacterial species are named after graecoroman mythical figures. The rules present for species named after a famous person do not apply, although some names are changed in the female nominative case, either by changing the ending to -a or to the diminutive -ella, depending on the name.[1]

- Acidianus and Janibacter: Janus, a god in Roman mythology with two faces.
- Amphritea: Amphitrite (Ἀμφιτρίτη), a sea-goddess and wife of Poseidon in Greek mythology and one of the 50 daughters of Nereus and Doris.
- Breoghania: Breogán, the first mythical Celtic king of Gallaecia in Celtic mythology.
- Chimaereicella: Chimaera (Χίμαιρα), a Greek mythological monstrous fire-breathing female creature with the fore part a lion, in the hinder a serpent, and in the middle a goat.
- Cronobacter: Cronos (Κρόνος), in Greco-roman mythology leader of the Titans who swallowed each of his children as soon as they were born, including Zeus.
- Demetria (genus): Demeter, the Greek goddess of harvest.
- Ekhidna (genus): Echidna (Ἔχιδνα), a slimy woman/snake sea creature in Greek mythology.
- Eudoraea: Eudora (Εὐδώρα), one of the Hyades in Greek mythology
- Haliea: Halie (Ἁλίη), a sea nymph, also one of the 50 daughters of Nereus and Doris.
- Hellea: Helle (Ἕλλη), a Greek sea goddess.
- Melitea: Melite (Μελίτη), one of the naiads, daughter of the river god Aegaeus, and one of the many loves of Zeus and his son Heracles. Her son was Hylas.
- Neptuniibacter and Neptunomonas: Neptunius, the Roman god of the sea, equivalent of the Greek Poseidon.
- Nereida: A Nereid, which are sea nymphs daughters of Nereus.
- Nisaea: Nicaea, a sea nymph and daughter of the river-god Sangarius and Cybele.
- Opitutus: Ops, a Roman Earth and harvest goddess married to Saturn. Equivalent of the Greek Rhea.
- Pandoraea: Pandora (Πανδώρα), the first woman who opened a jar, known as Pandora's box releasing evil into the world, in Greek mythology.
- Persephonella: Persephone (also known as Kore), is the daughter of Zeus and the harvest goddess Demeter, and queen of the underworld; she was abducted by Hades the king of the underworld.
- Pilimelia: Meliae (Μελίαι) were nymphs of the ash tree. Melia, one of them, was daughter of Oceanus and lover of her brother the river-god Inachus.
- Proteus and Thermoproteus: Proteus (Πρωτεύς), an early sea-god able to change himself into different shapes.
- Telluria: Tellus, a Roman goddess personifying the Earth.
- Vampirovibrio: A vampire, mythological beings who subsist by feeding on the life essence of other creatures.
- Vulcanibacillus, Vulcanisaeta and Vulcanithermus: Vulcanus, the Roman god of fire.

References

• names after mythology entry [2] in LPSN [Euzéby, J.P. (1997). "List of Bacterial Names with Standing in Nomenclature: a folder available on the Internet" [3]. *Int J Syst Bacteriol* **47** (2): 590-2. ISSN 0020-7713. PMID 9103655.]

[1] Help! Latin! How to avoid the most common mistakes while giving Latin names to newly discovered prokaryotes. Microbiología (Sociedad Española de Microbiología), 1996, 12, 473-475. http://www.bacterio.cict.fr/trueper.html

List of bacterial genera named after personal names

Many Bacterial species are named after people, either the discoverer or a famous person in the field of microbiology, for example Salmonella is after D.E. Salmon, who discovered it (albeit as "Bacillus typhi"[1]).[2]

For the generic epithet, all names derived from people must be in the female nominative case, either by changing the ending to -a or to the diminutive -ella, depending on the name.[3]

For the specific epithet, the names can be converted into either adjectival form (adding -nus (m.), -na (f.), -num (n.) according to the gender of the genus name) or the genitive of the latinised name.[3]

• Adlercreutzia: H. Adlercreutz, a Finnish professor.
• Afifella: S. Afif, a British philosopher and painter
• Agreia: Nina S. Agre, a Russian microbiologist.
• Ahrensia: Ahrens, a German microbiologist.
• Akkermansia: Antoon Akkermans, a Dutch microbiologist.
• Allisonella: M. J. Allison, an American microbiologist.
• Ameyamaea: Minoru Ameyama, a Japanese bacteriologist.
• Anderseniella: Valérie Andersen, a French bacteriologist.
• Andreprevotia: André R. Prévot, a French bacteriologist.
• Asaia: Toshinobu Asai, a Japanese bacteriologist.
• Neoasaia: Toshinobu Asai, a Japanese bacteriologist.
• Asanoa: Koso Asano, a Japanese microbiologist.
• Austwickia: Peter K.C. Austwick, a New Zealander botanist.
• Barnesiella: Ella M. Barnes, British microbiologist.
• Bartonella: Dr. A. L. Barton, Peruvian physician.
• Bauldia: John Bauld, an Australian microbiologist.
• Beggiatoa: F. S. Beggiato, a physician of Vicenza.
• Beijerinckia: Martinus W. Beijerinck, a Dutch microbiologist.
• Belliella: Russell Bell, a Swedish aquatic microbiologist.
• Belnapia: Jayne Belnap, an American microbiologist.
• Beneckea: W. Benecke, a German bacteriologist.
• Bergeriella: U. Berger, a German bacteriologist.
• Bergeyella: David H. Bergey, an American bacteriologist.
• Bermanella: Tom Berman, an aquatic microbial ecologist.
• Bhargavaea: Pushpa Mittra Bhargava, an Indian biologist.
• Bibersteinia: Ernst L. Biberstein, an American bacteriologist.
• Bizionia: Bartolomeo Bizio, an Italian naturalist.
• Blautia: Michael Blaut, a German microbiologist.
• Bordetella: Jules Bordet, a French microbiologist.

- Borrelia: A. Borrel, a French scientist.
- Bosea: J. C. Bose, the founder of the Bose Institute.
- Bowmanella: John P. Bowman, an Australian microbiologist.
- Brackiella: Manfred Brack, a German pathologist
- Branhamella: Sara Branham, an American microbiologist.
- Brenneria: Don J. Brenner, an American bacteriologist.
- Brucella: Sir Davis Bruce, a Scottish physician.
- Buchnera: Paul Buchner, a German biologist.
- Bulleidia: Arthur Bulleid, a British oral microbiologist.
- Burkholderia: W. H. Burkholder, an American bacteriologist.
- Buttiauxella: René Buttiaux, a French bacteriologist.
- Castellaniella: Sir Aldo Castellani, a British-Italian bacteriologist.
- Catonella: Elizabeth P. Cato, a United States microbiologist.
- Chainia: Ernst Boris Mikaelovich Chain, a German/British microbiologist.
- Clevelandina: L. R. Cleveland, an American biologist.
- Cobetia: Andre B. Cobet, an American bacteriologist.
- Cohnella: Ferdinand Cohn, a German microbiologist.
- Collinsella: Matthew D. Collins, a Bristish microbiologist.
- Colwellia: Rita R. Colwell, an American bacteriologist.
- Costertonia: J. W. Costerton, an American bacteriologist.
- Couchioplanes: J. N. Couch, an American mycologist.
- Cowdria: E. V. Cowdry, an American rickettsiologist.
- Coxiella: Herold R. Cox, an American microbiologist.
- Crabtreella: K. Crabtree, an American microbiologist.
- Crossiella: Thomas Cross, a Bristish microbiologist.
- Dasania: Dasan, a Korean scientist.
- Deleya: Jozef De Ley, a Belgian microbiologist.
- Derxia: H. G. Derx, a Dutch microbiologist.
- Devosia: Paul De Vos, a Belgian microbiologist.
- Devriesea: L. A. Devriese, a Belgian veterinary microbiologist.
- Dickeya: Robert S. Dickey, an American phytopathologist
- Dietzia: Alma Dietz, an American microbiologist.
- Dongia: Xiu-Zhu Dong, a Chinese bacteriologist and bacterial taxonomist.
- Dorea: Joël Doré, a French microbiologist.
- Duganella: P. R. Dugan, an American microbiologist.
- Dyella: Douglas W. Dye, a New Zealander microbiologist
- Edwardsiella: P. R. Edwards, an American bacteriologist.
- Eggerthella: Arnold H. Eggerth, an American bacteriologist.
- Paraeggerthella: Arnold H. Eggerth, an American bacteriologist.
- Ehrlichia: Paul Ehrlich, a German bacteriologist.
- Eikenella: M. Eiken, a Scandinavian biologist.
- Elioraea: Eliora Z. Ron, an Israeli microbiologist.
- Elizabethkingia: Elizabeth O. King, an American bacteriologist.
- Erwinia: Erwin Frink Smith, an American bacteriologist.
- Escherichia: Theodor Escherich, a German physician.
- Euzebya: Jean P. Euzéby, a French bacteriologist.
- Euzebyella: Jean P. Euzéby, a French bacteriologist.

- Ewingella: William H. Ewing, an American bacteriologist.
- Facklamia: Richard R. Facklam, an American bacteriologist.
- Fangia: Xinfang Fang, a Chinese microbiologist.
- Finegoldia: S. M. Finegold, an American bacteriologist.
- Francisella: Edward Francis, an American bacteriologist.
- Frankia: A. B. Frank, a Swiss microbiologist.
- Frateuria: Joseph Frateur, a Belgian microbiologist.
- Friedmanniella: E. Imre Friedmann, an American microbiologist.
- Gallionella: B. Gallion, a receiver of customs and zoologist (1782–1839) in Dieppe, France.
- Garciella: Jean-Louis Garcia, a French microbiologist.
- Gardnerella: H. L. Gardner, an American bacteriologist.
- Georgfuchsia: Georg Fuchs, a German bacteriologist.
- Gibbsiella: John N. Gibbs, a British forest pathologist.
- Giesbergeria: G. Giesberger, a Dutch microbiologist.
- Gillisia: Monique Gillis, a Belgian bacteriologist.
- Goodfellowiella (in place of the illegitimate nameGoodfellowia): Michael Goodfellow, a British microbiologist.
- Gordonia: Ruth E. Gordon, an American bacteriologist.
- Gordonibacter: Jeffrey I. Gordon, an American bacteriologist.
- Grahamella: George Stuart Graham Smith, a Bristish microbiologist.
- Gramella: Hans Christian Gram, a Danish pharmacologist and pathologist.
- Grimontia: Patrick A. D. Grimont, a French microbiologist.
- Guggenheimella: Bernhard Guggenheim, a Swiss microbiologist.
- Gulbenkiania: Calouste Gulbenkian, a Portuguese protector of the arts and sciences.
- Pseudogulbenkiania: alouste Gulbenkian, a Portuguese protector of the arts and sciences.
- Haemobartonella: Dr. A. L. Barton, Peruvian physician.
- Hahella: Yung Chil Hah, a Korean bacteriologist.
- Hallella: Ivan C. Hall, a United States microbiologist.
- Hamadaea: Masa Hamada, a Japanese microbiologist.
- Hansschlegelia: Hans G. Schlegel, a German microbiologist.
- Henriciella: Arthur T. Henrici, an American microbiologist.
- Hespellia: Robert B. Hespell, an American microbiologist.
- Hippea: Hans Hippe, a German microbiologist.
- Hirschia: Peter Hirsch, a German microbiologist.
- Hoeflea: Manfred Höfle, a German microbiologist.
- Holdemania: Lillian V. Holdeman Moore, an American microbiologist.
- Hollandina: André Hollande Jr., a French protistologist.
- Hongia: Soon-Woo Hong, a Korean microbiologist.
- Hongiella: Soon-Woo Hong, a Korean microbiologist.
- Howardella: Bernard Howard, a New Zealand microbiologist.
- Hoyosella: Manuel Hoyos, a pioneer in the research for the protection of Altamira Cave paintings.
- Hylemonella: Philip B. Hylemon, an American bacteriologist.
- Hyunsoonleella: Hyun-Soon Lee, a Korean microbiologist.
- Ignatzschineria (in place of the illegitimate name Schineria): Ignatz Rudolph Schiner, an Austrian entomologist, who first described the flyWohlfahrtia magnifica.
- Jahnella: Eduard Adolf Wilhelm Jahn.
- Jannaschia: Holger W. Jannasch, a German microbiologist.
- Jiangella: Cheng-Lin Jiang, a Chinese microbiologist

- Jishengella: Jisheng Ruan, a Chinese microbiologist.
- Johnsonella: John L. Johnson, a United States microbiologist.
- Jonesia: Dorothy Jones, a British microbiologist.
- Jonquetella: Professor Jonquet, a French clinician
- Joostella: P. J. Jooste, a South African bacteriologist.
- Kangiella: Kook Hee Kang, a Korean microbiologist.
- Kerstersia: Karel Kersters, a Belgian microbiologist.
- Kingella: Elizabeth O. King, an American bacteriologist.
- Kitasatoa: Shibasaburo Kitasato, a Japanese bacteriologist.
- Kitasatospora: Shibasaburo Kitasato, a Japanese bacteriologist.
- Klebsiella: Edwin Klebs, a German bacteriologist.
- Klugiella: Michael J. Klug, an American entomologist/microbiologist.
- Kluyvera: Albert Jan Kluyver, a Dutch microbiologist.
- Knoellia: Hans Knöll, a German pioneer in antibiotic research.
- Kocuria: Miroslav Kocur, a Slovakian microbiologist.
- Kofleria: Ludwig Kofler, an Austrian scientist.
- Koserella: Stewart A. Koser, an American bacteriologist.
- Kozakia: Michio Kozaki, a Japaneese microbiologist.
- Krasilnikovia: N. A. Krasil'nikov, a Russian actinomycetologist.
- Kriegella: Noel R. Krieg, an American microbiologist
- Kurthia: H. Kurth, a German bacteriologist.
- Kushneria: Donn J. Kushner, a Canadian microbiologist.
- Allokutzneria: Donn J. Kushner, a Canadian microbiologist.
- Kutzneria: Hans-Jürgen Kutzner, a German microbiologist.
- Labedella: David P. Labeda, an American bacteriologist.
- Labrenzia: Matthias Labrenz, a German marine microbiologist.
- Laceyella: John Lacey, a Bristish microbiologist.
- Larkinella: John M. Larkin, an American microbiologist.
- Lautropia: H. Lautrop, a Danish bacteriologist.
- Lawsonia: G. H. K. Lawson, an American bacteriologist.
- Leadbetterella: Edward R. Leadbetter, an American microbiologists.
- Lechevalieria: Hubert and Mary Lechevalier, an American microbiologists.
- Leclercia: H. Leclerc, a French bacteriologist.
- Leeia: Keho Lee, a Korean microbiologist.
- Leeuwenhoekiella: Antonie van Leeuwenhoek, a Dutch scientist.
- Leifsonia: Einar Leifson, an American microbiologist.
- Leisingera: Thomas Leisinger, a Swiss bacteriologist.
- Leminorella: Léon Le Minor, a French bacteriologist.
- Lentzea: Friedrich A. Lentze, a German microbiologist.
- Levinea: Max Levine, an American bacteriologist.
- Lewinella: Ralph Lewin, an American bacteriologist.
- Lishizhenia: Li Shizhen, a famous Chinese naturalist.
- Listeria: Lord Lister, a Bristish surgeon.
- Listonella: J. Liston, an American bacteriologist.
- Loktanella: Tjhing-Lok Tan from the Alfred Wegener Institute in Bremerhaven.
- Luedemannella: G. M. Luedemann, a Russian actinomycetologist.
- Mahella: Robert A. Mah, an American microbiologist.

- Malikia: Kuhrsheed A. Malik, a German microbiologist.
- Mannheimia: Walter Mannheim, a German microbiologist.
- Martelella: E. Martel, a French explorer
- Marvinbryantia (in place of the the illegitimate nameBryantella): Marvin P. Bryant, an American microbiologist.
- Millisia: Nancy F. Millis, an Australian microbiologist.
- Mitsuokella: T. Mitsuoka, a Japanese bacteriologist.
- Moellerella: V. Møller, a Danish microbiologist.
- Moorella: W. E. C. Moore, an American microbiologist.
- Moraxella: V. Morax, a Swiss ophthalmologist.
- Morganella: H. de R. Morgan, a Bristish bacteriologist.
- Moritella: Richard Y. Morita, an American microbiologist.
- Paramoritella: Richard Y. Morita, an American microbiologist.
- Moryella: Francine Mory, a French bacteriologist
- Murdochiella: David A. Murdoch, a British microbiologist.
- Nakamurella: Kazonuri Nakamura, a Japanese microbiologist.
- Neisseria: Dr. Albert Neisser, a German bacteriologist.
- Nesterenkonia: Olga Nesterenko, an Ukrainian microbiologist.
- Nicoletella: Jacques Nicolet, a Swiss microbiologist.
- Nocardia: Edmond Nocard, a French veterinarian and microbiologist.
- Nocardioides, Nocardiopsis, Pseudonocardia:
- Nonomuraea: H. Nonomura, a Japanese taxonomist of actinomycetes.
- Ohtaekwangia: Oh Tae-Kwang, a Korean microbiologist.
- Oerskovia: Jeppe Ørskov, a Danish microbiologist.
- Paraoerskovia: Jeppe Ørskov, a Danish microbiologist.
- Olleya: June Olley, a British bacteriologist.
- Olsenella: Ingar Olsen, a Norwegian microbiologist.
- Orenia: Aharon Oren, an Israeli bacteriologist.
- Ottowia: Johannes C. G. Ottow, a German bacteriologist.
- Owenweeksia: Owen B. Weeks, an American bacteriologist.
- Palleronia: Norberto Palleroni an American bacteriologist.
- Pasteurella: Louis Pasteur, a French scientist.
- Pasteuria: Louis Pasteur, a French scientist.
- Pelczaria: M. J. Pelczar, an American bacteriologist.
- Pfennigia: Norbert Pfennig, a German bacteriologist.
- Pillotina: J. Pillot, a French microbiologist.
- Piscirickettsia: Howard Taylor Ricketts, an American pathologist.
- Prauserella: Helmut Prauser, a German microbiologist.
- Prevotella: André R. Prévot, a French bacteriologist.
- Paraprevotella:
- Ruegeria: Rueger, a German microbiologist.
- Quinella: J. I. Quin, a South African microbiologist.
- Rahnella: Otto Rahn, a German-American microbiologist.
- Ralstonia: E. Ralston, an American bacteriologist.
- Raoultella: Didier Raoult, a French microbiologist.
- Rathayibacter: E. Rathay, an Australian plant pathologist.
- Reichenbachiella (in place of the the illegitimate nameReichenbachia): Hans Reichenbach, a German microbiologist.

- Rheinheimera: Gerhard Rheinheimer, a German marine microbiologist.
- Rickettsia: Howard Taylor Ricketts, an American pathologist.
- Neorickettsia, Rickettsiella: Howard Taylor Ricketts, an American pathologist.
- Riemerella: Riemer.
- Robinsoniella: Isadore M. Robinson, an American microbiologist.
- Rochalimaea: Henrique da Rocha-Lima, a Brazilian bacteriologist.
- Roseburia: Theodor Rosebury, an American microbiologist.
- Rothia: Genevieve D. Roth, an American bacteriologist.
- Ruania: Ji-Sheng Ruan, a Chinese microbiologist.
- Ruegeria: Rueger, a German microbiologist.
- Rummeliibacillus: John Rummel, an American astrobiologist.
- Salmonella: Daniel E. Salmon, a U.S. veterinary surgeon.
- Samsonia: Régine Samson, a French phytobacteriologist.
- Scardovia: Vittorio Scardovi, an Italian microbiologist.
- Aeriscardovia, Parascardovia, Alloscardovia,Metascardovia:
- Schineria: Ignatz Rudolph Schiner who first described the fly Wohlfahrtia magnifica.
- Schlegelella: H. G. Schlegel, a German microbiologist.
- Schlesneria: Heinz Schlesner, a German microbiologist.
- Schumannella: P. Schumann, a German microbiologist.
- Schwartzia: Helen M. Schwartz, a South African rumen physiologist.
- Sebaldella: Madeleine Sebald, a French bacteriologist.
- Seinonella: Akio Seino, a Japanese microbiologist.
- Seliberia: G. L. Seliber, a Russian microbiologist.
- Serratia: Serafino Serrati, an Italian physicist.
- Sharpea: Michaela E. Sharpe, a British bacteriologist.
- Shewanella: J. M. Shewan, a British bacteriologist.
- Alishewanella: J. M. Shewan, a British bacteriologist.
- Shigella: Kiyoshi Shiga, a Japanese bacteriologist.
- Shimazuella: Akira Shimazu, a Japanese microbiologist.
- Shimia: Jae H. Shim, a Korean microbiologist.
- Shimwellia: J. L. Shimwell.
- Shinella: Yong-Kook Shin, a Japanese microbiologist.
- Shuttleworthia: Cyril Shuttleworth, a British microbiologist.
- Simiduia: Usio Simidu, a Japanese microbiologist.
- Simkania: Arbitrary name formed from the personal name Simona Kahane.
- Simonsiella: Hellmuth Simons, a German bacteriologist..
- Skermanella: Victor B. D. Skerman, an Australian bacteriologist and taxonomist.
- Skermania: Victor B. D. Skerman, an Australian bacteriologist and taxonomist.
- Slackia: Geoffrey Slack, a British microbiologist and dental researcher.
- Smithella: Paul H. Smith, an American microbiologist.
- Sneathia: P. H. A. Sneath, a Bristish bacteriologist.
- Sneathiella: P. H. A. Sneath, a Bristish bacteriologist.
- Soehngenia: Nicolas L. Soehngen, a Dutch microbiologist.
- Soonwooa: Soon-Woo Hong, a Korean microbiologist.
- Stackebrandtia: Erko Stackebrandt, a German microbiologist.
- Staleya: James T. Staley, an American microbiologist.
- Stanierella: Roger Y. Stanier, a Canadian microbiologist.

- Stappia: Stapp, a Belgian microbiologist.
- Starkeya: Robert L. Starkey, an American bacteriologist.
- Stetteria: Karl Otto Stetter, a German biologist.
- Sutterella: Vera Sutter, an American bacteriologist.
- Parasutterella: Vera Sutter, an American bacteriologist.
- Suttonella: R. G. A. Sutton, a British bacteriologist.
- Swaminathania: Swaminathan, an Indian biologist.
- Tannerella: Anne C. R. Tanner, an American microbiologist.
- Tanticharoenia: Morakot Tanticharoen, a Thai bacteriologist.
- Tatlockia: Hugh Tatlock, an American microbiologist.
- Tatumella: Harvey Tatum, an American bacteriologist.
- Taylorella: C. E. D. Taylor, a British bacteriologist.
- Terasakiella: Y. Terasaki, a Japanese microbiologist.
- Thauera: R. Thauer, a German bacteriologist.
- Thorsellia: Walborg Thorsell, a Swedish biologist.
- Tindallia: Brian Tindall, a Bristish bacteriologist.
- Tistlia: Michael Tistl, a German geologist.
- Tissierella: P. H. Tissier, a French bacteriologist.
- Tomitella: Fusao Tomita, a Japanese microbiologist.
- Trabulsiella: L. R. Trabulsi, a Brazilian bacteriologist.
- Truepera: Hans G. Trüper, a German bacteriologist.
- Tsukamurella: Michio Tsukamura, a Japanese microbiologist.
- Turneriella: Leslie Turner, a Bristish microbiologist.
- Umezawaea: Hamao Umezawa, a Japanese bacteriologist.
- Uruburuella: Federico Uruburu, a Spanish microbiologist.
- Vasilyevaea: Lina Vasilyeva, a Russian microbiologist.
- Veillonella: Adrien Veillon, a French bacteriologist.
- Vogesella: Otto Voges, a German microbiologist.
- Volcaniella: B. Elazari-Volcani, an Israeli bacteriologist.
- Wautersia: Georges Wauters, a Belgian microbiologist.
- Wautersiella: Georges Wauters, a Belgian microbiologist.
- Weeksella: Owen B. Weeks, an American bacteriologist.
- Weissella: Norbert Weiss, a German bacteriologist.
- Wenxinia: Wen-Xin Chen, a Chinese microbiologist.
- Wigglesworthia: V. B. Wigglesworth, a British parasitologist.
- Williamsia: Stanley T. Williams, a British microbiologist.
- Winogradskyella: Sergey Winogradsky, a Russian microbiologist.
- Wolbachia: S. Burt Wolbach, an American bacteriologist.
- Wolinella: M. J. Wolin, an American bacteriologist.
- Yangia: H.-F. Yang, a Chinese microbiologist.
- Yaniella (in place of the the illegitimate name Yania): Xun-Chu Yan, a Chinese microbiologist.
- Yersinia: Alexandre J. E. Yersin, a Swiss bacteriologist.
- Yonghaparkia: Yong-Ha Park, a Korean microbiologist.
- Yuhushiella: Yuhu Shi, a Chinese microbiologist.
- Zavarzinella: Georgii A. Zavarzin, a Russian bacteriologist.
- Zavarzinia: Georgii A. Zavarzin, a Russian bacteriologist.
- Zhangella: Shu-Zheng Zhang, a Chinese biochemist.

- Zhihengliuella: Zhi-Heng Liu, a Chinese microbiologist.
- Zhouia: Pei-Jin Zhou, a Chinese microbiologist
- Zimmermannella: O.E.R. Zimmermann, a German microbiologist.
- Zobellella: Claude E. ZoBell, an American bacteriologist.
- Zobellia: Claude E. ZoBell, an American bacteriologist.
- Pseudozobellia: Claude E. ZoBell, an American bacteriologist.
- Zooshikella: Zoo Shik Lee, a Korean microbiologist.
- Zunongwangia: Zu-Nong Wang, a Chinese microbiologist.

References

- names after people entry [4] in LPSN [Euzéby, J.P. (1997). "List of Bacterial Names with Standing in Nomenclature: a folder available on the Internet" [3]. *Int J Syst Bacteriol* **47** (2): 590-2. ISSN 0020-7713. PMID 9103655.]

[1] SCHROETER (J.). In: F. COHN (ed.), Kryptogamenflora von Schlesien. Band 3, Heft 3, Pilze. J.U. Kern's Verlag, Breslau, 1885-1889, pp. 1-814.

[2] Salmonella entry (http://www.bacterio.cict.fr/s/salmonella.html) in LPSN [Euzéby, J.P. (1997). "List of Bacterial Names with Standing in Nomenclature: a folder available on the Internet" (http://ijs.sgmjournals.org/cgi/reprint/47/2/590). *Int J Syst Bacteriol* **47** (2): 590-2. ISSN 0020-7713. PMID 9103655. .]

[3] Help! Latin! How to avoid the most common mistakes while giving Latin names to newly discovered prokaryotes. Microbiología (Sociedad Española de Microbiología), 1996, 12, 473-475. http://www.bacterio.cict.fr/trueper.html

[4] http://www.bacterio.cict.fr/personalnames.html

Lucilina

Lucilina is an extinct genus of polyplacophoran mollusc.[1]

References

[1] van Belle, R. A. (1981). *Catalogue of Fossil Chitons*. ISBN 90 6279 018 6.

Lumpers and splitters

Lumping and **splitting** refers to a well-known problem in any discipline which has to place individual examples into rigorously defined categories. The lumper/splitter problem occurs when there is the need to create classifications and assign examples to them, for example schools of literature, biological taxa and so on. A "lumper" is an individual who takes a gestalt view of a definition, and assigns examples broadly, assuming that differences are not as important as signature similarities. A "splitter" is an individual who takes precise definitions, and creates new categories to classify samples that differ in key ways.

Origin of the terms

The earliest tandem use of the terms was by the biologist George G. Simpson in his 1945 work "The Principles of Classification and a Classification of Mammals." As he put it, "splitters see very small, highly differentiated units – their critics say that if they can tell two animals apart, they place them in different genera ... and if they cannot tell them apart, they place them in different species. ... Lumpers, on the other hand, see only large units – their critics say that if a carnivore is neither a dog nor a bear, they call it a cat." [1]

Another early use can be found in the title of a 1969 paper by the medical geneticist, Victor McKusick: "On lumpers and splitters, or the nosology of genetic disease."[2]

Reference to lumpers and splitters also appeared in a debate in 1975 between J. H. Hexter and Christopher Hill, in the *Times Literary Supplement*. It followed from Hexter's detailed review of Hill's book *Change and Continuity in Seventeenth Century England*, in which Hill developed Max Weber's argument that the rise of capitalism was facilitated by Calvinist Puritanism. Hexter objected to Hill's 'mining' of sources to find evidence that supported his theories. Hexter argued that Hill plucked quotations from sources in a way that distorted their meaning. Hexter explained this as a mental habit that he called 'lumping'. According to him, 'Lumpers' rejected differences and chose to emphasize similarities. Any evidence that did not fit their arguments was ignored as aberrant. 'Splitters', in contrast, emphasised differences, and resisted simple schemes. 'Lumpers' consistently tried to create coherent patterns. 'Splitters' preferred incoherent complexity.[3] In a similar vein, historian of ideas Isaiah Berlin categorized thinkers as 'Hedgehogs' (lumpers) and 'Foxes' (splitters) in his essay on Leo Tolstoy, 'The Hedgehog and the Fox'.

Usage in various fields

In industry

In the logistics business, it refers to the practice of unloading trucks and breaking down large shipments into smaller ones.

In biology

The categorization and naming of a particular species should be regarded as a *hypothesis* about the evolutionary relationships and distinguishability of that group of organisms. As further information comes to hand, the hypothesis may be confirmed or refuted. Sometimes, especially in the past when communication was more difficult, taxonomists working in isolation have given two distinct names to individual organisms later identified as the same species. When two named species are agreed to be of the same species, the older species name is almost always retained dropping the newer species name honoring a convention known as "priority of nomenclature". This form of lumping is technically called synonymization. Dividing a taxon into multiple, often new, taxa is called splitting. Taxonomists are often referred to as "lumpers" or "splitters" by their colleagues, depending on their personal approach to recognizing differences or commonalities between organisms.

In history

In history, lumpers are those who tend to create broad definitions that cover large periods of time and many disciplines, whereas splitters want to assign names to tight groups of inter-relationships. Each approach has its well-known problems. Lumping tends to create a more and more unwieldy definition, with members having less and less mutually in common. This can lead to definitions which are little more than conventionalities, or groups which join fundamentally different examples. Splitting often leads to "distinctions without difference", ornate and fussy categories, and failure to see underlying similarities.

For example, in the arts, "Romantic" can refer specifically to a period of German poetry roughly from 1780–1810, but would exclude the later work of Goethe, among other writers. In music it can mean every composer from Hummel through Rachmaninoff, plus many that came after.

In software modelling

Software engineering often proceeds by building models (sometimes known as model-driven architecture). A lumper is always keen to generalize, and produces models with a small number of broadly defined objects. A splitter is reluctant to generalize, and produces models with a large number of narrowly defined objects. For example, according to the lumpers, a subcontractor could be basically the same as any other supplier, and is therefore the same class; meanwhile the splitters would probably argue that there are significant differences between different groups of suppliers, justifying separate classes in the model.

In language classification

Language families with lumper-splitter controversies include Ural-Altaic, Altaic itself, Austric, Nostratic, and Joseph Greenberg's similar Eurasiatic, his Amerind languages, Indo-Pacific, and Nilo-Saharan, and above all Merritt Ruhlen's Proto-World. The splitting of mutually intelligible dialect continuums into different languages, or lumping them into one, is also an issue that continually comes up.

Splitters regard the comparative method (meaning not comparison in general, but only reconstruction of a common ancestor or protolanguage) as the only valid proof of kinship, and consider genetic relatedness to be the question of interest. American linguists of recent decades tend to be splitters.

Lumpers are more willing to admit techniques like mass lexical comparison or lexicostatistics, and mass typological comparison, and to tolerate the uncertainty of whether relationships found by these methods are the result of linguistic divergence (descent from common ancestor) or language convergence (borrowing). Much long-range comparison work has been from Russian linguists like Vladislav Illich-Svitych and Sergei Starostin. In the US, Greenberg's and Ruhlen's work has been well publicized, though it has met with little acceptance from linguists. Some well-known earlier American linguists like Morris Swadesh and Edward Sapir also pursued large-scale classifications like Sapir's 1929 scheme for the Americas, accompanied by controversy similar to that today.[4]

In liturgical studies

Paul F. Bradshaw suggests that the same principles of lumping and splitting apply to the study of early Christian liturgy. Lumpers, who tend to predominate, try to find a single (simple?) line of texts from the apostolic age to the fourth century (and later). Splitters see many parallel and overlapping strands which intermingle and flow apart so that there is not a single coherent path in development of liturgical texts. Liturgical texts must not be taken solely at face value; often there are hidden agendas in texts.[5]

The religion called Hinduism is essentially a lumper's concept, sometimes also known as Smartism. Hindu Splitters, and individual adherents, often identify themselves as adherents of a religion such as Shaivism, Vaishnavism, or Shaktism according to which deity they believe to be the supreme creator of the universe.

References

[1] Simpson, George G. "The Principles of Classification and a Classification of Mammals." Bulletin of the AMNH, vol. 85. 1945. American Museum of Natural History, New York.

[2] McKusick VA. On lumpers and splitters, or the nosology of genetic disease. Perspect Biol Med. 1969 Winter;12(2):298-312.

[3] Chase, Bob, 'Upstart Antichrist' *History Workshop Journal* - Issue 60, Autumn 2005, pp. 202-206

[4] http://www.nostratic.ru/books/(137)ruhlen12.pdf Merritt Ruhlen: Is Algonquian Amerind?

[5] Bradshaw, Paul F., *The Search for the Origins of Christian Worship*, Oxford Univ. Press, 2002, p. ix. ISBN 0195217322

External links

- Abstraction: Lumpers and Splitters (http://www.users.globalnet.co.uk/~rxv/infomgt/abstraction.htm#lumpersplitter)
- Lumper Vs. Splitter (http://www.tvtropes.org/pmwiki/pmwiki.php/Main/LumperVsSplitter) on TV Tropes, a wiki dedicated to recurring themes in fiction, metafiction, and real life

Mesochiton

Mesochiton is an extinct genus of polyplacophoran mollusc. Mosochiton became extinct during the Jurassic period. [1]

References

[1] van Belle, R. A. (1981). *Catalogue of Fossil Chitons*. ISBN 90 6279 018 6.

Military taxonomy

Military taxonomy encompasses the domains of weapons, equipment, organizations, strategies, and tactics.[1] The use of taxonomies in the military extends beyond its value as an indexing tool or record-keeping template.[2]

Blink of an eye

Military theorist Carl von Clausewitz stressed the significance of grasping the fundamentals of any situation in the "blink of an eye" (*coup d'œil*). In a military context, the astute tactician can immediately grasp a range of implications and can begin to anticipate plausible and appropriate courses of action.[4] Clauzewitz' conceptual "blink" represents a tentative ontology which organizes a set of concepts within a domain.

A conventional military taxonomy might be an hierarchical set of classifications for a given set of objects; and the progress of reasoning is developed from the general to the more specific. In such taxonomic schema, a conflative term is always a polyseme.[5]

In contrast, a less conventional approach might employ an open-ended contextual military taxonomy—a taxonomy holding only with respect to a specific context; and the progress of reasoning is developed form the specific to the more general.[6]

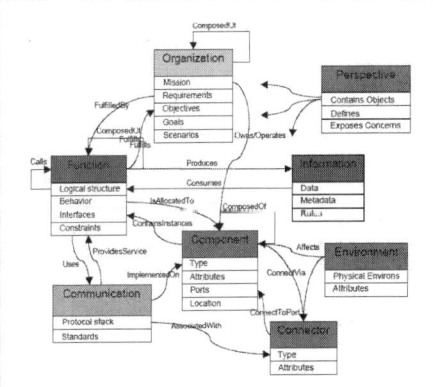

This NASA-generated chart expresses a framework for modeling non-military space systems architectures; but it could be construed as a military taxonomy -- modeling military space systems architectures.[3]

Descriptive paradigm

A taxonomy of terms to describe various types of military operations is fundamentally affected by the way all elements are defined and addressed—not unlike framing.

In terms of a specific military operation, a taxonomic approach based on differentiation and categorization of the entities participating would produce results which were quite different from an approach based on functional objective of an operation (such as peacekeeping, disaster relief, or counter-terrorism). An incidental advantage which flows from give-and-take in refining taxonomic terms more accurately and efficiently becomes more than a worthwhile objective in terms of anticipated outcomes or results. In today's nontraditional operations, the discussion about fundamentals also generates greater precision in how the defense and security community understands and discusses integrated operations.[7]

Hyūga class helicopter destroyer

Military taxonomy in Japan is circumscribed by Japan's pacifist post-war constitution. For example, this affects classification of the *Hyūga* class helicopter carriers, which are ships of the Japan Maritime Self-Defense Force (JMSDF).[8]

This type of helicopter carrier was formally identified as a helicopter destroyer (DDH) to comply with explicit constitutional limitations written in Article 9 of the Japanese Constitution.[9]

The two ships of this class, the JS *Hyūga* and the JS *Ise* resemble a light aircraft carrier or amphibious assault ship such as the Italian Navy's 13,850-ton *Giuseppe Garibaldi*, the Spanish Navy's 17,000-ton *Principe de Asturias* or the Royal Navy's 21,000-ton *Invincible*-class carriers.[10] According to a PBS documentary, JS *Hyūga* is the "first Japanese aircraft carrier built since WWII;"[11] but this label is controversial. A taxonomic label of "aircraft carrier" is legally proscribed.[12]

Each ship in this class has attracted media and Diet attention because of its resemblance to an aircraft carrier. Until the 1970s, US Navy taxonomy categorized large-scale flattops as "attack aircraft carriers" and small flattops as "antisubmarine aircraft carriers." In Japan, the constitutional prohibition against having "attack" aircraft carries has been construed to encompass small aircraft carriers but not helicopter carriers.[13]

A uniquely Japanese taxonomic template is applied to these ships and to their missions, which are limited to "military operations other than war" (MOOTW).[13]

Strategic paradigm

A number of military strategies can be parsed using a taxonomy model. The comparative theoretical framework might posit a range of criteria, e.g., the character of envisaged political goals, the type of military strategy preferred, and the scope of forces engaged; and this template suggests discrete modes of force. The taxonomy-model analysis suggests a useful depiction of the spectrum of the use of military force in a political context.[14]

Parsing terrorism

In the 21st century, the ambit of a subset taxonomy of terrorism would include terms related to terrorists, terrorist groups, terrorist attacks, weapons, venues, and characteristics of terrorists and terrorist groups.[1]

Limitations

Taxonomies offer useful, but incomplete means of structuring information.[15]

Taxonomies are a necessary but not sufficient condition for adequate evaluation of a given data set. While the taxonomic categorizations and sub-categorizations do enhance understanding, it may be significant that the lack of detail in describing objects or elements creates room for ambiguity.[15]

Notes

[1] Cycorp: Structured information (http://www.cyc.com/products/overview)

[2] Fenske, Russell W. "A Taxonomy for Operations Research," (http://www.jstor.org/pss/168881) *Operations Research,* Vol. 19, No. 1 (Jan.-Feb., 1971), pp. 224-234;] United Nations. "Taxonomy for Recordkeeping in Field Missions of UN Peacekeeping Operations." (http://archives.un.org/unarms/doc/taxonomy/20060609_Taxonomy_-_Version_1.pdf) June 2006.

[3] Shames, Peter and Joseph Skipper. (2006). "Toward a Framework for Modeling Space Systems Architectures." (http://trs-new.jpl.nasa.gov/dspace/bitstream/2014/39851/1/06-0876.pdf) NASA, JPL.

[4] Calusewitz, Carl. (1982). *On War,* p. 141; (http://books.google.com/books?id=_La4qTgECD0C&pg=PA141&lpg=PA141&dq=clausewitz+coup+d'oeil&source=web&ots=8UCKTI28o4&sig=0ntr9cQoagmpsJVuulXii533H8U&hl=en&sa=X&oi=book_result&resnum=10&ct=result) "Defining 'Taxonomy'," (http://www.greenchameleon.com/gc/blog_detail/defining_taxonomy/) Straights Knowledge website.

[5] Malone, Joseph L. (1988). *The Science of Linguistics in the Art of Translation: Some Tools from Linguistics for the Analysis and Practice of Translation,* p. 112. (http://books.google.com/books?id=PEY0U3umLRkC&pg=PA112&dq=conflation&client=firefox-a)

[6] Grossi, Davide, Frank Dignum and John-Jules Charles Meyer. (2005). "Contextual Taxonomies" in *Computational Logic in Multi-Agent Systems,* pp. 33-51 (http://www.springerlink.com/content/9yj2lfa5cy67c78m/fulltext.pdf?page=1).

[7] Downie, Richard D. "Defining integrated operations," (http://findarticles.com/p/articles/mi_m0KNN/is_38/ai_n15631260/pg_3?tag=artBody;col1) *Joint Force Quarterly* (Washington, D.C.). July, 2005.

[8] "16DDH "13,500 ton" ton Class" (http://www.globalsecurity.org/military/world/japan/ddh-x.htm). Globalsecurity.org (http://www.globalsecurity.org/index.html). . Retrieved 2008-07-13.; "Hyuga class (CVHG) (Japan), Helicopter Destroyers" (http://www.janes.com/extracts/extract/jfs/jfs_5730.html). *Jane's Fighting Ships (online extract).* Jane's Information Group (http://catalog.janes.com/index.cfm?fuseaction=home.ProductInfoBrief&product_id=96770). 2008-03-14. . Retrieved 2008-07-13.

[9] ["Japan's Largest 'Helicopter Carrier' Commissioned Amid Concerns," Kyodo News International. March 18, 2009.

[10] Hutchison, Harold C. (2007-08-25). "Japan's Secret Aircraft Carriers" (http://www.strategypage.com/htmw/htnavai/articles/20070825.aspx). Strategypage.com (http://www.strategypage.com/default.asp). . Retrieved 2008-07-13.; (Japanese) JMSDF's new carrier, launch video. (http://www.liveleak.com/view?i=cae_1188504476)

[11] PBS/WNET, NYC: "Japan's About-Face: The military's shifting role in post-war society." (http://www.pbs.org/wnet/wideangle/episodes/japans-about-face/introduction/746/) July 8, 2008; Teslik, Lee Hudson. "Backgrounder; Japan and Its Military," (http://www.cfr.org/publication/10439/japan_and_its_military.html) *Council on Foreign Relations.* April 13, 2006; Hsiao, Russell. "China navy floats three-carrier plan," (http://www.atimes.com/atimes/China/JA08Ad01.html) *Asia Times* (Hong Kong). January 8, 2008; "Meet Japan's New Destroyer - Updated," (http://informationdissemination.blogspot.com/search?q=hyuga) Information Dissemination (blog). August 23, 2007.

[12] "Japan Commissioned Its Biggest Helicopter Carrier," (http://www.avionews.com/index.php?corpo=see_news_home.php&news_id=1101427&pagina_chiamante=corpo=index.php) *AvionNews* (World Aeronautical Press Agency). March 18, 2009.

[13] "16DDH "13,500 ton" ton Class" (http://www.globalsecurity.org/military/world/japan/ddh-x.htm). Globalsecurity.org (http://www.globalsecurity.org/index.html). . Retrieved 2008-07-13.

[14] Cohen, Stuart A. and Efraim Inbar. "A taxonomy of Israel's use of military force," (http://www.informaworld.com/smpp/content~content=a782379359~db=all~order=page) *Journal Comparative Strategy,* Vol. 10, No. 2 (April 1991), pp. 121 - 138.

[15] Electronic Mapping Systems: taxonomy (http://www.e-mapsys.com/Taxonomy1.htm)

References

- Carbonell, J. G. and J. Siekmann, eds. (2005). *Computational Logic in Multi-Agent Systems,* Vol. 3487. (http://www.springerlink.com/content/fb5lq38pu0c7/?p=55d6f2e6622046f5909b8b3d31994ddb&pi=0) Berlin: Springer-Verlag. 13-ISBN 978-3-540-28060-6
- Clausewitz, Carl. (1982). *On War* (http://books.google.com/books?id=_La4qTgECD0C&dq=clausewitz+coup+d'oeil&source=gbs_summary_s&cad=0) (editor, Anatol Rapoport). New York: Penguin Classics. 10-ISBN 0-140-44427-0; 13-ISBN 978-0-140-44427-8
- Malone, Joseph L. (1988). *The Science of Linguistics in the Art of Translation: Some Tools from Linguistics for the Analysis and Practice of Translation.* (http://books.google.com/books?id=PEY0U3umLRkC&client=firefox-a) Albany, New York: State University of New York Press. 10-ISBN 0-887-06653-4; 13-ISBN 978-0-887-06653-5; OCLC 15856738 (http://www.worldcat.org/wcpa/oclc/15856738)

Mopaliidae

Mopaliidae is an extinct family of polyplacophoran mollusc.[1]

References

[1] van Belle, R. A. (1981). *Catalogue of Fossil Chitons.* ISBN 90 6279 018 6.

Multi-access key

In biology or medicine, a **multi-access key** is an identification key which overcomes the problem of the more traditional single-access keys (dichotomous or polytomous identification keys) of requiring a fixed sequence of identification steps. A multi-access key enables the user to freely choose the set and characteristics that are convenient to evaluate for the item to be identified. [1] [2]

Although good single-access keys will try to start with characters that are reliable, convenient to observe and generally available throughout most of the year, it is often impossible to achieve this for all taxa in a key. A multi-access key lets the user adapt the key to the particular organism that is being identified and to the circumstances of identification (e.g. field or laboratory).

Multi-access keys may be printed in various way (tabular, matrix, formula style, etc.) but are more commonly used as computer-aided, interactive keys.

Alternative terms

Alternative terms used for multi-access keys are "random-access key", "multi-entry key", polyclave, "matrix key", "tabular key", "synoptic key". Some of these terms should be avoided in this sense, however:

- True "multi-entry keys" exist.
- The terms "tabular key" and "matrix key" are best limited to a tabular presentation format of multi-access keys.[3]
- The term "synoptic key" has an older definition, defining it as a key reflecting taxonomic classification and opposed to diagnostic keys arranged solely for the convenience of identification. [4]

History

Interactive multi-access keys are a high-tech descendent of "card keys". Historically various styles of encoding features of species (such as flower color) on computer punch cards were used. Holes or notches in these cards would allow the user to eliminate cards based on characters observed in a specimen until only one card remained, yielding a tentative identification.[1] [2] [5]

Advantages and disadvantages

Multi-access keys largely serve the same purpose as single-access (dichotomous or polytomous) keys, but have many advantages, especially in the form of computer-aided, interactive keys [6]. The user of an interactive key may select or enter information about an unidentified specimen in any order, allowing the computer to interactively rule out possible identifications of the entity and present the user with additional helpful information and guidance on what information to enter next. Full-featured interactive keys may readily be equipped with images, audio, video, supplemental text, much-simplified language in conjunction with technical language and hyperlinks to assist the user with understanding of both entities and features[5].

Interactive keys remedy some of the problems outlined above. The problem of language translations is made easier in interactive keys because characters and states frequently are simplified with less reliance on the intricate nuances of long strings of words. The problem above where only one sex of an unknown specimen is at hand is mitigated because the user can simply use other characters. The problem of not having a reliable and complete description to compare a specimen with is alleviated by full service interactive keys that include or link to such descriptions and authoritatively identified images. The problem above about complete descriptions not being available in the field is also remedied if the interactive key is on a laptop or handheld computer. With paper-based dichotomous keys the discovery of a new species renders the key incomplete; interactive keys are easily updated by adding information for newly discovered species and reposting computer files on the internet[5].

Many different computer programs for interactive keys are currently available[7], with widely varying features, capacities, and sources. A popular full-featured commercial product is Lucid[8]. Popular full-featured free software packages are DELTA [9] and Discover Life[10]. An example of an open-source package is SLIKS [11]. A comparison of several interactive key software packages is available at [12].

References

[1] Pankhurst, R. J. 1991. Practical Taxonomic Computing.

[2] Winston, J. 1999. Describing Species. Columbia University Press.

[3] Fig. 19.6 in Winston, J. 1999. Describing Species. Columbia University Press.

[4] Pankhurst, R. J. 1992. Practical Taxonomic Computing.

[5] Brasher, J. W. 2006. The Southern Rocky Mountain Interactive Flora (SRMIF) and factors correlated with recognition of plants and mammals. University of Northern Colorado, Ph. D. Thesis. (http://worldcat.org/oclc/122551481?tab=details)

[6] Dallwitz, M.J., Paine, T.A. and Zurcher, E.J. 2000 onwards. Principles of interactive keys (http://delta-intkey.com/www/interactivekeys. htm).

[7] Dallwitz, M.J. 1996 onwards. Programs for interactive identification and information retrieval (http://delta-intkey.com/www/idprogs. htm).

[8] Lucidcentral: Home Page (http://www.lucidcentral.org)

[9] DELTA - DEscription Language for TAxonomy (http://delta-intkey.com)

[10] Discover Life (http://www.discoverlife.org)

[11] SLIKS Stinger's Lightweight Interactive Key Software. WWW.STINGERSPLACE.COM (http://www.stingersplace.com/SLIKS)

[12] Dallwitz, M.J. 2000 onwards. A comparison of interactive identification programs (http://delta-intkey.com/www/comparison.htm).

Multi-entry key

In biology or medicine, a **multi-entry key** is an identification key that allows the free choice of characters only in the first step. Whereas in a typical multi-access key the choice of characters used for identification can be repeated multiple times (reducing the number of remaining taxa each time), in literally multi-*entry* keys only the first step involves a free choice of characters. Examples for multi-entry keys are the keys created by the FRIDA software, where a single step of selecting one or multiple criteria is followed by a dichotomous key for the species remaining after this step. Several **multi-entry keys** are available in the pages of project *Dryades*, section *identification tools*.

External links

- project *Dryades* [1]

References

[1] http://www.dryades.eu

Neoloricata

The **Neoloricata** comprise the living representatives of the polyplacophoran molluscs.[1]

References

[1] van Belle, R. A. (1981). *Catalogue of Fossil Chitons*. ISBN 90 6279 018 6.

NRANK

NRANK, or **National Rank**, is a ranking of the rarity of a species within a nation. Each nation can assign their own NRANK, based on information from conservation data centres, natural heritage programmes and expert scientists.

Numerical taxonomy

Numerical taxonomy is a classification system in biological systematics which deals with the grouping by numerical methods of taxonomic units based on their character states.[1] . It aims to create a taxonomy using numeric algorithms like cluster analysis rather than using subjective evaluation of their properties. The concept was first developed by Robert R. Sokal & Peter H.A. Sneath in 1963[2] and later elaborated by the same authors[3] . They divided the field into phenetics in which classifications are formed based on the patterns of overall similarities and cladistics in which classifications based on the branching patterns of the estimated evolutionary history of the taxa. Note: in recent years many authors treat numerical taxonomy and phenetics as synonyms despite the distinctions made by those authors.

Although intended as an objective classification method, in practice the choice and implicit weighing of characteristics is, of course, influenced by available data and research interests of the investigator. What was made objective was the introduction of explicit steps to be used to create phenograms and cladograms using numerical methods rather than subjective synthesis of data.

References

[1] ""Numerical Taxonomy"" (http://www.accessscience.com/abstract.aspx?id=461900&referURL=http://www.accessscience.com/ content.aspx?id=461900). *www.accessscience.com*. McGraw Hill Ltd.. . Retrieved 13 April 2010.

[2] Sokal & Sneath: *Principles of Numerical Taxonomy*, San Francisco: W.H. Freeman, 1963

[3] Sneath and Sokal: *Numerical Taxonomy*, San Francisco: W.H. Freeman, 1973

Ocellochiton

Ocellochiton is an extinct genus of polyplacophoran mollusc.[1]

References

[1] van Belle, R. A. (1981). *Catalogue of Fossil Chitons*. ISBN 90 6279 018 6.

Olingechiton

Olingechiton is an extinct genus of polyplacophoran mollusc. Olingechiton became extinct at the end of the Cretaceous period.[1]

References

[1] van Belle, R. A. (1981). *Catalogue of Fossil Chitons*. ISBN 90 6279 018 6.

Oochiton

Oochiton is an extinct genus of polyplacophoran mollusc. Oochiton became extinct during the Miocene period. [1]

References

Open nomenclature

Open nomenclature involves the use of abbreviated taxonomic expressions in biological classification.[1] The most common expressions used are *aff.*, *cf.*, *?*, and *sp.*. Although there can be variation in where researchers place expressions such as *aff.* and *cf.* in the Latin name of a species, the way they are interpreted is the most significant unsettled issue. The International Code of Zoological Nomenclature (ICZN) does not make reference to open nomenclature, leaving its use and meaning open for interpretation by taxonomists.[2]

The expression *aff.* is generally used to express affinity of a potentially new but undescribed species with a known species.[1] To indicate a potentially new species without showing affinity, *sp.* is used. This suggests that identification has either not been attempted or the specimen cannot be closely related to established species or subspecies.[2] The expressions *cf.* and *?* signify varying degrees of uncertainty.[1]

References

[1] Bengtson 1988, p. 223.
[2] Bengtson 1988, p. 224.

Literature cited

- Bengtson, Peter (1988). "Open nomenclature" (http://www.webcitation.org/5vxR3btgz) (PDF). *Palaeontology* **31** (1): 223–227. Archived from the original (http://palaeontology.palass-pubs.org/pdf/Vol 31/Pages 223-227. pdf) on 23 January 2011. Retrieved 23 January 2011.

Paleochiton

Paleochiton is an extinct genus of polyplacophoran mollusc.[1]

References

[1] van Belle, R. A. (1981). *Catalogue of Fossil Chitons*. ISBN 90 6279 018 6.

Parachiton

Parachiton is an extinct genus of polyplacophoran mollusc.[1]

References

[1]   van Belle, R. A. (1981). *Catalogue of Fossil Chitons*. ISBN 90 6279 018 6.

Parapatric speciation

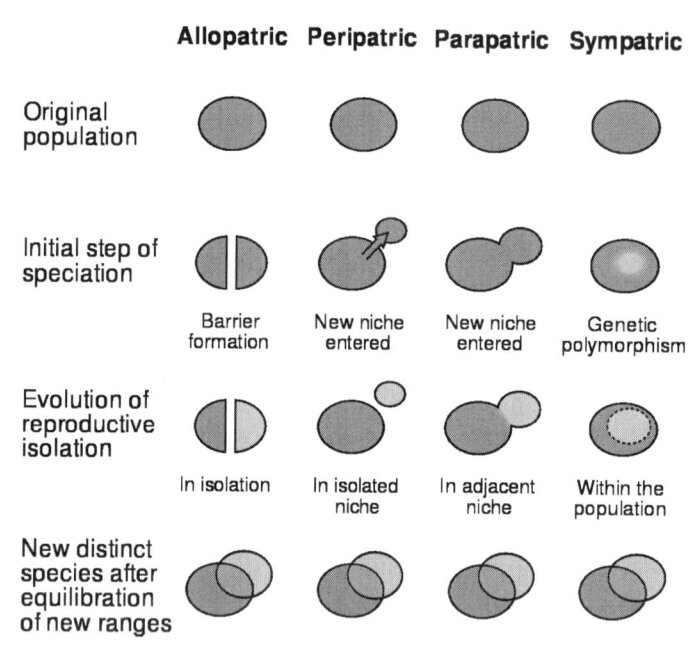

Comparison of allopatric, peripatric, parapatric and sympatric speciation.

Parapatric and **parapatry** are terms from biogeography, referring to organisms whose ranges do not significantly overlap but are immediately adjacent to each other; they only occur together in the narrow contact zone, if at all. Such organisms are usually closely related (e.g. sister species), their distribution being the result of **parapatric speciation**.

Parapatric speciation is a form of speciation that occurs due to variations in the mating habits of a population within a continuous geographical area. In this model, the parent species lives in a continuous habitat, in contrast with allopatric speciation and peripatric speciation where subpopulations become geographically isolated. Niches in this habitat can differ along an environmental gradient, hampering gene flow, and thus creating a cline. In parapatric speciation there is no specific extrinsic barrier to gene flow. The population is continuous, but nonetheless, the population does not mate randomly. Individuals are more likely to mate with their geographic neighbors than with individuals in a different part of the population's range. In this mode, divergence may happen because of reduced gene flow within the population and varying selection pressures across the population's range.[1]

An example[2] of this is the grass *Anthoxanthum*, which has been known to undergo parapatric speciation in such cases as mine contamination of an area. This creates a selection pressure for tolerance to those metals. Flowering time generally changes (tending toward character displacement—strong selection against interbreeding—as the hybrids are generally ill-suited to the environment) and often plants will become self-pollinating.

Similarly, a recent study provided evidence for parapatric speciation in Tennessee cave salamanders, involving divergence with gene flow between cave and surface populations.[3]

Another example are ring species.

References

[1] http://evolution.berkeley.edu/evosite/evo101/VC1dParapatric.shtml

[2] Antonovics J (July 2006). "Evolution in closely adjacent plant populations X: long-term persistence of prereproductive isolation at a mine boundary". *Heredity* **97** (1): 33–7. doi:10.1038/sj.hdy.6800835. PMID 16639420.

[3] MATTHEW L. NIEMILLER, BENJAMIN M. FITZPATRICK, BRIAN T. MILLER (2008). "Recent divergence with gene flow in Tennessee cave salamanders (Plethodontidae: Gyrinophilus) inferred from gene genealogies". *Molecular Ecology* **17** (9): 2258–2275. available online (http://www.blackwell-synergy.com/doi/abs/10.1111/j.1365-294X.2008.03750.x)

"Parapatric speciation." (http:/ / evolution. berkeley. edu/ evolibrary/ article/ _0_0/ speciationmodes_04) in *Understanding Evolution* at evolution.berkeley.edu

available online (http://www.blackwell-synergy.com/doi/abs/10.1111/j.1365-294X.2008.03750.x)

External links

• Berkeley evolution 101 (http://evolution.berkeley.edu/evosite/evo101/VC1dParapatric.shtml)

Peripatric speciation

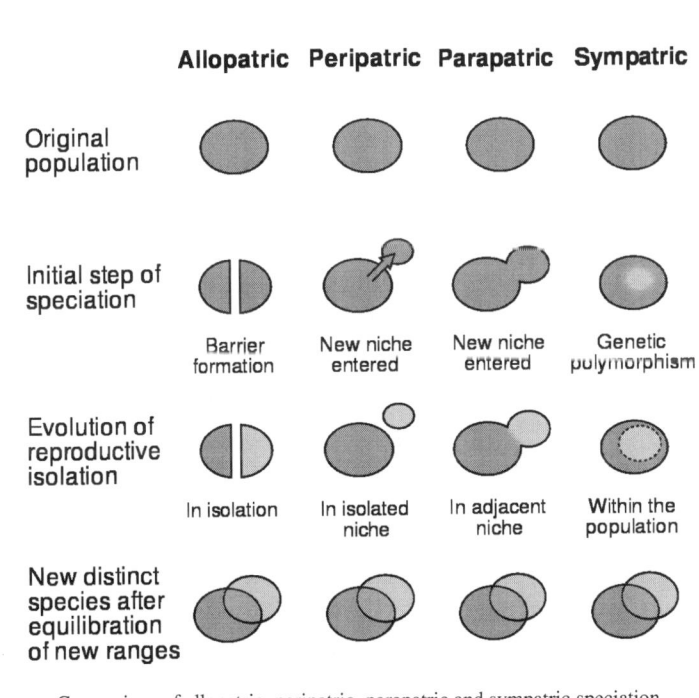

Comparison of allopatric, peripatric, parapatric and sympatric speciation.

Peripatric and **peripatry** are terms from biogeography, referring to organisms whose ranges are closely adjacent but do not overlap, being separated where these organisms do not occur – for example a wide river or a mountain range. Such organisms are usually closely related (e.g, sister species), their distribution being the result of **peripatric speciation**.

Peripatric speciation is a form of speciation, the formation of new species through evolution. In this form, new species are formed in isolated peripheral populations; this is similar to allopatric speciation in that populations are isolated and prevented from exchanging genes. However, peripatric speciation, unlike allopatric speciation, proposes that one of the populations is much smaller than the other.

Peripatric speciation was originally proposed by Ernst Mayr, and is related to the founder effect, because small living populations may undergo selection bottlenecks.[1] Genetic drift is often proposed to play a significant role in peripatric speciation.[2]

References

[1] Provine WB (1 July 2004). "Ernst Mayr: Genetics and speciation" (http://www.genetics.org/cgi/content/full/167/3/1041). *Genetics* **167** (3): 1041–6. PMC 1470966. PMID 15280221. .

[2] Templeton AR (1 April 1980). "The theory of speciation via the founder principle" (http://www.genetics.org/cgi/reprint/94/4/1011). *Genetics* **94** (4): 1011–38. PMC 1214177. PMID 6777243. .

Permochiton

Permochiton is an extinct genus of polyplacophoran mollusc. Permochiton became extinct during the Permian period. [1]

References

[1] van Belle, R. A. (1981). *Catalogue of Fossil Chitons*. ISBN 90 6279 018 6.

Protochiton

Protochiton is an extinct genus of polyplacophoran mollusc. Protochiton became extinct during the Eocene period.[1]

References

[1] van Belle, R. A. (1981). *Catalogue of Fossil Chitons*. ISBN 90 6279 018 6.

Pseudischnochiton

Pseudischnochiton is an extinct genus of polyplacophoran mollusc. Pseudischnochiton became extinct during the Miocene period.[1]

References

[1] van Belle, R. A. (1981). *Catalogue of Fossil Chitons*. ISBN 90 6279 018 6.

Pterochiton

Pterochiton is an extinct genus of polyplacophoran mollusc.[1]

References

[1] van Belle, R. A. (1981). *Catalogue of Fossil Chitons*. ISBN 90 6279 018 6.

Pterygochiton

Pterygochiton is an extinct genus of polyplacophoran mollusc. Pterygochiton became extinct during the Carboniferous period.[1]

References

[1] van Belle, R. A. (1981). *Catalogue of Fossil Chitons*. ISBN 90 6279 018 6.

Records management taxonomy

Records management taxonomy is the classification of data within an organization identifying what data is being generated by each department and where the data is stored. For instance, one department may create sales invoices in a Microsoft Word format. The marketing department may create sales brochures in PDF format and another department may have a different format.

Records management taxonomy is a sort of business process work flow for data that is generated.

Records Management specialists often may go inside a company as consultants and create a taxonomy report for the company. The taxonomy report is in the form of a spreadsheet showing each department, business process, function, types of data generated, retention policy for each type of material, records classification name for each item and many other fields.

References

• 8 Steps to Develop a Taxonomy [1] from Information Management Journal, Nov/Dec 2006 by Choksy, Carol E B

References

[1] http://findarticles.com/p/articles/mi_qa3937/is_200611/ai_n16871474

Reticulation (single-access key)

In biology, a **reticulation** of a single-access identification key connects different branches of the identification tree to improve error tolerance and identification success [1] [2] [3]. In a reticulated key multiple paths lead to the same result; the tree data structure thus changes from a simple tree to a directed acyclic graph.

Two forms of reticulation can be distinguished: Terminal reticulation and inner reticulation.

- In a terminal reticulation a single taxon or next-level-key is keyed out in several locations in the key. This type of reticulation is normally compatible with any printable presentation format of identification keys and normally does not require special precautions in software used for branching keys.
- In an inner reticulation a couplet with further leads can be reached through more than one path. Depending on the software or printable presentation format, this be more challenging. For the linked (= "parallel" or "bracketed") format, where each lead points to a numbered couplet, inner reticulations present no special challenge. However, for the nested (= "indented") presentation format, where all following couplets immediately follow their lead, a cross-connection to a different subtree in the key requires a special mechanisms.

Reticulations generally improve the usability of a key, but may also diminish the overall probability of correct identification averaged over all taxa [4].

References

[1] Osborne, D. V. 1963. Some Aspects of the theory of dichotomous keys. New Phytologist, 62 (2): 144-160.
[2] Payne, R. W. & Preece, D. A. 1977. Incorporating checks against observer error into identification keys. New Phytol. 79: 203-209.
[3] Payne, R. W. 1977. Reticulation and other methods of reducing the size of printed diagnostic keys. J. Gen. Microbiol. 98: 595-597.
[4] Osborne, D. V. 1963. Some Aspects of the theory of dichotomous keys. New Phytologist, 62 (2): 144-160.

Royal Entomological Society Handbooks

Handbooks for the Identification of British Insects is a series of books produced by the Royal Entomological Society of London (RES). The aim of the Handbooks is to provide illustrated identification keys to the insects of Britain, together with concise morphological, biological and distributional information. The series also includes several Check Lists of British Insects. All books contain line drawings, with the most recent volumes including colour photographs. In recent years, new volumes in the series have been published by Field Studies Council, and benefit from association with the AIDGAP identification guides and Synopses of the British Fauna.

Full list of titles

Volume 12 Part 5: The Staphylinidae (rove
beetles) of Britain and Ireland

Vol : 1 - Small Orders

Title	Edition	Vol	Date	Auth	Pages
Thysanura and Diplura		Vol 1 Pt 2	1954	Delany, M.J.	
Dermaptera and Orthoptera	1st	Vol 1 Pt 5	1949	Hincks, W.D.	
Dermaptera and Orthoptera	2nd	Vol 1 Pt 5	1956	Hincks, W.D.	24
Plecoptera		Vol 1 Pt 6	1950	Kimmins, D.E.	18
Psocids Psocoptera (Booklice and Barklice)	1st	Vol 1 Pt 7	1974	New, T.R.	102
Psocids Psocoptera (Booklice and Barklice)	2nd	Vol 1 Pt 7	2006	New, T.R.	146
Ephemeroptera		Vol 1 Pt 9	1950	Kimmins, D.E.	18
Odonata	1st	Vol 1 Pt 10	1949	Fraser, F.C.	48
Odonata	2nd	Vol 1 Pt 10	1956	Fraser, F.C.	
Thysanoptera		Vol 1 Pt 11	1976	Mound, L.A.,; Morison, G.D.; Pitkin, B.R. & Palmer, J.M.	76
Mecoptera, Megaloptera and Neuroptera		Vol 1 Pt 12-13	1959	Fraser, F.C.	40
Trichoptera, Hydroptilidae		Vol 1 Pt 14a	1978	Marshall, J.E.	31
Fleas (Siphonaptera)	1st	Vol 1 Pt 16	1957	Smit, F. G. A. M.	94
Fleas (Siphonaptera)	2nd	Vol 1 Pt 16	2007	Whitaker, A.P.	vi, 178

Vol : 2 - Hemiptera

Title	Edition	Vol	Date	Auth	Pages
Cicadomorpha-Cicadellidae, Membracidae, Cercopidae and Cicadellidae (except Deltocephaline and Typhlocybinae)		Vol 2 Pt 2a	1965	Le Quesne, W.J	64
Cicadomorpha-Cicadellidae (Deltocephaline)		Vol 2 Pt 2b	1969	Le Quesne, W.J	84
Cicadomorpha-Cicadellidae (Typhlocybinae)		Vol 2 Pt 2c	1981	Le Quesne, W.J.; Payne, K.R.	95
Fulgoromorpha		Vol 2 Pt 3	1960	Le Quesne, W.J.	68
Aphidoidea-Chaitophoridae and Callaphididae		Vol 2 Pt 4a	1976	Stroyan, H.L.G.	130
Psylloidea (Adults)		Vol 2 Pt 5a	1979	White, I.M.; Hodkinson, I.D.	79
Psylloidea (nymphal stages)		Vol 2 Pt 5b	1982	White, I.M.; Hodkinson, I.D.	50
Aphids - Pterocommatinae and Aphidinae (Aphidinae)		Vol 2 Pt 6	1984	Stroyan, H.L.G.	232
Aphids - Macrosiphini (Aphidinae)		Vol 2 Pt 7	2010	Blackman, R. L.	414

Vol : 4 - Coleoptera

Title	Edition	Vol	Date	Auth	Pages
Coleoptera. Introduction and Key to Families		Vol 4 Pt 1	1956	Crowson, R.A.	48
The Carabidae (ground beetles) of Britain and Ireland	1st	Vol 4 Pt 2	1974	Lindroth, C.H	148
The Carabidae (ground beetles) of Britain and Ireland	2nd	Vol 4 Pt 2	2007	Luff, M.	iv, 247
Coleoptera: Hydradephaga		Vol 4 Pt 3	1953	Balfour-Browne, F.	33
Coleoptera: Clambidae		Vol 4 Pt 6a	1966	Johnson, C.	13
Staphylinidae-Piestinae		Vol 4 Pt 8a	1954	Tottenham, C.E.	79
Paelaphidae		Vol 4 Pt 9	1957	Pearce, E.J.	32
Coleoptera: Histeroidea. Sphaeritidae and Histeridae		Vol 4 Pt 10	1963	Halstead, D.G.H.	16

Vol : 5 - Coleoptera

Title	Edition	Vol	Date	Auth	Pages
Buprestidae		Vol 5 Pt 1b	1977	Levey, B.	8
Heteroceridae		Vol 5 Pt 2c	1973	Clarke, R.O.S.	15
Dermestidae and Derodontidae		Vol 5 Pt 3	1993	Peacock, E.R.	144
Rhizophagidae		Vol 5 Pt 5a	1977	Peacock, E.R.	19
Phalacridae		Vol 5 Pt 5b	1958	Thompson, R.T.	17
Kateretidae & Nitidulidae: Meligethinae (Pollen beetles)		Vol 5 Pt 6a	1996	Kirk-Spriggs, A.H.	157
Coccinellidae and Sphindidae		Vol 5 Pt 7	1953	Pope, R.D.	12
Lagriidae-Meloidae		Vol 5 Pt 9	1954	Buck, F.D.	30
Tenebrionidae		Vol 5 Pt 10	1975	Brendell, M.J.D.	10
Dung Beetles and Chafers (Scarabaeoidea)	1st	Vol 5 Pt 11	1956	Britton, E.B.	
Dung Beetles and Chafers (Scarabaeoidea)	2nd	Vol 5 Pt 11	1986	Jessop, L	53
Cerambycidae		Vol 5 Pt 12	1952	Duffy, E.A.J.	18
Scolytidae & Platypodidae		Vol 5 Pt 15	1953	Duffy, E.A.J.	20
Orthocerous weevils (Curculionoidea - Nemonychidae, Anthribidae, Urodontidae, Attelabidae & Apionidae)		Vol 5 Pt 16	1990	Morris, M.G	108
Curculionidae: Entiminae (Broad-nosed weevils)		Vol 5 Pt 17a	1997	Morris, M.G	106
Curculionidae: Raymondionyminae - Smicronychinae (True weevils - part 1)		Vol 5 Pt 17b	2002	Morris, M.G	149
Curculionidae: Ceutorhynchinae (True weevils - part 2)		Vol 5 Pt 17c	2008	Morris, M.G	149
British Scraptiidae		Vol 5 Pt 18	2009	Levey, B.	32

Vol : 6 - Hymenoptera

Title	Edition	Vol	Date	Auth	Pages
Introduction and key to families		Vol 6 Pt 1	1977	Richards, O.W.	100
Symphyta (except Tenthredinidae)	1st	Vol 6 Pt 2a	1951	Benson, R.B.	
Symphyta (except Tenthredinidae)	2nd	Vol 6 Pt 2a	1981	Quinlan, J.; Gauld, I.D.	67
Hymenoptera Symphyta section (b)		Vol 6 Pt 2b	1951	Benson, R.B.	88
Hymenoptera Symphyta section (c)		Vol 6 Pt 2c	1958	Benson, R.B.	114
Bethyloidea-Embolemidae, Bethylidae and Dryinidae		Vol 6 Pt 3a	1976	Perkins, J.F.	38
Scolioidea, Vespoidea and Sphecoidea (Hymenoptera, Aculeata)		Vol 6 Pt 3b	1980	Richards, O.W.	118
Formicidae		Vol 6 Pt 3c	1975	Bolton, B.; Collingwood, C.A.	34
Spider wasps (Pompilidae)		Vol 6 Pt 4	1988	Day, M.C.	
Hymenoptera: Cuckoo wasps (Chrysididae)		Vol 6 Pt 5	1984	Morgan, D.	37

Vol : 7 - Hymenoptera: Ichneumonoidea

Title	Edition	Vol	Date	Auth	Pages
Pimpline ichneumon-flies (Ichneumonidae: Pimplinae)		Vol 7 Pt 1	1988	Fitton, M. G., M. R. Shaw & I. D. Gauld	
Ichneumonidae- key to subfamilies and Ichneumoninae (except Ichneumonini)		Vol 7 Pt2ai	1959	Perkins, J.F.	116
Ichneumonidae- Ichneumoninae (Ichneumonini), Alomyinae, Agriotypinae and Lycorininae		Vol 7 Pt2aii	1960	Perkins, J.F.	96
Ichneumonidae- Orthopelmatinae and Anomaloninae		Vol 7 Pt2b	1977	Gauld, I.D. & Mitchell, P.A.	32
Classification and Biology of Braconid Wasps (Hymenoptera: Braconidae)		Vol 7 Pt11	1991	Shaw, M.R.; Huddleston, T.	126

Vol : 8 - Hymenoptera: Cynipoidea, Chalcidoidea & Proctotrupoidea

Title	Edition	Vol	Date	Auth	Pages
Cynipoidea- key to families and subfamilies and Cynipidae (Cynipinae)		Vol 8 Pt 1a	1963	Eady, R.D. & Quinlan, J.	81
Cynipoidea-Eucoilidae		Vol 8 Pt 1b	1978	Quinlan, J.	58
Cynipoidae - Charipidae, Ibaliidae & Figitidae		Vol 8 Pt 1c	1986	Fergusson, N.D.M.	55
Chalcidoidea - Chalicidoidea		Vol 8 Pt 2a	1968	Ferriere, C.; Kerrich, G.J.	40
Chalcidoidea - Ealsmidae & Eulophidae		Vol 8 Pt 2b	1968	Askew, R.R.	39
Proctotrupoidea - Diapriidae (Diapriinae)		Vol 8 Pt 3di	1980	Nixon, G.E.J.	55
Proctotrupoidea - Diapriidae (Belytinae)		Vol 8 Pt 3dii	1957	Nixon, G.E.J.	107

Vol : 9 - Diptera: Nematocera & Brachycera

Title	Vol	Date	Auth	Pages
Diptera. Introduction and key to families	Vol 9 Pt 1	1949	Oldroyd, H.	49
Diptera. Introduction and key to families	Vol 9 Pt 1	1954 (2nd ed)	Oldroyd, H.	49
Diptera. Introduction and key to families	Vol 9 Pt 1	1970 (3rd ed)	Oldroyd, H.	104
Tipulidae to Chironomidae	Vol 9 Pt 2	1950	Coe, R.L, Freeman, P. & Mattingly, P.F.	216
Mycetophilidae (Bolitophilinae, Ditomyiinae, Diadocidiinae, Keroplatinae, Sciophilinae & Manotinae)	Vol 9 Pt 3	1980	Hutson, A.M.; Ackland, D.M.; Kidd, L.N.	111
Tabanoidea and Asiloidea	Vol 9 Pt 4	1969	Oldroyd, H.	132
Dolichopodidae	Vol 9 Pt 5	1978	d'Assis-Fonseca, E.C.M.	90
Sciarid flies (Sciaridae)	Vol 9 Pt 6	1983	Freeman, P.	68
Scatopsidae & Bibionidae	Vol 9 Pt 7	1985	Freeman, P.; Lane, R.P	74

Vol : 10 - Diptera: Cyclorrhapha

Title	Vol	Date	Auth	Pages
Syrphidae	Vol 10 Pt 1	1953	Coe, R.L.	98
Lonchopteridae	Vol 10 Pt 2ai	1969	Smith, K.G.V.	9
Pipunculidae	Vol 10 Pt 2c	1966	Coe, R.L.	83
Conopidae	Vol 10 Pt 3a	1969	Smith, K.G.V.	19
Tachinidae and Calliphoridae	Vol 10 Pt 4a	1954	van Emden, F.I.	133
Tachinidae	Vol 10 Pt 4ai	1993	Belshaw, R.	170
Muscidae	Vol 10 Pt 4b	1968	d'Assis-Fonseca, E.C.M.	118
Tephritidae	Vol 10 Pt 5a	1988	White, I	134
Sepsidae	Vol 10 Pt 5c	1979	Pont, A.C.	35
Lesser dung flies (Sphaeroceridae)	Vol 10 Pt 5e	1988	Pitkin, B.R.	175
Agromyzidae	Vol 10 Pt 5g	1972	Spencer, K.A.	136
Scuttle flies (Phoridae, except Megaselia)	Vol 10 Pt 6	1983	Disney, R.H.L	81
Keds, flat-flies & bat-flies (Hippoboscidae & Nycteribiidae)	Vol 10 Pt 7	1984	Hutson, A.M	84
Scuttle-flies (Megaselia)	Vol 10 Pt 8	1989	Disney, R.H.L	155
Immature stages of British flies	Vol 10 Pt 14	1989	Smith	80
British Lonchaeidae	Vol 10 Pt 15	2008	MacGowan & Rotheray	142

Vol : 11 & 12 - Checklists of British Insects

Title	Vol	Date	Auth	Pages
Checklist of British Insects, pt. 1: Small Orders and Hemiptera	Vol 11 Pt 1	1964	Kloet, G.S.; Hincks, W.D.	xv, 119
Checklist: Lepidoptera	Vol 11 Pt 2	1972	Kloet, G.S.; Hincks, W.D	viii, 153
Checklist: Coleoptera and Strapsiptera	Vol 11 Pt 3	1977	Pope, R.D	xiv, 105
Checklist: Hymenoptera	Vol 11 Pt 4	1978	Kloet, G.S.; Hincks, W.D.; Fitton, M.G. et al.	x, 159.
Checklist: Diptera & Siphonoptera	Vol 11 Pt 5	1976	Kloet, G.S.; Hincks, W.D.	ix, 139
Checklist: Diptera	Vol 12 Pt 1	1998	Chandler, Peter J.	234
The Staphylinidae (rove beetles) of Britain and Ireland: Part 5. Scaphidiinae, Piestinae, Oxytelinae	Vol 12 Pt 5	2009	Lott, Derek A.	100

External links

- Royal Entomological Society [1]
- Full list of RES Handbooks in print [2]

References

[1] http://www.royensoc.co.uk/publications.shtml

[2] http://www.field-studies-council.org/publications/res.aspx

Scanochiton

Scanochiton is an extinct genus of polyplacophoran mollusc. Scanochiton became extinct during the Cretaceous period.[1]

References

[1] van Belle, R. A. (1981). *Catalogue of Fossil Chitons*. ISBN 90 6279 018 6.

Scanochitonidae

Scanchitonidae is an extinct family of polyplacophoran mollusc.[1]

References

[1] van Belle, R. A. (1981). *Catalogue of Fossil Chitons*. ISBN 90 6279 018 6.

Schizochiton

Schizochiton is an extinct genus of polyplacophoran mollusc. Schizochiton became extinct during the Miocene period.[1]

References

Schizochitonidae

Schizochitonidae is an extinct family of polyplacophoran mollusc.[1]

References

[1] van Belle, R. A. (1981). *Catalogue of Fossil Chitons.* ISBN 90 6279 018 6.

Septemchiton

Septemchiton is an extinct genus of polyplacophoran mollusc. Septemchiton became extinct during the Ordovician period.[1]

References

[1] van Belle, R. A. (1981). *Catalogue of Fossil Chitons.* ISBN 90 6279 018 6.

Septemchitonina

Septemchitonina is an extinct suborder of polyplacophoran mollusc.[1]

References

[1] van Belle, R. A. (1981). *Catalogue of Fossil Chitons.* ISBN 90 6279 018 6.

Serotype

Serotype or **serovar** refers to distinct variations within a subspecies of bacteria or viruses. These microorganisms, viruses, or cells are classified together based on their cell surface antigens. Determining serotypes, the process of **serotyping**, can be based on a variety of factors, including virulence, lipopolysaccharides (LPS) in Gram-negative bacteria, presence of an exotoxin (such as pertussis toxin in *Bordetella pertussis*), plasmids, phages, genetic profile (such as determined by polymerase chain reaction), or other characteristics which differentiate two members of the same species,[1] [2] allowing the epidemiologic classification of organisms to the sub-species level.[1] [3] A group of serovars with common antigens is called a **serogroup**.

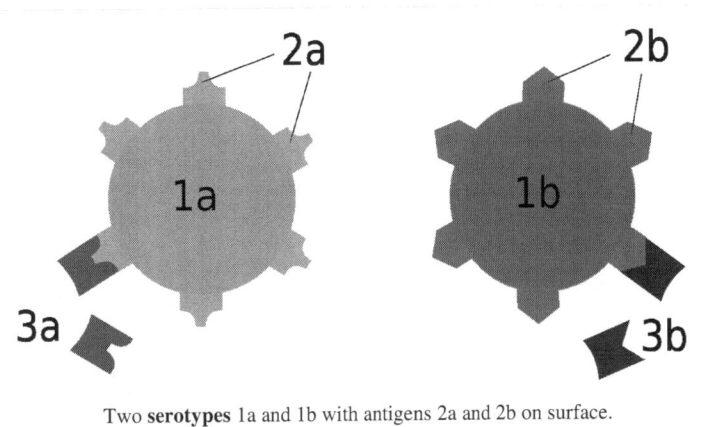

Two **serotypes** 1a and 1b with antigens 2a and 2b on surface.

Serotyping often plays an essential role in determining species and subspecies. The *Salmonella* genus of bacteria, for example, has been determined to have over 4400 serotypes, including *Salmonella enterica* serovar Typhimurium, *S. enterica* serovar Typhi, and *S. enterica* serovar Dublin.[2] *Vibrio cholerae*, the species of bacteria that causes cholera, has over 200 serotypes, based on cell antigens. Only two of them have been observed to produce the potent enterotoxin that results in cholera: 0:1 and 0:139.

Serotypes were discovered by the American microbiologist Rebecca Lancefield in 1933.[4]

Role in organ transplantation

The immune system is capable of discerning a cell as being 'self' or 'non-self' according to that cell's serotype. In humans, that serotype is largely determined by human leukocyte antigen (HLA), the human version of the major histocompatibility complex. Cells determined to be non-self are usually recognized by the immune system as foreign, causing an immune response, such as hemagglutination. Serotypes differ widely between individuals; therefore, if cells from one human (or animal) are introduced into another random human, those cells are oftentimes determined to be non-self because they do not match the self-serotype. For this reason, transplants between genetically non-identical humans often induce a problematic immune response in the recipient, leading to transplant rejection. In some situations this effect can be reduced by serotyping both recipient and potential donors to determine the closest HLA match.[5]

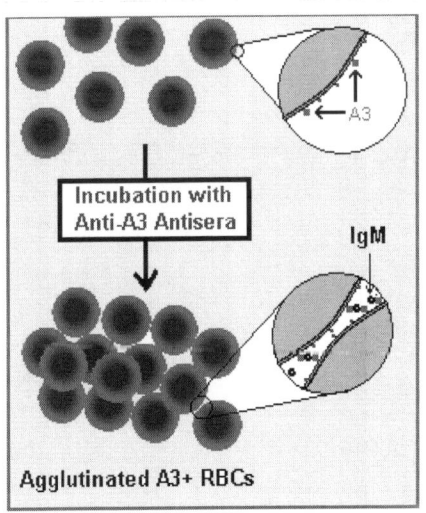

Agglutination of HLA-A3 positive red blood cells (RBCs) with anti-A3 alloreactive antisera containing Anti-A3 IgM

Human leukocyte antigens

Serotypes according the HLA (MHC) locus

HLA Locus	# of Serotypes	Broad Antigens	Split Antigens
A	25	4	15
B	50	9	
C*	12	1	
DR	21	4	
DQ	8	2	
DP*			
*DP and many Cw require SSP-PCR for typing.			

References

[1] Baron EJ (1996). *Classification.* In: *Baron's Medical Microbiology* (Baron S *et al.*, eds.) *(4th ed.). Univ of Texas Medical Branch. (via NCBI Bookshelf)* (http://www.ncbi.nlm.nih.gov/books/bv.fcgi?rid=mmed.section.352) *ISBN 0-9631172-1-1.*

[2] Ryan KJ; Ray CG (editors) (2004). *Sherris Medical Microbiology* (4th ed.). McGraw Hill. ISBN 0-8385-8529-9.

[3] "serovar." The American Heritage Medical Dictionary. 2007. Houghton Mifflin Company 24 Oct. 2009 http://medical-dictionary. thefreedictionary.com/serovar

[4] Lancefield RC (1933). "A serological differentiation of human and other groups of hemolytic streptococci" (http://www.jem.org/cgi/content/abstract/57/4/571) (abstract). *J Exp Med* **57** (4): 571–95. doi:10.1084/jem.57.4.571. PMC 2132252. PMID 19870148. .

[5] Christoph Frohn, Lutz Fricke, Jan-Christoph Puchta, and Holger Kirchner. The effect of HLA-C matching on acute renal transplant rejection. Nephrol. Dial. Transplant. 16: 355-360. http://ndt.oxfordjournals.org/cgi/content/full/16/2/355

External links

- HLA Allele and Haplotype Frequency Database (http://www.allelefrequencies.net)

Sibley-Ahlquist taxonomy of birds

The **Sibley-Ahlquist taxonomy** is a bird taxonomy proposed by Charles Sibley and Jon Edward Ahlquist. It is based on DNA-DNA hybridization studies conducted in the late 1970s and throughout the 1980s.[1]

DNA-DNA hybridization is among a class of comparative techniques in molecular biology that produce distance data (versus character data) and that can be analyzed to produce phylogenetic reconstructions only using phenetic tree-building algorithms. In DNA-DNA hybridization, the percent similarity of DNA between two species is estimated by the reduction in hydrogen bonding between nucleotides of imperfectly complemented heteroduplex DNA (i.e., double stranded DNAs that are experimentally produced from single strands of two different species), compared with perfectly matched homoduplex DNA (both strands of DNA from the same species).

This revolutionary reordering was initially widely accepted by North American ornithologists, and the American Ornithologists' Union adopted some of its provisions. In other parts of the world its adoption has been more deliberative: it has been a major influence on existing classification schemes but hardly any authority adopted it in its entirety.

Characteristics

The classification appears to be an early example of cladistic classification because it codifies many intermediate levels of taxa: the "trunk" of the family tree is the class Aves, which branches into subclasses, which branch into infraclasses, and then "parvclasses", superorders, orders, suborders, infraorders, "parvorders", superfamilies, families, subfamilies, tribes, subtribes and finally genera and species. However the classification study did not employ modern cladistic methods, as it relies strictly on DNA-DNA hybridization as the sole measure of similarity.

The Sibley-Ahlquist arrangement differs greatly from the more traditional approach used in the Clements taxonomy. More recently published phylogenetic reconstructions based on cladistic and maximum likelihood analyses of DNA sequences lend credence to some of the DNA-DNA hybridization-based taxonomy, e.g. the recognition of palaeognathous birds as monophyletic and sister to all others. However, later studies failed to support many of the rearrangements in the Sibley-Ahlquist classification, such as the monophyly of the Corvida.

Basal divergences of modern birds
in the Sibley-Ahlquist taxonomy

The major changes at order level are as follows:

- Enlarged **Struthioniformes** replaces the ratite orders Rheiformes (rheas), Casuariiformes (cassowaries), and Apterygiformes (kiwis) and Struthioniformes (ostriches).

- **Tinamiformes** (tinamous) is unchanged.
- A new, greatly enlarged **Ciconiiformes** includes the previous Sphenisciformes (penguins), Gaviiformes (divers), Podicipediformes (grebes), Procellariiformes (tubenoses), Pelecaniformes (pelicans and allies), Ciconiiformes (storks and allies), Falconiformes (birds of prey), Charadriiformes (waders, gulls, terns, and auks), and the family Pteroclidae (sandgrouse).
- **Anseriformes** (ducks and allies) is unchanged.
- New **Craciformes** chachalacas etc. Previously Galliformes
- New **Ralliformes** rails and crakes (this was eventually changed back to the traditional inclusion in Gruiformes)
- New **Gruiformes** Cranes
- New **Turniciformes** button-quails etc. Previously Gruiformes
- **Columbiformes** doves. Sandgrouse moved to Ciconiiformes.
- **Psittaciformes** cockatoos and parrots unchanged
- New **Musophagiformes** turacos. Previously Cuculiformes.
- New **Cuculiformes** rest of cuckoos
- New **Strigiformes** owls enlarged to include Caprimulgiformes nightjars
- New **Apodiformes** swifts
- New **Trochiliformes** hummingbirds. Previously Apodiformes.
- **Coliiformes** mousebirds unchanged
- **Trogoniformes** trogons unchanged
- New **Coraciiformes** rollers
- New **Upupiformes** Hoopoe, previously Coraciiformes
- New **Bucerotiformes** hornbills, previously Coraciiformes
- New **Galbuliformes** jacamars and puffbirds, previously Piciformes
- New **Piciformes** woodpeckers
- **Passeriformes** perching birds unchanged.

Some of these changes are minor adjustments. For instance, instead of putting the swifts, treeswifts, and hummingbirds in the same order that includes nothing else, Sibley and Ahlquist put them in the same superorder that includes nothing else, consisting of one order for the hummingbirds and another for the swifts and treeswifts. In other words, they still regard the swifts as the hummingbirds' closest relatives.

Other changes are much more drastic. The penguins were traditionally regarded as distant from all other living birds. For instance, Wetmore put them in a superorder by themselves, with all other non-ratite birds in a different superorder. Sibley and Ahlquist, though, put penguins in the same superfamily as divers (loons), tubenoses, and frigatebirds. According to their view, penguins are closer to those birds than herons are to storks.

The new research suggested that the ducks and gallinaceous birds are each other's closest relatives and together form the basal lineage of neognathous (non-ratite) birds, distinct from the others which are collectively called Neoaves. The ratites and tinamous are followed by the ducks and their allies and the pheasants and their allies. Penguins, grebes and divers are placed with other groups that were traditionally considered more modern.

The Galloanseres (waterfowl and landfowl) has found widespread acceptance. The DNA evidence of Sibley-Ahlquist for the monophyly of the group is supported by the discovery of the fossil bird *Vegavis iaai*, an essentially modern but most peculiar waterfowl that lived near Cape Horn some 66-68 million years ago, still in the age of the dinosaurs.[2]

On the other hand, penguins, grebes, divers, and so on (colloquially sometimes called "higher waterbirds") are still considered very ancient neoavian orders – quite possibly together with the shorebirds (waders) which seem a bit older still, the most ancient ones. The supposed distinctness of the storks and herons as well as at least the supposed degree of closeness of penguins to frigatebirds have been refuted. They, as well as the "Ciconiiformes" assemblage, appear to be due to the shortcomings, both methodological and analytical, of DNA-DNA hybridization.

In the light of more recent studies, the AOU, starting in the late 1990s, moved away from advocating the Sibley-Ahlquist taxonomy as originally published and today advocates the Howard-Moore taxonomy as baseline.

Classification

Palaeognathae

Ratitae	**Struthioniformes**	1. Struthionidae
		2. Rheidae
		3. Casuariidae
		4. Apterygidae
	Tinamiformes	1. Tinamidae

Neognathae

Galloanserae

Galloanserae	Gallomorphae	**Craciformes**	1. Cracidae
			2. Megapodiidae
		Galliformes	1. Phasianidae
			2. Numididae
			3. Odontophoridae
	Anserimorphae	**Anseriformes**	1. Anhimidae
			2. Anseranatidae
			3. Dendrocygnidae
			4. Anatidae

Turnicae

| Turnicae | **Turniciformes** | 1. Turnicidae |

Picae

Picae	**Piciformes**	1. Indicatoridae
		2. Picidae
		3. Megalaimidae
		4. Lybiidae
		5. Ramphastidae

Coraciae

Coraciae	Galbulimorphae	**Galbuliformes**	1. Galbulidae
			2. Bucconidae
	Bucerotimorphae	**Bucerotiformes**	1. Bucerotidae
			2. Bucorvidae
		Upupiformes	1. Upupidae
			2. Phoeniculidae
			3. Rhinopomastidae
	Coraciimorphae	**Trogoniformes**	1. Trogonidae
		Coraciiformes	1. Coraciidae
			2. Brachypteraciidae
			3. Leptosomidae
			4. Momotidae
			5. Todidae
			6. Alcedinidae
			7. Halcyonidae
			8. Cerylidae
			9. Meropidae

Coliae

| Coliae | **Coliiformes** | 1. Coliidae |

Passerae

PasseraePsittacimorphaeApodimorphaeTrochiliformesStrigimorphaeStrigiformesPasserimorphaeGruiformesCiconiiformesPasseriformesCuculimorphaePsittaciformesApodiformes
1. Trochilidae

Musophagiformes

1. Tytonidae
2. Strigidae
3. Aegothelidae
4. Podargidae
5. Batrachostomidae
6. Steatornithidae
7. Nyctibiidae
8. Eurostopodidae
9. Caprimulgidae

Columbiformes

1. Eurypygidae
2. Otididae
3. Gruidae
4. Aramidae
5. Heliornithidae
6. Psophiidae
7. Cariamidae
8. Rhynochetidae
9. Rallidae

10. Mesitornithidae

1. Pteroclidae
2. Thinocoridae
3. Pedionomidae
4. Scolopacidae
5. Rostratulidae
6. Jacanidae
7. Chionidae
8. Pluvianellidae
9. Burhinidae
10. Charadriidae
11. Glareolidae
12. Laridae
13. Accipitridae
14. Sagittariidae
15. Falconidae
16. Podicipedidae
17. Phaethontidae
18. Sulidae
19. Anhingidae
20. Phalacrocoracidae
21. Ardeidae
22. Scopidae
23. Phoenicopteridae
24. Threskiornithidae
25. Pelecanidae
26. Ciconiidae
27. Fregatidae
28. Spheniscidae
29. Gaviidae
30. Procellariidae

1. Acanthisittidae
2. Pittidae
3. Eurylaimidae
4. Philepittidae
5. Tyrannidae
6. Thamnophilidae
7. Furnariidae
8. Formicariidae
9. Conopophagidae
10. Rhinocryptidae
11. Climacteridae
12. Menuridae
13. Ptilonorhynchidae
14. Maluridae
15. Meliphagidae
16. Pardalotidae

17. Petroicidae
18. Irenidae
19. Orthonychidae
20. Pomatostomidae
21. Laniidae
22. Vireonidae
23. Corvidae
24. Callaeatidae
25. Picathartidae
26. Bombycillidae
27. Cinclidae
28. Muscicapidae
29. Sturnidae
30. Sittidae
31. Certhiidae
32. Paridae
33. Aegithalidae
34. Hirundinidae
35. Regulidae
36. Pycnonotidae
37. Hypocoliidae
38. Cisticolidae
39. Zosteropidae
40. Sylviidae
41. Alaudidae
42. Nectariniidae
43. Melanocharitidae
44. Paramythiidae
45. Passeridae
46. Fringillidae

Cuculiformes

1. Psittacidae

1. Apodidae
2. Hemiprocnidae

1. Musophagidae

1. Raphidae
2. Columbidae

1. Cuculidae
2. Centropodidae
3. Coccyzidae
4. Opisthocomidae
5. Crotophagidae
6. Neomorphidae

References

[1] Sibley & Ahlquist (1990)

[2] Clarke *et al.'* (2005)

- Clarke, J.A.; Tambussi, C.P.; Noriega, J.I.; Erickson, G.M. & Ketcham, R.A. (2005): Definitive fossil evidence for the extant avian radiation in the Cretaceous. *Nature* **433**: 305-308. DOI:10.1038/nature03150 PDF fulltext (http://www.digimorph.org/specimens/Vegavis_iaai/nature03150.pdf) Supporting information (http://www.nature.com/nature/journal/v433/n7023/suppinfo/nature03150.html)

- Sibley, Charles Gald & Ahlquist, Jon Edward (1990): *Phylogeny and classification of birds.* Yale University Press, New Haven, Conn.

- On the Phylogeny and Classification of Living Birds (http://digilander.libero.it/avifauna/classificazione/sequence5.htm), by Charles G. Sibley

- The Early History of Modern Birds Inferred from DNA Sequences of Nuclear and Mitochondrial Ribosomal Genes (http://mbe.oxfordjournals.org/cgi/content/full/17/3/451), by Marcel van Tuinen, Charles G. Sibley, and S. Blair Hedges

- Sibley's Classification of Birds (http://www.scricciolo.com/classificazione/sequence4.htm), by Eric Salzman, *Birding*, December 1993. The Web version lacks the illustrations, which show parts of the family tree, and includes only a partial bibliography, but adds a sequence down to the tribe level with detail on intermediate taxa (especially for the passerines).

Simplischnochiton

Simplischnochiton is an extinct genus of polyplacophoran mollusc.[1]

References

[1] van Belle, R. A. (1981). *Catalogue of Fossil Chitons*. ISBN 90 6279 018 6.

Species affinis

A **Species affinis** (**Affinis**, abbreviations: **sp. aff.**, **Aff.**, or **Affin.**) is a species related to but not identical with the named species.[1]

Reference

[1] "Species affinis (Affinis)" (http://www.cactus-art.biz/note-book/Dictionary/Dictionary_S/dictionary_species_affinis.htm). *Dictionary of botanic terminology*. cactus-art.biz. . Retrieved 2010-12-13.

Species description

A **species description** or **type description** is a formal description of a newly discovered species, usually in the form of a scientific paper. Its purpose is to give a clear description of a new species of organism and explain how it differs from species which have been described previously, or are related. The species description also contains photographs or other illustrations of the type material and explains in which museums the holotype (and other types such as paratypes) have been deposited.

It is customary for scientists to introduce all relevant new findings and research in a scientific paper, which is scrutinised by other scientists (peer review) and, if accepted, published in a scientific journal of the appropriate discipline; this applies to the discovery and naming of a new species or other taxon. In many cases the scientific community will not formally accept the existence of a new species (with a scientific name) until a species description has been published, even when it may seem obvious that the species is indeed new.

History of species descriptions

Early biologists often published entire volumes or multiple-volume works of descriptions in an attempt to catalog all known species. These catalogs typically featured extensive descriptions of each species and were often illustrated upon reprinting.

The first of these large catalogs was Aristotle's *History of Animals*, published around 343 B.C. Aristotle included descriptions of creatures, mostly fish and invertebrates, in his homeland, and several mythological creatures rumored to live in far-away lands, such as the manticore.[1]

In 77 A.D. Pliny the Elder dedicated several volume of his *Natural History* to the description of all life forms he knew to exist. He appears to have read Aristotle's work, since he writes about many of the same far-away mythological creatures.[2]

However, the earliest recognized species authority is Linnaeus, who standardized the modern taxonomy system beginning with his *Systema Naturae* in 1735.[3]

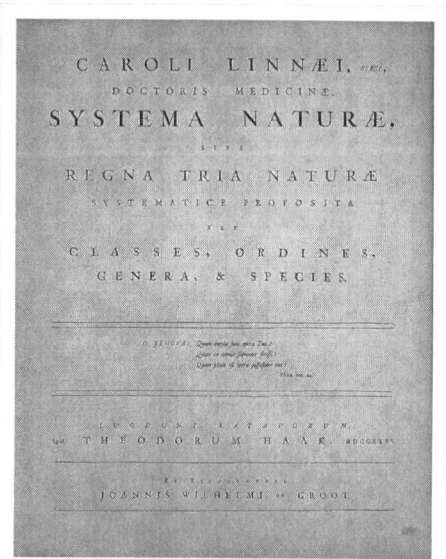

Original title page of Linnaeus's *Systema Naturae*, published in 1735.

As the catalog of known species was increasing rapidly, it became impractical to maintain a single work documenting every species. Publishing a paper documenting a single species was much faster and could be done by scientists with less broadened scopes of study. For example, a scientist who discovered a new species of insect would not need to understand fish or frogs, or even insects which did not resemble the species; he would only need to understand closely related insects.

Modern species descriptions

Formal species descriptions today follow strict guidelines set forth by the International Code of Zoological Nomenclature (ICZN) and International Code of Botanical Nomenclature (ICBN). Very detailed formal descriptions are made by scientists, who usually study the organism closely for a considerable time. These descriptions must specify the distinction between the new taxon and other taxa, and provide a name for it.

The description is submitted to a scientific journal, where it is peer-reviewed before publication. The taxon is accepted formally by science on publication.

References

[1] Aristotle (343 B.C.). *History of Animals*.

[2] Pliny the Elder (77). *Natural History*.

[3] Linnaeus, C. (1735). *Systema Naturae*.

Other sources

• Winston, Judith E. 1999. Describing Species: Practical Taxonomic Procedure For Biologists. Columbia University Press. ISBN 0231068247

Species group

A **species group** is an informal taxonomic rank into which an assemblage of closely-related species within a genus are grouped because of their morphological similarities[1] [2] and their identity as a biological unit with a single monophyletic origin.[3]

Use

The use of the term reduces the need to use a higher taxonomic category in cases with taxa that exhibit sufficient differentiation to be recognized as separate species but possess inadequate variation to be recognized as subgenera. Defining species groups is a convenient way of subdividing well-defined genera with a large number of recognized species. The use of species groups have enabled systematists to consolidate polytypic species species into nominal species which in turn can be grouped into the larger array of the species group.[3]

Range

In regards to whether or not members of a species group share a range, sources differ. A source from Iowa State University Department of Agronomy says that members of a species group usually have partially overlapping ranges but do not interbreed with each other.[1] *A Dictionary of Zoology* (Oxford University Press 1999) describes a species group as complex of related species that exist allopatrically and explains that this "grouping can often be supported by experimental crosses in which only certain pairs of species will produce hybrids."[2] The examples given below may support both uses of the term "species group."

Arthropod examples

- The fruit fly subgenus *Sophophora* contains the *Drosophila melanogaster* species group which itself contains 12 subgroups. The *Drosophila obscura* species group belongs to the same subgenus and contains 6 subgroups.[4]

- In *Vespula*, a genus of wasps, only a few species have a scavenging habit (as opposed to a strictly predatory habit) and thus are considered major pests. The most abundant and bothersome of these are the three species belonging to the "Vespula vulgaris species group" which includes the "common wasp" or "yellowjacket" (*Vespula vulgaris*), the "German wasp" or "European wasp" (*Vespula germanica*), and the "western wasp" or "western yellowjacket" (*Vespula pensylvanica*).[5]

- The Central American bark scorpions *Centruroides limbatus* and *Centruroides bicolor* belong to the "Gracilis species group". All of the species in this group are characterized by their long, narrow pedipalps and overall relatively large size.[6]

- The arachnids to which the common name "Black widow spider" is given are in a species group that includes the "southern black widow" (*Latrodectus mactans*), the "northern black widow" (*Latrodectus variolus*), and the "western black widow" (*Latrodectus hesperus'*).[7] [8]

- The Neotropical butterfly *Morpho adonis* is in a species group with *Morpho eugenia* and *Morpho uraneis*. *Morpho marcus* is also included in the group but might actually be the same species as *Morpho adonis*[9]

Vertebrate examples

- *Brachygobius*, a small genus of gobies which are popular as aquarium fish, are informally divided by taxonomists into two species groups. The dwarf "Brachygobius nunus species group" contains *Brachygobius nunus*, *Brachygobius aggregatus*, and *Brachygobius mekongensis* while the bigger "*Brachygobius doriae* species group" contains the bigger species of *Brachygobius doriae*, *Brachygobius sabanus*, and *Brachygobius xanthomelas*.[10]

- The chameleon *Brookesia minima* has been characterized as belonging to a species group with other "Madagascan Dwarf Chameleons" such as *Brookesia dentata*, *Brookesia tuberculata*, and other new or unidentified species such as a recently described chameleon from Tsingy de Bemaraha Strict Nature Reserve.[11]

- *Peromyscus*, a genus of deer mice, has been divided into subgenera *Peromyscus* and *Haplomylomys* and these subgenera are subdivided further into thirteen species groups.[3]

- Recent cytogenetic studies have shown that the Middle East Blind Mole Rat (*Spalax ehrenbergi*) may actually be a species group containing several cryptic species that can be distinguished by chromosome numbers.[12]

Other uses

The term "species group" is also used in a different way so as to describe the manner in which individual organisms group together. In this non-taxonomic context one can refer to "same-species groups" and "mixed-species groups." While same-species groups are the norm, examples of mixed-species groups abound. For example, zebra (*Equus burchelli*) and wildebeest (*Connochaetes taurinus*) can remain in association during periods of long distance migration across the Serengeti as a strategy for thwarting predators. *Cercopithecus mitis* and *Cercopithecus ascanius*, species of monkey in the Kakamega Forest of Kenya, can stay in close proximity and travel along exactly the same routes through the forest for periods of up to 12 hours. These mixed-species groups are cannot be explained by the coincidence of sharing the same habitat. Rather, they are created by the active behavioural choice of at least one of the species in question.[13]

References

[1] Iowa State University Department of Agronomy (http://www.agron.iastate.edu/~weeds/Ag317-99/id/define.html)

[2] Michael Allaby. "species group." *A Dictionary of Zoology* (Oxford University Press 1999) (http://www.encyclopedia.com/doc/1O8-speciesgroup.html)

[3] Molecular systematics of the *Peromyscus boylii* species group (http://etd.lib.ttu.edu/theses/available/etd-10272008-31295014212541/)

[4] Ranz JM, Maurin D, Chan YS, *et al.* (June 2007). "Principles of genome evolution in the *Drosophila melanogaster* species group". *PLoS Biol.* **5** (6): e152. doi:10.1371/journal.pbio.0050152. PMC 1885836. PMID 17550304.

[5] World- Wide Distribution of Pestiferous Social Wasps(Vespidae) (http://www.murraygula.com/Dr.Jack D.waspinator.pdf)

[6] Walter Reed Biosystematics Unit "Scorpion of the Day":*Centruroides limbatus* (http://wrbu.si.edu/scorpions/SC_du_jour/c_limbatus.html)

[7] Kaston, B. J. (1970). "Comparative biology of American black widow spiders". *Transactions of the San Diego Society of Natural History* **16** (3): 33–82.

[8] Anderson Tully Worldwide (http://www.andersontully.com/species/willow.htm)

[9] Le Moult (E.) & Réal (P.), 1962-1963. *Les Morpho d'Amérique du Sud et Centrale*, Editions du cabinet entomologique E. Le Moult, Paris]]

[10] Schäfer F (2005). *Brackish Water Fishes*. Aqualog. pp. 49–51. ISBN 3-936027-82-X.

[11] AdCham.com: *Brookesia minima* by E. Pollak (http://www.adcham.com/html/taxonomy/species/bminima.html)

[12] Sözen M, Matur F, Çolak E, Özkurt Ş, Karataş A (2006). "Some karyological records and a new chromosomal form for Spalax (Mammalia: Rodentia) in Turkey" (http://www.ivb.cz/folia/55/3/247-256.pdf) (PDF). *Folia Zool.* **55** (3): 247–256. .

[13] Tosh CR, Jackson AL, Ruxton GD (March 2007). "Individuals from different-looking animal species may group together to confuse shared predators: simulations with artificial neural networks". *Proc. Biol. Sci.* **274** (1611): 827–32. doi:10.1098/rspb.2006.3760. PMC 2093981. PMID 17251090.

Spongioradsia

Spongioradsia is an extinct genus of polyplacophoran mollusc. Spongioradsia became extinct during the Oligocene period.[1]

References

[1] van Belle, R. A. (1981). *Catalogue of Fossil Chitons*. ISBN 90 6279 018 6.

Standard Business Reporting

Standard Business Reporting is a group of international programs instigated by a number of governments to reduce the regulatory burden for business.

The concept is to make business the centre when it comes to managing business-to-government reporting obligations. Businesses conduct their own financial administration; the facts they record and decisions they make should drive their reporting. The government should be able to receive and process this information without imposing undue constraints on how businesses administer their finances.

The method used to achieve this goal is to define a "common language" (or taxonomy) using XBRL, then provide systems to process information classified under the taxonomy.

History

The **Dutch Taxonomy Project** (**Nederlandse Taxonomie Project**) or **NTP** began in 2004 as part of the Dutch cabinet's objectives to reduce the administrative burdens on businesses. The project was sponsored jointly by the Dutch Ministries of Finance and Justice. The NTP created an XBRL taxonomy that "enables businesses to generate the required reporting information directly from their own records and the government to then process this information efficiently and effectively".[1]

The Dutch approach was adopted by the Australian government in 2006, which established the **Standard Business Reporting** (SBR) Program. In addition to Australia, other countries (including New Zealand) are also planning to apply this approach. This approach has since been internationally designated as *Standard Business Reporting*.

In December 2008, the Dutch government decided to rename the NTP to the Standard Business Reporting (SBR) Programme, thus adopting the name introduced by Australia. The Dutch SBR programme has been tasked with deepening and embedding the results obtained so far and broadening the scope to other domains and applications.[2]

Implementations

Dutch Implementation

As of the first of January 2007, businesses and intermediaries can report their financial data to the government using the Dutch XBRL taxonomy.[3]

Australian Implementation

The 2006 report of the *Taskforce on Reducing Regulatory Burdens on Business*, "Rethinking Regulation" (the Banks report), recognised that government reporting requirements impose a significant burden on Australian business.[4]

The objective of the SBR Program in Australia is to reduce the cost of reporting for business by A$800 million over six years at a cost of A$320 million over the same period.[5]

The key activity of the SBR Program is to work across agencies and jurisdictions to standardise the reporting approach and language – developing the taxonomy. As well as the reporting language, SBR is developing a new e-channel for business which will include a single sign-on to on-line services across the agencies that are in scope.[6]

Scope

The agencies in scope are:

- Australian Tax Office (ATO)
- Australian Bureau of Statistics (ABS)
- Australian Securities and Investments Commission (ASIC)
- Australian Prudential Regulation Authority (APRA)
- State and Territory Revenue Offices (8 of them)

More than 75 government forms are in scope to be rationalised and replaced by electronic lodgments.[7]

Planned Solution

The Australian SBR solution is planned to be developed as follows[8] :

- Rationalise and harmonise the reporting terms and definitions in use
- Develop a Reporting Taxonomy
- Map the Reporting Taxonomy to a chart of accounts (provided via a software package)
- Develop IT capabilities and infrastructure, including:
  - Whole of Government authentication/single sign on process; and
  - System for secure on-line interactions
- Connect government systems to the IT capabilities and infrastructure
- Connect businesses to government systems via third-party software

Business Advisory Forum

The SBR program also created the SBR Business Advisory Forum as a way to provide ongoing consultation to the project. It is made up of 18 representatives drawn from industry groups (e.g. Council of Small Business Organisations of Australia [9]), professional associations (e.g. CPA Australia) and the SBR program itself.

The chair is Peter Strong, of the Council of Small Business Organisations of Australia.

Initial Support for SBR

A small number of Australian Companies already offer support for the various SBR forms, especially Business Activity Statement and Tax file Declaration forms, which are amongst the most popular forms. One such small business accounting software is Nominal Accounting

NZ implementation

In May 2008 the New Zealand Ministry of Economic Development published a business case for adopting an SBR program. The business case states that success relies on a high take-up rate by intermediaries such as accountants and lawyers. This is because many owner-operators and small businesses (68% and 21% of businesses, respectively) conduct their reporting via these third-parties.[5]

The business case states that "SBR will deliver compliance cost reductions to business by reducing the need for them to submit information to multiple agencies, standardising data definitions and implementing a standard communication language.".[5]

Notes

[1] van Burg et al, Foreword, p iii.
[2] van Burg et al, p 1
[3] Dutch Taxonomy Project, home page
[4] Madden, slide 2.
[5] Hodgson, p 2
[6] Madden, slide 3
[7] Madden, slide 4
[8] Madden, slide 5
[9] http://www.cosboa.org/

References

* Madden, Paul (3 June 2008). "Standard Business Reporting" (http://www.dama.org.au/canberra/docs/ SBR_June_2008.ppt) (PowerPoint). *Canberra DAMA Chapter*. DAMA Australia. Retrieved 7 July 2009.

* "Standard Business Reporting Program" (http://www.sbr.gov.au) (Web site). Commonwealth of Australia. 2002. Retrieved 14 October 2010. "Reducing the reporting burden for business."

* Hodgson, Minister for Economic Development, (Hon.) Pete; Dalziel, (Hon.) Lianne, Minister of Commerce; Cosgrove, (Hon.) Clayton, Minister for Small Business (16 May 2008). "Standard Business Reporting - Business Case" (http://www.med.govt.nz/upload/58241/SBR.pdf) (PDF). *Ministry of Economic Development*. New Zealand Government. Retrieved 7 July 2009. "This document proposes that New Zealand proceed with the implementation of Standard Business Reporting (SBR) as a whole-of-government work programme aimed at reducing reporting costs, and thereby compliance costs, for business."

* van Burg, Harm Jan; Lokin, Mariette (December 2008). "From NTP to SBR - perspectives on a special project" (http://www.xbrl-ntp.nl/english/ntptosbr) (PDF). *Het Nederlandse Taxonomie Project* (http://www.xbrl-ntp. nl) *(English version* (http://www.xbrl-ntp.nl/english)*)*. het Ministerie van Justitie & het Ministerie van Financiën (Nederlandse). Retrieved 7 July 2009. "Commentary on the occasion of the transition from the Dutch Taxonomy Project to Standard Business Reporting Programme."

* "Het Nederlandse Taxonomie Project [The Dutch Taxonomy Project]" (http://www.xbrl-ntp.nl) (in Dutch) (Web site). het Ministerie van Justitie & het Ministerie van Financiën (Nederlandse). December 2008. Retrieved 7 July 2009.

* "The Dutch Taxonomy Project (English version)" (http://www.xbrl-ntp.nl/english) (Web site). *Het Nederlandse Taxonomie Project*. het Ministerie van Justitie & het Ministerie van Financiën (Nederlandse). December 2008. Retrieved 7 July 2009.

* "Dutch SBR program" (http://www.sbr-nl.nl/item/dutch_standard_business_reporting) (Web site). *Dutch Standard Business Reporting Program*. Logius (http://www.logius.nl/). Retrieved 11 February 2010.

Stenoplax

Stenoplax is genus of polyplacophoran mollusc[1] .

References

[1] "ITIS Standard Report Page: Stenoplax" (http://www.itis.gov/servlet/SingleRpt/SingleRpt?search_topic=TSN&search_value=78920). . Retrieved 12 May 2011.

Sympatric speciation

Sympatric speciation is the process through which new species evolve from a single ancestral species while inhabiting the same geographic region. In evolutionary biology and biogeography, sympatric and sympatry are terms referring to organisms whose ranges overlap or are even identical, so that they occur together at least in some places. If these organisms are closely related (e.g. sister species), such a distribution may be the result of sympatric speciation. Etymologically, sympatry is derived from the Greek roots συν (together, with) and πατρίς (homeland or fatherland).[1] The term was invented by Poulton in 1904, who explains the derivation.[2]

Sympatric speciation is one of three traditional geographic categories for the phenomenon of speciation.[3] [4] Allopatric speciation is the evolution of geographically isolated populations into distinct species. In this case, divergence is facilitated by the absence of interbreeding (gene flow), which tends to keep populations genetically similar. Parapatric speciation is the evolution of geographically adjacent populations into distinct species. In this case, divergence occurs despite limited interbreeding where the two diverging groups come into contact. In sympatric speciation, there is no geographic constraint to interbreeding. It has been pointed out that these categories are special cases of a continuum from zero (sympatric) to complete (allopatric) spatial segregation of diverging groups.[4]

In multicellular eukaryotic organisms, sympatric speciation is thought to be an uncommon but plausible process by which genetic divergence (through reproductive isolation) of various populations from a single parent species and inhabiting the same geographic region leads to the creation of new species.[5] In bacteria, however, the analogous process (defined as "the origin of new bacterial species that occupy definable ecological niches") might be more common because bacteria are less constrained by the homogenizing effects of sexual reproduction and prone to comparatively dramatic and rapid genetic change through horizontal gene transfer.[6]

Evidence

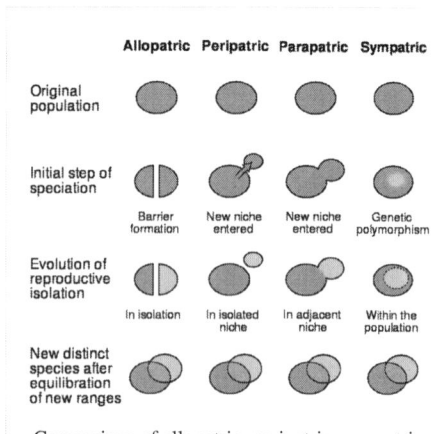

Comparison of allopatric, peripatric, parapatric and sympatric speciation

A number of models have been proposed to account for this mode of speciation. The most popular, which invokes the disruptive selection model, was first put forward by John Maynard Smith in 1966.[7] Maynard Smith suggested that homozygous individuals may, under particular environmental conditions, have a greater fitness than those with alleles heterozygous for a certain trait. Under the mechanism of natural selection, therefore, homozygosity would be favoured over heterozygosity, eventually leading to speciation. Sympatric divergence could also result from the sexual conflict.[8]

Disruption may also occur in multiple-gene traits. The Medium Ground Finch (*Geospiza fortis*) is showing gene pool divergence in a population on Santa Cruz Island. Beak morphology conforms to two different size ideals, while intermediate individuals are selected against. Some characteristics (termed magic traits) such as beak morphology may drive speciation because they also affect mating signals. In this case, different beak phenotypes may result in different bird calls, providing a barrier to exchange between the gene pools.[9]

A well studied circumstance of sympatric speciation is when insects feed on more than one species of host plant. In this case insects become specialized as they struggle to overcome the various plants' defense mechanisms. (Drès and Mallet, 2002)[10]

Rhagoletis pomonella, the apple maggot, may be currently undergoing sympatric or, more precisely, heteropatric (see heteropatry) speciation. The apple feeding race of this species appears to have spontaneously emerged from the hawthorn feeding race in the 1800 - 1850 AD time frame, after apples were first introduced into North America. The apple feeding race does not now normally feed on hawthorns, and the hawthorn feeding race does not now normally feed on apples. This may be an early step towards the emergence of a new species. [11] [12] [13] Isolated and relatively homogeneous habitats such as crater lakes and islands are among the best geographical settings in which to demonstrate sympatric speciation. For example, Nicaragua crater lake cichlid fishes include at least one species that has evolved by sympatric speciation [14]

Allochrony offers some empirical evidence that sympatric speciation has taken place, as many examples exist of recently diverged (sister taxa) allochronic species.

Sympatric speciation events are vastly more common in plants, as they are prone to developing multiple homologous sets of chromosomes, resulting in a condition called polyploidy. The polyploidal offspring occupy the same environment as the parent plants (hence sympatry), but are reproductively isolated.

A rare example of sympatric speciation in animals is the divergence of "resident" and "transient" Orca forms in the northeast Pacific.[15] Resident and transient orcas inhabit the same waters, but avoid each other and do not interbreed. The two forms hunt different prey species and have different diets, vocal behaviour, and social structures. Some divergences between species could also result from contrasts in microhabitats.

The polecat *Mustela putorius* exhibited a rare dark phenotype similar to the European mink *Mustela lutreola* phenotype which is directly influenced by peculiarities of forest brooks.[16]

Controversy

Debated almost since the beginning of popular evolutionary thought, sympatric speciation is still a highly contentious issue. By 1980 the theory was largely unfavourable given the void of empirical evidence available, and more critically the conditions scientists expect to be required. Ernst Mayr, one of the foremost thinkers on evolution, completely rejected sympatry outright, ushering in a climate of hostility towards the theory. While still debatable, well documented empirical evidence now exists, and the development of sophisticated theories incorporating multilocus genetics has followed.

References

[1] http://www.greek-language.gr/greekLang/index.html

[2] Poulton, E. B. 1904. What is a species? Proceedings of the Entomological Society of London 1903:lxxvii-cxvi.

[3] Futuyma, D. J. 2009. Evolution (2nd edition). Sinauer Associates, Inc.

[4] Fitzpatrick, B. M., J. A. Fordyce, and S. Gavrilets. 2008. What, if anything, is sympatric speciation? Journal of Evolutionary Biology 21: 1452-1459.

[5] Bolnick, D. I. and B. M. Fitzpatrick. 2007. Sympatric speciation: Models and empirical evidence. Annual Review of Ecology, Evolution and Systematics 38: 459-487.

[6] King, Stansfield, Mulligan (2006). *Dictionary of Genetics* (7th ed.). Oxford University Press.

[7] John Maynard Smith (1966). "Sympatric Speciation". *American Naturalist* **100 (916)**: 637–650. (http://www.jstor.org/stable/2459301)

[8] Thierry Lodé "La guerre des sexes chez les animaux" Eds O Jacob, Paris, 2006

[9] *Huber, SK; De León, LF; Hendry, AP; Bermingham, E; Podos, J (2007). "Reproductive isolation of sympatric morphs in a population of Darwin's finches". *Proc. Biol. Sci.* **274** (1619): 1709–14. doi:10.1098/rspb.2007.0224. PMC 2493575. PMID 17504742

[10] Begon, Townsend, Harper: Ecology - From individuals to ecosystems, 4th ed., p.10

[11] McPheron et al. 1988. *Nature* 336:64-66 (http://www.nature.com/nature/journal/v336/n6194/abs/336064a0.html)

[12] Smith, D.C. 1988. *Nature* 336:66-67 (http://www.nature.com/nature/journal/v336/n6194/abs/336066a0.html)

[13] Feder et al. 1988. *Nature* 336:61-64 (http://www.nature.com/nature/journal/v336/n6194/abs/336061a0.html)

[14] Sympatric speciation in Nicaraguan crater lake cichlid fish. By: Barluenga, Marta; Stölting, Kai N.; Salzburger, Walter; Muschick, Moritz; Meyer, Axel. Nature, 2/9/2006, Vol. 439 Issue 7077, p719-723.

[15] Hoetzel et al. 1998, Low genetic variation among killer whales (Orcinus orca) in the eastern North Pacific and genetic differentiation between foraging specialists, *J Hered* (http://jhered.oxfordjournals.org/content/89/2/121.full.pdf)

[16] Thierry Lodé "Genetic divergence without spatial isolation in polecat Mustela putorius populations". J Evol Biol 14:228-236, 2001

External links

- Berkeley evolution 101 (http://evolution.berkeley.edu/evosite/evo101/VC1eSympatric.shtml)

Synopses of the British Fauna

Synopses of the British Fauna is a series of identification guides, published by The Linnean Society and The Estuarine and Coastal Sciences Association. Each volume in the series provides and in-depth analysis of a group of animals and is designed to bridge the gap between the standard field guide and more specialised monograph or treatise. The series is now published by The Field Studies Council on behalf of The Linnean Society and The Estuarine and Coastal Sciences Association.

The series is designed for use in the field and is kept as user friendly as possible with technical terminology kept to a minimum and a glossary of terms provided, although the complexity of the subject matter makes the books more suitable for the more experienced practitioner.

History of the series

On 11 March 1943, at a meeting of The Linnean Society in Burlington House, TH Savoy presented his 'Synopsis of the Opiliones' (Harvestmen). It was so well received that a decision was made there and then to publish it as the first of a series of 'ecological fauna lists'.

Re-launched by Dr Doris Kermack in the mid-1960s, the New Series of Synopses of the British Fauna went from strength to strength. From number 13, the series had been jointly sponsored by The Estuarine and Coastal Sciences Association and Dr RSK Barnes became co-editor.

From 1993, the series has been published by The Field Studies Council and benefits from association with the extensive testing undertaken as part of the AIDGAP project.

Cover of Sea-Spiders (2010)

Volumes

The series contains the following volumes, many of which are out of print. Many of the volumes have been updated and reprinted under slightly different names to reflect either taxonomic changes or advances in the understanding of a group.

- Volume 58: Centipedes (AD Barber) 2009
- Volume 57: Barnacles (AJ Southward) 2008
- Volume 56: Echinoderms (EC Southward and AC Campbell) 2005
- Volume 55: Lobsters, Mud Shrimps and Anomuran Crabs (RW Ingle and ME Christiansen) 2004
- Volume 54: Polychaetes: British Chrysopetaloidea, Pisionoidea and Aphroditoidea (SJ Chambers and AI Muir) 1998
- Volume 53: Free Living British Nematodes, Part 3 Monohysterids (RM Warwick, HM Platt and PJ Somerfield) 1998
- Volume 52: Ticks of North-West Europe (Paul D Hillyard) 1996
- Volume 51: Marine and Brackish Water Harpacticoid Copepods, Part 1 (R Huys, JM Gee, CG Moore and R Hamond) 1996
- Volume 50: North-west European Thecate Hydroids and Their Medusae (PFS Cornelius) 1995
- Volume 49: Woodlice Keys and Notes for Identification of the Species (PG Oliver and CJ Meechan) 1993
- Volume 48: Marine Planktonic Ostracods (MV Angel) 1993
- Volume 47: Copepods Parasitic on Fishes (Z Kabata) 1992

- Volume 46: Commensal and Parasitic Copepods Associated with Marine Invertebrates (and Whales) (V Gotto) 1993
- Volume 45: Polychaetes British Phyllodocoideans, Typhloscolecoideans and Tomopteroideans (F Pleijel and RP Dales) 1991
- Volume 44: Polychaetes: Interstitial Families (Second Edition) (W Westheide) 2008
- Volume 44: Polychaetes: Interstitial Families (W Westheide) 1990
- Volume 43: Marine and Brackish Water Ostracods (Superfamilies Cypridacea and Cytheracea) (J Athersuch, DJ Horne and JE Whittaker) 1990
- Volume 42: Freshwater Ostracoda (PA Henderson) 1990
- Volume 41: Entoprocts (C Nielsen) 1989
- Volume 40: Pseudoscorpions (G Legg and RE Jones) 1988
- Volume 39: Chaetognatha (AC Pierrot-Bults and KC Chidghey) 1988
- Volume 38: Free Living Marine Nematodes Part II British Chromadorids (HM Platt and RM Warwick) 1988
- Volume 37: Molluscs Caudofoveata, Solenogastres, Polyplacophora and Scaphopoda (AM Jones and JM Baxtyer) 1987
- Volume 36: Halacarid Mites (J Green and M Macquitty) 1987
- Volume 35: Millipedes (J Gordon Blower) 1985
- Volume 34: Cyclostome Bryozoans (PJ Hayward and JS Ryland) 1985
- Volume 33: Ctenostome Bryozoans (PJ Hayward) 1985
- Volume 32: Polychaetes British Amphinomida, Spintherida and Eunicida (JD George and G Hartmann-Schroder) 1985
- Volume 31: Earthworms (RW Sims and BM Garard) 1985
- Volume 30: Euphasiid, Stomatopod and Leptostracan Crustaceans (J Mauchline) 1984
- Volume 29: Siphonophores and Velellids (PA Kirkpatrick and PR Pugh) 1984
- Volume 28: Free-Living Marine Nematodes Pt 1: British Enoplids Free Living Marine Nematodes (HM Platt and RM Warwick) 1983
- Volume 27: Tanaids (DM Holdich and JA Jones) 1983
- Volume 26: British Polyclad Turbellarians (S Prudhoe) 1983
- Volume 25: Shallow Water Crabs Keys and notes for identification of the species (RW Ingle) 1983
- Volume 24: Nemerteans R Gibson 1982
- Volume 23: British and Other Freshwater Ciliated Protozoa (Part 2) Ciliophora: Oligohymenophora & Polyhymenophora (CR Curds, MA Gates and D McRoberts) 1982
- Volume 22: British and Other Freshwater Ciliated Protozoa (Part 1) Ciliophora: Kinetofragminophora (CR Curds) 1982
- Volume 21: British Other Marine Estuarine Oligochaetes (Brinkhurst) 1982
- Volume 20: British Pelagic Tunicates (JH Fraser) 1982
- Volume 19: British Planarians (IR Ball and TB Reynoldson) 1981
- Volume 18: British Anthozoa (RL Manuel) 1981
- Volume 17: British Brachiopods (C Howard, C Brunton and GB Curry) 1979
- Volume 16: British Nearshore Foraminiferids (JW Murray) 1979
- Volume 15: Coastal Shrimps and Prawns Keys and Notes for Identification of the Species (Ed. G Smaldon, LB Holthius and CHJM Fransen) 1994
- Volume 15: British Coastal Shrimps Prawns (G Smaldon) 1979
- Volume 14: Cheilostomatous Bryozoa, Part 2 Hippothooidea - Celleporoidea (PJ Hayward and JS Ryland) 1999
- Volume 14: British Ascophoran Bryozoans (PJ Hayward, JS Ryland) 1979
- Volume 13: British and Other Phoronids (CC Emig) 1979
- Volume 12: British Sipunculans (PE Gibbs) 1978

- Volume 11: British Freshwater Bivalve Mollusca (AE Ellis) 1978
- Volume 10: Cheilostomatous Bryozoa, Part 1: Aeteoidea-Cribrilinoidea (PJ Hayward and JS Ryland)
- Volume 8: Molluscs: Benthic Opisthobranchs (Mollusca: Gastropoda) (TE Thompson) 1989
- Volume 8: British Opisthobranch Molluscs (TE Thompson, GH Brown) 1976
- Volume 7: British Cumaceans (NS Jones) 1976
- Volume 6: British Land Snails (RAD Cameron, M Redfern) 1976
- Volume 5: Sea-Spiders (Pycnogonida) of the north-east Atlantic (RN Bamber) 2010
- Volume 5: British Sea Spiders (PE King) 1974
- Volume 4: Harvestmen (PD Hillyard) 2005
- Volume 4: British Harvestmen (J Sankey, TH Savory) 1974
- Volume 3: British Marine Isopods (E Naylor) 1972
- Volume 2: Molluscs: Prosobranch and Pyramidellid Gastropods Keys and Notes for the Identification of the Species
- Volume 1: British Ascidians (R Millar) 1970

External links

- Linnean Society [1]
- Full list of Synopses in print [2]

References

[1] http://linnean.org/
[2] http://www.field-studies-council.org/publications/synopses.aspx

Tagspace

Tagspace is the space containing a plurality of metadata tags wherein there is visually illustrated at least one aspect of the metadata tags interrelatedness. The simplest tagspace is two dimensional in which the tags are sized to indicate relative importance, or popularity. More complex tagspaces extend to three or four dimensions and visually illustrate multiple aspects of metadata interrelatedness.

Tagspace is a Wordpress plugin available for download at Wordpress.org [1].

A **tagspace** is a list of tags used to describe an object. There are different ways of depicting the tagspace either by using a flat list or a tag cloud. The term tagspace is derived from namespace as it shares the same idea of disambiguation.

References

[1] http://wordpress.org/extend/plugins/tagspace/

Tautonym

In biology

In biology, **tautonym** is an informal term to indicate a scientific name of a species in which both parts of the name have the same spelling, for example *Bison bison*. The first part of the name is the name of the genus and the second part is referred to as the *specific epithet* in the *International Code of Botanical Nomenclature* and the *specific name* in the *International Code of Zoological Nomenclature*.

From a formal perspective, in the rules of nomenclature as laid down in the Nomenclature Codes, no tautonym exists. In past editions of the zoological Code the term was used, but it has now been replaced by the more inclusive "tautonymous names"; these include names such as *Gorilla gorilla gorilla*. Tautonymy (i.e., the usage of tautonymous names) is permissible in zoological nomenclature (see List of tautonyms for examples).

In the rules for botanical nomenclature, tautonyms are explicitly prohibited (*ICBN*, Art 23.4 [1]) . An example of a botanical tautonym that does not exist is 'Larix larix'. The earliest name for the European larch is *Pinus larix* L. (1753) but Gustav Karl Wilhelm Hermann Karsten did not agree with the placement of the species in *Pinus* and decided to move it to *Larix*. His proposed name would have created a tautonym, not acceptable under the rules (1906 onwards; the rules are retroactive): it does not and cannot exist (as a formal name). In such a case either the next earliest validly published name must be found, in this case *Larix decidua* Mill. (1768), or (in its absence) a new epithet must be published.

However, it is allowed for both parts of the name of a species to mean the same, without being identical in spelling. For instance, *Arctostaphylos uva-ursi* means bearberry twice, in Greek and Latin respectively; *Picea omorica* uses the Latin and Serbian terms for a pine. There are also instances of an almost repeat of the genus name, with a slight modification, such as *Lycopersicon lycopersicum* (Greek and Latinized Greek, a rejected name for the tomato). Differences as small as a single letter are permissible, as in the name *Ziziphus zizyphus*.

In linguistics

In general English, a tautonym is sometimes considered to be any word or term made from two identical parts or syllables, such as bonbon or dada. The origin of this usage is uncertain, but it has been suggested that it is of relatively recent derivation. The general term in linguistics for such double words is reduplicants.

External links

- *International Code of Botanical Nomenclature*, Art. 23.4 [1]
- *International Code of Zoological Nomenclature*, Art. 18 [2] and Art. 23.3.7 [3]

References

[1] http://www.bgbm.fu-berlin.de/iapt/nomenclature/code/SaintLouis/0027Ch3Sec4a023.htm

[2] http://www.iczn.org/iczn/includes/page.jsp?nfv=&article=18

[3] http://www.iczn.org/iczn/includes/page.jsp?nfv=&article=23#3.7

Taxome

The **taxome** is the sum of all the described species and higher groups such as genera, families, phyla of all life, or the sum of all valid taxa. The documenting of all this biodiversity is still very incomplete.

Many organisms have already been documented (it is guessed that around 1-2 million species have been described — see Species Inventory in biodiversity article), but probably around nine-tenths of existing species have never been described, and those that have been described may have been redescribed, many times, under different names. Thus, the state of the science of taxonomy (the systematic organization of life) is somewhat confused.

There system of Linnean nomenclature (named after the 18th century Swedish pioneer Carolus Linnaeus) is such that, in principle, the correct scientific name of all organisms described could be adjudicated, by means of historical priority. However, the names of many organisms are published in such obscure books and journals that very little of this information is available to most people. Thus, not only do we have little idea how many species there are, but we are even ignorant of the number of supposedly known species that have been described.

However, the situation is not as bad as it is sometimes painted. The sum total of all existing taxonomic and nomenclatural documentation of living things is not large by today's data-rich standards. We know where the books and journals are where species might have been described. We simply need to put in the work to make the text and graphics of species descriptions available in databases, particularly electronic databases. In many groups, species are poorly known, but it is now rare to discover a major undetected phylum or family, so coverage of the kinds of diversity of life is probably good, even if all species are not described. Most of the undiscovered groups are probably reasonably closely related to something we have described. Thus if we could document the existing knowledge, we would have a useful, albeit somewhat pixellated map of the diversity of life.

Just as a sequenced genome of an organism is a map of its DNA, a database documenting the complete taxome would form a map of the described biodiversity of the entire planet. Existing projects are mapping the positions of moons, planets and stars in the universe, as well as the physical geography of our own planet, and the genomes of selected organisms. Projects are now being set up to take advantage of information technology to document and make available the entire body of taxonomy on line. When this information becomes more complete, it should be possible to link this taxome information to all other information about biology.

Taxonomic database

A **taxonomic database** is a database created to hold information related to biological taxa - for example groups of organisms organized by species name or other taxonomic identifier - for efficient data management and information retrieval as required. Today, taxonomic databases are routinely used for the automated construction of biological checklists such as floras and faunas, both for print publication and online; to underpin the operation of web based species information systems; as a part of biological collection management (for example in museums and herbaria); as well as providing, in some cases, the taxon management component of broader science or biology information systems. They are also a fundamental contribution to the discipline of biodiversity informatics.

Goal

The goal of a taxonomic database is (or should be) to accurately model the characteristics of interest that are relevant to the organisms which are in scope for the intended coverage and usage of the system. For example, databases of fungi, algae, bryophytes and higher plants would need to encode conventions from the International Code of Botanical Nomenclature while their counterparts for animals and most protists would encode equivalent rules from the International Code of Zoological Nomenclature; in both cases modelling the relevant taxonomic hierarchy for any taxon is a natural fit with the relational model employed in almost all database systems. In additional to encoding organism identifiers (most frequently a combination of scientific name, author, and - for zoological taxa - year of original publication), a taxonomic database may frequently incorporate additional taxonomic information such as synonyms and taxonomic opinions, literature sources or citations, plus a range of biological of attributes as desired for each taxon such as geographic distribution, ecology, descriptive information, threatened or vulnerable status, etc.

History

Possibly the earliest documented management of taxonomic information in computerised form comprised the taxonomic coding system developed by Richard Swartz et al. at the Virginia Institute of Marine Science for the Biota of Chesapeake Bay and described in a published report in 1972[1] . This work led directly or indirectly to other projects with greater profile including the NODC Taxonomic Code system[2] which went through 8 versions before being discontinued in 1996, to be subsumed and transformed into the still current Integrated Taxonomic Information System (ITIS). A number of other taxonomic databases specializing in particular groups of organisms that appeared in the 1970s through to the present jointly contribute to the Species 2000 project, which since 2001 has been partnering with ITIS to produce a combined product, the Catalogue of Life. While the Catalogue of Life currently concentrates on assembling basic name information as a global species checklist, numerous other taxonomic database projects such as Fauna Europaea, the Australian Faunal Directory[3] , and more supply rich ancillary information including descriptions, illustrations, maps, and more. Many taxonomic database projects are currently listed at the TDWG "Biodiversity Information Projects of the World" site[4] .

Issues

The representation of taxonomic information in machine-encodable form raises a number of issues not encountered in other domains, such as variant ways to cite the same species or other taxon name, the same name used for multiple taxa (homonyms), multiple non-current names for the same taxon (synonyms), changes in name and taxon concept definition through time, and more. One forum that has promoted discussion and possible solutions to these and related problems since 1985 is the Taxonomic Database Working Group.

References

[1] Swartz, RC., Wass ML., Boesch DF. (1972). *A taxonomic code for the biota of the Chesapeake Bay. Special scientific report no. 62 of the Virginia Institute of Marine Science* (http://www.vims.edu/GreyLit/VIMS/ssr062.pdf). Gloucester Point, Va: Virginia Institute of Marine Science. pp. 117. .

[2] "NODC Taxonomic Code" (http://www.nodc.noaa.gov/General/CDR-detdesc/taxonomic-v8.html). . Retrieved 2009-08-06.

[3] "Australian Faunal Directory" (http://www.environment.gov.au/biodiversity/abrs/online-resources/fauna/afd/index.html). . Retrieved 2009-08-06.

[4] "TDWG "Biodiversity Information Projects of the World" database" (http://www.tdwg.org/biodiv-projects/). . Retrieved 2009-08-06.

External links

- TDWG (Taxonomic Database Working Group) website (http://www.tdwg.org/)

Taxonomic homonym

In biology, a **homonym** (**taxonomic homonym**) is a name for a taxon that is identical in spelling to another such name, that belongs to a different taxon.

The rule in the International Code of Zoological Nomenclature is that the first such name to be published is the **senior homonym** and is to be used (it is "valid"); any others are **junior homonyms** and must be replaced with new names. It is, however, possible that if a senior homonym is archaic, and not in "prevailing usage," it may be declared a *nomen oblitum* and rendered unavailable, while the junior homonym is preserved as a *nomen protectum*.

For example:

- Cuvier proposed the genus *Echidna* in 1797 for the spiny anteater.
- However, Forster had already published the name *Echidna* in 1777 for a genus of moray eels.
- Forster's use thus has priority, with Cuvier's being a junior homonym.
- Illiger published the replacement name *Tachyglossus* in 1811.

Similarly, the International Code of Botanical Nomenclature specifies that the first published of two or more homonyms is to be used: a **later homonym** is "illegitimate" and is not to be used unless conserved.

Example: the later homonym *Myroxylon* L.f. (1782), in the *Leguminosae*, is conserved against the earlier homonym *Myroxylon* J.R.Forst. & G.Forst. (1775), in the *Flacourtiaceae*.

Under the botanical code, names that are similar enough that they are likely to be confused, are also considered to be homonymous (article 53.3). For example, *Astrostemma* Benth. (1880) is an illegitimate homonym of *Asterostemma* Decne. (1838). The zoological code has a set of spelling variations (article 58) that are considered to be identical.

Both Codes only consider taxa that are in their respective scope (animals for the ICZN; primarily plants for the ICBN). Therefore, if an animal taxon has the same name as a plant taxon, both names are valid. For example, the name *Erica* has been given to both a genus of spiders, *Erica* Peckham & Peckham, 1892, and to a genus of heaths, *Erica* L.

References

Taxonomic inflation

Taxonomic inflation is a pejorative term for what is perceived to be an excessive increase in the number of recognised taxa in a given context, due not to the discovery of new taxa but rather to putatively arbitrary changes to how taxa are delineated.

The best known case is the elevation of a group of subspecies to species rank, through the arbitrary decision that the differences between the various taxa warrant distinguishing them at species rank.

Taxonomic inflation is often claimed to occur for conservation reasons. It may be difficult to make a case for the protection of an isolated and unusual population of a common and widespread species, but it becomes much easier to do so if that population is recognised as a rare subspecies or species.[1] [2]

References

[1] Isaac, Nick; Mallet, James; Mace, Georgina (2004). "Taxonomic inflation: its influence on macroecology and conservation" (http://www. ucl.ac.uk/taxome/jim/pap/isaac04.pdf). *TRENDS in Ecology and Evolution* **19** (9): 464–469. . Retrieved 2011-02-23.

[2] "Hail Linnaeus" (http://www.economist.com/node/9191545?story_id=9191545). *The Economist* (May 17, 2007). . Retrieved 2011-02-23.

Identification key

In biology, an **identification key** is a printed or computer-aided device that aids the identification of biological entities, such as plants, animals, fossils, microorganisms, and pollen grains. Identification keys are also used in many other scientific and technical fields to identify various kinds of entities, such as diseases, soil types, minerals, or archaeological and anthropological artifacts.

Traditionally identification keys have most commonly taken the form of **single-access keys**. These work by offering a fixed sequence of *identification steps*, each with multiple alternatives, the choice of which determines the next step. If each step has only two alternatives, the key is said to be **dichotomous**, else it is **polytomous**. Modern **multi-access** or **interactive** keys allow the user to freely choose the identification steps and their order.

At each step, the user must answer a question about one or more features (*characters*) of the entity to be identified. For example, a step in a botanical key may ask about the color of flowers, or the disposition of the leaves along the stems. A key for insect identification may ask about the number of bristles on the rear leg.

Principles of good key design

Identification errors may have serious consequences in both pure and applied disciplines, including ecology, medical diagnosis, pest control, forensics, etc..[1] Therefore, identification keys must be constructed with great care in order to minimize the incidence of such errors.

Whenever possible, the character used at each identification step should be *diagnostic*; that is, each alternative should be common to all members of a group of entities, and unique to that group. It should also be *differential*, meaning that the alternatives should separate the corresponding subgroups from each other. However, characters which are neither differential nor diagnostic may be included to increase comprehension (especially characters that are common to the group, but not unique).

Whenever possible, redundant characters should be used at each step. For example, if a group is to be split into two subgroups, one characterized by six black spots and the other by four brown stripes, the user should be queried about all three characters (number, shape, and color of the markings) — even though any single one of them would be sufficient in theory. This redundancy improves the reliability of identification, provides a consistency check against user errors, and allows the user to proceed even if some of the characters could not be observed. In this case, the characters should be ordered according to their reliability and convenience. Further error tolerance can be achieved by using reticulation.

The terminology used in the identification steps should be consistent in meaning and should be uniformly used. The use of alternative terms for the same concept to achieve more "lively prose" should be avoided. Positive statements should be used in preference to negative statements. The wording of the alternatives should be completely parallel sentences; alternatives like "flowers red, size 10-40 cm" versus "flowers yellow" should be avoided.

Geographic distribution characters should be used with caution. Species that have not been observed in a region may still occasionally occur there. Also, the organism may have been transported, particularly to locations near ports and airports, or it may have changed its range (e. g., due to global warming). For Europe and, probably, North Africa a Palaearctic key is advisable.

Rarity is not a viable character. An identification may be correct even though a species is very rare.

Common problems in key usage

Key users must overcome many practical problems, such as:

- *Variant forms*: The key may identify only some forms of the species, such as adult males (or, more rarely, females). Keys for larvae identification may consider only the final instar. (This is not the case, however, of keys used in forensic identification of fly larvae.)

- *Incomplete coverage*: Species and groups that are difficult to identify or that have been poorly characterized may have been left out of the key, or may be mentioned only in introductory text.

- *Lighting and magnification*: Very few keys give details of how the specimen was viewed (the magnification, lighting system, angle of view etc.). This can cause problems. The author may, for instance refer to tiny bristles, hairs or chaetae--but how tiny?

- *Language*: Very few keys are multilingual.[2] Translations of a key may be incorrect or misleading. Many keys contain vague words that do not translate..

- *Obsolescence*: Older keys may not include more recently described species. They may also use outdated species names, which must then be mapped to the current ones.

Verifying identifications

The identification obtained from a key should be viewed as only a suggestion of the species's real identity. Full identification requires comparison of the specimen with some authoritative source, such as a full and accurate description of the species, preferably in a monograph. Many keys contain brief descriptions to allow more certain identification, but these should not be assumed sufficient for verification.

Comparison with a monographic description is often difficult in practice, as many monographs are expensive, out of print, written in foreign languages, or hard to obtain. Monographs are often several decades old, so that often the species names used in the key do not match those used in the monograph.

Another alternative is comparison with authoritatively identified specimens in natural history museums or other relevant repositories. Authoritatively identified images are becoming more common on the internet. To qualify, the image must be labeled with a *voucher specimen* number, the name of the scientist who identified the photographed specimen, and the name of the public institution where the specimen is housed (so that interested parties can re-examine the specimen themselves).

External links

- Xper2 - Interactive identification and descriptive data management software [3]
- Principles of interactive keys [4]
- Programs for interactive identification and information retrieval [5]
- Lucid - Interactive Identification and Diagnostics key software [6]
- Visual Identification to *Carices* of North America at LSU Herbarium [7]
- Discover Life - Interactive Guides and free online guide development space [8]
- Bioimages [9] Comments on Royal Entomological Society of London Keys

References

[1] Steve Marshall, (http://www.biology.ualberta.ca/bsc/news_19_2/error_rates.htm)

[2] Commercial Timbers (http://delta-intkey.com/wood/index.htm), an example of a key in five languages.

[3] http://lis-upmc.snv.jussieu.fr/lis/?q=en/resources/software/xper2

[4] http://delta-intkey.com/www/interactivekeys.htm

[5] http://delta-intkey.com/www/idprogs.htm

[6] http://www.lucidcentral.org/

[7] http://www.herbarium2.lsu.edu/aba/index.html

[8] http://www.discoverlife.org/

[9] http://www.bioimages.org.uk/html/B147338.HTM

Subspecies of *Canis lupus*

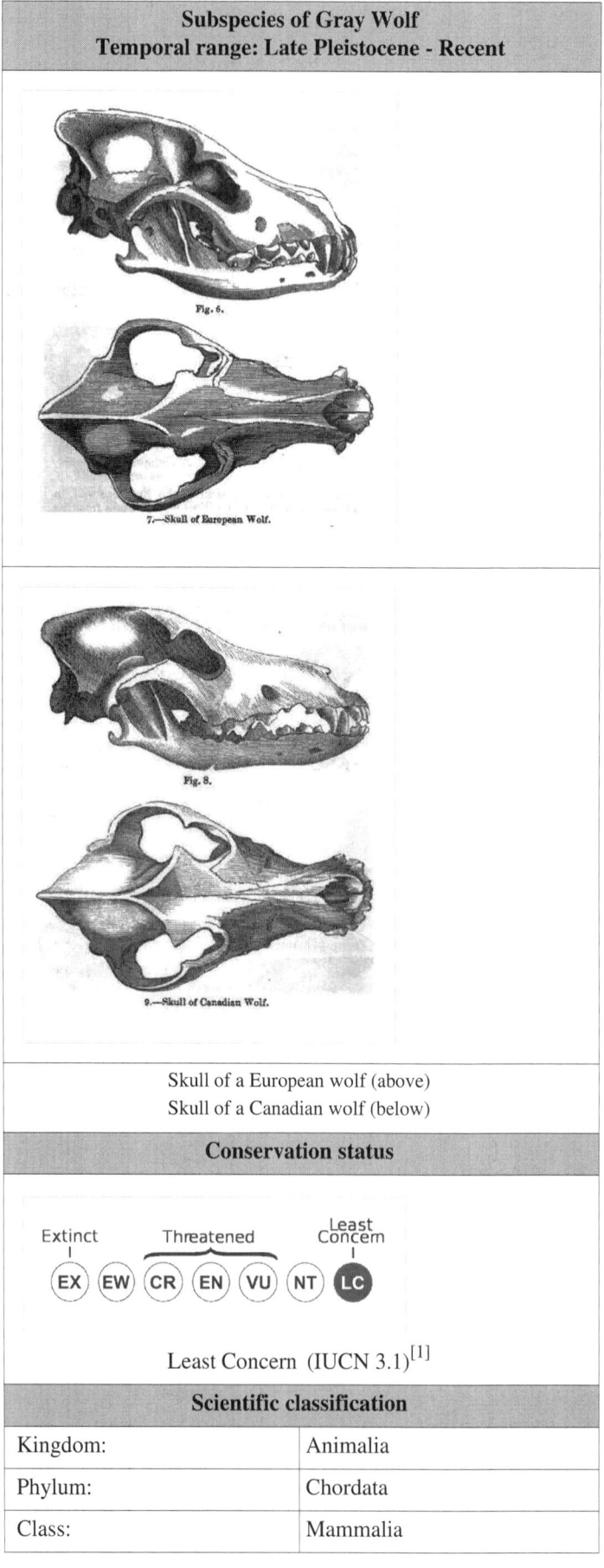

Subspecies of Gray Wolf Temporal range: Late Pleistocene - Recent	
Skull of a European wolf (above) Skull of a Canadian wolf (below)	
Conservation status	
Least Concern (IUCN 3.1)[1]	
Scientific classification	
Kingdom:	Animalia
Phylum:	Chordata
Class:	Mammalia

Order:	Carnivora
Family:	Canidae
Genus:	*Canis*
Species:	**C. lupus**
Binomial name	
Canis lupus Linnaeus, 1758	

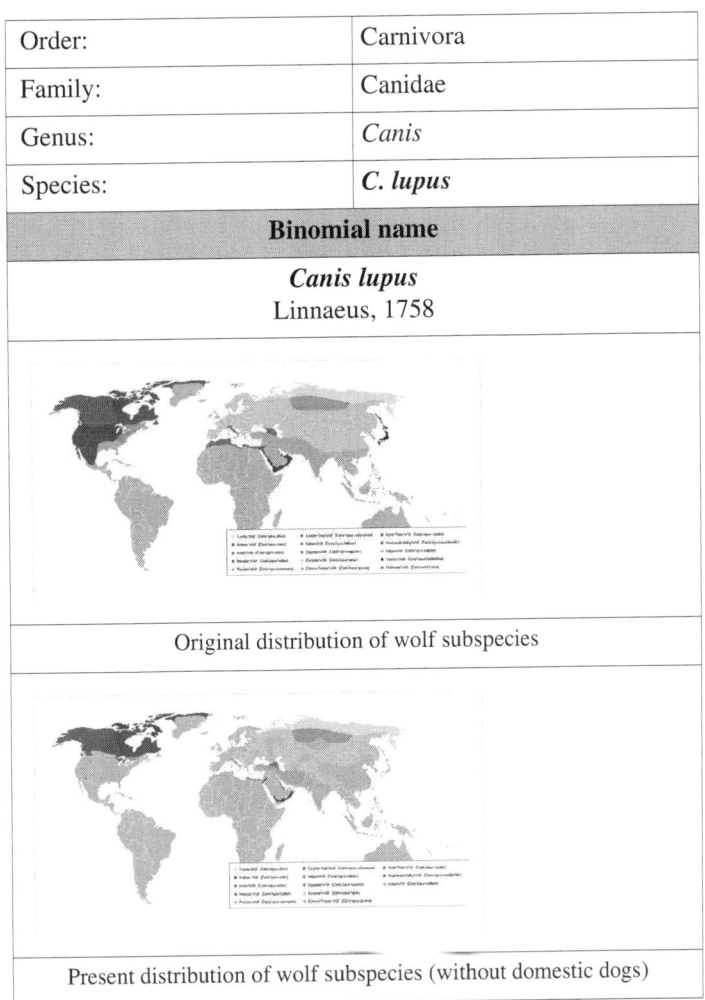

Original distribution of wolf subspecies
Present distribution of wolf subspecies (without domestic dogs)

Canis lupus has 39 subspecies currently described, including two subspecies of domestic dog, *Canis lupus dingo* and *Canis lupus familiaris*, and many subspecies of wolf throughout the Northern hemisphere. The nominate subspecies is *Canis lupus lupus*.

Canis lupus is assessed as Least Concern by the IUCN, as its relatively widespread range and stable population trend mean that the species, at global level, does not meet, or nearly meet, any of the criteria for the threatened categories.[1]

Biological taxonomy is not fixed, and placement of taxa is reviewed as a result of new research. The current categorization of subspecies of *Canis lupus* is shown below. Also included are synonyms, which are now discarded duplicate or incorrect namings. Common names are given but may vary, as they have no set meaning.

Geographical variations

Wolves show a great deal of dimorphism geographically, though they can interbreed. The Zoological Gardens of London for example once successfully managed to mate a male European wolf to an Indian female, resulting in a cub bearing an almost exact likeness to its sire.[2]

Europe

European wolves tend to have coarse fur with less soft wool intermixed than American wolves. Their heads are narrower, their ears longer, higher placed and somewhat closer to each other. Their loins are more slender, their legs longer, their feet narrower, and their tails more thinly clothed with fur.[3] Pelt colour in European wolves ranges from white, cream, red, grey and black, sometimes with all colours combined. Wolves in central Europe tend to be more richly coloured than those in Northern Europe. Eastern European wolves tend to be shorter and more heavily built than Northern Russian ones.[4]

North America

North American wolves are generally the same size as European wolves, but have shorter legs, larger, rounder heads, broader, more obtuse muzzles, and a sensible depression at the union of nose and forehead, which is more arched and broad. Their ears are shorter and have a more conical form. They typically lack the black mark on the forelegs, as is the case in European races. They have long and comparatively fine fur, mixed with a shorter wooly hair, and are more robust.[3] Fur colour in American wolves ranges from white, black, red, yellow, brown, gray, and grizzled skins, and others representing every shade between, although usually each locality has its prevailing tint. There are pronounced differences in North American wolves of different localities; wolves from Texas and New Mexico are comparatively slim animals with small teeth.[5] Mexican wolves in particular resemble some European wolves in stature, though their heads are usually broader, their necks thicker, their ears longer and their tails shorter.[6] Wolves of the central and northern chains of the Rocky Mountains and coastal ranges are more formidable animals than the more southern plains wolves, and resemble Russian and Scandinavian wolves in size and proportions.[5]

List of subspecies

Canis lupus subspecies as of 2005[7]

Subspecies	Authority	Description	Range	Synonyms
Eurasian wolf *Canis lupus lupus* (nominate subspecies)	Linnaeus 1758[8]	Generally a large subspecies measuring 105–160 cm in length and weighing 40–80 kg. The pelt is usually a mix of rusty ocherous and light grey.[9]	Has the largest range among wolf subspecies and is the most common in Europe and Asia, ranging through Western Europe, Scandinavia, Russia, China, Mongolia, and the Himalayan Mountains	*altaicus* (Noack, 1911), *argunensis* (Dybowski, 1922), *canus* (Sélys Longchamps, 1839), *communis* (Dwigubski, 1804), *deitanus* (Cabrera, 1907), *desertorum* (Bogdanov, 1882), *flavus* (Kerr, 1792), *fulvus* (Sélys Longchamps, 1839), *italicus* (Altobello, 1921), *kurjak* (Bolkay, 1925), *lycaon* (Trouessart, 1910), *major* (Ogérien, 1863), *minor* (Ogerien, 1863), *niger* (Hermann, 1804), *orientalis* (Wagner, 1841), *orientalis* (Dybowski, 1922), *signatus* (Cabrera, 1907)[10]
Tundra wolf *Canis lupus albus*	Kerr 1792[11]	A large subspecies, with adults measuring 112–137 cm, and weighing 36.6–52 kg. The fur is very long, dense, fluffy and soft and is usually very light and grey in colour. The lower fur is lead-grey and the upper fur is reddish-grey.[9]	Northern tundra and forest zones in the European and Asian parts of Russia and Kamchatka. Outside Russia, its range includes the extreme north of Scandinavia[9]	*dybowskii* (Domaniewski, 1926), *kamtschaticus* (Dybowski, 1922), *turuchanensis* (Ognev, 1923)[12]
† Kenai Peninsula wolf *Canis lupus alces*	Goldman 1941[13]	A large wolf measuring over 180 cm in length and weighing 45–63 kg. It is thought that its large size was an adaptation to hunting the extremely large moose of the Kenai Peninsula.[14]	Kenai Peninsula	

Arabian wolf *Canis lupus arabs* 	Pocock 1934[15]	A small, "desert adapted" wolf that is around 66 cm tall and weighs, on average, about 18 kg.[16] Its fur coat varies from short in the summer and long in the winter, possibly because of solar radiation.[17]	Southern Israel, Southern and western Iraq, Oman, Yemen, Jordan, Saudi Arabia, and probably some parts of the Sinai Peninsula	
Arctic wolf *Canis lupus arctos* 	Pocock 1935[18]	A medium sized wolf that is between 64 and 79 cm tall and 89 to 189 cm long, weighing between 35 and 45 kg on average, though there have been specimens found weighing up to 68 kg.[19][20]	Canadian Arctic, Alaska and northern Greenland	
Mexican wolf *Canis lupus baileyi* 	Nelson and Goldman 1929[21]	A small subspecies which weighs 25–45 kg and measures 140–170 cm in total length (nose to tip of tail), and 72–80 cm in shoulder height. The pelt contains a mix of gray, black, brown, and rust colors in a characteristic pattern, with white underparts[22]	Northern Mexico, western Texas, southern New Mexico, and southeastern and central Arizona[22]	
† Newfoundland wolf *Canis lupus beothucus*	G. M. Allen and Barbour 1937	A white coloured subspecies typically measuring 180 cm in length and weighing 45 kg[14]	Newfoundland	
† Bernard's wolf *Canis lupus bernardi*	Anderson 1943	This subspecies became extinct in 1934, though it was described as "white with black-tipped hair along the ridge of the back".[23]	Limited to Banks and Victoria Islands in the arctic	*banksianus* (Anderson, 1943)[24]
Steppe wolf *Canis lupus campestris*	Dwigubski 1804	A wolf of average size with short, coarse and sparse fur. The fur is light grey on the sides and rusty, brownish grey on the back[9]	Northern Ukraine, southern Kazakhstan, Caucasus and Trans-Caucasus[9]	*bactrianus* (Laptev, 1929), *cubanenesis* (Ognev, 1923), *desertorum* (Bogdanov, 1882)[25]
Tibetan wolf *Canis lupus chanco* 	Gray 1863	A small subspecies rarely exceeding 45 kg in weight. It is of a light, whitish-grey colour, with an admixture of brownish tones on the upper part of the body[9]	Central Asia from Turkestan, Tien Shan throughout Tibet to Mongolia, Northern China, Shensi, Sichuan, Yunnan, the Western Himalayas in Kashmir from Chitral to Lahul.[26] Also occurs in the Korean peninsula[27]	*coreanus* (Abe, 1923), *dorogostaiskii* (Skalon, 1936), *ekloni* (Przewalski, 1883), *filchneri* (Matschie, 1907), *karanorensis* (Matschie, 1907), *laniger* (Hodgson, 1847), *niger* (Sclater, 1874), *tschiliensis* (Matschie, 1907)[28]

† British Columbia wolf *Canis lupus columbianus*	Goldman 1941		Yukon, British Columbia, and Alberta	
Vancouver Island wolf *Canis lupus crassodon* 	Hall 1932	A medium sized subspecies, it is generally greyish-white or white in fur color. It is a very social subspecies and can usually be found roaming in packs of five to thirty-five individuals.[29]	Vancouver Island, British Columbia	
Dingo *Canis lupus dingo* 	Meyer 1793	Generally 52–60 cm tall at the shoulders and measures 117 to 124 cm from nose to tail tip. The average weight is 13 to 20 kg.[30] Fur color is mostly sandy to reddish brown, but can include tan patterns and be occasionally black, light brown, or white[31]	Australia, Thailand, India, Indonesia and New Guinea	*antarcticus* (Kerr, 1792), *australasiae* (Desmarest, 1820), *australiae* (Gray, 1826), *dingoides* (Matschie, 1915), *macdonnellensis* (Matschie, 1915), *novaehollandiae* (Voigt, 1831), *papuensis* (Ramsay, 1879), *tenggerana* (Kohlbrugge, 1896), *harappensis* (Prashad, 1936), *hallstromi* (Troughton, 1957)[32]
Domestic dog *Canis lupus familiaris* [domestic dog] 	Linnaeus 1758	Tends to have a 20% smaller skull and a 30% smaller brain,[33] as well as proportionately smaller teeth than other wolf subspecies[34] The paws of a dog are half the size of those of a wolf, and their tails tend to curl upwards, another trait not found in wolves[16]	Worldwide	*aegyptius* (Linnaeus, 1758), *alco* (C. E. H. Smith, 1839), *americanus* (Gmelin, 1792), *anglicus* (Gmelin, 1792), *antarcticus* (Gmelin, 1792), *aprinus* (Gmelin, 1792), *aquaticus* (Linnaeus, 1758), *aquatilis* (Gmelin, 1792), *avicularis* (Gmelin, 1792), *borealis* (C. E. H. Smith, 1839), *brevipilis* (Gmelin, 1792) *cursorius* (Gmelin, 1792) *domesticus* (Linnaeus, 1758) *extrarius* (Gmelin, 1792), *ferus* (C. E. H. Smith, 1839), *fricator* (Gmelin, 1792), *fricatrix* (Linnaeus, 1758), *fuillus* (Gmelin, 1792), *gallicus* (Gmelin, 1792), *glaucus* (C. E. H. Smith, 1839), *graius* (Linnaeus, 1758), *grajus* (Gmelin, 1792), *hagenbecki* (Krumbiegel, 1950), *haitensis* (C. E. H. Smith, 1839), *hibernicus* (Gmelin, 1792), *hirsutus* (Gmelin, 1792), *hybridus* (Gmelin, 1792), *islandicus* (Gmelin, 1792), *italicus* (Gmelin, 1792), *laniarius* (Gmelin, 1792), *leoninus* (Gmelin, 1792), *leporarius* (C. E. H. Smith, 1839), *major* (Gmelin, 1792), *mastinus* (Linnaeus, 1758), *melitacus* (Gmelin, 1792), *melitaeus* (Linnaeus, 1758), *minor* (Gmelin, 1792), *molossus* (Gmelin, 1792), *mustelinus* (Linnaeus, 1758), *obesus* (Gmelin, 1792), *orientalis* (Gmelin, 1792), *pacificus* (C. E. H. Smith, 1839), *plancus* (Gmelin, 1792), *pomeranus* (Gmelin, 1792), *sagaces* (C. E. H. Smith, 1839), *sanguinarius* (C. E. H. Smith, 1839), *sagax* (Linnaeus, 1758), *scoticus* (Gmelin, 1792), *sibiricus* (Gmelin, 1792), *suillus* (C. E. H. Smith, 1839), *terraenovae* (C. E. H. Smith, 1839), *terrarius* (C. E. H. Smith, 1839), *turcicus* (Gmelin, 1792), *urcani* (C. E. H. Smith, 1839), *variegatus* (Gmelin, 1792), *venaticus* (Gmelin, 1792), *vertegus* (Gmelin, 1792)[35]

† Florida Black wolf Canis lupus floridanus	Miller 1912	A jet black wolf that is described as being extremely similar to the Red wolf in both size and weight.[36] This subspecies became extinct in 1908.[37]		
† Cascade Mountain wolf Canis lupus fuscus	Richardson 1839	A cinnamon coloured wolf measuring 165 cm and weighing 36–49 kg[14]	Cascade Range	
† Gregory's wolf Canis lupus gregoryi	Goldman 1937[38]	A medium sized subspecies, though slender and tawny, its coat contains a mixture of various colors, including black, grey, white, and cinnamon.[38]		*gigas* (Townsend, 1850)[39]
†Manitoba wolf Canis lupus griseoalbus	Baird 1858		North Alberta, Saskatchewan, and Manitoba	*knightii* (Anderson, 1945)[40]
†Hokkaidō wolf Canis lupus hattai	Kishida 1931		Hokkaidō	*rex* (Pocock, 1935)[41]
†Honshū wolf Canis lupus hodophilax	Temminck 1839		Honshū, Shikoku, and Kyūshū	*hodopylax* (Temminck, 1844), *japonicus* (Nehring, 1885)[42]
Hudson Bay wolf Canis lupus hudsonicus	Goldman 1941		Northern Manitoba and the Northwest Territories	
Northern Rocky Mountains wolf Canis lupus irremotus	Goldman 1937[38] [43]		Northern Rocky Mountains	
Labrador wolf Canis lupus labradorius	Goldman 1937[38]		Labrador and northern Quebec	
Alexander Archipelago wolf Canis lupus ligoni	Goldman 1937[38]		Alexander Archipelago	

Eastern wolf *Canis lupus lycaon*	Schreber 1775		Mainly occupies the area in and around Algonquin Provincial Park in Ontario, and also ventures into adjacent parts of Quebec, Canada. It also may be present in Minnesota and Manitoba	*canadensis* (de Blainville, 1843), *ungavensis* (Comeau, 1940)[44]
Mackenzie River wolf *Canis lupus mackenzii*	Anderson 1943		Northwest Territories	
Baffin Island wolf *Canis lupus manningi*	Anderson 1943		Baffin Island	
† Mogollon Mountain wolf *Canis lupus mogollonensis*	Goldman 1937[38]	A dark coloured wolf measuring 135–150 cm in length, and weighing 27–36 kg[14]	Arizona and New Mexico	
†Texas wolf *Canis lupus monstrabilis*	Goldman 1937[38]	Similar in size and colour to *C. lupus mogollonensis*[14]	Texas and New Mexico	*niger* (Bartram, 1791)[45]
Buffalo wolf *Canis lupus nubilus*	Say 1823		Minnesota, Michigan, and Wisconsin. Single wolves have been reported in the Dakotas and as far south as Nebraska	*variabilis* (Wied-Neuwied, 1841)[46]
Mackenzie Valley wolf *Canis lupus occidentalis*	Richardson 1829		Western Canada	*sticte* (Richardson, 1829), *ater* (Richardson, 1829)[47]
Greenland wolf *Canis lupus orion*	Pocock 1935		Greenland	
Indian wolf *Canis lupus pallipes*	Sykes 1831	A small wolf with pelage shorter than that of northern wolves, and with little to no underfur.[48] Fur colour ranges from greyish red to reddish white with black tips. The dark V shaped stripe over the shoulders is much more pronounced than in northern wolves. The underparts and legs are more or less white.[49]	Western India, Iran, Turkey, Saudi Arabia and southern Israel	

Yukon wolf *Canis lupus pambasileus*	Elliot 1905		Alaska and the Yukon	
Red wolf *Canis lupus rufus*	Audubon and Bachman 1851	Has a brownish or cinnamon pelt, with grey and black shading on the back and tail. Generally intermediate in size between other American wolf subspecies and coyotes. Like other wolves, it has almond-shaped eyes, a broad muzzle and a wide nosepad, though like the coyote, its ears are proportionately larger. It has a deeper profile, a longer and broader head than the coyote, and has a less prominent ruff than wolves[50]	Eastern North Carolina[51]	
Alaskan tundra wolf *Canis lupus tundrarum*	Miller 1912	Has heavier dentition than *pambasileus*		
†Southern Rocky Mountains wolf *Canis lupus youngi*	Goldman 1937[38]		Southern Rocky Mountains	

Disputed subspecies and species

Two subspecies not mentioned in the list above are the Italian Wolf (*Canis lupus italicus*) and the Iberian Wolf (*Canis lupus signatus*). The wolves of the Italian and Iberian peninsulas have morphologically distinct features from other Eurasian wolves and each are considered by their researchers to represent their own subspecies.[52] [53] [54]

The genetic distinction of the Italian wolf subspecies was recently supported by analysis which consistently assigned all the wolf genotypes of a sample in Italy to a single group. This population also showed a unique mitochondrial DNA control-region haplotype, the absence of private alleles and lower heterozygosity at microsatellite loci, as compared to other wolf populations.[55]

Italian (Apennine) Wolf from the National Park of Abruzzo, Lazio e Molise

Recent genetic research suggests that the Indian Wolf populations in the Indian subcontinent may represent a distinct species from their conspecifics. Similar results were obtained for the Himalayan wolf, which is traditionally placed under the Tibetan wolf (*Canis lupus laniger*).[56]

References

[1] Mech, L.D., Boitani, L. (2008). *Canis lupus*. 2006. *IUCN Red List of Threatened Species*. IUCN 2006. www.iucnredlist.org (http://www.iucnredlist.org). Retrieved on 2006-05-05.

[2] *The Living Age*, published by Littell, Son and Co., 1851

[3] Richardson, J., Swainson, W., Kirby, W. (1829) *Fauna Boreali-americana, Or, The Zoology of the Northern Parts of British America: Containing Descriptions of the Objects of Natural History Collected on the Late Northern Land Expeditions, Under Command of Captain Sir John Franklin, R.N.* J. Murray, London book preview (http://www.archive.org/details/faunaborealiamer01rich)

Iberian Wolves

[4] *Hutchinson's animals of all countries: the living animals of the world in picture and story. Volume I.* 1923. p. 384.

[5] Hunting the Grisly and Other Sketches by Theodore Roosevelt - Full Text Free Book (Part 3/3) (http://www.fullbooks.com/Hunting-the-Grisly-and-Other-Sketches3.html)

[6] *The Natural History of Dogs: Canidæ Or Genus Canis of Authors. Including Also the Genera Hyæna and Proteles* by Charles Hamilton Smith, contributor William Home Lizars, Samuel Highley, W. Curry, Junr. & Co, Published by W.H. Lizars, ... S. Highley, ... London; and W. Curry, jun. and Co. Dublin., 1839

[7] Wozencraft, W. Christopher (16 November 2005). "Order Carnivora (pp. 532-628)" (http://www.bucknell.edu/msw3/browse. asp?id=14000738). In Wilson, Don E., and Reeder, DeeAnn M., eds. *Mammal Species of the World: A Taxonomic and Geographic Reference* (http://google.com/books?id=JgAMbNSt8ikC&pg=PA532) (3rd ed.). Baltimore: Johns Hopkins University Press, 2 vols. (2142 pp.). ISBN 978-0-8018-8221-0. OCLC 62265494. .

[8] "*Canis lupus lupus* Linnaeus, 1758" (http://www.itis.gov/servlet/SingleRpt/SingleRpt?search_topic=TSN&search_value=180598). Integrated Taxonomic Information System. .

[9] *Mammals of the Soviet Union* Vol.II Part 1a, SIRENIA AND CARNIVORA (Sea cows; Wolves and Bears), V.G Heptner and N.P Naumov editors, Science Publishers, Inc. USA. 1998. ISBN 1886106819

[10] Wozencraft, W. Christopher (16 November 2005). "Order Carnivora (pp. 532-628)" (http://www.bucknell.edu/msw3/browse. asp?id=14000739). In Wilson, Don E., and Reeder, DeeAnn M., eds. *Mammal Species of the World: A Taxonomic and Geographic Reference* (http://google.com/books?id=JgAMbNSt8ikC&pg=PA532) (3rd ed.). Baltimore: Johns Hopkins University Press, 2 vols. (2142 pp.). ISBN 978-0-8018-8221-0. OCLC 62265494. .

[11] "*Canis lupus albus* Kerr, 1792" (http://www.itis.gov/servlet/SingleRpt/SingleRpt?search_topic=TSN&search_value=726809). Integrated Taxonomic Information System. .

[12] Wozencraft, W. Christopher (16 November 2005). "Order Carnivora (pp. 532-628)" (http://www.bucknell.edu/msw3/browse. asp?id=14000740). In Wilson, Don E., and Reeder, DeeAnn M., eds. *Mammal Species of the World: A Taxonomic and Geographic Reference* (http://google.com/books?id=JgAMbNSt8ikC&pg=PA532) (3rd ed.). Baltimore: Johns Hopkins University Press, 2 vols. (2142 pp.). ISBN 978-0-8018-8221-0. OCLC 62265494. .

[13] "*Canis lupus alces* Goldman, 1941" (http://www.itis.gov/servlet/SingleRpt/SingleRpt?search_topic=TSN&search_value=726810). Integrated Taxonomic Information System. .

[14] *The Encyclopedia of Vanished Species* by David Day, Universe Books ltd. 1981. ISBN 0947889302

[15] "*Canis lupus arabs* Pocock, 1934" (http://www.itis.gov/servlet/SingleRpt/SingleRpt?search_topic=TSN&search_value=726811). Integrated Taxonomic Information System. .

[16] Lopez, Barry (1978). *Of wolves and men*. New York: Scribner Classics. p. 320. ISBN 0743249364.

[17] Fred H. Harrington, Paul C. Paquet (1982). *Wolves of the World: Perspectives of Behavior, Ecology, and Conservation*. p. 474. ISBN 0815509057.

[18] "*Canis lupus arctos* Pocock, 1935" (http://www.itis.gov/servlet/SingleRpt/SingleRpt?search_topic=TSN&search_value=726812). Integrated Taxonomic Information System. .

[19] "White wolf of the North" (http://wwf.panda.org/about_our_earth/species/profiles/mammals/arcticwolf/), World Wide Fund for Nature

[20] "Arctic wolf" (http://www.torontozoo.com/ExploretheZoo/AnimalDetails.asp?AnimalId=403), Toronto Zoo

[21] "*Canis lupus baileyi* Nelson and Goldman, 1929" (http://www.itis.gov/servlet/SingleRpt/SingleRpt?search_topic=TSN&search_value=726813). Integrated Taxonomic Information System. .

[22] *"Green Fire" Returns to the Southwest: Reintroduction of the Mexican Wolf* (http://www.eebweb.arizona.edu/Courses/Ecol406R_506R/Parsons1998-MexWolf.pdf)- Author(s): David R. Parsons. Source: Wildlife Society Bulletin, Vol. 26, No. 4, Commemorative Issue Celebrating the 50th Anniversary of *"A Sand County Almanac"* and the Legacy of Aldo Leopold (Winter, 1998), pp. 799-807. Published by: Allen Press

[23] "Bernard, P. and J." (http://books.google.com/books?id=I-kSmWLc6vYC&pg=PA40&lpg=PA40&dq="Bernard's+Wolf"& source=bl&ots=WondBDY25l&sig=Md1LSHTckWuxTFfUGIR6h_94sfc&hl=en&ei=wetRTIHOH4GknQf4iOCPBA&sa=X&

oi=book_result&ct=result&resnum=7&ved=0CCMQ6AEwBjgK#v=onepage&q="Bernard's Wolf"&f=false), *The Eponym Dictionary of Mammals* by Bo Beolens, Michael Watkins and Michael Grayson, JHU Press, 2009, Pg. 40

[24] Wozencraft, W. Christopher (16 November 2005). "Order Carnivora (pp. 532-628)" (http://www.bucknell.edu/msw3/browse. asp?id=14000746). In Wilson, Don E., and Reeder, DeeAnn M., eds. *Mammal Species of the World: A Taxonomic and Geographic Reference* (http://google.com/books?id=JgAMbNSt8ikC&pg=PA532) (3rd ed.). Baltimore: Johns Hopkins University Press, 2 vols. (2142 pp.). ISBN 978-0-8018-8221-0. OCLC 62265494. .

[25] Wozencraft, W. Christopher (16 November 2005). "Order Carnivora (pp. 532-628)" (http://www.bucknell.edu/msw3/browse. asp?id=14000747). In Wilson, Don E., and Reeder, DeeAnn M., eds. *Mammal Species of the World: A Taxonomic and Geographic Reference* (http://google.com/books?id=JgAMbNSt8ikC&pg=PA532) (3rd ed.). Baltimore: Johns Hopkins University Press, 2 vols. (2142 pp.). ISBN 978-0-8018-8221-0. OCLC 62265494. .

[26] *Fauna of British India: Mammals Volume 2* by R. I. Pocock, printed by Taylor and Francis, 1941 (http://ia341313.us.archive.org/0/ items/PocockMammalia2/pocock2.pdf)

[27] Walker, Brett L. (2005). *The Lost Wolves Of Japan*. p. 331. ISBN 0295984929.

[28] Wozencraft, W. Christopher (16 November 2005). "Order Carnivora (pp. 532-628)" (http://www.bucknell.edu/msw3/browse. asp?id=14000748). In Wilson, Don E., and Reeder, DeeAnn M., eds. *Mammal Species of the World: A Taxonomic and Geographic Reference* (http://google.com/books?id=JgAMbNSt8ikC&pg=PA532) (3rd ed.). Baltimore: Johns Hopkins University Press, 2 vols. (2142 pp.). ISBN 978-0-8018-8221-0. OCLC 62265494. .

[29] "Preliminary Investigations of the Vancouver Island Wolf" (http://books.google.com/books?id=LX5qi4qTs0UC&pg=PA54& lpg=PA54&dq="vancouver+island+wolf"&source=web&ots=zdNQ8bwOQt& sig=XOGNPDTqmkKYDaX7Uf2MpW53_Lc#v=onepage&q="vancouver island wolf"&f=false), *Wolves of the world: perspectives of behavior, ecology, and conservation* by Fred H. Harrington and Paul C. Paquet, William Andrew, 1982, Pg. 54

[30] Ben Allen (2008). "Home Range, Activity Patterns, and Habitat use of Urban Dingoes" (http://www.invasiveanimals.com/downloads/ Final-proceedings-with-cover.pdf). *14th Australasian Vertebrate Pest Conference*. Invasive Animals CRC. . Retrieved 2009-04-29.

[31] Fleming, Peter; Laurie Corbett, Robert Harden, Peter Thomson (2001). *Managing the Impacts of Dingoes and Other Wild Dogs*. Commonwealth of Australia: Bureau of Rural Sciences.

[32] Wozencraft, W. Christopher (16 November 2005). "Order Carnivora (pp. 532-628)" (http://www.bucknell.edu/msw3/browse. asp?id=14000751). In Wilson, Don E., and Reeder, DeeAnn M., eds. *Mammal Species of the World: A Taxonomic and Geographic Reference* (http://google.com/books?id=JgAMbNSt8ikC&pg=PA532) (3rd ed.). Baltimore: Johns Hopkins University Press, 2 vols. (2142 pp.). ISBN 978-0-8018-8221-0. OCLC 62265494. .

[33] Serpell, James (1995). *The Domestic Dog; its evolution, behaviour and interactions with people*. Cambridge: Cambridge Univ. Press. p. 35. ISBN 0-521-42537-9.

[34] Coppinger, Ray (2001). *Dogs: a Startling New Understanding of Canine Origin, Behavior and Evolution*. New York: Scribner. ISBN 0684855305.

[35] Wozencraft, W. Christopher (16 November 2005). "Order Carnivora (pp. 532 628)" (http://www.bucknell.edu/msw3/browse. asp?id=14000752). In Wilson, Don E., and Reeder, DeeAnn M., eds. *Mammal Species of the World: A Taxonomic and Geographic Reference* (http://google.com/books?id=JgAMbNSt8ikC&pg=PA532) (3rd ed.). Baltimore: Johns Hopkins University Press, 2 vols. (2142 pp.). ISBN 978-0-8018-8221-0. OCLC 62265494. .

[36] "The Wolf" (http://books.google.com/books?id=90eEeae4rmIC&pg=PA42&lpg=PA42&dq="Florida+Black+wolf"&source=bl& ots=2LTI5F9fiY&sig=5Y9gM4mEGHqHXcNMT59XYYOxOms&hl=en&ei=CTdTTNbRForanAfPudH-Ag&sa=X&oi=book_result& ct=result&resnum=8&ved=0CDEQ6AEwBw#v=onepage&q="Florida Black wolf"&f=false), *Alsatian Shepalute's: A New Breed for a New Millennium* by Lois Denny, AuthorHouse, 2004, Pg. 42

[37] Klinkenberg, Jeff, "For saving the Florida panther, it's desperation time" (http://pqasb.pqarchiver.com/sptimes/access/50193046. html?dids=50193046:50193046&FMT=ABS&FMTS=ABS:FT&type=current&date=Feb+11,+1990&author=JEFF+KLINKENBERG& pub=St.+Petersburg+Times&desc=For+saving+the+Florida+panther,+it's+desperation+time&pqatl=google), St. Petersburg Times, February 11, 1990

[38] "The Wolves of North America" (http://www.jstor.org/stable/1374306?seq=8), E. A. Goldman, *Journal of Mammalogy*, Vol. 18, No. 1 (Feb., 1937), pp. 37-45

[39] Wozencraft, W. Christopher (16 November 2005). "Order Carnivora (pp. 532-628)" (http://www.bucknell.edu/msw3/browse. asp?id=14000754). In Wilson, Don E., and Reeder, DeeAnn M., eds. *Mammal Species of the World: A Taxonomic and Geographic Reference* (http://google.com/books?id=JgAMbNSt8ikC&pg=PA532) (3rd ed.). Baltimore: Johns Hopkins University Press, 2 vols. (2142 pp.). ISBN 978-0-8018-8221-0. OCLC 62265494. .

[40] Wozencraft, W. Christopher (16 November 2005). "Order Carnivora (pp. 532-628)" (http://www.bucknell.edu/msw3/browse. asp?id=14000756). In Wilson, Don E., and Reeder, DeeAnn M., eds. *Mammal Species of the World: A Taxonomic and Geographic Reference* (http://google.com/books?id=JgAMbNSt8ikC&pg=PA532) (3rd ed.). Baltimore: Johns Hopkins University Press, 2 vols. (2142 pp.). ISBN 978-0-8018-8221-0. OCLC 62265494. .

[41] Wozencraft, W. Christopher (16 November 2005). "Order Carnivora (pp. 532-628)" (http://www.bucknell.edu/msw3/browse. asp?id=14000757). In Wilson, Don E., and Reeder, DeeAnn M., eds. *Mammal Species of the World: A Taxonomic and Geographic Reference* (http://google.com/books?id=JgAMbNSt8ikC&pg=PA532) (3rd ed.). Baltimore: Johns Hopkins University Press, 2 vols. (2142 pp.). ISBN 978-0-8018-8221-0. OCLC 62265494. .

[42] Wozencraft, W. Christopher (16 November 2005). "Order Carnivora (pp. 532-628)" (http://www.bucknell.edu/msw3/browse. asp?id=14000758). In Wilson, Don E., and Reeder, DeeAnn M., eds. *Mammal Species of the World: A Taxonomic and Geographic Reference* (http://google.com/books?id=JgAMbNSt8ikC&pg=PA532) (3rd ed.). Baltimore: Johns Hopkins University Press, 2 vols. (2142 pp.). ISBN 978-0-8018-8221-0. OCLC 62265494. .

[43] "*Canis lupus irremotus* Goldman, 1937" (http://www.itis.gov/servlet/SingleRpt/SingleRpt?search_topic=TSN&search_value=726829). Integrated Taxonomic Information System. .

[44] Wozencraft, W. Christopher (16 November 2005). "Order Carnivora (pp. 532-628)" (http://www.bucknell.edu/msw3/browse. asp?id=14000763). In Wilson, Don E., and Reeder, DeeAnn M., eds. *Mammal Species of the World: A Taxonomic and Geographic Reference* (http://google.com/books?id=JgAMbNSt8ikC&pg=PA532) (3rd ed.). Baltimore: Johns Hopkins University Press, 2 vols. (2142 pp.). ISBN 978-0-8018-8221-0. OCLC 62265494. .

[45] Wozencraft, W. Christopher (16 November 2005). "Order Carnivora (pp. 532-628)" (http://www.bucknell.edu/msw3/browse. asp?id=14000767). In Wilson, Don E., and Reeder, DeeAnn M., eds. *Mammal Species of the World: A Taxonomic and Geographic Reference* (http://google.com/books?id=JgAMbNSt8ikC&pg=PA532) (3rd ed.). Baltimore: Johns Hopkins University Press, 2 vols. (2142 pp.). ISBN 978-0-8018-8221-0. OCLC 62265494. .

[46] Wozencraft, W. Christopher (16 November 2005). "Order Carnivora (pp. 532-628)" (http://www.bucknell.edu/msw3/browse. asp?id=14000768). In Wilson, Don E., and Reeder, DeeAnn M., eds. *Mammal Species of the World: A Taxonomic and Geographic Reference* (http://google.com/books?id=JgAMbNSt8ikC&pg=PA532) (3rd ed.). Baltimore: Johns Hopkins University Press, 2 vols. (2142 pp.). ISBN 978-0-8018-8221-0. OCLC 62265494. .

[47] Wozencraft, W. Christopher (16 November 2005). "Order Carnivora (pp. 532-628)" (http://www.bucknell.edu/msw3/browse. asp?id=14000769). In Wilson, Don E., and Reeder, DeeAnn M., eds. *Mammal Species of the World: A Taxonomic and Geographic Reference* (http://google.com/books?id=JgAMbNSt8ikC&pg=PA532) (3rd ed.). Baltimore: Johns Hopkins University Press, 2 vols. (2142 pp.). ISBN 978-0-8018-8221-0. OCLC 62265494. .

[48] *NATURAL HISTORY OF THE MAMMALIA OF INDIA AND CEYLON* by Robert A. Sterndale, THACKER, SPINK, AND CO. BOMBAY: THACKER AND CO., LIMITED. LONDON: W. THACKER AND CO. 1884. (http://www.gutenberg.org/files/19550/19550-h/19550-h. htm#245)

[49] *A monograph of the canidae* by St. George Mivart, F.R.S, published by Alere Flammam. 1890

[50] "Red Wolf" (http://www.canids.org/species/Red_wolf.pdf). *canids.org*. .

[51] Red Wolf Recovery Project (http://www.fws.gov/alligatorriver/redwolf.html) from the U.S. Fish and Wildlife Services

[52] The wolf in Spain (http://www.signatus.org/docs/situation.pdf)

[53] Canis lupus italicus (http://www.animalcorner.co.uk/wildlife/wolves/wolf_italian.html)

[54] J. Vos: *Food habits and livestock depredation of two Iberian wolf packs (*Canis lupus signatus*) in the north of Portugal.* Journal of Zoology (2000), 251: 457-462 Cambridge University Press. online abstract (http://journals.cambridge.org/action/ displayAbstract?fromPage=online&aid=54315)

[55] V. LUCCHINI, A. GALOV and E. RANDI *Evidence of genetic distinction and long-term population decline in wolves (Canis lupus) in the Italian Apennines.* Molecular Ecology (2004) 13, 523–536. abstract online (http://www3.interscience.wiley.com/journal/118794860/ abstract)

[56] R. K. Aggarwal, T. Kivisild, J. Ramadevi, L. Singh:*Mitochondrial DNA coding region sequences support the phylogenetic distinction of two Indian wolf species.* Journal of Zoological Systematics and Evolutionary Research, Volume 45 Issue 2 Page 163-172, May 2007 online (http:/ /www.blackwell-synergy.com/doi/abs/10.1111/j.1439-0469.2006.00400.x)

External links

- Canis lupus on the ITIS (http://www.itis.gov/servlet/SingleRpt/SingleRpt?search_topic=TSN& search_value=180596) (Integrated Taxonomic Information System)
- Citations for Mammal Species of the World, as a PDF (http://www.bucknell.edu/msw3/documents/ MSW3Citations.pdf)
- Ancient origin and evolution of the Indian wolf (http://genomebiology.com/2003/4/6/P6) including discussion on naming.
- Wolf subspecies list with photos and maps (http://www.wolfhowl.org/subspecies.php)
- Animal Corner, UK list of wolves (http://www.animalcorner.co.uk/wildlife/wolves/wolf_species.html)
- A very detailed hobbyist's site (http://www.lioncrusher.com/animalinfo.asp)

Taxonomy of commonly fossilised invertebrates

Although the phylogenetic classification of sub-vertebrate animals (both extinct and extant) remains a work-in-progress, the following taxonomy attempts to be useful by combining *both* traditional (old) *and* new (21st-century) paleozoological termonology.

So the paleobiologic systematics which follows is *not* intended to be all-inclusive or completely comprehensive. For practical reasons and relevancy, the below classification and annotations *emphasize invertebrates* that (a) are popularly collected as fossils and/or (b) no longer continue alive on this planet. Therefore, as a result, some phyla, classes, and orders of invertebrates are not listed. [1]

If a non-vertebrate animal is mentioned below using its common, vernacular, *everyday* name, the creature is usually a living, present-day invertebrate. But if, on the other hand, a non-vertebrate is cited below

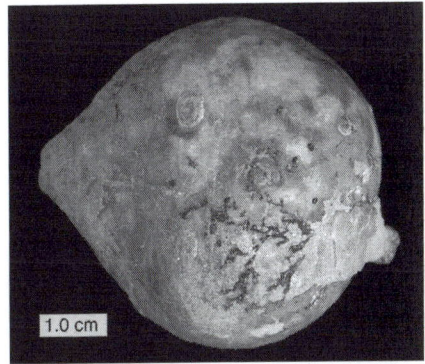

The Ordovician cystoid *Echinosphaerites* (an extinct echinoderm of the Class Rhombifera) from northeastern Estonia; encrusted by a graptolite (black branches).

by its scientific, taxonomic *genus* (in *italics*), then it is typically an extinct invertebrate, known only from the fossil record. [2]

Invertebrate clades that are (a) *very important* as fossils (for example, ostracods frequently used as index fossils), and/or (b) *very abundant* as fossils (for example, crinoids easily found in crinoidal limestone), [3] are highlighted with a bracketed exclamation mark [**!**].

Invertebrate groups that (a) are now *substantially* extinct, and/or (b) contain a *large proportion* of extinct species, are followed by a dashed notation [**--** such as this]. But invertebrate clades which are now *totally* -- that is, 100 percent -- *extinct* are designated with a bracketed dagger/cross [**†**]:

Domain of EUKARYOTA / EUKARYA

(eukaryotes / eukaryans / all cellular organisms bearing a central, organized nucleus with DNA)

- comprises *most* of the species of life which have been documented by biologists and paleontologists as either living or deceased
- includes a wide variety of single-celled protists, all algae, most plankton, most molds, the green plants, and *all* animal-related kingdoms
  - but does *not* include the primal, sub-nuclear, prokaryotic domains of Archaea and Bacteria -- nor the enigmatic domain of Viruses

Sub-domain of OPISTHOKONTA

(opisthokonts / the animal-related kingdoms / the proto-spongal choanoflagellates, proto-fungal microsporidians, true fungi, and true animals

- comprises most life forms documented as either living or deceased
  - excludes many molds, all one-celled protists (or protoctists), all algae, and all green plants

Kingdom of ANIMALIA / METAZOA

(metazoans / many-celled true animals / all invertebrates and vertebrates / multi-cellular creatures that grab and ingest their organic food)

- comprises most living and deceased species which have ever been recorded by paleontological and life scientists
  - excludes all unicellular and fungal opisthokonts

Sub-kingdom of PARAZOA

(parazoans / typically-sessile, basal non-eumetazoans / the most-primitive animals / the simplest, colonial, attached, bottom-dwelling, marine invertebrates)

Phylum Archaeocyatha / Archeocyatha / Archaeocyathida / Archeocyathida / Pleospongia [†]

(cone-shaped archaeocyathids/archeocyathids / cup-shaped archaeocyathans/archeocyathans / reef-building pleosponges / calcareous "ancient-cups")

(includes fossil genera such *Archaeocyathus*, *Cambrocyathus*, *Atikonia*, *Tumuliolynthus*, *Kotuyicyathus*, *Metaldetes*, *Ajacicyathus* and *Paranacyathus*)

(Archaeocyatha is sometimes classified as a class of Porifera below)

Phylum Porifera / Nuda / Spongia

(quintessential true sponges / marine, colonial, pore-bearing animals / organized collar-flagellates / poriferans; today mostly siliceous) -- *half* of all documented species of Porifera are fossils and extinct [4]

(Porifera may eventually be broken up into separate phyla)

- Sub-phylum Calcarea / Calcispongiae (primitive calcareous poriferans such as yellow lemon sponge, sphinctozoans, pharetronids, *Scypha*, *Leucetta*, *Gravestockia*, *Grantia*, *Astraeospongium*, *Clathrina*, *Lelapia*, *Rhaphidonema*, and *Girtyocoelia*)
  - Class Calcinea
  - Class Calcaronea
  - Class Stromatoporoidea / Stromatoporata / Stromatoporida / Spongliomorphida [†] (lime-layered stromatoporoids / reef-building stromatoporates / button-shaped stromatoporids / disc-shaped spongliomorphids; e.g., *Stromatopora*, *Aulacera*, *Stromatactis*, *Actinostroma*, *Discophyllum*, *Parallelopora* and *Amphipora*)
  - Class Heteractinida [†] (Paleozoic calcitic heteractinids such as *Eiffelia*)
- Sub-phylum Silicea / Silicospongia (siliceous poriferans)
  - Class Demospongea / Demospongiae (most living sponges hardened by opaline silica or spongin; for instance, horny sponge, bath sponge, stove-pipe sponge, yellow boring sponge, carnivorous sponge, bristle sponge, chaetids, lithistids, *Astroclera*, *Ceractinomorpha*, *Clionoides*, *Hindia*, *Ventriculites*, *Laosoiadia*, *Clionolithes*, *Tetractinella*, and *Astylospongia*)

- Class Hexactinellida / Hyalospongiae / Sclerospongiae (siliceous, deep-sea glass sponges, e.g. glassy-latticed Venus flower basket, bird's nest sponge, cloud sponge, *Hexactinella*, *Hydroceras*, *Dictyonina*, *Brachiospongia*, *Titusvillea*, and *Rhizopoterion*)

Sub-kingdom of EUMETAZOA

(eumetazoans / true metazoans / typically-mobile, multicellular animals)

(Eumetazoa contains *most* of the living and deceased species of recorded life, including *most* invertebrates (alive and extinct), as well as *all* vertebrate animals)

Super-phylum of RADIATA

(radiates / non-bilaterian eumetazoans)

Phylum Cnidaria / Coelenterata

(cnidarians / coelenterates)

- Class Hydrozoa (hydra or hydroid group)
  - Subclass Stromatoporoidea [†] (lime-layered stromatoporoids)
  - Subclass Conulata [†] (four-sided, pyramidal conularians)
- Class Anthozoa (corals / polyps)
  - Subclass Receptaculidea [†] (receptaculites, a.k.a. sunflower corals)
  - Subclass Octocorallia / Alcyonaria (soft corals and sea pens)
  - Subclass Zoantharia [!] (sea anemones and most extant corals)
    - Order Rugosa / Tetracoralla [†] [!] (wrinkled, horn-shaped tetracorals such as Petoskey coral, *Caninia* and *Heliophyllum*)
    - Order Tabulata / Schizocoralla [†] [!] (tabulate corals, for instance, *Favosites* and *Aulopora*)
    - Order Scleractinia / Hexacoralla [!] (stony corals such as brain coral, *Favia*, *Meandrina*, and most living corals)

Super-phylum of LOPHOTROCHOZOA / PROTOSTOMIA # 1

(lophotrochozoan bilaterians, such as flatworms, ribbon worms, lophophorates, and molluscs)

Phylum Bryozoa / Ectoprocta / Polyzoa

(bryozoans / moss animals) -- *half* of all documented species of Bryozoa are fossils *and* extinct [5]

- Class Stenolaemata / Gymnolaemata [!] (mostly marine, calcareous bryozoans)
  - Order Cheilostomata [!] (living, rimmed-mouthed moss animals)
  - Order Cyclostomatida (uncontracted, round-mouthed bryozoans including fossil *Stomatopora*)
  - Order Cystoporata [†] (extinct, minor group of moss animals)
  - Order Trepostomata [†] [!] (changed-mouthed bryozoans such as extinct *Constellaria* and *Monticulipora*)
  - Order Cryptostomata [†] [!] (round hidden-mouthed bryozoans such as *Archimedes*, *Fenestrellina* and *Rhombopora*)
  - Order Ctenostomata [†] (uncommon, comb-mouthed bryozoans)
  - Order Phylactolaemata (living, fresh-water bryozoans)

Phylum Brachiopoda

(lampshells, brachiopods or "brachs," not to be confused with the hard-shelled marine mollusks below) -- *99 percent* of all documented species of Brachiopoda are now extinct

- Subphylum Linguliformea (inarticulate atremates, such as "living fossil" *Lingula*) -- but mostly extinct
- Subphylum Craniiformea (inarticulate neotremates, such as extant *Crania*) -- but mostly extinct
- Subphylum Rhynchonelliformea [!] (articulate brachiopods with hinged valves; includes most extinct *and* living brachs)

  - Class Rhynchonellata [!]

    - Order Orthida [†] [!] (orthid brachs such as fossil *Orthis*)
    - Order Pentamerida [†] (pentamerid brachs such as *Conchidium*)
    - Order Rhynchonellida [!] (rhynchonellid brachs such as fossils *Rhynchotrema* and *Rhynchonella*)
    - Order Spiriferida [†] [!] (spiriferid brachs)

      - Suborder Spiriferinida [†] [!] (spiriferid brachs such as *Spirifer* and *Eospirifer*)
      - Suborder Atrypida [†] [!] (atrypid brachs such as *Atrypa*)
    - Order Terebratulida [!] (most living brachiopods; includes fossil *Dielasma*)
  - Class Strophomenata [†] [!] (so-called petrified butterflies)

    - Order Strophomenida [†] [!] (strophomenid brachs)
    - Order Productida [†] [!] (spiny or productid brachs)

      - Suborder Chonetidina [†] [!]
      - Suborder Productidina [†] [!]

Rhynchotrema dentatum, a rhynchonellid brachiopod from the Cincinnatian (Upper Ordovician) of southeastern Indiana.

Phylum Annelida

(segmented worms such as earthworms and leeches)

- Class Polychaeta (marine annelids / polychaetes)

  - Order Scolecodonta [!] (mostly chitinous jaws of scolecodonts)

Phylum Mollusca

(molluscs or mollusks, not to be confused with the hard-shelled marine brachiopods above)

- Class Monoplacophora (extinct, except for "living fossil" Neopilina)
- Class Bivalvia / Pelecypoda (bivalves / pelecypods) -- *half* of all documented species of Bivalvia are fossils *and* extinct [6]

  - Subclass Lamellibranchia [!] (clams, oysters, mussels and scallops)
- Class Gastropoda (gastropods / snail group)

  - Subclass Prosobranchia (marine snails and conches)
  - Subclass Opisthobranchia (sea slugs)
  - Subclass Pulmonata (land snails)
- Class Cephalopoda (cephalopods) -- *97 percent* of all documented species of Cephalopoda are now extinct

  - Subclass Nautiloidea (mostly extinct, but includes "living fossil" *Nautilus*)

    - Order Orthocerida [†] [!] (long, straight-shelled nautiloids)
  - Subclass Ammonoidea [†] [!] (generally coiled-shelled ammonoids)

- Agoniatitic (agoniatites) [†]
- Goniatitic (goniatites) [†] [!] (ammonoids with simple sutures)
- Ceratitic (ceratites) [†]
- Ammonitic [†] [!] (the true ammonites, bearing complex sutures)
- Subclass Coleoidea (includes the living squid, cuttlefish, and octopus)

  - Order Belemnoidea [†] (extinct orthoconic belemnoids)

Super-phylum of ECDYSOZOA / PROTOSTOMIA # 2

(ecdysozoans, such as nematodes, horsehair worms, and molting bilaterians / panarthropods))

Phylum Tardigrada

(panarthropodic water bears)

Phylum Onychophora

(panarthropodic velvet worms, including proto-arthropodic fossils of *Arthropleura* and *Aysheaia*)

Phylum Arthropoda

(arthropods; jointed legged creatures with an exoskeleton)

- Subphylum Crustacea (crustaceans)

  - Class Ostracoda (ostracods)
  - Class Malacostraca (true crabs, lobster and most shrimp)
  - Class Branchiopoda (brine shrimp)

    - Order Notostraca
  - Class Cirripedia (barnacles)
  - Class Arachnoidea
- Subphylum Trilobitomorpha [†] (extinct trilobite group)

  - Class Trilobita [†] (the armored trilobites)
- Subphylum Hexapoda

  - Class Insecta (insects, best preserved in amber)
- Subphylum Chelicerata

  - Class Arachnida (spiders, best preserved in amber)
  - Class Merostomata ("living fossil" horseshoe crab and extinct eurypterid)
- Subphylum Myriapoda

  - Class Diplopoda
  - Class Chilopoda

Super-phylum of DEUTEROSTOMIA / ENTEROCOELOMATA

(second-mouthed bilaterians called deuterostomians, such as chordates and echinoderms)

Phylum Echinodermata

(echinoderms) -- *72 percent* of all documented species of Echinodermata are fossils *and* extinct [7]

- Subphylum Crinozoa (sessile echinoderms) -- *91 percent* of all documented species of Crinozoa are now extinct
  - Class Crinoidea (crinoids / sea lilies) -- See Crinozoa above
- Subphylum Blastozoa [†] (extinct blastoids)
  - Class Diploporita
  - Class Rhombifera
- Subphylum Echinozoa (mobile echinoderms) -- *89 percent* of all documented species of Echinozoa are now extinct
  - Class Echinoidea (echinoids or sea urchins) -- See Echinozoa above
- Subphylum Asterozoa
  - Class Asteroidea (sea stars / starfish)
  - Class Ophiuroidea

Phylum Hemichordata

(hemichordates such as extant acorn worms) -- *Less than half* of the documented species of Hemichordata are fossils *and* extinct

- Class Graptoloidea [†] (extinct graptolites)
  - Order Dendroidea [†]
  - Order Graptoloidea [†]
    - Suborder Didymograptina [†]
    - Suborder Diplograptina [†]
    - Suborder Monograptina [†]

Phylum Chordata

(*both* invertebrate *and* vertebrate chordates; animals possessing a notochord)

Invertebrate subphyla

- Subphylum Urochordata (invertebrate tunicate such as sea squirts)
- Subphylum Cephalochordata (invertebrate lancelets)

Subphylum Vertebrata

- (vertebrates such as hagfishes, lampreys, conodonts [†], ostracoderms [†], placoderms [†], sharks, ray-finned fishes, lobe-finned fishes, amphibians, reptiles, dinosaurs [†], birds and mammals)

Footnotes

[1] For superb anatomical illustrations and much-more comprehensive information, the aspiring paleozoologist should scan *Volume E* (*Archaeocyatha / Porifera*) through *Volume V* (*Graptolithina*), published 1953 to 2006 (and continuing), of *the Treatise on Invertebrate Paleontology*, long-edited by Raymond C. Moore and Roger L. Kaesler (Boulder, Colorado: Geological Society of America; and Lawrence, Kansas: University of Kansas Press). But be warned that some terms therein employed -- such as supersubphylum -- can be unnecessarily wordy or obstruse. Incidentally, *revised* volumes have been recently published regarding the sponges/archaeocyatha (2004, ISBN 08137 31313) and the brachiopods (2006, ISBN 0813731356).

[2] The names of genera, orders, classes and phyla have been culled from dozens of sources, both current and decades-old. See the International Code of Zoological Nomenclature (ICZN), as well as *Volume 1* and *Volume 2* of *Grzimek's Animal Life Encyclopedia* (Farmington Hills, Michigan: Gale Group), edited by zoologists Michael Hutchin, Dennis A. Thorney and Sean F. Craig (2003).

[3] For correspondingly-ancient ecosystems, see the *Treatise on Ecology and Paleoecology, Volume 2: Paleoecology*, edited for years by Harry S. Ladd (1957 / 1971), and published by both the Geological Society of America (Boulder, Colorado) and the Waverly Press (Washington, D.C.).

[4] The rates of extinction for sponges and other phyla are derived from W. H. Easton, 1960, *Invertebrate Paleontology* (New York: Harper and Brothers) and various modern sources.

[5] For bryozoans and brachiopods, the same footnote as above.

[6] For bivalves and cephalopods (both mollusks), see the above notation.

[7] For the echinoderms, see the above footnote regarding W. E. Easton, 1960, *Invertebrate Paleontology*, and other sources.

Taxonomy of scorpions

The **taxonomy of scorpions** deals with the classification of this predatory arthropod into thirteen extant families and approximately 1,400 described species and subspecies. In addition, there are 111 described taxa of extinct scorpions.[1]

The classification is based on that of Soleglad and Fet (2003),[2] which replaced the older, unpublished classification of Stockwell.[3] Additional taxonomic changes are from papers by Soleglad et al. (2005).[4] [5] The classification proposed by Fet and Soleglad in 2003 and subsequent papers has not been universally accepted; some authorities have challenged their methodology as invalid.[5]

Taxonomy

Order Scorpiones

- Infraorder Orthosterni Pocock, 1911

  - Parvorder Pseudochactida Soleglad et Fet, 2003

    - Superfamily Pseudochactoidea Gromov, 1998

      - Family Pseudochactidae Gromov, 1998

  - Parvorder Buthida Soleglad et Fet, 2003

    - Superfamily Buthoidea C. L. Koch, 1837

      - Family Buthidae C. L. Koch, 1837 (thick-tailed scorpions)

      - Family Microcharmidae Lourenço, 1996

  - Parvorder Chaerilida Soleglad et Fet, 2003

    - Superfamily Chaeriloidea Pocock, 1893

      - Family Chaerilidae Pocock, 1893

        - Subfamily Chearilinae Pocock, 1893

        - † Subfamily Electrochearilinae Fet, Soleglad et Anderson 2004 (extinct)

  - Parvorder Iurida Soleglad et Fet, 2003

    - Superfamily Chactoidea Pocock, 1893

- Family Chactidae Pocock, 1893
  - Subfamily Chactinae Pocock, 1893
    - Tribe Chactini Pocock, 1893
    - Tribe Nullibrotheini Soleglad et Fet, 2003
  - Subfamily Brotheinae Simon, 1879
    - Tribe Belisariini Lourenço, 1998
    - Tribe Brotheini Simon, 1879
      - Subtribe Brotheina Simon, 1879
      - Subtribe Neochactina Soleglad et Fet, 2003
  - Subfamily Uroctoninae
- Family Euscorpiidae Laurie, 1896
  - Subfamily Euscorpiinae Laurie, 1896
  - Subfamily Megacorminae Kraepelin, 1905
    - Tribe Chactopsini Soleglad et Sissom, 2001
    - Tribe Megacormini Kraepelin, 1905
  - Subfamily Scorpiopinae Kraepelin, 1905
    - Tribe Scorpiopini Kraepelin, 1905
    - Tribe Troglocormini Soleglad et Sissom, 2001
- Family Superstitioniidae Stahnke, 1940
  - Subfamily Superstitioniinae Stahnke, 1940
  - Subfamily Typlochactinae Mitchell, 1971
- Family Vaejovidae Thorell, 1876
- Superfamily Iuroidea Thorell, 1876
  - Family Caraboctonidae Kraepelin, 1905 (hairy scorpions)
    - Subfamily Caraboctoninae Kraepelin, 1905
    - Subfamily Hadrurinae Stahnke, 1974
  - Family Iuridae Thorell, 1876
- Superfamily Scorpionoidea Latreille, 1802
  - Family Bothriuridae Simon, 1880
    - Subfamily Bothriurinae Simon, 1880
    - Subfamily Lisposominae Lawrence, 1928
  - Family Hemiscorpiidae Pocock, 1893 (= Ischnuridae, =Liochelidae) (rock scorpions, creeping scorpions, or tree scorpions)
    - Subfamily Hemiscorpiinae Pocock, 1893
    - Subfamily Heteroscorpioninae Kraepelin, 1905
    - Subfamily Hormurinae Laurie, 1896
  - † Family Protoischnuridae Carvalho et Lourenço 2001 (extinct)
  - Family Scorpionidae Latreille, 1802 (burrowing scorpions or pale-legged scorpions)
    - Subfamily Diplocentrinae Karsch, 1880
      - Tribe Diplocentrini Karsch, 1880
      - Tribe Nebini Kraepelin, 1905
    - Subfamily Scorpioninae Latreille, 1802
    - Subfamily Urodacinae Pocock, 1893
- Superfamily *incertae sedis*

- • † Family Palaeoeuscorpiidae Lourenço 2003 (extinct)
- • Parvorder *incertae sedis*
  - • † Family Archaeobuthidae Lourenço 2003 (extinct)
  - • † Family Palaeopisthacanthidae Kjellesvig-Wæring 1986 (extinct)
  - • † Family Protobuthidae Lourenço et Gall 2003 (extinct)
  - • † Family *incertae sedis* (contains genera *Corniops* Jeram 1994; *Palaeoburmesebuthus* Lourenço 2002; *Sinoscorpius* Hong 1983).

References

[1] Dunlop, Jason A.; Penney, David; Tetlie, O. Erik; and Anderson, Lyall I. (2008). "How many species of fossil arachnids are there" (http://www.bioone.org/doi/abs/10.1636/CH07-89.1). *Journal of Arachnology* (BioOne) **36** (2): 262–272. doi:10.1636/CH07-89.1. . Retrieved 2010-04-07.

[2] Soleglad, Michael E.; Fet, Victor (2003). "High-level systematics and phylogeny of the extant scorpions (Scorpiones: Orthosterni)" (http://www.science.marshall.edu/fet/euscorpius/pubs.htm) (multiple parts). *Euscorpius* (Marshall University) **11**: 1–175. . Retrieved 2008-06-13.

[3] Stockwell, Scott A., 1989. Revision of the Phylogeny and Higher Classification of Scorpions (Chelicerata). Ph.D. Dissertation, University of California, Berkeley

[4] Soleglad, Michael E.; Fet, Victor; and Kovařík, F. (2005). "The systematic position of the scorpion genera *Heteroscorpion* Birula, 1903 and *Urodacus* Peters, 1861 (Scorpiones: Scorpionoidea)" (http://www.science.marshall.edu/fet/euscorpius/p2005_20.pdf). *Euscorpius* (Marshall University) **20**: 1–38. . Retrieved 2008-06-13.

[5] Fet, V.; Soleglad, Michael E. (2005). "Contributions to scorpion systematics. I. On recent changes in high-level taxonomy." (http://www.science.marshall.edu/fet/euscorpius/p2005_31.pdf). *Euscorpius* (Marshall University) (31): 1–13. ISSN 1536-9307. . Retrieved 2010-04-07.

Trachypleura

Trachypleura is an extinct genus of polyplacophoran mollusc. Trachypleura became extinct during the Triassic period.[1]

References

[1] van Belle, R. A. (1981). *Catalogue of Fossil Chitons*. ISBN 90 6279 018 6.

Type (biology)

In biology, a **type** is one particular specimen (or in some cases a group of specimens) of an organism to which the scientific name of that organism is formally attached. In other words, a type is an example that serves to anchor or centralize the defining features of that particular taxon.

A taxon is a scientifically named grouping of organisms with other like organisms, a set that includes some organisms and excludes others, based on a detailed published description (for example a species description) and on the provision of type material, which is usually available to scientists for examination in a major museum research collection, or similar institution.

Type specimen for *Cimbrophlebia brooksi*, a fossil scorpion fly. By convention, the red label denotes a type specimen.

Type specimen

According to a precise set of rules laid down by the ICZN and the ICBN, the scientific name of every taxon is almost always based on one particular *specimen*, or in some cases specimens. Types are of great significance to biologists, especially to taxonomists. Types are usually physical specimens that are kept in a specially designated *type collection* in a museum research collection, or are a particular plant sample in a herbarium. Usually types are a physical example of the taxon, but failing that, an image of an individual of that taxon can be used. This material is the "type" or "types" of that taxon. Describing species and appointing type specimens is part of scientific nomenclature and alpha taxonomy.

When identifying material, a scientist attempts to apply a taxon name to a specimen or group of specimens based on his or her understanding of the relevant taxa, based on (at least) having read the type description(s), preferably based on an examination of all the type material of all of the relevant taxa. If there is more than one named type that all appear to be the same taxon, then the oldest name takes precedence, and is considered to be the correct name of the material in hand. If on the other hand the taxon appears never to have been named at all, then the scientist or another qualified expert picks a type specimen and publishes a new name and an official description.

This process is crucial to the science of biological taxonomy. People's ideas of how living things should be grouped changes and shifts over time. How do we know that that that we call "*Canis lupus*" is the same thing, or approximately the same thing, as what they will be calling "*Canis lupus*" in 200 years time? It is possible to check this because there is a particular wolf specimen preserved in a museum somewhere, and everyone who uses that name--no matter what else they may mean by it--will mean that particular specimen.

Depending on the nomenclature code applied to the organism in question, a type can be a specimen, a culture, an illustration, a description, or a taxon.

For example, in the research collection of the Natural History Museum in London, there is a bird specimen numbered 1886.6.24.20. This is a specimen of a kind of bird commonly known as the Spotted Harrier, which currently bears the scientific name *Circus assimilis*. This particular specimen is the holotype for that species; the name *Circus assimilis* refers, by definition, to the species of that particular specimen. That species was named and described by Jardine and Selby in 1828, and the holotype was placed in the museum collection so that other scientists might refer to it as necessary.

Note that at least for type specimens there is no requirement for a "typical" individual to be used. When describing new species, this is often impossible to tell anyway until more research has been done. Genera and families, particularly those established by early taxonomists, tend to be named after species that are more "typical" for them, but here too this is not always the case and due to changes in systematics *cannot* be. Hence, the term name-bearing type or onomatophore is sometimes used, to denote the fact that biological types do not define "typical" individuals or (in zoology) taxa, but rather fix a scientific name to a specific operational taxonomic unit. Type specimens are theoretically even allowed to be aberrant or deformed individuals or color variations, though this is rarely chosen to be the case, as it makes it hard to determine to which population the individual belonged.

The usage of the term *type* is somewhat complicated by slightly different uses in botany and zoology. In the *PhyloCode*, type-based definitions are replaced by phylogenetic definitions.

Types in botany

In botanical nomenclature, a *type* (*typus*, *nomenclatural type*), "is that element to which the name of a taxon is permanently attached."[1]

A botanical name, by itself, is only a phrase (of one to three words). For a name to be meaningful it is necessary to be sure what it applies to. A type fixes a botanical name to a taxon. In botany a type is either a specimen or an illustration. A specimen is a real plant (or one or more parts of a plant or a lot of small plants), dead and kept safe, "curated", in a herbarium (or the equivalent for fungi). Notable cases of where an illustration may serve as a type are (this is not an exclusive listing):

- A detailed drawing, painting, etc., depicting the plant, from the early days of plant taxonomy (as we now know it). In those days a dried plant was difficult to transport and hard to keep safe for the future: many specimens that famous botanists looked at have since been lost or damaged. However, there were devoted botanical artists who upon assignment by a botanist (or naturalist) could make a faithful and detailed work of botanical art, for inclusion in a costly book.
- A detailed picture of something that can be seen only through a microscope. A tiny 'plant' on a microscope slide makes for a poor type: the microscope slide may be lost or damaged, or it may be very difficult to find the 'plant' in question among whatever else is on the microscope slide. An illustration makes for a much more reliable type (Art 37.5 of the *Vienna Code*, 2006).

Note that a type fixes only a name to a single representative of the taxon. A type does not determine the circumscription (therefore a taxon is independent of its type species or specimen) of the taxon. For example, the common dandelion is a controversial taxon: some botanists consider it to consist of over a hundred species, although most botanists regard it to be a single species. The type of the name *Taraxacum officinale* is the same whether the circumscription of the species includes all those small species (*Taraxacum officinale* is a 'big' species) or whether the circumscription is limited to only one small species among the other hundred (*Taraxacum officinale* is a 'small' species). In this case the name *Taraxacum officinale* is the same and the type of the name is the same, but the extent of what the name actually applies to varies strongly. Setting the circumscription of a taxon is done by a taxonomist in a publication.

Miscellaneous notes:

1. Usually, only a species or an infraspecific taxon can have a type of its own. For a new taxon (published on or after 1 January 1958) at these ranks a type should not be an illustration.
2. A genus (almost always) has the same type as that of one of its species. Because the mere name of the species is considered equivalent to that species's type, this species is frequently called the type species, a phrase that has no standing under the *ICBN*.
3. A family has the same type as that of one of its genera (that is, almost always the type of a species). The term *"type genus"* in much the same way as "type species" is widely used in practice.
4. The *ICBN* provides a listing of the various kinds of type in Art 9 [2], the most important of which is the holotype. Note that the word "type" appears in botanical literature as a part of several terms that have no status under the *ICBN*: for example a clonotype, an herbarium specimen vegetatively propagated from (and thus a clone of) the same plant from which a type specimen was made that is used for documenting the type collection.

Types in zoology

In zoological nomenclature, the type of a species (or subspecies) is a specimen (or series of specimens), the type of a genus (or subgenus) is a species, and the type of a suprageneric taxon (e.g., family, etc.) is a genus. Names higher than superfamily rank do not have types. A "name-bearing type" "provides the objective standard of reference whereby the application of the name of a nominal taxon can be determined."

Figs 1-4. *Jamides elioti* sp. nov. 1,2. Holotype, ♂. 3, 4. Paratype, ♀. 1, 3. Upperside. 2, 4. Underside.

Gossamer-winged butterfly *Jamides elioti*, upper pair is upper and lower surface of the holotype, lower pair is the paratype

Definitions

- A type specimen is a vernacular term (not a formally defined term) typically used for an individual or fossil that is any of the various name-bearing types for a species. For example, the type specimen for the species *Homo neanderthalensis* was the specimen "Neanderthal-1" discovered by Johann Karl Fuhlrott in 1856 at Feldhofer in the Neander Valley in Germany, consisting of a skullcap, thigh bones, part of a pelvis, some ribs, and some arm and shoulder bones. There may be more than one type specimen, but there is (at least in modern times) only one holotype.

- A type species is the nominal species that is the name-bearing type of a nominal genus or subgenus.
- A type genus is the nominal genus that is the name-bearing type of a nominal family-group taxon.
- The type series are all those specimens included by the author in a taxon's formal description, unless the author explicitly or implicitly excludes them as part of the series.

Use of types

Although in reality biologists may examine many specimens (when available) of a new taxon before writing an official published species description, nonetheless, under the formal rules for naming species (the International Code of Zoological Nomenclature), a single type must be designated, as part of the published description.

When a single specimen is clearly designated in the original description, this specimen is known as the holotype of that species. The holotype is typically placed in a major museum, or similar well-known public collection, so that it is freely available for later examination by other biologists. Type illustrations have also been used by zoologists, as in the case of the Réunion Parakeet, which is known only from historical illustrations and descriptions.[3] :24

A type description must include a diagnosis (typically, a discussion of similarities to and differences from closely related species), and an indication of where the type specimen or specimens are deposited for examination. The geographical location where a type specimen was originally found is known as its type locality. In the case of parasites, the term type host (or symbiotype) is used to indicate the host organism from which the type specimen was obtained.[4]

Zoological collections are maintained by universities and museums. Ensuring that types are kept in good condition and made available for examination by taxonomists are two important functions of such collections. And, while there is only one *holotype* designated, there can be other "type" specimens, the following of which are formally defined:

- **Paratype** – Any additional specimen other than the holotype, listed in the type series, where the original description designated a holotype. These are not name-bearing types.
- **Neotype** – A specimen later selected to serve as the single type specimen when an original holotype has been lost or destroyed, or where the original author never cited a specimen.
- **Syntype** – Any of two or more specimens listed in a species description where a holotype was not designated; historically, syntypes were often explicitly designated as such, and under the present Code this is a requirement, but modern attempts to publish species description based on syntypes are generally frowned upon by practicing

taxonomists, and most are gradually being replaced by lectotypes. Those that still exist are still considered name-bearing types.

- **Lectotype** – A specimen later selected to serve as the single type specimen for species originally described from a set of syntypes.
- **Paralectotype** – Any additional specimen from among a set of syntypes, after a lectotype has been designated from among them. These are not name-bearing types.
- **Hapantotype** – A special case in Protistans where the type consists of two or more specimens of "directly related individuals representing distinct stages in the life cycle"; these are collectively treated as a single entity, and lectotypes cannot be designated from among them.

The various types listed above are necessary because many species were described one or two centuries ago, when a single type specimen, a holotype, was often not designated. Also, types were not always carefully preserved, and intervening events such as wars and fires have resulted in destruction of original type material. The validity of a species name often rests upon the availability of original type specimens; or, if the type cannot be found, or one has never existed, upon the clarity of the description.

The ICZN has existed only since 1961, when the first edition of the Code was published. The ICZN does not always demand a type specimen for the historical validity of a species, and many "type-less" species do exist, perhaps the most notable being *Homo sapiens*. This example is instructive: the current edition of the Code, Article 75.3, prohibits the designation of a neotype unless there is "an exceptional need" for "clarifying the taxonomic status" of a species; as the status and identity of *H. sapiens* is not questioned, there is no exceptional need for clarification, and "any such neotype designation is invalid" (Article 75.2).

Recently, some species have been described where the type specimen was released alive back into the wild, such as the Bulo Burti Boubou (a bushshrike), described as *Laniarius liberatus*, in which the species description included DNA sequences from blood and feather samples. Assuming there is no future question as to the status of such a species, the absence of a type specimen does not invalidate the name, but it may be necessary in the future to designate a neotype for such a taxon, should any questions arise. However, in the case of the bushshrike, ornithologists have argued that the specimen was a rare and hitherto unknown color morph of a long-known species, using only the available blood and feather samples. While there is still some debate on the need to deposit actual killed individuals as type specimens, it can be observed that given proper vouchering and storage, tissue samples can be just as valuable even in case disputes about the validity of a species arise.

There are many other permutations and variations on terms using the suffix "-type" (e.g., allotype, cotype, topotype, generitype, isotype, isoneotype, etc.) but these are not formally regulated by the Code, and a great many are obsolete and/or idiosyncratic. However, some of these categories can potentially apply to genuine type specimens, such as a neotype; e.g., isotypic/topotypic specimens are preferred to other specimens, when they are available at the time a neotype is chosen (because they are from the same time and/or place as the original type).

The term fixation is used by the Code for the declaration of a name-bearing type, whether by original or subsequent designation.

Type species

Each genus must have a designated type species (the term "genotype" was once used for this but has been abandoned because the word has been co-opted for use in genetics and is much better known in that context). The description of a genus is usually based primarily on its type species, modified and expanded by the features of other included species. The generic name is permanently associated with the name-bearing type of its type species.

Ideally, a type species best exemplifies the essential characteristics of the genus to which it belongs, but this is subjective and, ultimately, technically irrelevant, as it is not a requirement of the Code. If the type species proves, upon closer examination, to belong to a pre-existing

The common toad, *Bufo bufo* described by Linnaeus, is the type species for the genus *Bufo*, and indeed for the whole family Bufonidae

genus (a common occurrence), then all of the constituent species must be either moved into the pre-existing genus, or disassociated from the original type species and given a new generic name; the old generic name passes into synonymy and is abandoned unless there is a pressing need to make an exception (decided case-by-case, via petition to the International Commission on Zoological Nomenclature).

Type genus

A type genus is that genus from which the name of a family or subfamily is formed. As with type species, the type genus is not necessarily the most representative, but is usually the earliest described, largest or best known genus. It is not uncommon for the name of a family to be based upon the name of a type genus that has passed into synonymy; the family name does not need to be changed in such a situation.

References

[1] Art 7.1 *International Code of Botanical Nomenclature.*

[2] http://www.bgbm.fu-berlin.de/iapt/nomenclature/code/SaintLouis/0013Ch2Sec2a009.htm

[3] Hume, Julian Pender (25 June 2007). "Reappraisal of the parrots (Aves: Psittacidae) from the Mascarene Islands, with comments on their ecology, morphology, and affinities" (http://julianhume.co.uk/wp-content/uploads/2010/07/Hume-Mascarene-Parrots.pdf). *Zootaxa* (1513): 1–76. ISSN 1175-5334. . Retrieved 13 January 2011.

[4] Jennifer K. Frey, Terry L. Yates, Donald W. Duszynski, William L. Gannon and Scott L. Gardner (1992). "Designation and Curatorial Management of Type Host Specimens (Symbiotypes) for New Parasite Species" (http://jstor.org/stable/3283335). *The Journal of Parasitology* **78** (5): 930–993. doi:10.2307/3283335. .

External links

- *ICZN Code*: International Code of Zoological Nomenclature (http://www.iczn.org/), the official website
- Fishbase (http://filaman.uni-kiel.de/LarvalBase/Glossary/Glossary.cfm?TermEnglish=type species) Glossary section.
- A compendium of terms (http://pages.unibas.ch/museum/microfossils/Colls_NMB/GENERALS/COMTYPES.HTML)

Type genus

In biological classification, a **type genus** is a representative genus, as with regard to a biological family. The term and concept is used much more often and much more formally in zoology than it is in botany, and the definition is dependent on the nomenclatural *Code* that applies:

- In zoological nomenclature, a type genus is "The nominal genus that is the name-bearing type of a nominal family-group taxon."

- In botanical nomenclature, the phrase "type genus" is used, unofficially, as a term of convenience. In the *ICBN* this phrase has no status. Although the code also uses type specimens for ranks up to family (all ranks must bear the name of the genus in which their types are placed), but does not refer to the genus containing that type as a "Type genus". Names above the rank of family are not under any nomenclatural restriction according to the ICBN, except where it comes to their endings.

> Example: "*Faba* is the type genus of the family Fabaceae" is another way of saying that the family name Fabaceae is based on the generic name *Faba*.

References

Type species

In biological nomenclature, a **type species** is a species to which the name of a genus is permanently linked. It comes into play whenever taxon containing multiple species must be divided; the type species automatically assigns the name of the original taxon to one of the resulting new taxons, reducing the potential for confusion. Under both the zoological and botanical nomenclature codes, every named genus or subdivision of a genus, whether or not currently recognized as valid or correct, should ideally have a type species, but in practice there is a backlog of untypified names.

A similar concept is used for supregeneric groups: the type genus.

In zoology

The term type species is regulated in zoological nomenclature by article 42.3 of the *International Code of Zoological Nomenclature*, which defines type species as the name-bearing type of the name of a genus or subgenus (a "genus-group name") is the "type species". In the Glossary, type species is defined as

> "The nominal species that is the name-bearing type of a nominal genus or subgenus".

The type species permanently attaches a genus to its formal name (its generic name) by providing just one species within that genus to which the genus is permanently linked (i.e. the genus must include that species if it is to bear the name). The species name in turn is fixed, in theory, to a type specimen.

For example, the type species for the land snail genus *Monacha* is *Monacha cartusiana*. That genus is currently placed within the family Hygromiidae. The type genus for that family is the genus *Hygromia*.

The concept of the type species in zoology was introduced by Pierre André Latreille.[1]

In botany

In botanical nomenclature, the type for any given taxonomic name - if it has a type - is technically a specimen (or illustration).[2] In the case of the name of a genus (or of a subdivision of a genus), its type will usually be the type for a species included within it and can be indicated by the name of this species alone.[3]

In modern nomenclature, the type of a genus (often referred to as the **generitype**) is systematically that of a published species (although that specific name might be currently regarded as a synonym), and thus only a species name is cited. As a result, despite the provisions of the code, it is not unusual to designate a genus' type without regard as to whether that species itself has a type (be in an holotype, lectotype or neotype). The term "type species", although of no formal standing under the Code (beyond performing an operation a code allows), has thus been borrowed from zoological nomenclature.

References

[1] Claude Dupuis (1974). "Pierre André Latreille (1762–1833): the foremost entomologist of his time" (http://www.annualreviews.org/doi/pdf/10.1146/annurev.en.19.010174.000245) (PDF). *Annual Review of Entomology* **19**: 1–14. doi:10.1146/annurev.en.19.010174.000245. .

[2] *ICBN*, articles 10.1, 8.1 and 10.4 (Vienna Code, 2005)

[3] ICBN Art 10.1 (Vienna Code, 2005)

ViralZone

ViralZon

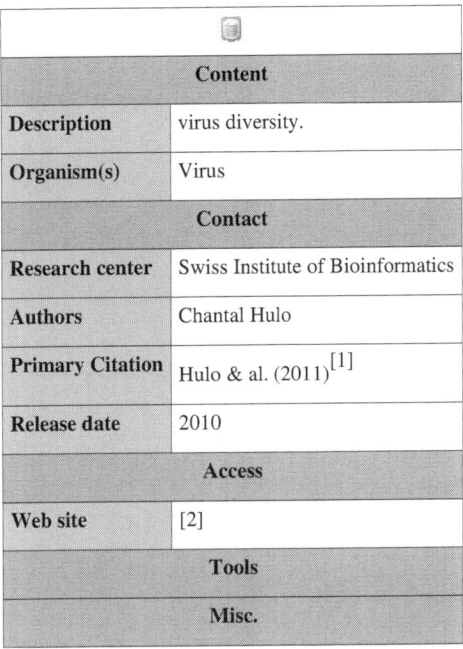

Content		
Description	virus diversity.	
Organism(s)	Virus	
Contact		
Research center	Swiss Institute of Bioinformatics	
Authors	Chantal Hulo	
Primary Citation	Hulo & al. (2011)[1]	
Release date	2010	
Access		
Web site	[2]	
Tools		
Misc.		

ViralZone is a Swiss Institute of Bioinformatics web-resource for all viral genus and families, providing general molecular and epidemiological informations, along with virion and genome figures.[1]

References

[1] Hulo, Chantal; de Castro Edouard, Masson Patrick, Bougueleret Lydie, Bairoch Amos, Xenarios Ioannis, Le Mercier Philippe (Jan 2011).
"ViralZone: a knowledge resource to understand virus diversity" (in eng). *Nucleic Acids Res.* (England) **39** (Database issue): D576-82.
doi:10.1093/nar/gkq901. PMC 3013774. PMID 20947564.

[2] http://www.expasy.org/viralzone/

External links

* http://www.expasy.org/viralzone/

Wastebasket taxon

Wastebasket taxon (also called a **wastebin taxon**, **dustbin taxon**[1] or **catch-all taxon**[2]) is a term used in some taxonomic circles to refer to a taxon that has the sole purpose of classifying organisms that do not fit anywhere else. They are typically defined by their *lack* of one or more distinct character states or by their *not* belonging to one or more other taxa. Wastebasket taxa are by definition either paraphyletic or polyphyletic, and are therefore not considered to be valid taxa under strict cladistic rules of taxonomy. The name of a wastebasket taxon may in some cases be retained as the designation of an evolutionary grade, however.

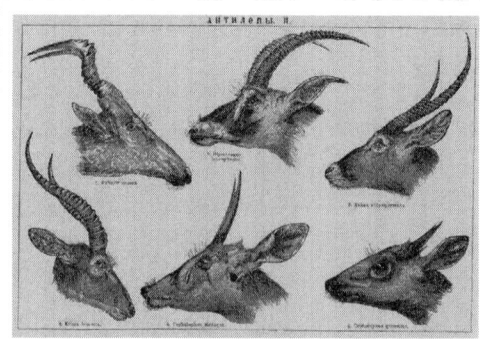

Antelopes are assorted groups of bovids that are not goats, sheep or cattle.

The familiar category of invertebrates is an "everything-else" category, comprising all animals without backbones. Other examples of wastebasket taxa include the Protista, Carnosauria, Thecodontia, Palaeoptera and Tricholomataceae. Fossil groups that are poorly known due to fragmentary remains are sometimes grouped together on gross morphology or stratigraphy, only later to be found to be wastebasket taxa, such as the more or less crocodile like Triassic group Rauisuchia.[3] Sometimes, during taxonomic revisions, the wastebasket taxa can be salvaged after doing thorough research on its members, and then imposing tighter restrictions on what continues to be included. Such techniques "saved" Carnosauria and *Megalosaurus*. Other times, the taxonomic name contains too much unrelated "baggage" to be successfully salvaged. As such, it is usually dumped in favour of a new, more restrictive name (for example, Rhynchocephalia or Thecodontia), or abandoned altogether (for example, *Simia*).

A related concept is that of **form taxon**, "wastebasket" groupings that are united by gross morphology. This is often result of a common mode of life, often one that is generalist, leading to generally similar body shapes by convergent evolution.

References

[1] Hallam, A.; Wignall, P. B. (1997). *Mass extinctions and their aftermath* (http://books.google.com/?id=06yrErJt_NsC&lpg=PA107& dq="dustbin taxon"&pg=PA107). Oxford [England]: Oxford University Press. p. 107. ISBN 978-0-19-854916-1. .

[2] Monks, N. (2002). "Cladistic analysis of a problematic ammonite group: the Hamitidae (Cretaceous, Albian-Turonian) and proposals for new cladistic terms". *Palaeontology,* **45**: 689–707. doi:10.1111/1475-4983.00255.

[3] Nesbitt, S. J. (2003). "*Arizonasaurus and its implications for archosaur divergence*" (http://www.journals.royalsoc.ac.uk/content/ 2vetg3w8xha9e992). *Proceedings of the Royal Society B* **270** (Suppl. 2): S234–S237. doi:10.1098/rsbl.2003.0066. ISSN 0962-8452. PMC 1809943. PMID 14667392. .

Web-based taxonomy

Web-based taxonomy is the effort by taxonomists to use the World Wide Web in order to create unified, consensus taxonomies of life on Earth.

In his 2002 paper on the subject[1] , H. Charles J. Godfray called for the creation of Web-based organisations to collect all the accumulated literature on a taxonomic group into a centralized knowledge base and make this data available through the Web as a unified taxonomy, so that it can be more easily examined and revised. Such a platform would be owned and maintained by a taxonomic working group, governed by an editor or an editorial board. An example of such a platform is FishBase.

The notion of Web-based consensus taxonomies remains controversial because, as two Australian researchers pointed out[2] , taxonomic names are not fixed but hypotheses, and therefore in constant change.

References

[1] Godfray, H.C.J (2002). Challenges for taxonomy. *Nature* 417: 17-19 (http://www.nature.com/nature/journal/v417/n6884/full/417017a. html)

[2] Thiele, Kevin and David Yeates (2002). "Tension arises from duality at the heart of taxonomy". *Nature* **419** (6905): 337. doi:10.1038/419337a. PMID 12353005.

External links

- CATE Project (http://www.cate-project.org/)
- Encyclopedia of Life (http://www.eol.org/)
- Species 2000 / ITIS Catalogue of Life (http://www.catalogueoflife.org)

West American Digest System

The **West American Digest System** is a system of identifying points of law from reported cases and organizing them by topic and key number. The system was developed by West Publishing to organize the entire body of American law. This extensive taxonomy makes the process of doing case law legal research less time consuming as it directs the researcher to cases that are similar to the legal issue under consideration.

History

The problem of finding cases on a particular topic was a large problem for the rapidly growing American legal system of the 19th century. John B. West, the founder of West Publishing, described this problem in his article *A multiplicity of reports* [1]. To solve the problem, he developed a system with two major parts. First, his company published cases in many American jurisdictions in bound volumes called reporters (the West National Reporter System now covers all state and federal courts). Second, he put together a classification system in which he divided the law into major categories which he called topics (such as "Contracts"). He then created hundreds of subcategories. To save space in printing, these were given a number called a key number. He then applied this "topic and key number" system to the cases he published. The key number is identified in the books with a key number and a key symbol graphic.

Early digests

How the Digest System works

Each case published in a West reporter is evaluated by an editor who identifies the points of law cited or explained in the case. The editor places the summaries of the points of law covered in the case at the beginning of the case. These summaries are usually a sentence long, and are called **headnotes**. Each headnote is then assigned a topic and key number. The headnotes are arranged according to their topic and key number in multi-volume sets of books called Digests. A digest serves as a subject index to the case law published in West reporters. Headnotes are merely editorial guides to the points of law discussed or used in the cases, and the headnotes themselves are not legal authority.

West publishes *West's Analysis of American Law*, which is a complete guide to the topic and key number system, and it is revised periodically.

Print Digest

In print, a digest works like an encyclopedia, in that the topics are listed in alphabetical order and printed on the spines. The "Descriptive Word Index" provides guidance as to the proper topics and key numbers.

The digest system includes digests for the individual states (except for Delaware, Nevada and Utah). The U.S. Supreme Court, Bankruptcy Courts, Federal Claims Court, and military courts each have an individual digest, as well as their decisions being included in the *Federal Practice Digest* with the notes of decisions from the federal District Courts and Courts of Appeals. Digests are also published for West's National Reporter System. Specialty subject digests exist, such as the Education Law Digest, and the Social Security Digest.

For nationwide research, about once a month, West publishes a *General Digest* volume, which incorporates classified digest notes from all reporters of the West National Reporter System. These are then cumulated into a *Decennial Digest*. Decennial implies that this occurs every ten years, but in the past several decades, there have been Decennial Digest Parts I and II (the 11th Series now has Part III[2]), so the cumulation is now more frequent. However, the various Decennial Digests are not cumulated. Thus, completing such a search over several decades requires consulting the Decennial Digests, and then updating that work with the most recent series of the General Digest.

Some of the state and topical digests are revised to include the first cases in the jurisdiction, while the spines of the books of some of the other digests indicate that they are from "1933 to date," for instance, indicating that one must consult a prior series for references to earlier cases. The state, federal, regional, and topical digests are updated by interim pamphlets, pocket parts, replacement volumes, or a new series.

The Digest on Westlaw

Researchers can also search the digest electronically using Westlaw:

- with the "Key Number Search Tool," which uses a word search to identify up to five key numbers,
- with the "Key Numbers and Digest" feature (browse by subject using an expandable tree - no search terms required),
- by a key number search using the "Terms and Connectors" method (with a known topic and key number - in the form of 134k261; topic 134 is Divorce and the key number is 261 for "Enforcement, In general"),
- by using the KeySearch feature (a menu of hierarchical links that automatically generates a search without the need to see the key numbers or the terms and connectors query), or
- by finding a relevant case using keyword searching and then using the key number hyperlinks in the document to find related cases.

Most secondary sources published by Thomson West, such as Corpus Juris Secundum and American Jurisprudence, also have key number hyperlinks in their on-line Westlaw versions.

The "Key Numbers and Digest" feature and the hyperlinks create a "Custom Digest."

The Custom Digest allows:

- selection of the jurisdiction of interest (so that headnotes from cases in that jurisdiction will appear in the results);
- limiting the time frame of the search; and
- adding additional search terms.

Selecting key numbers and jurisdictions in the "Key Number Search Tool" results in a similar display of digest headnotes.

Since all West headnote annotations are merged on Westlaw into a single database from which each Custom Digest is generated, there is no need to consult each separate series of the hard copy Decennial Digest. Full text of the cases may be accessed from the Custom Digest by clicking on the underlined case citation. The key number search or KeySearch will retrieve entire cases from a case law database.

Other digest systems

Other digest systems exist, including Butterworth's Digest[3] for the United Kingdom (also containing references to cases decided in other Commonwealth countries), the Canadian Abridgment,[4] digests associated with official state reports, such as in California and Wisconsin, and digests associated with topical reporters, such as the Uniform Commercial Code Case Digest. Most of these use a topic and section format, while some, like the U.C.C. Case Digest, use a section format based on the statute or rules being annotated. The A.L.R. Digest, accompanying the American Law Reports, formerly had its own classification system, but was replaced in 2004 by *West's American Law Reports Digest,* which follows West's topic and key number system.

External references

- West Topic & Key Number System - Westlaw Quick Reference Guide [5](.pdf)
- West product search for Key Number Digest [6]
- *West's Analysis of American Law* product description [7]
- *West's A.L.R. Digest* product description [8]

References

[1] http://www.hyperlaw.com//90-99-docs/1909-multiplicity_of_reports_jbwest.html

[2] http://west.thomson.com/productdetail/147058/40591956/productdetail.aspx

[3] http://rimer.butterworths.co.uk/webcat/enquiry/product/prodInfo.asp?ProdID=460&Text=First&i=cat&Acca=0

[4] http://www.carswell.com/areasofinterest/law/print/abridgment.htm

[5] http://west.thomson.com/documentation/westlaw/wlawdoc/wlres/keynmb06.pdf

[6] http://west.thomson.com/store/Results.aspx?n=4294966990&ntt=+key&pagesize=20&no=0&ntk=KEYWORD-SEARCH

[7] http://west.thomson.com/product/17304137/product.asp

[8] http://west.thomson.com/store/product.asp?product_id=13503637

Wikispecies

Wikispecies

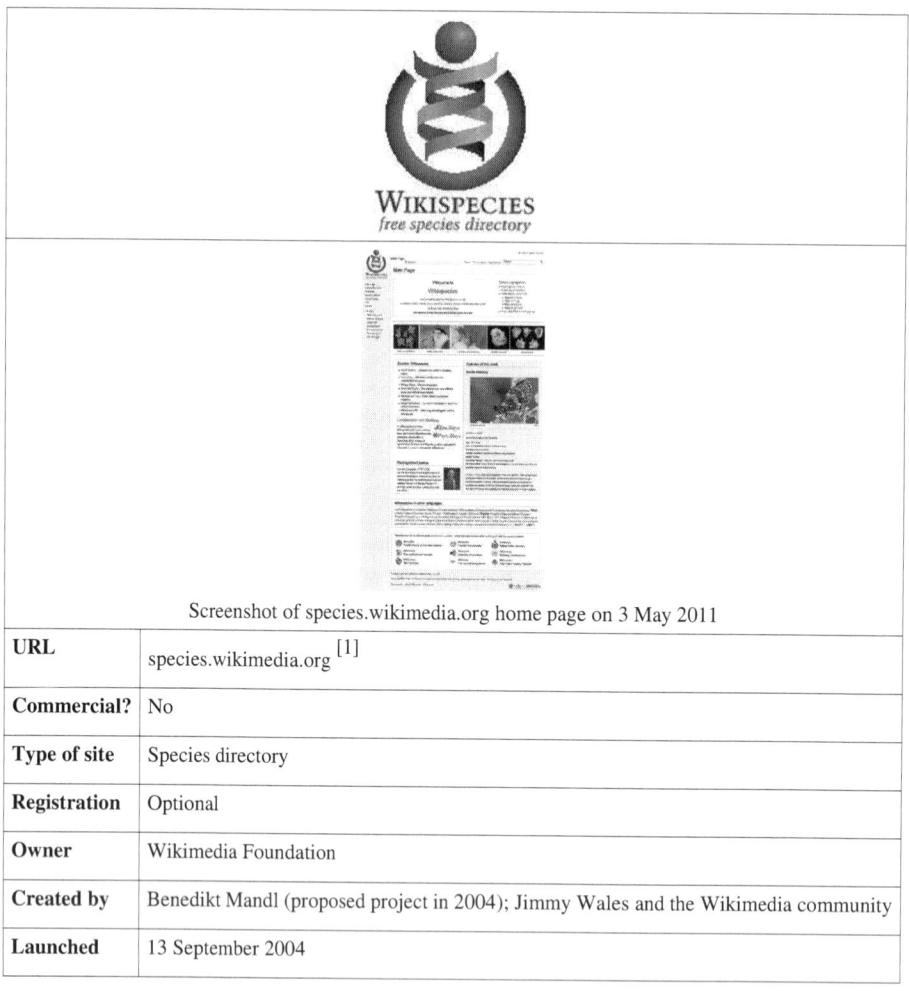

Screenshot of species.wikimedia.org home page on 3 May 2011

URL	species.wikimedia.org [1]
Commercial?	No
Type of site	Species directory
Registration	Optional
Owner	Wikimedia Foundation
Created by	Benedikt Mandl (proposed project in 2004); Jimmy Wales and the Wikimedia community
Launched	13 September 2004

Wikispecies is a wiki-based online project supported by the Wikimedia Foundation. Its aim is to create a comprehensive free content catalogue of all species and is directed at scientists, rather than at the general public. Jimmy Wales—chairman emeritus of the Wikimedia Foundation—stated that editors are not required to fax in their degrees, but that submissions will have to pass muster with a technical audience.[2] [3] Wikispecies is available under the GNU Free Documentation License and CC-BY-SA 3.0.

Started in September 2004, with biologists across the world invited to contribute,[4] the project had grown a framework encompassing the Linnaean taxonomy with links to Wikipedia articles on individual species by April 2005.[3]

History

Benedikt Mandl co-ordinated the efforts of several people who are interested in getting involved with the project and contacted potential supporters in early summer 2004. Databases were evaluated and the administrators contacted, some of them have agreed on providing their data for Wikispecies. Benedikt Mandl defined two major tasks:

1. Figure out how the contents of the data base would need to be presented — by asking experts, potential non-professional users and comparing that with existing data bases.
2. Figure out how to do the software, which hardware is required and how to cover the costs — by asking experts, looking for fellow volunteers and potential sponsors.

Advantages and disadvantages were widely discussed by the wikimedia-I mailing list. The board of directors of the wikimedia foundation voted by 4 to 0 in favor of the establishment of a Wikispecies. The project was launched in August 2004 and is hosted at species.wikimedia.org [5]. It was officially merged to a sister project of Wikimedia Foundation on September 14, 2004.

On October 10, 2006, the project exceeded 75,000 articles. On May 20, 2007, the project exceeded 100,000 articles with a total of 5,495 registered users. On September 8, 2008, the project exceeded 150,000 articles with a total of 9,224 registered users.

Policies

Wikispecies has disabled local upload and asks users to use images from Wikimedia Commons. Wikispecies does not allow the use of content that does not conform to a free license.

References

[1] http://species.wikimedia.org/
[2] "Calling all taxonomists" (http://www.sciencemag.org/cgi/reprint/307/5712/1021d.pdf). *Science* **307** (5712): 1021. 2005. doi:10.1126/science.307.5712.1021a. .
[3] "WikiSpecies" (http://www.americanscientist.org/template/SiteOfTheWeekTypeDetail/assetid/43122). *American Scientist Online*. 25 April 2005. .
[4] Mark Peplow (2005). "Species list reaches half-million mark". *Nature*. doi:10.1038/news050314-6.
[5] http://species.wikimedia.org

External links

- Official site (http://species.wikimedia.org/wiki/Main_Page)
- Species Community Portal (http://species.wikimedia.org/wiki/Wikispecies:Community_Portal)
- The Wikispecies Charter (http://species.wikimedia.org/wiki/Wikispecies:Wikispecies_Charter), written by Wales.

Zootaxa

Zootaxa	
Abbreviated title (ISO)	*Zootaxa*
Discipline	Taxonomy
Language	English
Edited by	Zhi-Qiang Zhang
Publication details	
Publisher	Magnolia Press (New Zealand)
Publication history	2001–present
Impact factor	0.891 (2009)
Indexing	
ISSN	1175-5326 [1] (print) 1175-5334 [2] (web)
OCLC number	49030618 [3]
Links	
	• Journal homepage [4] • Online access [5]

Zootaxa is a peer-reviewed scientific journal for animal taxonomists. It is published by Magnolia Press (Auckland, New Zealand). The journal was established by Zhi-Qiang Zhang in 2001 and new issues are published multiple times a week. As of November 2010 more than 16,000 new species have been described in the journal.[6]

Zootaxa gained international notice when it published a paper announcing the discovery of the Cypriot Mouse in October of 2006.[7]

References

[1] http://www.worldcat.org/issn/1175-5326

[2] http://www.worldcat.org/issn/1175-5334

[3] http://www.worldcat.org/oclc/49030618

[4] http://www.mapress.com/zootaxa/

[5] http://www.mapress.com/zootaxa/content.html

[6] Zootaxa Statistics (http://www.mapress.com/zootaxa/support/Statistics.htm)

[7] "Mighty mouse! Rare discovery in Europe" (http://web.archive.org/web/20061013035349/http://www.cnn.com/2006/TECH/science/ 10/12/new.mouse.ap/index.html). Associated Press. October 12, 2006. Archived from the original (http://www.cnn.com/2006/TECH/ science/10/12/new.mouse.ap/index.html) on 2006-10-13. . Retrieved 2006-10-12.

External links

• Official website (http://http://www.mapress.com/zootaxa/)

Article Sources and Contributors

Folksonomy *Source*: http://en.wikipedia.org/w/index.php?oldid=431604403 *Contributors*: Abdullais4u, Andy Dingley, Apothecia, Artw, Basswulf, BioPupil, Bjankuloski06en, Brillybean, Chaojoker, Courcelles, Cybercobra, Ddcarnage, Delcnsltmd, Edgar181, Everything counts, JV Smithy, Jeffrey04, Kgwiki, Markuspony, McGeddon, Nabeth, Navalg, Ocean Shores, Papertiger, Pigsonthewing, Ronz, Schalliol, The Thing That Should Not Be, Toussaint, Wireless friend, 35 anonymous edits

Card sorting *Source*: http://en.wikipedia.org/w/index.php?oldid=430528485 *Contributors*: Andres, Andy Dingley, Briansuda, Bruce Esrig, Cennydd, Daltxn, Diego Moya, Dobrien, Eallik, Edward, Flanneljammies, Fram, Jpbowen, Maniacgeorge, Orangejon, Rballou, ShaunOgg, 7 anonymous edits

steve.museum *Source*: http://en.wikipedia.org/w/index.php?oldid=414050965 *Contributors*: Alansohn, Amarkov, Bladeswin, Brewcrewer, Brookie, Iridescent, IronGargoyle, Keeper76, Malcolma, Rayshah, Rjwilmsi, Robert Leopold, SarahStierch, Silensor, Sils660, Star Mississippi, Trialsanderrors, Tubezone, Vegaswikian, Verrai, ZimZalaBim, 6 anonymous edits

Tag management *Source*: http://en.wikipedia.org/w/index.php?oldid=385542874 *Contributors*: Gculpin, 1 anonymous edits

Vocabulary OneSource *Source*: http://en.wikipedia.org/w/index.php?oldid=426496383 *Contributors*: Buckshot06, Cybercobra, Daswani.Amit, Dharma Initiative, Fabrictramp, Jacobsatterfield, Ndunruh, 6 anonymous edits

Comparison of enterprise bookmarking platforms *Source*: http://en.wikipedia.org/w/index.php?oldid=407093123 *Contributors*: Ben Ben, Chowbok, Gculpin, Haakon, JLaTondre, Malcolma, MarekMahut, Nagle, Pnm, Rabbasher, 27 anonymous edits

Enterprise bookmarking *Source*: http://en.wikipedia.org/w/index.php?oldid=422214112 *Contributors*: Aperdaens, Art LaPella, Erianna, Gculpin, Mild Bill Hiccup, Nagle, Punja2002, Raja2002, Ttonyb1, 11 anonymous edits

List of social bookmarking websites *Source*: http://en.wikipedia.org/w/index.php?oldid=431042381 *Contributors*: Acroterion, Alexf, Bonadea, DOHill, Dkg, GoingBatty, Golkow, HJ Mitchell, JoelDowns, Kris1911, Lachelt, MrOllie, Mrwebby1122, Paul A, Plausmi, Pnm, Poromenos, Ppolsinelli, Rinnku, Rubisco67, Salsan.edakkalathur, Skingston1024, Socialmysite, Teddytop, Victor falk, Zachlipton, 28 anonymous edits

Social bookmark link generator *Source*: http://en.wikipedia.org/w/index.php?oldid=404917011 *Contributors*: Dreamyshade, Fribbler, Islander, MrOllie, Pnm, Samughal786, Vishvax, 5 anonymous edits

Social bookmarking *Source*: http://en.wikipedia.org/w/index.php?oldid=429116712 *Contributors*: 16@r, 7, A. B., AbsolutDan, Acslab, Ajobin, Akendall, Ali'i, Alkasingh, Allstarecho, Alun6680, Alvin-cs, Andrea Parri, Andrejj, Andrewrp, Andy Dingley, Anetode, Angela, Anna Lincoln, Annarchy, AntonioDsouza, Arichnad, Athuljayaram, Atiteu, Azimof, Baronnet, Bcuser, Beatyou, Beowulf314159, Bigpinkthing, Bobblunt80, Bonadea, Cbauckhage, Champmark, Chaojoker, Chrisch, Chriswaterguy, Chuck369, Colonies Chris, Cool Blue, Courcelles, Cy21, CynicalMe, Dan aka jack, Danski14, Davenaff, Davitof, Deepkraft, DelineJY, Delpino, Dgrey, Discospinster, Dmlandfair, Dolly Setia, Downwards, Dposse, Dr.alf, Dreamyshade, Dylan Lake, Egmontaz, Elwikipedista, Emx, Eptin, Erickaakcire, Evanreyes, Everything counts, Firsfron, FlyHigh, Fpfp, Frap, FromanylanD, GTBacchus, Gaius Cornelius, GeoFan49, George Hernandez, Ghewgill, Gogo Dodo, Golkow, Gorx, Gracefool, GraemeL, Greenrd, Grimlock, Haakon, Holdtheonions95, Hu12, I already forgot, IDNexpert, Iahead, Ilasiene, Infododge, Ipsingh, Irrbloss, Itsonlychand, JForget, JHP, Jackfork, Jasoncalacanis, Jebba, JeffMHoward, Jemima29, Jenshibuya, Jeremy04, Jglaysher, Joe Jarvis, JoeSmack, JonHarder, Jonas Olson, Jpservicez, Jugger90, Jusdafax, JzG, Kariteh, Kathleenchester, Kharissa, Kjlewis, Kledy, Ksero, Kuchiguchi, Langec, Lcarscad, Lectiodifficilior, LimeHat, Llywrch, Lowdeo1, Lquerel, Lun4tic, MPS, MacManX, Macrakis, Manop, Masterzora, MatthewKarlsen, Mavhc, McGeddon, Mdog, Megri12, Merlion444, MichaK, Mietchen, Mindmatrix, MissDanni, MuthuKutty, Myvenner, Nabeth, Narutodude000, Nathanyarnold, Neil9327, NeilN, Nickrice, Nlu, Noctibus, Notinasnaid, NuclearWarfare, Nysus, Octahedron80, Ohnoitsjamie, Oliviaanderson, Papertiger, Paranoid, Paulscho36, PhilKnight, Phuonglien 2002, Pingveno, Planetoid, Pnm, Priddle, Pschemp, Punja2002, Quintonm, Rajaryanmalhotra, Rbraunwa, Resin8, ResortLabs, Rich Farmbrough, Robertfalco, Rony888, RoodyAlien, RoyBoy, Ruud Koot, S Gladkova, SGGH, Samw, SarahGriffiths, Sdavis0830, Se76889, Seojoint, Shaahin, SheffieldSteel, Sietse Snel, Sjunaidali, Sjö, Sleepyhead81, Smilodon, Snipehack, Sporsho, SpuriousQ, Stephenb, StephenfromIBM, Steven Walling, Swpb, Tacx, Tagtooga, Tariqabjotu, Tedstanton, ThePup, TheRingess, Thecheesykid, Theshufflelist, Tobias Bergemann, Tony1, Toussaint, Tregoweth, Trentonknight, TreveX, Ukmediaroom, Vasil', Vegas Bleeds Neon, Versageek, Victor falk, Vishvax, Vlaze, Vodnokon4e, Voyage2mail, Vsithasa, WebWonderGal, Webdesign2011, West.andrew.g, Willi1634, William Avery, Y, ZZyXx, Zacheos, Zhitelew, ZimZalaBim, Zymose, 张丹丰, 616 anonymous edits

2collab *Source*: http://en.wikipedia.org/w/index.php?oldid=424844310 *Contributors*: Apokrif, Ginsta, Harold Philby, John Vandenberg, Jvhertum, Karnesky, Peter4more, Rich257, Yen Zotto, 1 anonymous edits

A.nnotate *Source*: http://en.wikipedia.org/w/index.php?oldid=424150495 *Contributors*: Barrylb, CharlesC, CommonsDelinker, DreamGuy, Enloopa, Felisdomesticus, Glosses100, Greenrd, Ironholds, JLaTondre, Juliancolton, LilHelpa, Markus10, Note6200, Qda500, Sarah Hubbard 15, Skomorokh, 4 anonymous edits

AddThis *Source*: http://en.wikipedia.org/w/index.php?oldid=431586990 *Contributors*: BillyPreset, Calmer Waters, Dabomb87, Garazy, Gary King, Gobonobo, Jennifer55, Jhartmann, Jojalozzo, Pnm, 4 anonymous edits

AddToAny *Source*: http://en.wikipedia.org/w/index.php?oldid=399358223 *Contributors*: CommonsDelinker, Stevendsaunders

Areapal *Source*: http://en.wikipedia.org/w/index.php?oldid=399379345 *Contributors*: JForget, Ohnoitsjamie, Rich Farmbrough, Spoiltsport, UtherSRG, 2 anonymous edits

BibSonomy *Source*: http://en.wikipedia.org/w/index.php?oldid=359297988 *Contributors*: 16@r, Dreamyshade, Free Software Knight, Hotlio, JakobVoss, Muozek, Rjobeton, Ryan Roos, Shinkolobwe, 8 anonymous edits

BookmarkSync *Source*: http://en.wikipedia.org/w/index.php?oldid=397922970 *Contributors*: 1ForTheMoney, Alex Ruddick, AlistairMcMillan, Aviator67, Beginnersview, Cmdrjameson, DMG413, Dflax@yahoo.com, Dreamyshade, Esowteric, Exyst Internet Agentur, Gahanaedits, Highpriority, Karnesky, Mabdul, No11akersfan, Omstedall, Rich257, Rjwilmsi, Roaxth, Skylights76, Superninja, Waggers, 27 anonymous edits

Broowaha *Source*: http://en.wikipedia.org/w/index.php?oldid=430878000 *Contributors*: Masem, Morgana's POV, RedCoat10, Rjwilmsi, Thelionofgod, 8 anonymous edits

CiteULike *Source*: http://en.wikipedia.org/w/index.php?oldid=431622859 *Contributors*: (:Julien:), AbsolutDan, Booyabazooka, DGG, Delirium, Dialectric, Duncan.Hull, Greenrd, Hoffmeier, Imz, Irishguy, JLaTondre, Jakob Suckale, Jennekef, Jerixo, Johnbibby, Karnesky, LA2, Mboverload, MichaK, Nabeth, Neolithic66, NotFromUtrecht, Phauly, Pro bug catcher, R'n'B, Rettetast, Shinkolobwe, Taylor5053, Wesley fair, Y2kcrazyjoker4, 19 anonymous edits

Cleeng *Source*: http://en.wikipedia.org/w/index.php?oldid=422564352 *Contributors*: Bearcat, Donald.res, Gildo GD, Nick Wilson, Yworo, 11 anonymous edits

Connotea *Source*: http://en.wikipedia.org/w/index.php?oldid=400816295 *Contributors*: Booyabazooka, Felix Folio Secundus, Gaius Cornelius, Imz, Irishguy, Jaxl, JoannaScott, Karnesky, Karol Langner, KnowledgeOfSelf, MaxEnt, MichaK, Mike Linksvayer, MuthuKutty, Philthecow, PuerExMachina, Rashford, Reinyday, Shinkolobwe, Shortride, Sleepyhead81, Sunny256, Vsithasa, Ysyoon, 22 anonymous edits

Delicious (website) *Source*: http://en.wikipedia.org/w/index.php?oldid=428832985 *Contributors*: -Majestic-, Ahogan2, Aksi great, Akumiszcza, Alansohn, Alerante, Alex43223, AndrewLovesComputing, Anisotropic inversion, AnnaAniston, AtticusX, AxelBoldt, Babajobu, Barek, Bender235, Bentler, Biblbroks, Bigboy1184, Bigfella332, BlankVerse, Booyabazooka, Boris Kaiser, Boyandin, BrianKnez, Bryan Derksen, Btx40, C3o, Calton, Carlosguitar, Chaitanya.lala, Christopherlin, Cleared as filed, Coccyx Bloccyx, Computerjoe, CoolKid1993, Coolbeck, CyberSkull, D, Darranc, Deodar, Dgeiser13, Dmholmes, Dreamyshade, Drizzit12, ENeville, Earlypsychosis, Ebyabe, Edward, Edward Vielmetti, Edward301, Eluchil404, Erianna, Eric.frederich, Ericg, Etienne.navarro, EurekaLott, Everything counts, Evil Monkey, Fcendejas, Flash200, Flyamerica, Frankieroberto, Frosted14, George100, GiovanniS, Green caterpillar, Gyre, Gywst, HairyPotter, Hao2lian, Heisencat, Holek, Ian Moody, Iant, Iknowyourider, InverseHypercube, Isarian, IvanLanin, J.delanoy, JMowery, JanH-KA, Jareha, Jatkins, Jessehlittle, Jestar12345, Jluismarin, Joeschmoe, Kafuffle, Kanamekun, Kelvinj, Kingturtle, Koavf, KyraVixen, LauriO, Leif, Lightmouse, Liloukc, Lotje, Lunkwill, Lurlock, M1ss1ontomars2k4, M4rkphillips, MER-C, MIT Trekkie, Mahemoff, Manop, Marco Krohn, Marcus Qwertyus, Martinroell, Master of Puppets, Mboverload, McGeddon, Measure for Measure, Melesse, Meow, Mets501, MichaK, Minghong, Moonbeast, Mortense, Mountainash, MuZemike, Munboy, NB2000, Nakon, Nifky?, Nikai, Nohat, Nonpareility, Nubiatech, Ohnoitsjamie, Oscarthecat, Otisg, Ottawahitech, Oxymoron83, PIrish, PRRfan, Pakaran, Palnatoke, Pchere, Pearle, Phil Boswell, Philip Trueman, Phocks, Proofreader77, Pxma, Qwerty0, RainbowOfLight, Rajaryanmalhotra, Reifman, Rgedwards, Rhe br, Riotnrrd, RockMFR, SPUI, Sameeersingh, SarekOfVulcan, Selath, Shadowjams, Shii, Sietse Snel, Simeon H, Singpolyma, Sleepyhead81, Sobaka, Soetermans, Sorcerer13, Spencer195, Sshoberi, Steven Walling, Sue Gardner, Tedder, The Gnome, The Missing Hour, The Thing That Should Not Be, Tide rolls, Tim1357, Tom harrison, Toussaint, Tregoweth, Trevor Burnham, Trevor MacInnis, Trivialist, Vahid83, Vincentblanc, Vsithasa, WCityMike, Waldir, Weareallone, Yurik, Zac934, Zazpot, ZooFari, 274 anonymous edits

Digg *Source*: http://en.wikipedia.org/w/index.php?oldid=431599424 *Contributors*: -Majestic-, A333, Aaron Brenneman, Abqwildcat, After Midnight, Agentmori, Aido2002, Aikisenshi, Aircorn, Ajmint, Aka042, Akamad, Akonews, AlabamaSteve, Alansohn, AlbrechtH, Alerante, Alex d 76, Alexius08, Alexjohnc3, Allholy1, Amitparikh, Amouge, AnOddName, Anarchopedia, Andrewlp1991, Angoodkind, Aniish72, Anonymousdigger, Anotherworld2, Antandrus, Anthony Appleyard, Antispammer, Anton1234, Anwar saadat, Appl3zealot, Arctic.gnome, AriaStar, Arichnad, Article709 f9 11 02 9d 74 e3 5b d8 41 56 c5 63 56 88 c0, Artistography, As847618, Ascii27, Asdfasdf1231234, Ash211, AskWill, Atif.t2, AuburnPilot, AussieNickuss, Autoerrant, Az1568, Azimuth1, BCube, Baavaa, Barek, Baronnet, Bash, Bcasterline, Bdude, Beamerized, Bear.owned, Ben Laufer, Bender235, Benqmonitor, Bevo, Bewildebeast, Bgpaulus, Bhny, Bill37212, BillWSmithJr, Black and White, Bleek II, Bluestriker, Boarder8925, Bobrayner, Bodragon, Bonadea, Bookofjude, Boomshadow, Boothy443, Borch1jc, Boredzo, Boris Kaiser, Bossanueva, Bovineone, BradM, Brak710101, Brandon, BrokenSegue, Bryan Derksen, Bwats2, Cacycle, Calwatch, Capricorn42, CarlaJanssen9, Carotids, Cerejota, Chillzkid, Chris the speller, Chrislk02, Clarkhuke, Clydeiii, Coccyx Bloccyx, Comic J, Commander, CommonsDelinker, ConradKilroy, CoolKid1993, Corevette, Cosmotron, Cptspiffy, Crash Underride, Crumb, Cryptic, Curps, Cy21, CyberSkull, Cybercat, Cyberoidx, Cyde, Cziltang Brone, Czj, DCJoeDog, DCrazy, DK4, DMCer, Daigboboh, Dan428, Danieljackson, Dannymilner, Danzik, Dapsycho, DarkZealot89, Darkstar949, Dash-2, Dataneger, DaveTheRed, Daveswagon, David Levy, Dea1ctivate, Deepakoberoi, Delechrom, Demers.alex, Denelson83, DerHexer, Deramisan, Dick Brandt, Digg, DiggKiller, Disavian, DiscordantJellyfish, Discospinster, Djtripp, Dmarom, DocWatson42, Dompody, Donwilson, Doubl3d, Downwards, Dr. WTF, Dr.alf, Drderail, Dreaded Walrus, Dreamyshade, Drizzit12, DropDeadGorgias, Dudeman13142002, Dumaka, Dwayne, Dynomites, ESkog, Ebashatly, Einsensteiner, ElTyrant, Enbeeone3, Enkrates, Erianna, ErrantX, Ethicalhacker, Everyking, Evilpig, Exoendo, Faisal.akeel, Falcon9x5, Fangfufu, Farry, Fayenatic london, FayssalF, Fendenhowzen, Fiber-optics, Finlay McWalter, FireMouseHQ, Firien, Fletchsliver, Floaterfluss, Flydpnkrtn, Foo bar, Foolfromhell, Fosibodu, Fran Rogers, FrancoGG, Frankbkkcam1, Frederic Friedel, Frederikton, Fuhghettaboutit, Fullmetalape, Functionofxy, FuturePastTwo, Fæ, G-RaZoR, GVOLTT, Gamaliel, Gary King, Gavia immer, Gayhomolib, Geilt, Gfoley4, Ghewgill, Ghost650, Glenn W, Gman890890, Gobonobo, Golbez, Gonei72, Goodolclint, Gotyear, GraemeL, Grahamu, Granburguesa, Grouse, Gscshoyru, Gudeldar, Gyutae, Haakon, Hackit12, HalHal, Halbared, Hammer Raccoon, Hamtechperson, HandsomeRob1977, Hawaiian717, Helland, HelloAnnyong, Henry W. Schmitt, Hermie2007, Herostratus, Hit bull, win steak, Hoovernj, Howabout1, Hu12, IRP, Iahead, Ieure, Ihatecrayons, Ilyag, Informationrulz, Interiot, Iridescent, Irish Souffle, Irishguy, Ishdarian, Isyoucrazyson, J.delanoy, JCHall, JDavis680, JTASD111111, JYOuyang, JabberWok, Jacj, Jakewaage, Jamdonut, Jayjg, Jazzgrl, Jcm267, Jdavidb, Jdelamater, JebusbJS, Jeff94, Jennica, Jeremy Banks, Jeremy Visser, Jersey Devil, Jessehlittle, Jfb392, Jjafuller, Jkelly, Jmccorm, Jmlk17, Jnp2109, JoanneB, Joeblakesley, Joelgermeister, John Bokma, John.n-irl, John5170, Johnteslade, Johntheentrepreneur, Jonathan Hardin', Joshua H, Js1234, Jstohler, Julesd, Julienroger, JustinBlank, KBi, Kadavill, Ke5crz, Kellan, Kerttie, Kesal, Kev585, Kevin143, Khalid hassani, Kirils, Kirkio, Komitsuki, Koogunmo, Koregaonpark, Korimickster, Kotepho, Kross, Ksspauld, Kukini, L Kensington, LOL, Labbaipierre, Lancealot4, LancerEvolution ;, Larsinio, LatencyRemixed, Latka, LauriO, Lbh1402, Lcarscad, LeCorrector, Leki, Leszek Jańczuk, Liamdaly620, Liberal00Q1, Life, Liberty, Property, Lightmouse, Linuxcluster, LiquidGUI, Longhair, Lorian, Lotje, Louislonc, Lstanley, LtPowers, Luckyluke, Luigi30, Lumping, Luna Santin, Lurker, MZMcBride, Mabisa, Mace, Madskjaer, Magister Mathematicae, Mahanga, Major optics, Malfourmed, Malo, Man with one red shoe, Mangyan88, MarkKB, Marsala, Mastiland, Masturnate, Mathiastck, Matt Gies, Mattarata, MatttK, Maxamegalon2000, Mazdapickup89, Mc hammerutime, McGeddon, Mechamind90, Melaen, Mercury888, Merope, MicahDCochran, Micahmn, MichaelBillington, Michaelbeckham, MightyWarrior, Mike Rosoft, Mikelima, Mikesolow, Mikm, Miles32, Minerclub, Mipadi, Misterdiscreet, MonkeyMan, Monkeykiss, MonsterShouter, MonstrousBone, Mookiefurr, Mossman93, Mporcheron, Mr.Kennedy1, MrRacistMan, MrWhipple, Mrand, Mrmiscellanious, Msikma, Mtmelendez, Muchness, Muhandes, Mundlapati, Mushroom King, Mysidia, N3c, NCSS, Nakon, Nareek, Narniaexpert, Nathan8225, NawlinWiki, Nemilar, Netscape Navigator, Netsnipe, Neurolysis, New Bully on the Block, Nick Garvey, NickBush24, NigariaKingo, Nima1024, NinaOdell, Nintendo Revolution, Nitrodist, Noclip, Norsktroll, Notared, Nothlit, NouvusOrdoSeclorum, Novangelis, Nrbelex, Nuclear Treason, NuclearWarfare, Nulall, Numbo3, O.neill.kid, OMGsplosion, Ohnoitsjamie, One, Ood, Operating, Oren0, Orlady, Otchster, Ourai, OutPhase, OverlordQ, P3net, PJY, PSWG1920, Pats1237, Paul1991, Paulish, Pearle, Penelopepope, Perceval, Persian Poet Gal, Peter McGinley, Pgan002, Phil Boswell, Philwiki, Piano non troppo, Pifvyubjwm, Plastic editor, Pmsyyz, Policeforcer, President Skroob, Prettyxvacant, Progressivenazism, Psamathos, Psykus, Pufnstuf, Pupster21, Q-cue, Queen.zeal, Qwyrxian, Rack88, Raiz, Randolph, RandomStringOfCharacters, Randomusername331, Randy Johnston, RaseaC, RattleMan, Ray4389, Rd232, Rdsmith4, Red Thrush, Reedy, Reefsurfer226, RejoicingPoet, Remember the dot, ReyBrujo, Rhobite, Rich Farmbrough, Ricky81682, Riksweeney, Rivemont, Rjwilmsi, Rm999, Robofish, Robust Physique, RockMFR, Rodeosmurf, Ronjohn, Rt sachin, Rtcpenguin, Rterminator69, Rubenarslan, Ruckgesicht, Rufous, Ruy Pugliesi, Ryankearney, S33k3r, SCZenz, SF007, SWAdair, Sahaskatta, Saintlink, SamJunior, Sammi84, Saralk, Satori Son, SaxTeacher, Schlichtm, Schzmo, Scott3, Scottyslist, Scryptographyk, Scy1192, Sdfisher, Seaphoto, Seinman, Sentineneve, Shadowblade, Shanel, Siamesed, Sideburns Sam, Signalhead, Simeon, Singee15, Sir Gladspoke, SirGrant, SirNuke, SlapAyoda, SlashDot, Sleepyhead81, Slicing, Smeggysmeg, Smmgeek, Snake 89, Someguyonearth, Soumyasch, Soupy sautoy, Spiffyxd, Spleeyah, SpuriousQ, Squids and Chips, Squink999, Sshoberi, Steel, Stephen, Stephenb, Steveharoz, Steveoeo, Steviedpeele, Strznc, Styckx, StyroPro, SummonerMarc, Superm401, Svetovid, Szoltys, Szzuk, THEN WHO WAS PHONE?, Taciturnip, Tanman627, Tawlboy, Tc.edit, Techietim, TehBrandon, Tempodivalse, TerraFrost, Texture, Th1rt3en, Th3un4g1v3n, Thatguy0900, The Psycho, The Thing That Should Not Be, The red diter, The undertow, The wub, TheDJ, TheParanoidOne, TheSaladCaper, TheTrueEditor247, TheWizard, Thefriedone, Thepulse2007, Thorpe, Thryduulf, Thue, Tim333, TimBentley, Tiptoety, Tobey, Todd661, Tokek, Toussaint, Tranix, TransUtopian, Treelovinhippie, Tregoweth, Truthdowser, Typatigertot, Ukt-zero, Uncle G, Unloud, Useight, Utcursch, Valwen, Van helsing, Varghesekishor, Vary, Vector4F, Veinor, Vereinigen, Versageek, Virtualnick, Vrapche, WJBscribe, WarMach, Wayne Slam, Weelijimmy, Weregerbil, Wiki.Tango.Foxtrot, WikiBone, Wikilost, Wikipedian06, William Graham, Wimt, Wm, Wolfeye90, XP1, Xanucia, Xaosflux, Xerves, Xeworlebi, Xeysz, Xxsonyboy4lfexx, YUL89YYZ, YanMill, Yavoh, Ynyfrik, Yoctobarryc, Yuckfoo, Zeality, Zeke pbuh, ZimZalaBim, Zincyams, Zoe, Ό οἶστρος, 1167 anonymous edits

Diigo *Source*: http://en.wikipedia.org/w/index.php?oldid=430973483 *Contributors*: 16@r, Aflm, Catgut, Danny lost, Dontdoit, Dr.drej, Dreamyshade, Fences and windows, Greenrd, Kwamikagami, Loyola, Marawe, MrJayZee, Redvers, Rich Farmbrough, Rilkas, Royote, SpuriousQ, Sunny256, Tuckerresearch, WeisheitSuchen, Zeldafan777, 22 anonymous edits

Faves.com *Source*: http://en.wikipedia.org/w/index.php?oldid=420243231 *Contributors*: Axi030, Biivii, Black-Velvet, Crzrussian, DigitalEnthusiast, Dreamyshade, Epolk, Mailer diablo, Pnm, RedLavaLamp, Refsworldlee, Rivemont, RockMFR, Satori Son, Twas Now, UnitedStatesian, 6 anonymous edits

Flattr *Source*: http://en.wikipedia.org/w/index.php?oldid=427453578 *Contributors*: Bensin, Cander0000, Clamiax, CommonsDelinker, Cuaxdon, Devourer09, Eeekster, Greenrd, HaeB, Hontogaichiban, IGEL, Intgr, Jacob Lundberg, Jamiew, Jbening, Kocio, Mabdul, Malcolma, Manuelzs, MatiasSingers, MichaelSchoenitzer, Mortense, Nsaa, Obhave, OlivierMehani, PabloCastellano, Piglop, Polarbearjack, Rjwilmsi, Robbo1337, Ruud Koot, Skizzik, Smartse, Sonicsuns, Stassats, SuNotísima, Toussaint, Tuggler, Uwe Dedering, WakiMiko, Xeno, 14 anonymous edits

Folkd *Source*: http://en.wikipedia.org/w/index.php?oldid=420348675 *Contributors*: Acather96, Michaeldsuarez, Timetrax23, 2 anonymous edits

Furl *Source*: http://en.wikipedia.org/w/index.php?oldid=404333920 *Contributors*: Arungoodboy, AxelBoldt, Betacommand, Carl.bunderson, Chriswaterguy, Cimon Avaro, D6, Dreamyshade, Eug, Fmccown, Gary King, GeoFan49, Hu12, Jczeledonp, Jwillbur, Kenb215, Leolaursen, Meco, Melaen, Nerdytenor, Probuzz, Rakerman, Rl, Robertvan1, Steve Bob, Thunderbrand, WikiLeon, 41 anonymous edits

GiveALink.org *Source*: http://en.wikipedia.org/w/index.php?oldid=404412607 *Contributors*: BlueAzure, Booyabazooka, Dreamyshade, Grey Horse, Perfecto, Uzma Gamal, 13 anonymous edits

Gnolia *Source*: http://en.wikipedia.org/w/index.php?oldid=422089332 *Contributors*: Btipling, Colfer2, Dreamyshade, EnTerr, Frin, Guaka, Kak, KathrynLybarger, Lalcorn, Mattmorgan, Mpt, MrBoo, Orangemike, Paraphrased, SamJohnston, Trivialist, Zazpot, 10 anonymous edits

Google Bookmarks *Source*: http://en.wikipedia.org/w/index.php?oldid=409023545 *Contributors*: A Nobody, Angrysockhop, AnthonyMastrean, Bonadea, Bongwarrior, Darkwind, Devadhasi, Fences and windows, Forestflyer, Greenrd, Jareha, John225, Kenyon, Khalid hassani, MamboJambo, Marawe, Matekm, Mporcheron, Pfc432, SAMADPOOMANGALAM, TFCforever, Tobias Bergemann, Toddst1, Trevor Burnham, Unfgreen, Yidisheryid, 15 anonymous edits

Hacker News *Source*: http://en.wikipedia.org/w/index.php?oldid=429450039 *Contributors*: Alexrexpvt, AllTheGoodUsernamesHaveAlreadyBeenTaken, Apoc2400, CaptainMorgan, Cheesy, Chrisbolt, Dreamyshade, Edward, ErrantX, Hao2lian, Harpastum, Jevansen, John Millikin, Kevin143, Maximisedk, Pipedreamergrey, Spiritfox12, Stiang, Thirashima, 31 anonymous edits

Licorize *Source*: http://en.wikipedia.org/w/index.php?oldid=397277067 *Contributors*: Fæ, Ppolsinelli

Linkwad *Source*: http://en.wikipedia.org/w/index.php?oldid=388271757 *Contributors*: Artw, Clementina, Davitof, Dreamyshade, Eeera, Jonh tomas, Maralia, Markiewp, R'n'B, Rjwilmsi, Thorenn, Woohookitty, Zenlax, 9 anonymous edits

MemeStreams *Source*: http://en.wikipedia.org/w/index.php?oldid=389812482 *Contributors*: Disavian, Jayron32, 2 anonymous edits

Menéame *Source*: http://en.wikipedia.org/w/index.php?oldid=404505591 *Contributors*: Locos epraix, 2 anonymous edits

Mister Wong *Source*: http://en.wikipedia.org/w/index.php?oldid=421776450 *Contributors*: Bender235, Dreamyshade, HenrikWL, Luckyz, Quadcoresparky, Skomorokh, The Gnome, 3 anonymous edits

Models of collaborative tagging *Source*: http://en.wikipedia.org/w/index.php?oldid=427419342 *Contributors*: Acslab, KenWalker, Nabeth, Papertiger, Reywas92, Tedder, Zorroz, 11 anonymous edits

NewsTrust *Source*: http://en.wikipedia.org/w/index.php?oldid=379200990 *Contributors*: Apostle12, Ettrig, Ironholds, Kzar, 1 anonymous edits

Newsvine *Source*: http://en.wikipedia.org/w/index.php?oldid=422267117 *Contributors*: A. B., AndrewTH, Anetode, AniMate, Arak80, Arpingstone, Artw, Astigmatism, AtlantaSantos, Auxblood, CaelumArisen, Corey.spring, CyberSkull, Czj, Darrelljon, Dean1970, DotShell, Dreamyshade, Drone007, ElinorD, Gobonobo, Haniff, HarcourtArms, Hayfordoleary, JHP, Jatkins, Jesusfreak84, Jjjchang, KillerAsteroids, Lbneal, Mathwixzp, Mets501, Michaelczhang, Mipadi, MrArcadian, N cody46, Nono64, Obeattie, Ottawahitech, Peter, PigFlu Oink, Randy Johnston, Rappo11, RegBarc, SDC, Scarequotes, Sdalmonte, SpuriousQ, Tagus, TakuyaMurata, Tangfish, TheRegicider, TheTrueSora, Tiredandold, Tmcw, Unimaxium, UnitedStatesian, Walkiped, WikiLeon, Zorcon1617, 76 anonymous edits

Ngbot mobile *Source*: http://en.wikipedia.org/w/index.php?oldid=430968271 *Contributors*: Namzo, Nono64, R'n'B, Woohookitty

Oneview *Source*: http://en.wikipedia.org/w/index.php?oldid=344654801 *Contributors*: Brianpreuss, Dreamyshade, LimeHat, NeF, 1 anonymous edits

PopUrls *Source*: http://en.wikipedia.org/w/index.php?oldid=393371457 *Contributors*: Bpier, ChrisFields, Computerjoe, DavidSJ, Dreamyshade, Hailey C. Shannon, LinguistAtLarge, Sen amitava, Sunny256, Victor falk, 5 anonymous edits

Propeller.com *Source*: http://en.wikipedia.org/w/index.php?oldid=398530547 *Contributors*: Alex d 76, Auric, Dreamyshade, FatLester, Humanisticmystic, IPAddressConflict, Koavf, LancerEvolution ;, Mixthenet, NisseSthlm, Ohconfucius, Rjwilmsi, ScottyBerg, Shortride, TheGiftedOne, ZimZalaBim, 9 anonymous edits

Reddit *Source*: http://en.wikipedia.org/w/index.php?oldid=431951910 *Contributors*: 7, A-lo, Aaaaapos, AaronSw, Acdx, Alansohn, Alex d 76, Alexis.ohanian, Allstarecho, Amitparikh, Andytags, Ansible81, Antrikshy, Ashanda, Avono, B7342, Babank, BarryWood, Benshelock, Bobbyllama, Bonadea, Bongwarrior, Boppin3, Boris Kaiser, Brandon, Brinkost, Callidior, Camr, Camw, Canley, Cap'n Refsmmat, Cerberus12, Chandler, ChristianH, Chuq, Chwilliam, Clibble, Closetoeuphoria, Coccyx Bloccyx, CommonsDelinker, Crysb, Cusscakes, Cybercobra, Czj, Daedalus969, Dancter, Danlev, Darkmeerkat, Darrenhusted, Dasony, Dave420, David Levy, David.rand, Dawdler, Dbmikus, DeadEyeArrow, DefenseSupportParty, Denelson83, DominatorMatrix, DonSlice, Dreish, Dreiss2, Drewerd, Drilnoth, Drizzit12, Eatwithaspork, Ebelular, Edward, Enigmocracy, Everard Proudfoot, Everything counts, Excaelestis, Falcon8765, Falcon9x5, Fargliv, Favonian, Fbg1111, Fever008, Figs, Finlay McWalter, Firefighter60115, Fiskbil, Flarrp, Forever Dusk, Frankthewho, Freshyill, GOD ACRONYM, Gary King, Ghewgill, Gioto, Glane23, Gobonobo, Goodnightmush, Grafen, Grammarxxx, Greenrd, Grue, Haakon, Hans Adler, Hao2lian, HappyPrism, Henrik, Henry W. Schmitt, Herbythyme, Highway Hitchhiker, Hmm..., HorseloverFat, Hue White, Hydrogen Iodide, Iahead, Ilyag, Imperi, Imz, IndiWebPirate, Inklein, InternetMeme, JCDenton2052, JEN9841, JForget, Jacobolus, JarritoFJ, Jarro 2783, Jasenlee, Jason404, Jaydec, Jeffrey Mall, Jehochman, Jellevc, Joe2832, Jomynow, Jonah Stein, Jonathan.s.kt, Jreferee, Judge373, Juggaleaux, Juliamae, KGasso, Karam.Anthony.K, King of Hearts, Kingboyk, Kingpin13, Kingturtle, KirbyWallace, Kirrages, Kkm010, Klow, Koavf, Kpjas, Kross, Kubigula, Kubigulo, Kwamikagami, L Kensington, LauriO, Lawrencekhoo, Lear's Fool, Lebowbowbowski, Leki, Lemmingway, Libertyaboveallelse, LightSpeed3, Looptvc, Luna Santin, M.nelson, Malo, Man with one red shoe, Marie flwr, Marioo2, Marokwitz, Master of Puppets, Mato, Melmignone, MerchantofSoul, Michaelczhang, Midgrid, Mike Schiraldi, Moldysasquatch, Mordgier, Mortense, MotoFly1675, Mptb3, MrAmoeba, Mrand, Mtrinque, Muboshgu, Mudwater, Mundlapati, MyrddinEmrys, Mythrilfan, N5iln, Nae'blis, Nightscream, NisseSthlm, Nmnogueira, Norlik, NorthernChaosGod, Notwist, Npdbls, Olsoncal, OnePt618, Onomatopoeiaieopotamono, Orphan Wiki, Paul1991, Peer-LAN, Pgan002, Phantomsteve, Phenomena00, Philip Trueman, Philwiki, Piano non troppo, Picklegnome, Piet Delport, Playdagame6991, Ponydepression, Pretzels, Priiiiit, Psantora, Pstuart, Psyced, QEDQEDQED, Quriously unquenched, RainbowOfLight, Rainer Wasserfuhr, RarkCyrg, Razzairpina, Reddit sucks, ReyBrujo, Ripst420, Rogerbrent, Rory O'Kane, Rubicon, Ryangoff, SF007, Sad squirrel, Sam Hughes, Sapfan, Satxer, Sawta, ScottyBerg, Seaphoto, SelfStudyBuddy, Sempf, Ser Amantio di Nicolao, Seriouslyshouldjustbe, Shortride, Simxp, Slark, Smurfjones, Somehippo, Sopoforic, SpuriousQ, Stephen, Stocksy, Studenttempacc, Supersonic^, Svgalbertian, Tabletop, Tanner Swett, TechMology, The Inedible Bulk, The red diter, The wub, TheArcologist, Thrill going up, Throwaway85, Tide rolls, Tin03gin, Tivate, Tobias Bergemann, Tobyw87, Territorri, Toussaint, TrbleClef, Tty29a, Tykauffman, Uberciter, Useight, Utcursch, Vcelloho, Veinor, Victor falk, ViperSnake151, Vusdude, WatchAndObserve, Wedittor, Wes!, Whoisjohngalt, Wickethewok, Wikiwiderworld, Wwwwolf, XDanielx, Xaje, Ysangkok, ZimZalaBim, Zsero, Zwilson, 579 anonymous edits

Scuttle (software) *Source*: http://en.wikipedia.org/w/index.php?oldid=423300294 *Contributors*: Levin, Repat

ShareThis *Source*: http://en.wikipedia.org/w/index.php?oldid=412939952 *Contributors*: BorderStyle12, Deepak ST, Gary King, Just plain Bill, Killiondude, Me-123567-Me, Mudallal, Oknazevad, Pnm, Prashanthns, 5 anonymous edits

Simpy *Source*: http://en.wikipedia.org/w/index.php?oldid=427714013 *Contributors*: AlastairBurt, B7T, Bebenko, BruceMagnus, Chrike, Dittaeva, Dreamyshade, Imz, Isilanes, Kocio, Magic Speller, Otisg, 3 anonymous edits

SiteBar *Source*: http://en.wikipedia.org/w/index.php?oldid=421457621 *Contributors*: 16@r, Aecis, ConcernedVancouverite, Djmckee1, Dreamyshade, Drpickem, Frap, Imz, Petr V, Thegibbie, 23 anonymous edits

StumbleUpon *Source*: http://en.wikipedia.org/w/index.php?oldid=431869140 *Contributors*: ACREW, AVRS, AceMyth, Airconswitch, Alex132, Alvinjaques, Andoru, Angela, Asdfasdjkl;a, Assyrio, AxG, Barek, Benji1304, Bensci54, Betacommand, Betterusername, Billso, BlankVerse, Bloggerprod, Blumster, Bonadea, Boneheadmx, Booyabazooka, Bridies, Bronwyn in sf, Brucevdk, Canadaworker, Captain panda, Castorquinn, Cdyron37, Chasingamy, Chops76, Chrisbolt, Cinderelly007, Colmt3, Corvus cornix, Crystal Linux, Cs302b, Cunado19, Cybe, Dancter, Danlev, Dantheman223, Darrenhusted, Dave Runger, Debresser, Deramisan, Discospinster, Dogadvicer, DominatorMatrix, Doyle73, Dvd Avins, Edgar181, Editor2020, Egoldber, Enivid, Evil Eccentric, Evil saltine, Eviljojo, Finnegar, Flowanda, FlyingToaster, Frazzydee, Fuzzycasserole, Gail, Gmc, Gobonobo, GraemeL, Grafen, Graham87, Grey Horse, Guitarhhero, Gyrferret, Halbared, Hebrides, Hoo man, Hu12, IanManka, Isyoucrazyson, JAStewart, JLaTondre, Jefflithe, Jholis, Jhsounds, Jim7907, Jkonner, Jordantheking, Jtwall12, Karolinger, KarthikKakarala, Kevin W., Kinu, Konradc, KrakatoaKatie, Krelle, Kuru, Labnol, Lambo2409, LilHelpa, LinguistAtLarge, M4bwav, Mabuse, Magister Mathematicae, ManiacalMonkey, Marcus Qwertyus, Mark alfred, Mathiastck, MattKeegan, MatthewMastracci, McGeddon, Meaghan, Melancholie, Meno25, Michaelbeckham, Michaelsuarez, Micru, MikeCapone, Molinari, MrBussi, Mrdude, N Yo FACE, Ncmvocalist, Nicolae6, Nixeagle, Nogwa, Notinasnaid, Oneforfortytwo, Pixelface, Playdagame6991, Probuzz, Profitline, Raerth, Raithesoft, Rajah, RapPhenom, RazorICE, Rdsmith4, Receshenproof, ReinforcedReinforcements, Remember the dot, Rjwilmsi, Rm w a vu, Rvalles, Ryankrameretc, SMMcintyre, Samwaltz, Sastopeit, Scriberius, Shishir0610, Simbamangu, Sketchee, Skier Dude, Slon02, Some jerk on the Internet, Somnlaut, Sshoberi, Starwed, Stevietheman, SyberGod, T3xs, Tafinucane, Tbone762, TheGreatEd, Theanphibian, Thumperward, Timanderso, Tkgd2007, Toddcourt1, TonyW, Tregowoth, True Pagan Warrior, Trusilver, UkPaolo, Undergroundindeepthought, Unmerklich, UserDoe, VJ Emsi, Verrai, Vitriden, Vlad, Widefox, Wikinewguy, Wimt, Woohookitty, WorldlyWebster, Xenophod, Xiner, Yiwen017, Zackaback, Zoe, Zvn, 319 anonymous edits

Sturvs *Source*: http://en.wikipedia.org/w/index.php?oldid=351587700 *Contributors*: Hmains, Malcolma, Robofish, Temi2004, Toytown Mafia, 4 anonymous edits

Taringa! *Source*: http://en.wikipedia.org/w/index.php?oldid=431922935 *Contributors*: 93 lfedroa, Adegbnhryryry, Alemaniagrryryry, Antarctic-adventurer, Awgtwat, Benjamin breaking, Blueboy96, Bob diablo, CMBJ, Carlossuarez46, CommonsDelinker, Cypher.ar, Enza a manif, Fabrictramp, February 2004 in used, Fixman, Fma12, Fma12 chupalala, Fma12difamador, Fma12eldifamador, Fma12gringo, Fma12rojo, G2.0 USA, GB fan, Gangaz, Garnet 753, Gobonobo, Hairhorn, Hugo 87, Immunize, Ivc392, JForget, Macpl, Mate92, Materialscientist, Mcsee, Mild Bill Hiccup, Neutralmancadt, Nneonneo, Pablo323, Phil Bridger, Rockk3r, Ron Ritzman, Ronk01, Schmloof, Theda, Usb10, Wikispan, Woohookitty, ZZeBaH Punk, 54 anonymous edits

Twine (website) *Source*: http://en.wikipedia.org/w/index.php?oldid=387727088 *Contributors*: Artw, Hthth, JustAGal, MRSC, MiddleOfNowhere, Mjroots, SoWhy, 5 anonymous edits

Wink Technologies *Source*: http://en.wikipedia.org/w/index.php?oldid=371041360 *Contributors*: 16@r, Aaron Brenneman, Betacommand, ChemGardener, Chowbok, Clicketyclack, Fram, Jjcrawford, MER-C, Melancholie, Mtanne, Rktur, Thingg, Trivialist, Vicaya, WereSpielChequers, XDanielx, 7 anonymous edits

Yahoo! Buzz *Source*: http://en.wikipedia.org/w/index.php?oldid=430272641 *Contributors*: Bender235, Colonies Chris, CoolKid1993, Cpt ricard, Dreamyshade, Dumaka, Fastily, Gaius Cornelius, InverseHypercube, Jayen466, Kgoarany, Logan, MattKeegan, Mixthenet, Moxfyre, Ottawahitech, Owl order, Persian Poet Gal, Recurian, Reddog X2000, Superm401, Swellesley, Themfromspace, Waacstats, White 720, 21 anonymous edits

Yardbarker *Source*: http://en.wikipedia.org/w/index.php?oldid=422940334 *Contributors*: Andrewlasken, Aspects, Ecoleetage, Gateman1997, Gwen Gale, Jamesontai, Lightmouse, Mattgirling, OllieFury, Pelechati, RHaworth, Rjwilmsi, Ryulong, TexasAndroid, Themfromspace, 8 anonymous edits

Celestial Emporium of Benevolent Knowledge's Taxonomy *Source*: http://en.wikipedia.org/w/index.php?oldid=429897012 *Contributors*: AbbyKelleyite, AxelBoldt, Breed Zona, Chris Thompson, Chzz, Comtebenoit, Dominus, Gwern, Lankenau, Ligulem, Lola Voss, Lulu of the Lotus-Eaters, M5, Paul A, Pierremenard, Rjwilmsi, Shyamal, That Guy, From That Show!, Vagary, Zompist, 6 anonymous edits

Parataxonomy *Source*: http://en.wikipedia.org/w/index.php?oldid=423231580 *Contributors*: Hebrides, Jimmy Pitt, KenBailey, S.v.Mering

Taxonomy *Source*: http://en.wikipedia.org/w/index.php?oldid=432033513 *Contributors*: 01011000, 21655, 24.45.94.xxx, A Macedonian, ABMH, APH, Abercrombiexfellas, Adambro, Addit, Addy "The Welsh Plumber", Adhominem, Adibob, AdjustShift, Agencius, Ahoerstemeier, Airconswitch, Alansohn, Alcarreau, Alcmaeonid, Alex43223, Alexei Kouprianov, Alias Flood, Alphachimp, Altenmann, Amcbride, AnakngAraw, Anclation, Andres, Andrewpmk, AndriesVanRenssen, Andycjp, Anthere, Antonio Prates, Aretheysafe, Argav, Auminski, AxelBoldt, Ayla, Azzors, Baa, Bas3ball1, Bdbbigdaddybumpewewew, Beano, Bejnar, Bernd in Japan, Bittner, Blackburn.greg, Blanchardb, Blueboy96, Bobo192, Bodnotbod, Boomshadow, Bornslippy, Brandon, Brya, Bsadowski1, Bugboy52.40, Bugone, BullRangifer, C+C, C4duser, CallumDarch, Caltas, Cbrodersen, Chaleyer61, Chapiown, Charles Matthews, CharlotteWebb, Chase me ladies, I'm the Cavalry, Clone A, Cocytus, Cometstyles, ConfuciusOrnis, Conversion script, Courcelles, Cpl Syx, Craigy144, Cryptic, Cshapeshifter, Curtis Clark, DARTH SIDIOUS 2, DMacks, Dagwood Agonistes, Danger, DanielEng, Dank, Davidlchandler, Dbaird31919bnerq, Dbfirs, Deconstructhis, Den fjättrade ankan, Dendrid, Dfmchfhf, Discoleo, Discospinster, Diwas, Doulos Christos,

Dpotter, Dpv, Dyanega, Dycedarg, Dysepsion, Dysmorodrepanis, Dysprosia, Eclecticology, Elbbom, Ellywa, Emily Jensen, Emprovision, Epbr123, Erik9, Eug, Ewright12, Fastily, Francesco sclano, Frankenpuppy, Freakofnurture, Fusionmix, Future Perfect at Sunrise, Fæ, Gdr, George100, Gerrywhite, Gilliam, Gnorkel, Gnostrat, Godzig, Gogo Dodo, Golgofrinchian, Granitethighs, Greenguy1090, Grendelkhan, Grondemar, GrooveDog, Grundle2600, Guymacon, Gyrlapple, Hahahahakid, HalJor, Hassocks5489, Herbal Lemon, Hhedden, Hordaland, Huku-chan, Husond, Igoldste, Imcoolyeahyeahyeah, Invertzoo, Iridescent, IronChris, Ismedvedev, Ivan007, Ixfd64, J.delanoy, JALockhart, JPPINTO, Jabowery, Jag123, Jamenshively, Jamesontai, Jeff G., Jembooth, Jfab6, Jnk1, Jodi.a.schneider, JoeOnSunset, JosebaAbaitua, Josh Grosse, Jozif, Jtwang, Junnoske, Jusjih, Jwsmith708, Kane5187, Kanonkas, Karebh, Kedawa, Khatru2, Kingpin13, Krauss, Kupirijo, Kuru, L Kensington, Langec, Lateg, Lauranrg, Lenov, Leptictidium, Lewisskinner, LilHelpa, Lindsay658, Little Mountain 5, LizardJr8, Llull, Looktothis, Loren.wilton, Lyoko is Cool, MPF, MPerel, Macrakis, Mandarax, Marek69, Mark Dingemanse, Markus.zhang, Martarius, Masterjamie, Mastershubham, Mav, Maver1ck, MaxHund, Mdd, MeHereAtWiki, MickWest, Minneapolismark, Modify, Moreschi, Mozmac, Mtindia, Mxn, Myrvin, MythosRaconteur, Nabeth, NawlinWiki, Nekolady, NeoJustin, Neverquick, NewEnglandYankee, Nick, Nicknoltevstheworld, Nihiltres, No Junk, NorwegianBlue, Nrbelex, NuclearWarfare, Nurg, O, OMCV, Obryan.23, Ohnoitsjamie, Oodles of toodles, Orange Suede Sofa, OverlordQ, Paddles, Pascal.Tesson, Pavel Vozenilek, Pcb21, Philip Trueman, Philipp Wetzlar, Phishsauce, Picknchewz, Pihka, Pilotguy, Pinethicket, Piotrus, Pippu d'Angelo, Plantsurfer, Pleather, Plumbago, Pol098, Poor Yorick, PranksterTurtle, Premond, Proficient, Prolog, Quais indy, Quiddity, Qxz, R'n'B, R.O.C, RainbowOfLight, Random contributor, Ranna, Reaper Eternal, Redgolpe, Rettetast, RexNL, RichardF, Roberta F., Robykiwi, Ronhjones, Ronz, RoyBoy, Rtkw, Rulevoider, Rumphius, RupertMillard, Rursus, RxS, SHIMONSHA, Sam Korn, Sango123, Scarian, Scarpy, SchfiftyThree, Schmeitgeist, Scilit, Seglea, Segoeb, Sgt.Kallle, Shadowjams, Sheeana, Shirik, Shizane, Shizhao, ShurikenStar98, SiobhanHansa, Slrubenstein, Sluzzelin, SmurfyK, Snek01, Snoofleglax, SoCalSuperEagle, SpacemanSpiff, Spalding, Speedeep, Spitfire, Stanskis, StaticGull, Stemonitis, Steven Zhang, Styrofoam1994, Subwiz, Superiority, THE MIST, TLEberle, TUF-KAT, Tamaratrouts, Tannin, Tau666666, Taxonomyyeti, Template namespace initialisation script, Tempodivalse, Tenmei, TeunSpaans, The Cunctator, The Rambling Man, The Thing That Should Not Be, TheLeopard, Thewayforward, Tide rolls, TigerShark, Tinkerbell411, Tinton5, Tomisti, Tony1212, Treisijs, Tresiden, Vald, VashiDonsk, VictorChu, VictorianMutant, Vildricianus, Voyagerfan5761, Vrenator, Vsmith, Wavelength, Wb5hvh, WhatamIdoing, WhyAskWhyNot, Wi-king, Wikid77, WikipedianMarlith, Wimt, Woohookitty, Wtmitchell, XJamRastafire, Xueexueg, Yaco, Yamakiri, Yamamoto Ichiro, Zazazawewqedqwcdwsd, Zeno Gantner, Zidane tribal, Zippy, ZooFari, Zsinj, Zzuuzz, Ô, Александър, 雁太郎, 865 anonymous edits

Acanothochitonidae *Source*: http://en.wikipedia.org/w/index.php?oldid=400435702 *Contributors*: Boleyn, Mikemoral, Smith609

Acanthochitonina *Source*: http://en.wikipedia.org/w/index.php?oldid=407412655 *Contributors*: Guoguo12, Smith609

Acutichiton *Source*: http://en.wikipedia.org/w/index.php?oldid=401870432 *Contributors*: Smith609, Sumsum2010

Affinity (taxonomy) *Source*: http://en.wikipedia.org/w/index.php?oldid=426993170 *Contributors*: JonRichfield, KConWiki

Afossochiton *Source*: http://en.wikipedia.org/w/index.php?oldid=415765916 *Contributors*: Pjoef, Sadads, Smith609, Sumsum2010

Afossochitonidae *Source*: http://en.wikipedia.org/w/index.php?oldid=402138482 *Contributors*: Pjoef, Smith609

AIDGAP series *Source*: http://en.wikipedia.org/w/index.php?oldid=412886286 *Contributors*: Mrs foxall, Pnoble805, Princess Tiswas, Rich Farmbrough, SP-KP, Skapur, Wrucken

Allochiton *Source*: http://en.wikipedia.org/w/index.php?oldid=401865949 *Contributors*: Smith609, Sumsum2010

Alpha taxonomy *Source*: http://en.wikipedia.org/w/index.php?oldid=431486258 *Contributors*: AdamFunk, Arbitrarily0, Brya, CharlesC, Circeus, Closedmouth, CommonsDelinker, Curtis Clark, Dbromley, Discospinster, Donald Albury, Dysmorodrepanis, Escape Orbit, Eugene van der Pijll, Eugene-elgato, Fortdj33, Fplay, Hiplis, Hodja Nasreddin, Invertzoo, Iridescent, IronChris, Kctucker, Mario Žamić, Mark Renier, MaxHund, Meomena24, Michael Hardy, NorwegianBlue, ParticleMan, Petter Bøckman, Piano non troppo, R'n'B, Redgolpe, Richard New Forest, Rocket000, Rosarinagazo, Safay, Shiftchange, Stemonitis, Theuser, Wavelength, WhyAskWhyNot, WikiKherad, Yidisheryid, 49 anonymous edits

Analytical Profile Index *Source*: http://en.wikipedia.org/w/index.php?oldid=430370476 *Contributors*: Alan Liefting, Carohann, EagleFan, Eredrian, GeorgeLouis, Isenmouthe, Nicolas1981, Roto2esdios, 3 anonymous edits

Bacterial phyla *Source*: http://en.wikipedia.org/w/index.php?oldid=430115233 *Contributors*: Bender235, EoGuy, Foobarnix, Lavateraguy, Mgiganteus1, Podex, Rich Farmbrough, Smartse, Squidonius, 3 anonymous edits

Baraminology *Source*: http://en.wikipedia.org/w/index.php?oldid=430382616 *Contributors*: 8teenfourT4, Agapetos angel, Ajmmii, AltiusBimm, Andrewlp1991, Andycjp, Angr, Apokryltaros, Armchair info guy, Aunt Entropy, AxiomOfFaith, Azcolvin429, BD2412, BatteryIncluded, Belscb, Bonesiii, Brz7, CarlDrews, Cat Whisperer, Christian Skeptic, Chubbles, ConfuciusOrnis, Cpcheung, Crazycomputers, Cubbi, Curtis Clark, Cygnis insignis, Czar1991, DGG, DanielCD, Dave souza, David Gerard, Davidderiso, Dd 8630, Debresser, Dgri, Dougweller, Duae Quartunciae, Duncharris, EALacey, Ec5618, Emw, EvilFlyingMonkey, F00188846, Fastily, Filll, FisherQueen, FreezBee, Gabbe, Ged UK, Geometry guy, Glunt, Gniniv, Goodone121, Gracie Allan, Guettarda, Haikupoet, Hans Adler, Henrygb, HerrLoll, Homestarmy, Hrafn, IMSoP, Ian Pitchford, ImpartialCelt, J. Spencer, Ja 62, JamesBWatson, John Quiggin, Johnuniq, K, Karada, Keahapana, Kingoomieiii, LamondDaChristianMan, Linas, M, Mann jess, MartinPoulter, Maximus Rex, Mcebach, Metropolitan90, Michael Hardy, Micov, Mild Bill Hiccup, Mrappold, Mystman666, Nfli3596, Nightscream, Node ue, Oceanblue1492, Orangemarlin, PDD, Paulcoyne, Pbarnes, Perey, Peyre, PiCo, Pigman, Plumbago, ProGloriaDei, Quarl, Quietmarc, RadioFan2 (usurped), Raeky, Rainwarrior, Rdsmith4, Retired username, Rich Farmbrough, Richard001, Rjwilmsi, Rockfang, Roland Deschain, S Marshall, Saga City, Sapphic, Shalom1918, Shoemaker's Holiday, Silly rabbit, Sochwa, Spotfixer, Srich32977, Srleffler, Steven J. Anderson, Tassedethe, Tasty monster, Tavilis, Tbhotch, Teh Pulpo, Terper, Tgr, Thundermaker, TomS TDotO, Tony Sidaway, Trabucogold, Troberts2525, TruthIIPower, Ungtss, Vanished User 0001, Vanished user, VanishedUser314159, WikiWHOnow, Z10x, Zafiroblue05, Δ, 137 anonymous edits

Bayer Code *Source*: http://en.wikipedia.org/w/index.php?oldid=428008172 *Contributors*: Barticus88, Bissinger, CharlotteWebb, Maccheek, N4nojohn, PaulHanson, RJFJR, Roland2, Sebbi, Somanypeople, Taschenrechner, Twe315, 2 anonymous edits

Biodiversity informatics *Source*: http://en.wikipedia.org/w/index.php?oldid=419344833 *Contributors*: Chase me ladies, I'm the Cavalry, Chicoreus, Csstsrg, Ecorahul, Eep², Elonka, Erkan Yilmaz, FaEu, Hardistyar, Jackhynes, Jncraton, Jvhertum, Myrmoteras, Pegship, Petefrog, Ragnvald, Rjwilmsi, Robth, Snek01, Stho002, Stifle, Tassielee, Tony1212, Wavelength, Willem2007, Willemcoetzer, 29 anonymous edits

Biovar *Source*: http://en.wikipedia.org/w/index.php?oldid=431919461 *Contributors*: Jeppelbaum, Leptictidium, Mako098765, Michael Hardy, Nihiltres, Omnipaedista, Sabedon, Scharks, Senori, Steinsky, Thorwald, 4 anonymous edits

Body plan *Source*: http://en.wikipedia.org/w/index.php?oldid=424956051 *Contributors*: 13XIII, A.J.Clifford, Alcmaeonid, Anomie, AshLin, Bender235, Bobo192, BradBeattie, Chickenflicker, Coelacan, DCDuring, Dark Green, Donald Albury, Edavila, Enqamar, Escape Orbit, Euchiasmus, FT2, GetsEclectic, Gongoozler123, Goodnightmush, Gregfitzy, Hetar, Hynca-Hooley, Insanity Incarnate, J. Spencer, J.delanoy, Jeepday, Jrockley, KGasso, Lauranrg, Liberatus, Mangostar, MarnetteD, Matthew Brandon Yeager, Memestream, Mietchen, Mokele, Mr. Lefty, Oleg Alexandrov, PierreAbbat, PookeyMaster, ProGloriaDei, Radagast83, Rarara1111, Rjwilmsi, Saint yondo, Samsara, Sbluen, Some jerk on the Internet, Stephenb, Syp, The Anome, Violetriga, WikiCantona, Zureks, 60 anonymous edits

Branching identification key *Source*: http://en.wikipedia.org/w/index.php?oldid=423518210 *Contributors*: D6, Manitobamountie, PigFlu Oink, Vigilius, Virnuls, 1 anonymous edits

Calceochiton *Source*: http://en.wikipedia.org/w/index.php?oldid=401868703 *Contributors*: Smith609, Sumsum2010

Callistochiton *Source*: http://en.wikipedia.org/w/index.php?oldid=420983590 *Contributors*: Pjoef, Smith609, Sumsum2010, 1 anonymous edits

Catalogue of Life *Source*: http://en.wikipedia.org/w/index.php?oldid=425205760 *Contributors*: Alan Liefting, BirdHunters, Blackburn.greg, Donarreiskoffer, Erich gasboy, Erkan Yilmaz, Eynbein, Gaurav, Greatestrowerever, Green Squares, Hintss, Hodja Nasreddin, Lightmouse, MGSpiller, Madhero88, Monkeypuzzled, NatureA16, OhanaUnited, Physicistjedi, Quiddity, Rdmpage, Sp2000secretariat, Tmotommyo, Vanished User 4517, Versageek, 12 anonymous edits

Chelodidae *Source*: http://en.wikipedia.org/w/index.php?oldid=415373071 *Contributors*: Pjoef, Rich Farmbrough, Smith609, Sumsum2010

Chelodina (chiton) *Source*: http://en.wikipedia.org/w/index.php?oldid=415373118 *Contributors*: Pjoef, Rich Farmbrough, Smith609, Sumsum2010

Chitonina *Source*: http://en.wikipedia.org/w/index.php?oldid=415373238 *Contributors*: Pjoef, Rich Farmbrough, Smith609, Sumsum2010

Chresonym *Source*: http://en.wikipedia.org/w/index.php?oldid=418034240 *Contributors*: DavidRemsen, Doc Taxon, EastTN, JoJan, Kceq, Malpass93, Nadiatalent, Rdmpage, Richhoncho, Rpyle731, Shyamal, Snowmanradio, Techman224, Wavelength, WolfmanSF, 2 anonymous edits

Circumscription (taxonomy) *Source*: http://en.wikipedia.org/w/index.php?oldid=419440210 *Contributors*: Andycjp, Circeus, Nurg, Rosarinagazo, Una Smith

Cline (biology) *Source*: http://en.wikipedia.org/w/index.php?oldid=424856900 *Contributors*: -Strogoff-, 100110100, AnonMoos, Anthony Appleyard, Applejuicefool, Beland, Chatfecter, Drussey, Dysmorodrepanis, ENeville, Epipelagic, FilipeS, Innotata, La Pianista, Look2See1, Mausy5043, Maxim Gavrilyuk, Mgiganteus1, Muntuwandi, Nicke L, NuclearWarfare, Nø, Postdlf,

Psychohistorian, Ramdrake, Rich Farmbrough, Rickproser, Robin S, Samwb123, Snowmanradio, Switchercat, The Ogre, Tktktk, Varlet16, Victor falk, WBardwin, Wlodzimierz, Wobble, 17 anonymous edits

Cryptoplax Source: http://en.wikipedia.org/w/index.php?oldid=405078922 Contributors: Pjoef, Smith609, Sumsum2010

Cymatochiton Source: http://en.wikipedia.org/w/index.php?oldid=402021144 Contributors: Smith609, Sumsum2010

Deep homology Source: http://en.wikipedia.org/w/index.php?oldid=425890466 Contributors: Aciel, Addshore, Mietchen, RDBrown, Rinnenadtrosc, Robofish, 1 anonymous edits

DNA barcoding Source: http://en.wikipedia.org/w/index.php?oldid=429146135 Contributors: Abduallah mohammed, Aranae, Arga Warga, Ary29, Banus, Bataplai, Beetstra, CapitalR, Carlosp420, Ceyockey, Charles Matthews, Cmdrjameson, David Gale, Dratman, Dyanega, Dysmorodrepanis, Earthsky, Evolver, Florentino floro, G Colyer, Gioto, Gj7, HamburgerRadio, Hoffmeier, Horatio, Isilanes, Jlittlet, JoJan, Josh Grosse, Jyril, Kadoo, Kembangraps, Kingdon, Lexor, Mdhowe, Michael Hardy, Nbocs, Omarabid, Onco p53, One more night, Pengo, Physicistjedi, Pjvpjv, Plantsurfer, Pseudomyrmex, RDBrown, Rich Farmbrough, Rjwilmsi, Ronhjones, Samsara, Seglea, Shreth, Shyamal, Springbok26, Squids and Chips, StephenWeber, TastyPoutine, Tedernst, Toytoy, Yumegusa, 57 anonymous edits

Dustbin category Source: http://en.wikipedia.org/w/index.php?oldid=408958309 Contributors: Fabrictramp, Sam Weller

Encyclopedia of Life Source: http://en.wikipedia.org/w/index.php?oldid=430689441 Contributors: Alan Liefting, Alekperova, Alienlifeformz, Atrian, BirdHunters, Blackburn.greg, Bueller 007, Cenarium, Church of emacs, CieloEstrellado, DDima, DragonFire1024, Druidland, Duncan.france, Edsova, El C, Elfalem, Emerson7, Erich gasboy, Espoo, Gaurav, Georgeryp, Girl2k, Green Squares, GregorB, Hintss, Ianml, Jacobolus, James.harris.anderson, JamesMLane, Jeandré du Toit, Jerome Charles Potts, JosephHVilas, Kingdon, Kittybrewster, Korg, Kslays, LFaraone, Lyhana8, MGSpiller, Melly42, Mervyn, Mgiganteus1, Mingwangx, Myrmoteras, Nihiltres, Nishkid64, Nlu, OhanaUnited, OlEnglish, Pointillist, Postdlf, Quiddity, R'n'B, Ragesoss, RaymondYee, RekishiEJ, Richard001, RichardF, Rjwilmsi, Rkitko, Rossami, Scapler, Scarecroe, Silverdaemonskye, Stbalbach, Stepa, Stephantom, Surena, Svetovid, TakuyaMurata, The Mysterious El Willstro, Tmotommyo, Tomwithanh, Vanished User 4517, Versageek, Vigilius, Visor, Wadsworth, Xadith12, Yug, Zanimum, ZombieWacker, 37 anonymous edits

Enteromorpha Source: http://en.wikipedia.org/w/index.php?oldid=430192381 Contributors: Hamamelis, Kleopatra, MrLincoln, Njál, Rettetast, WereSpielChequers, Ykvach, 3 anonymous edits

Eochelodes Source: http://en.wikipedia.org/w/index.php?oldid=416183248 Contributors: Pjoef, Sadads, Smith609

Eriinae Source: http://en.wikipedia.org/w/index.php?oldid=427495172 Contributors: John Hill

Evolutionary grade Source: http://en.wikipedia.org/w/index.php?oldid=421611443 Contributors: Aitias, Alan Liefting, Arcadian, Curtis Clark, Darth Ag.Ent, J. Spencer, JamesAM, Josephholsten, Life of Riley, Peter coxhead, Petter Bøckman, Richerman, Rjwilmsi, Smith609, Stupid girl, Ucucha, Wickey-nl, Zeimusu, 2 anonymous edits

Figurative system of human knowledge Source: http://en.wikipedia.org/w/index.php?oldid=416502603 Contributors: A Nobody, AnonMoos, ArglebargleIV, Auntof6, BryanG, Ceyockey, Charles Matthews, DanMS, Dekimasu, Dreadstar, Either way, Everton1984, Eyrian, Fastfission, Grafen, Guaka, J04n, Jeff3000, KConWiki, Ken Gallager, Msrasnw, Naevus, Omnipaedista, Rjanag, Rmhermen, Sango123, Snoyes, Steve Quinn, Tekeek, Tomisti, VanishedUser314159, Vanisheduser12345, WOSlinker, 13 anonymous edits

Folk taxon Source: http://en.wikipedia.org/w/index.php?oldid=268490469 Contributors: Babajobu, Charles T. Betz, Duncharris, Dysmorodrepanis, Eequor, Except, IEdML, Ish ishwar, Itub, Ivan007, J Milburn, JimStyle61093475, Jokestress, Josh Parris, Jovianeye, Jwinius, Kh123, MPS, Mark Dingemanse, MarkHudson, Mdz, Nbarth, Pt36, Ragesoss, Ramdrake, Rich Farmbrough, Robojames, RyJones, Shyamal, The Anome, Ultramartin, Una Smith, Univer, 14 anonymous edits

Folk taxonomy Source: http://en.wikipedia.org/w/index.php?oldid=377897177 Contributors: Babajobu, Charles T. Betz, Duncharris, Dysmorodrepanis, Eequor, Except, IEdML, Ish ishwar, Itub, Ivan007, J Milburn, JimStyle61093475, Jokestress, Josh Parris, Jovianeye, Jwinius, Kh123, MPS, Mark Dingemanse, MarkHudson, Mdz, Nbarth, Pt36, Ragesoss, Ramdrake, Rich Farmbrough, Robojames, RyJones, Shyamal, The Anome, Ultramartin, Una Smith, Univer, 14 anonymous edits

Form classification Source: http://en.wikipedia.org/w/index.php?oldid=422895615 Contributors: Altzinn, Dysmorodrepanis, EncycloPetey, Jimfbleak, Mgiganteus1, Petter Bøckman, Smith609, Stemonitis, Una Smith, Woohookitty, 1 anonymous edits

Genetypes Source: http://en.wikipedia.org/w/index.php?oldid=427310705 Contributors: Ebe123, Jebus989, Melaen, Prosanta1, 5 anonymous edits

Glyptochiton Source: http://en.wikipedia.org/w/index.php?oldid=405075164 Contributors: Pjoef, Smith609, Sumsum2010

Gotlandochiton Source: http://en.wikipedia.org/w/index.php?oldid=402027614 Contributors: Smith609, Sumsum2010

Haeggochiton Source: http://en.wikipedia.org/w/index.php?oldid=404467107 Contributors: Pjoef, Smith609

Hanleya Source: http://en.wikipedia.org/w/index.php?oldid=425847325 Contributors: Pjoef, Smith609, Sumsum2010

Helminthochiton Source: http://en.wikipedia.org/w/index.php?oldid=405240416 Contributors: Pjoef, Smith609, Sumsum2010

Heterochiton Source: http://en.wikipedia.org/w/index.php?oldid=407447334 Contributors: Smith609, Sumsum2010

Holophyletic group Source: http://en.wikipedia.org/w/index.php?oldid=392123493 Contributors: Gosox5555, Menvall, RayAYang, Sjö, T@nn, Why Not A Duck, 7 anonymous edits

Human genetic variation Source: http://en.wikipedia.org/w/index.php?oldid=425888708 Contributors: ACSE, Acroterion, Agathman, Alatari, AnonMoos, Atomic blunder, Aucaman, Bryan Derksen, DBZROCKS, Dark Tichondrias, Darth Mike, Dbachmann, Dratman, Ehrenkater, Emw, Epf, Ettrig, Evolauxia, Fat Cigar, Fences and windows, FilipeS, Forluvoft, Fred Hsu, Gerkinstock, Giornorosso, Grow60, Gwicky, Heardlarge2, Hectorguinness, Helgus, Hennessey, Patrick, Hewhocauses, Hobartimus, J04n, JWB, Jamoche, John Vandenberg, Johnuniq, Jose448, Jrockley, Kernow, Knowledgge, Lambiam, Little Professor, Livingrm, Lukas19, Maklinovich, Maproom, Maunus, Medical geneticist, Michaelkourlas, Mikihiko, Millstoner, Miradre, Moxy, Muntuwandi, Neko-chan, Nentrex, Oost, Oxymoron83, Paul A. Newman, Paul Clapham, Petiatil, Ph.eyes, Philwelch, Pigman, Pjvpjv, Pseudomyrmex, Puellanivis, R'n'B, RDBrown, Ramdrake, RetiredWikipedian789, Rich Farmbrough, Richard001, Rjwilmsi, Runcero, Samsara, Sasha l, Saul Greenberg, Semmler, Shalom Yechiel, Showtime2009, Sisodia, SpaceFlight89, Superm401, Surachit, Tassedethe, Tgr, The Thing That Should Not Be, Tide rolls, Tijfo098, WeijiBaikeBianji, Wet dog fur, Wknight94, Wobble, Woohookitty, Xezbeth, Yamagishi, 83 anonymous edits

Identification (biology) Source: http://en.wikipedia.org/w/index.php?oldid=362791081 Contributors: EagleFan, Fschoenm, Lotje, Vigilius, 8 anonymous edits

Ischnochitonidae Source: http://en.wikipedia.org/w/index.php?oldid=415380034 Contributors: Pjoef, Rich Farmbrough, Smith609, Sumsum2010

Ivoechiton Source: http://en.wikipedia.org/w/index.php?oldid=405237169 Contributors: Pjoef, Smith609, Sumsum2010

Kindbladochiton Source: http://en.wikipedia.org/w/index.php?oldid=401870118 Contributors: Smith609, Sumsum2010

Lavenachiton Source: http://en.wikipedia.org/w/index.php?oldid=405498181 Contributors: Pjoef, Smith609

LawMoose Source: http://en.wikipedia.org/w/index.php?oldid=393110362 Contributors: BrokenSegue, Eastlaw, Mailer diablo, V3rt1g0, Wavelength, 29 anonymous edits

Lepidochiton Source: http://en.wikipedia.org/w/index.php?oldid=415288614 Contributors: Pjoef, Smith609, 1 anonymous edits

Lepidopleurina Source: http://en.wikipedia.org/w/index.php?oldid=415382092 Contributors: Pjoef, Rich Farmbrough, Smith609, Sumsum2010

Leptochiton Source: http://en.wikipedia.org/w/index.php?oldid=405240991 Contributors: Pjoef, Smith609, Sumsum2010

Leptochitonidae Source: http://en.wikipedia.org/w/index.php?oldid=415382137 Contributors: Pjoef, Rich Farmbrough, Smith609, Sumsum2010

Lewontin's Fallacy Source: http://en.wikipedia.org/w/index.php?oldid=430671138 Contributors: AnonMoos, Bueller 007, Captain Occam, CharlesHR101, Chris Capoccia, Ciphergoth, Conscious, Coubure, DGG, DJ Clayworth, Danny Yee, Dbachmann, Doubting thomas, Duncharris, Ernham, Felsenst, Fortdj33, Guettarda, Gwicky, Jabowery, Jamesr74x, Jdcooper, JereKrischel, Lethiere, MarSch, MayerG, Michael Hardy, Miradre, Muntuwandi, Nectarflowed, Pascal666, Quizkajer, Rjwilmsi, Runcero, Saul Greenberg, Tabletop, Terry Longbaugh, Tijfo098, User2004, Victor Chmara, WeijiBaikeBianji, Wobble, Woohookitty, 15 anonymous edits

Linnaean enterprise Source: http://en.wikipedia.org/w/index.php?oldid=399122498 Contributors: Bearcat, Bender235, Eupedia, Georgeryp, Malcolma, SeamusSweeney, 2 anonymous edits

Lirachiton *Source*: http://en.wikipedia.org/w/index.php?oldid=401862498 *Contributors*: Smith609, Sumsum2010

List of Bacteria genera *Source*: http://en.wikipedia.org/w/index.php?oldid=421972199 *Contributors*: Afacerop, Ahoerstemeier, D6, Ezhuks, Littlealien182, Nono64, Rich Farmbrough, Sabedon, WOSlinker, Wwm101, 8 anonymous edits

List of bacterial genera named after geographical names *Source*: http://en.wikipedia.org/w/index.php?oldid=430481595 *Contributors*: Squidonius

List of bacterial genera named after institutions *Source*: http://en.wikipedia.org/w/index.php?oldid=431854155 *Contributors*: Khazar, Squidonius

List of bacterial genera named after mythological figures *Source*: http://en.wikipedia.org/w/index.php?oldid=430633294 *Contributors*: Squidonius

List of bacterial genera named after personal names *Source*: http://en.wikipedia.org/w/index.php?oldid=430481610 *Contributors*: Squidonius

Lucilina *Source*: http://en.wikipedia.org/w/index.php?oldid=414759785 *Contributors*: Pjoef, Smith609

Lumpers and splitters *Source*: http://en.wikipedia.org/w/index.php?oldid=431692679 *Contributors*: 4pq1injbok, Aaron Schulz, Alpha Quadrant (alt), Balazs.varadi, CRGreathouse, Charles Matthews, Chris the speller, Circeus, Cmdrjameson, DMG413, De.Gerbil, Garion96, Grafen, Infrogmation, JWB, Jahsonic, Keenan Pepper, Khym Chanur, Kwamikagami, Longhair, Metanoid, Missmarple, Monedula, Mr Stephen, Objectivesea, Paul Barlow, Rbrwr, Rich Farmbrough, RichardVeryard, Rousse, SMcCandlish, SP-KP, Samsara, Spettro9, Stirling Newberry, Tamfang, Teorth, The Claw, Tktktk, Tony May, Tothebarricades.tk, Uncle Bill, VoA, XQ fan, Zafiroblue05, 27 anonymous edits

Mesochiton *Source*: http://en.wikipedia.org/w/index.php?oldid=401863342 *Contributors*: Smith609, Sumsum2010

Military taxonomy *Source*: http://en.wikipedia.org/w/index.php?oldid=390674900 *Contributors*: Bart133, Eastlaw, R'n'B, Tenmei

Mopaliidae *Source*: http://en.wikipedia.org/w/index.php?oldid=415395210 *Contributors*: Pjoef, Rich Farmbrough, Smith609, Sumsum2010

Multi-access key *Source*: http://en.wikipedia.org/w/index.php?oldid=360229721 *Contributors*: Chris the speller, Mike Dallwitz, Thibbs, Vigilius, 2 anonymous edits

Multi-entry key *Source*: http://en.wikipedia.org/w/index.php?oldid=260460933 *Contributors*: Flechte, Vigilius

Neoloricata *Source*: http://en.wikipedia.org/w/index.php?oldid=407410926 *Contributors*: AndrewvdBK, Smith609, 1 anonymous edits

NRANK *Source*: http://en.wikipedia.org/w/index.php?oldid=295496651 *Contributors*: Dialectric, Grutness, Jrockley, Super cyclist

Numerical taxonomy *Source*: http://en.wikipedia.org/w/index.php?oldid=391869370 *Contributors*: Anupam, AshLin, Bender235, Dysmorodrepanis, EagleFan, Fjrohlf, GTBacchus, Jabowery, Laureapuella, Lavateraguy, Pairwise, Vigilius, 4 anonymous edits

Ocellochiton *Source*: http://en.wikipedia.org/w/index.php?oldid=415489238 *Contributors*: Pjoef, Smith609

Olingechiton *Source*: http://en.wikipedia.org/w/index.php?oldid=401859755 *Contributors*: Smith609, Sumsum2010

Oochiton *Source*: http://en.wikipedia.org/w/index.php?oldid=404932416 *Contributors*: Pjoef, Smith609, Sumsum2010

Open nomenclature *Source*: http://en.wikipedia.org/w/index.php?oldid=409753699 *Contributors*: Jackhynes, Random User 937494, Visionholder

Paleochiton *Source*: http://en.wikipedia.org/w/index.php?oldid=397321807 *Contributors*: DanielCD, Smith609

Parachiton *Source*: http://en.wikipedia.org/w/index.php?oldid=416823157 *Contributors*: Pjoef, Sadads, Smith609

Parapatric speciation *Source*: http://en.wikipedia.org/w/index.php?oldid=430819817 *Contributors*: A.Ou, Anthon.Eff, Azcolvin429, BenB4, Dysmorodrepanis, EncycloPetey, GoEThe, Greeneto, Ilmari Karonen, Johann Wolfgang, John0101ddd, Johnuniq, Joriki, Jrockley, Levineps, Lycurgus, M1ss1ontomars2k4, Mchavez, Midgley, Ockendeni, PatrickFisher, Qmwne235, Quicksilvre, RDBrown, Samsara, Tedtoal, Victor falk, VirtualDelight, Wikipediamaniac14, WurmWoode, 12 anonymous edits

Peripatric speciation *Source*: http://en.wikipedia.org/w/index.php?oldid=422652706 *Contributors*: Azcolvin429, BenB4, Delirium, Dysmorodrepanis, EncycloPetey, GoEThe, Greeneto, Heron, Ilmari Karonen, JoshuaZ, Jrockley, Levineps, Lexor, Qmwne235, RJFJR, Raul654, Rich Farmbrough, Samsara, Tedtoal, TimVickers, Tsackton, Victor falk, WurmWoode, 7 anonymous edits

Permochiton *Source*: http://en.wikipedia.org/w/index.php?oldid=401868122 *Contributors*: Smith609, Sumsum2010

Protochiton *Source*: http://en.wikipedia.org/w/index.php?oldid=404932678 *Contributors*: Pjoef, Smith609, Sumsum2010

Pseudischnochiton *Source*: http://en.wikipedia.org/w/index.php?oldid=415629016 *Contributors*: Pjoef, Smith609, Sumsum2010

Pterochiton *Source*: http://en.wikipedia.org/w/index.php?oldid=407442357 *Contributors*: Avocado, Smith609

Pterygochiton *Source*: http://en.wikipedia.org/w/index.php?oldid=402023076 *Contributors*: Smith609, Sumsum2010

Records management taxonomy *Source*: http://en.wikipedia.org/w/index.php?oldid=394148474 *Contributors*: Bearian, Farmerman, Harvey the rabbit, Kevinxml007, Smiller933, Snek01, Stifle, Triwbe, Whpq, Wyatt Riot, 1 anonymous edits

Reticulation (single-access key) *Source*: http://en.wikipedia.org/w/index.php?oldid=202515136 *Contributors*: Vigilius

Royal Entomological Society Handbooks *Source*: http://en.wikipedia.org/w/index.php?oldid=419818015 *Contributors*: Conops, Maias, Mark-mitchell-aldershot, Mrs foxall, Neilmarj, Rich Farmbrough, SP-KP, Simuliid, Stemonitis, 1 anonymous edits

Scanochiton *Source*: http://en.wikipedia.org/w/index.php?oldid=401865026 *Contributors*: Smith609, Sumsum2010

Scanochitonidae *Source*: http://en.wikipedia.org/w/index.php?oldid=415400881 *Contributors*: Pjoef, Smith609, Sumsum2010

Schizochiton *Source*: http://en.wikipedia.org/w/index.php?oldid=405111314 *Contributors*: Pjoef, Smith609, Sumsum2010

Schizochitonidae *Source*: http://en.wikipedia.org/w/index.php?oldid=415400929 *Contributors*: Pjoef, Smith609, Sumsum2010

Septemchiton *Source*: http://en.wikipedia.org/w/index.php?oldid=404934320 *Contributors*: Pjoef, Smith609, Sumsum2010

Septemchitonina *Source*: http://en.wikipedia.org/w/index.php?oldid=413672706 *Contributors*: Pjoef, Smith609

Serotype *Source*: http://en.wikipedia.org/w/index.php?oldid=429602898 *Contributors*: BD2412, Bradkittenbrink, Chowbok, Classicalclarinet, David Markun, Forluvoft, Gnetter, JeffreyN, Kengzy, LeCire, MarcoTolo, Myceteae, Pdeitiker, Raul654, Rjwilmsi, Thorwald, Timemutt, WriterHound, 18 anonymous edits

Sibley-Ahlquist taxonomy of birds *Source*: http://en.wikipedia.org/w/index.php?oldid=423249026 *Contributors*: 4444hhhh, ACW, Alan Pascoe, Andycjp, Bobo192, Chinasaur, ClockworkLunch, Curtis Clark, Daph Chloe, Debresser, Docu, Dolfin, Dyanega, Dysmorodrepanis, Firsfron, Foobar, Grafen, Grant Gussie, Haplochromis, HorsePunchKid, Jbdy, JerryFriedman, Jimbreed, Jimfbleak, JoJan, John Trapp, JohnOwens, Joseph Solis in Australia, Kaldari, Matz, Medeis, Mgiganteus1, Miss Madeline, Moriori, Muriel Gottrop, Nikai, Omnipaedista, Peter Isotalo, PierreAbbat, Ravedave, Richard D. LeCour, Sabine's Sunbird, Sardanaphalus, Shell Kinney, Shyamal, Smallweed, SudlonrA, Tannin, Totnesmartin, Tuxedo junction, UtherSRG, Velociraptor888, Vicki Rosenzweig, Vicpeters, Wrenthrush, 18 anonymous edits

Simplischnochiton *Source*: http://en.wikipedia.org/w/index.php?oldid=409259205 *Contributors*: Pjoef, Smith609

Species affinis *Source*: http://en.wikipedia.org/w/index.php?oldid=404467380 *Contributors*: GoingBatty, Nono64, Pjoef

Species description *Source*: http://en.wikipedia.org/w/index.php?oldid=398954685 *Contributors*: Bob the Wikipedian, Debivort, Eugene van der Pijll, Invertzoo, KnowledgeRequire, Pol098, Shyamal, Snek01, ZooPro

Species group *Source*: http://en.wikipedia.org/w/index.php?oldid=427628252 *Contributors*: Bender235, Boston, Danger, Editor at Large, Gnostrat, GoingBatty, J. Spencer, J04n, Jacqueshb, JamesAM, KimvdLinde, KrakatoaKatie, RDBrown, Spinningspark, Ucucha, 1 anonymous edits

Spongioradsia *Source*: http://en.wikipedia.org/w/index.php?oldid=407462459 *Contributors*: Pjoef, Smith609, Sumsum2010

Standard Business Reporting *Source*: http://en.wikipedia.org/w/index.php?oldid=404350832 *Contributors*: AussieSBR, Edward, Hyphen DJW, LilHelpa, Ohconfucius, 8 anonymous edits

Stenoplax *Source*: http://en.wikipedia.org/w/index.php?oldid=428792103 *Contributors*: Kueda, Pjoef, Smith609, Sumsum2010

Sympatric speciation *Source*: http://en.wikipedia.org/w/index.php?oldid=428385829 *Contributors*: AC+79 3888, Addshore, Andrew Forbes, Andycjp, Angela, Arch dude, Attys, Azcolvin429, Bcorr, BenB4, Bendzh, Boreal99, Bosmon, CRGreathouse, Clayoquot, Collegekdr, Cryptic C62, Dyanega, Dysmorodrepanis, EEBCVB, EncycloPetey, Eratosignis, GoEThe, Graft, Greeneto, Hans Dunkelberg, Ilmari Karonen, Jason.grossman, John0101ddd, Johnuniq, JoshuaZ, Jrockley, Keoormsby, KnightRider, Koavf, Levineps, Lexor, Lowellian, Maurajbo, Mendaliv, Mutlydog, Nicke L, Nowa, Nurg, OS2Warp, Ockendeni, Peter Chastain, Peter Kaminski, Pspealman, Rednblu, Rich Farmbrough, Rickproser, Rusty Cashman, Sacquebout, Samsara, Seb951, Shao, SilenceDoGood, Stemonitis, Superborsuk, Sverdrup, Tedtoal, Thumperward, Tofof, Trigaranus, Ucucha, Victor falk, Visionholder, William Avery, Wmgetz, Zgheng, 56 anonymous edits

Synopses of the British Fauna *Source*: http://en.wikipedia.org/w/index.php?oldid=426167570 *Contributors*: Bobbyboyuk, Brenont, Edward, Fastilysock, Jafeluv, John of Reading, Lightmouse, Mrs foxall, Open2universe, Rolf Schmidt, 1 anonymous edits

Tagspace *Source*: http://en.wikipedia.org/w/index.php?oldid=420251565 *Contributors*: Cgingold, Gilliam, Rockfang, Zidonuke, Zorroz, 3 anonymous edits

Tautonym *Source*: http://en.wikipedia.org/w/index.php?oldid=396498300 *Contributors*: Branddobbe, Brya, CubicFeet, Delta422869, Dysmorodrepanis, Egmontaz, Eu-151, General Wesc, Hamamelis, Jeremiah Mountain, KarlM, Kingdon, MrDarwin, Otto4711, PubliusTacitus, Radagast83, SB Johnny, SP-KP, Sergio Macías, Slon02, The Tom, UrsusArctos, 工口口口, 8 anonymous edits

Taxome *Source*: http://en.wikipedia.org/w/index.php?oldid=387335919 *Contributors*: Avalon, Dysmorodrepanis, Lawrence Cohen, Look2See1, Melaen, Pearle, TheLateDentarthurdent, Travelbird, 6 anonymous edits

Taxonomic database *Source*: http://en.wikipedia.org/w/index.php?oldid=425191043 *Contributors*: FaEu, Gaurav, Tony1212

Taxonomic homonym *Source*: http://en.wikipedia.org/w/index.php?oldid=300315699 *Contributors*: Bff, Brya, Dyanega, Edcolins, Hesperian, Invertzoo, Jwo3, Mgiganteus1, Nadiatalent, Una Smith, 2 anonymous edits

Taxonomic inflation *Source*: http://en.wikipedia.org/w/index.php?oldid=422131380 *Contributors*: First Light, Hesperian, Jncraton, Phlounder

Identification key *Source*: http://en.wikipedia.org/w/index.php?oldid=431869103 *Contributors*: Abeg92, Animeronin, AxelBoldt, Ben Ram, Berton, Bobo192, Brya, Burzmali, Cavrdg, Clicketyclack, Curtis Clark, DeadEyeArrow, Duncharris, Dysmorodrepanis, Eleazar, Eug, Fredrik, Fryed-peach, Hardyplants, Hut 8.5, Jacek Kendysz, Jaknouse, Jorge Stolfi, Krynitzkia-typing, LegCircus, LilHelpa, Lisamh, MPF, Mendel, Mike Dallwitz, Mild Bill Hiccup, Minghong, Moltenblue, Notafly, Nuno Tavares, Osborne, Pedro Onativia, Qxz, RJFJR, Richard001, SB Johnny, ST47, Scientific29, Steven Zhang, Sthuh1, Stwalkerster, Tpolonski2, Triwbe, Vigilius, 70 anonymous edits

Subspecies of *Canis lupus* *Source*: http://en.wikipedia.org/w/index.php?oldid=431979039 *Contributors*: 2help, Altaileopard, Anna, Anna Frodesiak, BhagyaMani, Chrisrus, Clasqm, Coaster1983, Conversion script, Dark hyena, Dger, Eliezg, EoGuy, Feyre, Gatorgirl7563, Gene Nygaard, Greatestrowerever, Hafwyn, Inugami-bargho, Izvora, LedgendGamer, LilHelpa, Lothar von Richthofen, Maphobbyist, Mariomassone, Mdd4696, Mgiganteus1, Mirlen, Ntennis, ONEder Boy, PFHLai, Phatom87, Pmaas, RANDREWF7777, Raul654, Rich Farmbrough, Rlendog, Ryulong, Scarykitty, Secret Squïrrel, Shadowjams, Silver seren, Smitty, Superluser, TenPoundHammer, UtherSRG, Vanbasten 23, Vortex Dragon, 66 anonymous edits

Taxonomy of commonly fossilised invertebrates *Source*: http://en.wikipedia.org/w/index.php?oldid=428125396 *Contributors*: Bry9000, D6, Dr.Bastedo, Epsilon60198, Euchiasmus, Hqb, Kwamikagami, Legis, Lumos3, Miss Madeline, MrKIA11, Neelix, Nihiltres, Nono64, Rjd0060, Smith609, Stemonitis, Wilson44691, 5 anonymous edits

Taxonomy of scorpions *Source*: http://en.wikipedia.org/w/index.php?oldid=417851379 *Contributors*: AshLin, Kevmin, Rrostrom, Tinton5

Trachypleura *Source*: http://en.wikipedia.org/w/index.php?oldid=404933436 *Contributors*: Pjoef, Smith609, Sumsum2010

Type (biology) *Source*: http://en.wikipedia.org/w/index.php?oldid=422143320 *Contributors*: Alan Liefting, Anthony Appleyard, Argo Navis, Aroatron, Ava, Ballista, Brya, Cfilorvv, Chrisminter, Circeus, Cymru.lass, Danger, Dyanega, Dysmorodrepanis, Edward, Erdigenc, Fconaway, Fieldday-sunday, Figma, FunkMonk, Gdr, Hairy Dude, Huntster, Invertzoo, JerryFriedman, Jhobson1, JoanneB, JonRichfield, Julesd, Lavateraguy, Loew Galitz, MPF, Marshman, Mpulier, Nipisiquit, Nohat, Nsaa, Numbo3, Pembers, Permacultura, Petter Bøckman, SP-KP, Seascapeza, Selket, Shyamal, Stemonitis, Stho002, Tivedshambo, Ucucha, UtherSRG, Wedster, 30 anonymous edits

Type genus *Source*: http://en.wikipedia.org/w/index.php?oldid=411692964 *Contributors*: Alexei Kouprianov, BengMog, Brya, Circeus, ENeville, Invertzoo, L Kensington, Loew Galitz, Look2See1, Michael Hardy, Rkitko, Tkinias, Ucucha, Vigilius, 4 anonymous edits

Type species *Source*: http://en.wikipedia.org/w/index.php?oldid=430430088 *Contributors*: Brya, Circeus, CubicFeet, Curps, Cygnis insignis, Dbenbenn, Dysmorodrepanis, ENeville, Eequor, Favonian, GerardM, GoEThe, Halteres, Hixteilchen, IncognitoErgoSum, Invertzoo, Käärel, Kotniski, LeaveSleaves, Loew Galitz, Look2See1, Marshman, Nipisiquit, Peter G Werner, PhD Dre, Pro bug catcher, Rkitko, Sannab, Stemonitis, Susanibyvf, Ucucha, Umrguy42, Wachholder0, Wedster, WikipedianMarlith, 18 anonymous edits

ViralZone *Source*: http://en.wikipedia.org/w/index.php?oldid=425194662 *Contributors*: Plindenbaum

Wastebasket taxon *Source*: http://en.wikipedia.org/w/index.php?oldid=426966393 *Contributors*: Affinis, Auric, Brya, DanielCD, Dbachmann, Dysmorodrepanis, ElectricValkyrie, Florian Blaschke, Gdr, Jurassosaurus, Klon-immortal, Lexor, Maximilli, Mgiganteus1, Palfrey, Peter G Werner, Petter Bøckman, Phansen, Postglock, Smith609, TJRC, Tgoodwil, Wetman, АлександрВв, 5 anonymous edits

Web-based taxonomy *Source*: http://en.wikipedia.org/w/index.php?oldid=426556274 *Contributors*: Cybersally, Hesperian, Jvhertum, Rjwilmsi, 1 anonymous edits

West American Digest System *Source*: http://en.wikipedia.org/w/index.php?oldid=394802924 *Contributors*: Alex756, Branddobbe, Busjack, Coolcaesar, Dale Arnett, Dreftymac, Eaefremov, Eastlaw, Epbr123, Ice Cold Beer, Kevlar67, Kingturtle, L33th4x0rguy, Marloishomo, Mattlary, Mattsuksbalz, Michael Hardy, Skeezix1000, SteveSims, Tony Sidaway, Walshga, Wikifex, Yjones, 25 anonymous edits

Wikispecies *Source*: http://en.wikipedia.org/w/index.php?oldid=430165269 *Contributors*: Alan Liefting, Alex43223, AmZCi, Amberrock, Angela, AngoraFish, Anonymous Dissident, Anthony, Badbats, Belginusanl, BirdHunters, Bjankuloski06en, Borgx, Butko, Capt. James T. Kirk, Chuq, Donarreiskoffer, EncycloPetey, FaEu, Fabartus, FrummerThanThou, GangstaEB, Gaurav, Gavia immer, General Eisenhower, Georgeryp, Gnewf, GnuDoyng, Gobonobo, Grothmag, H sy, Hankyeol, Headbomb, Here, Holder, Hydriz, Hyjwei, Im.a.lumberjack, JamesR1701E, Jappoz, Jeandré du Toit, Joystick, Kevmin, King of Hearts, Kjoonlee, Koavf, Kotasik, Ksd5, Lachaume, Leeheonjin, LeonardoGregianin, Loupeter, M Johnson, MPF, Mahanga, Mailer diablo, Maitch, Mendaliv, Meno25, Mervyn, Metaspheres, Muzic2HeartO, NCurse, Nascar1996, Nishkid64, OhanaUnited, Oxymoron83, Pauli133, Picaroon, PuzzletChung, Ragesoss, Raichu, Ral315, Reguiieee, Retired username, SP-KP, Sade, Samwb123, Scapler, Shushruth, Sir Link, Stanqo, Stho002, Stux, TFCforever, Teh Rote, Tevonic, The editor1, Tree Biting Conspiracy, Twas Now, Ucucha, Uncle G, Violetriga, Vizzydix1, Wideangle, Xaosflux, Xelgen, Ybbor, Yerpo, Yonidebest, Yug, Zabanio, Zanimum, Zenohockey, Zvika, 49 anonymous edits

Zootaxa *Source*: http://en.wikipedia.org/w/index.php?oldid=415811247 *Contributors*: Crusio, Headbomb, Isfisk, John Vandenberg, Lasius, MrDarcy, R'n'B, Snek01, Stemonitis, Yerpo, 6 anonymous edits

Image Sources, Licenses and Contributors

License

Printed in Great Britain
by Amazon.co.uk, Ltd.,
Marston Gate.